PHILIP'S

C000259190

STREE

Cambridgeshire

Cambridge, Huntingdon, March, Peterborough, St Neots, Wisbech

www.philips-maps.co.uk

First published in 2001 by

Philip's, a division of
Octopus Publishing Group Ltd
www.octopusbooks.co.uk
2–4 Heron Quays, London E14 4JP
An Hachette Livre UK Company
www.hachettelivre.co.uk

Third colour edition 2008
First impression 2008
CAMCA

ISBN 978-0-540-09293-2 (pocket)

© Philip's 2008

Contents

II **Mobile safety cameras**

III **Key to map symbols**

IV **Key to map pages**

VI **Route planning**

X **Administrative and Postcode boundaries**

1 **Street maps** at 2⅔ inches to 1 mile

208 **Street maps** at 1⅓ inches to 1 mile

239 **Street maps** at 2⅔ inches to 1 mile

246 **Street map of Cambridge city centre** at 5⅓ inches to 1 mile

247 **Index** of towns, villages, streets, hospitals, industrial estates, railway stations, schools, shopping centres, universities and places of interest

Digital Data

The exceptionally high-quality mapping found in this atlas is available as digital data in TIFF format, which is easily convertible to other bitmapped (raster) image formats.

The index is also available in digital form as a standard database table. It contains all the details found in the printed index together with the National Grid reference for the map square in which each entry is named.

For further information and to discuss your requirements, please contact victoria.dawbarn@philips-maps.co.uk

On-line route planner

For detailed driving directions and estimated driving times visit our free route planner at www.philips-maps.co.uk

Mobile safety cameras

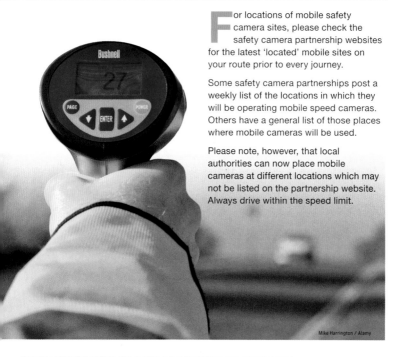

Mike Harrington / Alamy

For locations of mobile safety camera sites, please check the safety camera partnership websites for the latest 'located' mobile sites on your route prior to every journey.

Some safety camera partnerships post a weekly list of the locations in which they will be operating mobile speed cameras. Others have a general list of those places where mobile cameras will be used.

Please note, however, that local authorities can now place mobile cameras at different locations which may not be listed on the partnership website. Always drive within the speed limit.

Useful websites

Cambridgeshire Safety Camera Partnership
www.cambs.police.uk/camops/safetycameras

Hertfordshire Safety Camera Partnership
www.hertsdirect.org/envroads/roadstrans/rsu/driving/safetycameras

Further information
www.dvla.gov.uk
www.thinkroadsafety.gov.uk
www.dft.gov.uk
www.road-safe.org

Key to map symbols

III

(22a)	**Motorway** with junction number
	Primary route – dual/single carriageway
	A road – dual/single carriageway
	B road – dual/single carriageway
	Minor road – dual/single carriageway
	Other minor road – dual/single carriageway
	Road under construction
	Tunnel, covered road
(30) (30)	**Speed cameras** - single, multiple
	Rural track, private road or narrow road in urban area
	Gate or obstruction to traffic (restrictions may not apply at all times or to all vehicles)
	Path, bridleway, byway open to all traffic, restricted byway
	Pedestrianised area
DY7	**Postcode boundaries**
	County and unitary authority boundaries
	Railway, tunnel, railway under construction
	Tramway, tramway under construction
	Miniature railway
Walsall	**Railway station**
	Private railway station
South Shields	**Metro station**
	Tram stop, tram stop under construction
	Bus, coach station

◆	**Ambulance station**
◆	**Coastguard station**
◆	**Fire station**
◆	**Police station**
✚	**Accident and Emergency entrance to hospital**
H	**Hospital**
+	**Place of worship**
i	**Information Centre** (open all year)
	Shopping Centre
P P&R	**Parking, Park and Ride**
PO	**Post Office**
Δ ⌂	**Camping site, caravan site**
► ✕	**Golf course, picnic site**
Prim Sch	**Important buildings, schools, colleges, universities and hospitals**
	Built up area
	Woods
River Ouse	**Tidal water, water name**
	Non-tidal water – lake, river, canal or stream
	Lock, weir, tunnel
Church	**Non-Roman antiquity**
ROMAN FORT	**Roman antiquity**
87	**Adjoining page indicators and overlap bands** The colour of the arrow and the band indicates the scale of the adjoining or overlapping page (see scales below)
237	

Abbr	Full	Abbr	Full	Abbr	Full
Acad	Academy	Inst	Institute	Recn Gd	Recreation Ground
Allot Gdns	Allotments	Ct	Law Court		
Cemy	Cemetery	L Ctr	Leisure Centre	Resr	Reservoir
C Ctr	Civic Centre	LC	Level Crossing	Ret Pk	Retail Park
CH	Club House	Liby	Library	Sch	School
Coll	College	Mkt	Market	Sh Ctr	Shopping Centre
Crem	Crematorium	Meml	Memorial	TH	Town Hall/House
Ent	Enterprise	Mon	Monument	Trad Est	Trading Estate
Ex H	Exhibition Hall	Mus	Museum	Univ	University
Ind Est	Industrial Estate	Obsy	Observatory	W Twr	Water Tower
IRB Sta	Inshore Rescue Boat Station	Pal	Royal Palace	Wks	Works
		PH	Public House	YH	Youth Hostel

Enlarged mapping only

	Railway or bus station building
	Place of interest
	Parkland

■ The small numbers around the edges of the maps identify the 1 kilometre National Grid lines ■ The dark grey border on the inside edge of some pages indicates that the mapping does not continue onto the adjacent page

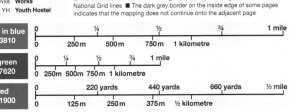

The scale of the maps on the pages numbered in blue is 4.2 cm to 1 km • 2⅔ inches to 1 mile • 1: 23810

0	¼	½	¾	1 mile
0	250 m	500 m	750 m	1 kilometre

The scale of the maps on the pages numbered in green is 2.1 cm to 1 km • 1⅓ inches to 1 mile • 1: 47620

0	¼	½	¾	1 mile
0	250m	500m	750 m	1 kilometre

The scale of the maps on the pages numbered in red is 8.4 cm to 1 km • 5⅓ inches to 1 mile • 1: 11900

0	220 yards	440 yards	660 yards	½ mile
0	125 m	250 m	375m	½ kilometre

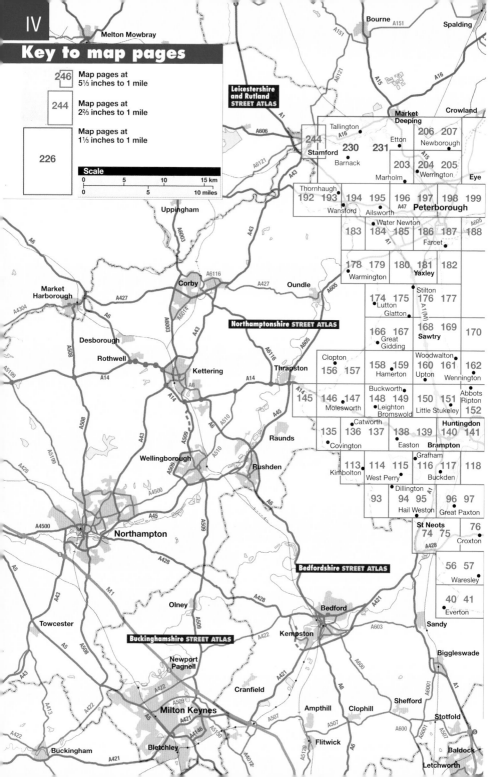

IV

Key to map pages

246	Map pages at 5⅓ inches to 1 mile
244	Map pages at 2⅔ inches to 1 mile
226	Map pages at 1⅓ inches to 1 mile

Scale

0   5   10   15 km
0   5   10 miles

Melton Mowbray

Bourne   A151

Spalding

A151   A151

A16

A1   A16

Leicestershire and Rutland STREET ATLAS

Market Deeping   Crowland

Tallington

A606   A16   Etton   206 207 Newborough

244   230   231

Stamford   Barnack   Marholm   203 204 205 Werrington   Eye

A6121   A43

Thornhaugh   192 193 194 195 196 197 198 199

Uppingham   Wansford   Ailsworth   A47   Peterborough

Water Newton   A605

183 184 185 186 187 188

A1   Farcet

A6116   A427   Oundle   A605

178 179 180 181 182

Warmington   Yaxley

Market Harborough   Corby   A6116   A427   Stilton

A6014   174 175 176 177

Lutton   Glatton   A1(M)

Desborough   166 167 168 169 170

Rothwell   Great Gidding   Sawtry

A14   Kettering   Thrapston   Woodwalton

Northamptonshire STREET ATLAS

Clopton   158 159 160 161 162

156 157   Hamerton   Upton   Wennington

A14   Buckworth   Abbots Ripton

145 146 147 148 149 150 151 152

Molesworth   Leighton Bromswold   Little Stukeley

Catworth   Huntingdon

Raunds   135 136 137 138 139 140 141

Covington   Easton   Brampton

Wellingborough   Grafham

Rushden   113 114 115 116 117 118

Kimbolton   West Perry   Buckden

Dillington   A1

93   94 95   96 97

Hail Weston   Great Paxton

A45   St Neots   76

74 75   Croxton

A428

Northampton   56 57

Waresley

Bedfordshire STREET ATLAS

40 41

Everton

Olney   Bedford   Sandy

Buckinghamshire STREET ATLAS

Towcester   Kempston   Biggleswade

Newport Pagnell   Cranfield   Shefford

Milton Keynes   Ampthill   Clophill   Stotfold

Bletchley   Flitwick   Baldock

Buckingham   Letchworth

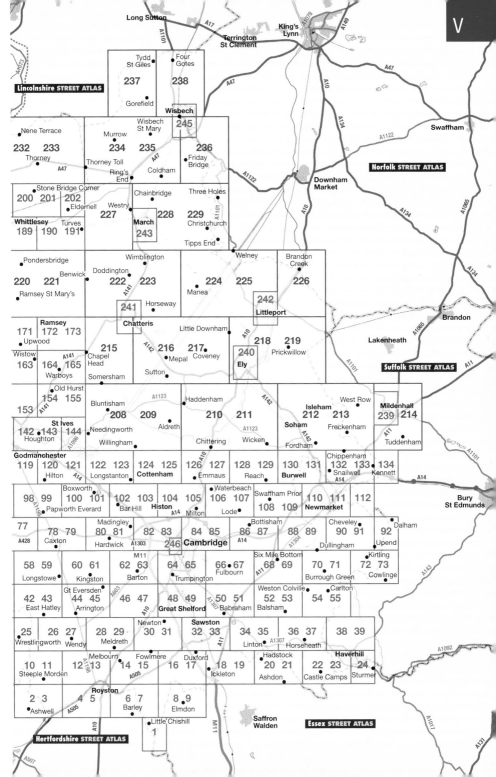

Route Planning

Scale

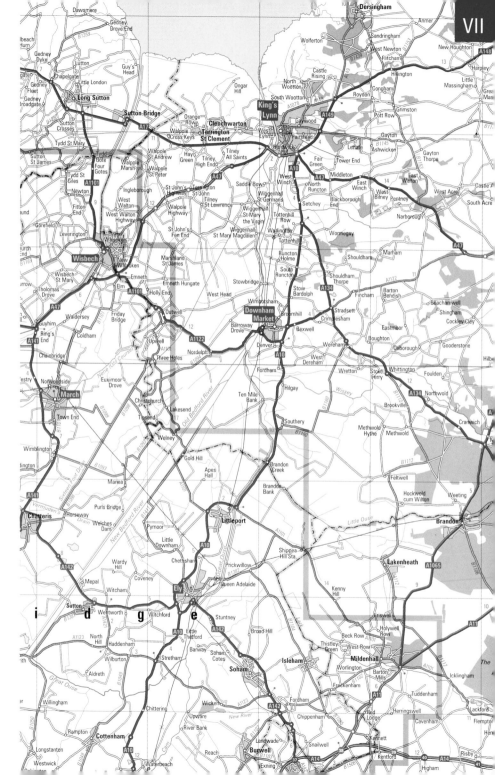

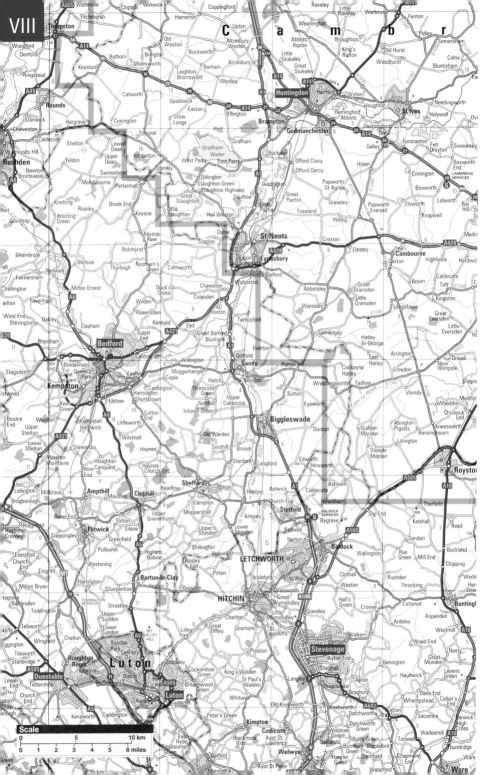

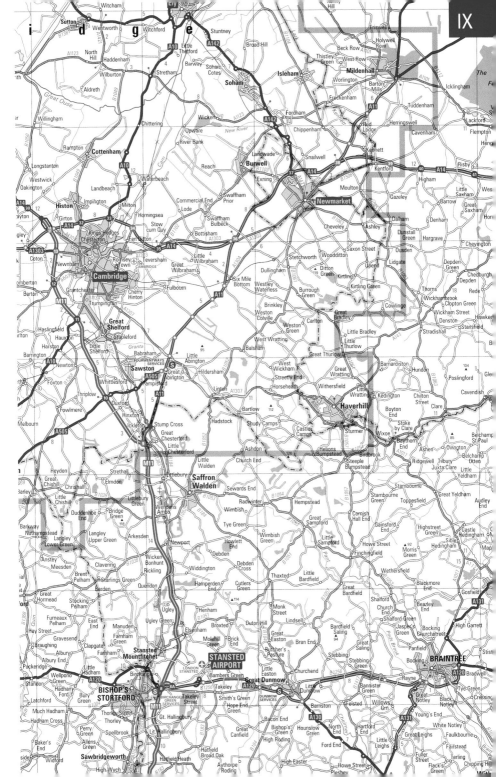

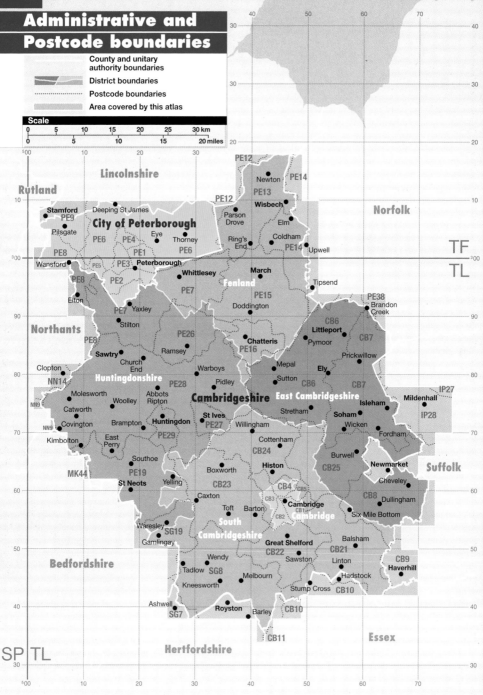

Administrative and Postcode boundaries

County and unitary authority boundaries
District boundaries
Postcode boundaries
Area covered by this atlas

Scale

0   5   10   15   20   25   30 km
0   5   10   15   20 miles

Lincolnshire

Rutland

Stamford
PE9
Pilsgate
PE8
Wansford
PE8
Elton
Northants
Clopton
NN14
Molesworth
Catworth
NN9
Covington
Kimbolton
MK44
Southoe
PE19
St Neots
Waresley
SG19
Gamlingay

Bedfordshire

Deeping St James

City of Peterborough
PE6   PE4   Eye   Thorney
PE1
PE5   PE3   Peterborough
PE2
PE7   Yaxley
Stilton
PE26
Sawtry   Ramsey
Church
End
PE28   Warboys
Pidley
Abbots
Ripton
Huntingdonshire
Woolley
Brampton   Huntingdon
PE27
PE29   Willingham
East
Perry
Boxworth
Yelling
Caxton
Toft   Barton
Wendy
Tadlow   SG8
Melbourn
Kneesworth
Ashwell
SG7   Royston   Barley

PE12
Newton
PE14
PE13
PE12   Wisbech
Parson
Drove
Elm
Ring's   Coldham
End   PE14   Upwell
March
Fenland
PE7   PE15
Doddington   Tipsend
Whittlesey
PE6

PE38
Brandon
Creek
C86
Littleport
PE16   Pymoor   CB7
Chatteris   Prickwillow
Mepal   Ely
Sutton   CB6   CB7
Cambridgeshire   East Cambridgeshire
Stretham   Isleham   Mildenhall
St Ives   Soham   IP28
Wicken
Cottenham   Fordham
CB24   Burwell
Histon   Newmarket
CB25   Cheveley
Boxworth   CB8   Dullingham
CB23   CB4   CB5
CB3   Cambridge   Six Mile Bottom
CB1   Cambridge
CB2
South
Cambridgeshire   Great Shelford   Balsham
CB22   CB21   CB9
Sawston   Linton   Haverhill
Hadstock
Stump Cross   CB10
CB10
CB11

Norfolk

TF
TL

IP27

Suffolk

Essex

SP   TL

Hertfordshire

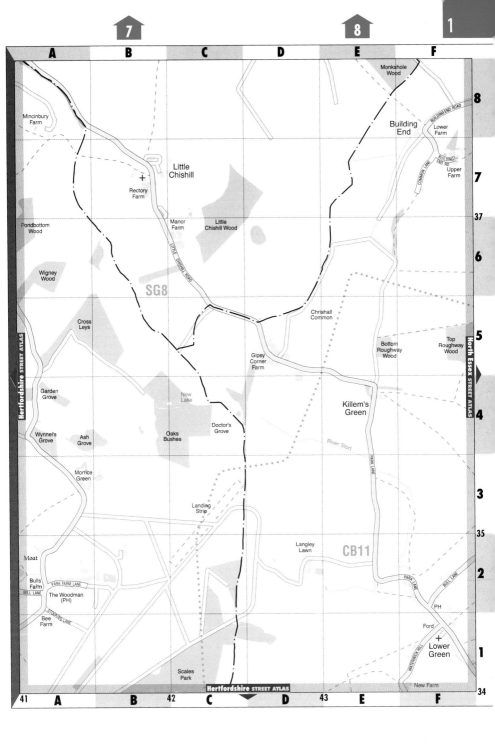

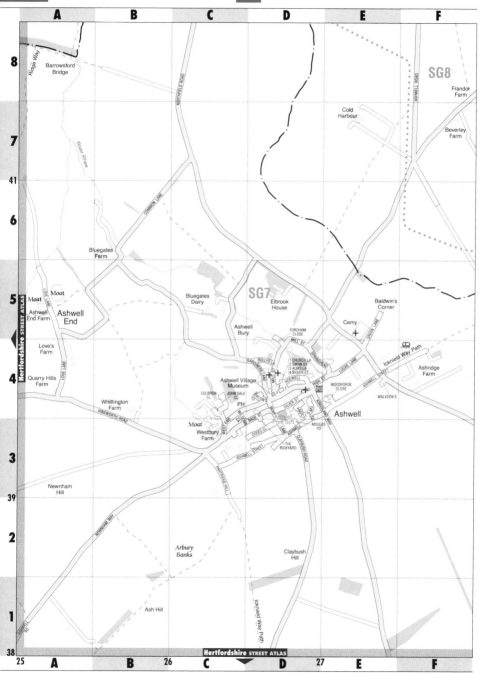

8

Ridge Way

Barrowsford
Bridge

SG8

Frandor
Farm

7

River Rhee

Cold
Harbour

Beverley
Farm

41

COMMON LANE

6

Bluegates
Farm

NORTHFIELD ROAD

ASHWELL ROAD

5

Moat
Moat

Ashwell
End Farm

Ashwell
End

LOVE LANE

Bluegates
Dairy

SG7

Elbrook
House

Ashwell
Bury

FORDHAM
CLOSE

MILL ST

Cemy

Baldwin's
Corner

GREEN LANE

Icknield Way Path

Ashridge
Farm

Love's
Farm

Quarry Hills
Farm

LOVE LANE

Ashwell Village
Museum

GARDENERS LA
ROLLYS LA

1 CHURCH LA
2 SWAN ST
3 ALMS LA
4 SILVER CT.

SPRINGHEAD

HODWELL

LUCAS LANE

HIGH ST

WOODFORDE
CLOSE

ASHWELL STREET

WALKDEN'S

4

Whittington
Farm

HINKWORTH ROAD

COLBRON
CL

JOHN SALE
CL

PH

SILVER ST

Ashwell
Prim Sch

MOULES
YD

Ashwell

Moat
Westbury
Farm

WEST END

BACK ST

DIXIES CL

ASHWELL STREET

THE
RICKYARD

KINGSLAND WAY

KIRBISH ROAD

3

Newnham
Hill

PARTRIDGE HILL

39

NEWNHAM WAY

2

Arbury
Banks

Claybush
Hill

1

Ash Hill

Icknield Way Path

38

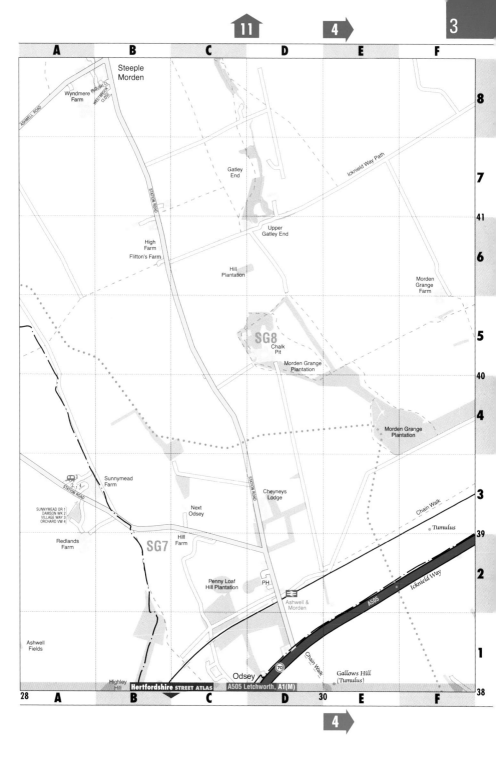

Steeple
Morden

Wyndmere
Farm

Gatley
End

Icknield Way Path

Upper
Gatley End

High
Farm
Flitton's Farm

Hill
Plantation

Morden
Grange
Farm

SG8

Chalk
Pit

Morden Grange
Plantation

Morden Grange
Plantation

Sunnymead
Farm

Cheyneys
Lodge

Chain Walk

SUNNYMEAD OR 1
DAMSON WK 2
VILLAGE WAY 3
ORCHARD VW 4

Next
Odsey

• Tumulus

Redlands
Farm

SG7

Hill
Farm

Penny Loaf
Hill Plantation

PH

Icknield Way

A505

Ashwell &
Morden

Ashwell
Fields

Highley
Hill

Odsey

Chain Walk

Gallows Hill
(Tumulus)

70

28   A   B   C   D   30   E   F   38

8
7
41
6
5
40
4
3
39
2
1

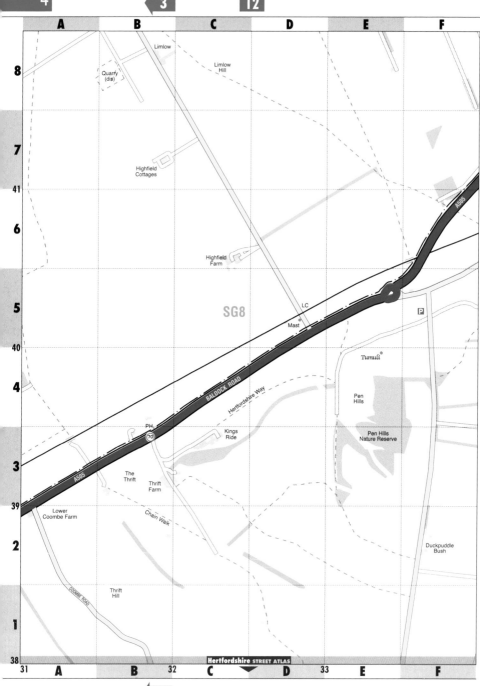

Limlow

Quarry
(dis)

Limlow
Hill

Highfield
Cottages

Highfield
Farm

SG8

LC

Mast

A505

BALDOCK ROAD

Hertfordshire Way

Tumuli

Pen
Hills

P

PH

70

Kings
Ride

Pen Hills
Nature Reserve

A505

The
Thrift

Thrift
Farm

Lower
Coombe Farm

Chain Walk

Duckpuddle
Bush

COOMBE ROAD

Thrift
Hill

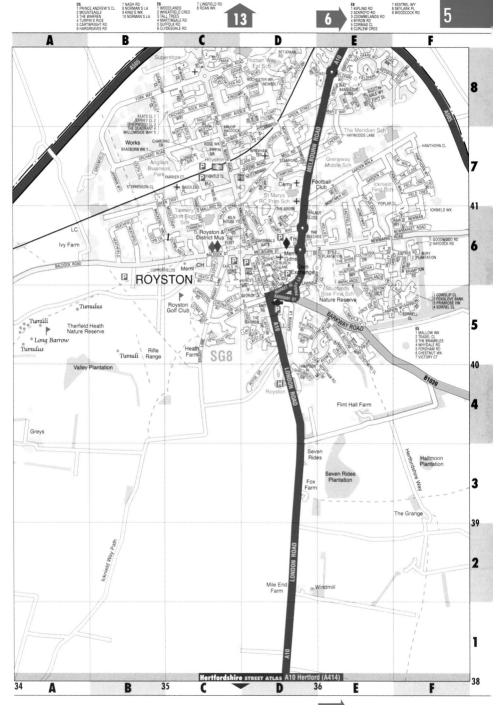

D5
1 PRINCE ANDREW'S CL
2 MOUNTEAGLE
3 THE WARREN
4 TURPIN'S RIDE
5 CARTWRIGHT RD
6 HARGREAVES RD

7 NASH RD
8 NORMAN'S LA
9 KING'S WK
10 NORMAN'S LA

E6
1 WOODLANDS
2 WHEATFIELD CRES
3 TALL TREES
4 MARTINGALE RD
5 SUFFOLK RD
6 CLYDESDALE RD

7 LINGFIELD RD
8 ROAN WK

13

6

E8
1 KIPLING RD
2 ACKROYD RD
3 COOMBELANDS RD
4 BYRON RD
5 DORMAS CL
6 CURLEW CRES

7 KESTREL WY
8 SKYLARK PL
9 WOODCOCK RD

5

5
14

	A	B	C	D	E	F

8

Heath Farm

A505

Ickneld Way Path

7

Hyde Hill Farm

Hillside Farm

Noon's Folly Farm

41

Mast

A505

NEWMARKET ROAD

Wardington Bottom

6

Burloes Plantation

Burloes Hall

Burloes Farm

5

Lowerfield

SG8

40

Cow Plantation

Poor's Land

4

Hillside Farm

B1039

New Stud Farm

Heath Farm

3

Whiteley Hill

ROYSTON RD

39

B1368

2

Valley Cottage

Barley +

HIGH ST

BAKERS LANE

Newsells Park Stud

Newsells Farm

HORSESHOE

THE MOUNT

LONDON ROAD

B1368

CROSSWAYS

1

Horseshoe Farm

38

37	A		B	38	C		D	39	E		F

5

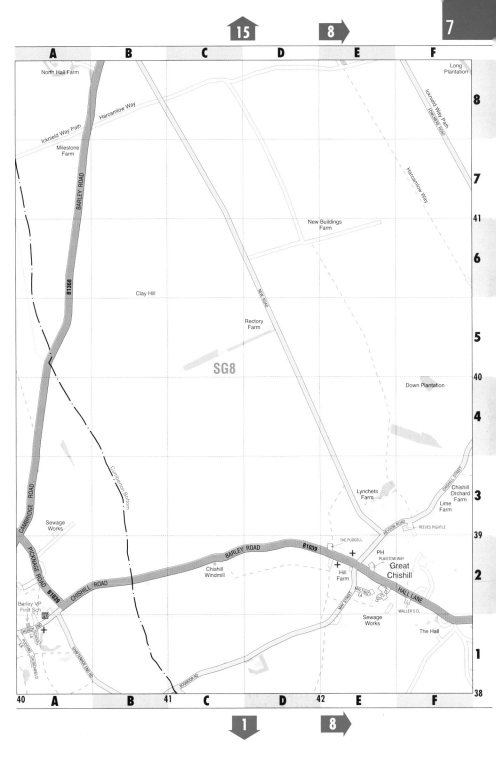

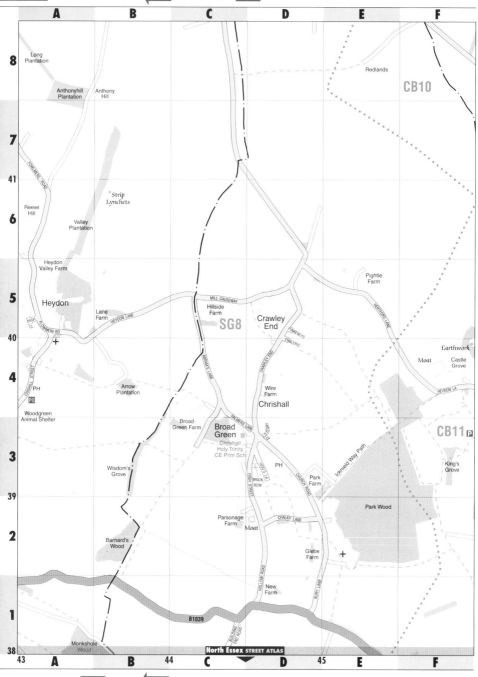

8 Long Plantation

Anthonyhill Plantation   Anthony Hill

Redlands

CB10

7

41

Strip Lynchets

Reeve Hill

6 Valley Plantation

Heydon Valley Farm

Pightle Farm

5 Heydon

Lane Farm   HEYDON LANE

MILL CAUSEWAY

Hillside Farm   SG8

Crawley End

PINKENEYS

ENGLERIC

HERTFORD LANE

Earthwork

Moat   Castle Grove

40

HIGH ST   FOWLMERE RD

CHISHILL STREET

PH

PO

Woodgreen Animal Shelter

KEMAR'S LANE

CRAWLEY END

Wire Farm

Chrishall

HEYDON LA

4 Arrow Plantation

PALMERS LANE

Broad Green Farm   Broad Green

Chrishall Holy Trinity CE Prim Sch

CB11 P

King's Grove

3 Wisdom's Grove

HIGH STREET   PIGG'S LA   BRICK ROW

PH

PIGG'S LA

CHURCH ROAD

Park Farm

Icknield Way Path

39

Parsonage Farm

CHALKY LANE

Park Wood

2 Barnard's Wood

Moat

Glebe Farm

HOLLOW ROAD

New Farm

BURY LANE

B1039

1

BULLENS END ROAD

38 Monkshole Wood

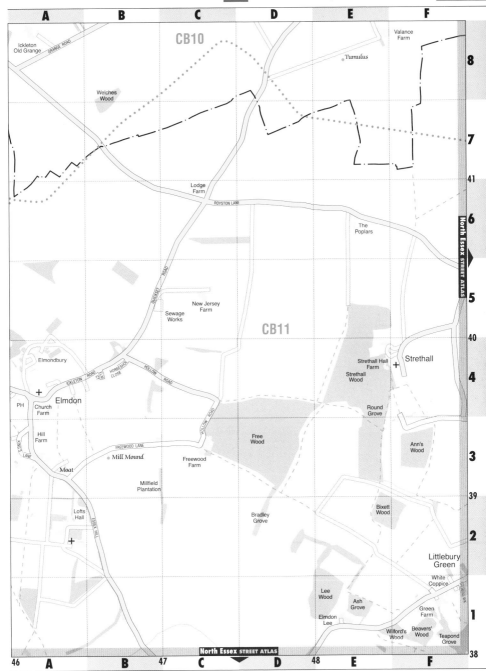

Ickleton
Old Grange

CB10

Valance
Farm

GRANGE ROAD

Welches
Wood

Tumulus

8

7

41

Lodge
Farm

ROYSTON LANE

6

The
Poplars

North Essex STREET ATLAS

5

CB11

New Jersey
Farm

Sewage
Works

DUKSET ROAD

40

Elmondbury

Strethall Hall
Farm

Strethall

Strethall
Wood

4

ICKLETON ROAD

HORSESHOE CLOSE

HOLLOW ROAD

PH

Church
Farm

Elmdon

Round
Grove

Hill
Farm

HOLLOW ROAD

Free
Wood

Ann's
Wood

3

KING'S LANE

FREEWOOD LANE

Mill Mound

Freewood
Farm

Moat

Millfield
Plantation

Bixett
Wood

39

Lofts
Hall

ESSEX HILL

Bradley
Grove

2

Littlebury
Green

White
Coppice

Lee
Wood

Ash
Grove

Green
Farm

1

STREES WAY

Elmdon
Lee

Wilford's
Wood

Beavers'
Wood

Teapond
Grove

38

46   A   B   47   C   48   D   E   F

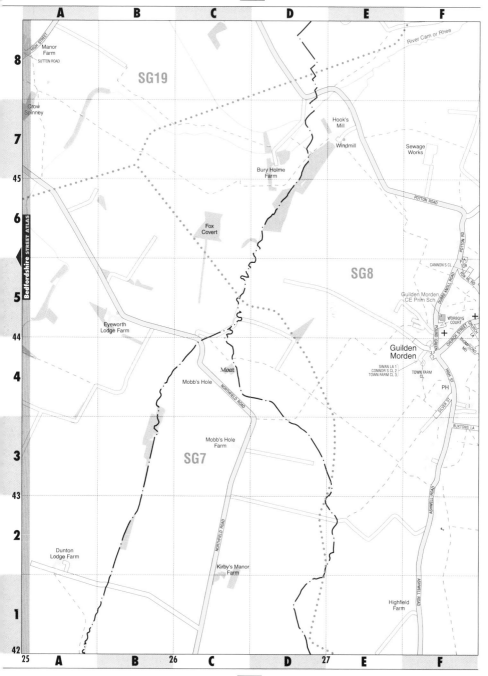

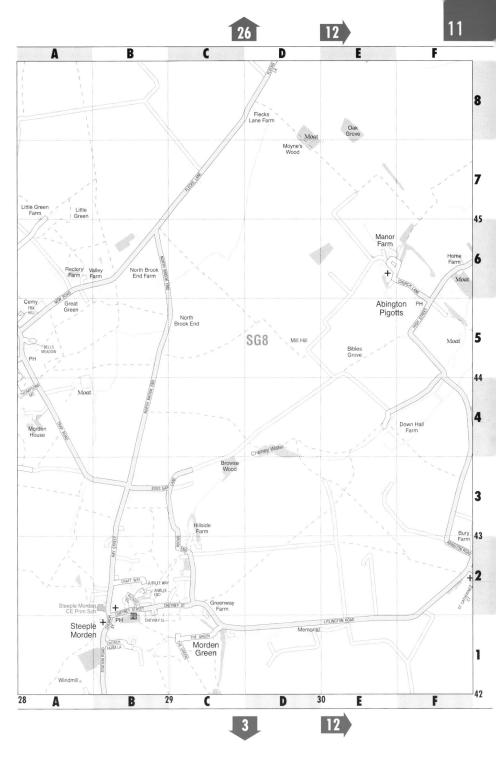

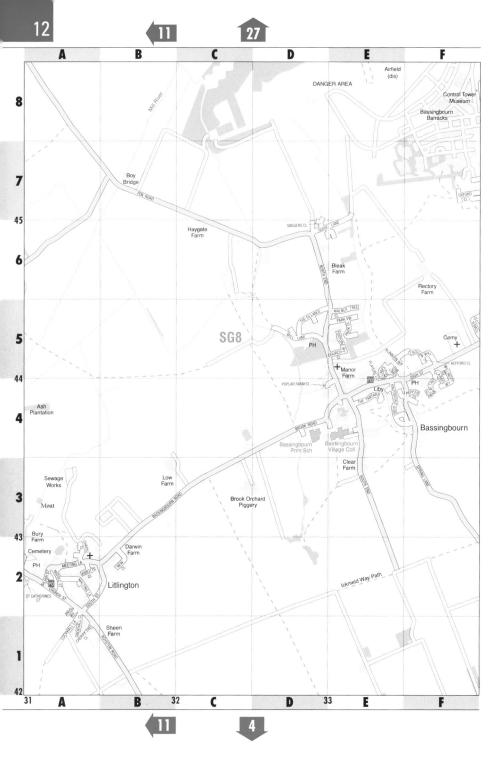

13 29

	A	B	C	D	E	F

Works
Meldreth Prim Sch
THE GRANGE
BELL
FLAMBARDS
DASHES
Meldreth
Foxfield Farm
WOODLANDS DR
A10
THE MOOR
Chiswick End
Meldreth
CH
THATCHER STANFORDS
Melbourn Science Park
Kingsway Golf Centre
CAMBRIDGE ROAD
Valley Farm
STATION ROAD
Melbourn Village Coll
The Moor
Solway Farm
St Johns Farm
STATION
McSplash Swimming Pool
Liby
Tostock Farm
Moat
VICARAGE
BARHAM
P
Melbourn Prim Sch
East Farm
Windpump
Moat
PO
Melbourn
SG8
Windpump
Bury Lane Fruit Farm
Melbourn Bury
THE LAWNS
Melda Farm
BACK LANE
GREENBANKS
Works
SAXON WAY
Long Barrow
Greenlow
A10
NEW ROAD
Harcomflow Way
Ickneild Way Path
Summer House Farm
Muncey's Farm
Goffers Knoll (Tumulus)
A505

37 38 39

A	B	C	D	E	F

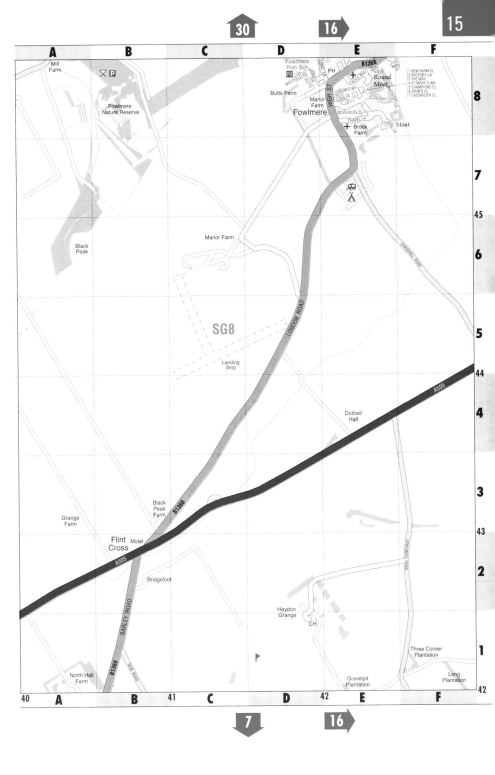

1 NEW FARM CL
2 RECTORY LA
3 THE WAY
4 ST MARY'S WK
5 CHAMPIONS CL
6 JOHN'S CL
7 CASSANDER CL

Mill Farm

Fowlmere Nature Reserve

Fowlmere Prim Sch

Butts Farm

Manor Farm

Fowlmere

Round Moat

Brook Farm

Moat

Black Peak

Manor Farm

SG8

Landing Strip

DRISSAILL ROAD

LONDON ROAD

HIGH ST

B1368

Dottrell Hall

A505

Black Peak Farm

B1368

Grange Farm

Flint Cross   Motel

A505

Bridgefoot

BARLEY ROAD

FOWLMERE ROAD

Heydon Grange

CH

NEW ROAD

B1368

North Hall Farm

Three Corner Plantation

Long Plantation

Gravelpit Plantation

40   A   B   41   C   D   42   E   F   42

8   7   45   6   5   44   4   3   43   2   1

A   B   C   D   E   F

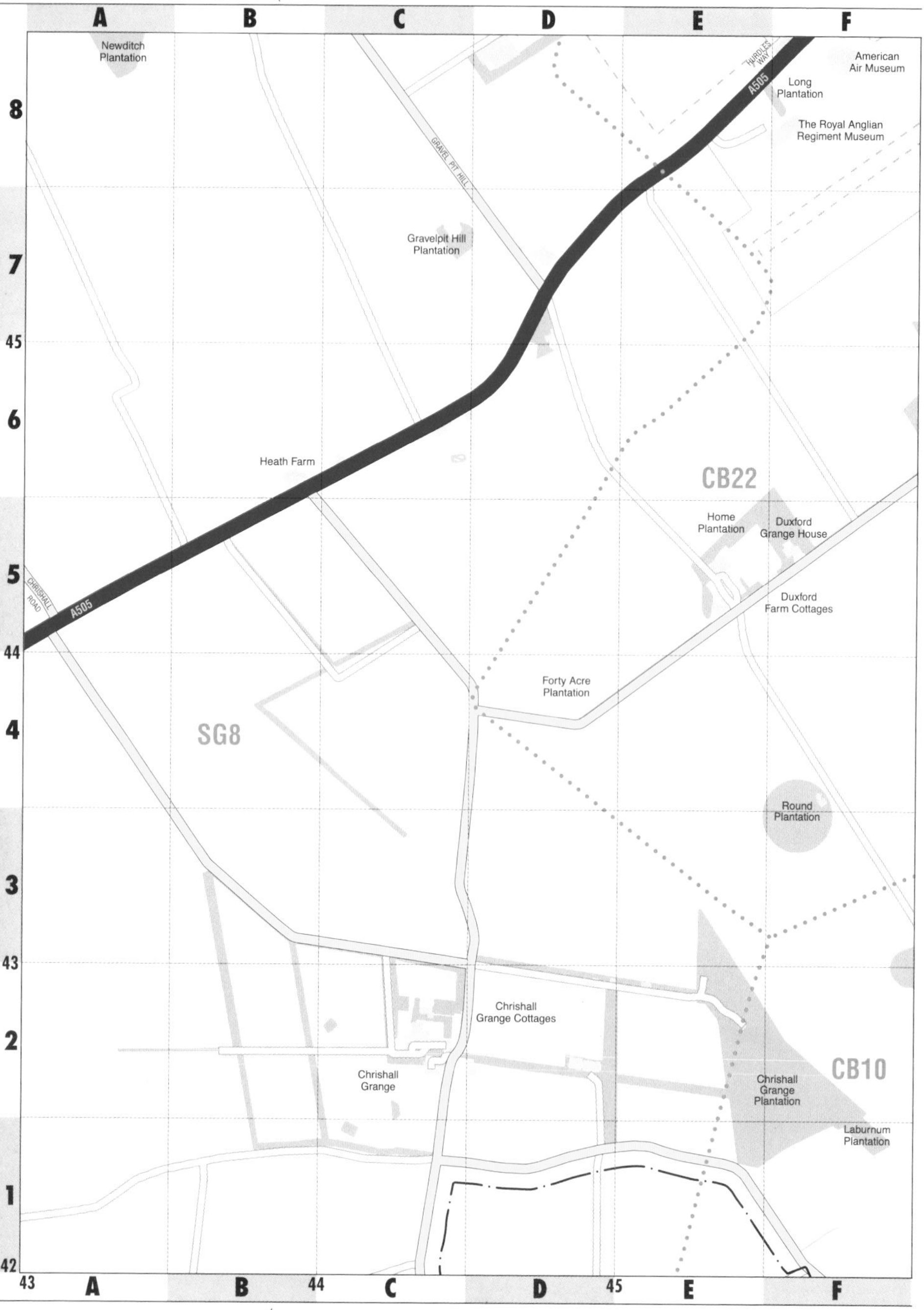

8

Newditch
Plantation

A505

Long
Plantation

American
Air Museum

The Royal Anglian
Regiment Museum

7

Gravelpit Hill
Plantation

GRAVEL PIT HILL

45

6

Heath Farm

CB22

Home
Plantation

Duxford
Grange House

5

A505

DRIFT HALL
ROAD

Duxford
Farm Cottages

44

4

SG8

Forty Acre
Plantation

Round
Plantation

3

43

2

Chrishall
Grange Cottages

Chrishall
Grange

Chrishall
Grange
Plantation

CB10

Laburnum
Plantation

1

42

43   A   B   44   C   D   45   E   F

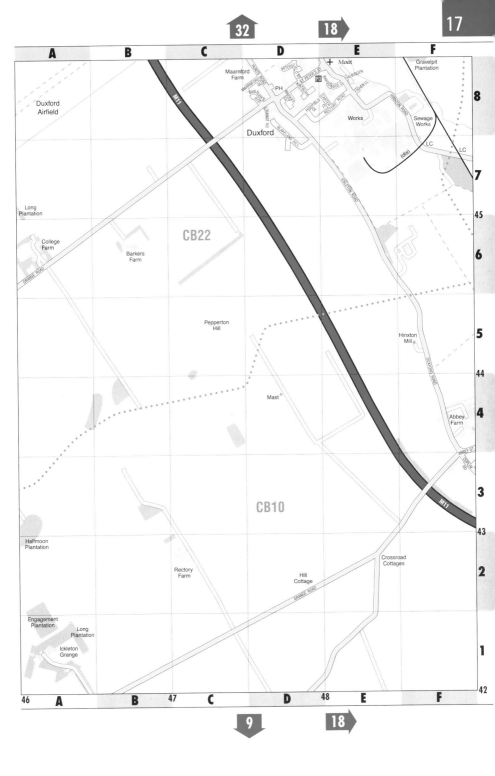

A   B   C   D   E   F

Duxford
Airfield

Maarnford
Farm

Moat

Gravelpit
Plantation

PH

Works

Duxford

8

Sewage
Works

(dis)   LC   LC

7

Long
Plantation

45

College
Farm

Barkers
Farm

CB22

6

GRANGE ROAD

Pepperton
Hill

5

Hinxton
Mill

44

Mast

4

Abbey
Farm

ABBEY ST

3

M11

43

Halfmoon
Plantation

Crossroad
Cottages

2

Rectory
Farm

Hill
Cottage

GRANGE ROAD

Engagement
Plantation

Long
Plantation

Ickleton
Grange

CB10

1

46   A   B   47   C   D   48   E   F   42

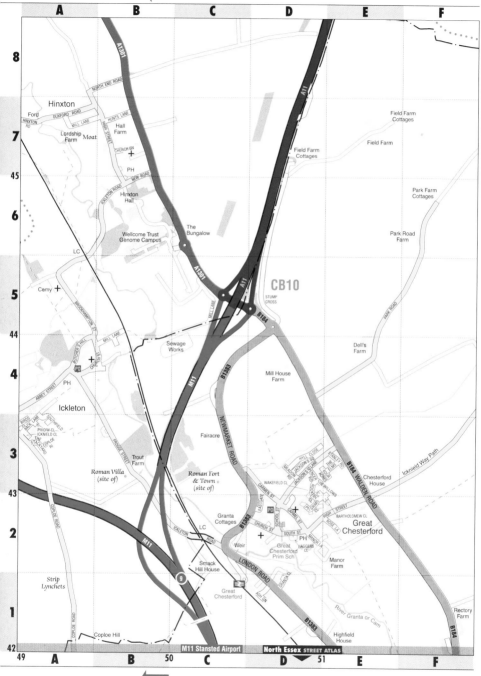

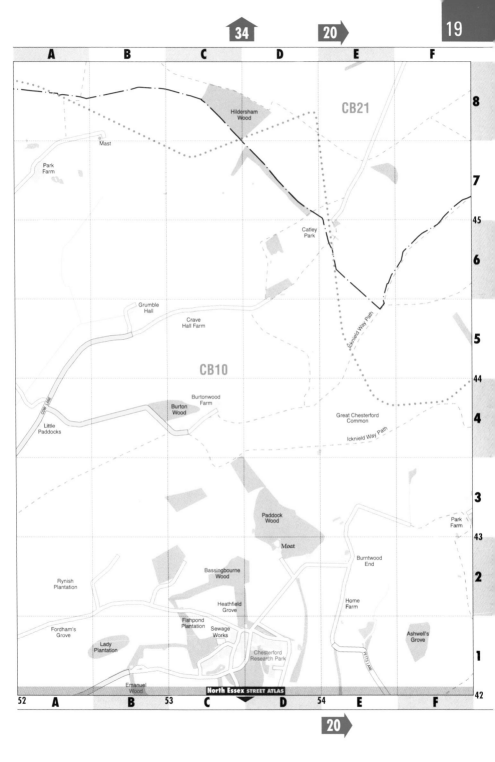

A B C D E F

8

CB21

Hildersham
Wood

Mast

Park
Farm

7

45

Catley
Park

6

Grumble
Hall

Crave
Hall Farm

5

Icknield Way Path

CB10

44

Burtonwood
Farm

BOW LANE

Burton
Wood

Great Chesterford
Common

4

Little
Paddocks

Icknield Way Path

3

Paddock
Wood

Park
Farm

43

Moat

Burntwood
End

2

Rynish
Plantation

Bassingbourne
Wood

Home
Farm

Heathfield
Grove

Fordham's
Grove

Fishpond
Plantation

Sewage
Works

Ashwell's
Grove

Lady
Plantation

Chesterford
Research Park

FITTS LANE

1

Emanuel
Wood

52 A B 53 C D 54 E F 42

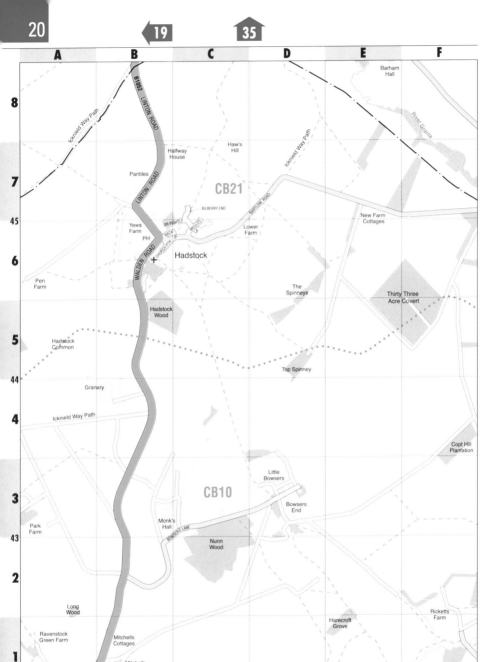

B1052 LINTON ROAD

Icknield Way Path

Barham
Hall

River Granta

Halfway
House

Haw's
Hill

Pantiles

Icknield Way Path

CB21

BILBERRY END

LINTON ROAD

BARTLOW ROAD

New Farm
Cottages

Yews
Farm

OR PIGHTLE

MOYES
LA

PH

BACK
LA

Lower
Farm

CHURCH PTH

Hadstock

WALDEN ROAD

Pen
Farm

The
Spinneys

Thirty Three
Acre Covert

Hadstock
Wood

Hadstock
Common

Top Spinney

Granary

Icknield Way Path

Copt Hill
Plantation

Little
Bowsers

CB10

Bowsers
End

Park
Farm

Monk's
Hall

BONHOEUSE LANE

Nunn
Wood

Ricketts
Farm

Long
Wood

Harecroft
Grove

Ravenstock
Green Farm

Mitchells
Cottages

Mitchells

Madge
Hobbs Wood

Ashdon Steet
Farm

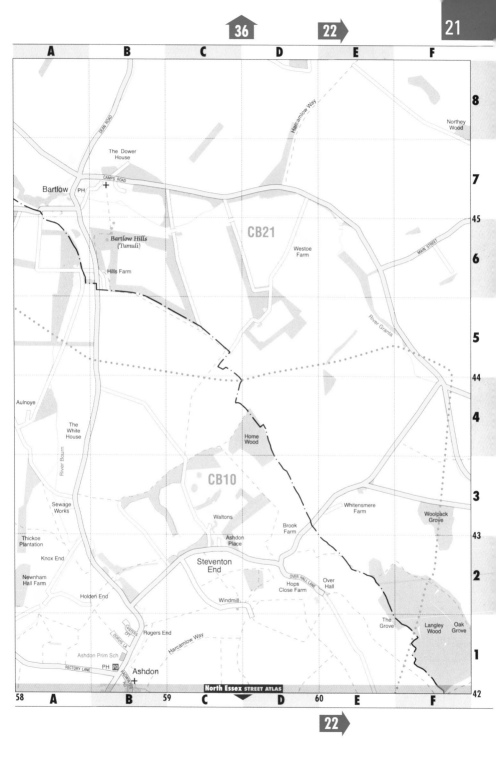

	A	B	C	D	E	F

8

Moat

Shardelow's
Farm

Northey
Wood

Moat

Grange
Farm

Mill
Green

7

Water
Tower

CB9

Barsey Farm
Moat

45

NEW ROAD

Tumulus

Priory
Farm

Lower
Farm

MAIN STREET

Carters
Farm

Priory
Plantation

6

Shudy
Camps Park

Lake
Plantation

DARDY HILL

HOOLEY CL

BLACKSMITHS LANE

Rumbold's
Chase Farm

Dairy
Farm

Shudy Camps +

CHURCH ROAD

Lordship
Farm

New
Plantation

HAVERHILL ROAD

Nosterfield
End

5

CB21

44

Park
Farm

HAVERHILL ROAD

4

Sewage
Works

BARTLOW ROAD

Hill
Farm

CLAYDON

HIGH ST

Castle Camps

Pond
Farm

PH +

3

Camps
Hall

Sangsters
Farm

CHURCH LANE

Castle
Camps
CE Prim Sch

PO

PARK LANE

43

Moat
Farm

2

Medieval Village
(site of)

+

Castle Camps
Motte &
Bailey

Castle
Farm

1

Langley
Wood

Camps
End

Little
Biggs
Farm

Fleet
Farm

Rectory
Farm

Coopers
Farm

42

61	A	B	62	C	D	63	E	F

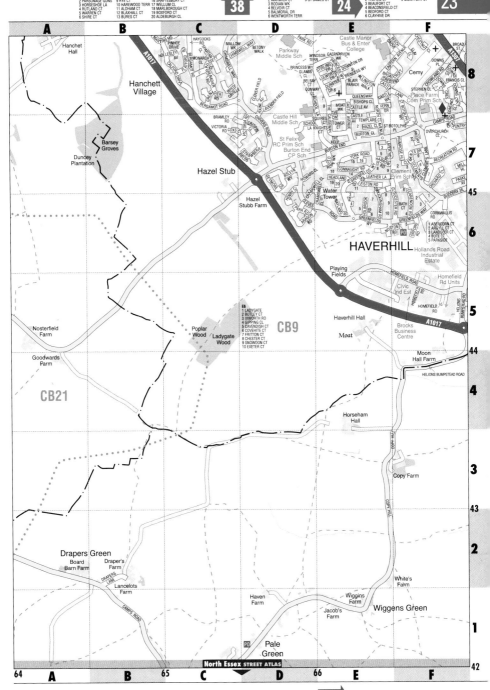

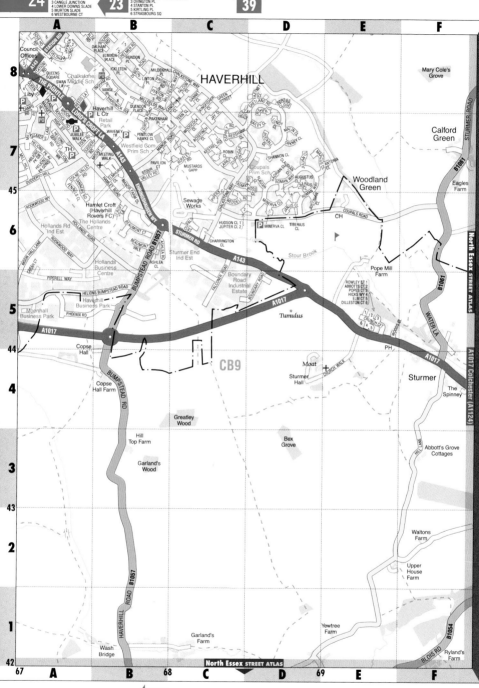

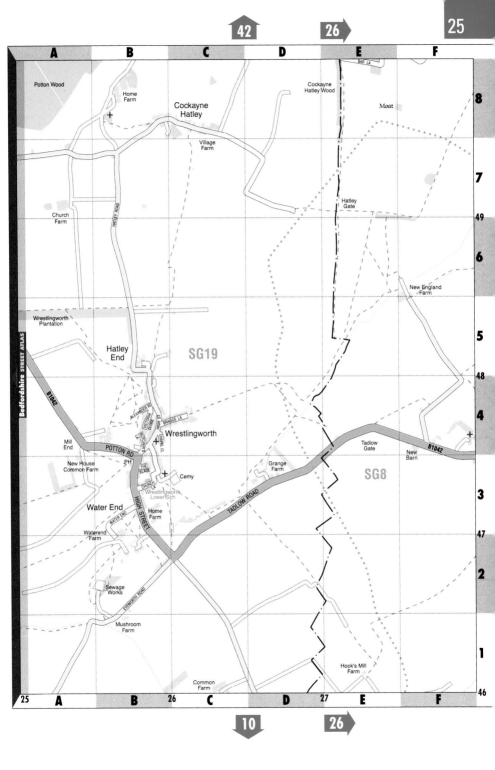

Potton Wood

Home Farm

Cockayne Hatley

Cockayne Hatley Wood

Moat

BAR LA

Village Farm

Hatley Gate

Church Farm

HATLEY ROAD

New England Farm

Wrestlingworth Plantation

Hatley End

SG19

B1042

Bedfordshire STREET ATLAS

ALEXANDER RD

BRAGGS LA

VICTORIA RD

GT DOB

LT HIGH

CHAPEL CL

Mill End

POTTON RD

BUTCHER'S

Wrestlingworth

Tadlow Gate

New Barn

B1042

SG8

New House Common Farm

PH

THE BLADE

Cemy

Grange Farm

TADLOW ROAD

CHURCH

LA

HIGH STREET

Water End

WATER END

Wrestlingworth Lower Sch

Home Farm

Waterend Farm

Sewage Works

EYEWORTH ROAD

Mushroom Farm

Hook's Mill Farm

Common Farm

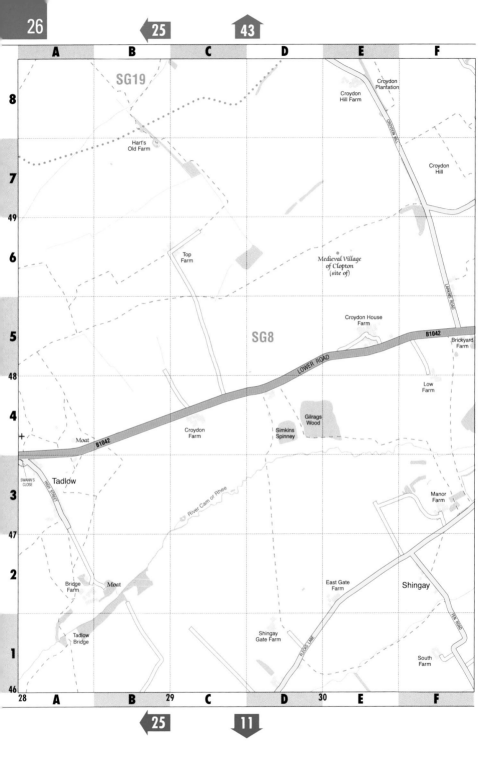

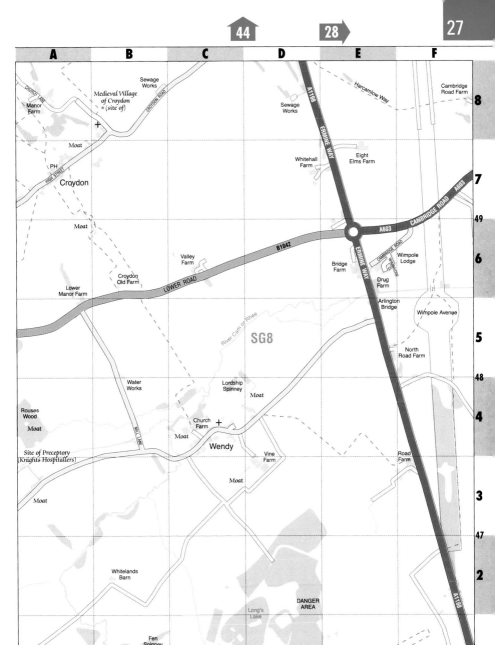

CHURCH LANE

Manor Farm

Sewage Works

Medieval Village of Croydon (site of)

CROYDON ROAD

Harcamlow Way

Cambridge Road Farm

8

Moat

PH

HIGH STREET

Croydon

A1198

ERMINE WAY

Sewage Works

Whitehall Farm

Eight Elms Farm

7

Moat

A603

CAMBRIDGE ROAD

49

B1042

A603

Valley Farm

LOWER ROAD

Bridge Farm

CAMBRIDGE ROAD

WOODBRIDGE

ERMINE WAY

Wimpole Lodge

Drug Farm

6

Croydon Old Farm

Lower Manor Farm

Arlington Bridge

Wimpole Avenue

River Cam or Rhee

SG8

North Road Farm

5

Water Works

Lordship Spinney

Moat

48

Rouses Wood

Moat

MILL LANE

Church Farm

Moat

Wendy

4

Site of Preceptory (Knights Hospitallers)

Moat

Vine Farm

Road Farm

Moat

Moat

3

47

Whitelands Barn

DANGER AREA

2

Long's Lake

A1198

Fen Spinney

1

Airfield (dis)

46

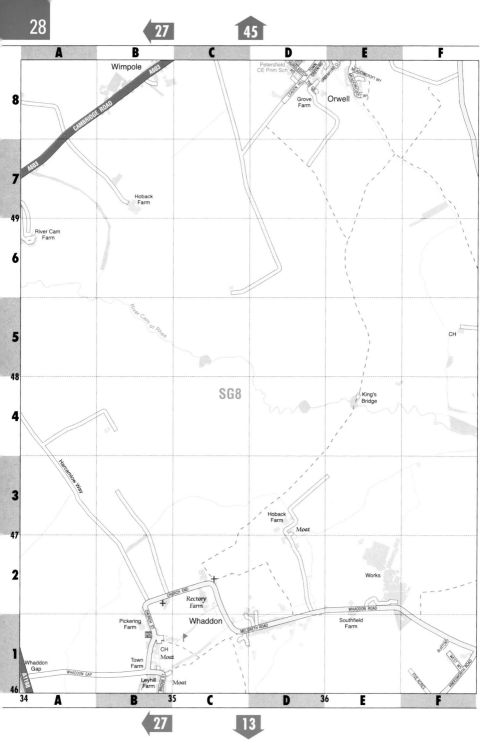

Wimpole

CAMBRIDGE ROAD

A603

A603

Petersfield
CE Prim Sch

Orwell

MEADOWCROFT WY

MEADOWCROFT WY

Grove
Farm

Hoback
Farm

River Cam
Farm

River Cam or Rhee

CH

SG8

King's
Bridge

Harcamlow Way

Hoback
Farm

Moat

Works

CHURCH END

Rectory
Farm

Whaddon

WHADDON ROAD

Southfield
Farm

Pickering
Farm

MELDRETH ROAD

CHURCH ST

PO

CH
Moat

Town
Farm

BRIDGE ST

Leyhill
Farm

Moat

Whaddon
Gap

A1198

WHADDON GAP

BURTONS

WEST WY

TIPE ACRES

KNEESWORTH ROAD

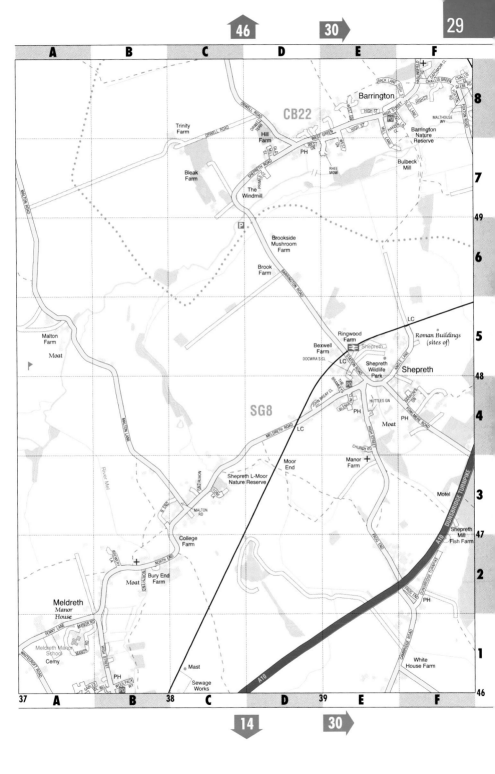

A B C D E F

8

7

49

6

5

48

4

3

47

2

1

46

GLEBE ROAD
LC
Foxton Road LC
Sewage Works
College Farm
BARRINGTON ROAD

River Cam of Rhee

Hoffers Brook Farm
Hoffer Bridge
Manor Farm

ROYSTON RD
A10

CAMBRIDGE ROAD

Strip Lynchets
Rowley's Hill

LC Foxton

Hoffer Brook

MILL CL
FENTON ROAD
Bury Farm
Moat
Mortimer's Farm

CB22

PH
Windmill
HIGH STREET
BARONS LA
HIGH ST
MORTIMERS
FOWLMERE ROAD
ST LAURENCE RD
Foxton

Beech Tree Farm
MALTING LA
CLAYTON LANE
Stocks Farm
WEST VIEW
SHEPRETH ROAD
HARDMAN RD
EDIS CL
PO
Foxton Prim Sch
ILLINGWORTH WY
ROWLANDS CL
HILLFIELD

A10
ROYSTON ROAD

West Hill

FOWLMERE ROAD

CAMBRIDGE ROAD

SHEPRETH ROAD

Rushmoor Plantation
Field Farm

SG8

Cerny

North Farm
Lower Farm
LONG LANE

Lower Farm
Fowlmere

RAYNER'S CL
RECTORY LA
CASSANDER CL
Works
THE MACT
B1368
THRIPLOW ROAD

40 A B 41 C D 42 E F

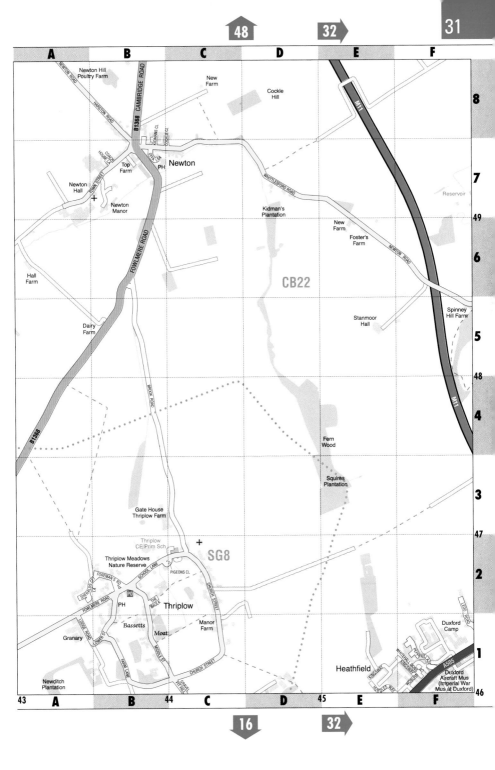

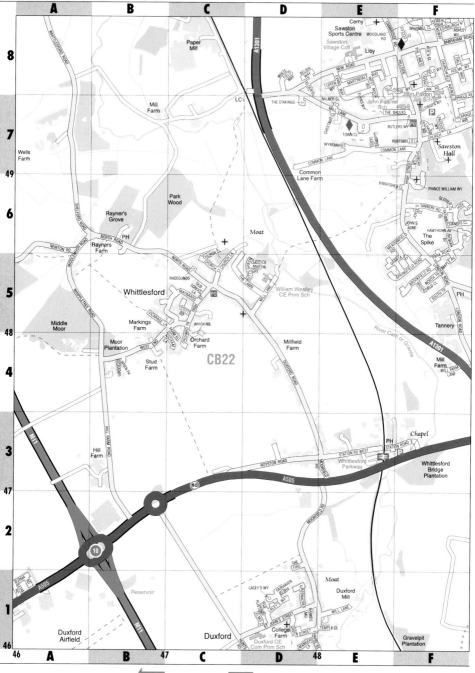

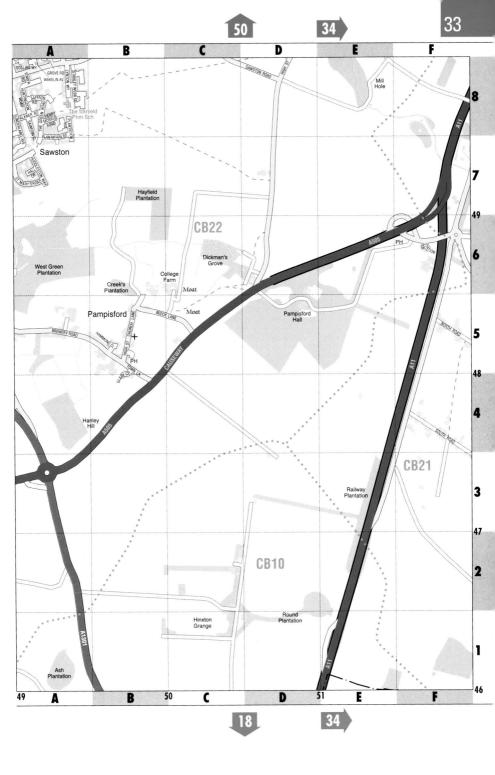

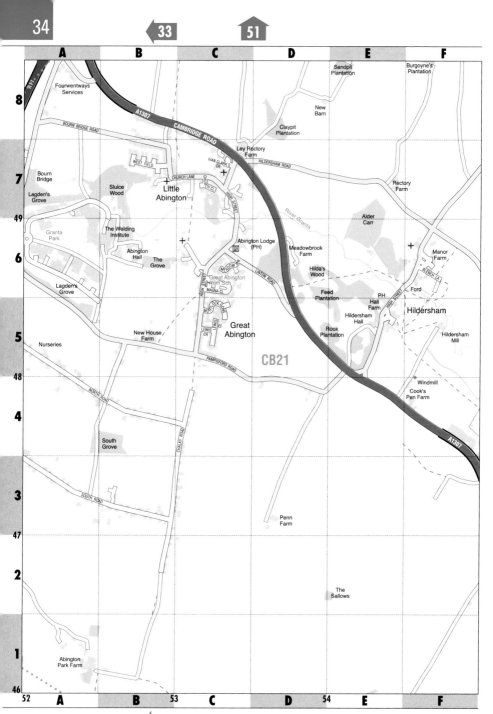

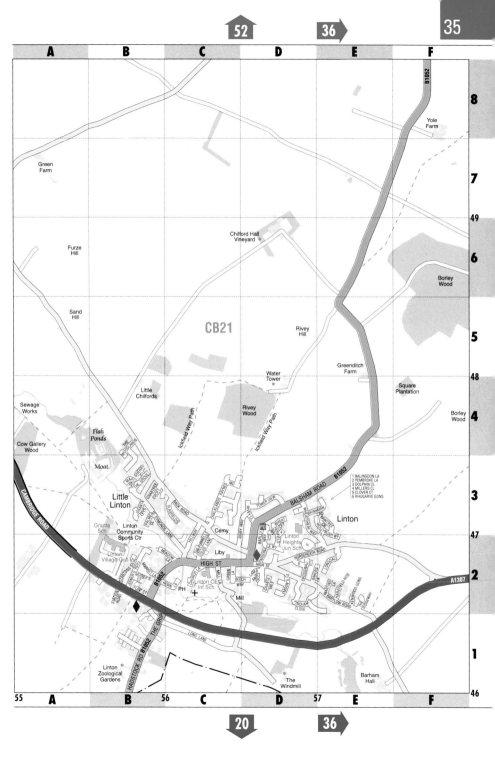

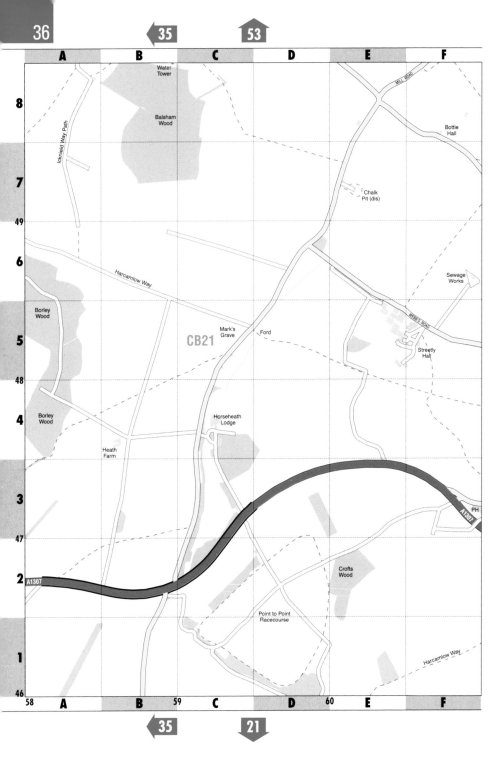

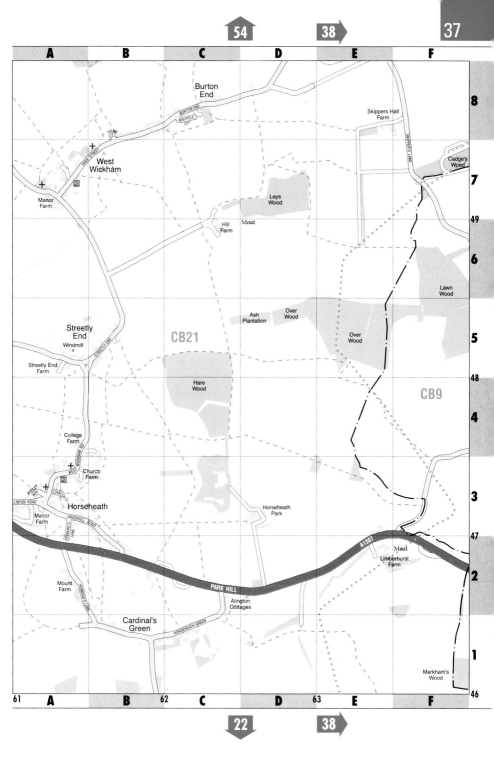

A B C D E F

8

CB21

The New Plantation

Dowsett Wood

Moat

Glebe Plantation

Smoothies Plantation

WEST END LANE

Cadge's Wood

North Wood

Tuffill's Plantation

Hunts Park Farm

7

The Spinney

WITHERSFIELD ROAD

49

Exhibition Farm

Littley Wood

6

High Noon Farm

SNOW'S LANE

Lawn Wood

Lawn Farm

Moat

Charity Farm

CB9

ROSE HILL

BURTON HILL

Paradise Farm

5

Bitton's Farm

CHURLOW ROAD

48

Silver Street Farm

SILVER STREET   HORSEHEATH ROAD

PH

HOLLOW HILL

Withersfield

Lilley Farm

TURNPIKE HILL

Recreation Ground

4

HOMESTALL DR

CHURCH STREET

Church Farm

QUEENE STREET

Hall Farm

Norney Plantation

Sewage Works

3

Howe Wood

47

HALES BARN RD

LOPHAMS CL 1
GANWICK CL 2
MONEYPIECE CL 3
SPERLING DR 4

Spring Grove Farm

A1307

APPROACH COTTAGES

FOREST GLADE

LEE CLOSE

2

A1307

Meldham Bridge

Superstore

LAUREL CL

HAWTHORN RD

CARLTON CL

TRUNDLEY CL

CHAPPLE DR

Hanchet House

SHARDLOW CL

BAINES CONEY

HAWTHORN RD

ROWAN CL

WILLIAM BLAKE CT

WITHERSFIELD ROAD A1307

ARRENDENE RD

New Cangle Com. Prim Sch

BANHAM MS 1
BENACRE 2
ELVEDON WY 3
FIELD VW 4

A1307

Hanchet End

HEMPSTEAD ROAD

HENDERSON'S WY

MUNNINGS CL

CAMBRIDGE CL

TOWN END CLOSE

WATERS EDGE

1

HANCHET END LANE

HOPTON RI

MELLIS

NOTLEY CL

ST MARTINS MEWS

SAXHAM CT

OLBY CL

BRYBANK

BUNNY

VETCH CL

CHIMSWELL

SWAN WALK

WILLOW

BRAMBLE

POPLAR

HONEYSUCKLE

CAMBRIDGE

EASTERN AV

46

Hanchet Hall

APPLE ACRE RD

SORREL WALK

CATKIN CL

Playing Fields

BEECH DR

64   A   B   65   C   D   66   E   F

D1
1 CONSTABLE RD
2 RUSKIN CL
3 STUBBS CL
4 REYNOLD'S CL
5 TEASEL CL

F1
1 MONEYPIECE CL
2 SHADOWBUSH CL
3 MARKHAMS CL
4 BLACKMORE CL
5 CARDINAL WY
6 CHAPLAINS CL

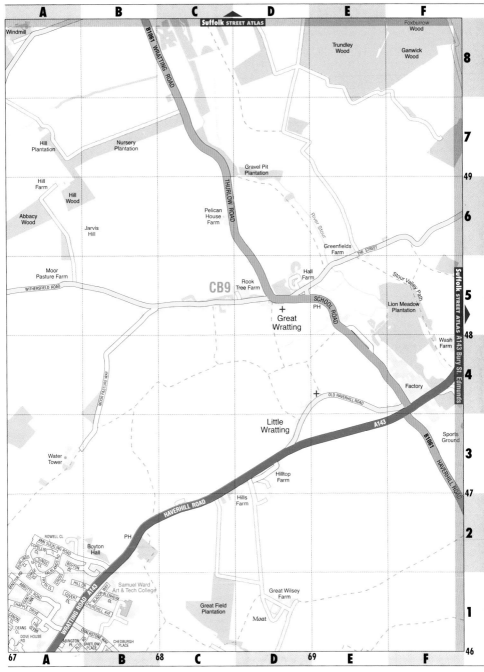

Windmill

Foxburrow Wood

Trundley Wood

Ganwick Wood

Hill Plantation

Nursery Plantation

Hill Farm

Hill Wood

Gravel Pit Plantation

Abbacy Wood

Jarvis Hill

Pelican House Farm

THURLOW ROAD

B1061 WRATTING ROAD

River Stour

Greenfields Farm

THE STREET

Moor Pasture Farm

WITHERSFIELD ROAD

CB9

Rook Tree Farm

Hall Farm

Stour Valley Path

Lion Meadow Plantation

+ Great Wratting

PH

SCHOOL ROAD

Wash Farm

Factory

Suffolk STREET ATLAS A143 Bury St. Edmunds

MOOR PASTURE WAY

+ OLD HAVERHILL ROAD

A143

B1061

Little Wratting

Water Tower

Sports Ground

HAVERHILL ROAD

Hilltop Farm

Hills Farm

ROWELL CL

ANN SUCKLING ROAD

CORELLI CL

GOLDINGS

PALKLA

Boyton Hall

PH

HAVERHILL ROAD

BOYTON

HILL DR

BLENHEIM

BEATON

COLVERT

CHURCHILL AVE

Samuel Ward Art & Tech College

Great Wilsey Farm

CHAPPLE DRIVE

CANON CL

THE GLEBE

DEANS CL

DOVE HOUSE RD

WRATTING ROAD A143

ABINGTON PL

CHALKSTONE WAY

BARTLOW PLACE

CHEDBURGH PLACE

Great Field Plantation

Moat

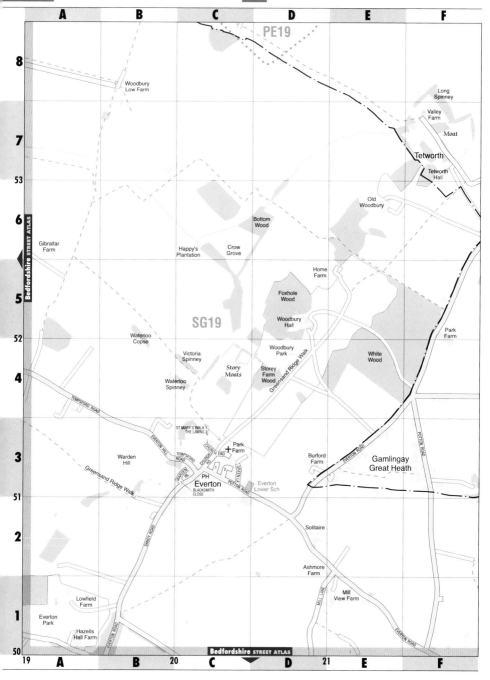

PE19

8

Woodbury
Low Farm

Long
Spinney

Valley
Farm

7

Moat

Tetworth

53

Tetworth
Hall

Old
Woodbury

6

Gibraltar
Farm

Bottom
Wood

Happy's
Plantation

Crow
Grove

Home
Farm

5

Foxhole
Wood

Woodbury
Hall

Park
Farm

52

Waterloo
Copse

SG19

Victoria
Spinney

Woodbury
Park

White
Wood

Waterloo
Spinney

Story
Moats

Storey
Farm
Wood

Greensand Ridge Walk

4

TEMPSFORD ROAD

ST MARY'S WALK 1
THE LAWNS 2

Park
Farm

Burford
Farm

EVERTON ROAD

**Gamlingay
Great Heath**

3

Warden
Hill

EVERTON HILL

TEMPSFORD
ROAD

CHURCH END

CHURCH RD

GREEN END

POTTON ROAD

Greensand Ridge Walk

WARDEN HILL

PH
Everton

BLACKSMITH
CLOSE

Everton
Lower Sch

POTTON ROAD

51

Solitaire

2

SANDY ROAD

Ashmore
Farm

MILL LANE

1

Lowfield
Farm

Mill
View Farm

Everton
Park

Hazells
Hall Farm

EVERTON ROAD

EVERTON ROAD

50

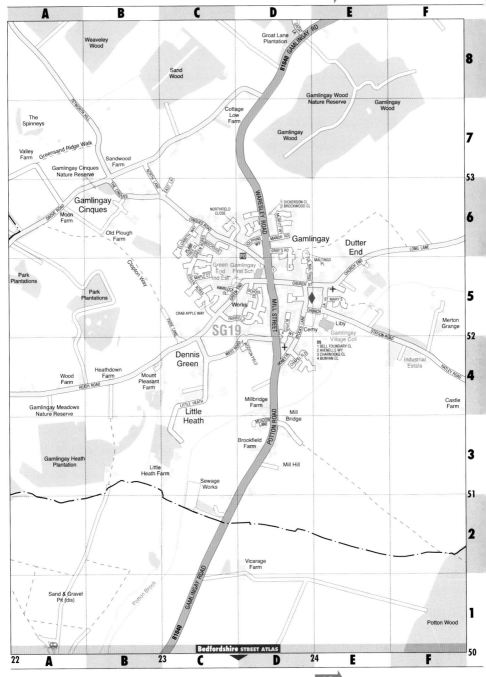

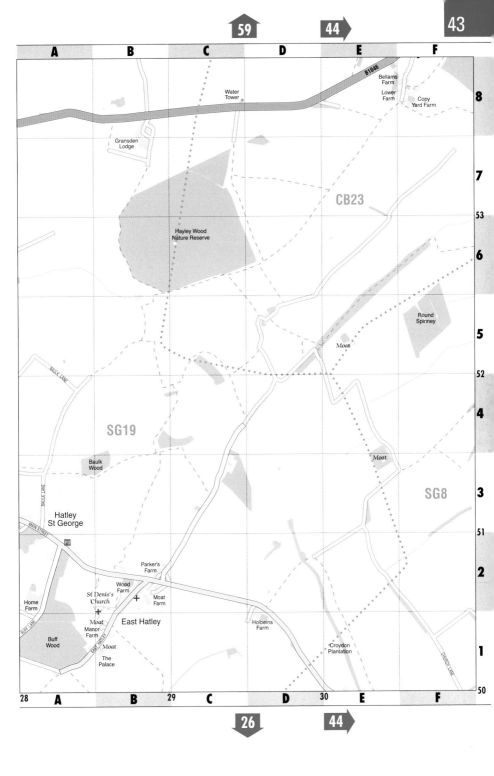

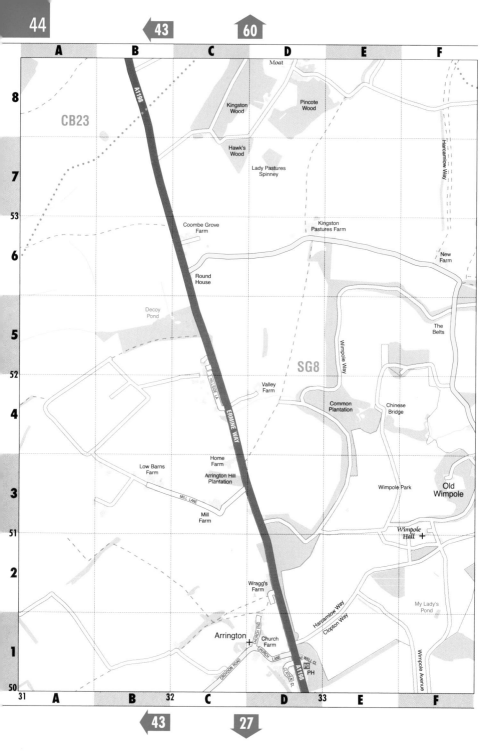

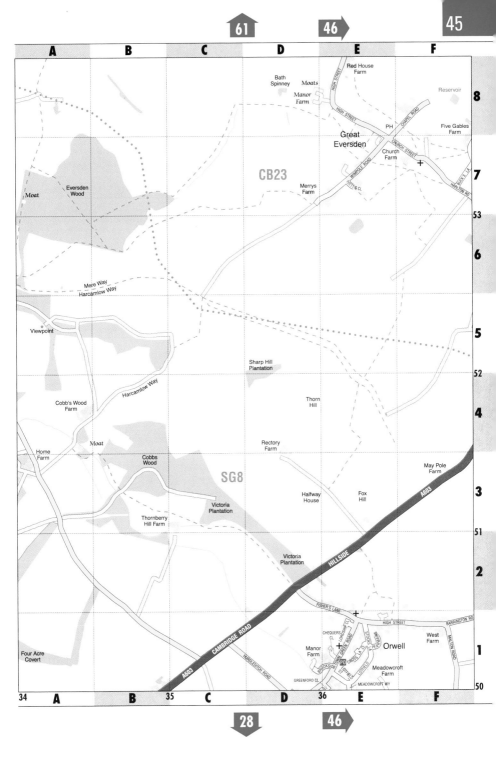

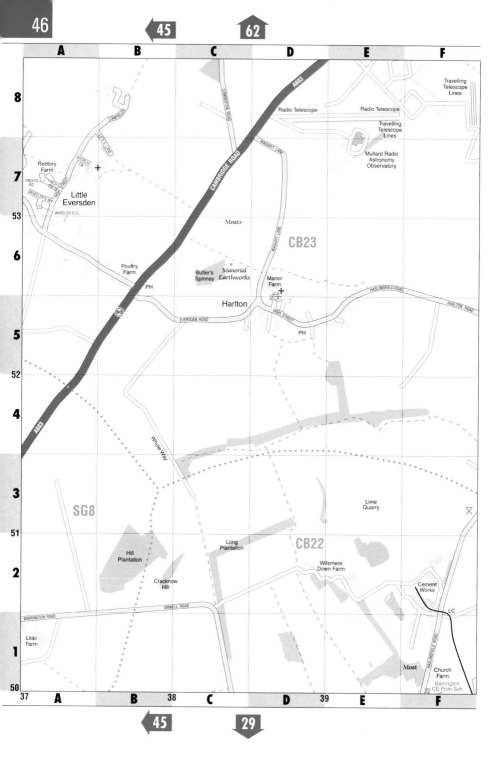

45
62

A   B   C   D   E   F

8

A603

Travelling
Telescope
Lines

Radio Telescope   Radio Telescope

Travelling
Telescope
Lines

7

Rectory
Farm

CAMBRIDGE ROAD

WASHPIT LANE

LOWER LOG

LACE'S LANE

CHURCH LA

FINCH STREET

FINCH'S
RD

FINCH'S
FIELD

WHEELER'S WY

Little
Eversden

WHEELER'S CL

53

Mullard Radio
Astronomy
Observatory

Moats

WASHPIT LANE

CB23

6

Poultry
Farm

PH

Butler's
Spinney

Manorial
Earthworks

Manor
Farm

COACH
DRIFT

HASLINGFIELD ROAD

HARLTON ROAD

60

EVERSDEN ROAD

Harlton

HIGH STREET

5

PH

52

4

A603

Whole Way

3

SG8

Lime
Quarry

51

Long
Plantation

CB22

2

Hill
Plantation

Cracknow
Hill

Wilsmere
Down Farm

Cement
Works

HASLINGFIELD ROAD

LC

ORWELL ROAD

BARRINGTON ROAD

1

Lilac
Farm

Moat

Church
Farm

Barrington
CE Prim Sch

50

37   A   B   38   C   D   39   E   F

45
29

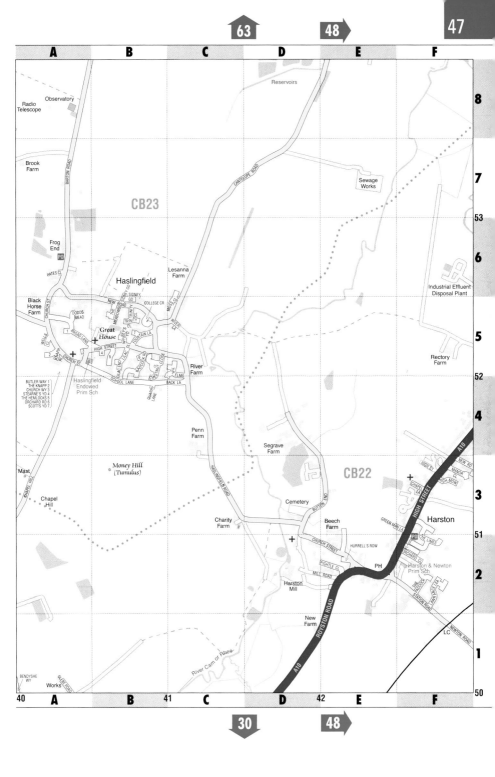

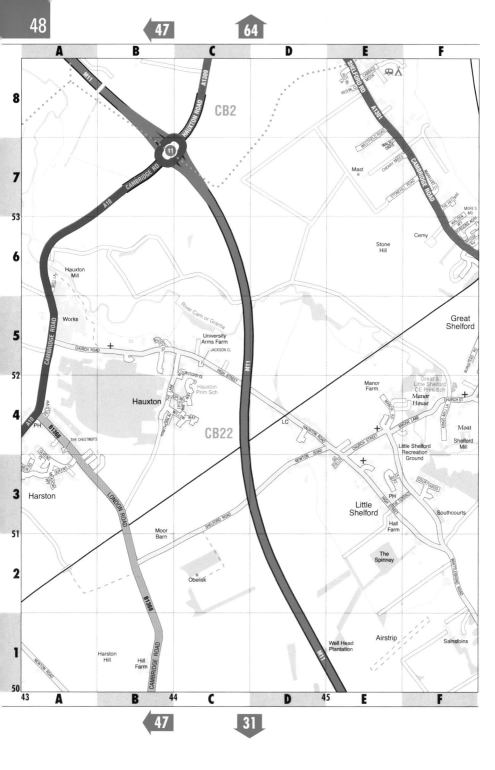

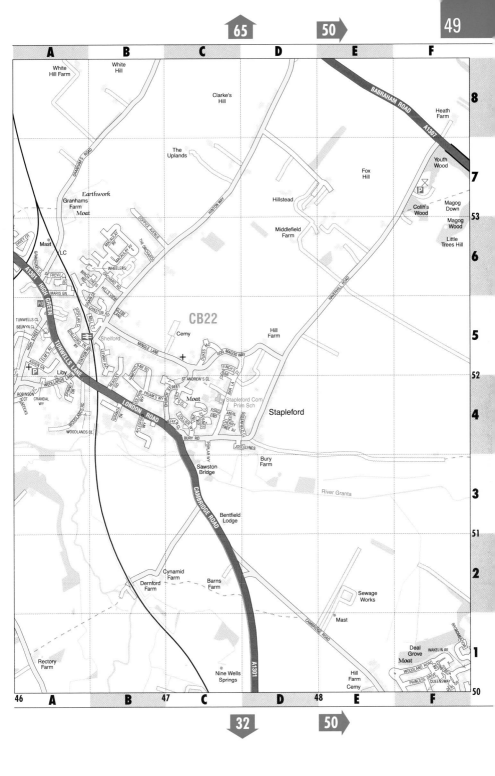

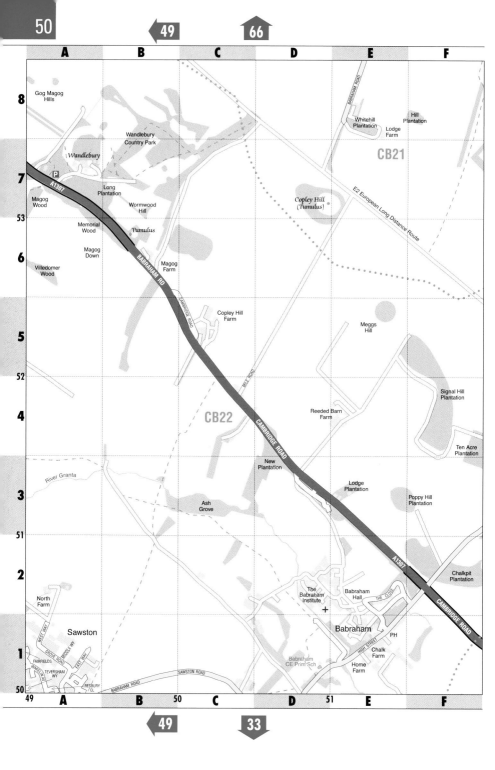

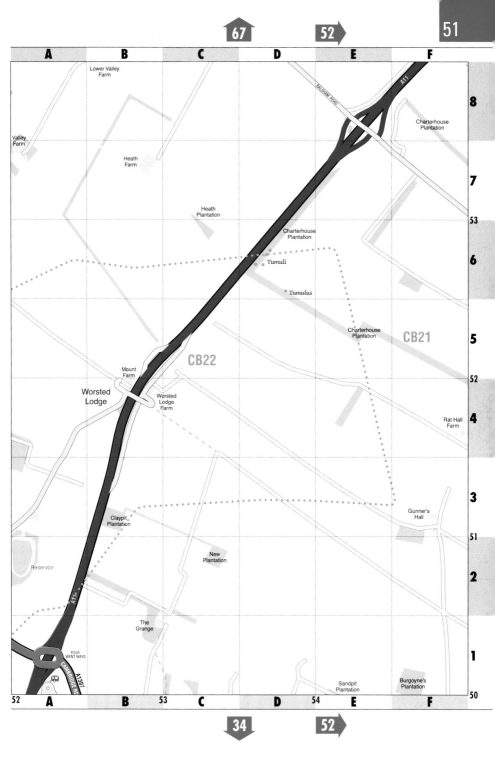

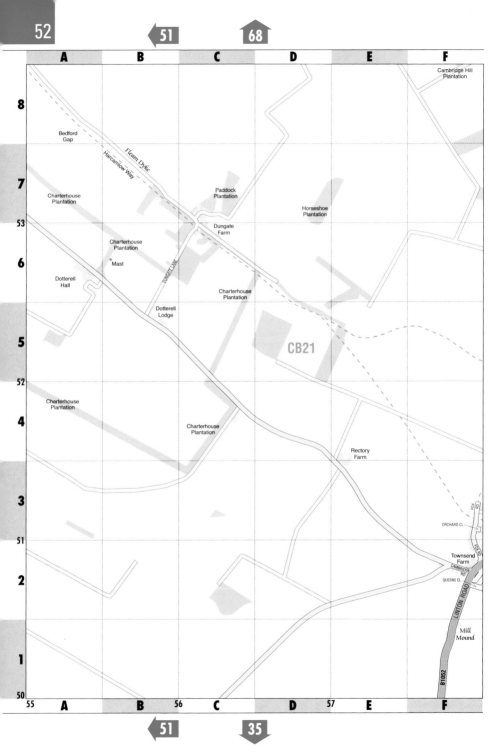

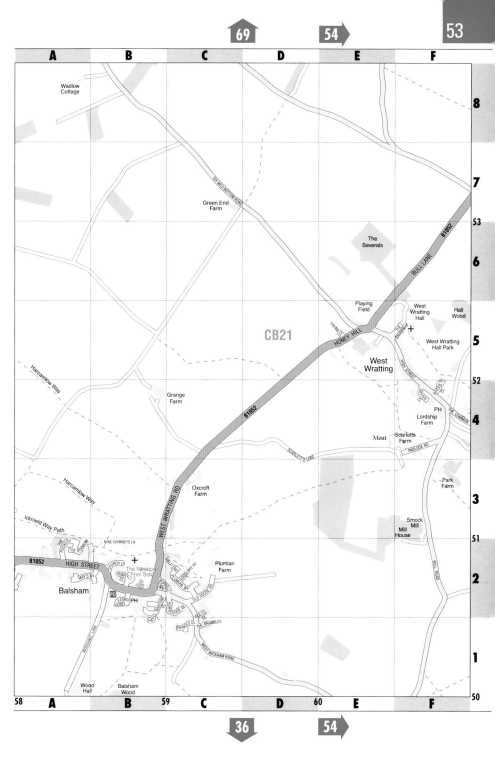

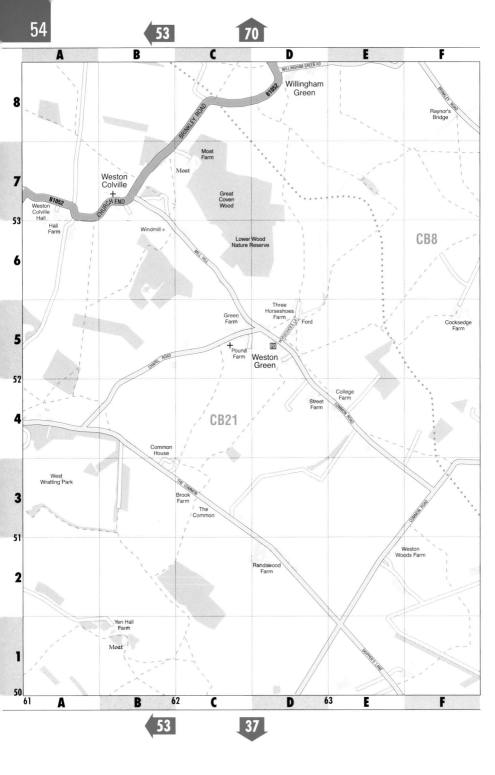

Willingham Green

WILLINGHAM GREEN RD

B1052

Raynor's Bridge

BRINKLEY ROAD

Moat Farm

Moat

Weston Colville

CHURCH END

B1052

Weston Colville Hall

Hall Farm

Great Coven Wood

Windmill

Lower Wood Nature Reserve

CB8

MILL HILL

CB21

Green Farm

Three Horseshoes Farm

Ford

HORSESHOES LA

Cocksedge Farm

CHAPEL ROAD

Pound Farm

PO

Weston Green

College Farm

Street Farm

COMMON ROAD

Common House

West Wratting Park

THE COMMON

Brook Farm

The Common

Randswood Farm

Weston Woods Farm

COMMON ROAD

Yen Hall Farm

Moat

SKIPPER'S LANE

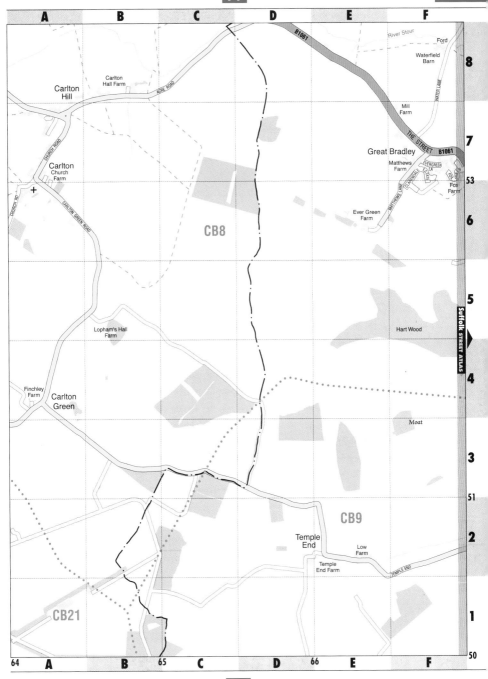

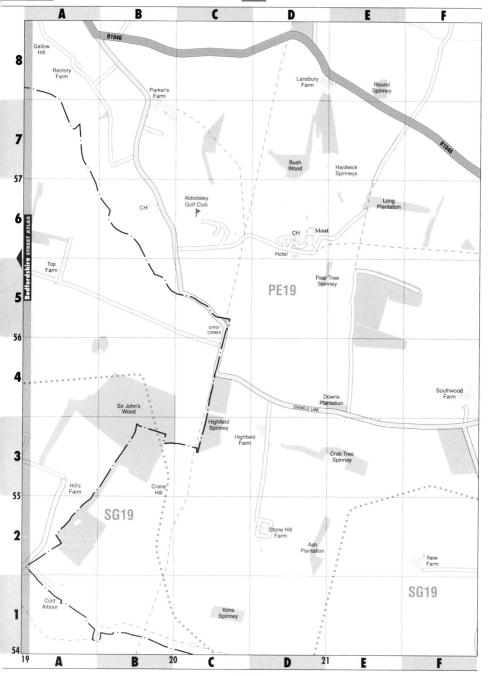

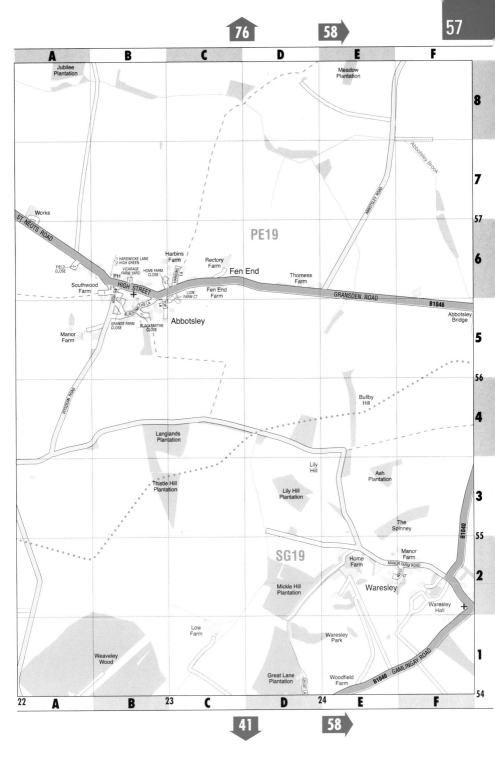

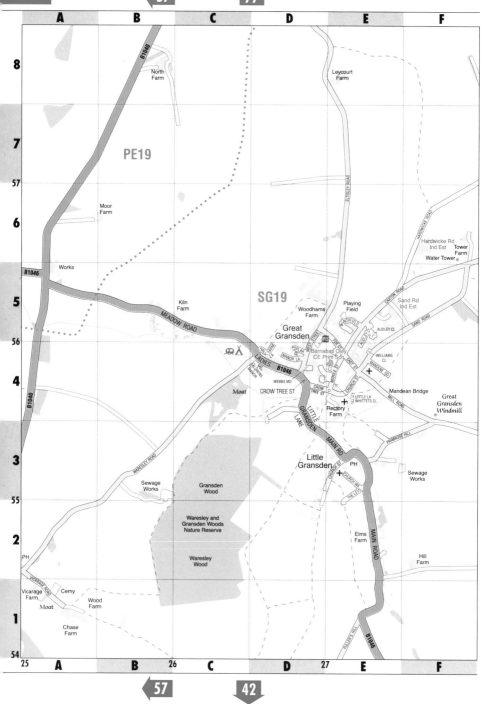

8

7

57

6

5

56

4

3

55

2

1

54

A B C D E F

PE19

B1040

North Farm

Moor Farm

Works

B1046

Kiln Farm

MEADOW ROAD

SG19

Leycourt Farm

ELTISLEY ROAD

Hardwicke Rd Ind Est
Tower Farm
Water Tower

Sand Rd Ind Est

CAXTON ROAD

SAND ROAD

Woodhams Farm

Playing Field

Great Gransden

WINCH HILL

POPLAR RD

MANOR LA

EAST ST

HALL ST

HIGH ST

B1046

Barnabas Oley
CE Prim Sch

WEBBS MD

CROW TREE ST

CROW TREE ST

AUDLEY CL

WILLIAMS CL

MANDENE RD

CHURCH ST

Mandean Bridge

MILL ROAD

Great Gransden Windmill

LADIES

HL THS

THE MANOR

Moat

1 LITTLE LA
2 WHITTETS CL

Rectory Farm

LITTLE GRANSDEN LANE

MAIN RD

PRIMROSE HILL

WARESLEY ROAD

Sewage Works

Gransden Wood

Waresley and Gransden Woods Nature Reserve

Waresley Wood

Little Gransden

GROVE ST

CHURCH WK

THE LEYS

PH

Sewage Works

Elms Farm

Hill Farm

MAIN ROAD

PH

VICARAGE ROAD

Vicarage Farm

Cemy

Moat

Wood Farm

Chase Farm

B1040

FULLERS HILL

B1046

A B C D E F

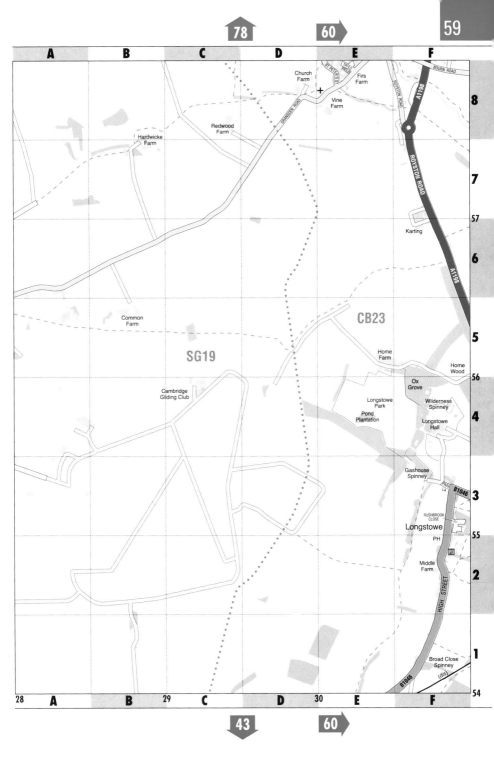

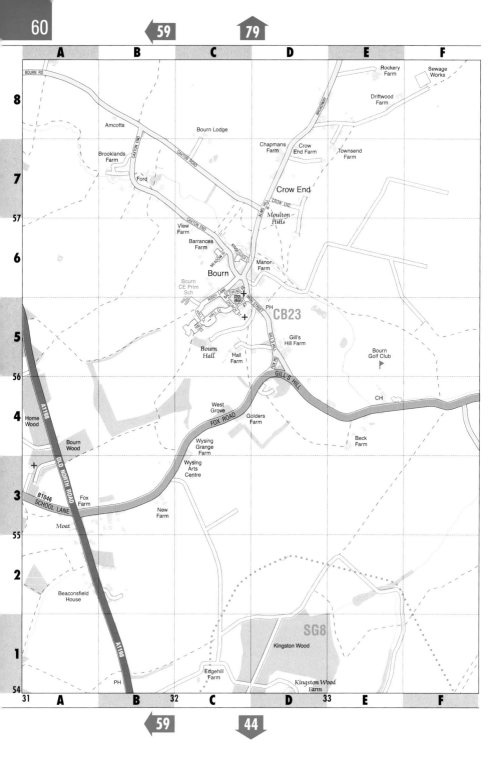

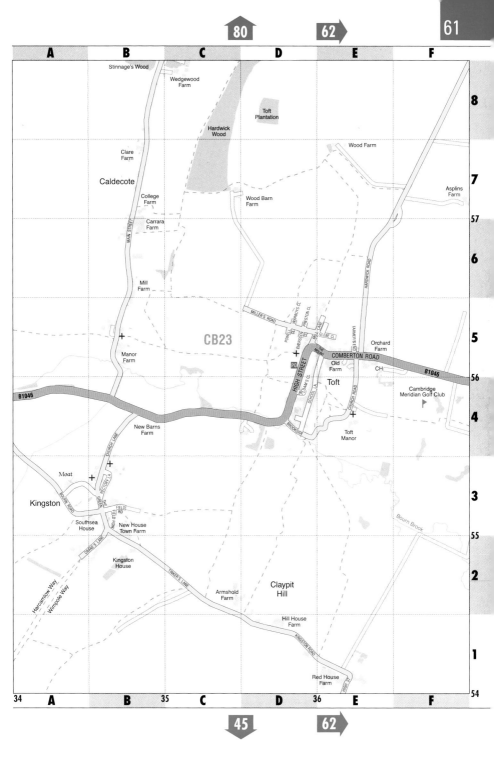

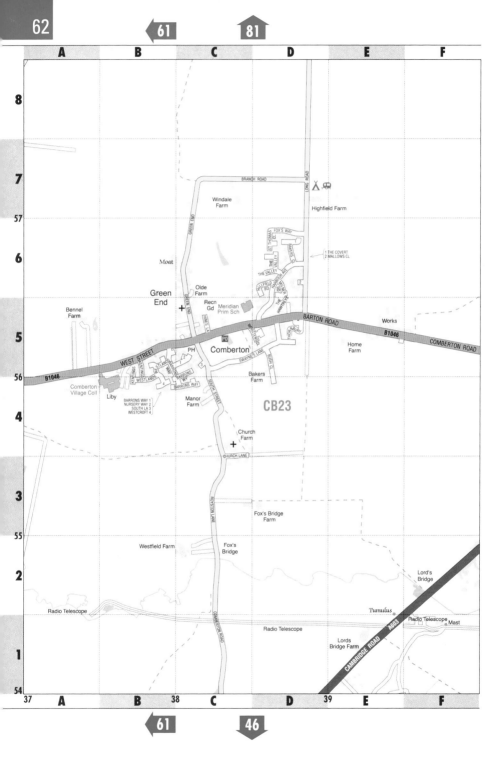

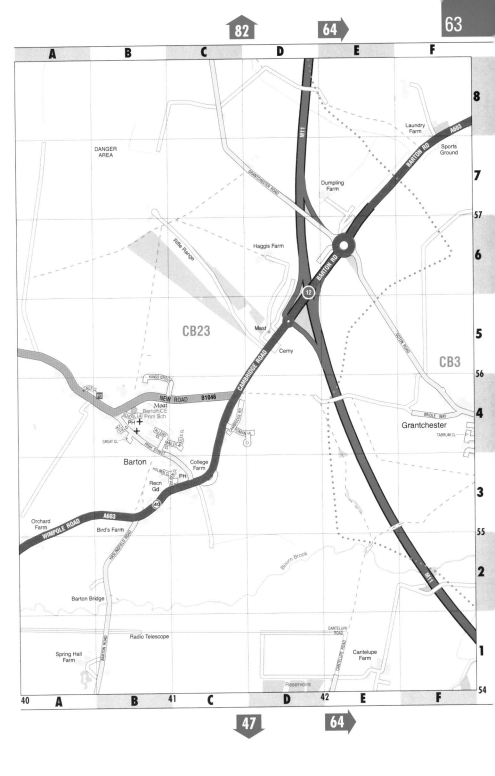

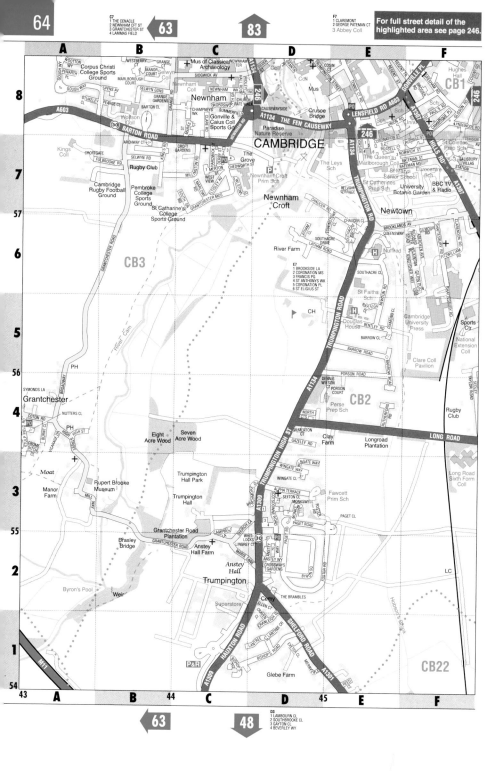

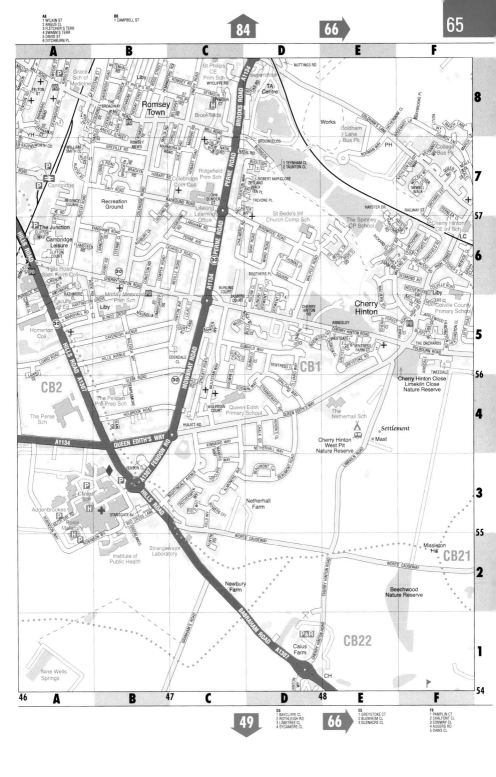

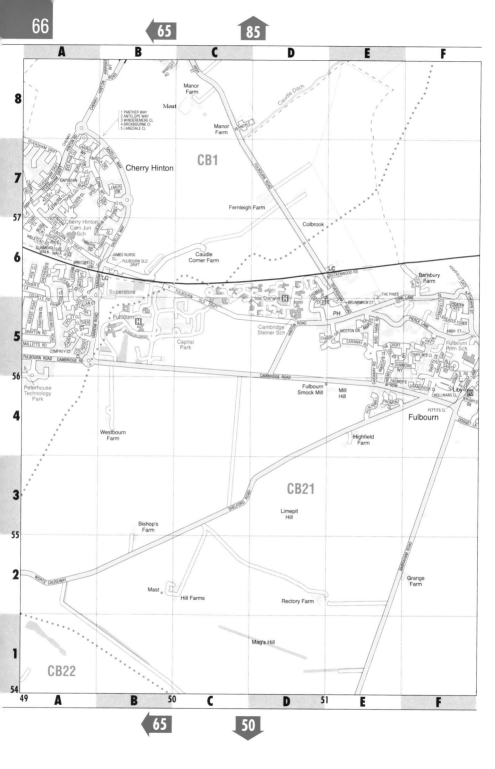

CB1

8

Manor Farm

Moat

Manor Farm

1 PANTHER WAY
2 ANTELOPE WAY
3 WINDERMERE CL
4 BROXBOURNE CI
5 LANGDALE CL

Caudle Ditch

7

Cherry Hinton

57

Fernleigh Farm

Colbrook

Cherry Hinton Com Jun Sch

6

James Nurse CL

Caudle Corner Farm

LC

Breckenwood Rd

Barnbury Farm

Superstore

Charles Darwin

The Pines

Brunswick Ct

Oval Lane

Greater Foxes

Greater Foxes

Fulbourn

PH

PH

Cambridge Steiner Sch

Weston Gr

Caraway Rd

Pierce Lane

High St

5

Capital Park

The Croft

Chaplin's Cl

Fulbourn Prim Sch

Mallets Rd

Comfrey Ct

Fulbourn Road   Cambridge Road

56

Cambridge Road

Peterhouse Technology Park

Fulbourn Smock Mill

Mill Hill

Hollmans Cl

Pettits Cl

Grandridge

Liby

Fulbourn

4

Westbourn Farm

Highfield Farm

Dogget La

CB21

3

Limepit Hill

Shelford Road

Bishop's Farm

55

Barnham Road

2

Worts' Causeway

Mast

Hill Farms

Rectory Farm

Grange Farm

1

CB22

Mag's Hill

54

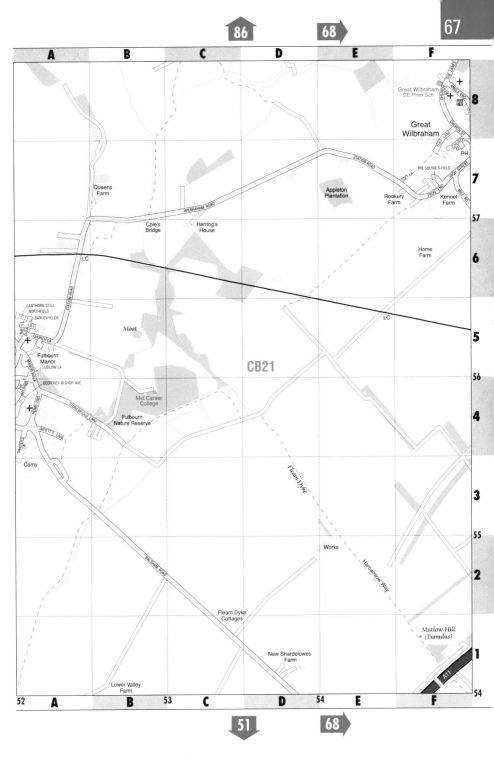

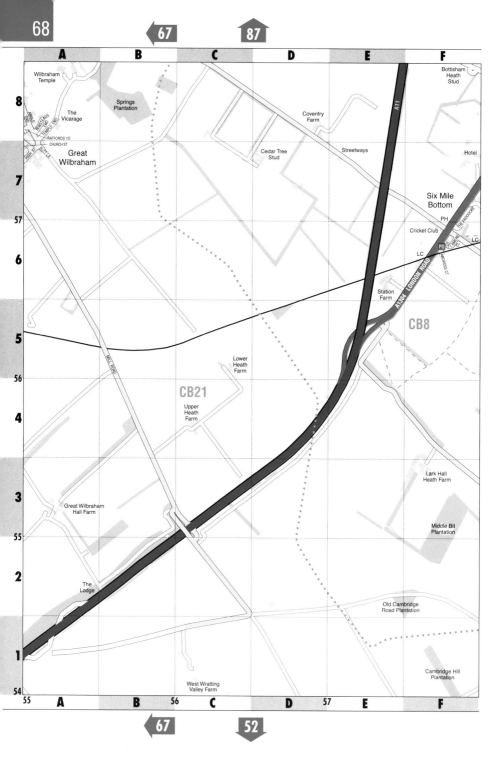

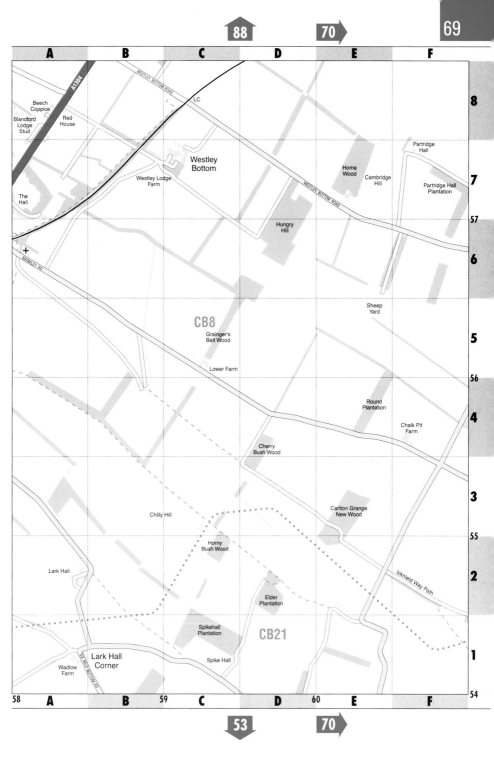

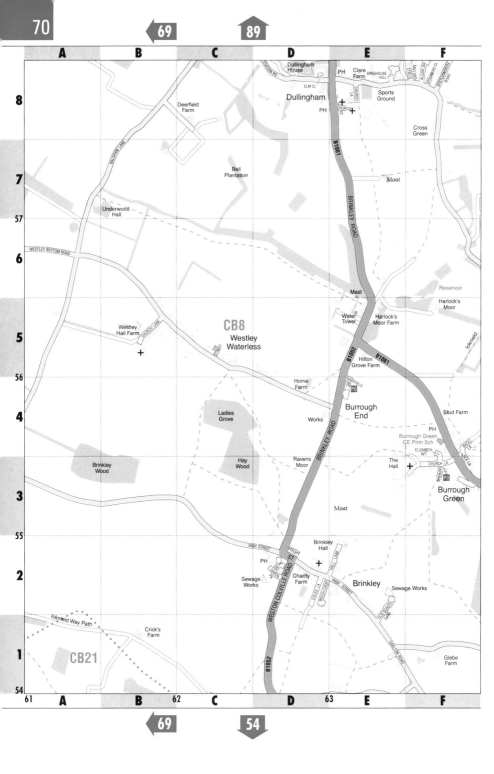

A B C D E F

8

7

57

6

5

56

4

3

55

2

1

54

STATION RD
Dullingham House
PH
Clare Farm
BAKEHOUSE HILL
Dullingham
ELM CL
PH
Sports Ground
CHURCH CL
Cross Green

Deerfield Farm

BALSHAM LANE

Bell Plantation

Underwood Hall

B1061

BRINKLEY ROAD

Moat

WESTLEY BOTTOM ROAD

Mast
Reservoir
Harlock's Moor

Westley Hall Farm
CHURCH LANE
CB8
Westley Waterless
THE STREET
Water Tower
Harlock's Moor Farm
Icknield

B1052
B1061
Hilton Grove Farm

Home Farm
CHARTFIELD RD
PO
Burrough End
Stud Farm

Ladies Grove
Works
PH
Burrough Green CE Prim Sch
ELIZABETH WY
BACK LA
Brinkley Wood
Hay Wood
Ravens Moor
BRINKLEY ROAD
The Hall
CHURCH LA
INGHERT LT
Burrough Green
PO

Moat

HIGH STREET
Brinkley Hall
HIGH ST
PH
GREEN
HALL LANE

Icknield Way Path
Crick's Farm
CB21
Sewage Works
Charity Farm
COLES LA
BEECH CROFT
HIGH STREET
Brinkley
Sewage Works
OLD SCHOOL LANE

WESTON COLVILLE ROAD
B1052
CARLTON ROAD
Glebe Farm

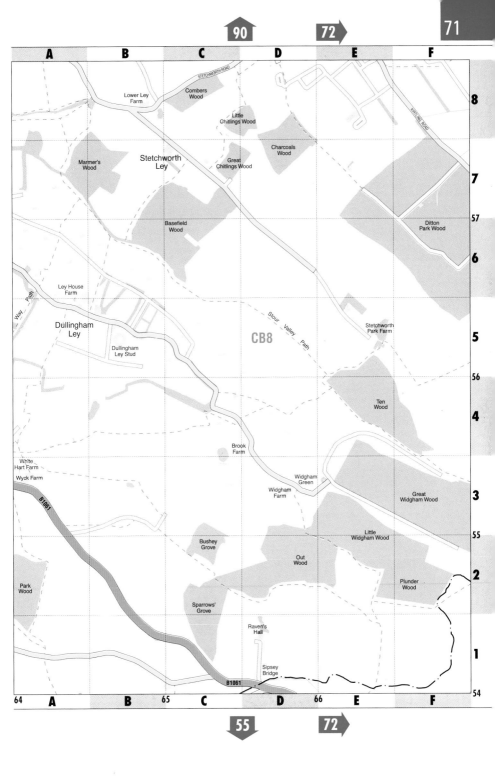

8

STETCHWORTH ROAD

Lower Ley
Farm

Combers
Wood

Little
Chitlings Wood

7

Marmer's
Wood

Stetchworth
Ley

Great
Chitlings Wood

Charcoals
Wood

Ditton
Park Wood

57

Basefield
Wood

6

Ley House
Farm

Way ── Path

Dullingham
Ley

Dullingham
Ley Stud

CB8

Stour Valley Path

Stetchworth
Park Farm

5

56

Ten
Wood

4

White
Hart Farm

Wyck Farm

Brook
Farm

Widgham
Green

Widgham
Farm

Great
Widgham Wood

3

B1061

Little
Widgham Wood

55

Bushey
Grove

Out
Wood

Plunder
Wood

2

Park
Wood

Sparrows'
Grove

Raven's
Hall

1

Sipsey
Bridge

B1061

54

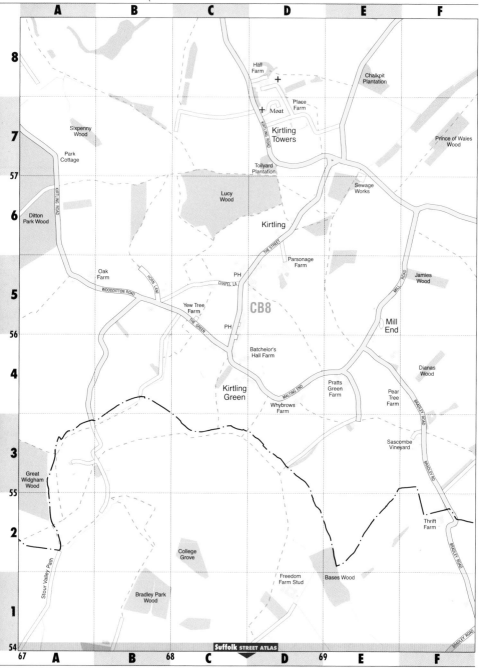

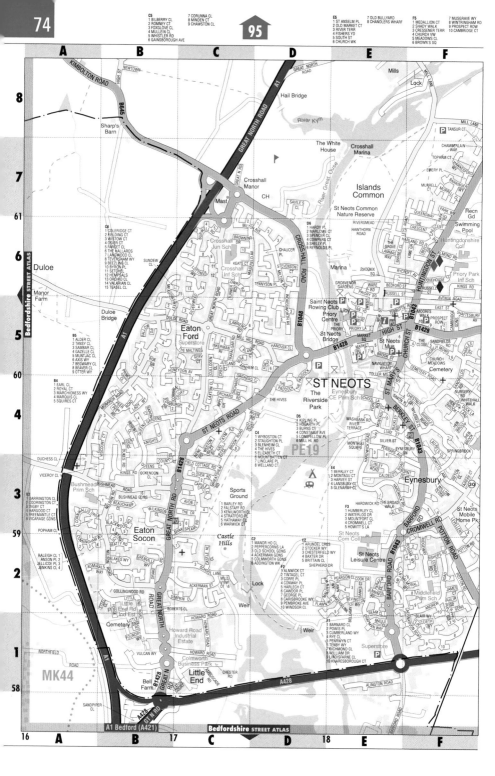

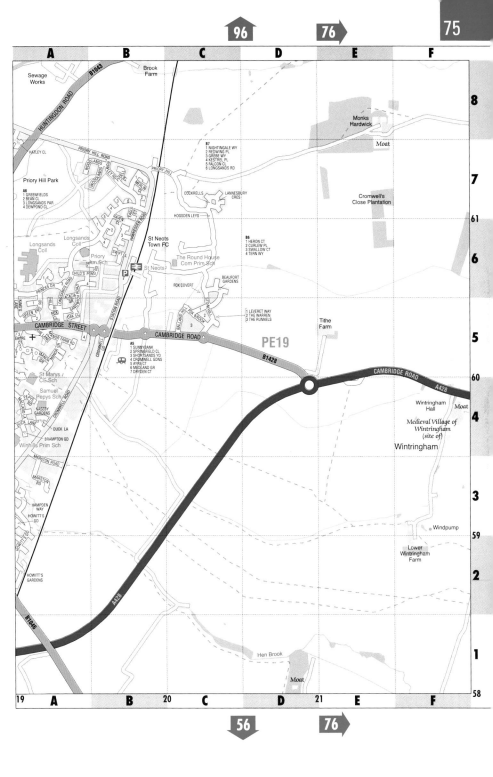

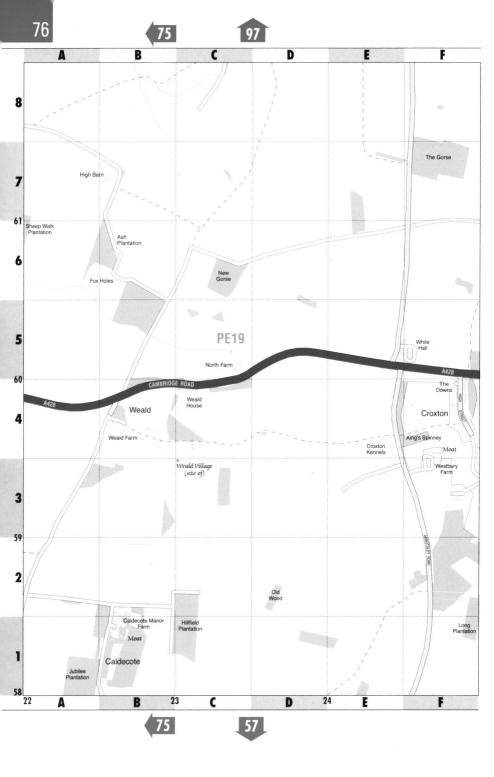

75
97

8

7

61

6

5

60

4

3

59

2

1

58

A B C D E F

The Gorse

High Barn

Sheep Walk
Plantation

Ash
Plantation

Fox Holes

New
Gorse

PE19

White
Hall

North Farm

CAMBRIDGE ROAD

A428

The
Downs

Weald

Weald
House

Croxton

Weald Farm

King's Spinney

Moat

Croxton
Kennels

Westbury
Farm

HIGH STREET

Weald Village
(site of)

Old
Wood

ABBOTSLEY ROAD

Caldecote Manor
Farm

Hillfield
Plantation

Long
Plantation

Moat

Caldecote

Jubilee
Plantation

22   A   B   23   C   D   24   E   F

75
57

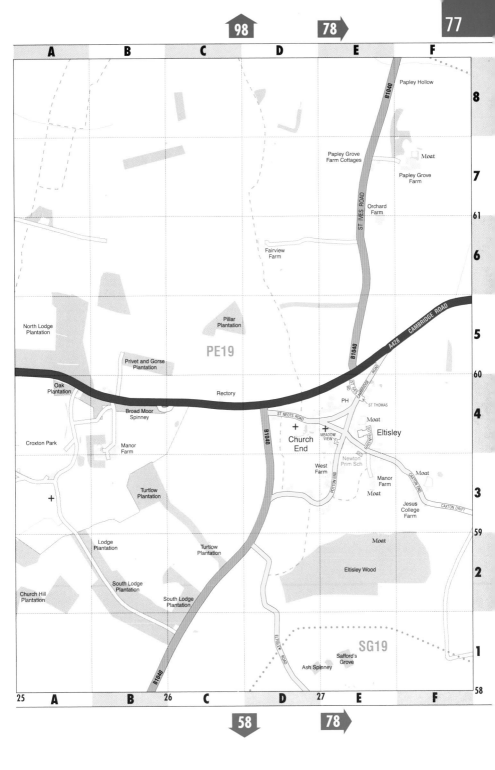

A B C D E F

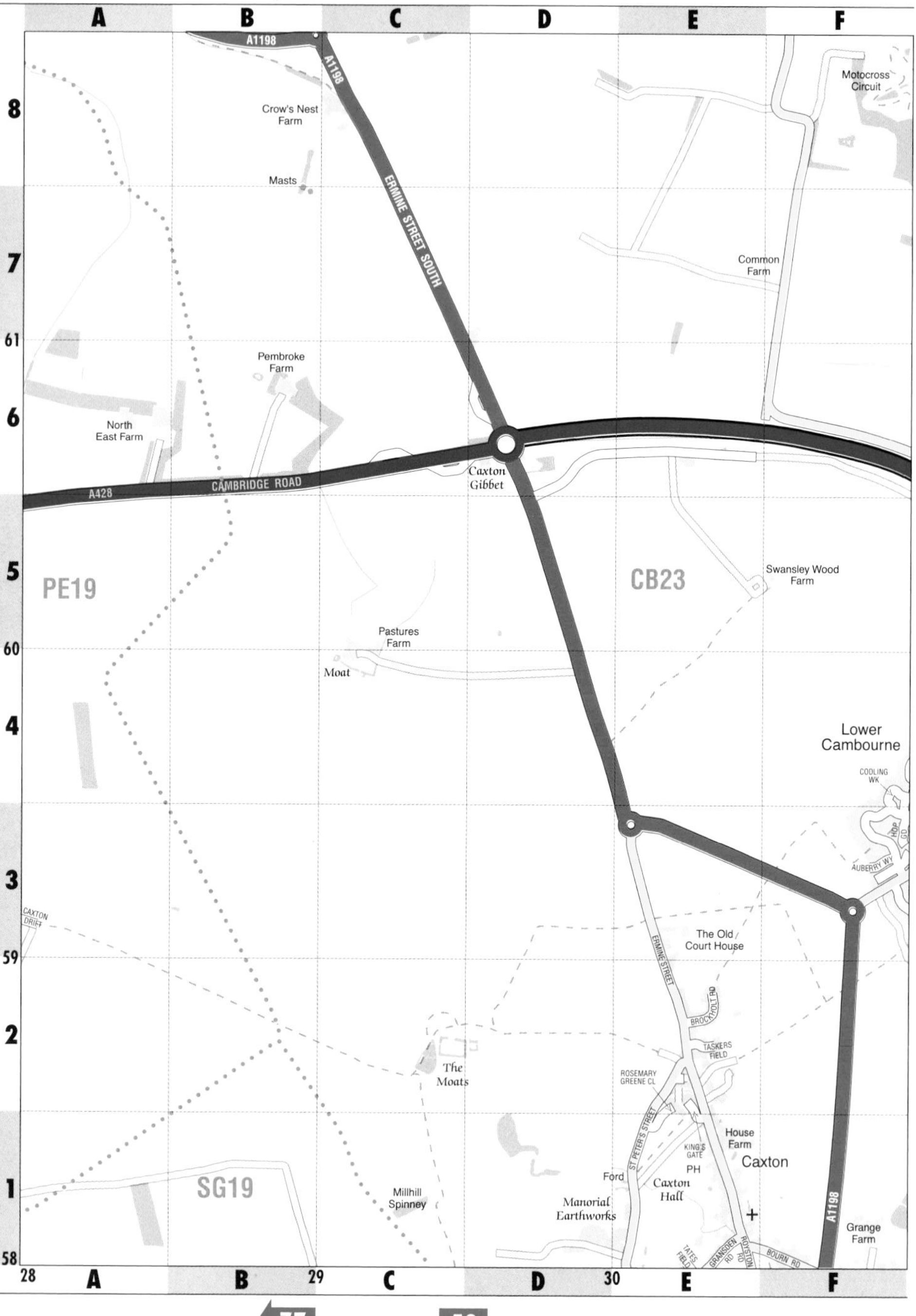

8

Motocross Circuit

Crow's Nest Farm

Masts

ERMINE STREET SOUTH

A1198

7

Common Farm

61

Pembroke Farm

6

North East Farm

A428 CAMBRIDGE ROAD

Caxton Gibbet

5

PE19

CB23

Swansley Wood Farm

60

Pastures Farm

Moat

4

Lower Cambourne

CODLING WK

HINDE

AUBERRY WY

3

CAXTON DRIFT

The Old Court House

59

ERMINE STREET

BROCKLEY END

2

The Moats

TASKERS FIELD

ROSEMARY GREENE CL

House Farm

Caxton

1

SG19

Millhill Spinney

Ford

ST PETER'S STREET

KING'S GATE

PH

Caxton Hall

Manorial Earthworks

GRANSDEN RD

BOURN RD

A1198

Grange Farm

58

28 A B 29 C D 30 E F

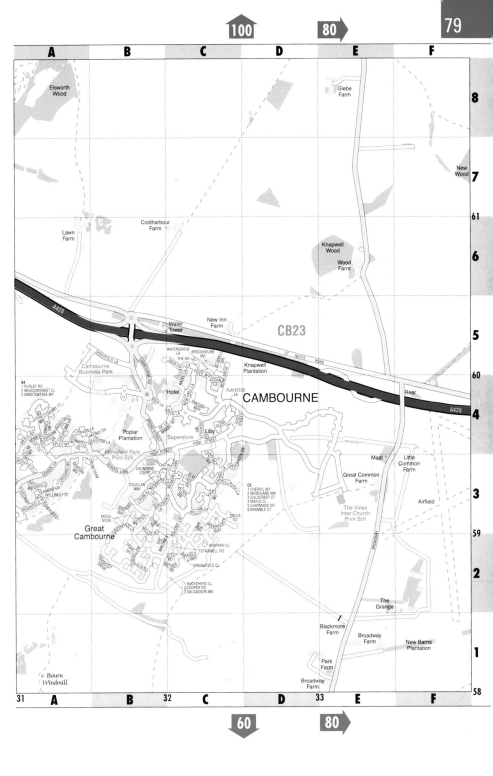

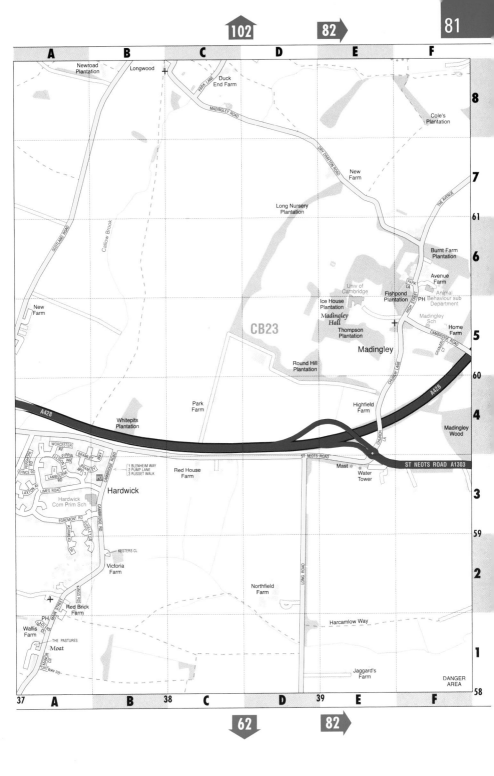

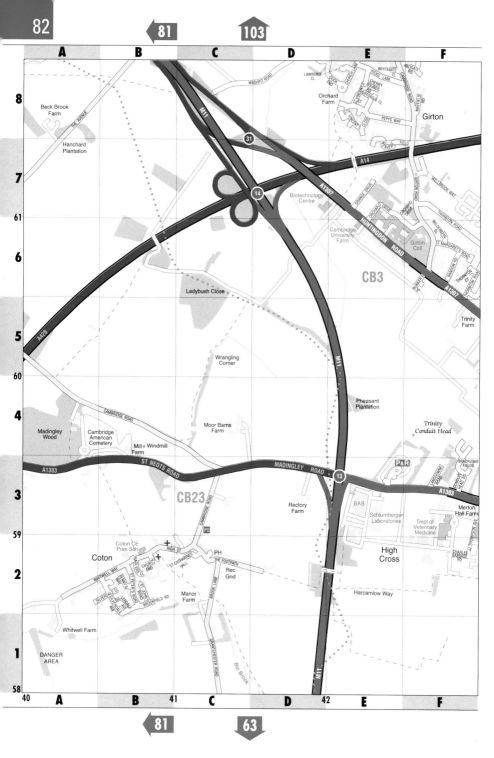

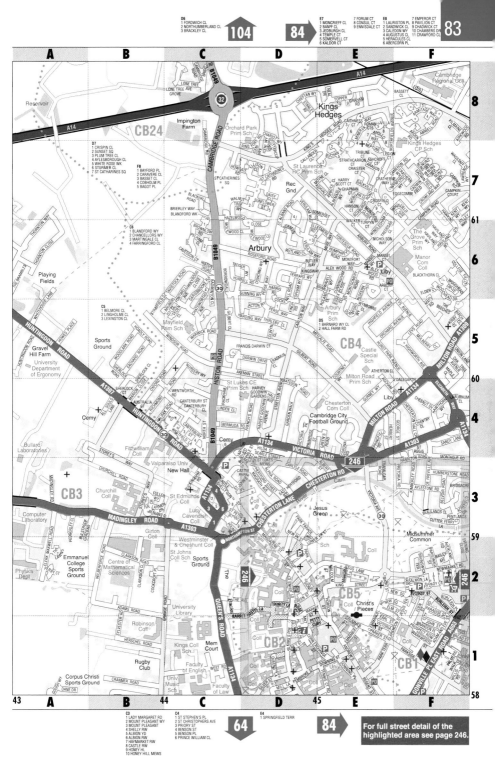

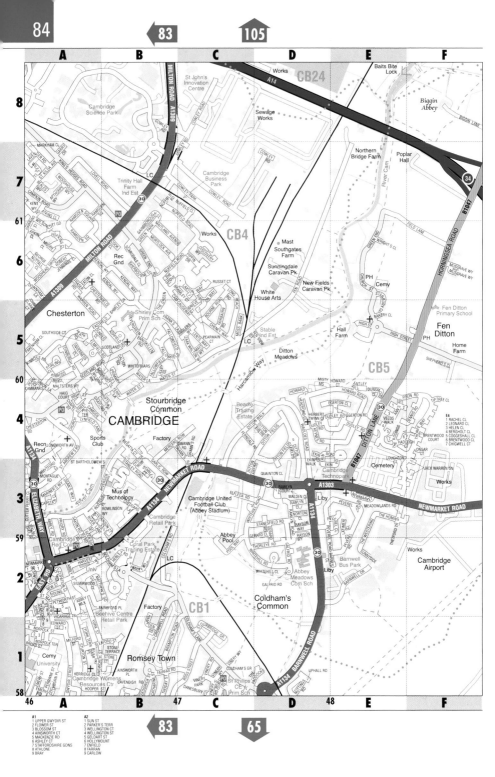

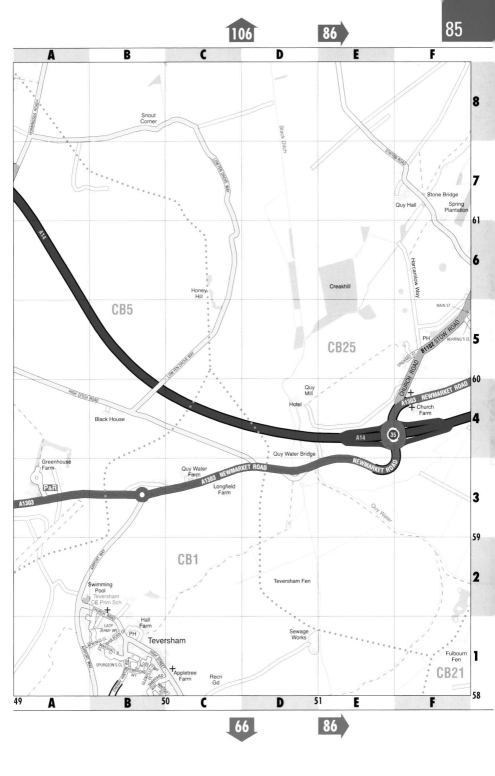

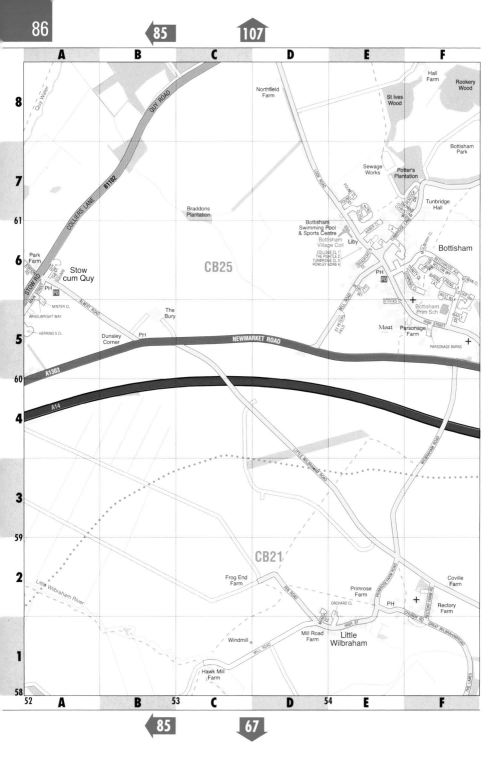

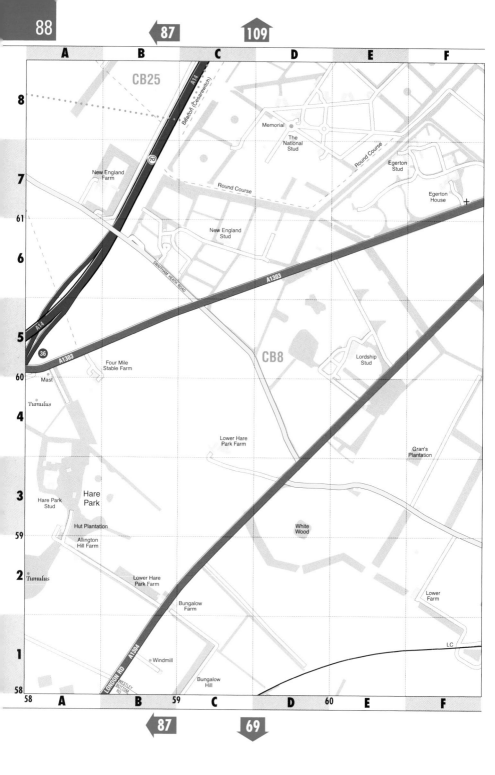

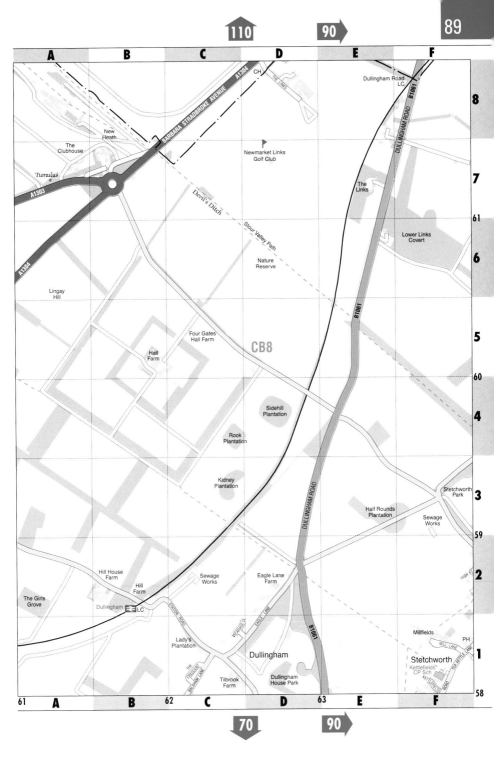

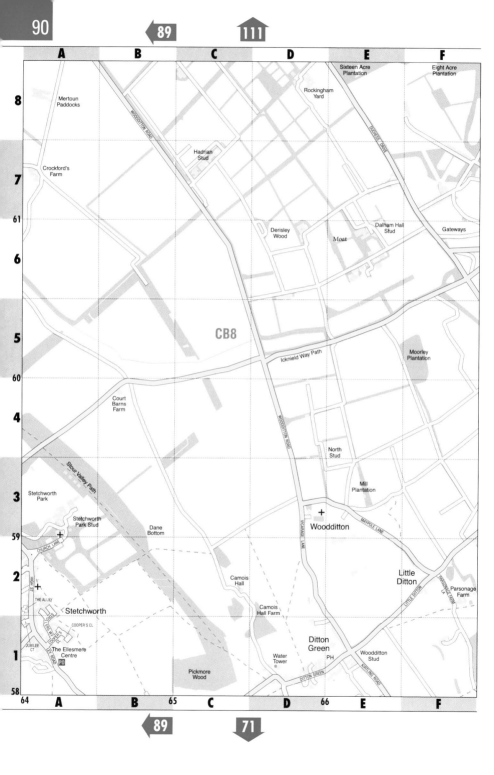

89
111

A **B** **C** **D** **E** **F**

8
Mertoun
Paddocks

Sixteen Acre
Plantation

Eight Acre
Plantation

Rockingham
Yard

7
Crockford's
Farm

Hadrian
Stud

61
Derisley
Wood

Dalham Hall
Stud

Gateways

6
Moat

5
CB8

Moorley
Plantation

Icknield Way Path

60
Court
Barns
Farm

4
WOODDITTON ROAD

North
Stud

3
Stetchworth
Park

Mill
Plantation

Stetchworth
Park Stud

Dane
Bottom

Woodditton

MAYPOLE LANE

59
CHURCH LANE

VICARAGE LANE

2
HIGH ST

THE ALLEY

Camois
Hall

Little
Ditton

PARSONAGE FARM LA

Parsonage
Farm

LITTLE DITTON

Stetchworth

COOPER'S CL

Camois
Hall Farm

1
JUBILEE
CT

COOPER'S
CL

The Ellesmere
Centre

PO

Ditton
Green

Woodditton
Stud

KIRTLING ROAD

Water
Tower

PH

Pickmore
Wood

DITTON GREEN

58
64 **A** **B** 65 **C** **D** 66 **E** **F**

89
71

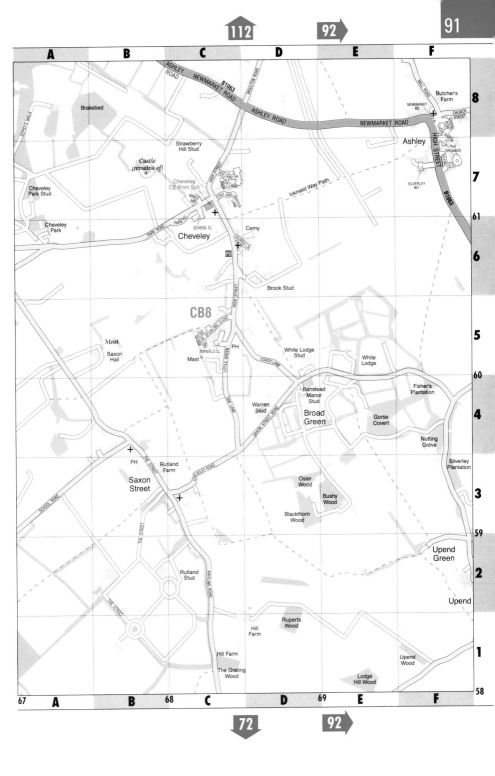

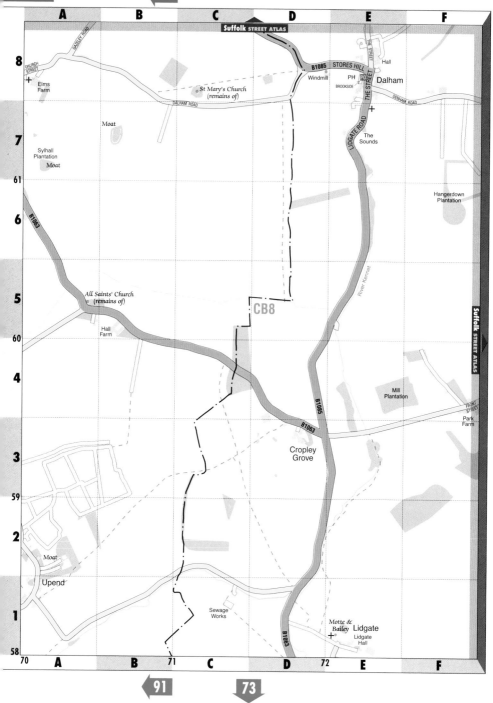

Suffolk STREET ATLAS

Suffolk STREET ATLAS

8

Church Street
Elms Farm

St Mary's Church (remains of)

GALLEY ROAD

DALHAM ROAD

B1085

STORES HILL

Windmill

Hall

Dalham

PH

BROOKSIDE

DENHAM ROAD

THE STREET

Moat

7

Sylhall Plantation

Moat

LIDGATE ROAD

The Sounds

61

Hangerdown Plantation

6

B1063

River Kennet

5

All Saints' Church (remains of)

CB8

60

Hall Farm

4

Mill Plantation

B1085

FRONT STREET

Park Farm

B1063

3

Cropley Grove

59

2

Moat

Upend

Sewage Works

1

Motte & Bailey

Lidgate

B1063

Lidgate Hall

58

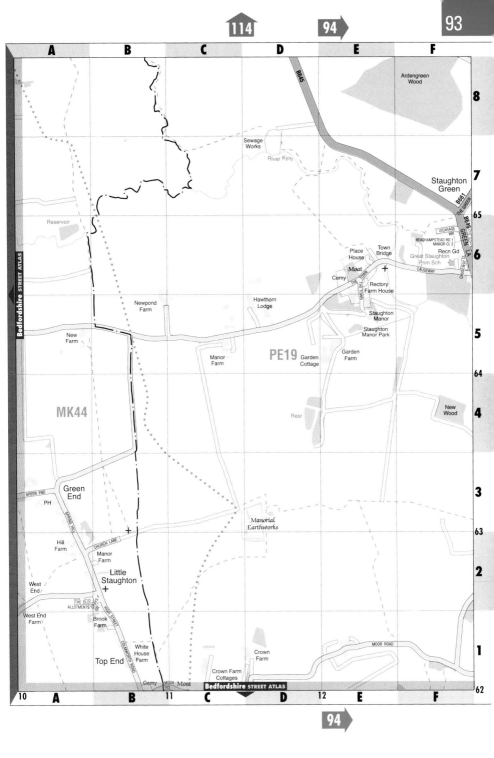

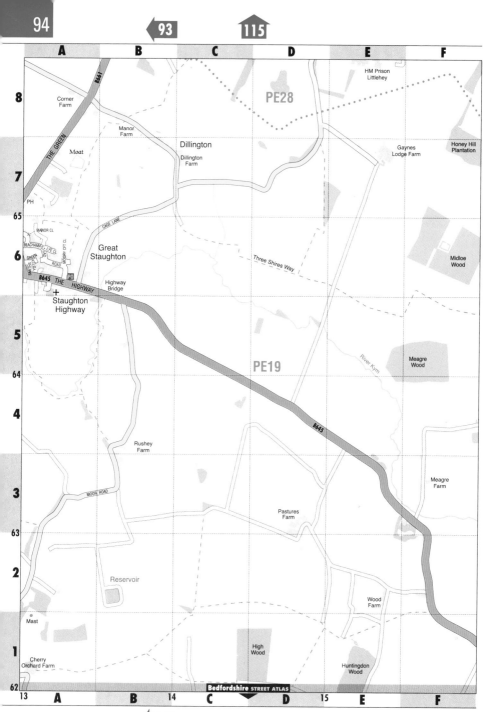

8

PE28

HM Prison
Littlehey

Corner
Farm

THE GREEN

B661

Manor
Farm

Moat

Dillington

Gaynes
Lodge Farm

Honey Hill
Plantation

Dillington
Farm

7

PH

65

CAGE LANE

MANOR CL

BEACHAMP

LYE CL

GREEN

MOOR CFT CL

Great
Staughton

Three Shires Way

Midloe
Wood

6

THE

HIGHWAY

ROAD

B645

Highway
Bridge

Staughton
Highway

5

PE19

River Kym

Meagre
Wood

64

B645

4

Rushey
Farm

Meagre
Farm

3

MOOR ROAD

Pastures
Farm

63

2

Reservoir

Wood
Farm

Mast

1

High
Wood

Huntingdon
Wood

Cherry
Orchard Farm

62

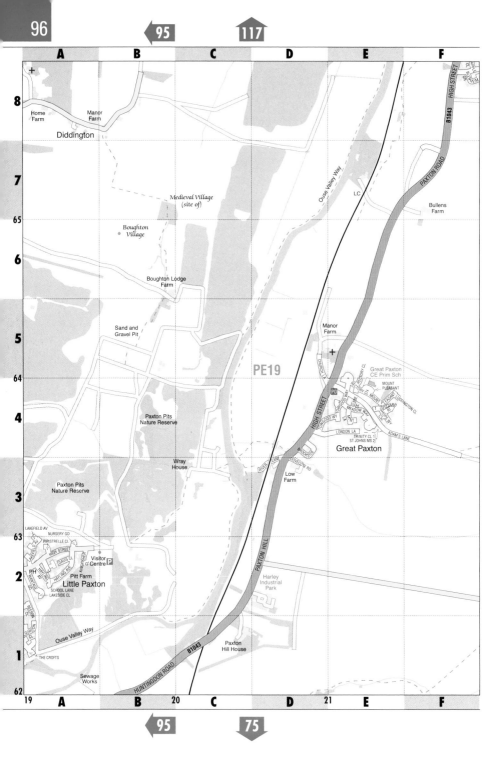

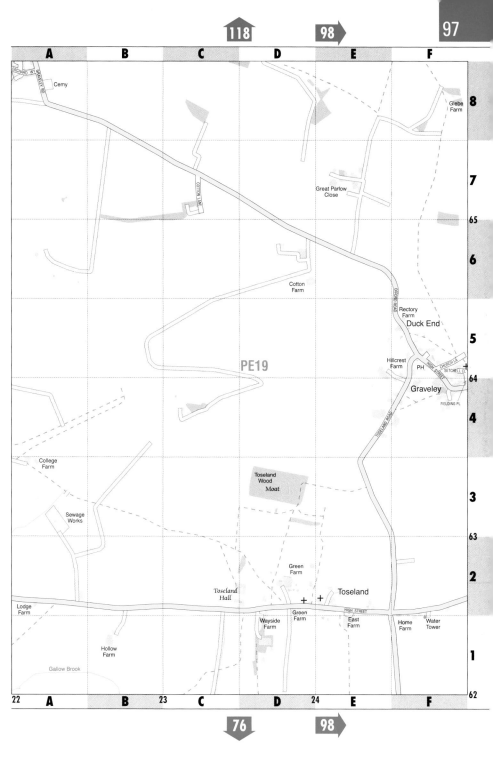

A   B   C   D   E   F

Cerny

8

Glebe
Farm

COTTON LANE

7

Great Parlow
Close

65

6

Cotton
Farm

Rectory
Farm
Duck End

ORFORD ROAD

5

PE19

Hillcrest
Farm

PH

HIGH STREET
CHURCH LA
SETCHELL CL

64

Graveley

FIELDING PL

TOSELAND ROAD

4

College
Farm

Toseland
Wood
Moat

3

Sewage
Works

63

Green
Farm

2

Toseland
Hall

Toseland

HIGH STREET

Lodge
Farm

Green
Farm

Wayside
Farm

East
Farm

Home
Farm

Water
Tower

Hollow
Farm

1

Gallow Brook

62

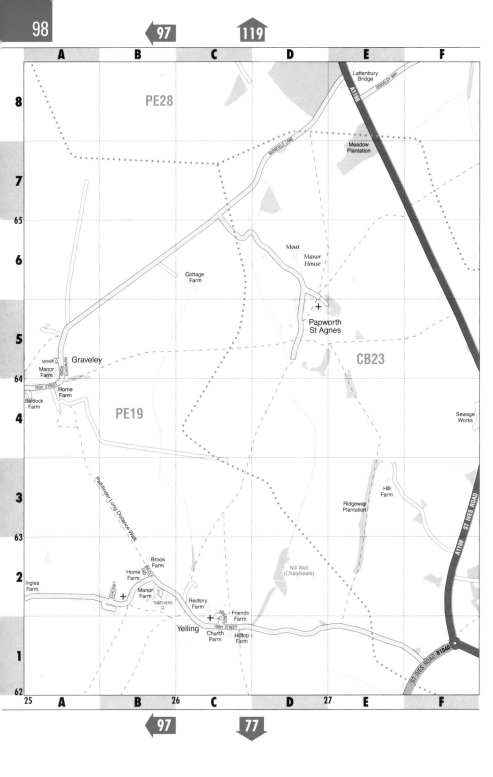

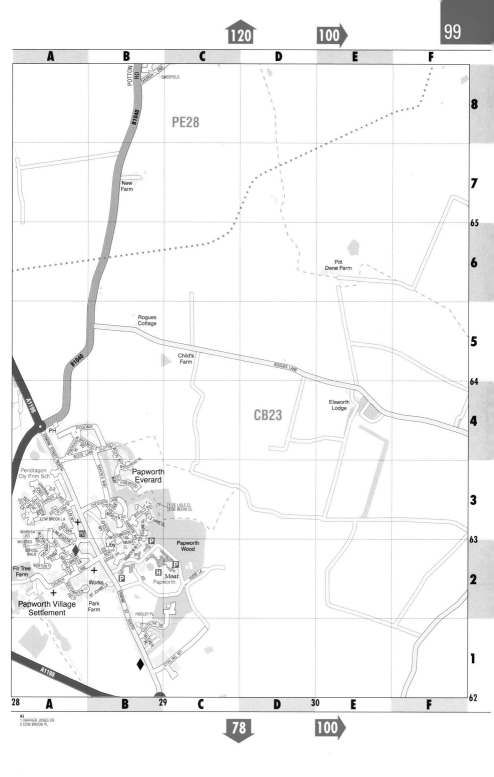

PE28

New Farm

Rogues Cottage

Child's Farm

ROGUES LANE

Pitt Dene Farm

CB23

Elsworth Lodge

RIDGEWAY

Pendragon Cty Prim Sch

Papworth Everard

1 DE LISLE CL
2 DE BECHE CL

Papworth Wood

WIMBISH RD
WIGSTED CL
SCHOOL WALK
MORTON CL

Fir Tree Farm

Liby

MURIEL CL

Works

Moat Papworth

FARM LA

Park Farm

Papworth Village Settlement

HOOLEY PL

STIRLING WY

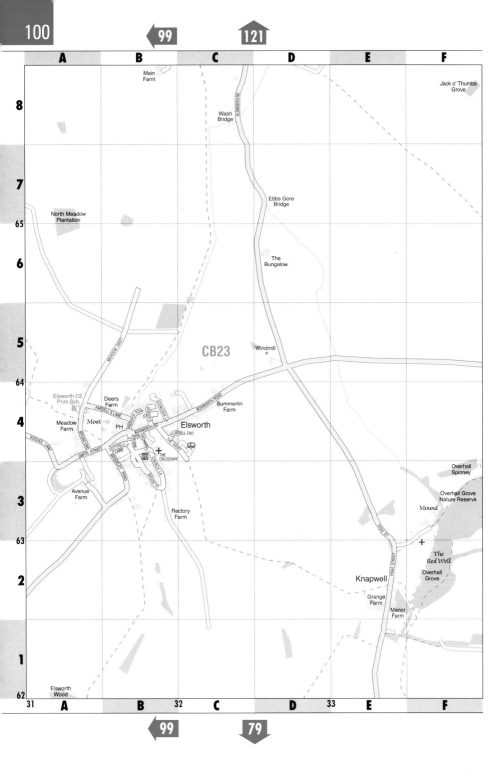

Main Farm

Jack o' Thumbs Grove

8

Wash Bridge

ELSWORTH RD

7

Ebbs Gore Bridge

North Meadow Plantation

65

The Bungalow

6

5

CB23

Windmill

64

Elsworth CE Prim Sch

MEADOW DRIFT

Deers Farm

Summerlin Farm

BOXWORTH ROAD

4

Meadow Farm

Moat

PH

BROAD END

FARDELL'S LANE

PAGE'S DRIFT

RIDER'S DRIFT

BOXWORTH RD

OLD STREET

Elsworth

WIDELL END

ROGUES LANE

SMITH STREET

BROADEND

COTTRELL'S LANE

BROUGHTON

BROCKLEY ROAD

THE CAUSEWAY

PO

Overhall Spinney

Avenue Farm

BROOK ST

Rectory Farm

Overhall Grove Nature Reserve

Mound

3

63

The Red Well

Overhall Grove

2

Knapwell

HIGH STREET

HIGH ST

Grange Farm

Manor Farm

1

62

Elsworth Wood

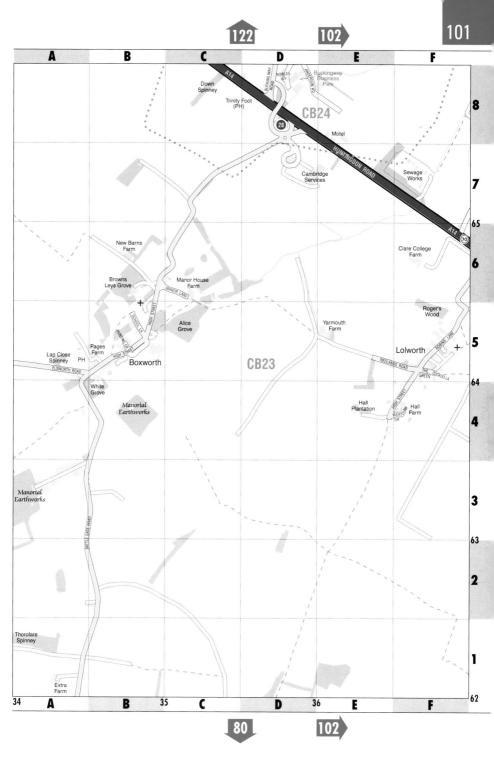

122
102

A B C D E F

8

7

65

6

5

64

4

3

63

2

1

62

A14

Down
Spinney

ROWLES WY

BUCKING WAY ROAD

ANDERSON RD

ROWLES WY

Buckingway
Business
Park

Trinity Foot
(PH)

CB24

28

Motel

HUNTINGDON ROAD

Sewage
Works

Cambridge
Services

A14

70

New Barns
Farm

Clare College
Farm

Browns
Leys Grove

Manor House
Farm

MANOR LANE

Roger's
Wood

SCHOOL

HIGH STREET

Alice
Grove

Yarmouth
Farm

ROBINS LANE

Lolworth

Pages
Farm

CB23

REDLANDS ROAD

THE
GREEN

CUCKOO LA

Lap Close
Spinney

PH

HIGH STREET

HUNTING ST

Boxworth

64

White
Grove

Hall
Plantation

HIGH STREET

MERTON
DR

Hall
Farm

ELSWORTH ROAD

Manorial
Earthworks

Manorial
Earthworks

BATTLE GATE ROAD

Thorofare
Spinney

Extra
Farm

34

A

B

35

C

D

36

E

F

80
102

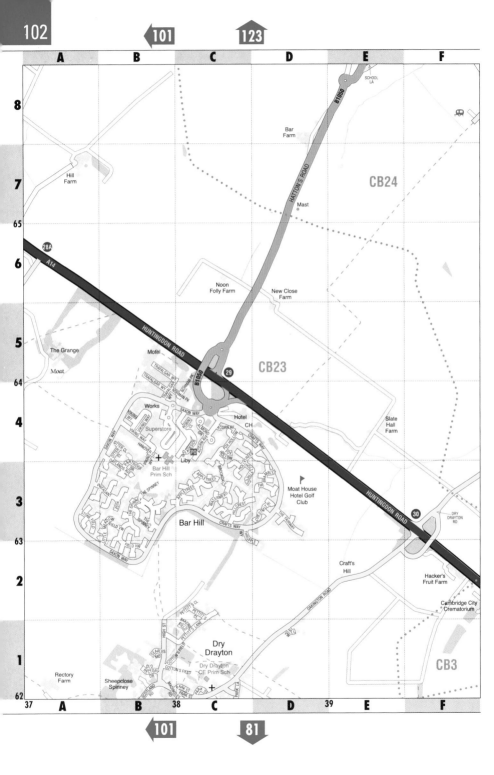

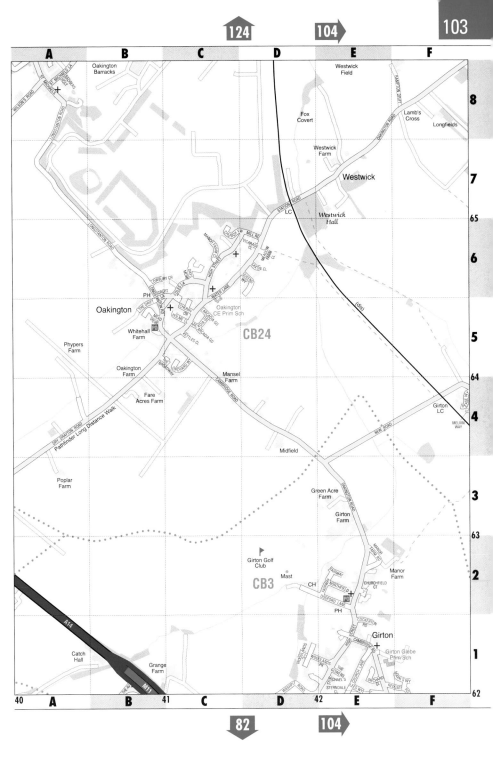

124
104

A   B   C   D   E   F

8

Oakington
Barracks

Westwick
Field

Fox
Covert

Lamb's
Cross

Longfields

Westwick
Farm

7

Westwick

65

Westwick
Hall

LC

6

CHURCH VW
MILL RD

VICARAGE
CL

MEADOW
CL

SAXON CL

GREENS
WY

Water Lane

Oakington
CE Prim Sch

(dis)

PH

Oakington

Whitehall
Farm

PO

Oakington
CE Prim Sch

CB24

5

Phypers
Farm

KETTLES CL

Oakington
Farm

Mansel
Farm

64

Fare
Acres Farm

CAMBRIDGE ROAD

Girton
LC

4

DRY DRAYTON ROAD
Pathfinder Long Distance Walk

NEW ROAD

MELVIN
WAY

Poplar
Farm

Midfield

3

Green Acre
Farm

Girton
Farm

63

Girton Golf
Club

Manor
Farm

2

CB3

Mast

CH

Churchfield
CT

PH

Girton

Girton Glebe
Prim Sch

1

Catch
Hall

Grange
Farm

A14

M11

62

40   A   41   B   C   D   42   E   F

82
104

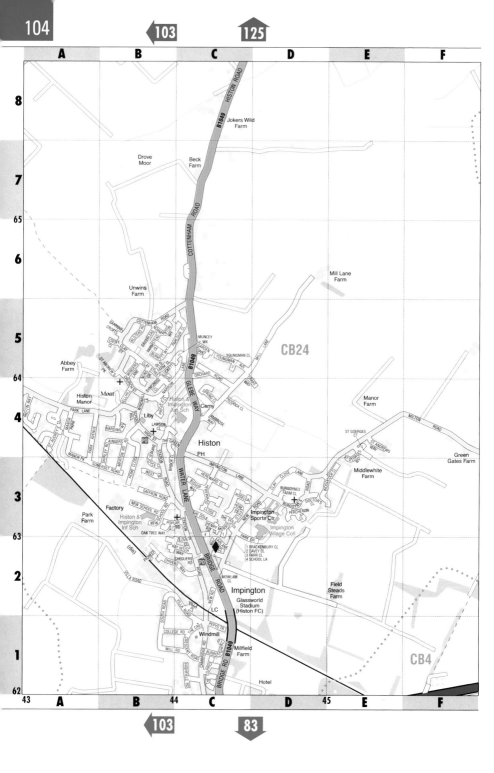

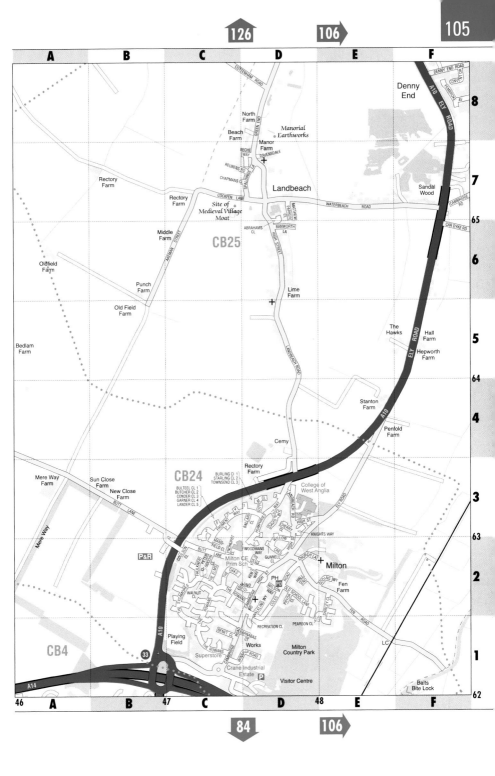

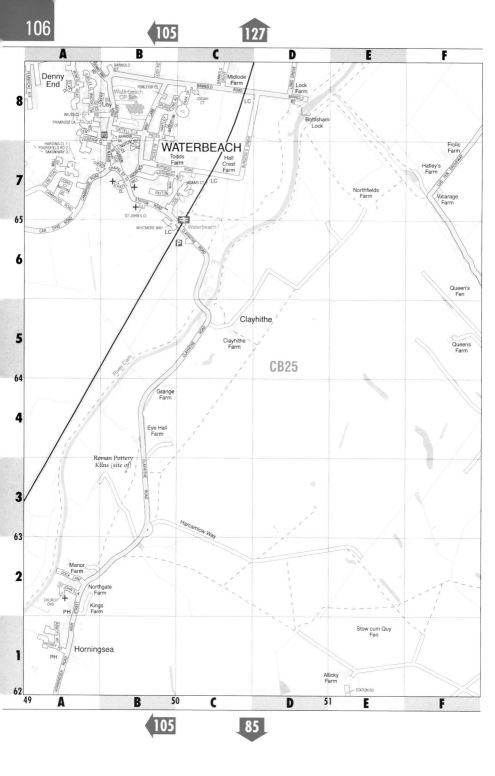

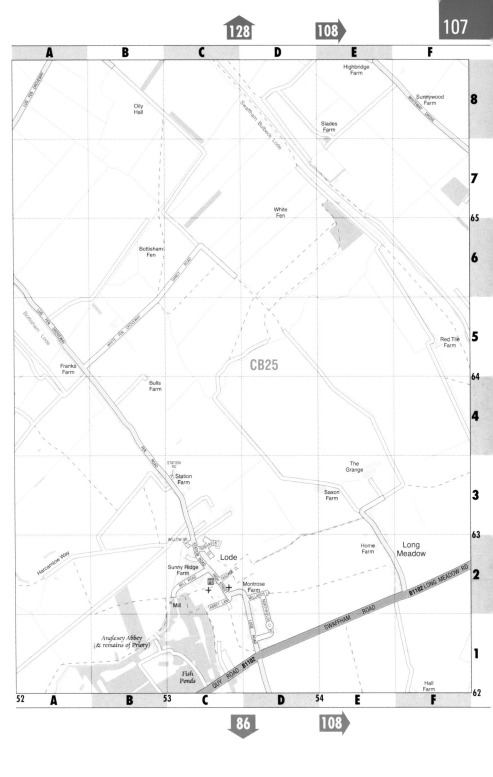

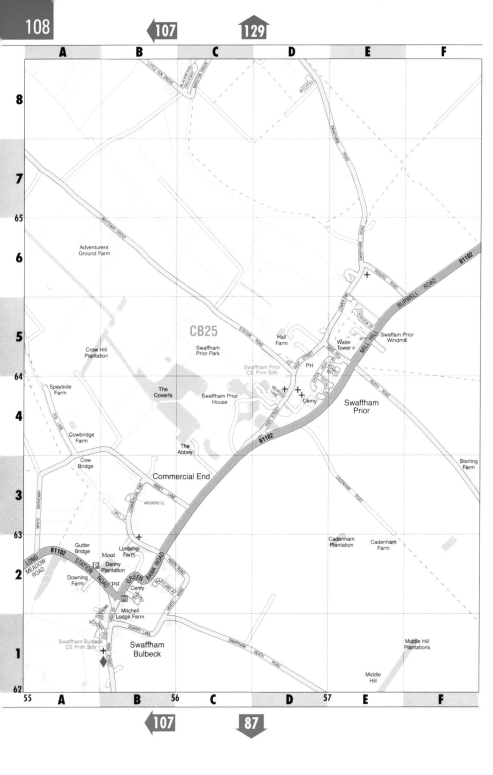

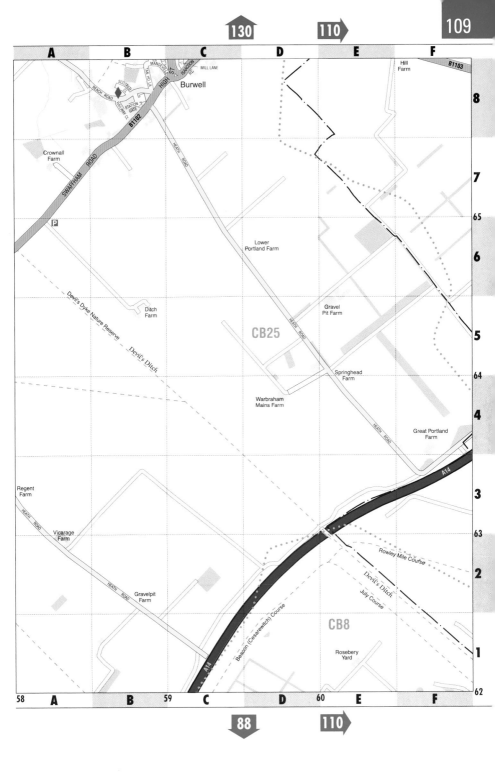

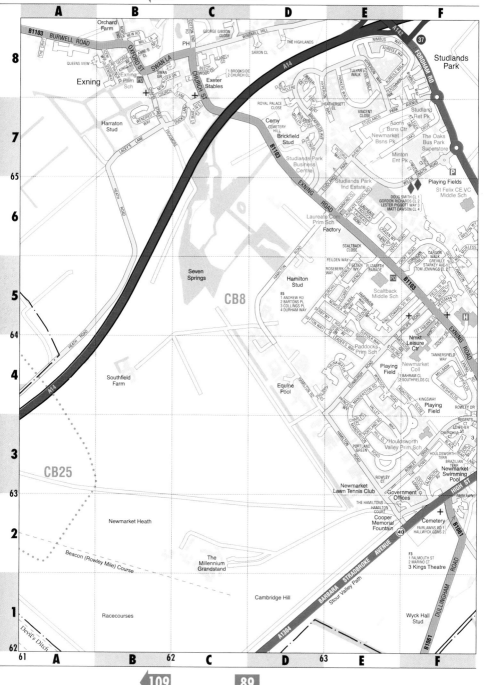

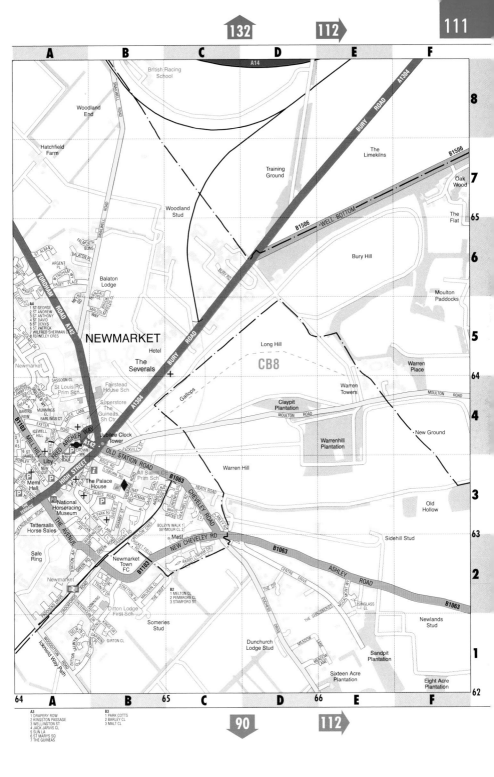

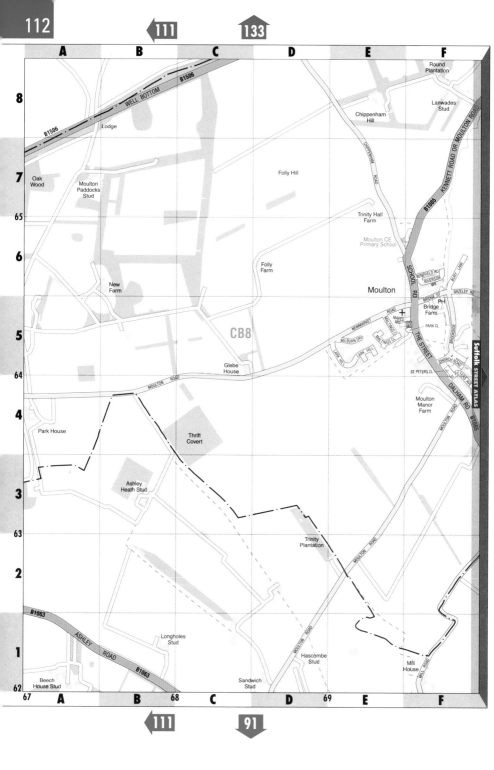

Suffolk STREET ATLAS

B1506

WELL BOTTOM

B1506

Round
Plantation

Lanwades
Stud

Chippenham
Hill

Lodge

Oak
Wood

Folly Hill

CHIPPENHAM ROAD

KENNETT ROAD OR MOULTON ROAD

Moulton
Paddocks
Stud

B1085

Trinity Hall
Farm

Moulton CE
Primary School

New
Farm

Folly
Farm

SCHOOL RD

BENEFIELD RD
RIVERSIDE
WK

BURY LANE

Moulton

GAZELEY RD

BRIDGE ST

CB8

MAYES
MDW

Bridge
Farm

PARK CL

NEWMARKET

MALTING CL

PH

MALTINGS CL

THE STREET

BROOKSIDE

Glebe
House

MILBURN DRO

LAWN HILL

LANE END

PARK CL

CHURCH ROAD

ST PETERS CL

PETERS CL

MOULTON ROAD

MOULTON ROAD

DALHAM RD

B1085

Moulton
Manor
Farm

Park House

Thrift
Covert

Ashley
Heath Stud

Trinity
Plantation

MOULTON ROAD

B1063

ASHLEY ROAD

B1063

Longholes
Stud

MOULTON ROAD

MILL ROAD

Hascombe
Stud

Mill
House

Beech
House Stud

Sandwich
Stud

67 A B 68 C D 69 E F

8 7 65 6 5 64 4 3 63 2 1 62

A B C D E F

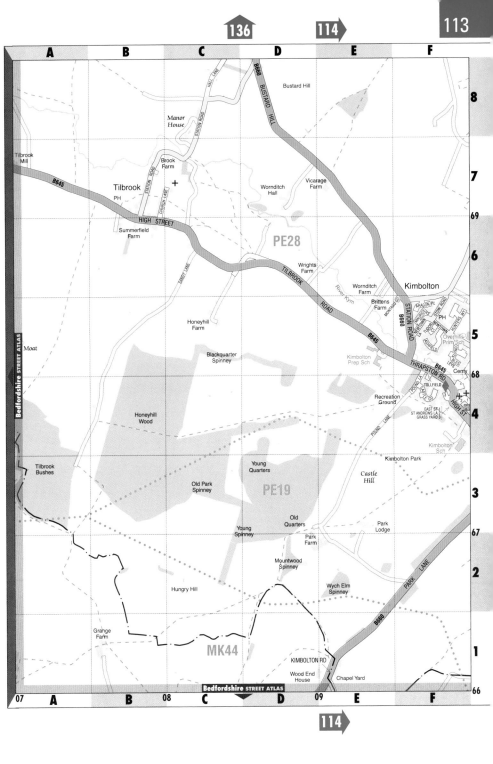

A   B   C   D   E   F

Bustard Hill

8

Manor
House

HALL LANE

B660

BUSTARD HILL

STATION ROAD

Tilbrook
Mill

Brook
Farm

7

B645

Tilbrook

PH

Wornditch
Hall

Vicarage
Farm

69

HIGH STREET

STATION ROAD

CHURCH LANE

Summerfield
Farm

PE28

6

Wrights
Farm

TILBROOK ROAD

Wornditch
Farm

Kimbolton

SANDY LANE

Honeyhill
Farm

River Kym

Brittens
Farm

MONTAGUE (D)

ARAGON PL

STATION ROAD

B660

NEWTOWN

PH

HUNTERS WAY

TILBROOK ROAD

Moat

Blackquarter
Spinney

Kimbolton
Prep Sch

B645

Oxerhills
Prim Sch

5

FAIRFIELD

68

THRAPSTON RD

B645

Cemy

Honeyhill
Wood

Recreation
Ground

TOLLFIELD

POUND LANE

CASTLE LA

HIGH ST

EAST ST 1
ST ANDREWS LA 2
GRASS YARD 3

4

Tilbrook
Bushes

Young
Quarters

Castle
Hill

Kimbolton
Sch

Kimbolton Park

Old Park
Spinney

PE19

3

Old
Quarters

Young
Spinney

Park
Lodge

67

Park
Farm

PARK LANE

Mountwood
Spinney

2

Hungry Hill

Wych Elm
Spinney

B660

Grange
Farm

MK44

1

KIMBOLTON RD

Wood End
House

Chapel Yard

66

07   A   B   08   C   D   09   E   F

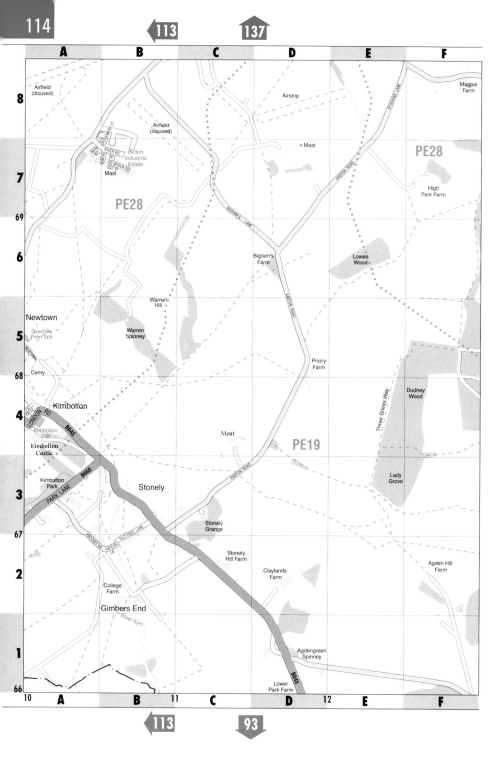

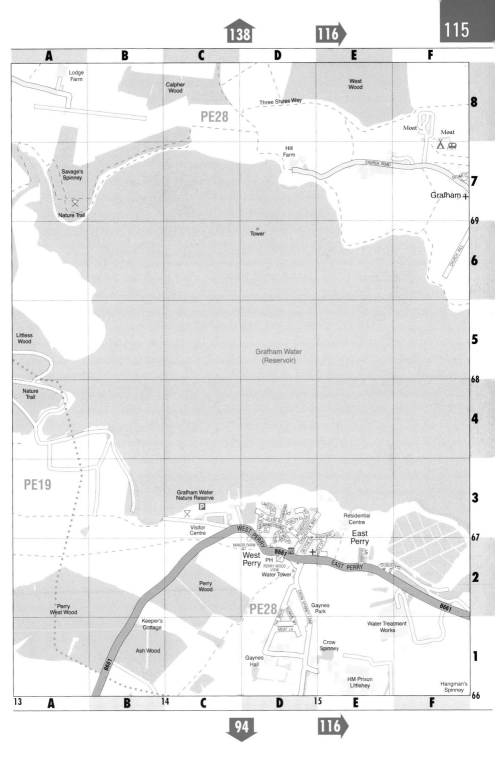

A B C D E F

8

Lodge
Farm

Calpher
Wood

West
Wood

PE28

Three Shires Way

Moat

Moat

Hill
Farm

CHURCH ROAD

Savage's
Spinney

CEDAR CL

7

Grafham

Nature Trail

69

Tower

CHURCH HILL

6

Littless
Wood

Grafham Water
(Reservoir)

5

Nature
Trail

68

4

PE19

3

Grafham Water
Nature Reserve

P

Residential
Centre

East
Perry

67

Visitor
Centre

LAKESIDE

GLEBE RD

OWLEY CL

HAWKINS

ARMSTRONG
CL

WHITE
HART

CHURCHILL CL

HOLYROOD CL

RIDGEWAY

BAKERS
WY

MANOR FARM

West
Perry

PH
PERRY WOOD
VIEW
Water Tower

EAST PERRY

DUBERLY CL

2

Perry
Wood

PE28

Gaynes
Park

Water Treatment
Works

B661

Perry
West Wood

Keeper's
Cottage

THE DRIVE

CROW SPINNEY LANE

MOAT LA

Crow
Spinney

1

Ash Wood

Gaynes
Hall

HM Prison
Littlehey

B661

Hangman's
Spinney

66

13 A B 14 C D 15 E F

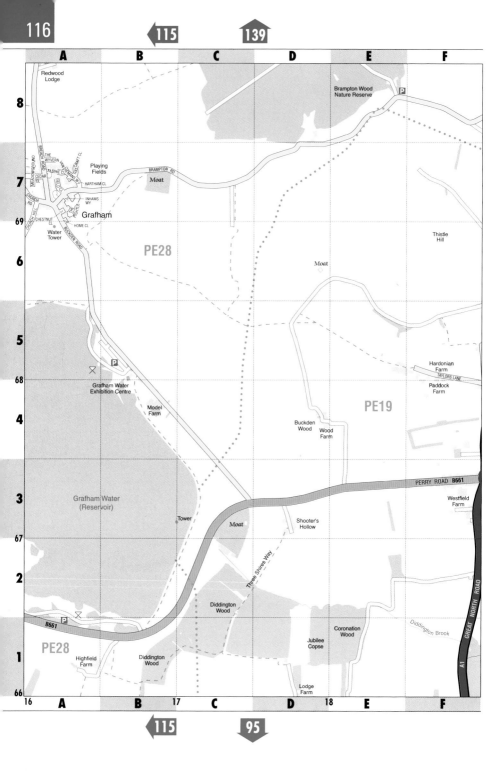

A | B | C | D | E | F

8

Redwood
Lodge

Brampton Wood
Nature Reserve

P

7

THE WYVERN
HALLSYKE CL
VINCENT CL

BRAMPTON RD

Playing
Fields

Moat

HARTHAM CL

MEADOWGROUND
BREACH CL
CEDAR CL
FIELD CL
CHURCH RD

INHAMS WY

THE PIGHTLE

69

CLOSE
CHESTNUT
HILL

Grafham

HOME CL

Thistle
Hill

PE28

6

Water
Tower

BUCKDEN ROAD

Moat

5

P
⚔

Hardonian
Farm

TAYLORS LANE

Paddock
Farm

68

Grafham Water
Exhibition Centre

Model
Farm

PE19

4

Buckden
Wood

Wood
Farm

3

Grafham Water
(Reservoir)

Tower

PERRY ROAD B661

Westfield
Farm

67

Moat

Shooter's
Hollow

2

Three Shires Way

Diddington
Wood

GREAT NORTH ROAD

Diddington Brook

B661
⚔

Coronation
Wood

1

PE28

Highfield
Farm

Diddington
Wood

Jubilee
Copse

A1

66

Lodge
Farm

16 | A | B | 17 | C | D | 18 | E | F

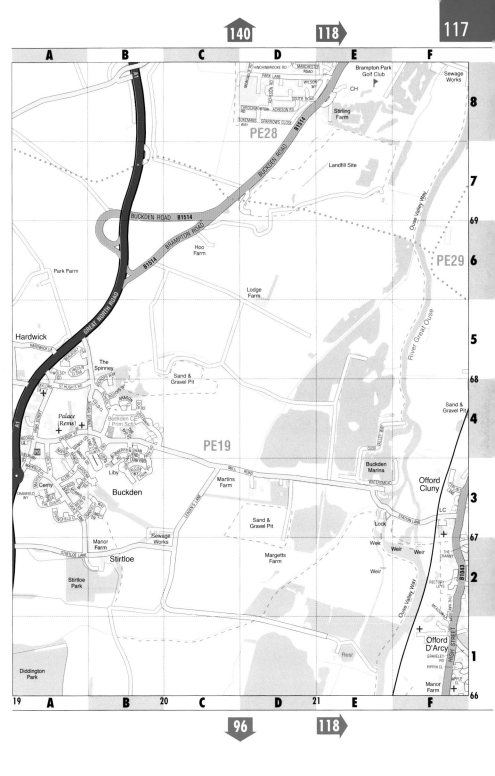

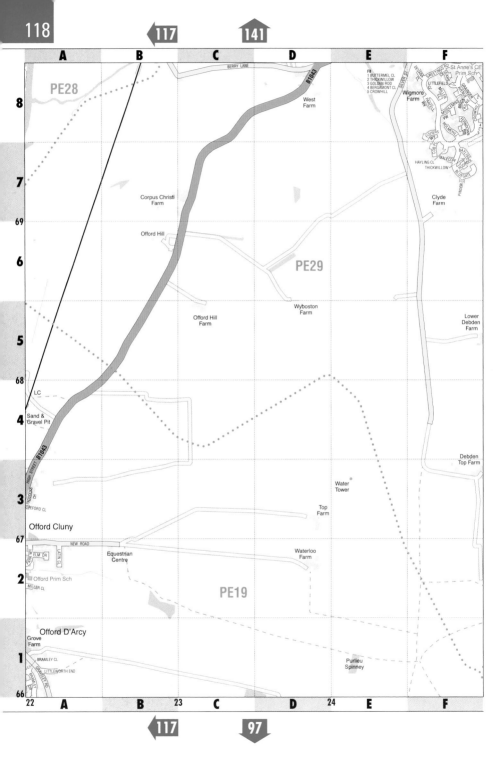

PE28

BERRY LANE

West Farm

FB
1 BUTTERMEL CL
2 THICKWILLOW
3 GOLDEN ROD
4 BERGAMONT CL
5 CROWHILL

St Anne's CE Prim Sch

Wigmore Farm

HAYLING CL
THICKWILLOW

Clyde Farm

Corpus Christi Farm

Offord Hill

PE29

Offord Hill Farm

Wyboston Farm

Lower Debden Farm

LC

Sand & Gravel Pit

B1043

PRIORY STREET

PADDOCK CH

CHIEFORD CL

Offord Cluny

Water Tower

Debden Top Farm

Top Farm

NEW ROAD

ELM DR

LATIN CL

Equestrian Centre

Waterloo Farm

PE19

Offord Prim Sch

MILLER CL

Offord D'Arcy

Grove Farm

BRAMLEY CL

LITTLEWORTH END

BRAMLEY RD

Purlieu Spinney

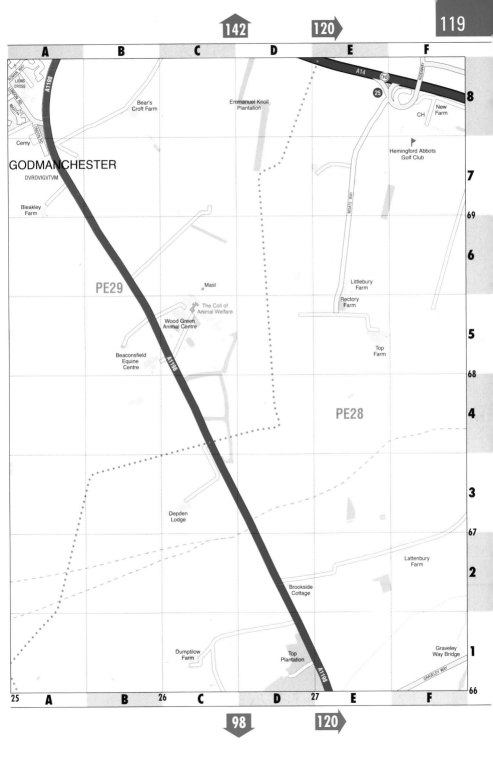

A14
70
25
8

New
Farm
CH

Bear's
Croft Farm

Emmanuel Knoll
Plantation

Hemingford Abbots
Golf Club

Cemy

GODMANCHESTER
DVROVIGVTVM

7

69

Bleakley
Farm

MOATS WAY

6

PE29

Mast

Littlebury
Farm

Rectory
Farm

The Coll of
Animal Welfare

Wood Green
Animal Centre

5

Beaconsfield
Equine
Centre

A1198

Top
Farm

68

PE28

4

Depden
Lodge

3

67

Lattenbury
Farm

2

Brookside
Cottage

Dumptilow
Farm

Top
Plantation

A1198

Graveley
Way Bridge

1

GRAVELEY WAY

66

119
143

A B C D E F

8

Douglas Farm

Rectory Farm

A14

PE27

Stepping Stone Bridge

Gore Tree Farm

GORE TREE ROAD

7

Arthur's Meadow Nature Reserve

The Grove

GROVE LANE

Galley Hill Farm

Galley Hill

LONDON ROAD

A1096

MARSH LANE

69

HUNTINGDON ROAD

A14

6

Woolpack Farm

26

Mast

B1040

West End Farm

5

Topfield Farm

MERE WAY

PE28

West Brook

68

Linton's Farm

4

POTTON ROAD

HILTON ROAD

3

Five Arch Bridge

67

Oxholme Farm

Clayfield Farm

2

THE PADDOCKS

NEW ENGLAND ROAD

WEST BROOK

CHEQUERS CFT

Moat

WEST BROOK CL

CROSS FARM CL

Punch's Grove

Hilton End Farm

GRAVELEY WAY

TYTHE

ECKS CL

The Green

Hilton

B1040

GREEN END

MALT RD

Turf Maze

PH

HOME FARM CLOSE

CHURCH END

Park Farm

FLACKDALE RD 1
RUTLAND GN 2
MILL HILL END 3

1

66

28 A 29 B C 30 D E F

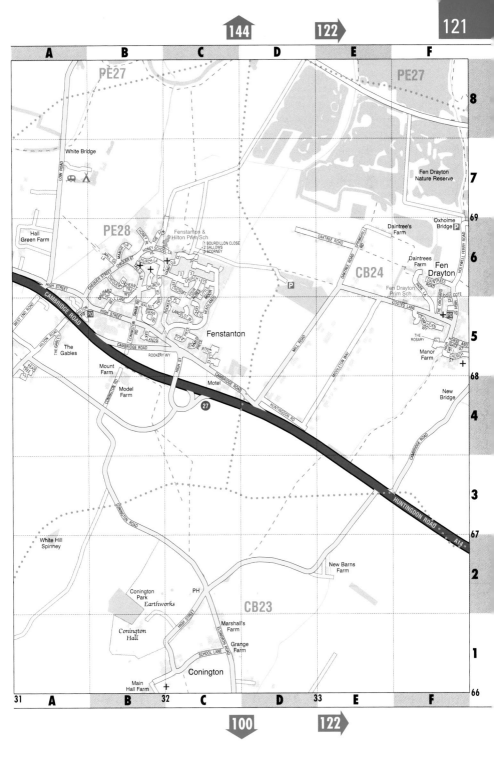

A | B | C | D | E | F

Sand & Gravel Works
Church Farm
HOLYWELL FERRY ROAD
PE27
Covells Bridge
Mare Fen Nature Reserve
Brownsfield Farm
High Causeway Bridge
Cloverfield Farm
ASER ROAD
STATION ROAD

8

(dis) LC LC
LC

7

Church Bridge
Church End
STATION RD

69

Friesland Farm
MILL WAY
Earthworks
TAYLOR'S LA
BLACK HORSE LA
CHEQUERS CT
MARKET ST
WALK
RD

6

Windmill
WHITEGATE CL
MOAT WAY
MOOR WAY
P
CENTRE
HEMBLEDODDS CL
GREENSIDE CL
Swavesey
Swavesey Prim Sch

SCHOOL LA
WHITTON'S LA

High Causeway Bridge
CB24
GATES WAY
GIBRALTER LANE

5

CHURCH ST
HORSE AND GATE LA
Swavesey Village Coll
Liby
Swavesey Sports Centre
MIDDLE WATCH
Mill Farm
FEN DRAYTON ROAD
WHITTON LA

68

CAMBRIDGE RD
SWAVESEY ROAD
St John's College Farm

4

ROSE AND CROWN ROAD
Dairy Farm
PINE GROVE

Works

3

BOXWORTH END
Boxworth End

67

A14
Boxworth End Farm

2

HUNTINGDON ROAD
TIPPLERS ROAD
Thorpes Farm
BUCKING WAY ROAD

CB23

1

Friesland Farm
A14
ANDERSON RD

66

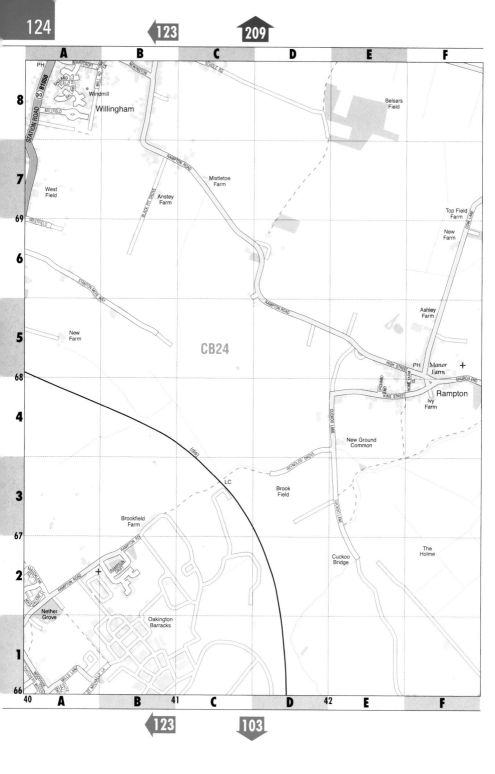

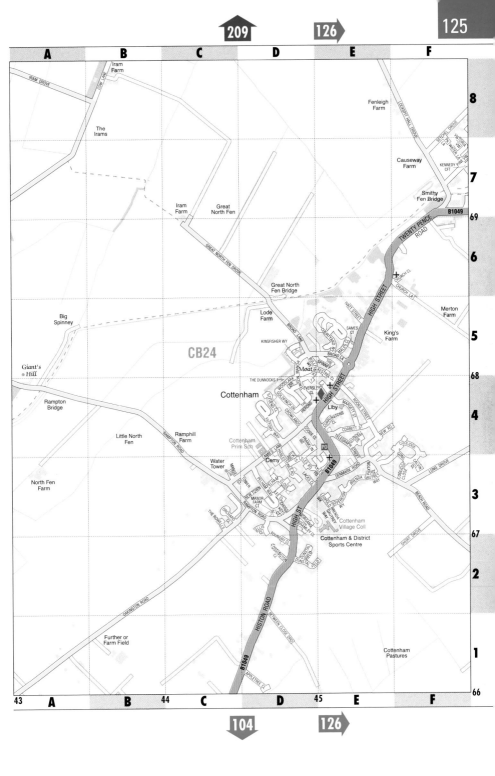

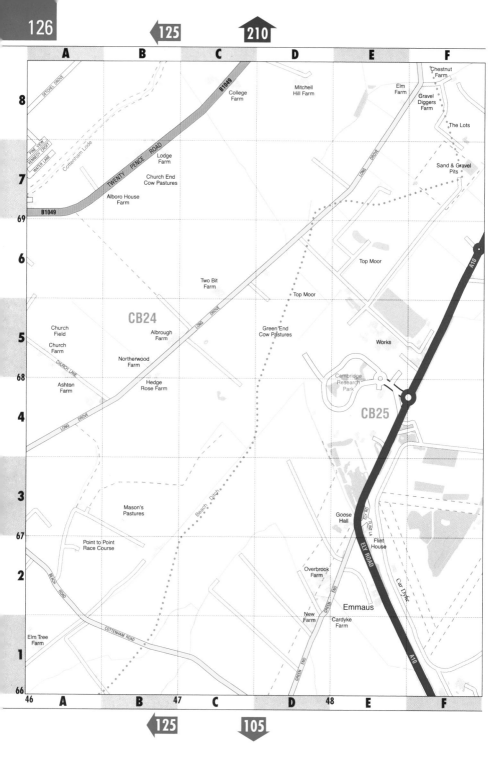

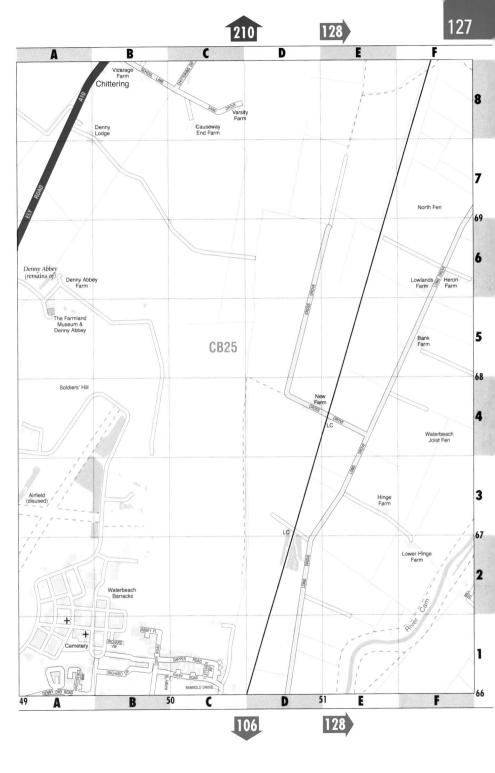

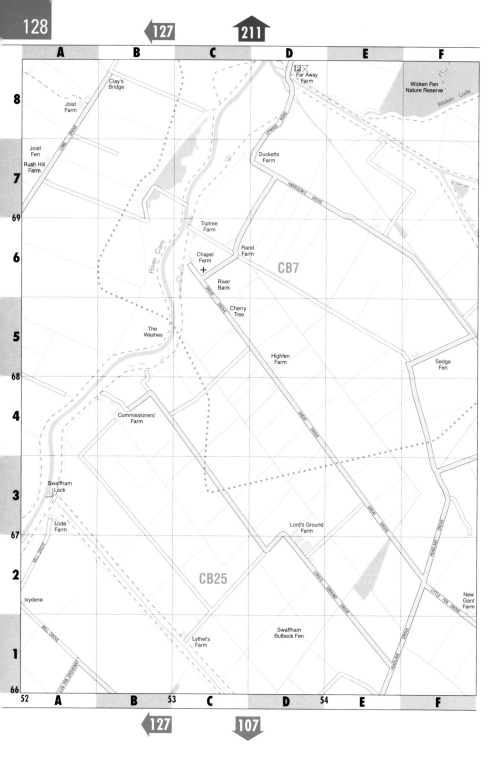

127
211

A   B   C   D   E   F

8

7

69

6

5

68

4

3

67

2

66

1

Joist
Farm

Clay's
Bridge

P ✕
Far Away
Farm

Wicken Fen
Nature Reserve

Wicken Lode

Joist
Fen
Rush Hill
Farm

LONG DROVE

UPWARE ROAD

Ducketts
Farm

HARRISON'S DROVE

Tiptree
Farm

Rand
Farm

Chapel
Farm
+

River
Bank

CB7

River Cam

Cherry
Tree

GREAT DROVE

The
Washes

Highfen
Farm

Sedge
Fen

Commissioners'
Farm

GREAT DROVE

Swaffham
Lock

Lode
Farm

MILL DROVE

Lord's Ground
Farm

GREAT DROVE

HEADLAKE DROVE

CB25

LONG'S GROUND DROVE

LITTLE FEN DROVE

New
Gant
Farm

Ivydene

MILL DROVE

LODE FEN DROVEWAY

Lythel's
Farm

Swaffham
Bulbeck Fen

HEADLAKE DROVE

52   A   B   53   C   D   54   E   F

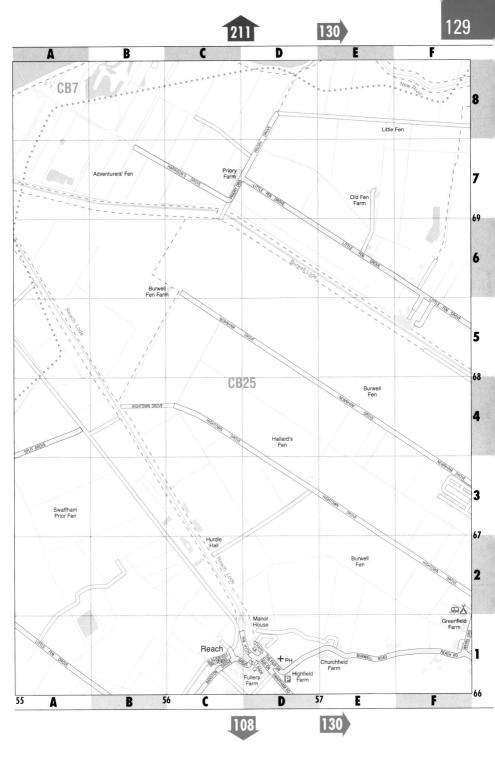

A B C D E F

CB7

New River

8

Little Fen

HARRISON'S DROVE

PRIORY DROVE

Adventurers' Fen

Priory
Farm

7

PRIORY LANE

LITTLE FEN DROVE

Old Fen
Farm

69

LITTLE FEN DROVE

6

Burwell Lode

Burwell
Fen Farm

LITTLE FEN DROVE

Reach Lode

NEWNHAM DROVE

5

68

CB25

Burwell
Fen

HIGHTOWN DROVE

NEWNHAM DROVE

4

SPLIT DROVE

HIGHTOWN DROVE

Hallard's
Fen

NEWNHAM DROVE

3

Swaffham
Prior Fen

HIGHTOWN DROVE

Hurdle
Hall

67

Reach Lode

Burwell
Fen

HIGHTOWN DROVE

2

Manor
House

Greenfield
Farm

LITTLE FEN DROVE

Reach

Churchfield
Farm

BURWELL ROAD

REACH RD

1

THE TYTHE LA.

BLACKBERRY DROVE/VIEW

BARSTON DRIVE

GREAT LA.

FAIR LA.

SWAFFHAM RD

PH

Fullers
Farm

Highfield
Farm

66

55 A 56 C 57 E F
B D

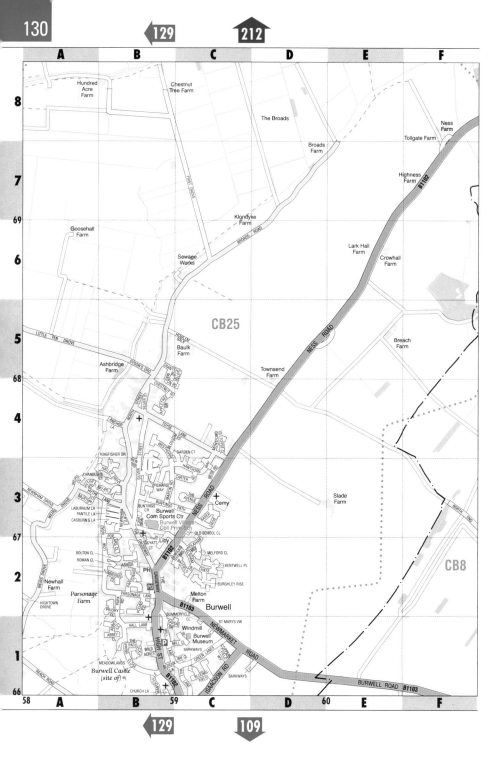

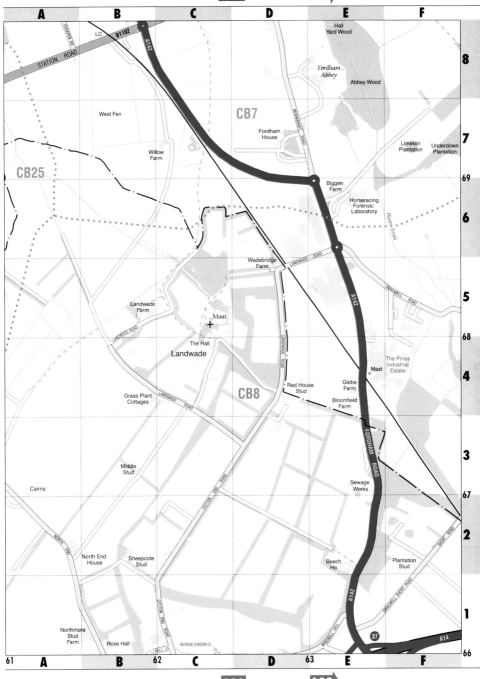

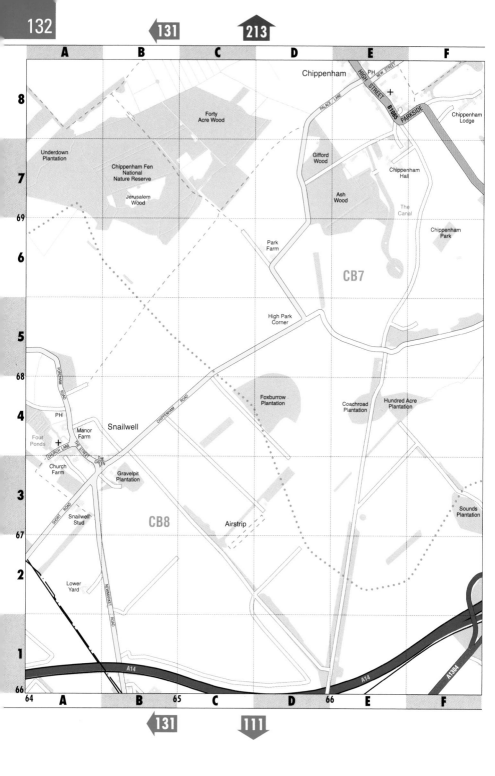

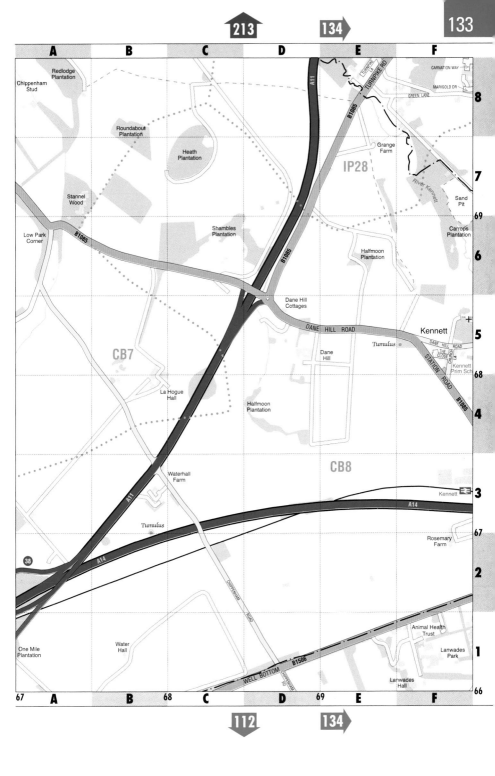

Honeysuckle Cl
Carnation Wy
Marigold Dr
Green Lane
Red Lodge
The Birches

Ickfield Way Path

Triangle Plantation

Blacklands Plantation

Sandpit Plantation

The Grange

Herringswell

Woodlands

Marl Pit Plantation

Warren Farm

Ella's Plantation

Shooting Lodge Plantation

Broomhill Plantation

Prince's Plantation

Three Sisters' Plantation

Sand Pit

George's Plantation

Duke's New Plantation

IP28

Saw Mill

Carrops Plantation

Forest End

The Carrops

Kennett Hall

Tubb's Plantation

Warrenhill Farm

Jubilee Plantation

Hallhill Farm

Court Farm

River Kennett

Home Farm

Kentford Heath

Ickfield Way Path

Anchor Farm

Long Plantation

Longstones Stud

Round Plantation

B1085

Herringswell Road

Moorland Stud

CB8

Tumulus

Slade Bottom

Pin Farm

Nuns Wood

A14

Catswood Farm

Mount Plantation

Station Road

Kennett End

Bury Road

B1506

Factory

B1506

PH

PH

Kentford

Moulton Rd

Edgeborough Cl

Barrett Road

39

A14

Kennett Rd Dr

Moulton Rd

Nursery Plantation

A14 Bury St. Edmunds

Suffolk STREET ATLAS

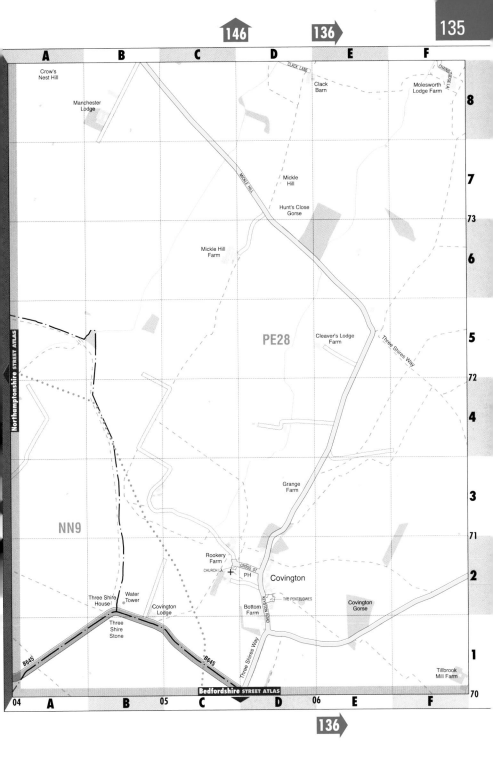

A   B   C   D   E   F

Crow's
Nest Hill

CLACK LANE

Clack
Barn

Molesworth
Lodge Farm

CHANGE-BRIDGE LA

8

Manchester
Lodge

Mickle
Hill

7

MICKLE HILL

Hunt's Close
Gorse

73

Mickle Hill
Farm

6

PE28

Cleaver's Lodge
Farm

Three Shires Way

5

72

4

Grange
Farm

3

71

NN9

Rookery
Farm

CROSS ST

Covington

2

CHURCH LA

PH

THE PENTELOWES

Three Shire
House

Water
Tower

KEYSOE ROAD

Covington
Gorse

Covington
Lodge

Bottom
Farm

Three
Shire
Stone

Three Shires Way

1

B645

B645

Tillbrook
Mill Farm

70

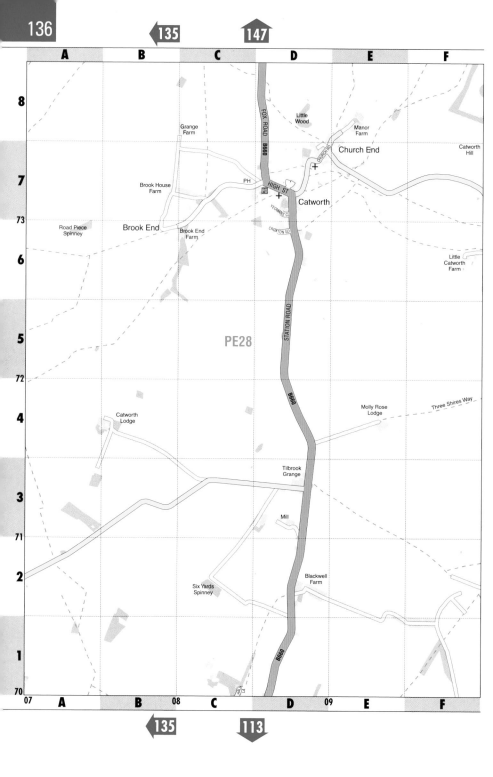

A   B   C   D   E   F

8

FOX ROAD

Little
Wood

Manor
Farm

Grange
Farm

B660

Catworth
Hill

Church End

7

Brook House
Farm

PH

HIGH ST

PO

YEOMANS CL

Catworth

73

Road Piece
Spinney

Brook End

Brook End
Farm

CROXTON RD

Little
Catworth
Farm

6

STATION ROAD

PE28

5

72

B660

Molly Rose
Lodge

Three Shires Way

4

Catworth
Lodge

Tilbrook
Grange

3

Mill

71

Six Yards
Spinney

Blackwell
Farm

2

B660

1

70

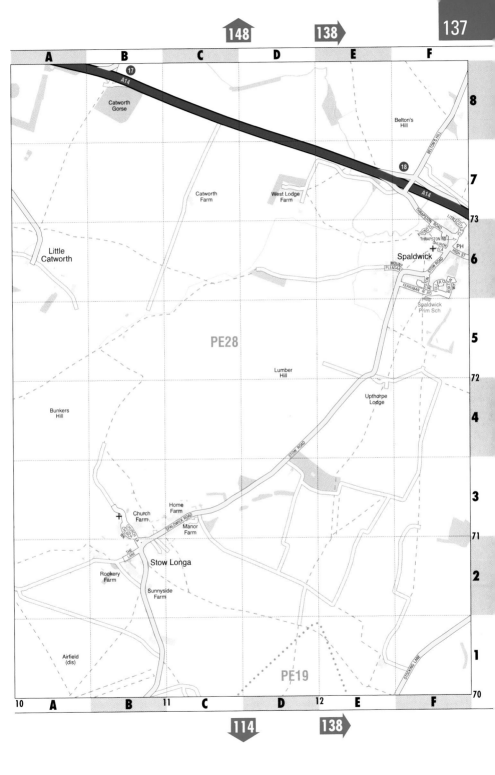

A14

17

Catworth Gorse

Belton's Hill

8

West Lodge Farm

Catworth Farm

18

A14

7

73

THRAPSTON ROAD

LITTLECOT CL

Little Catworth

THRAPSTON RD
CHURCH LA
HIGH ST

Spaldwick

PH

6

MOUNT PLEASANT

STOW ROAD

FERRIMAN

Spaldwick Prim Sch

PE28

5

Lumber Hill

72

Upthorpe Lodge

Bunkers Hill

4

STOW ROAD

3

Home Farm

Church Farm

SPALDWICK ROAD

71

CHURCH WK

Manor Farm

THE LANE

Stow Longa

2

Rookery Farm

Sunnyside Farm

1

Airfield (dis)

PE19

STOCKING LANE

70

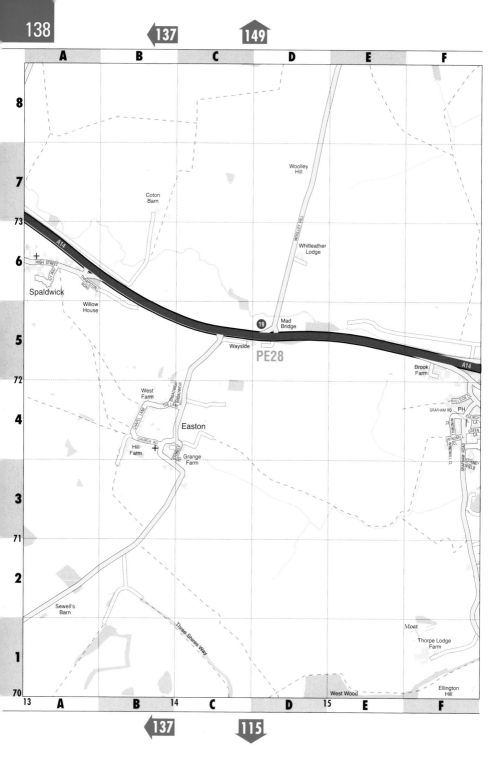

A B C D E F

8

7

73

6 High Street
Spaldwick

Coton Barn

Woolley Hill

Whitleather Lodge

Willow House

5 Wayside

19 Mad Bridge

PE28

Brook Farm

72

West Farm

Easton

Hillside CL

Grafham Rd

PH

4

Church La

Green La

Windmill CL

Chapel Lane

The Broadway

Church Rd

Hill Farm

Grange Farm

Windmill

Grafham Road

Spinney Field

3

71

2

Sewell's Barn

Moat

Thorpe Lodge Farm

Three Shires Way

1

70

West Wood

Ellington Hill

13 A B 14 C D 15 E F

A B C D E F

8

Moat

Weybridge
Lodge Farm

7

73

Weybridge
Farm

6

PE28

5

20

Grove
Bridge

Sand &
Gravel Pit

72

MALTING LA

THRAPSTON ROAD

Moat

A14

HIGH ST

COACHING LA

ST PETER'S WAY

Manor Farm

Woodhatch
Farm

Little
Meadow
Farm

4

Ellington

PARSON'S DR

Low
Harthay

Church
Farm

High
Harthay

3

71

Ellington
Thorpe

2

Moat

Underlands
Wood

Red
Wood

Redwood
Lodge

Brampton Wood
Nature Reserve

1

Madders
Hill

Sparrow's
Spinney

70

16 A B 17 C D 18 E F

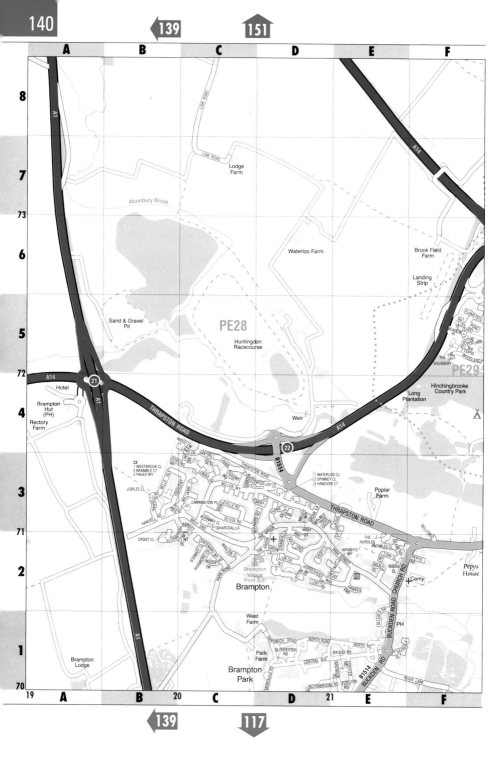

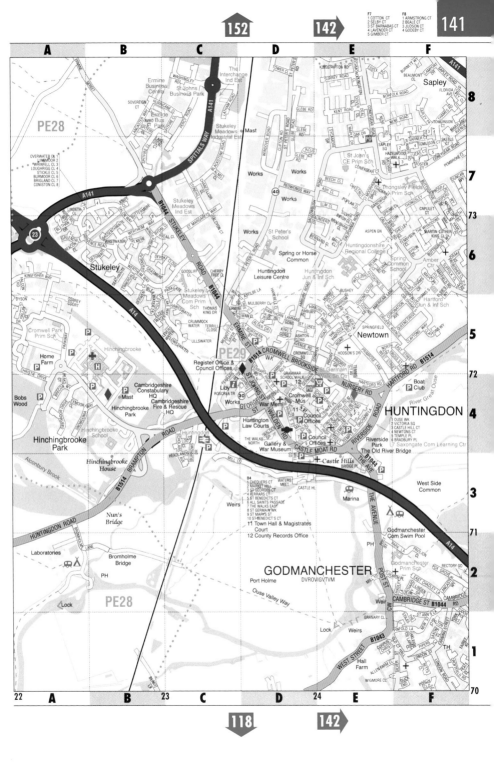

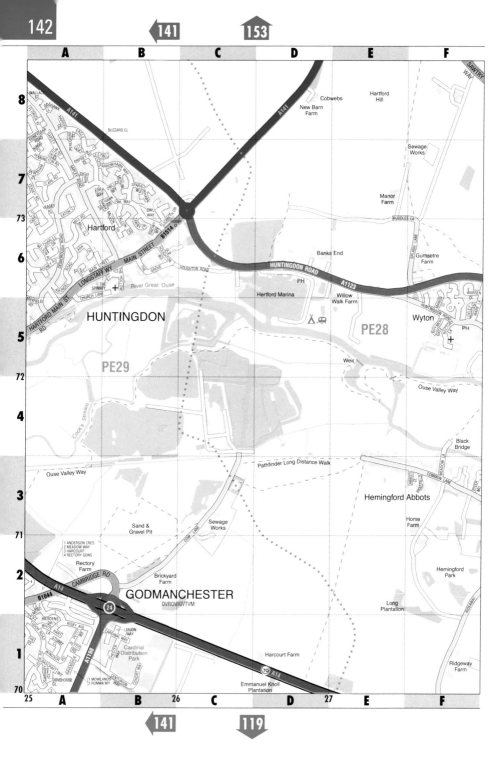

HUNTINGDON

Hartford

PE29

PE28

Wyton

Hemingford Abbots

GODMANCHESTER
DVROVIGVTVM

Cardinal
Distribution
Park

Rectory
Farm

Brickyard
Farm

Sand &
Gravel Pit

Sewage
Works

Hartford Marina

Willow
Walk Farm

Banks End

New Barn
Farm

Cobwebs

Hartford
Hill

Sewage
Works

Manor
Farm

Gumsetre
Farm

River Great Ouse

The Spinney

Weir

Ouse Valley Way

Ouse Valley Way

Pathfinder Long Distance Walk

Black
Bridge

Home
Farm

Hemingford
Park

Long
Plantation

Harcourt Farm

Ridgeway
Farm

Emmanuel Knoll
Plantation

Huntingdon Road

Cambridge Rd

Legion
Way

1 Anderson Cres
2 Meadow Way
3 Harcourt
4 Rectory Gdns

1 Mowlands
2 Roman Wy

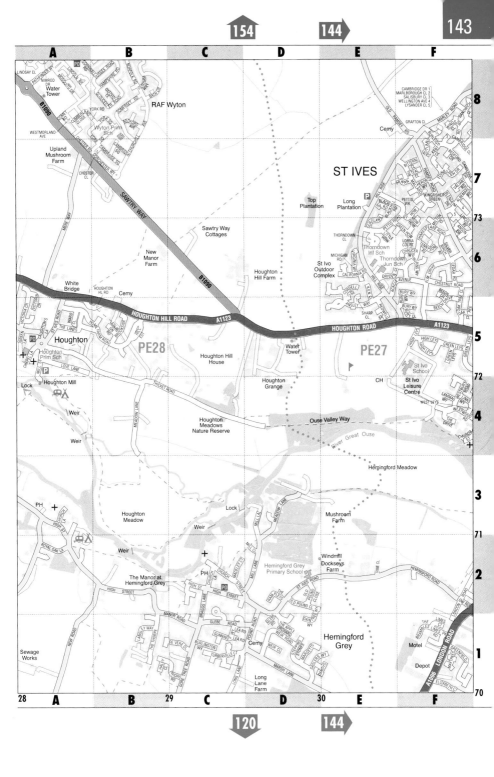

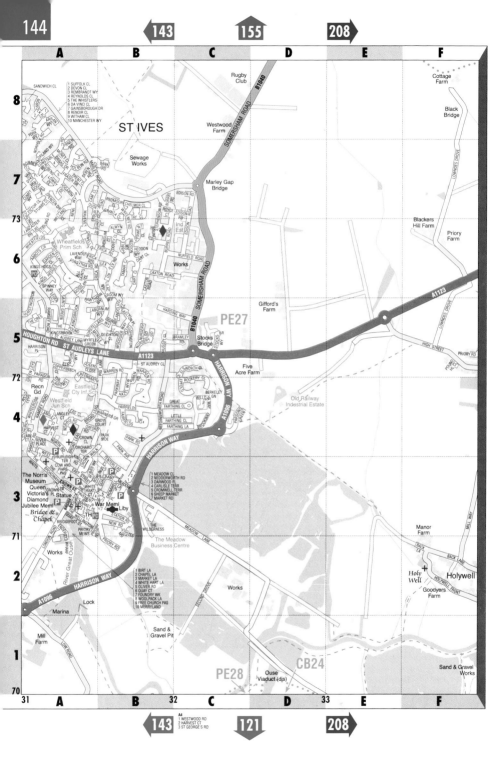

A   B   C   D   E   F

8

7

73

6

5

72

4

3

71

2

1

70

ST IVES

1 SUFFOLK CL
2 DEVON CL
3 REMBRANDT WY
4 REYNOLDS CT
5 THE WHISTLERS
6 DA VINCI CL
7 GAINSBOROUGH DR
8 RENOIR CL
9 WITHAM CL
10 MANCHESTER WY

SANDWICH CL

Sewage
Works

Rugby
Club

Westwood
Farm

Cottage
Farm

Black
Bridge

Marley Gap
Bridge

EDISON RD

CHELMER CL

ROYCE

Ind Est

Works

CAXTON ROAD

NUFFIELD ROAD

Wheatfields
Prim Sch

LAVENDER
WAY

HARDING WAY

KINGS HDGS

SPINNEY
WAY

HAWTHORN

LABURNUM

THE CRES

KINGSBROOKE

HOUGHTON RD   ST AUDLEYS LANE

HARRISON
PL

BRAMLEY

Stocks
Bridge

Blackers
Hill Farm

Priory
Farm

PE27

SOMERSHAM ROAD

B1040

B1040

A1123

A1123

Gifford's
Farm

Five
Acre Farm

HIGH STREET

PRIORY RD

ST AUDREY CL

WARREN RD

ROOKERY CT

GREAT
FARTHING CL

LITTLE
FARTHING CL
FARTHING LA

CROWN ST

BERKELEY
GN

WILLO

HARRISON WAY

Old Railway
Industrial Estate

Recn
Gd

Eastfield
City Inf Sch

Westfield
Jun Sch

FAIRFIELDS

WARNERS GR

GROVE
COURT

PARK
WIDE

PARK RD

Harvest

RIVER
PLACE

ORCHARD
TER

COW AND
HARE PAS

WHITE
HART

CROWN
WK

1 MEADOW CL
2 NEDDERWORTH RD
3 DARWOOD PL
4 CARLISLE TERR
5 CROMWELL TERR
6 SHEEP MARKET
7 MARKET RD

War Meml

Liby

The Norris
Museum
Queen
Victoria's
Diamond
Jubilee Meml
Bridge &
Chapel

TH

Statue

NEW RD

PRIORY RD

THE
WILDERNESS

The Meadow
Business Centre

MEADOW LANE

Manor
Farm

BACK
LA

BACK LA

Holy
Well

Holywell

Goodyers
Farm

MILL WAY

HOLYWELL FRONT

Works

1 BIRT LA
2 CHAPEL LA
3 MARKET LA
4 WHITE HART LA
5 OLIVER RD
6 QUAY CT
7 FOUNDRY WK
8 WOOLPACK LA
9 FREE CHURCH PAS
10 MERRYLAND

HARRISON WAY

A1096

River Great Ouse

Lock

Marina

Mill
Farm

LOW ROAD

Sand &
Gravel Pit

Works

SCOON DRIVE

PE28

Ouse
Viaduct (dis)

CB24

Sand & Gravel
Works

LOWNDES GROVE

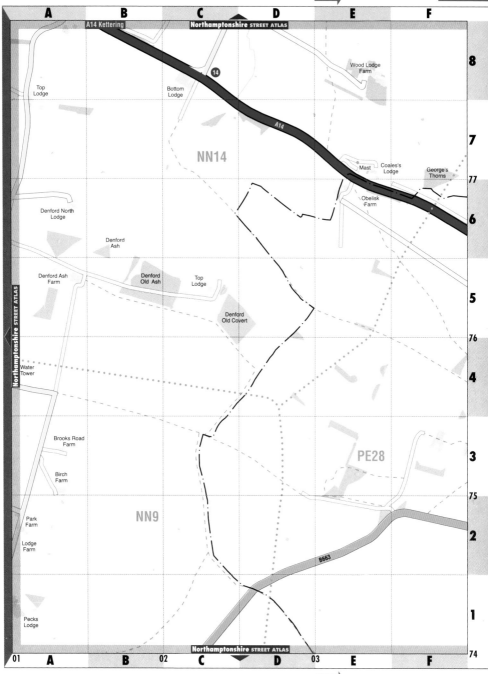

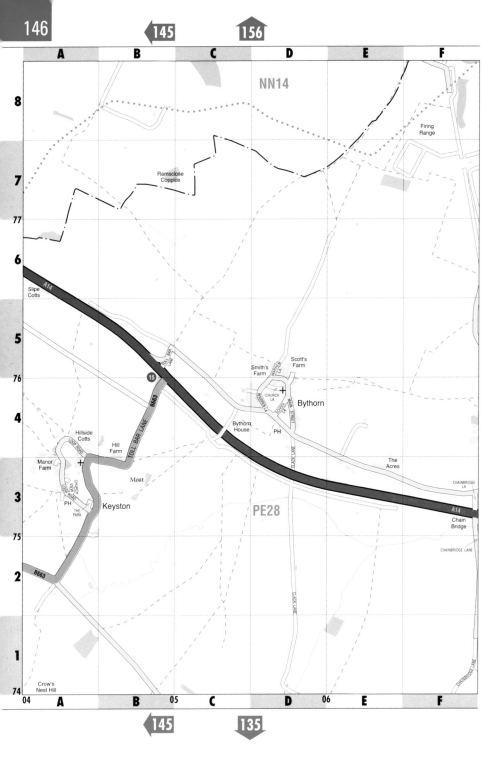

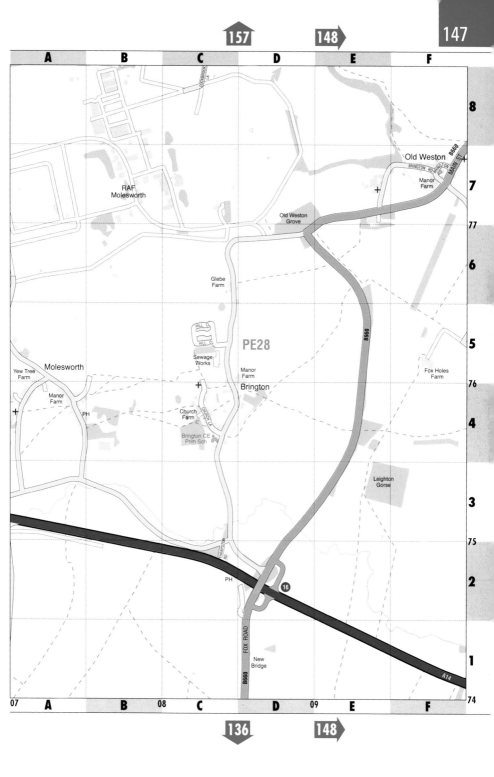

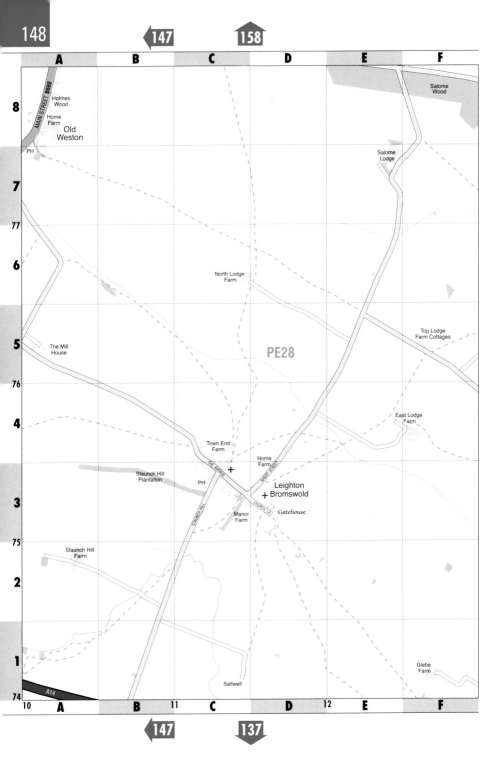

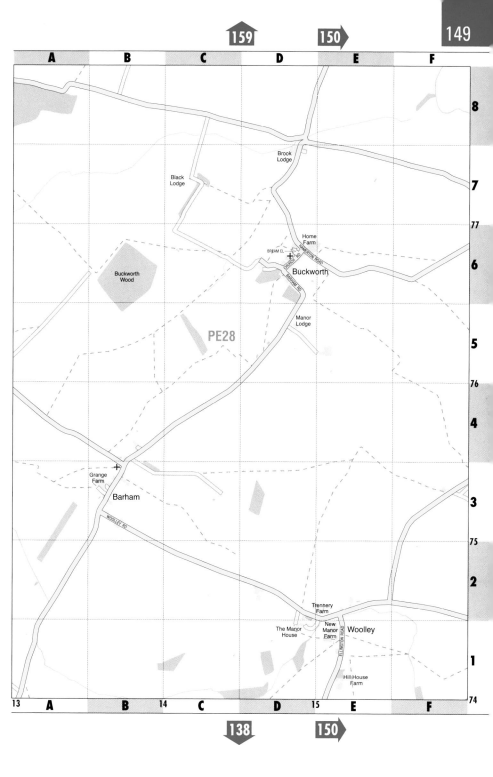

8

7

77

6

Brook
Lodge

Black
Lodge

Home
Farm

BREAM CL

Buckworth

Buckworth
Wood

PE28

Manor
Lodge

5

76

4

Grange
Farm

Barham

3

75

WOOLLEY RD

2

Trennery
Farm

New
Manor
Farm

Woolley

The Manor
House

ELLINGTON ROAD

Hill House
Farm

1

74

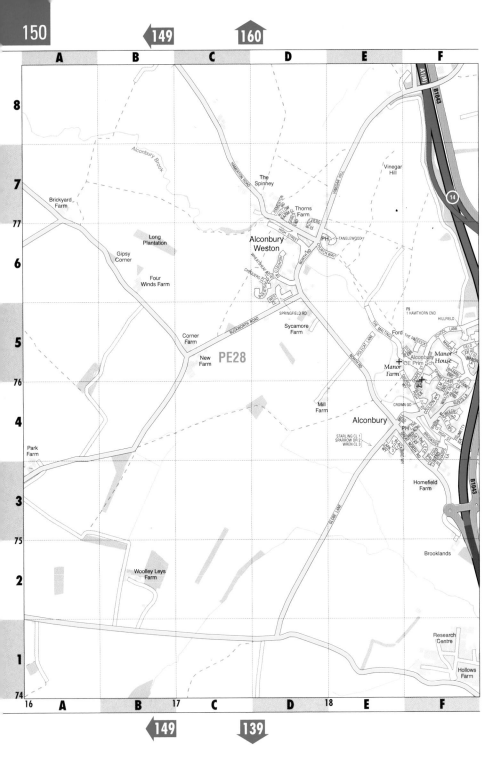

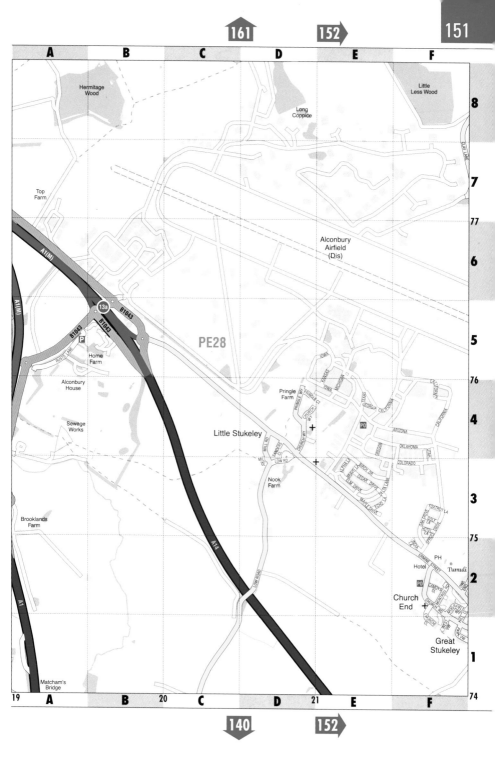

Hermitage
Wood

Little
Less Wood

8

Long
Coppice

7

Top
Farm

A1(M)

77

Alconbury
Airfield
(Dis)

6

A1(M)

13a B1043

B1043

B1043

P

PE28

5

BUSH LANE

Home
Farm

IOWA

76

Alconbury
House

Pringle
Farm

KANSAS

IOWA

MICHIGAN

TEXAS

GEORGIA

CALIFORNIA

CALIFORNIA

4

Sewage
Works

PRINGLE WY

PRINGLE CT

CHURCH

ARIZONA

OKLAHOMA

UTAH

COLORADO

Little Stukeley

MILL RD

CHURCH WY

OREGON

MILL
CL

GARDENS

LOW RD

Nook
Farm

S PETER LA

BIRCH DR

CEDAR DRIVE

DELTA LANE

MAPLE DRIVE

FORD LA

3

Brooklands
Farm

A14

ELM DRIVE

FOXTROT LA

OAK DRIVE

HOLLY

HOTEL DR

NOVA

75

PH

Hotel

Tumuli

ERMINE STREET

2

A1

PO

Church
End

CANDY'S

CHERRY WY

CHURCH

CHAPEL

DAIRY WY

Great
Stukeley

1

Matcham's
Bridge

19   20   21

74

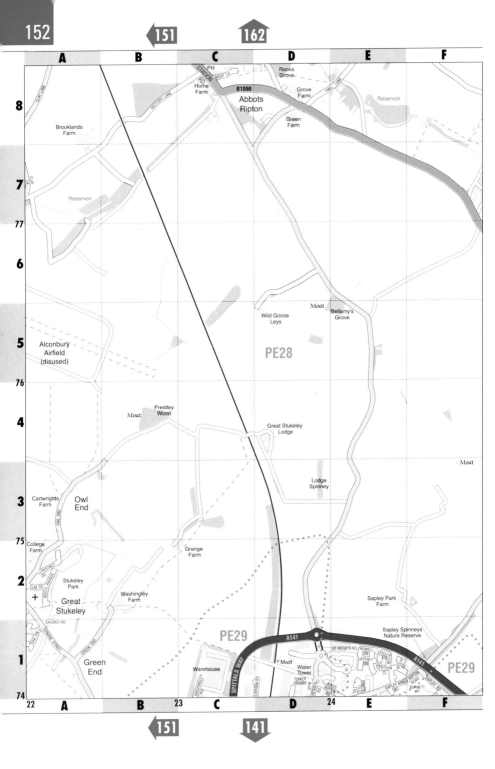

A B C D E F

8
Brooklands
Farm

Rooks
Grove

PH
STATION RD
MOAT LA.
Home
Farm
B1090
Abbots
Ripton

Grove
Farm
HALL LANE
Reservoir

Green
Farm

7
Reservoir
CLAY LA.

77

6

Wild Goose
Leys

Moat

Bellamy's
Grove

5
Alconbury
Airfield
(disused)

PE28

76

4
Moat
Prestley
Wood

Great Stukeley
Lodge

Moat

3
Cartwrights
Farm
Owl
End
OWL END

Lodge
Spinney

75
College
Farm

Grange
Farm

2
CHESTNUT GR
ELM RD
BEECH AVENUE
Stukeley
Park

Washingley
Farm

Sapley Park
Farm

+
Great
Stukeley

PE29
A141

Sapley Spinneys
Nature Reserve

PE29

CHURCH RD

1
BROOK
THRAPE STREET
GREEN END
Green
End

Warehouse

SPITTALS WAY
HALLINGLEY RD
CATHIELD RD

Mast
Water
Tower

St PETER'S RD
HOWELL
DR
JEFFREY
DR

SAPLEY KINGS RIPTON RD
A141

BURNETT
WY

TOWER
SQUARE
KINGS
RIPTON
RD

74
22 A 23 B C 24 D E F

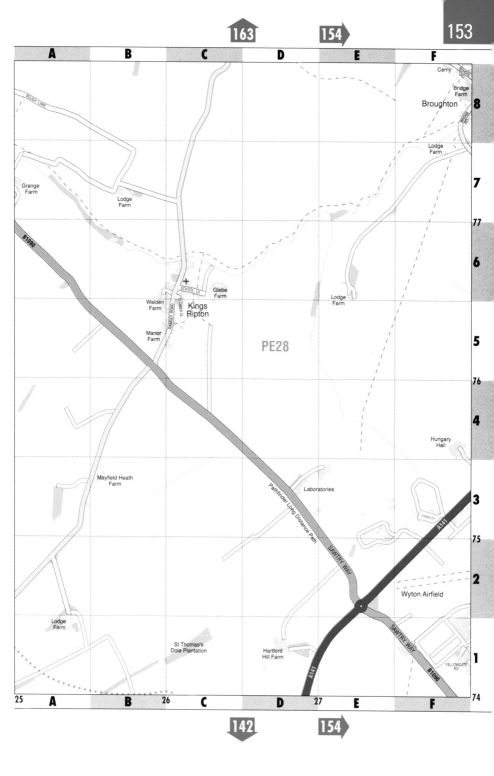

A B C D E F

8 7 77 6 5 76 4 75 2 1 74

Rough Lane

B1090

Grange Farm

Lodge Farm

Walden Farm

SCHOOL LA.
Kings Ripton
Glebe Farm

RAMSEY RD.
HITHER CL.

Manor Farm

Cemy

Bridge Farm

Broughton

SCHOOL WY

BRIDGE RD

Lodge Farm

Lodge Farm

PE28

Hungary Hall

Mayfield Heath Farm

Pathfinder Long Distance Path

Laboratories

SAWTRY WAY

A141

75

Wyton Airfield

Lodge Farm

St Thomas's Dole Plantation

Hartford Hill Farm

SAWTRY WAY

B1090

YELLOWGATE RD

25 A B 26 C D 27 E F

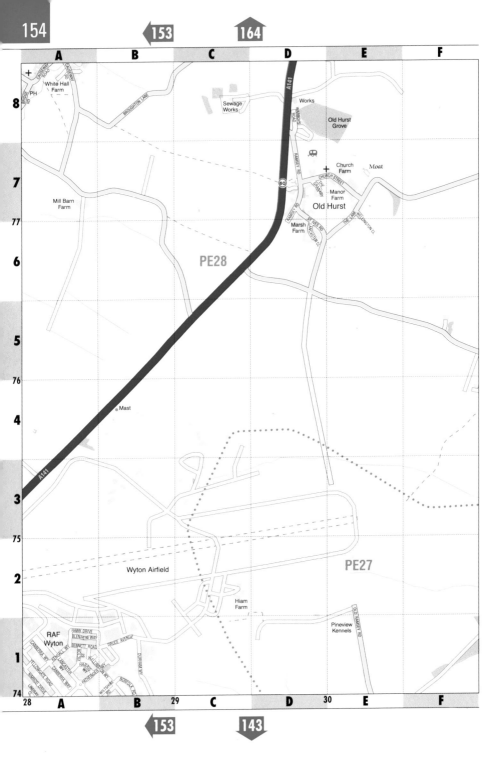

A B C D E F

8

White Hall Farm

PH

Sewage Works

Works

Old Hurst Grove

A141

BROUGHTON LANE

RAMSEY RD

WARBOYS ROAD

7

Mill Barn Farm

60

Church Farm

Moat

CHURCH STREET

Manor Farm

Old Hurst

THE GRANARY

THE LANE

WELLINGTON CL.

77

RAMSEY RD

ST IVES RD

Marsh Farm

LEICESTER CL.

PE28

6

5

76

4

Mast

3

A141

75

Wyton Airfield

PE27

2

Hiam Farm

Pineview Kennels

OLD RAMSEY RD

HAWK DRIVE

BLENHEIM WAY

RAF Wyton

CANBERRA WY

TEDHAM WY

JAVELIN WY

LANCASTER WY

HARRIER WY

WELLINGTON

BENNETT ROAD

DRUCE AVENUE

DURHAM WY

NORFOLK RD

WILTSHIRE RD

PATHFINDER WY

CANBERRA WY

VIMROD DRIVE

ANGLESEY

1

74

28 A B 29 C D 30 E F

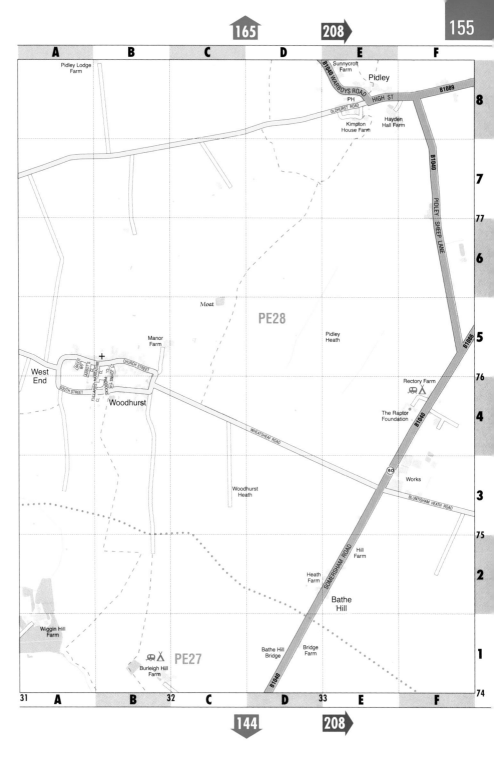

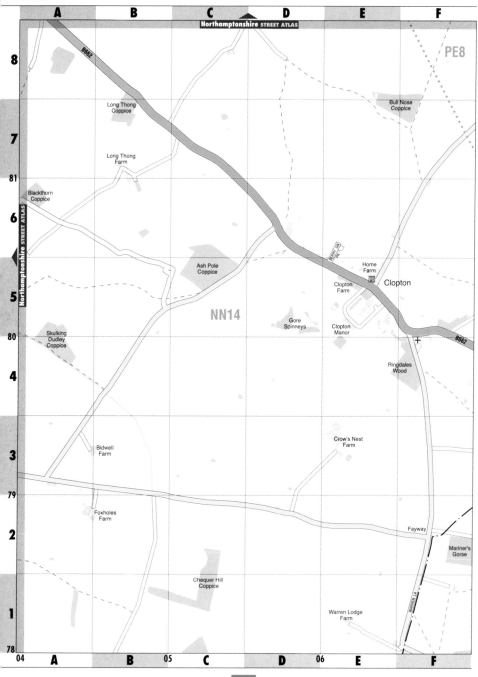

PE8

B662

Long Thong
Coppice

Long Thong
Farm

Blackthorn
Coppice

Bull Nose
Coppice

Ash Pole
Coppice

NN14

Gore
Spinneys

BURY LA

Home
Farm

Clopton
Farm

Clopton

Clopton
Manor

B662

Skulking
Dudley
Coppice

Ringdales
Wood

Bidwell
Farm

Crow's Nest
Farm

Foxholes
Farm

Fayway

Mariner's
Gorse

Chequer Hill
Coppice

Warren Lodge
Farm

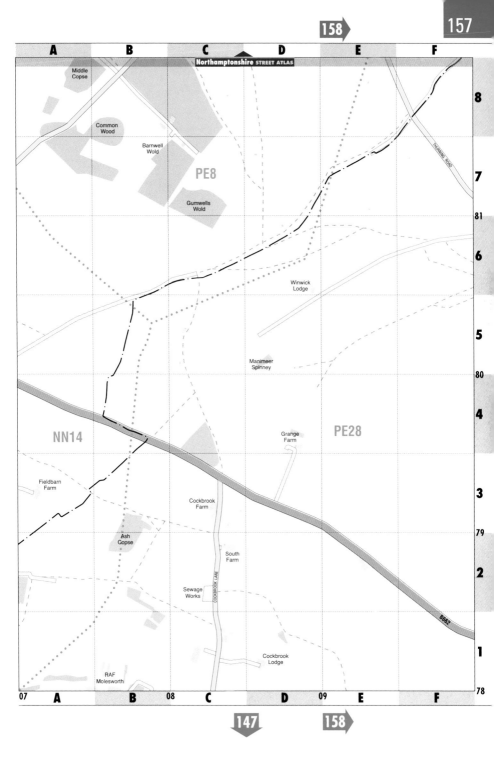

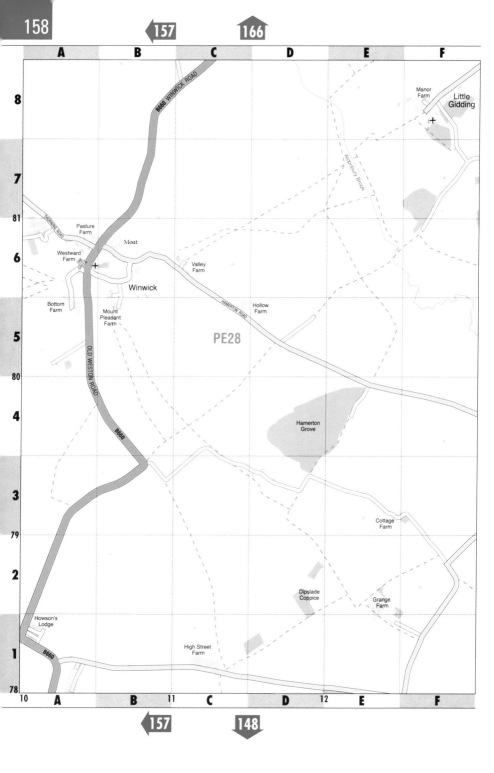

157
166

A **B** **C** **D** **E** **F**

8

Manor Farm

Little Gidding

7

81

Pasture Farm

Turnpike Road

Moat

Westward Farm

Green Lane

Winwick

B660 WINWICK ROAD

Valley Farm

HAMERTON ROAD

Hollow Farm

Alconbury Brook

6

Bottom Farm

Mount Pleasant Farm

PE28

5

80

OLD WESTON ROAD

B660

Hamerton Grove

4

3

79

Cottage Farm

2

Dipslade Coppice

Grange Farm

Howson's Lodge

B660

High Street Farm

1

78

10 **A** **B** 11 **C** **D** 12 **E** **F**

157
148

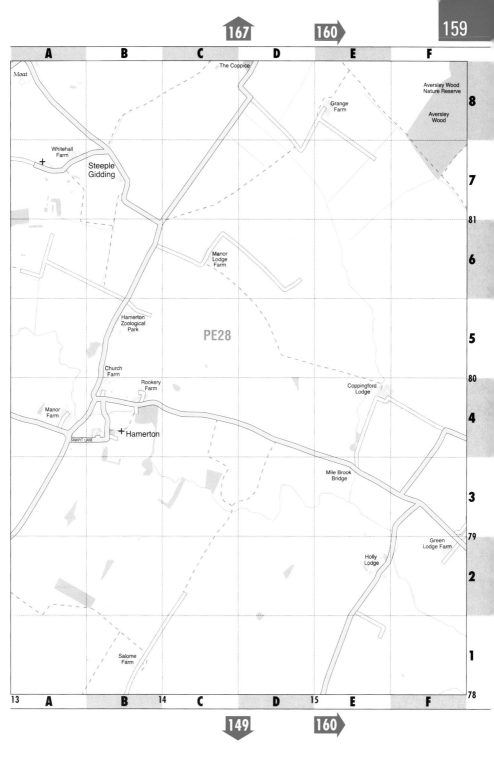

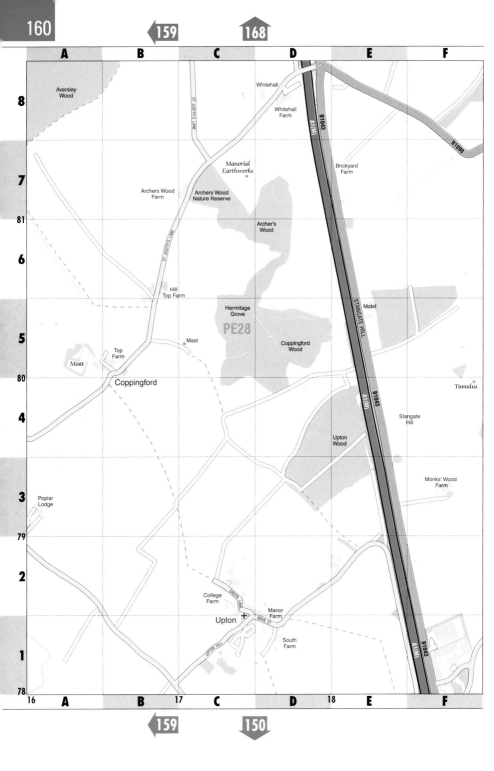

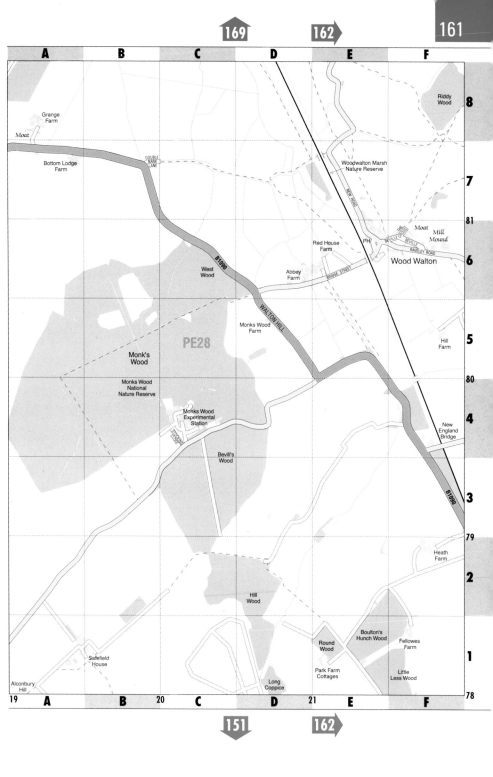

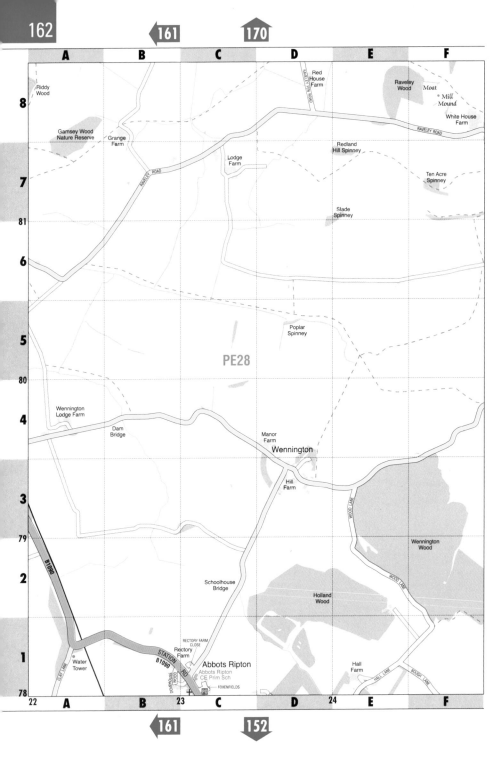

Riddy Wood

Gamsey Wood Nature Reserve

Grange Farm

RAVELEY ROAD

Lodge Farm

Red House Farm

BARLEYTHE ROAD

Raveley Wood

Moat

Mill Mound

White House Farm

RAVELEY ROAD

Redland Hill Spinney

Ten Acre Spinney

Slade Spinney

Poplar Spinney

PE28

Wennington Lodge Farm

Dam Bridge

Manor Farm

Wennington

Hill Farm

Wood Lane

Wennington Wood

WOOD LANE

Schoolhouse Bridge

Holland Wood

B1090

Water Tower

CLAY LANE

STATION RD

B1090

DOVEHOUSE WOOD

RECTORY FARM CLOSE

Rectory Farm

Abbots Ripton
Abbots Ripton CE Prim Sch

FOXENFIELDS

Hall Farm

HALL LANE

BOUGH LANE

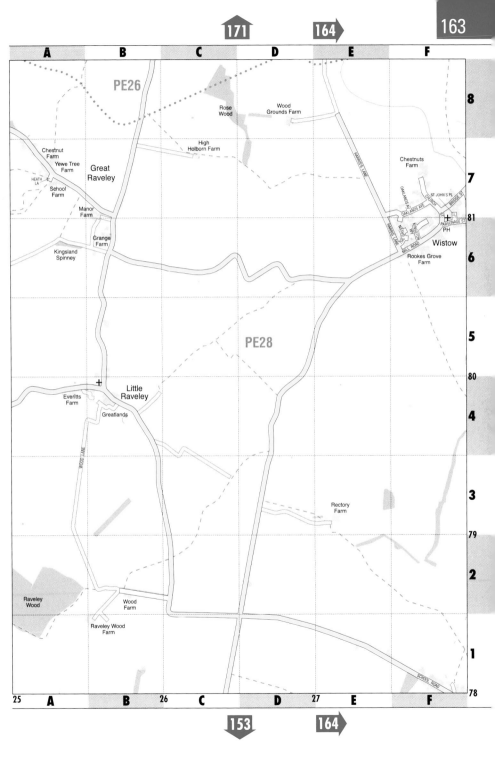

A   B   C   D   E   F

PE26

8

Rose
Wood

Wood
Grounds Farm

High
Holborn Farm

Chestnut
Farm
Yewe Tree
Farm

Great
Raveley

HEATH
LA

School
Farm

Chestnuts
Farm

7

NARISS'S LANE

OAKLANDS AV

ST JOHN'S PL

BRIDGE ST

Manor
Farm

PARSONAGE ST   81

KINGSTON
WAY

PH

Grange
Farm

Wistow

Kingsland
Spinney

HARRIS'S LANE

MILL ROAD

Rookes Grove
Farm

6

PE28

5

80

Everitts
Farm

Little
Raveley

4

Greatlands

WOOD LANE

3

Rectory
Farm

79

2

Raveley
Wood

Wood
Farm

Raveley Wood
Farm

1

SCHOOL ROAD

78

25   A   B   26   C   D   27   E   F

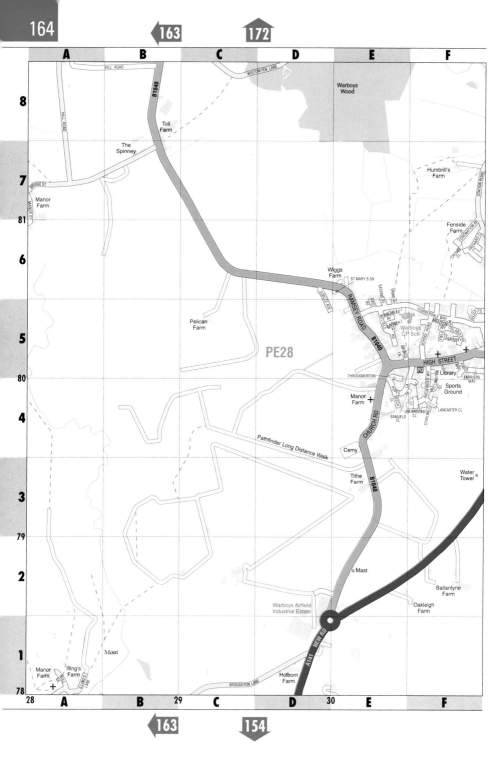

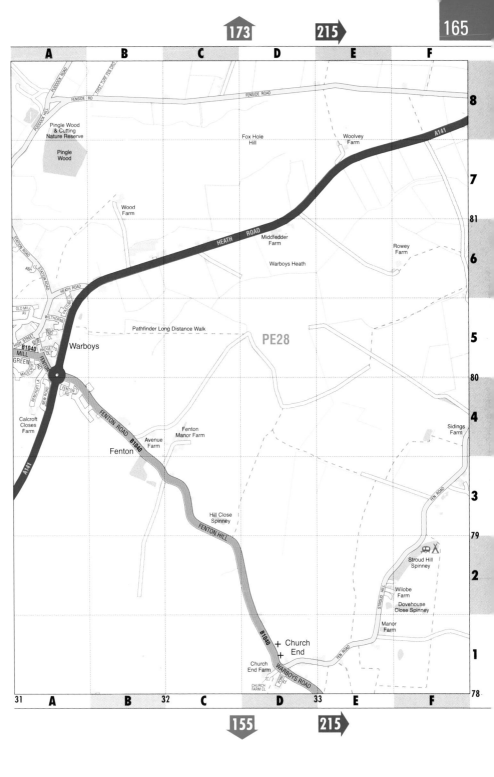

174

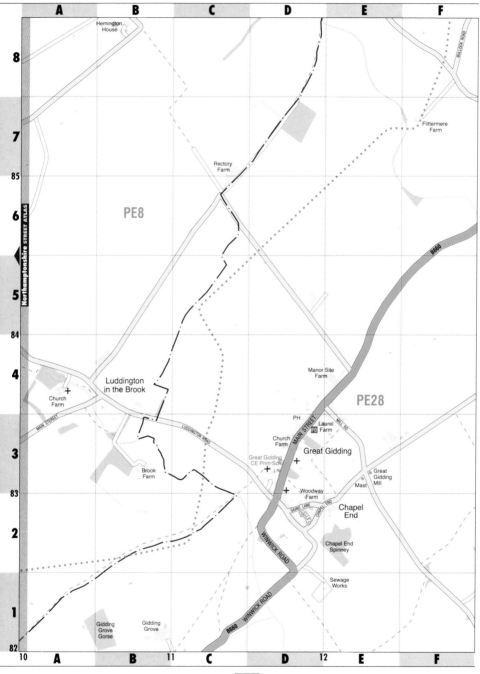

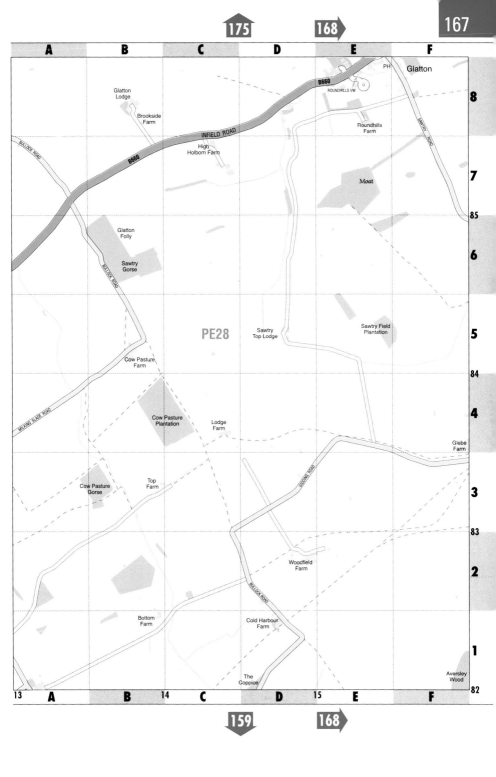

A B C D E F

Glatton

B660

Glatton
Lodge

Brookside
Farm

ROUNDHILLS VW

PH

8

INFIELD ROAD

Roundhills
Farm

SAWTRY ROAD

B660

High
Holborn Farm

7

BULLOCK ROAD

Moat

85

Glatton
Folly

6

BULLOCK ROAD

Sawtry
Gorse

PE28

Sawtry
Top Lodge

Sawtry Field
Plantation

5

84

Cow Pasture
Farm

MILKING SLADE ROAD

Cow Pasture
Plantation

Lodge
Farm

4

Glebe
Farm

Cow Pasture
Gorse

Top
Farm

GROOME ROAD

3

83

Woodfield
Farm

2

BULLOCK ROAD

Bottom
Farm

Cold Harbour
Farm

1

The
Coppice

Aversley
Wood

82

13 A B 14 C D 15 E F

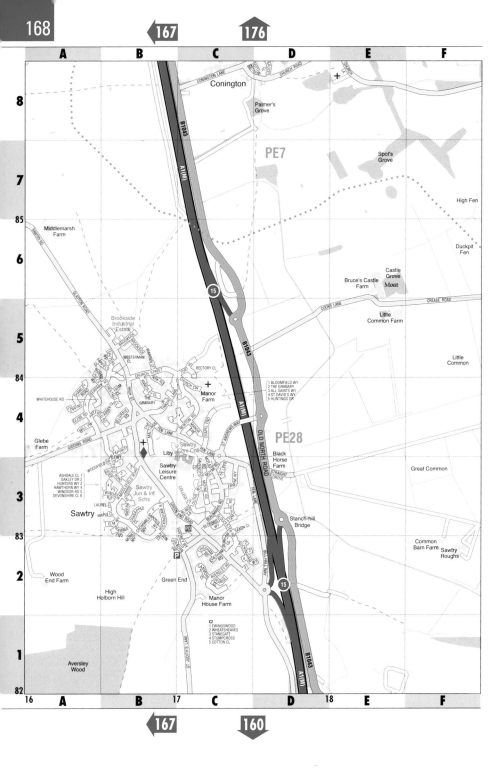

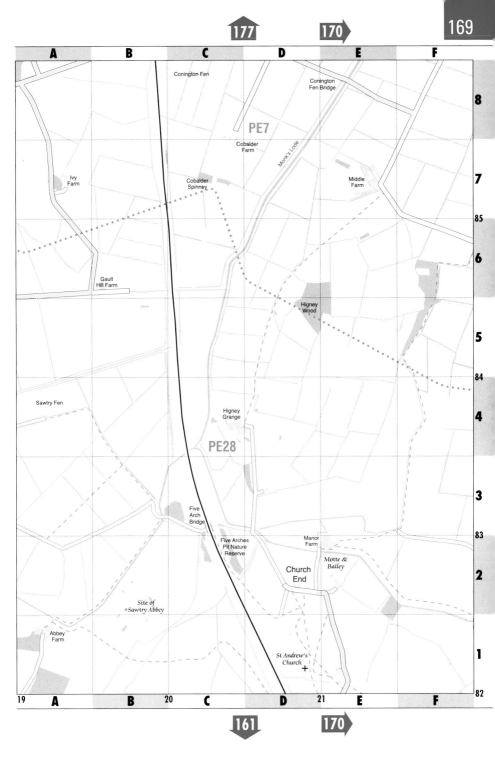

169
220

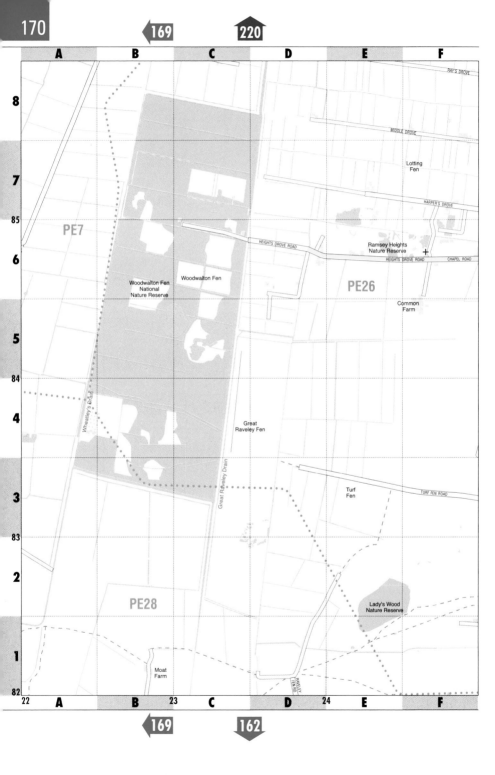

169
162

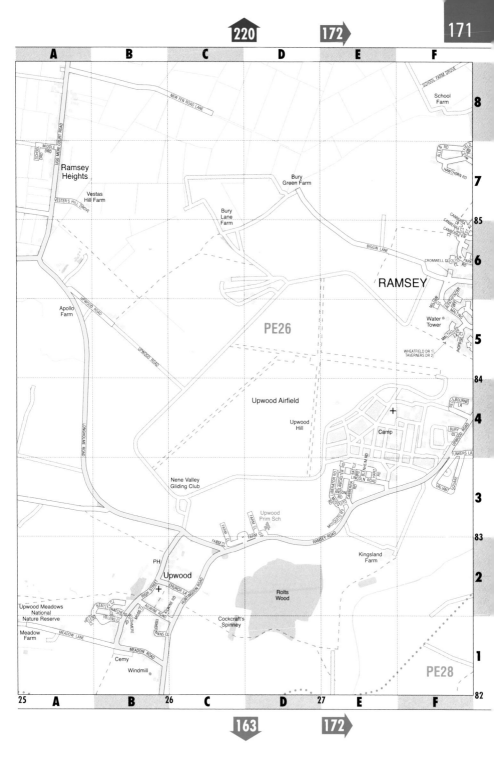

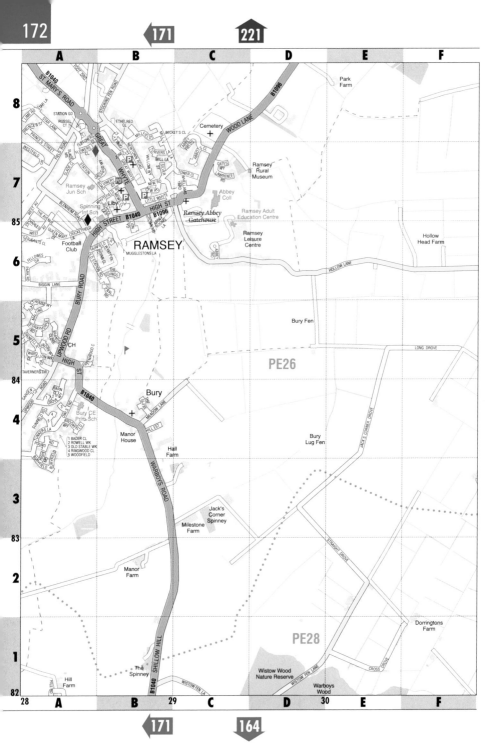

Map labels

B1040 ST MARY'S ROAD

STATION GD

RUSSEL CT

ETHELRED CL

Cemetery

WOOD LANE

B1096

Park Farm

Ramsey Rural Museum

Abbey Coll

Ramsey Jun Sch

Spinning Inf Sch

Lib

HIGH ST

LITTLE WHYTE

Ramsey Abbey Gatehouse

B1040

B1096

Ramsey Adult Education Centre

Football Club

RAMSEY

MUGGLESTONS LA

Ramsey Leisure Centre

Hollow Head Farm

BIGGIN LANE

HOLLOW LANE

BURY ROAD

Bury Fen

UPWOOD RD

HIGH ST

PE26

LONG DROVE

TAVERNERS DR

Bury CE Prim Sch

Bury

MEADOW LANE

HILL EST

Bury Lug Fen

JACK'S CORNER DRIVE

B1040

1 BADER CL
2 ROWELL WK
3 OLD STABLE WK
4 RINGWOOD CL
5 WOODFIELD

Manor House

Hall Farm

WARBOYS ROAD

Jack's Corner Spinney

Milestone Farm

STRAIGHT DROVE

Manor Farm

PE28

Dorringtons Farm

SHILLOW HILL

CROSS DROVE

The Spinney

B1040

WISTOW FEN LA

Wistow Wood Nature Reserve

WISTOW FEN LANE

Hill Farm

Warboys Wood

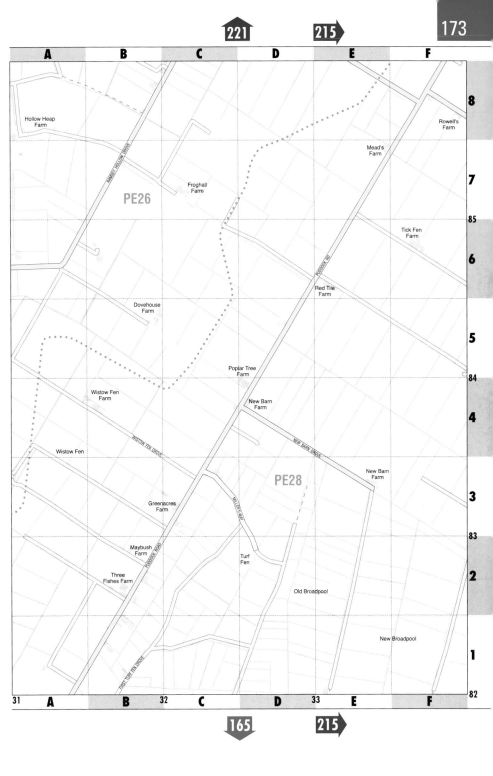

A   B   C   D   E   F

8

Hollow Heap
Farm

Rowell's
Farm

Mead's
Farm

7

PE26

Froghall
Farm

85

Tick Fen
Farm

6

Red Tile
Farm

Dovehouse
Farm

5

Poplar Tree
Farm

84

Wistow Fen
Farm

New Barn
Farm

4

WISTOW FEN DROVE

NEW BARN DROVE

Wistow Fen

New Barn
Farm

PE28

3

Greenacres
Farm

83

Maybush
Farm

Turf
Fen

2

Three
Fishes Farm

Old Broadpool

New Broadpool

1

82

31   A   B   32   C   D   33   E   F

RAMSEY HOLLOW DROVE

RUDDOCK RD

MILLER'S WAY

RUDDOCK ROAD

FIRST TURF FEN DROVE

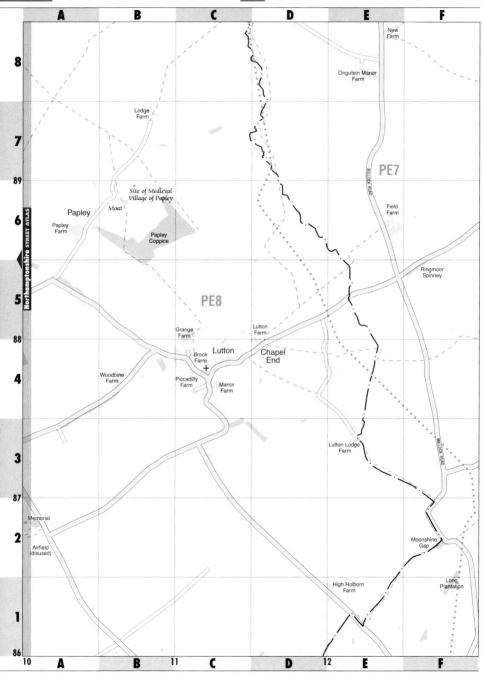

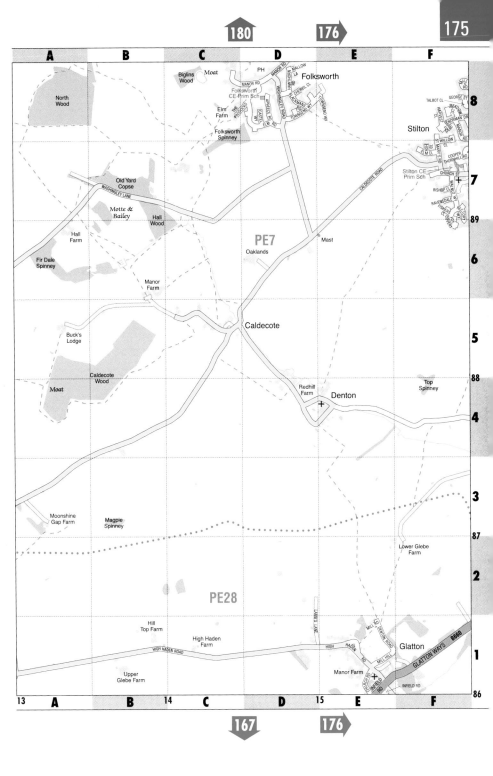

A **B** **C** **D** **E** **F**

North Wood

Biglins Wood

Moat

PH

MANOR RD

MANOR RD

MALLOW

NORTH PATH

Folksworth

8

Folksworth CE Prim Sch

Elm Farm

THE MEADOWS

CHERVIL CL

MANOR WY

CASTLE WY

APPLECE RD

ELM RD

WASHINGLEY ROAD

TOWNSEND WY

TOWNSEND WY

Folksworth Spinney

TALBOT CL

GEORGE ST

MEADOW CL

HARFORD CL

BENFORD DR

WILLOW RD

Stilton

7

ST MARY'S RD

WILLOW CL

COOPER THORNHILL RD

CHURCH ST

Stilton CE Prim Sch

BISHOP CL

WALL NUT WY

RECTORY

RAVENSDALE

FENWICK'S CT

89

Old Yard Copse

WASHINGLEY LANE

Motte & Bailey

Hall Wood

CALDECOTE ROAD

PE7

Mast

Hall Farm

Oaklands

6

Fir Dale Spinney

Manor Farm

Buck's Lodge

5

Caldecote

Caldecote Wood

Redhill Farm

Denton

Top Spinney

88

Moat

4

Moonshine Gap Farm

Magpie Spinney

3

Lower Glebe Farm

87

PE28

2

Hill Top Farm

High Haden Farm

LAMB'S LANE

MILL RD

DENTON ROAD

MILL HILL

Glatton

B660

GLATTON WAYS

1

HIGH HADEN ROAD

HIGH HADEN

Manor Farm

BRIDGE RD

INFIELD RD

INFIELD RD

Upper Glebe Farm

86

13 **A** 14 **B** **C** 15 **D** **E** **F**

175
181

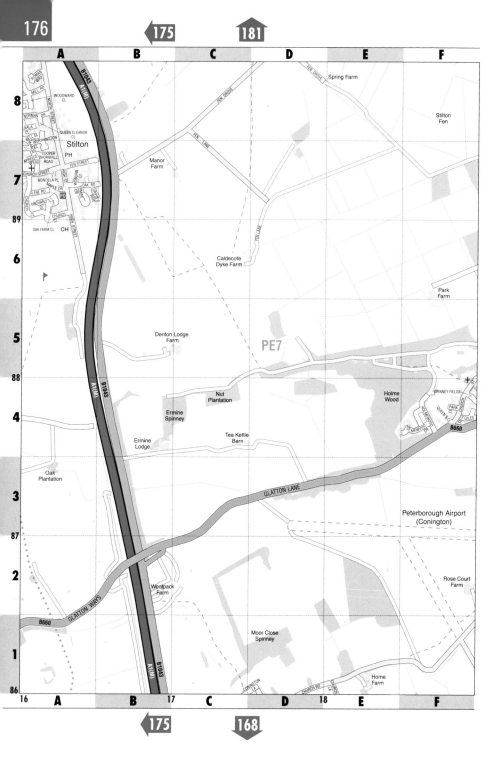

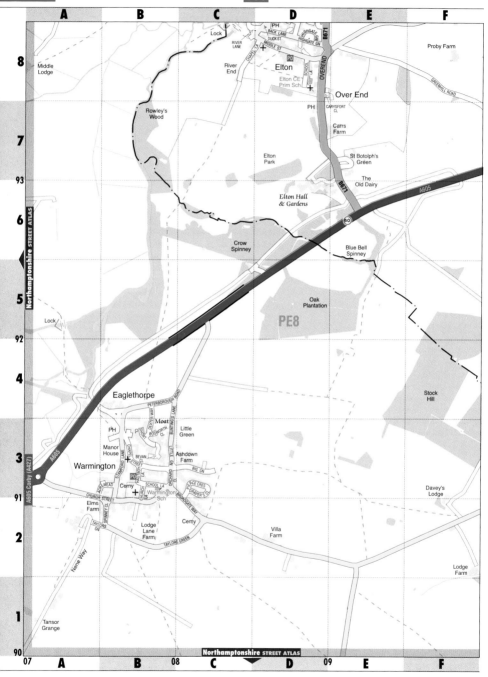

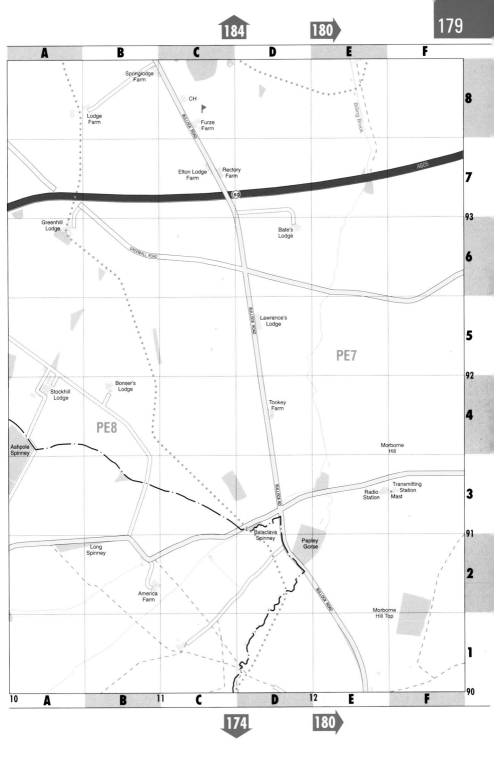

A B C D E F

8

Springlodge
Farm

CH

Lodge
Farm

Furze
Farm

BULLOCK ROAD

Billing Brook

A605

Elton Lodge
Farm

Rectory
Farm

7

60

93

Greenhill
Lodge

GREENHILL ROAD

Bate's
Lodge

6

Lawrence's
Lodge

5

PE7

92

Stockhill
Lodge

Bonser's
Lodge

BULLOCK ROAD

Tookey
Farm

PE8

4

Morborne
Hill

Ashpole
Spinney

3

Transmitting
Station
Mast

Radio
Station

BULLOCK RD

Balaclava
Spinney

91

Long
Spinney

Papley
Gorse

2

America
Farm

BULLOCK ROAD

Morborne
Hill Top

1

10 A   B   11   C   D   12   E   F

90

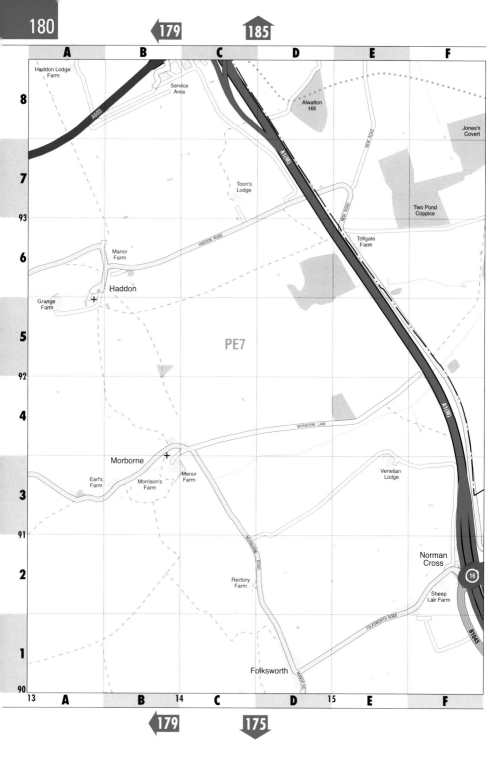

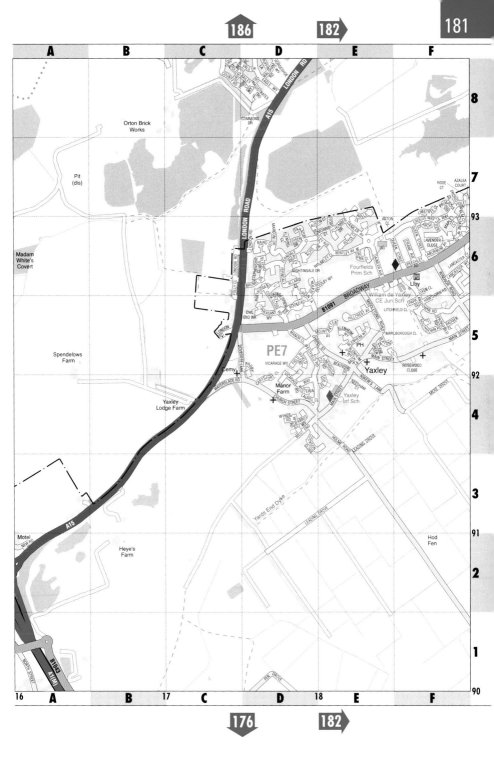

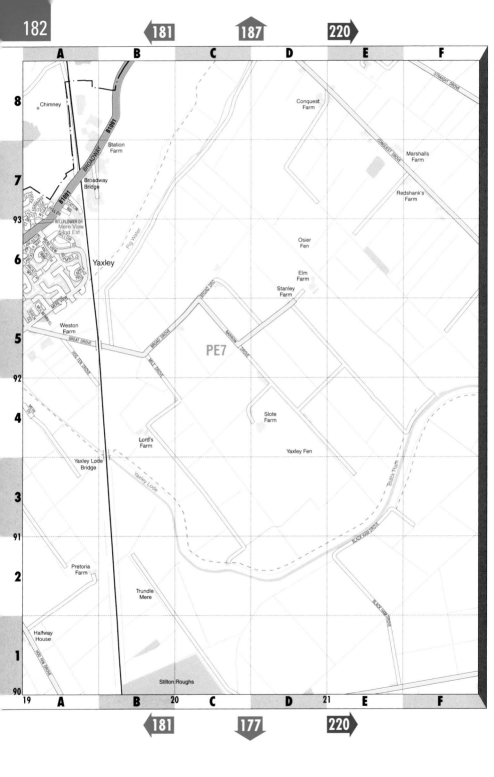

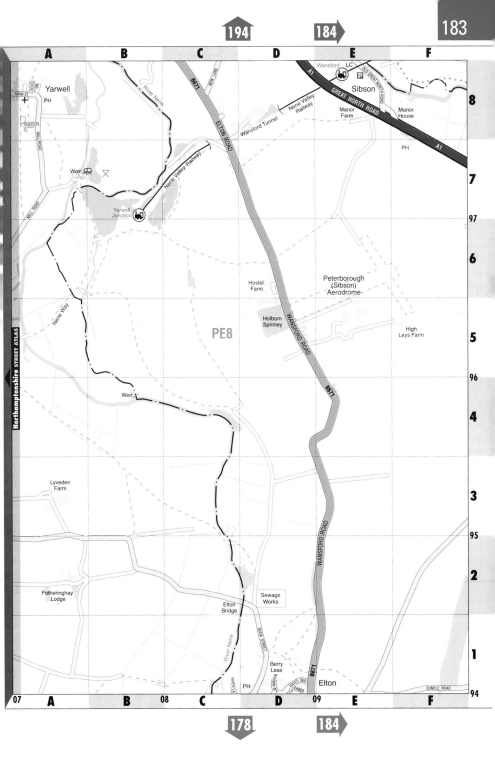

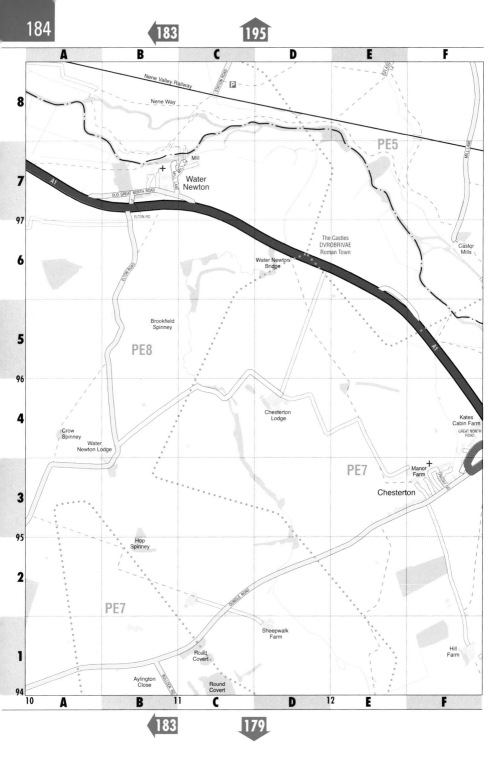

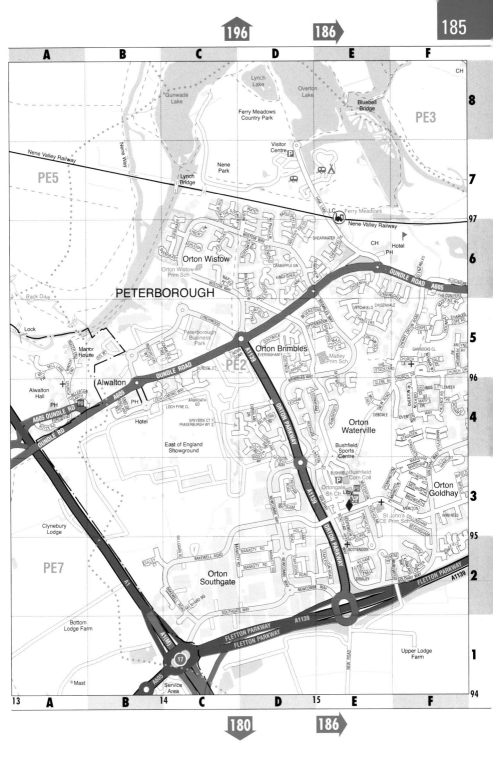

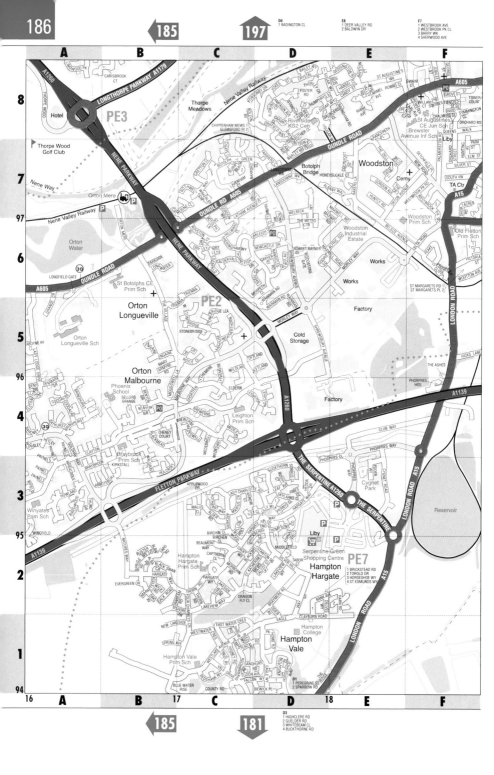

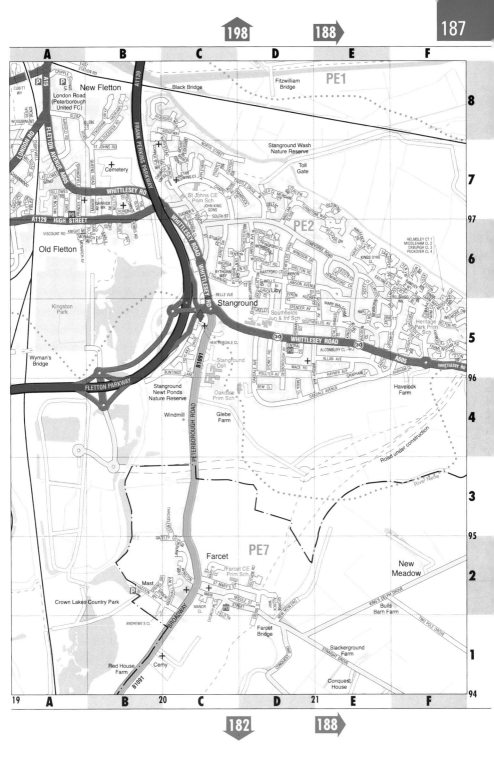

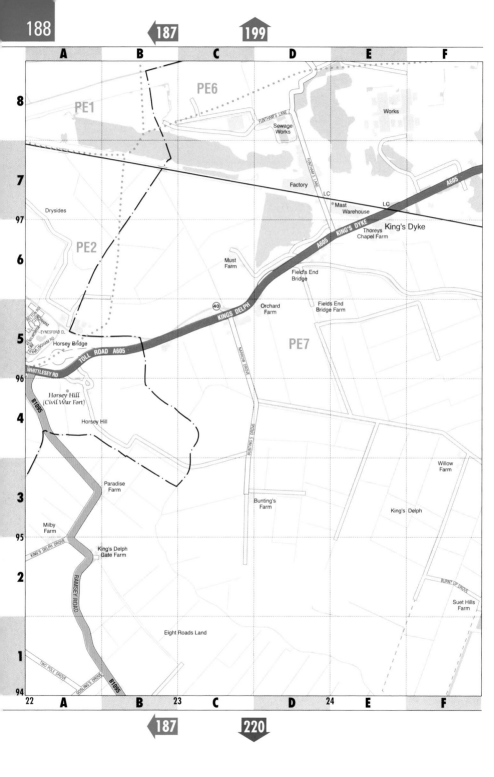

A   B   C   D   E   F

8

PE6

PE1

Works

TUNTHAM'S LANE

Sewage
Works

7

Factory

FENTHAM'S LANE

A605

LC

Drysides

Mast
Warehouse

LC

97

King's Dyke

KING'S DYKE

Thoreys
Chapel Farm

King's Dyke

PE2

A605

6

Must
Farm

Field's End
Bridge

5

40   KINGS DELPH

Orchard
Farm

Fields End
Bridge Farm

PE7

BELTISHGHAM

EYNESFORD CL

FRINGHAM RD

TOLL ROAD A605

Horsey Bridge

MARROW DROVE

WHITTLESEY RD

96

B1095

Horsey Hill
(Civil War Fort)

4

Horsey Hill

Willow
Farm

3

Paradise
Farm

BUNTING'S DROVE

Bunting's
Farm

King's Delph

Milby
Farm

95

KING'S DELPH DROVE

King's Delph
Gate Farm

BURNT UP DROVE

2

RAMSEY ROAD

Suet Hills
Farm

Eight Roads Land

1

TWO POLE DROVE

GOSLING'S DROVE

B1095

94

22   A   B   23   C   D   24   E   F

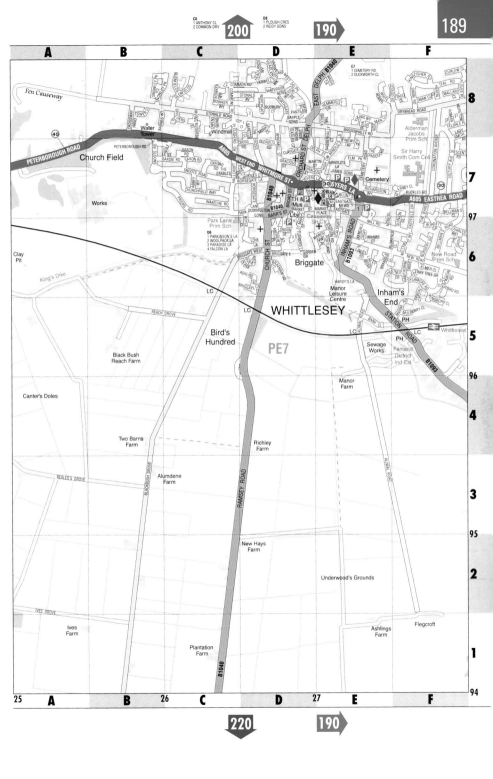

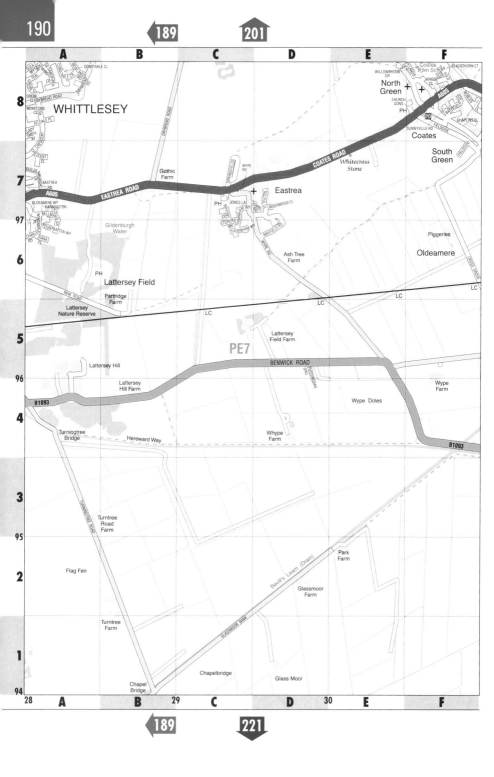

WHITTLESEY

North Green

Coates

South Green

Gothic Farm

COATES ROAD

Whitecross Stone

EASTREA ROAD

A605

Eastrea

PH

Piggeries

Oldeamere

Gildenburgh Water

Ash Tree Farm

PH

Lattersey Field

Partridge Farm

Lattersey Nature Reserve

NEW ROAD

LC

LC

LC

LC

LC

PE7

Lattersey Field Farm

BENWICK ROAD

Lattersey Hill

Lattersey Hill Farm

Wype Farm

B1093

Wype Doles

B1093

Turningtree Bridge

Hereward Way

Whype Farm

Turntree Road Farm

Flag Fen

Bevill's Leam (Drain)

Park Farm

Glassmoor Farm

Turntree Farm

GLASSMOOR BANK

Chapelbridge

Glass Moor

Chapel Bridge

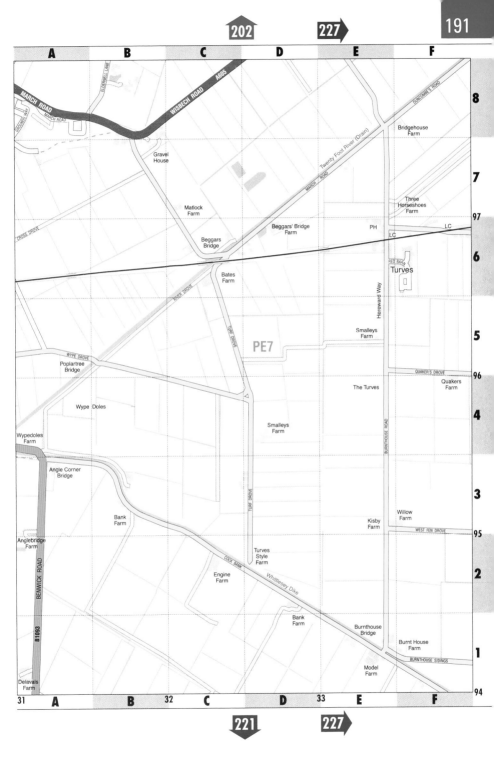

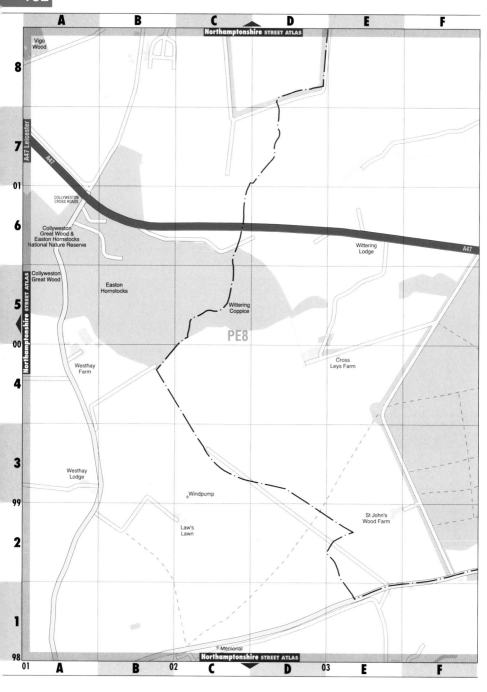

Vigo
Wood

A47 Leicester

A47

COLLYWESTON
CROSS ROADS

Collyweston
Great Wood &
Easton Hornstocks
National Nature Reserve

Collyweston
Great Wood

Easton
Hornstocks

Wittering
Coppice

PE8

Wittering
Lodge

A47

Cross
Leys Farm

Westhay
Farm

Westhay
Lodge

Windpump

St John's
Wood Farm

Law's
Lawn

Memorial

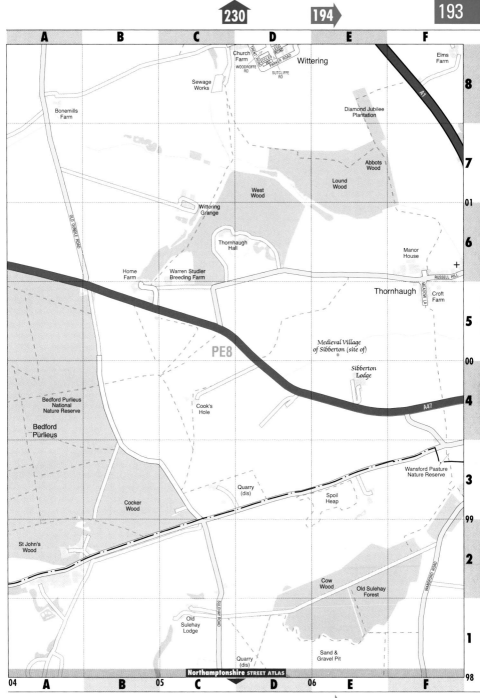

A | B | C | D | E | F

Church Farm
WOODROFFE RD
BECCLES
PARKER ROAD
SUTCLIFFE RD
Wittering

Elms Farm

Sewage Works

Bonemills Farm

Diamond Jubilee Plantation

A1

8

7

01

Abbots Wood

Lound Wood

West Wood

Wittering Grange

Thornhaugh Hall

Manor House

6

Home Farm

Warren Studler Breeding Farm

RUSSELL HILL

MEADOW LA

Thornhaugh

Croft Farm

5

PE8

Medieval Village of Sibberton (site of)

Sibberton Lodge

00

Bedford Purlieus National Nature Reserve

Cook's Hole

A47

4

Bedford Purlieus

Wansford Pasture Nature Reserve

3

Quarry (dis)

Spoil Heap

Cocker Wood

99

St John's Wood

WANSFORD ROAD

2

Cow Wood

Old Sulehay Forest

SULEHAY ROAD

Old Sulehay Lodge

1

Quarry (dis)

Sand & Gravel Pit

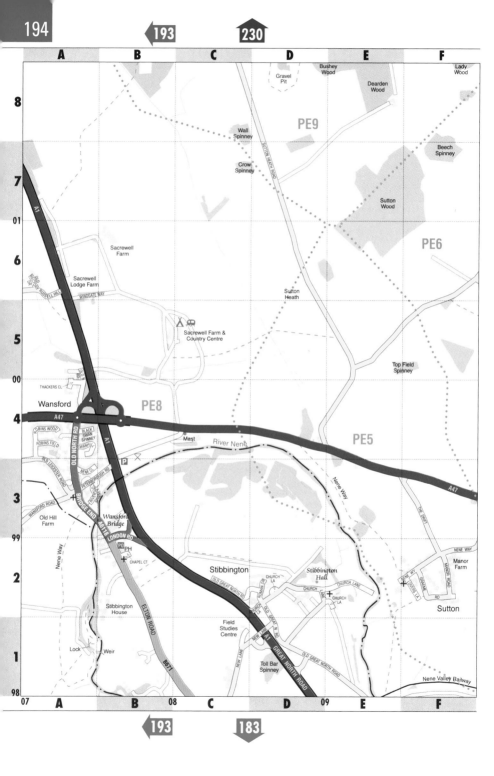

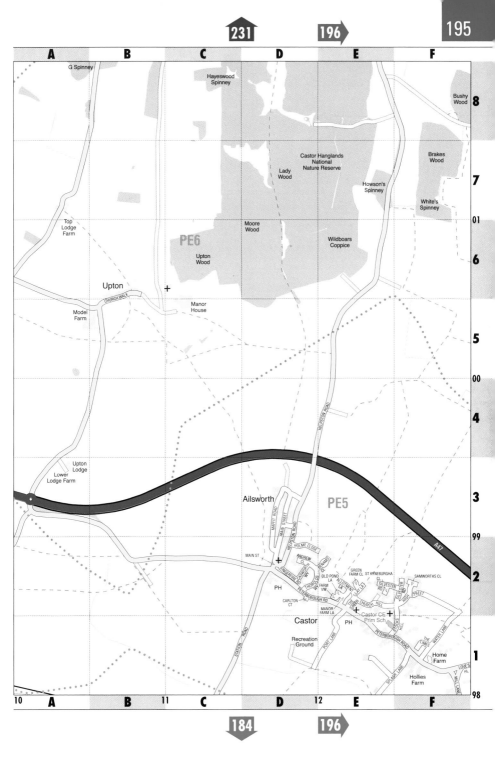

204
198

A5
1 BRETTON GN
2 KING HENRY CH
3 MUNTJAC CL

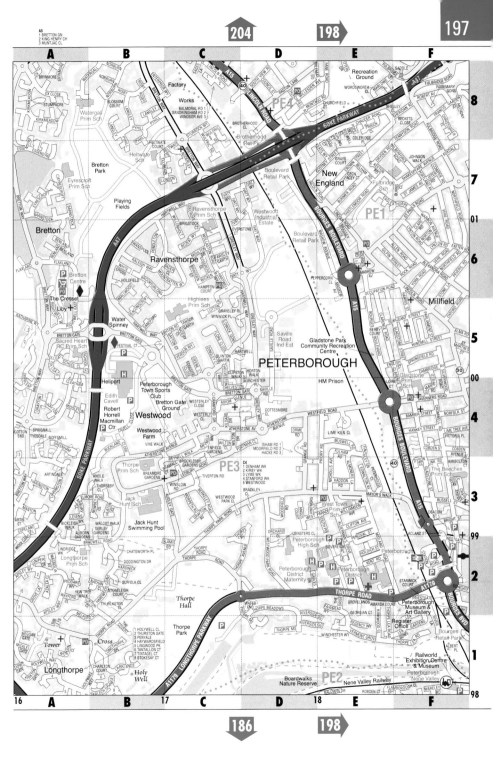

A   B   C   D   E   F

8
7
01
6
5
00
4
99
2
1
98

PE4

SOKE PARKWAY

New
England

PE1

Millfield

PETERBOROUGH

Bretton

Ravensthorpe

BOURGES BOULEVARD

Westwood

PE3

Gladstone Park
Community Recreation
Centre

HM Prison

Jack Hunt
Swimming Pool

Thorpe
Hall

Thorpe
Park

Longthorpe

THORPE ROAD

Peterborough
District
Maternity

Peterborough
District

Peterborough
High Sch

Peterborough
Museum &
Art Gallery

Boardwalks
Nature Reserve

Nene Valley Railway

PE2

Railworld
Exhibition Centre
& Museum

C4
1 DENHAM WK
2 KIRBY WK
3 LYME WK
4 STANFORD WK
5 WESTWOOD

1 HOLYWELL CL
2 THURSTON GATE
3 PENYALE
4 HAYWARDSFIELD
5 LINGWOOD PK
6 TANTALLON CT
7 TINTAGEL CT
8 STOKESAY CT

16   A   17   B   17   C   18   D   E   18   F   98

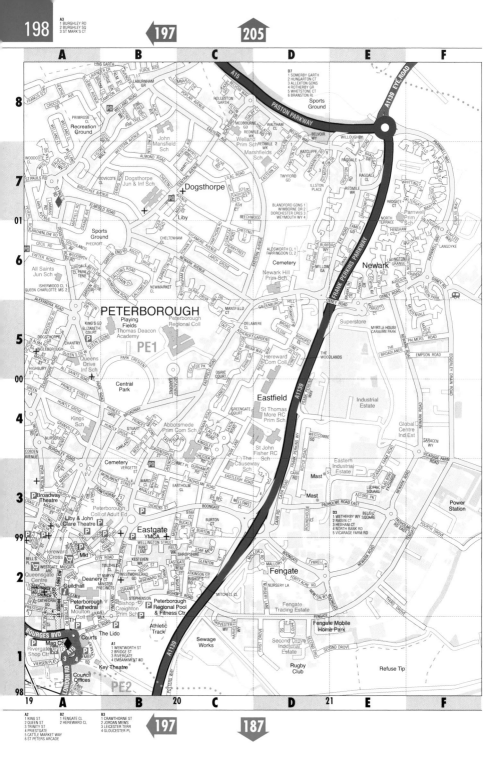

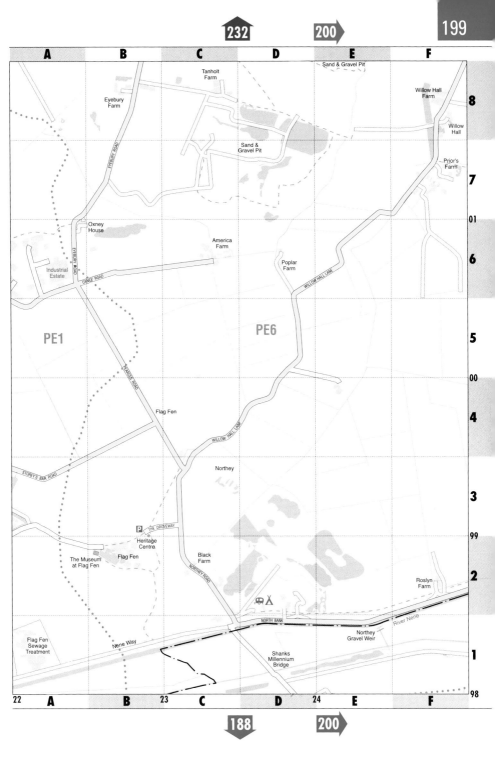

The Gores

Gore's Farm

THE CHASE

Stone Bridge Corner

Stone Bridge

Prior's Fen

PE6

Teakettle Hall Farm

Teakettle Hall Bridge

NORTH SIDE

GREEN DROVE

Prior's Fen Farm

Bank Farm

North Side

LEVITT'S DROVE

Dog-in-a-Doublet Farm

Dog-in-a-Doublet Bridge

North Fen

PH

Nature Reserve

Lock

Nene Way

LONG DROVE

The Wash

Gull Farm

NORTH BANK

Delph Dike

Plum Tree Farm

River Nene

PE7

Little Bridge

B1040

EAST DELPH

Morton's Leam

YARWELLS HEADLANDS

WHITLESEY ROAD

B1040

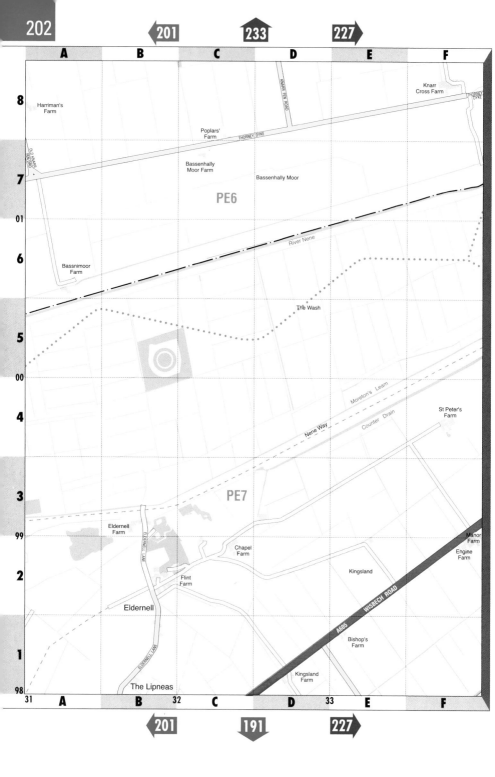

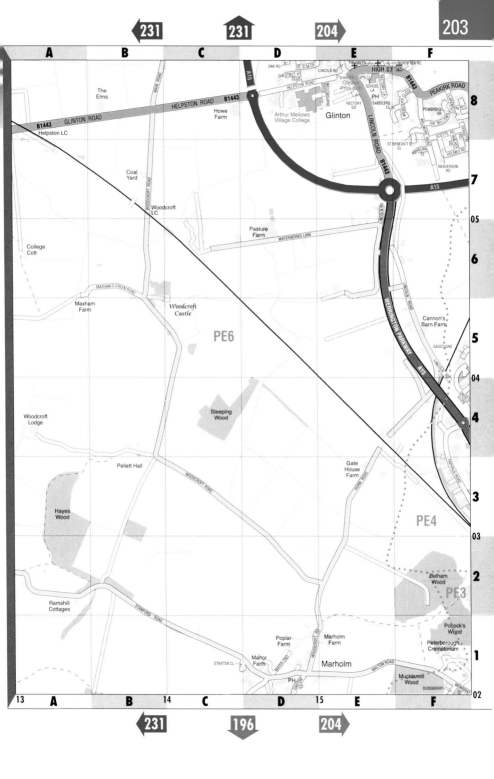

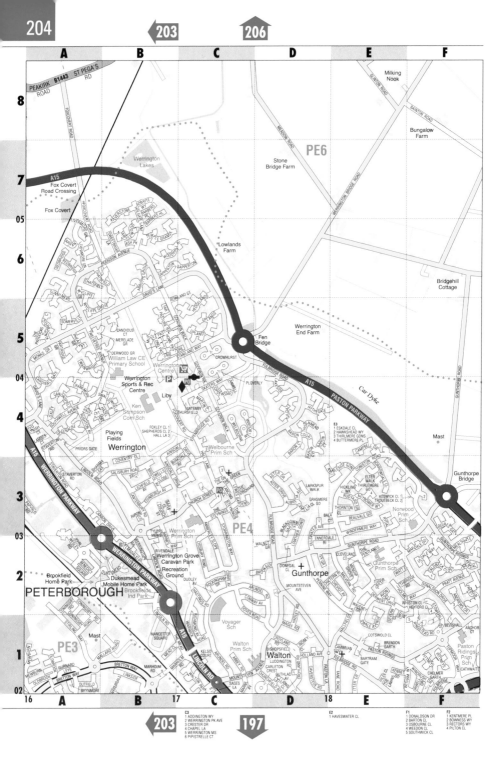

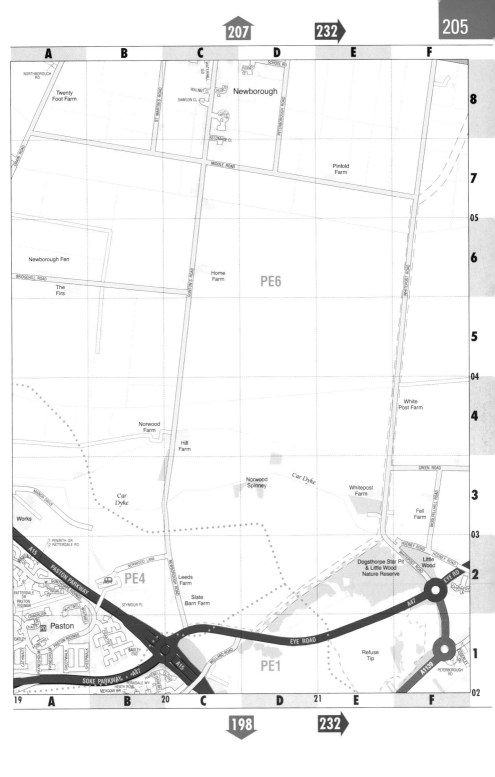

A B C D E F

NORTHBOROUGH RD

Twenty Foot Farm

DRAIN ROAD

ST MARTIN'S ROAD

WATERHALL GDNS

WALNUT CL

DAWSON CL

CHURCH CL

FERN CL

SCHOOL RD

Newborough

PETERBOROUGH ROAD

REEDMADE CL

MIDDLE ROAD

Pinfold Farm

Newborough Fen

BRIDGEHILL ROAD

The Firs

GUNTON'S ROAD

Home Farm

PE6

WHITEPOST ROAD

White Post Farm

Norwood Farm

Hill Farm

Car Dyke

Norwood Spinney

Car Dyke

Whitepost Farm

GREEN ROAD

Works

MANOR DRIVE

Car Dyke

WOOLFELL LANE ROAD

Fell Farm

1 PENRITH GR
2 PATTERDALE RD

A15

PASTON PARKWAY

NORWOOD LANE

Leeds Farm

NEWBOROUGH ROAD

HOONEY ROAD

HOONEY ROAD

Dogsthorpe Star Pit & Little Wood Nature Reserve

WHITEPOST ROAD

Little Wood

EYE RD

GRANGERY LA

PE4

GUNTHORPE RIDINGS

PATTERDALE DR
PASTON RIDINGS

WHITWELL

TINGDALE

SEYMOUR PL

Slate Barn Farm

A47

CHADBURN

CHADS

CATLEY

20

Paston

HONEYDELL

PASTON RIDINGS

BRIEF

BRIEF

WELLAND ROAD

EYE ROAD

A47

Refuse Tip

A1139

ROSELEY CL

PETERBOROUGH RD

CATTWAITE

PAYNESHOLM

PAYNESHOLM

SHEEPWALK

SHEEPWALK

SHEEPWALK

BAGLEY END

A15

A47

SOKE PARKWAY

HAREBELL CLOSE

HEATH ROW

FERNDALE WY

MEADOW GR

PE1

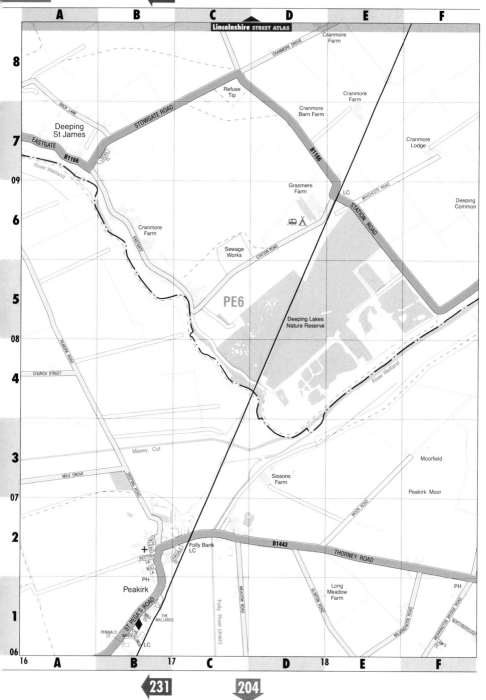

Lincolnshire STREET ATLAS

A **B** **C** **D** **E** **F**

8

Cranmore
Farm

CRANMORE DRIVE

Refuse
Tip

Cranmore
Farm

Cranmore
Barn Farm

STOWGATE ROAD

BACK LANE

Deeping
St James

7

EASTGATE

B1166

B1166

Cranmore
Lodge

River Welland

09

LC

WHICHGATE ROAD

STATION ROAD

Grasmere
Farm

Deeping
Common

6

Cranmore
Farm

EASTGATE

Sewage
Works

STATION ROAD

5

PE6

Deeping Lakes
Nature Reserve

08

PRIOR'S ROAD

CHURCH STREET

4

River Welland

Maxey Cut

3

MILE DROVE

DEEPING ROAD

Moorfield

Sissons
Farm

07

MOOR ROAD

Peakirk Moor

2

Folly Bank
LC

B1443

THORNEY ROAD

RECTORY
LA

BULL
LA

PH

Long
Meadow
Farm

PH

Peakirk

ST PEGA'S ROAD

MILL
LC

THE MALLARDS

PENWALD
CT

THE
SANDERS

LC

MEADOW ROAD

Folly River (drain)

GLINTON ROAD

MILKINGNOOK ROAD

WERRINGTON BRIDGE ROAD

NORTHBOROUGH ROAD

ST PEGA'S

1

06

16 **A** **B** 17 **C** **D** 18 **E** **F**

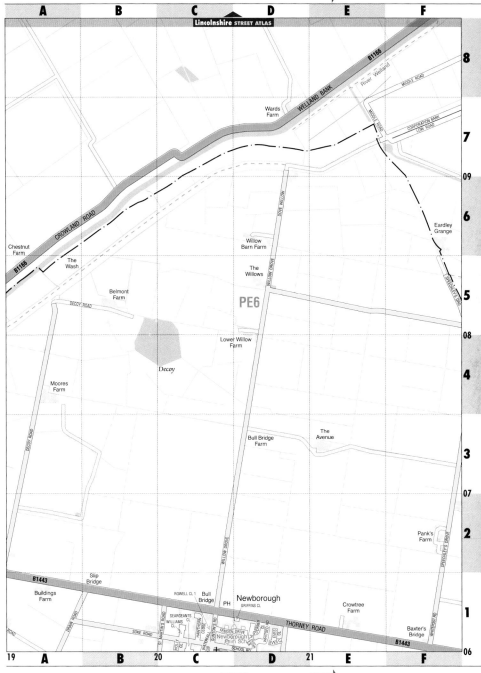

Lincolnshire STREET ATLAS

8

B1166

River Welland

MIDDLE ROAD

WELLAND BANK

Wards
Farm

MIDDLE ROAD

CORPORATION BANK
LOW ROAD

7

09

CROWLAND ROAD

DOVE WILLOW

Willow
Barn Farm

Eardley
Grange

6

Chestnut
Farm

B1166

The
Wash

The
Willows

WILLOW DROVE

SPALDGATE'S RD

5

08

Belmont
Farm

DECOY ROAD

PE6

Lower Willow
Farm

Decoy

4

Moores
Farm

DECOY ROAD

3

Bull Bridge
Farm

The
Avenue

07

WILLOW DROVE

Pank's
Farm

2

SPECHLEY'S DROVE

B1443

Slip
Bridge

Buildings
Farm

ROWELL CL 1

Bull
Bridge

Newborough

PH

GRIFFINS CL

Crowtree
Farm

WHITPOST RD

Baxter's
Bridge

1

DELPH ROAD

ROAD

SEARGEANTS
CL

WILLIAMS
CL

SOKE ROAD

HOLLY CL

HAWTHORN CLOSE

GUNTHER'S RD

FENSIDE DRIVE

Newborough
Prim Sch

SCHOOL RD

WHITTRED RD

WHITTRED RD

ELVES CL

THORNEY ROAD

B1443

06

19   A   B   20   C   D   21   E   F

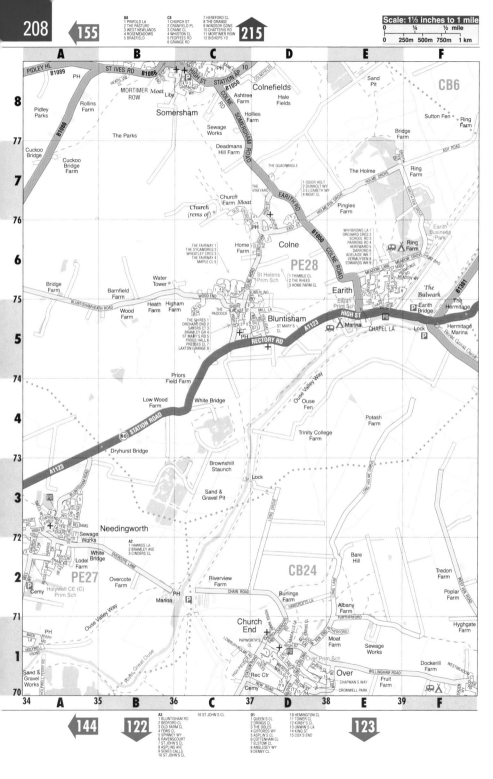

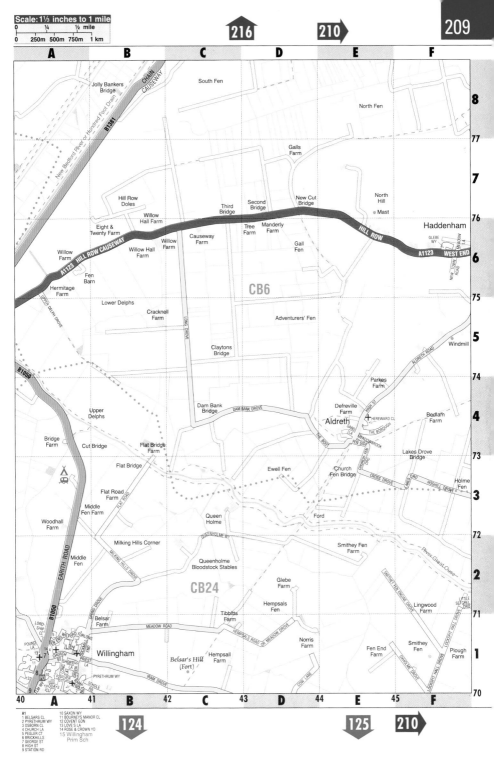

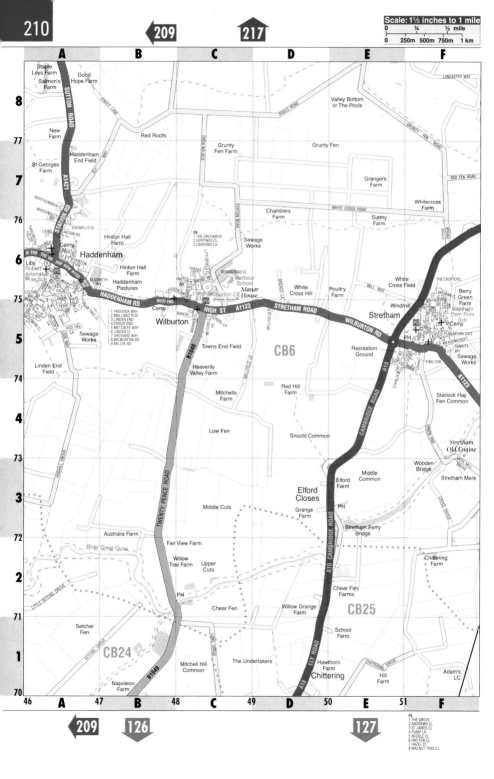

Scale: 1½ inches to 1 mile

0   ¼   ½ mile
0   250m 500m 750m 1 km

A **B** **C** **D** **E** **F**

Staple
Leys Farm
Salmon's
Farm

Good
Hope Farm

LANCASTER WAY

8

New Farm

Red Roofs

Valley Bottom
or The Pools

77

St Georges
Farm

Haddenham
End Field

Grunty
Fen Farm

Grunty Fen

RED FEN ROAD

7

Grangers
Farm

Whitecross
Farm

WHITE CROSS ROAD

76

Chambers
Farm

Sunny
Farm

Cemy

Haddenham

Hinton Hall
Farm

Sewage
Works

White
Cross Hill

White
Cross Field

6

Liby
Robert
Arkenstall
Prim Sch

Hinton Hall
Farm

Harbour
School

Manor
House

Poultry
Farm

Windmill

Berry
Green
Farm
Stretham
Com Prim
Sch

HADDENHAM RD

WEST END

Wilburton CE
Prim Sch

STRETHAM ROAD

Stretham

PH

75

Cemy

Bakery

WILBURTON RD

Sewage
Works

Wilburton

1 PADDOCK WAY
2 MALLARD RISE
3 LINDEN END
4 FROIZE END
5 METCALFE WAY
6 LINDEN CL
7 ORCHARD WAY
8 WILBURTON RD
9 MILLYA RD

Towns End Field

CB6

Recreation
Ground

KING COB

Starlock Hay
Fen Common

5

Sewage
Works

Linden End
Field

Heavenly
Valley Farm

Mitchells
Farm

Red Hill
Farm

74

Stretham
Old Engine

4

Low Fen

Snoots Common

Stretham Mere

73

Wooden
Bridge

Middle Cuts

Middle
Common

Elford
Farm

3

Elford
Closes

PH

Australia Farm

Grange
Farm

Stretham Ferry
Bridge

Chittering
Farm

72

Fair View Farm

Willow
Tree Farm

Upper
Cuts

CAMBRIDGE ROAD

2

TWENTY PENCE ROAD

PH

Chear Fen

Willow Grange
Farm

Chear Fen
Farms

CB25

Little Setchel Drove

Setchel
Fen

71

School
Farm

1

CB24

Mitchell Hill
Common

The Undertakers

Hawthorn
Farm

Hill
Farm

Adam's
LC

ELY ROAD

Napoleon
Farm

Chittering

70

F5
1 THE GROVE
2 ANDREWS CL
3 ST JAMES CL
4 PUMP LA
5 MIDDLE CL
6 HAY FEN CL
7 HAZEL CT
8 WALNUT TREE CL

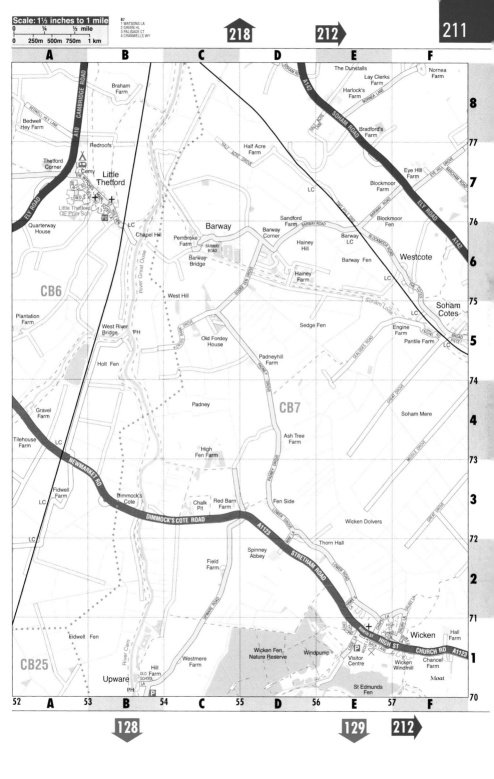

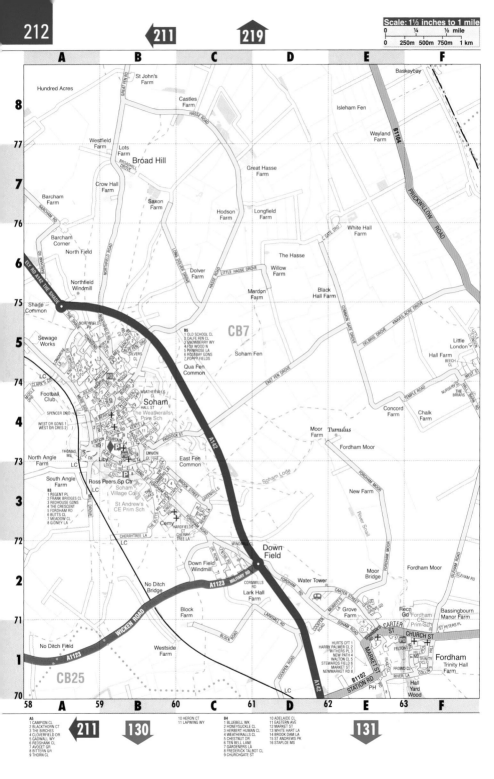

Scale: 1⅓ inches to 1 mile

0   ¼   ½ mile
0   250m 500m 750m 1 km

Baskeybay

Hundred Acres

St John's Farm

Castles Farm

Isleham Fen

HASSE ROAD

Wayland Farm

Westfield Farm

Lots Farm

Broad Hill

BROADHILL DRIVE

GREAT FEN RD

Great Hasse Farm

White Hall Farm

Crow Hall Farm

Barcham Farm

Saxon Farm

Hodson Farm

Longfield Farm

The Hasse

BARCHAM RD

Barcham Corner

North Field

Dolver Farm

Willow Farm

Black Hall Farm

Northfield Windmill

Mardon Farm

LITTLE HAISSE DROVE

HASSE ROAD

LONG DOLVER DRIVE

NORTHFIELD ROAD

Shade Common

CB7

Sewage Works

Soham Fen

COMMON GATE DROVE

KNAVES ACRE DROVE

Little London

Hall Farm

BEECH

Football Club

Qua Fen Common

EAST FEN DROVE

DELVING DROVE

TEMPLE ROAD

The Briars

NURSERY RD

WEST DR GDNS 1
WEST DR CRES 2

SPENCER DRO

Soham

The Weatheralls Prime Sch

Concord Farm

Chalk Farm

B5
1 OLD SCHOOL CL
2 CALFE FEN CL
3 SNOWBERRY WY
4 FOX WOOD N
5 PRIMROSE LA
6 ROSEBAY GDNS
7 POPPY FIELDS

Moor Farm

Tumulus

Fordham Moor

North Angle Farm

THOMAS MS

Liby

East Fen Common

Soham Lode

River Snail

FORDHAM MOOR

South Angle Farm

Ross Peers Sp Ctr

Soham Village Colls

BROOK STREET

GREENHILLS

New Farm

B3
1 REGENT PL
2 FRANK BRIDGES CL
3 REDHOUSE GDNS
4 THE CRESCENT
5 FORDHAM RD
6 BUTTS CL
7 MEADOW CL
8 GIDNEY LA

St Andrew's CE Prim Sch

Cemy

HARDFIELDS LA

THE BUTTS

FORDHAM RD

CHERRY TREE LA

CHERRYTREE LA

WINDMILL ST

Down Field

MILITARY RD

Moor Bridge

Fordham Moor

Down Field Windmill

A1123

CORNMILLS RD

Water Tower

Moor Farm

ISLEHAM RD

No Ditch Bridge

Lark Hall Farm

CARTER STREET

Grove Farm

Recn Gd

Fordham CE Prim Sch

Bassingbourn Manor Farm

Block Farm

LANDALE RD

FORDHAM RD

MURFITTS LA

ST PETERS PL

STAPLOE RD

CARTER ST

CHURCH ST

No Ditch Field

A1123

WICKEN ROAD

Westside Farm

BLOCK DROVE

COOPERS ROAD

SOHAM ROAD

HURTS CFT 1
HARRY PALMER CL 2
WITHERS PL 3
NEW PATH 4
WALTON CL 5
STEWARDS FIELD 6
MARKET ST 7
NEWMARKET RD 8

FELTONS

TRINITY PL

FROWD CL

Fordham

Trinity Hall Farm

CB25

A1123

B1102

STATION RD

MARKET ST

Hall Yard Wood

A5
1 CAMPION CL
2 BLACKTHORN CT
3 THE BIRCHES
4 CLOVERFIELD DR
5 GADWALL WY
6 REDSHANK CL
7 AVOCET GR
8 BITTERN GR
9 THORN CL

10 HERON CT
11 LAPWING WY

B4
1 BLUEBELL WK
2 HONEYSUCKLE CL
3 HERBERT HUMAN CL
4 WEATHERALLS CL
5 CHESTNUT DR
6 TEN BELL LANE
7 GARDENERS CL
8 FREDERICK TALBOT CL
9 CHURCHGATE ST

10 ADELAIDE CL
11 EASTERN AVE
12 MARKET ST
13 WHITE HART LA
14 BROOK DAM LA
15 ST ANDREWS PK
16 STAPLOE MS

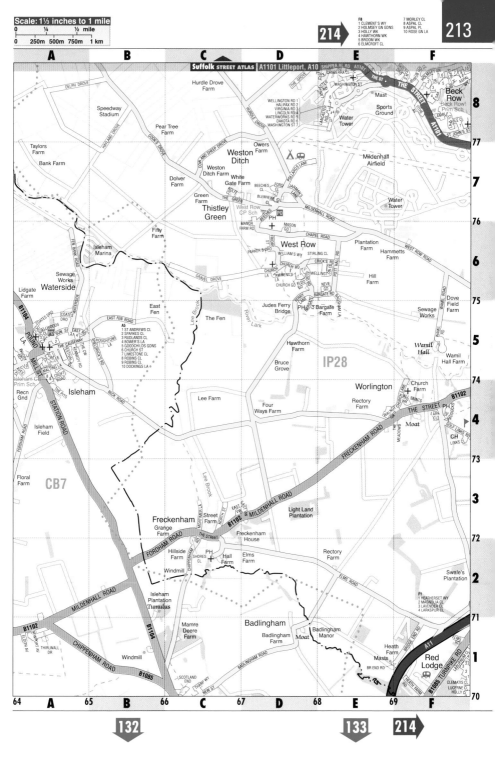

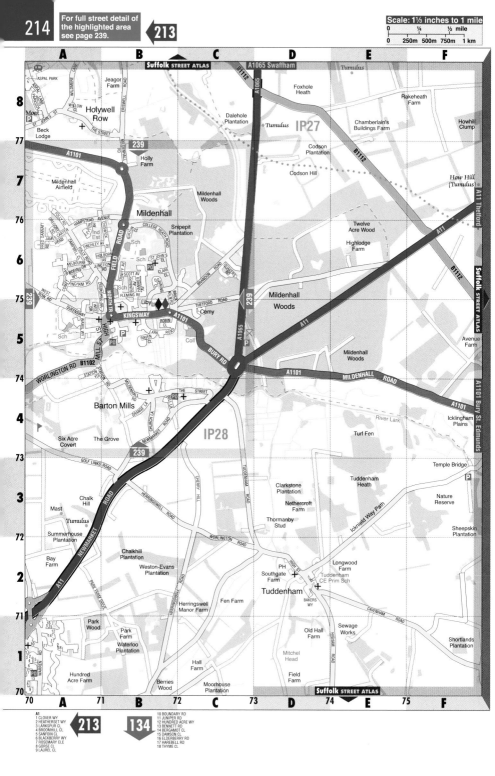

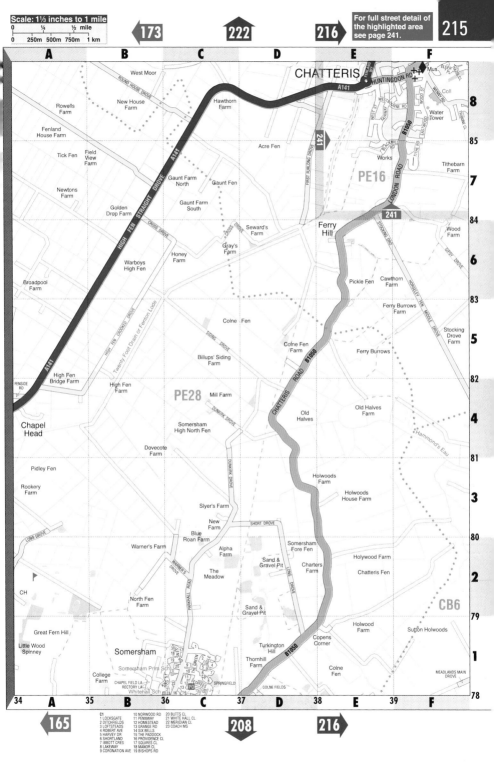

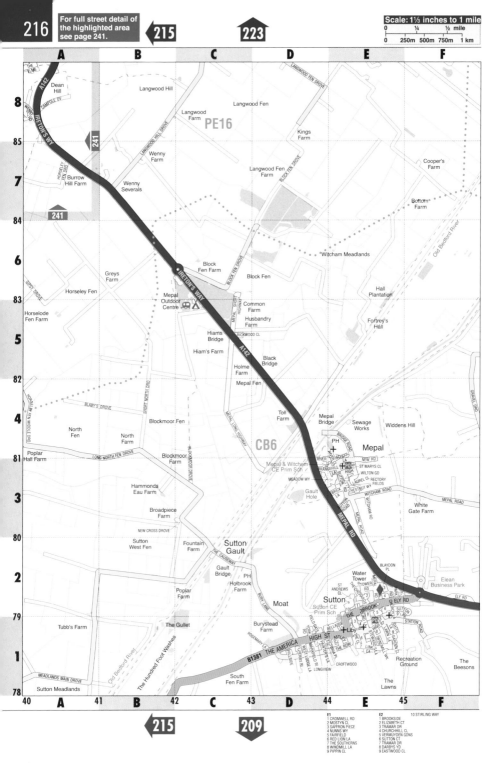

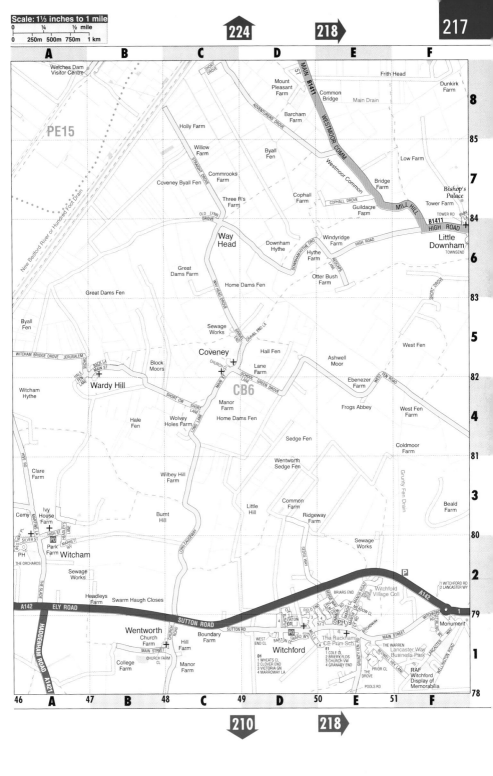

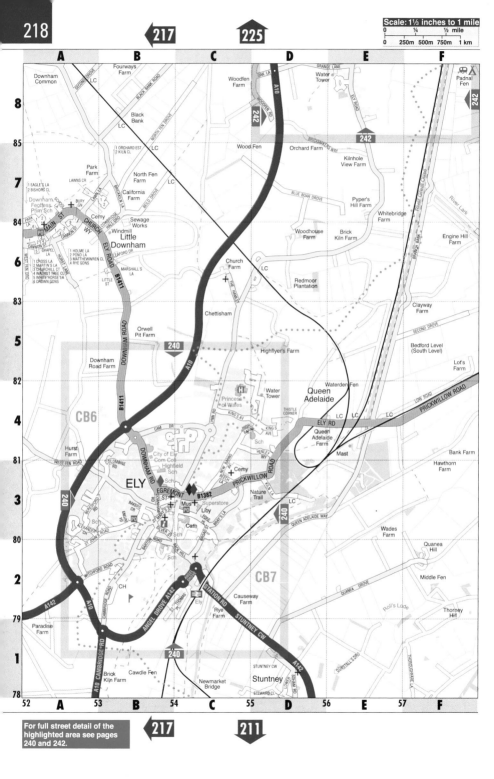

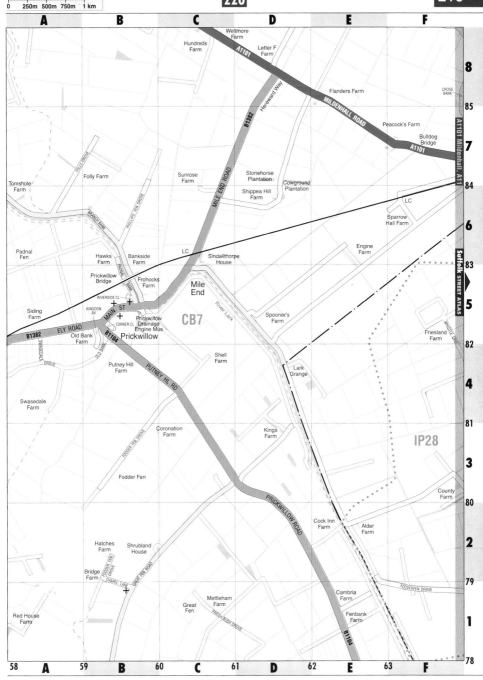

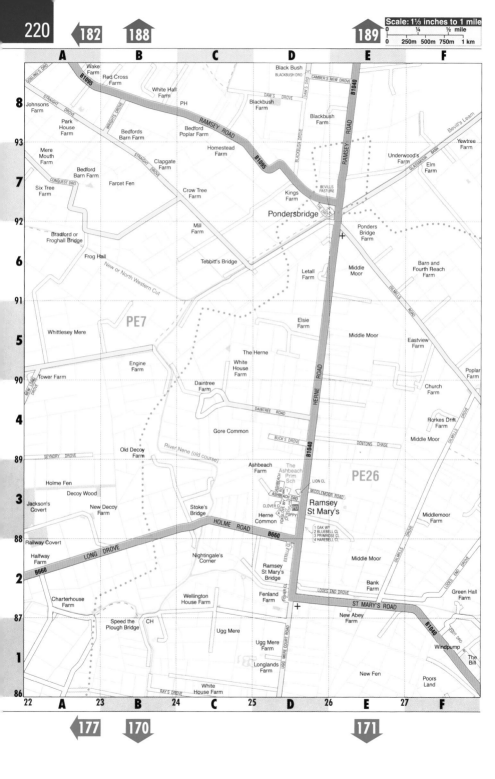

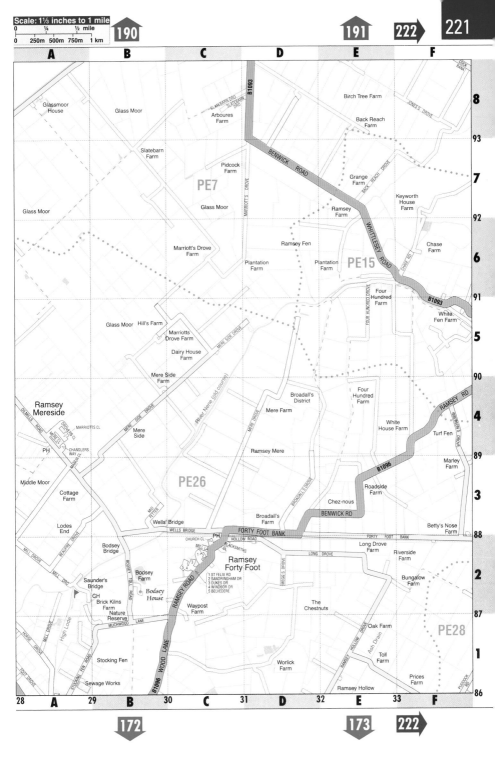

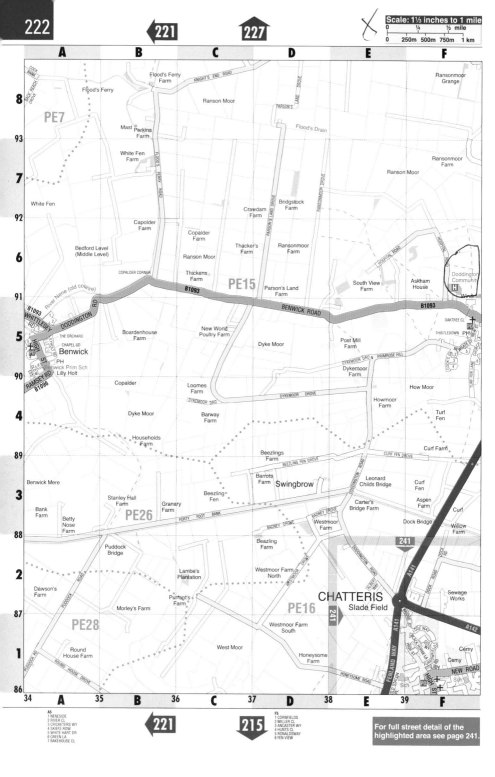

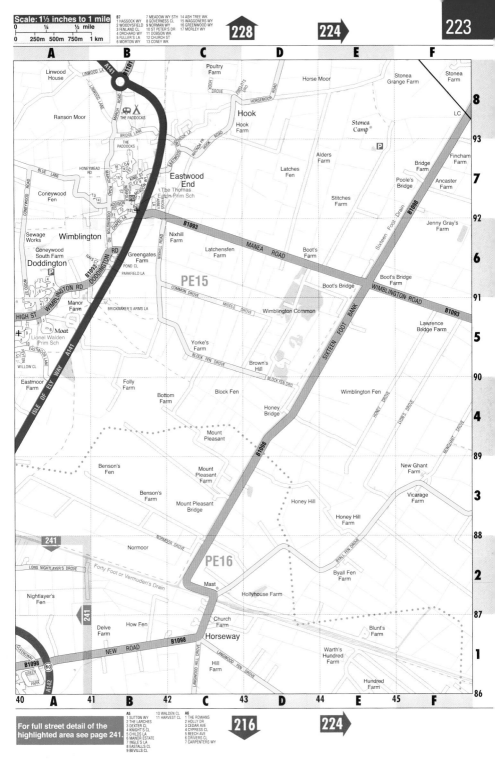

Scale: 1½ inches to 1 mile

0   ¼   ½ mile
0   250m 500m 750m 1 km

B7
1 HASSOCK WY
2 WOODYSFIELD
3 FENLAND CL
4 ORCHARD WY
5 FULLER'S LA
6 MORTON CL

7 MEADOW WY STH
8 GOVERNESS CL
9 NORMAN WY
10 ST PETER'S DR
11 DOBSON WK
12 CHURCH ST
13 CONEY WK

14 ASH TREE WK
15 WAGGONERS WY
16 GREENWOOD WY
17 MORLEY WY

228   224   223

A   B   C   D   E   F

Linwood
House

Ranson Moor

THE PADDOCKS

Poultry
Farm

Hook

Hook
Farm

Horse Moor

Stonea
Grange Farm

Stonea
Farm

LC

Stonea
Camp

8

93

BRIDGE LANE

THE
PADDOCKS

HONEYMEAD
RD

Coneywood
Fen

Eastwood
End

The Thomas
Eaton Prim Sch

Latches
Fen

Alders
Farm

Stitches
Farm

Bridge
Farm

Poole's
Bridge

Ancaster
Farm

Fincham
Farm

7

92

Sewage
Works

Wimblington

Coneywood
South Farm

Doddington

Greengates
Farm

POND CL

PARKFIELD LA

Nixhill
Farm

B1093

Latchensfen
Farm

MANEA ROAD

Boot's
Farm

Boot's
Bridge

Jenny Gray's
Farm

Boot's Bridge
Farm

WIMBLINGTON ROAD

6

91

PE15

Manor
Farm

BRICKMAKER'S ARMS LA

COMMON DROVE

MIDDLE DROVE

Wimblington Common

Boot's Bridge
Farm

Lawrence
Bridge Farm

B1093

HIGH ST

Lionel Walden
Prim Sch

Moat

EASTMOOR LANE

WILLOW CL

Yorke's
Farm

BLOCK FEN DROVE

Brown's
Hill

BLOCK FEN DRO

SIXTEEN FOOT BANK

5

90

Eastmoor
Farm

Folly
Farm

Bottom
Farm

Block Fen

Honey
Bridge

Wimblington Fen

HONEY DROVE

NEWGHANT DROVE

4

89

Benson's
Fen

Mount
Pleasant

Mount
Pleasant
Farm

B1098

New Ghant
Farm

Vicarage
Farm

3

88

Benson's
Farm

Mount Pleasant
Bridge

Honey Hill

Honey Hill
Farm

241

Normoor

NORMOOR DROVE

PE16

BYALL FEN DROVE

Byall Fen
Farm

2

LONG NIGHTLAYER'S DROVE

Forty Foot or Vermuden's Drain

Mast

Hollyhouse Farm

87

Nightlayer's
Fen

241

Delve
Farm

How Fen

Church
Farm

Horseway

B1098

LANDWOOD FEN DROVE

Blunt's
Farm

Warth's
Hundred
Farm

1

B1098

A142

GREEN
PARK

60

NEW ROAD

B1098

Hill
Farm

LANDWOOD HILL DROVE

Hundred
Farm

86

40   A   41   B   42   C   43   D   44   E   45   F

241   216   224

For full street detail of the
highlighted area see page 241.

A5
1 SUTTON WY
2 THE LARCHES
3 DEXTER CL
4 KNIGHT'S CL
5 CHILDS LA
6 MANOR ESTATE
7 INGLE'S LA
8 EASTALLS CL
9 BEVILLS CL

10 WALDEN CL
11 HARVEST CL

A6
1 THE ROWANS
2 HOLLY DR
3 CEDAR AVE
4 CYPRESS CL
5 BEECH AVE
6 DRIVERS CL
7 CARPENTERS WY

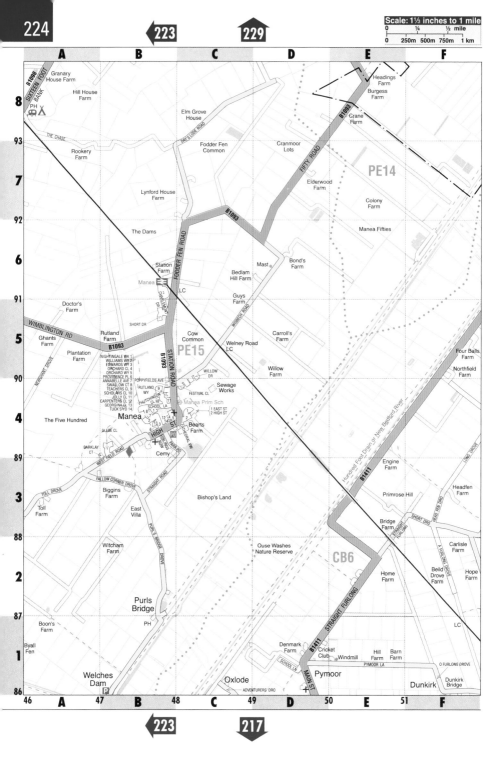

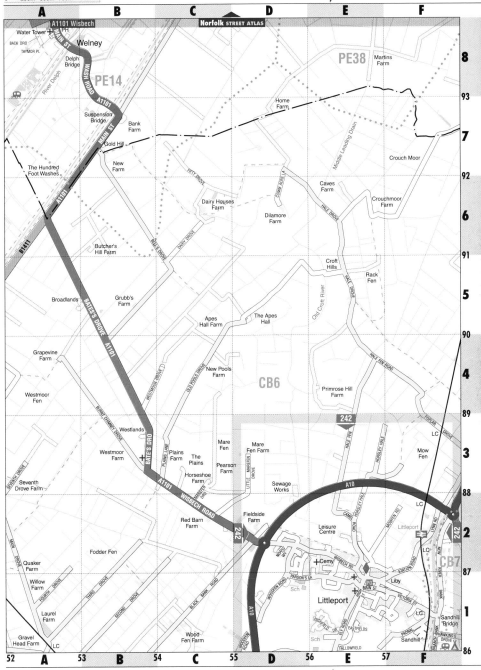

Scale: 1⅓ inches to 1 mile

0 ¼ ½ mile
0 250m 500m 750m 1 km

Norfolk STREET ATLAS

A1101 Wisbech
Water Tower
PH
BACK DRO
TAYMOR PL
Welney
Delph Bridge
PE14
WASH ROAD
MAIN ST
Suspension Bridge
A1101
Gold Hill
Bank Farm
New Farm
The Hundred Foot Washes
River Delph
PE38
Martins Farm
Home Farm
Crouch Moor
Middle Leading Drain
FIFTY DROVE
CONNA ACRE LA
HALE DROVE
Caves Farm
Crouchmoor Farm
Dilamore Farm
Dairy Houses Farm
BATE'S DROVE
DAIRY DROVE
Butcher's Hill Farm
B1411
A1101
Broadlands
Grubb's Farm
Croft Hills
Rack Fen
Old Croft River
HALE DROVE
Apes Hall Farm
The Apes Hall
Grapevine Farm
BATE'S DROVE
A1101
WESTMOOR DROVE LD
OLD POOLS DROVE
New Pools Farm
CB6
HALE FEN ROAD
Primrose Hill Farm
Westmoor Fen
BURNT CHIMNEY DROVE
Westlands
Westmoor Farm
BATE'S DRO
PLAINS LANE
Plains Farm
The Plains
Mare Fen
Mare Fen Farm
LITTLE MAREFEN
Pearson Farm
MARE FEN DROVE
242
HALE FEN
MORLEY HALE
Mow Fen
POPLAR DROVE
LC
89
SEVENTH DROVE
Seventh Drove Farm
A1101
WISBECH ROAD
Horseshoe Farm
MARSH DRO
Sewage Works
A10
LC
88
242
Fieldside Farm
Red Barn Farm
CAMEL ROAD
MORLEY HALE
MOW FEN
STATION ROAD
MAIN RD
NEW RD
RIVER BANK
242
CB7
MAIN DROVE
FOURTH DROVE
Quaker Farm
Willow Farm
THIRD DROVE
SECOND DROVE
Fodder Fen
BLACK BANK ROAD
242
MOSS WAY
WOODFEN ROAD
Leisure Centre
WISBECH RD
PARSON'S LA
Cemy
Sch
Liby
VICTORIA ST
LC
87
Laurel Farm
Gravel Head Farm
LC
Wood Fen Farm
A10
WOODFEN ROAD
Littleport
Littleport
MAIN ST
EASTFIELDS
EUCLID
PINFOLD
FALLOWFIELD
Sch
PRIORY
PRONAL
Sandhill
Sandhill Bridge
HAWKING'S DROVE
HAWKING'S DROVE
86

52 A 53 B 54 C 55 D 56 E 57 F

8
93
7
92
6
91
5
90
4
89
3
88
2
87
1
86

218
226
For full street detail of the highlighted area see page 242.

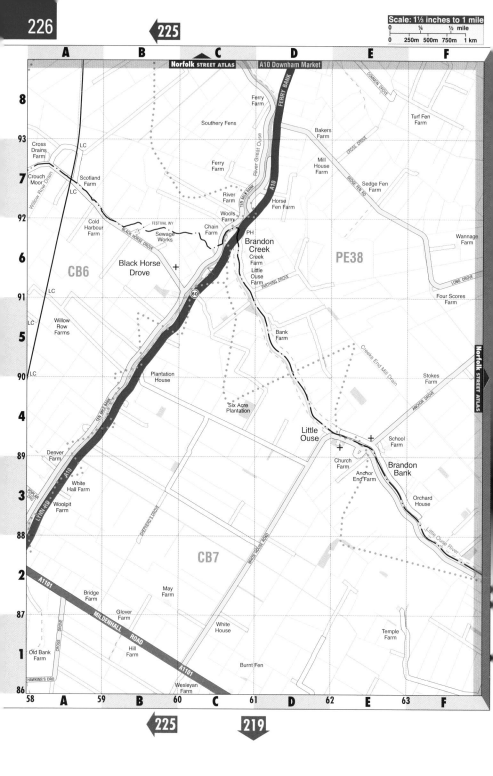

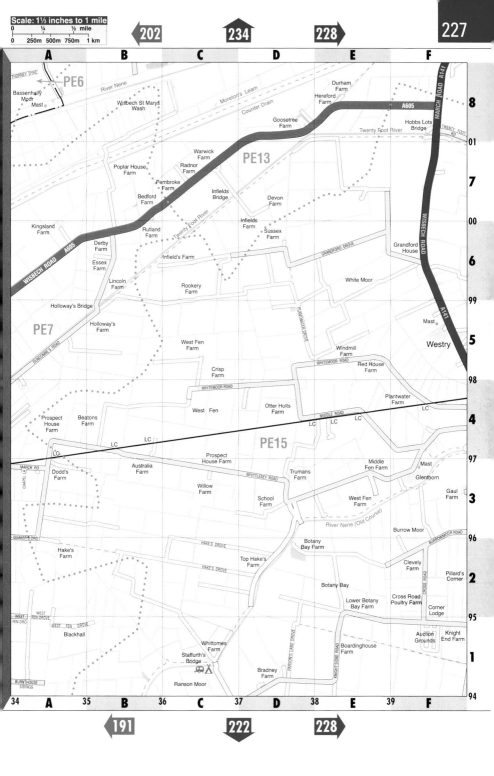

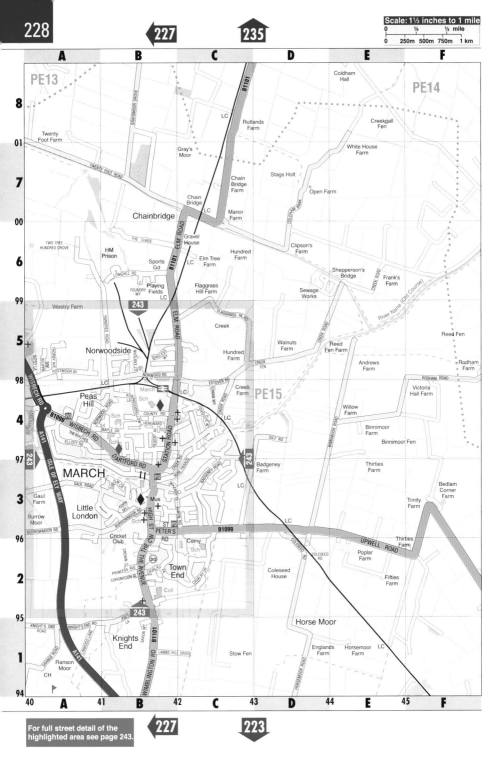

227

235

Scale: 1⅓ inches to 1 mile

0   ¼   ½   mile
0   250m 500m 750m 1 km

PE13

8

01

Twenty
Foot Farm

7

00

Chainbridge

6

Coldham
Hall

PE14

Creekgall
Fen

Rutlands
Farm

White House
Farm

Gray's
Moor

Chain
Bridge
Farm

Stags Holt

Open Farm

Chain
Bridge

LC

Manor
Farm

Gravel
House

Clipson's
Farm

TWO TREE
HUNDRED DROVE

THE CHASE

HM
Prison

Sports
Gd

Elm Tree
Farm

Hundred
Farm

Shepperson's
Bridge

Frank's
Farm

Longhill Rd

FOUNDRY
WY

Playing
Fields

LC

Flaggrass
Hill Farm

Sewage
Works

99

Westry Farm

243

FLAGGRASS HILL RD

Creek

River Nene (Old Course)

Reed Fen

5

Norwoodside

Hundred
Farm

Walnuts
Farm

Reed
Fen Farm

Reed
Fen

Rodham
Farm

THORPE AVE

HOSTMOOR AV

NORWOOD RD

CREEK
FEN

Andrews
Farm

RODHAM ROAD

98

WISBECH RD

LC

March

Sch

LC

ESTOVER RD

ROMAN WY

Creek
Farm

PE15

Victoria
Hall Farm

Peas
Hill

Willow
Farm

4

B1099

WISBECH RD

THE BIRCHES

MAPLE GA

HEREWARD

COUNTY RD

STATION ROAD

Binnimoor
Farm

Binnimoor Fen

A141

ISLE OF ELY WAY

ELLIOTT RD

SILT RD

97

243

DARTFORD RD

Sch

BROADWAY

BADGENEY ROAD

243

BINNIMOOR ROAD

Badgeney
Farm

Thirties
Farm

Bedlam
Corner
Farm

MARCH

GAUL ROAD

Sch

Mus

HIGH ST

LC

Trinity
Farm

3

Gaul
Farm

Little
London

BURROWMOOR RD

PETER'S

B1099

UPWELL ROAD

Thirties
Farm

Burrow
Moor

BURROWMOOR RD

Cricket
Club

Cemy

Sch

RD

COLESEED RD

Poplar
Farm

96

PRINCESS AVE

CORONATION GT

THE AVENUE

30

Town
End

Coll

Coleseed
House

Coleseed

Fifties
Farm

2

95

243

KNIGHTS END
ROAD

Knights End Rd

WIMBLINGTON RD

Horse Moor

Knights
End

Stow Fen

Englands
Farm

Horsemoor
Farm

LC

A141

GRANGE ROAD

B1101

LAMBS HILL DROVE

HORSEMOOR RD

1

Ranson
Moor

CH

94

40   A   41   B   42   C   43   D   44   E   45   F

227

223

For full street detail of the
highlighted area see page 243.

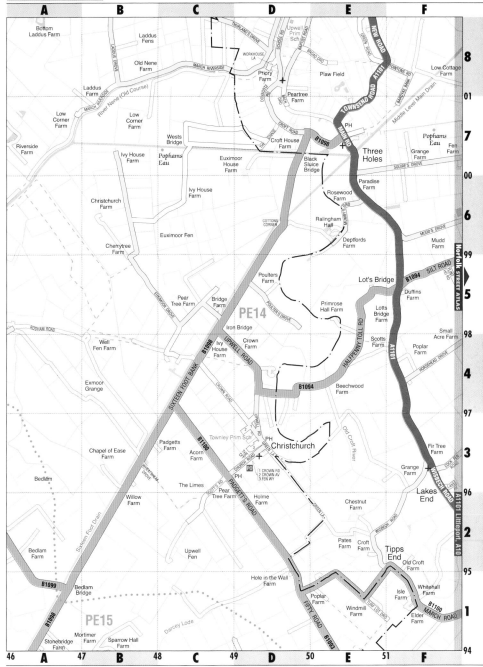

Scale: 1⅓ inches to 1 mile

Norfolk STREET ATLAS

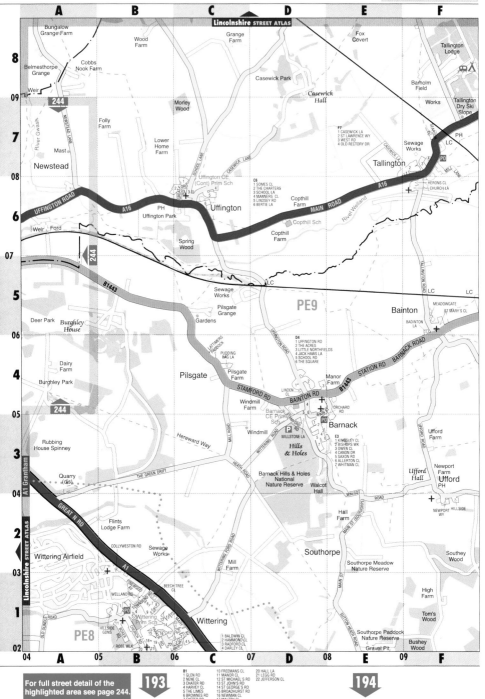

Scale: 1⅓ inches to 1 mile

0   ¼   ½ mile
0   250m 500m 750m 1 km

Bungalow Grange Farm

Wood Farm

Grange Farm

Fox Covert

Tallington Lodge

Belmesthorpe Grange

Cobbs Nook Farm

Casewick Park

Barholm Field

Weir

Morley Wood

Casewick Hall

Works

Tallington Dry Ski Slope

River Gwash

Folly Farm

Lower Home Farm

F7
1 CASEWICK LA
2 ST LAWRENCE WY
3 WEST RD
4 OLD RECTORY DR

Sewage Works

PH

Newstead

Mast

Uffington CE (Cont) Prim Sch

Tallington

LC

PO

UFFINGTON ROAD

A16

A16

C6
1 SOMES CL
2 THE CHARTERS
3 SCHOOL LA
4 MANNERS CL
5 LINDSEY RD
6 BERTIE LA

MAIN ROAD

HERONS CL
CHURCH LA

Uffington

PH

Copthill Farm

Copthill Farm

MILL LANE

Uffington Park

River Welland

Weir Ford

Spring Wood

Copthill Farm

Copthill Sch

244

B1443

Sewage Works

LC

PE9

Bainton

MEADOWGATE
ST MARY'S CL

Deer Park

Burghley House

Pilsgate Grange

Gardens

UPPINGTON ROAD

BADINTON LA

TALLINGTON ROAD

LC

LC

LATTIMENS PADDOCK

Dairy Farm

PUDDING BAG LA

Pilsgate

Pilsgate Farm

STAMFORD RD

D4
1 UFFINGTON RD
2 THE ACRES
3 LITTLE NORTHFIELDS
4 JACK HAWS LA
5 SCHOOL RD
6 THE SQUARE

Manor Farm

STATION RD

BARNACK ROAD

Burghley Park

244

Windmill Farm

LINDEN CL

BAINTON RD

ORCHARD RD

B1443

Ufford Farm

Rubbing House Spinney

Hereward Way

MILL ROAD

Windmill

Barnack CE Prim Sch

MILLSTONE LA

PO

Barnack

E3
1 KIMBSLEY CL
2 BISHOPS WK
3 OWEN CL
4 CANON DR
5 SAXON RD
6 ALLERTON CL
7 WHITMAN CL

Ufford Hall

Newport Farm

Ufford
PH

AT Grantham

Quarry (dis)

THE GREEN DRIFT

HEATH ROAD

WITTERING ROAD

Hills & Holes

Barnack Hills & Holes National Nature Reserve

Walcot Hall

WALCOT ROAD

Hall Farm

NEWPORT HILLSIDE WY

GREAT N RD

Flints Lodge Farm

COLLYWESTON RD

Sewage Works

Mill Farm

WITTERING ROAD

MAIN ST SOUTHORPE

Southorpe

Southorpe Meadow Nature Reserve

Southey Wood

AT

Wittering Airfield

BEECH TREE CL

WELLAND RD

Wittering Prim Sch

Wittering

MAIN ST

SUTTON HEATH ROAD

High Farm

Tom's Wood

PE8

HILLSIDE GDNS

ROSE WLK

1 BALDWIN CL
2 HAMMOND CL
3 RADFORD CL
4 DARLEY CL

Southorpe Paddock Nature Reserve

Gravel Pit

Bushey Wood

For full street detail of the highlighted area see page 244.

193

194

B1
1 GLEN RD
2 NENE CL
3 CHATER RD
4 HARVEY CL
5 THE LIMES
6 BROWNES RD
7 EXETER RD
8 THE HOLT
9 BURGHLEY AVE
10 FREEMANS CL
11 MANOR CL
12 ST MICHAEL S RD
13 ST JOHN'S RD
14 ST GEORGE S RD
15 BROADHURST RD
16 NEWMAN CL
17 MALTBY CL
18 CARNEGIE RD
19 EMBRY RD
20 HALL LA
21 LEGG RD
22 JEFFERSON CL

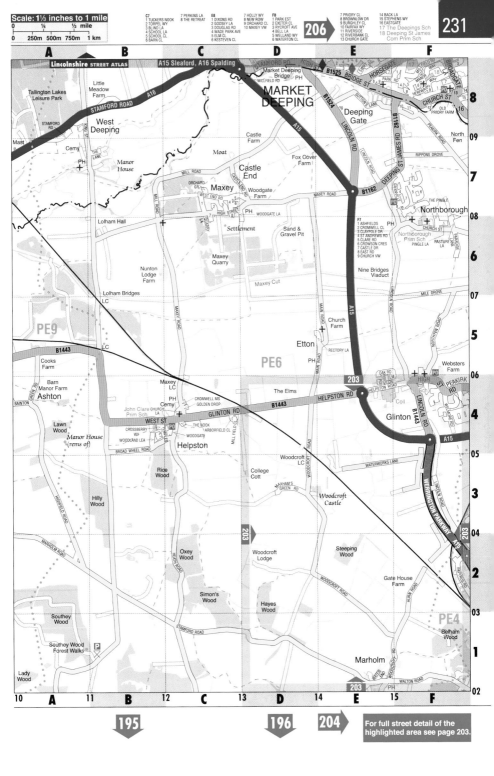

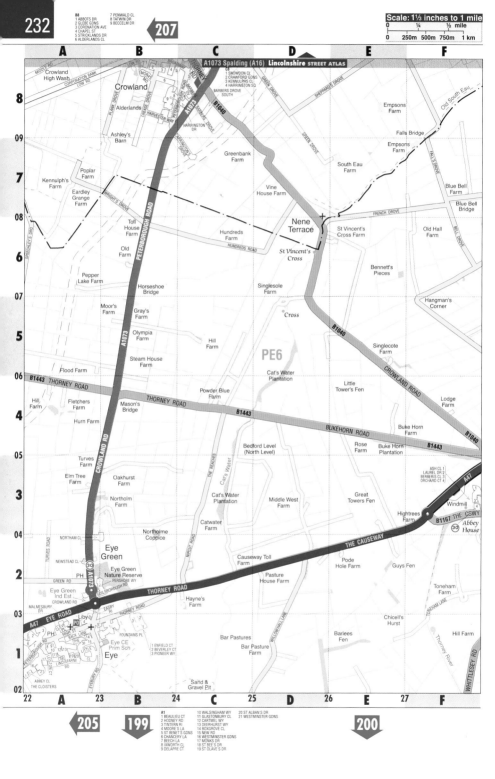

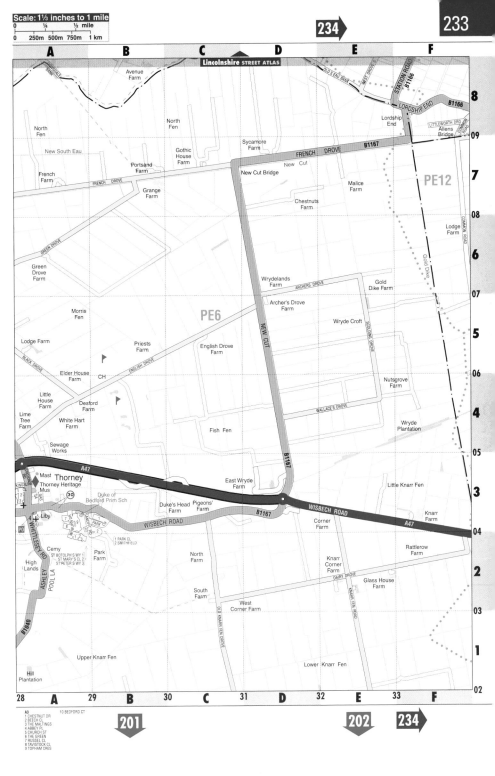

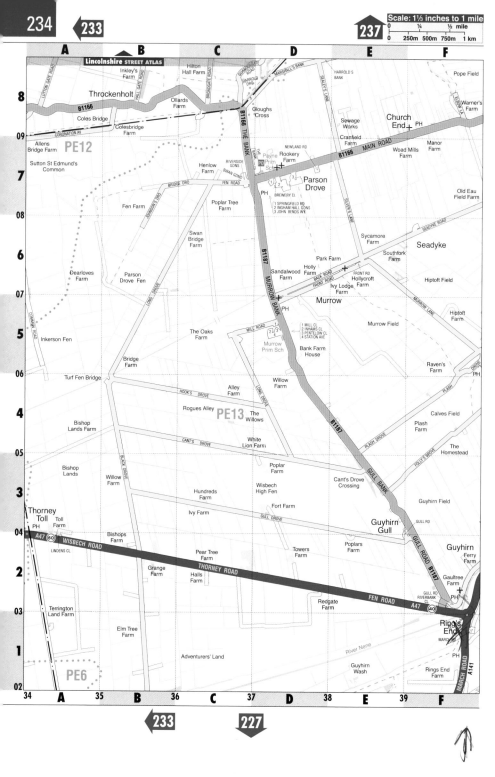

Scale: 1⅓ inches to 1 mile

¼ ½ mile
0 250m 500m 750m 1 km

Lincolnshire STREET ATLAS

8

Inkley's Farm
Hilton Hall Farm
Pope Field

Throckenholt
B1166
Ollards Farm
Gloughs Cross
HARROLD DRO
Harrold's Bank
Church End + PH
Warner's Farm

09
Coles Bridge
Coles Bridge
Colesbridge Farm
Sewage Works
MAIN ROAD
B1166
Woad Mills Farm
Manor Farm

Allens Bridge Farm
PE12
Cranfield Farm
NEWLAND RD
Rookery Farm
Payne Prim Sch

7
Sutton St Edmund's Common
Henlow Farm
RIVERSIDE GDNS
SWAN GDNS
FEN ROAD
Parson Drove
Old Eau Field Farm

08
Fen Farm
Poplar Tree Farm
PH
1 SPRINGFIELD RD
2 INGHAM HALL GDNS
3 JOHN BENDS WY
SILVER'S LANE
SEADYKE ROAD

Swan Bridge Farm
Sycamore Farm
Seadyke

6
Dearloves Farm
Parson Drove Fen
B1187
Park Farm
Southfork Farm

Sandalwood Farm
Holly Farm
BACK ROAD
FRONT RD
Hollycroft Farm
Hiptoft Field

07
LONG DROVE
BRIDGE DRO
MURROW BANK
FRONT ROAD
Ivy Lodge Farm
Murrow
MURROW LANE

Inkerson Fen
PH
Hiptoft Farm

5
CRANWAY ROAD
MILL ROAD
2/3
1 MILL CL
2 INGHAMS CL
3 PENTELOW CL
4 STATION AVE
Murrow Field

The Oaks Farm
Murrow Prim Sch
Bank Farm House
Raven's Farm

06
Turf Fen Bridge
Bridge Farm
HOOK'S DROVE
Alley Farm
LONG DROVE
Willow Farm
PLASH
PH
DROVE

Rogues Alley
PE13
The Willows
B1187
Calves Field

4
Bishop Lands Farm
CANT'S DROVE
White Lion Farm
Plash Farm

05
BLACK DROVE
Poplar Farm
Cant's Drove Crossing
GULL BANK
PLASH DROVE
FOLLY'S DROVE
The Homestead

Bishop Lands
Willow Farm
Wisbech High Fen
Guyhirn Field

3
Hundreds Farm
Fort Farm
Guyhirn Gull
GULL RD

Thorney Toll
Ivy Farm
GULL DROVE
Poplars Farm
Guyhirn

04
PH
A47
Toll Farm
WISBECH ROAD
Bishops Farm
Guyhirn Ferry Farm

LINDENS CL
Pear Tree Farm
THORNEY ROAD
Towers Farm
GULL RD RIVERBANK CL
Gaultree Farm
PH

2
Grange Farm
Halls Farm
FEN ROAD
A47
MARCH ROAD
A141

Terrington Land Farm
Redgate Farm
Rings End

03
Elm Tree Farm
River Nene
PH

1
Adventurers' Land
Guyhirn Wash
Rings End Farm

02
PE6

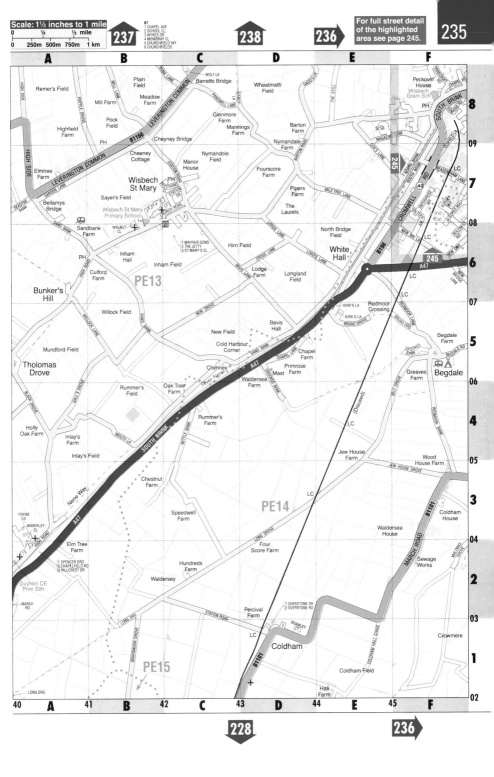

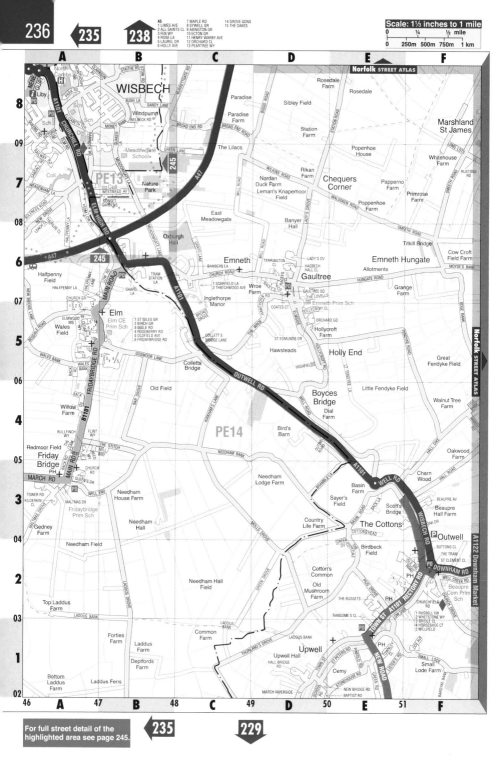

236

235 238

A5
1 LIMES AVE
2 ALL SAINTS CL
3 FEN WY
4 ROSE LA
5 LAUREL DR
6 HOLLY AVE
7 MAPLE RD
8 SYWELL GR
9 ABINGTON GR
10 ECTON GR
11 HENRY WARBY AVE
12 ORCHARD CL
13 PEARTREE WY
14 GROVE GDNS
15 THE OAKES

Scale: 1½ inches to 1 mile
0   ¼   ½ mile
0 250m 500m 750m 1 km

Norfolk STREET ATLAS

WISBECH

Norfolk STREET ATLAS

PE13

PE14

Emneth

Emneth Hungate

Gaultree

Holly End

Boyces Bridge

The Cottons

Friday Bridge

Upwell

Outwell

Elm

A47

A1101

A1101

A1122 Downham Market

For full street detail of the highlighted area see page 245.

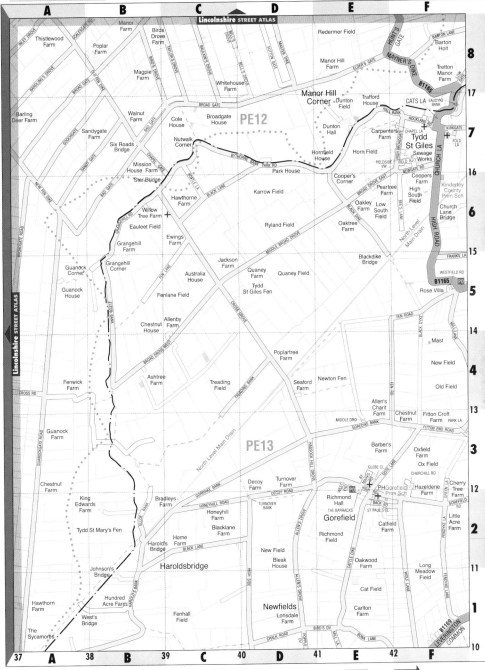

Lincolnshire STREET ATLAS

Lincolnshire STREET ATLAS

234
235
238

PE12

PE13

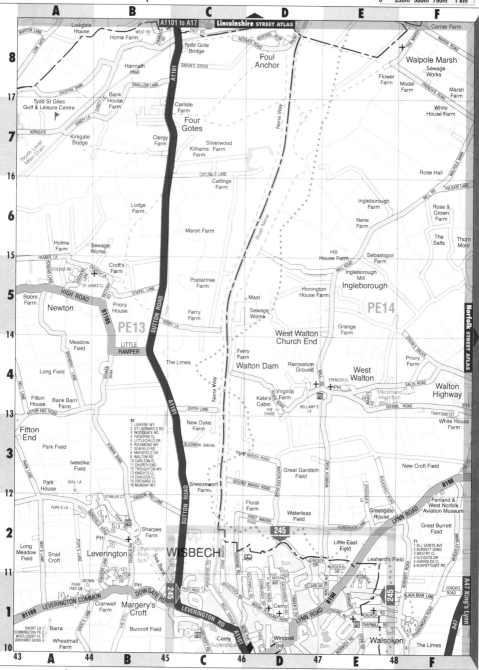

Lincolnshire STREET ATLAS

Norfolk STREET ATLAS

237

235

236

For full street detail of the
highlighted area see page 245.

B2
1 LEAFERE WY
2 ST LEONARD'S RD
3 WOODGATE RD
4 IVESDYKE CL
5 LITTLECHILD DR
6 RICHMOND WY
7 SEAFIELD RD
8 MAYSFIELD DR
9 WALTON RD
10 CARLTON CL
11 CHURCH END
12 TROUGHTON WY
13 KNIGHTS CL
14 CHAUCER CL
15 ORCHARD CL
16 MUNDAY WY

F1
1 ALL SAINTS AVE
2 BURRETT GDNS
3 SLEIGHTS DR
4 HARROLDS CL
5 BURRETTGATE RD

SHORT LA 1
DONNINGTON PK 2
WOOLCROFT CL 3
ORCHARD GDNS 4

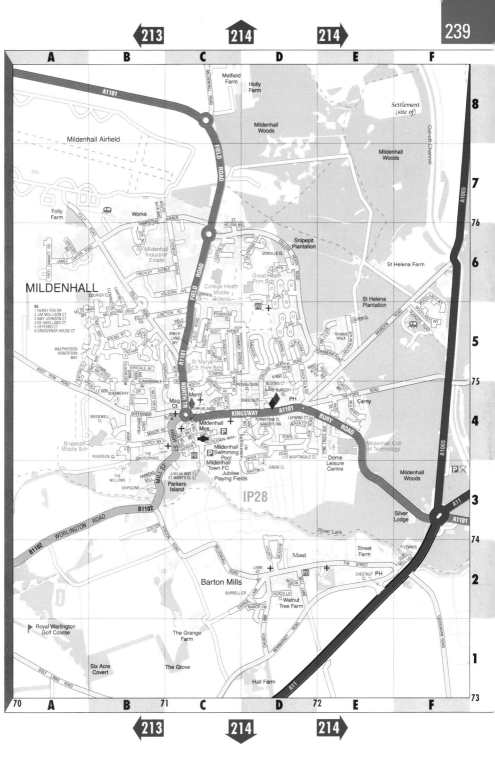

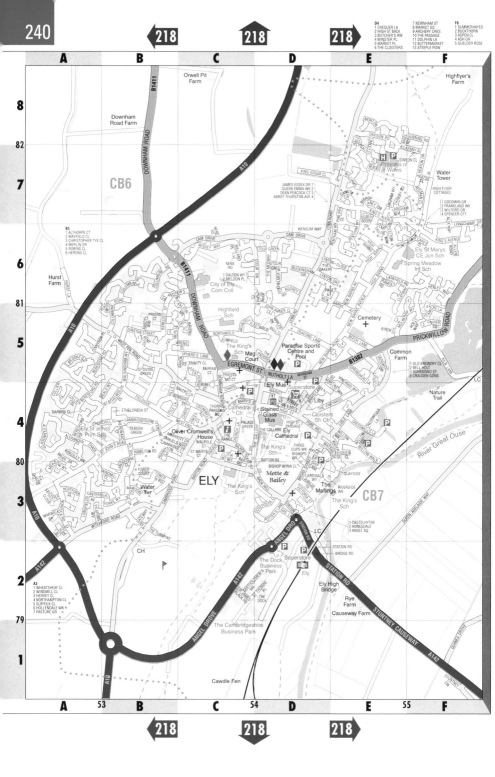

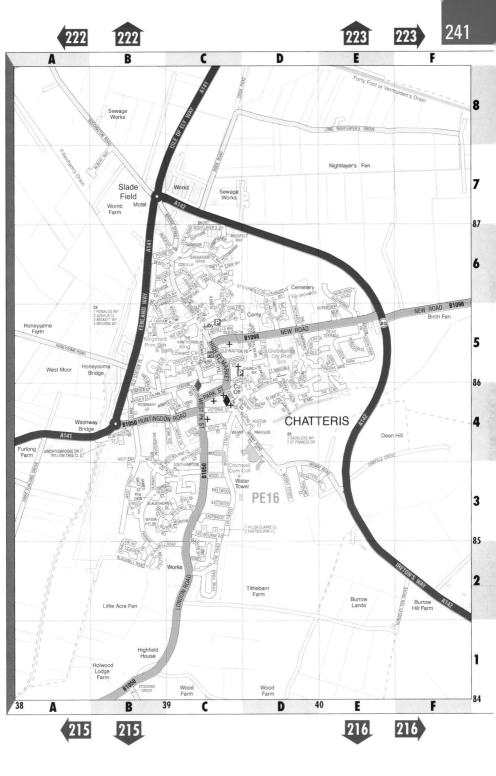

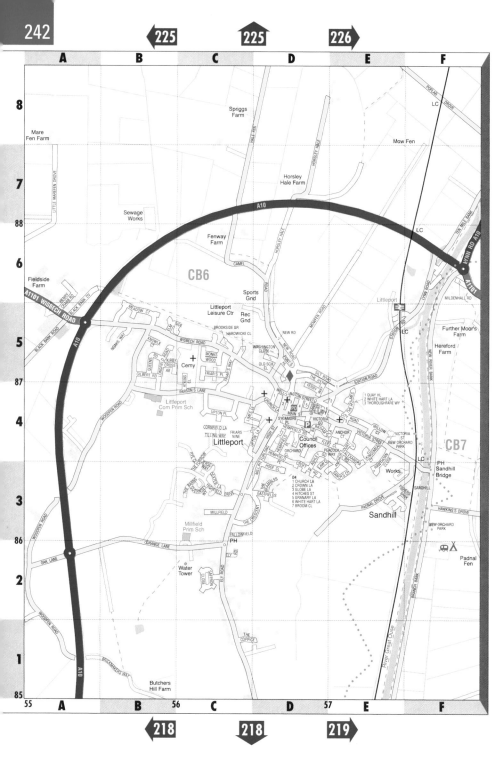

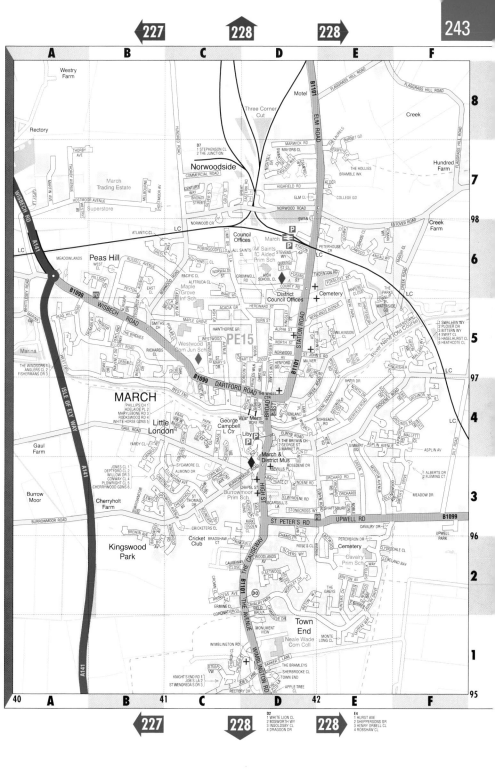

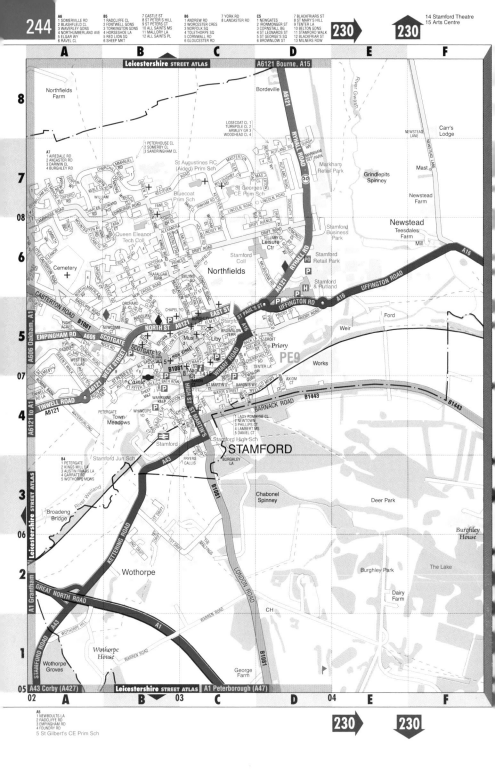

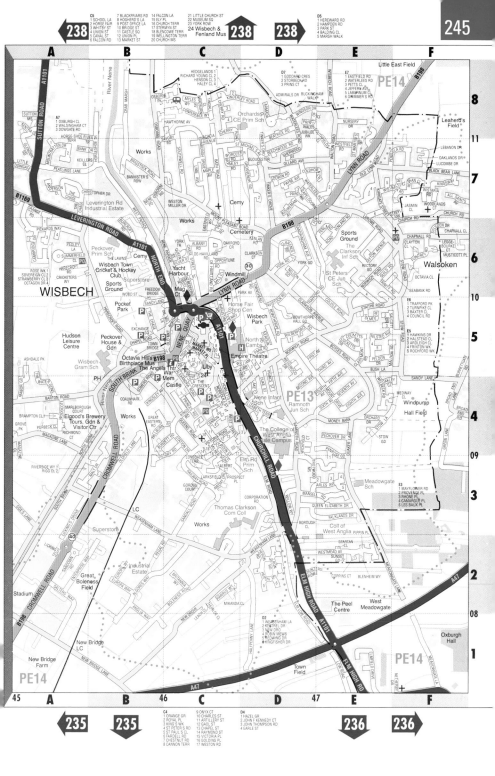

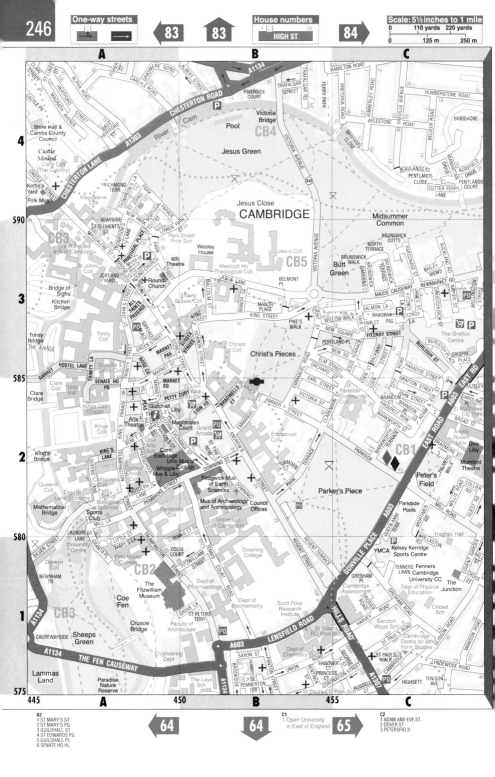

Index

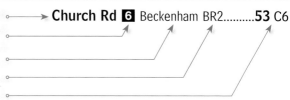

Place name May be abbreviated on the map

Location number Present when a number indicates the place's position in a crowded area of mapping

Locality, town or village Shown when more than one place has the same name

Postcode district District for the indexed place

Page and grid square Page number and grid reference for the standard mapping

Church Rd **6** Beckenham BR2..........**53** C6

Cities, towns and villages are listed in CAPITAL LETTERS
Places of interest are highlighted in blue with a star★

Public and commercial buildings are highlighted in magenta

Abbreviations used in the index

Acad	**Academy**	Comm	**Common**	Gd	**Ground**	L	**Leisure**
App	**Approach**	Cott	**Cottage**	Gdn	**Garden**	La	**Lane**
Arc	**Arcade**	Cres	**Crescent**	Gn	**Green**	Liby	**Library**
Ave	**Avenue**	Cswy	**Causeway**	Gr	**Grove**	Mdw	**Meadow**
Bglw	**Bungalow**	Ct	**Court**	H	**Hall**	Meml	**Memorial**
Bldg	**Building**	Ctr	**Centre**	Ho	**House**	Mkt	**Market**
Bsns, Bus	**Business**	Ctry	**Country**	Hospl	**Hospital**	Mus	**Museum**
Bvd	**Boulevard**	Cty	**County**	HQ	**Headquarters**	Orch	**Orchard**
Cath	**Cathedral**	Dr	**Drive**	Hts	**Heights**	Pal	**Palace**
Cir	**Circus**	Dro	**Drove**	Ind	**Industrial**	Par	**Parade**
Cl	**Close**	Ed	**Education**	Inst	**Institute**	Pas	**Passage**
Cnr	**Corner**	Emb	**Embankment**	Int	**International**	Pk	**Park**
Coll	**College**	Est	**Estate**	Intc	**Interchange**	Pl	**Place**
Com	**Community**	Ex	**Exhibition**	Junc	**Junction**	Prec	**Precinct**

Prom	**Promenade**		
Rd	**Road**		
Recn	**Recreation**		
Ret	**Retail**		
Sh	**Shopping**		
Sq	**Square**		
St	**Street**		
Sta	**Station**		
Terr	**Terrace**		
TH	**Town Hall**		
Univ	**University**		
Wk, Wlk	**Walk**		
Wr	**Water**		
Yd	**Yard**		

Index of towns, villages, streets, hospitals, industrial estates, railway stations, schools, shopping centres, universities and places of interest

A

Abbey Cl
Burwell CB25 . . . . **130** B1
Eye PE6 . . . . **232** A1
Sawtry PE28 . . . . **168** B4
Abbey Coll PE26 . . . . **172** C7
Abbey Coll Cambridge **3**
CB1 . . . . **64** F7
Abbey Fields PE26 . . . . . . **172** C7
Abbeygate Ct PE15 . . . . . **243** D3
Abbey La
Lode CB25 . . . . **107** C2
Swaffham Bulbeck CB25 . . **108** B3
Abbey Meadows Com Sch
CB5 . . . . **84** D2
Abbey Pl
4 Thorney PE6 . . . . **233** A3
Waterbeach CB25 . . . . . . **127** B1
Abbey Rd
Cambridge CB5 . . . . **84** A3
Peterborough PE4 . . . . . . **204** C1
Ramsey PE26 . . . . **172** C6
Abbey Rooms La PE26 . . **172** B6
Abbey St
Cambridge CB1 . . . . **84** A2
Ickleton CB10 . . . . **17** F3
Abbey Way PE7 . . . . **189** C7
Abbey Wlk CB1 . . . . **84** A2
Abbotsbury PE2 . . . . **186** A3
Abbots Cl
Cambridge CB4 . . . . **83** E7
Hemingford Abbots PE28 . . **142** F3
Ramsey PE26 . . . . **172** C7
Abbot's Cl PE28 . . . . **155** A5
Abbots Cres PE27 . . . . . . **144** A6
Abbots Dr **1** PE6 . . . . . . **232** B8
ABBOTSLEY **57** C5
Abbotsley Rd PE19 . . . . . . **57** E8
Abbotsmede Prim Com Sch
PE1 . . . . **198** C4
ABBOTS RIPTON **162** C1
Abbots Ripton CE Prim Sch
PE28 . . . . **162** C1
Abbots Way
Ely CB6 . . . . **240** B5
Horningsea CB25 . . . . **106** A4
Abbott Cl PE28 . . . . **140** C3
Abbot Thurston Ave CB6 **240** C4
Abbotts Cl SG8 . . . . **12** A2
Abbotts Cl PE9 . . . . **244** D4
Abbotts Ct **2** CB9 . . . . . . **24** E5

Abbotts Gr PE4 . . . . **204** B6
Abbott's Grove Cotts CB9 . **24** F3
Abbotts Rd CB9 . . . . **39** A1
Abbot Way PE7 . . . . **181** D4
Abercorn Ct CB9 . . . . **23** F6
Abercorn Pl **6** CB4 . . . . . . **83** E8
Aberdeen Ave CB2 . . . . **64** F6
Abington Gr **8** PE14 . . . . **236** A5
ABINGTON PIGGOTTS **11** E5
Abington Pl CB9 . . . . **39** A1
Abington Rd SG8 . . . . **11** F2
Aboyne Ave PE2 . . . . **185** F5
Abrahams Cl CB25 . . . . . . **105** D6
Abram's La SG8 . . . . **8** C4
Acacia Ave
Peterborough PE1 . . . . . . **198** B8
St Ives PE27 . . . . **143** E6
Wisbech PE13 . . . . **245** C8
Acacia Gr
March PE15 . . . . **243** C5
St Neots PE19 . . . . **75** A6
Acer Rd PE1 . . . . **198** B6
Acheson Rd PE28 . . . . **117** B8
Ackerman Gdns **4** PE19 . . **74** C2
Ackerman St PE19 . . . . **74** C2
Ackroyd Rd **2** SG8 . . . . **5** E8
Acland St PE1 . . . . **197** F3
Acorn Ave CB23 . . . . **102** C4
Acorn La CB23 . . . . **79** C4
Acrefield Dr CB4 . . . . **246** C4
Acremead PE15 . . . . **178** A3
Acre Rd
Carlton CB8 . . . . **55** B8
March PE15 . . . . **243** D4
Acres The **2** PE9 . . . . **230** D4
Acton Way CB4 . . . . **83** D5
Adam & Eve St **1** CB1 . . **246** C1
Adams Ct CB25 . . . . **106** C7
Adam's La PE19 . . . . **96** E4
Adams Rd
Cambridge CB3 . . . . **83** B2
Swaffham Prior CB25 . . . . **108** D5
Adastral Cl CB8 . . . . **110** E4
adc Theatre★ CB1 . . . . . . **246** A3
Adderley PE3 . . . . **197** C7
Addington Way **1** PE4 . . **204** C3
Addington Wlk **6** PE19 . . **74** C2
Addison Rd PE15 . . . . **223** B7
Adelaide Cl **10** CB7 . . . . . **212** B4
Adelaide Pl PE15 . . . . **243** C4
Adelaide St PE9 . . . . **244** C5

Adelaide Wlk PE28 . . . . . . **208** E6
Admirals Dr PE13 . . . . **245** D8
Admirals Way PE19 . . . . **74** A2
Adventurers' Dro CB6 . . . . **224** C1
A Furlong Dro CB6 . . . . . . **224** F2
AILSWORTH **195** D3
Ailwine Rd PE26 . . . . **171** B2
Aingers Rd CB24 . . . . **104** B4
Ainsdale CB1 . . . . **65** F5
Ainsdale Dr PE4 . . . . **204** B4
Ainsworth Ct **4** CB1 . . . . . **84** A1
Ainsworth Pl CB1 . . . . **84** B1
Ainsworth St CB1 . . . . **84** A1
Aintree Rd SG8 . . . . **5** F6
Airedale Cl PE1 . . . . **198** A6
Airedale Rd **1** PE9 . . . . . . **244** A7
Airport Way CB1 . . . . **85** B2
Akeman Cl CB6 . . . . **210** F6
Akeman St
Cambridge CB4 . . . . **83** C5
Landbeach CB25 . . . . **105** C6
Akerly Dr CB23 . . . . **79** A4
Alamein Ct PE19 . . . . **74** C5
Albany Rd PE13 . . . . **245** C6
Albany Wlk PE2 . . . . **186** D7
Alba Rd PE7 . . . . **186** B4
Albemarle Rd PE27 . . . . . . **143** F7
Albemarle Way CB4 . . . . . . **83** E7
Alberta Cres PE29 . . . . **141** E5
Albert Ct PE13 . . . . **245** C3
Albert Pl PE3 . . . . **197** F1
Albert Rd
Stamford PE9 . . . . **244** C5
Albert's Dr PE15 . . . . **243** F3
Albert St CB4 . . . . **246** B4
Albert Way PE16 . . . . **241** B7
Albion Row **6** CB3 . . . . . . **83** C3
Albion Yd **5** CB3 . . . . **83** C3
ALCONBURY **150** E4
Alconbury CE Prim Sch
PE28 . . . . **150** F5
Alconbury Rd PE2 . . . . **187** E5
ALCONBURY WESTON . . . **150** D6
Aldeburgh Cl **21** CB9 . . . . **23** E7
Alder Cl
1 Eaton Socon PE19 . . . . **74** B5
January PE15 . . . . **243** E7
Alde Rd CB9 . . . . **39** A1
Alder Dr
Bourn CB23 . . . . **79** C3
Huntingdon PE29 . . . . **141** D5
Alderlands PE6 . . . . **232** B8

Alderlands Cl **6** PE6 . . . . . **232** B8
Alderman Jacobs Prim Sch
PE7 . . . . **189** F8
Alderman's Dr PE3 . . . . . . **197** E3
Alder Rd PE7 . . . . **186** C3
Alderton Cl CB9 . . . . **38** E2
Aldham Ct **12** CB9 . . . . **23** E7
Aldous Ct SG8 . . . . **15** E8
Aldreth CB6 . . . . **209** F4
Aldreth Rd CB6 . . . . **209** F5
Aldsworth Cl PE1 . . . . **198** D6
Alec Rolph Cl CB21 . . . . **66** C5
Alexander Chase CB6 . . . . **240** A4
Alexander Rd SG19 . . . . **25** B4
Alexandra Rd
Littleport CB6 . . . . **242** E4
Peterborough PE1 . . . . . . **197** F6
Stamford PE9 . . . . **244** B6
Wisbech PE13 . . . . **245** C5
Alex Wood Rd CB4 . . . . **83** E6
Alfric Sq PE2 . . . . **186** D6
Alftruda Cl PE15 . . . . **243** C6
Algar Dr CB8 . . . . **70** F8
Algores Way PE13 . . . . **245** B2
Alington Rd PE19 . . . . **74** F1
Aliwal Rd PE7 . . . . **189** E3
Alix Way CB7 . . . . **240** F7
Allan Ave PE2 . . . . **187** E5
Allard Cl PE7 . . . . **181** D6
Allen Cl CB2 . . . . **64** D2
Allen Farm Cl PE29 . . . . . . **141** E1
Allen Rd
Ely CB6 . . . . **240** F6
Peterborough PE1 . . . . . . **197** E6
Ramsey PE26 . . . . **171** F7
Allens Cl CB23 . . . . **63** B4
Allen's Dro PE13 . . . . **237** D1
Allen's Orch PE28 . . . . **140** E1
Allens Yd PE16 . . . . **241** D4
Allerton Cl **6** PE29 . . . . . **230** D3
Allerton Garth PE7 . . . . . . **185** A4
Allexton Gdns **3** PE1 . . . **198** D7
Allington Wlk CB8 . . . . **23** E8
Allotment La PE5 . . . . **195** E2
Allotments Dro CB6 . . . . . . **211** B7
All Saints Ave PE13 . . . . . . **245** F7
All Saints CE Prim Sch
CB8 . . . . **111** B3
All Saints Cl
January PE15 . . . . **243** D6
St Ives PE27 . . . . **144** A6
2 Wisbech PE14 . . . . . . **236** A5

Abb–Amb

All Saints Gn PE27 . . . . . . **144** A6
All Saints IC Aided Prim Sch
PE15 . . . . **243** D6
All Saints Jun Sch PE1 . . **198** A6
All Saints Mews **10** PE9 . **244** B5
All Saints Pas
Cambridge CB2 . . . . **246** A3
6 Huntingdon PE29 . . . . **141** D4
All Saints' Pl **12** PE9 . . . **244** B5
All Saints Rd
Fulbourn CB21 . . . . **66** F5
Newmarket CB8 . . . . **111** A3
Peterborough PE1 . . . . . . **198** A5
All Saints' St PE9 . . . . **244** B5
All Saints Way PE28 . . . . . **168** C4
All Saints Wlk IP28 . . . . . . **213** F4
All Souls La CB3 . . . . **83** B4
Alma Rd PE1 . . . . **197** F5
Alma Terr PE16 . . . . **241** B6
Almond Cl PE29 . . . . **142** A1
Almond Dr PE15 . . . . **243** C3
Almond Gr CB23 . . . . **102** C4
Almond Rd
Peterborough PE1 . . . . . . **198** B7
St Neots PE19 . . . . **74** F6
Almoners' Ave CB1 . . . . **65** C3
Almoners La PE3 . . . . **197** E3
Alms Cl PE29 . . . . **141** C7
Alms Hill CB23 . . . . **60** D7
Alms La SG7 . . . . **2** D4
Alnwick Ct **1** PE19 . . . . . . **74** F2
Alpha La PE28 . . . . **151** E3
Alpha Rd CB4 . . . . **246** A4
Alpha St PE15 . . . . **243** D5
Alpha Terr CB2 . . . . **64** D3
Alstead Rd CB24 . . . . **104** B5
Alsyke Cl PE15 . . . . **116** A7
Althorpe Ct **1** CB6 . . . . . **240** B5
Alvis Dr PE7 . . . . **181** D6
ALWALTON **185** B4
Alwin Cl PE28 . . . . **117** B8
Alwyn Cl PE27 . . . . **144** B6
Alwyne Rd PE1 . . . . **65** C2
Amanda Ct PE3 . . . . **197** E2
Amber Ctr PE29 . . . . **141** F6
Amberley Slope PE4 . . . . . **204** C3
Ambleside Gdns PE4 . . . . . **204** C3
Ambrose Way CB24 . . . . . . **104** C4
Ambury Hill PE29 . . . . **141** E5
Ambury Rd PE29 . . . . **141** D5

248 Amb–Bar

Ambury Road S PE29.... 141 D5
Ambuscade Rd PE19 .... 74 C1
Amcotts CB23 .... 60 B8
American Air Mus* CB22 .16 F8
American La PE29 .... 141 E5
America The CB6 .... 216 D1
Amwell Rd CB4 .... 83 F8
Amy Johnson Ct 3 IP28 .239 B5
Ancaster Rd 2 PE9 ..... 244 A7
Ancaster Way
  Cambridge CB1 .... 65 C7
  3 Doddington/Wimblington
  PE15.................. 222 F5
Anchor Ct
  Littleport CB6 .... 242 E3
  Peterborough PE4 ..... 205 F1
Anchor Dro PE38 .... 226 F4
Anchor La CB25......... 130 B4
Anderson Cl PE13....... 245 A7
Andersons Cres PE29 ... 142 A2
Anderson Rd
  Boxworth CB4 .... 101 D8
  Swavesey CB24 .... 122 D1
Andrea Cl PE2 .... 187 C6
Andrew Cl PE5 .... 195 D2
Andrew's Cl PE7....... 187 B1
Andrew Rd
  Newmarket CB8........ 110 E5
  1 Stamford PE9........ 244 B6
  St Neots PE19 .... 74 F2
Andrews Cl 2 CB6...... 210 F5
Andrews Cres PE4 ...... 204 F2
Angel Dro CB7 .... 240 D2
Angell's Mdw SG7 ...... 2 D4
Angel Sq CB7........... 240 D3
Angle End CB21 .... 67 F8
Angle La SG8 .... 29 E5
Anglers Cl PE15........ 243 A5
Anglers Way CB4 .... 84 C5
Anglesey Abbey (& remains
  of Priory)* CB25........ 107 B1
Anglesey Way 6 CB24 ..208 D1
Angles Theatre The*
  PE13.................. 245 C5
Anglian Bsns Pk SG8..... 5 B7
Anglian Cl PE2 .... 187 D6
Anglia Ruskin Univ CB1 .246 C2
Anglia Way PE13........ 245 B2
Angoods La PE16 .... 241 B6
Angus Cl 2 CB1........ 65 A8
Angus Ct PE3........... 197 D3
Annabelle Ave PE15.... 224 B4
Anne Rd PE9 .... 244 A6
Anne's Cl CB8 .... 110 B8
Annesdale CB7 .... 240 D3
Annesley CB1........... 65 E5
Annesley Cl PE28 ...... 168 B4
Annington Cres SG8 ..... 13 A8
Ann's Rd CB5........... 84 E4
Ann Suckling Rd CB9 .... 39 A2
Ansley Way PE27........ 143 E5
Anson Cl PE26......... 171 E3
Anson Dr PE27.......... 143 F6
Anson Pl PE19 .... 74 A2
Anstey Way CB2 .... 64 D2
Antelope Way CB1 ...... 66 A7
Anthony Cl
  1 Whittlesey PE7 ..... 189 C8
Antonia Cl CB9 .... 24 E7
Anvil Ave SG8 .... 12 A2
Anvil Cl
  Chatteris PE16........ 241 E5
  Great Shelford CB22 ... 49 C4
Apeldoorn Wlk PE13 ... 245 D7
Apley Way CB23 .... 79 A4
Apollo Way CB4 .... 83 E8
Apple Acre Rd CB9 ..... 38 C1
Appleby Pk CB6 .... 240 D5
Apple Cl PE19 .... 96 F8
Apple Gr PE19 .... 74 C4
Apple Orch The PE28... 143 D2
Appletree Cl CB24 ..... 125 D1
Apple Tree Cl
  Hardwick CB23 .... 80 F3
  January PE15......... 243 D1
  Yaxley PE7............ 211 C6
Appletree Gr CB25 ..... 130 B4
Appletrees CB23 .... 102 C3
Applewood Cl CB1 ..... 65 F5
Applewood Dr PE7 .... 186 C3
Appleyard PE2 .... 187 C2
Approach Cotts CB9 .... 38 D2
Apreece Rd PE7 .... 175 D8
Apreece Way PE7...... 176 A7
Apsley Way PE3 .... 197 A2
Apthorpe St CB21...... 66 F6
Apthorpe Way CB4 ..... 84 A7
Aragon Cl
  Buckden PE19 .... 117 B4
  Cambridge CB4 .... 83 E7
Aragon Pl PE28 .... 113 F5
Aragon Rd CB9 .... 23 D6
Arbor Cl CB25.......... 86 E6
Arborfield Cl PE6...... 230 E4
Arbour La CB23 .... 79 A4
Arbroath Gdns PE2 .... 185 C4
ARBURY 83 D6
Arbury Banks* SG7...... 2 C2
Arbury Cl PE3 .... 197 A3
Arbury Ct CB4.......... 83 E6
Arbury Prim Sch CB4 ... 83 E5
Arbury Rd CB4 .... 83 E6
Arcadia Gdns CB24 .... 103 C5
Archers Cl CB25........ 108 B3

Archers Dro PE6....... 233 D6
Archers Wood PE7 .... 186 C3
Archers Wood Nature
  Reserve* PE28........ 160 C7
Archery Cres 8 CB7... 240 D4
Archway Ct CB3 .... 64 B7
Arden Rd CB4 .... 83 F8
Ardleigh Cl 3 PE13.... 245 E5
Ardross Ct CB8 .... 68 F6
Argent Pl CB8 .... 111 A6
Argyle St CB1.......... 65 B8
Argyll Ct CB9 .... 23 F6
Arizona PE28 .... 151 F4
Arizona Way CB24 ..... 125 D1
Armada Cl PE13 .... 245 D8
Armingford Cres SG8 ... 14 E7
Armitage Way CB4 ..... 83 F8
Armley Gr PE9......... 244 B7
Armshold La CB23 ..... 61 D2
Armstrong Cl
  Newmarket CB8........ 111 B3
  Perry PE28........... 115 D3
Armstrong Ct 1 PE29...141 F8
Arnhem Cl PE19 .... 74 C5
Arnold's La PE7 .... 189 E7
Arran Cl CB1........... 65 F6
Arran Way PE27 .... 144 A8
Arrendene Rd CB9...... 38 F1
ARRINGTON............. 44 C1
Arrow Ct PE2........... 186 C3
Art Gall & War Mus*
  PE29................. 141 D4
Arthur Mellows Village Coll
  PE6.................. 203 D8
Arthur's Meadow Nature
  Reserve* PE28........ 120 C7
Arthur St CB4 .... 83 C4
Artillery St 11 PE13 .... 245 E4
Artindale PE3.......... 197 A3
Artis Ct PE3........... 197 A3
Arundel Cl CB4 .... 83 C5
Arundel Cres PE19 ..... 74 E2
Arundell CB6 .... 240 C5
Arundel Rd
  Huntingdon PE29...... 142 A6
  Peterborough PE4 .... 204 C1
Arundel Wlk 11 CB9... 23 E8
Ascham La CB22........ 32 B4
Ascham Rd CB4........ 83 E4
Ascot Dr PE1 .... 198 B6
Ascot Rd SG8.......... 5 F6
Ashbeach Dro PE26 ... 220 D3
Ashbeach Prim Sch The
  PE26................. 220 D3
Ashbeach Rd
  Huntingdon PE28 .... 243 D4
  Ramsey PE26......... 220 D3
Ashburn Cl PE6........ 203 F7
Ashbury Cl CB1........ 65 B6
Ash Cl
  Huntingdon PE29..... 141 E7
  Peterborough PE7 .... 198 C2
  Stilton PE7........... 175 F7
  Thorney PE6.......... 232 F3
  Warboys PE28 .... 165 A6
Ashcroft PE19 .... 98 B2
Ashcroft Ct CB4 .... 83 E7
Ashcroft Gdns PE1..... 198 C5
Ash Ct
  Brampton PE28 ...... 140 C3
  Peterborough PE1 .... 198 C2
Ashdale Cl PE28 .... 168 B3
Ashdale Pk PE13....... 245 A5
ASHDON................ 21 B1
Ashdon Pl CB10........ 21 C2
Ashdon Prim Sch CB10...21 B1
Ashen Gn CB22 .... 49 A5
Ashes The PE2......... 186 F5
Ashfield PE28.......... 113 F5
Ashfield Rd CB4 .... 84 B5
Ashfields 1 PE6....... 231 F7
Ash Gr
  Burwell CB25.......... 130 B2
  Chatteris PE16........ 241 C5
  4 Ely CB7............ 240 F5
  Haverhill CB9......... 38 E1
  March PE15........... 243 C5
  Melbourn SG8 .... 14 C5
Ashlea Cl CB9 .... 24 B6
Ashlea Rd CB9........ 24 B6
Ashleigh PE2 .... 185 C6
ASHLEY................ 91 F7
Ashley Ct 9 CB1 ...... 84 A1
Ashley Gdns CB6...... 242 D3
Ashley Pool La PE7 .... 233 A2
Ashley Rd
  Cheveley CB8......... 112 A1
  Newmarket CB8....... 111 E2
Ashley Way CB22 ...... 32 F8
Ashline Gr PE7 .... 189 D6
Ashmead Dr CB23..... 81 A3
Ash Pk PE4............ 204 B6
Ash Pl CB6............ 210 F5
Ash Rd
  Earith PE28........... 208 F7
  Peterborough PE1 .... 198 C2
ASHTON............... 231 A4
Ashton Cl PE27 .... 208 A2
Ashton Gdns PE29 .... 141 D5
Ashton Rd PE3......... 197 B5
Ash Tree Cl 14 PE15...223 B7
Ashvale CB4........... 83 D7
Ash Way SG8 .... 5 F6
ASHWELL............... 2 E4
Ashwell Bury SG7...... 2 C5
ASHWELL END.......... 2 A5
Ashwell & Morden Sta SG7 3 D2

Ashwell Prim Sch SG7 ...2 D4
Ashwell Rd
  Guilden Morden SG8 ...10 F2
  Newnham SG7......... 2 A1
Ashwell St
  Ashwell SG7........... 2 D3
  Bassingbourn cum Kneesworth
  SG8.................. 13 A3
Ashwell Village Mus* SG7..2 D4
Askers Field CB23...... 78 E2
Askew's La PE7........ 181 E4
Aspal Cl 8 IP28...... 213 F8
Aspal Hall Rd IP28.... 213 F8
Aspal La IP28.......... 214 A8
Aspal Pk
  Beck Row, Holywell Row &
  Kenny Hill IP28....... 214 A8
  Mildenhall IP28....... 213 F8
Aspal Pl 9 IP28....... 213 F8
Aspen Cl
  8 Ely CB7........... 240 E5
  Haverhill CB9......... 38 E1
Aspen Gn PE29 .... 141 E6
Asplin Ave PE15 ...... 243 E4
Asplins Ave 6 PE27... 208 A3
Asplin's Cl CB24 ...... 208 D1
Asplin's La PE19 ...... 117 F3
Aster Dr PE4 .... 204 D3
Astilbe La PE29....... 141 D5
Astley Cl CB6......... 216 E1
Astore Pk PE1......... 198 F5
Atherstone Ave PE11 .. 197 B4
Atherton Cl CB4 .... 83 E5
Athlone 7 CB1........ 84 A1
Athlone Cl CB23 .... 99 A3
Atkins Cl
  Cambridge CB4 .... 84 A7
  Littleport CB6 .... 242 C5
Atkinson St PE1 .... 198 C2
Atlantic Cl PE15 ...... 243 B6
Atterton Rd CB9 .... 38 D1
Auberry Way CB23 ..... 78 F3
Auborn Gdns PE3...... 193 A3
Aubretia Ave PE4 ..... 204 D3
Auckland Rd CB5...... 246 C3
Audley Cl SG19 .... 58 E4
Audley Gate PE3...... 197 C3
Audley Way CB21 ...... 37 A3
Augers Rd 4 CB1 ..... 65 F6
Augusta Cl PE1 .... 198 E6
Augustus Cl
  4 Cambridge CB4 .... 83 E8
  Haverhill CB9......... 24 D7
Augustus Way PE16 ... 241 D6
Aureole Wlk CB8 ...... 110 D8
Austin Cl PE7......... 181 D6
Austin Friars La 3 PE9 .244 A4
Austin St PE9......... 244 B4
Australia Cl CB3 ...... 243 A6
Avenells Way 2 SG19...41 D5
Avenue Rd
  Huntingdon PE29..... 141 D5
  St Neots PE19 .... 74 F6
Avenue The
  Borough Fen PE6..... 207 E3
  Burwell CB25.......... 130 C3
  Cambridge CB3 .... 246 A3
  Girton CB3........... 103 B1
  Godmanchester PE29 ..141 E3
  Leighton PE28 .... 148 C3
  Madingley CB23....... 81 F7
  March PE15........... 243 D2
  Newmarket CB8....... 111 A3
  Ramsey PE26......... 172 A7
Aversley Wood Nature
  Reserve* PE28....... 159 F8
Aves Cl PE7........... 213 A5
Avocet Gr CB7......... 212 A5
Avon Ct
  Eaton Socon PE19 .... 74 C3
  Peterborough PE4 .... 204 D2
Avro Ct PE29 .... 141 B8
Awdry Dr PE13 .... 245 C3
Axiom Ave PE3 .... 197 C4
Axis Way 6 PE19 ..... 74 B5
Aydon Rd PE7........ 209 A4
Aylesborough Cl 4 CB4..83 D7
Aylesford Way CB22 ... 49 B4
Aylestone Rd CB4..... 246 C4
Aylington Cl PE8 ...... 184 B1
Ayre Ct 5 PE19....... 75 A5
Ayres Dr PE2......... 187 C6
Azalea Cl PE3 .... 197 A2
Azalea court PE7...... 181 F6

B

Babble Cl PE15 .... 243 C4
BABRAHAM............. 50 E1
Babraham CE Prim Sch
  CB22................. 50 D1
Babraham Rd
  Babraham CB22....... 50 B1
  Cambridge CB2........ 65 C2
  Fulbourn CB21........ 50 E8
  Great Shelford CB22 ... 49 E8
  Sawston CB22........ 32 F8
  Stapleford CB22 ..... 50 B1
Back Dro
  Upwell PE14.......... 229 D8
  Welney PE14......... 225 A8
Back Hill
  Ely CB7.............. 240 D3
  Hadstock CB21........ 20 B6

Back La
  Barrington CB22 ...... 29 E8
  Bourn CB23........... 79 B4
  Burrough Green CB8 .. 70 F4
  Cambourne CB23...... 79 C4
  Coveney CB6.......... 217 B5
  14 Deeping St James PE6..231 F8
  Elton PE8............ 178 D8
  Ely CB7.............. 240 D4
  Eye PE6.............. 232 A1
  Haslingfield CB23..... 47 B4
  Holywell-cum-Needingworth
  PE27................. 144 F2
  Ickleton CB10 .... 18 A3
  Market Deeping PE6 .. 206 A7
  Melbourn SG8 .... 14 C4
  Outwell PE14......... 236 E3
  Stamford PE9......... 244 C5
  Wicken CB7........... 211 E1
  Yaxley PE7........... 181 E5
Back Rd
  Elm PE14............ 236 A5
  Gorefield PE13....... 237 E2
  Linton CB21.......... 35 C3
  Murrow PE13......... 234 D6
  Wisbech PE14......... 236 A3
Back Reach Dro PE15...221 E7
Back St SG7.......... 2 D3
Bacon's Yd SG7....... 2 D4
Badcock Rd CB23...... 47 B5
Bader Cl
  Peterborough PE3 .... 197 B6
  Ramsey PE26......... 172 A4
Bad Gate PE12........ 237 B7
Badgeney Rd PE15.... 243 E4
Badger Cl PE7........ 181 F5
Badgers Holt CB24.... 103 A8
Badinton La PE9...... 230 F5
BADLINGHAM......... 213 C6
Badlingham Rd CB7.... 213 C1
Badminton Cl CB4..... 83 C6
Badney Dro PE16 ..... 222 D3
Bagley End PE4....... 205 B1
Bagot Pl 5 CB4....... 83 F8
Bagsham La IP28...... 213 E6
Bahram Cl CB8........ 110 E4
Bailey Cl CB9......... 24 C8
Bailey Mews CB5..... 246 C3
Bailey Way PE2....... 186 D8
Bain Cl PE9.......... 244 C7
Baines Coney CB9..... 38 D1
BAINTON............. 230 F5
Bainton Green Rd PE9 .231 A4
Bainton Rd
  Barnack PE9......... 230 D4
  Newborough PE6..... 204 F8
Baird Cl PE7......... 181 D6
Bakehouse Cl 7 PE25...222 A5
Bakehouse Hill CB8 ... 70 E8
Baker Dr CB25........ 130 C3
Bakers Cl CB23........ 62 D6
Bakers Field CB23 .... 102 C1
Bakers La
  Barley SG8.......... 6 F3
  Linton CB21......... 35 D2
  Peterborough PE2.... 186 E7
Bakers Link PE19 ..... 74 E2
Bakers Row CB8...... 111 A4
Bakers Way
  Perry PE28.......... 115 E2
  Tuddenham IP28 .... 214 D2
Bakery Cl
  Fen Ditton CB5....... 84 E5
  Wilburton CB6....... 210 C5
Bakewell Rd PE2...... 185 C2
Bala Ct PE4........... 204 E3
Balaton Pl CB8 .... 111 A6
Balding Cl 4 PE13.... 245 D5
Baldock Rd SG8....... 4 C4
Baldock St SG8....... 5 D6
Baldock Way CB1..... 65 B5
Baldwin Cl PE8....... 184 D2
Baldwins Cl CB23 .... 60 C5
Baldwin's Cnr SG7.... 2 E5
Balingdon La CB21.... 35 D3
Balintore Rise PE2.... 185 D4
Balland Field CB24.... 124 A8
Balland Hill PE19..... 75 C5
Ballantine Gate PE6... 204 B8
Balmoral Dr 5 CB9... 23 F8
Balmoral Rd PE4...... 197 C8
Balmoral Way PE19 ... 74 E2
BALSHAM............. 53 A2
Balsham La CB8....... 70 B7
Balsham Rd
  Fulbourn CB21........ 67 B2
  Linton CB21.......... 35 D3
Bambers La PE14..... 236 C6
Bamber St PE1....... 197 F4
Bancroft Cl PE1....... 65 B6
Bancroft La CB7...... 212 B5
Bandon Rd CB3...... 82 F6
Banff Cl 2 CB4....... 83 E7
Banham Mews CB9.... 38 B1
Banhams Cl CB4..... 246 C4
Bank Ave
  Hampton Hargate PE7..186 D2
  Somersham PE28 .... 208 C8
Bank Cl PE7.......... 189 E5
Bank Dr PE13......... 245 A7
Bankes Mead CB22.... 32 D1
Bank Rd PE27........ 144 B7
Banks Cnr CB6....... 240 C4
Banks Ct PE19........ 74 E2
Bank's End PE28..... 142 D6
Bank The PE13....... 234 C7
Bannister Gdns SG8 ... 5 E8

Bannister's Row PE13...245 B7
Bannold Ct CB25...... 106 B8
Bannold Dro CB25 .... 106 C8
Bannold Rd CB25..... 106 B8
Banworth La CB25 .... 105 D6
Baptist Rd PE14...... 229 D7
Barbara Stradbroke Ave
  CB8................. 89 B7
Barber Cl PE2........ 187 C7
Barbers Dro PE6...... 232 C8
Barbers Drove S PE6... 232 C8
Barbers Hill CB4..... 204 B7
Barcham Rd CB7...... 211 F7
Bar Cl CB22.......... 49 C5
Bardling's Dro PE12... 237 A8
Bardney PE2......... 186 A4
Bar Dro PE14........ 236 B4
Bardyke Bank PE14 ... 229 F7
Baretts Cl PE7....... 189 D8
Barford Cl PE2....... 186 C7
Barford Rd PE19...... 74 E2
Bargate La IP28...... 213 D5
Bargate Rd IP28...... 213 D6
BARHAM.............. 149 B3
Barham Cl PE2....... 187 F5
Barham Ct SG8....... 14 D6
Barham Rd PE28..... 149 D6
Bar Hill Prim Sch CB23 ..102 C3
Barker Cl
  Hail Weston PE19 .... 95 A1
  Waterbeach CB25 .... 106 A1
Barker's La PE15..... 243 D1
Barkham's La CB6 .... 242 D4
Barklay Ct PE15...... 224 A4
Barkston Dr PE1..... 198 B6
Barkway Rd SG8...... 5 E5
Barkways CB25....... 130 C1
Barkway St SG8...... 5 D5
Bar La
  Hatley SG19.......... 42 E2
  Stapleford CB22 ..... 49 C4
  Tadlow SG19......... 25 E8
BARLEY.............. 6 F2
Barley Cl 2 CB8...... 111 B3
Barleyfields CB21 .... 67 A5
Barley Mews PE2 .... 186 D7
Barley Rd
  Eaton Socon PE19 .... 74 C3
  Great & Little Chishill SG8..7 A7
Barley VP Fst Sch SG8 ...7 A2
Barley Way CB21...... 35 D2
Barlings Ct PE28 ..... 111 A4
Barnabas Ct CB24.... 105 D1
Barnabas Oley CE Prim Sch
  SG19................. 58 E4
BARNACK.............. 230 E3
Barnack CE Prim Sch
  PE9................. 230 D4
Barnack Gr SG8....... 5 C7
Barnack Hills & Holes
  National Nature Reserve*
  PE9................. 230 D3
Barnack Rd
  Bainton PE9.......... 230 E4
  St Martin's Without PE9 .244 C4
Barnard Ct 1 PE19 ... 74 F1
Barnard Way
  1 Cambridge CB4..... 83 D5
  Peterborough PE1 .... 196 F3
Barn Cl
  Huntingdon PE29..... 142 A7
  6 Maxey PE6........ 231 C7
  Peterborough PE4.... 204 B3
  Ramsey PE26......... 172 A4
  Stilton PE7.......... 175 F8
Barnes Cl
  Cambridge CB5....... 84 D2
  St Neots PE19........ 74 E6
Barnes Way
  Peterborough PE4.... 204 B3
  Whittlesey PE7 ...... 189 B8
Barnfield Gdns PE7 ... 190 F8
Barnfield La PE28..... 98 D7
Barn Hill PE9........ 244 B5
Barns Cl CB24........ 208 D1
Barns The
  Buckden PE19 .... 117 B4
  Littleport CB6........ 242 C3
Barnstock PE3........ 197 A7
Barnwell Dr CB1...... 84 E2
Barnwell Rd CB1..... 84 E2
Baron Ct
  Eaton Socon PE19 .... 74 B4
  2 Paston PE4........ 204 D4
  Peterborough PE4.... 204 D4
Barons La CB22....... 30 C5
Baron's Way
  Papworth Everard CB23 ..99 B3
  Stamford PE9........ 244 C4
Baros Cl CB1......... 22 A7
Barra PE13........... 238 A1
Barracks The PE13.... 237 E2
Barringer Way PE19...74 F7
BARRINGTON......... 29 E8
Barrington CE Prim Sch
  CB22................. 46 F1
Barrington Nature Reserve*
  CB22................. 29 E8
Barrington Rd
  Orwell SG8.......... 45 F1
  Shepreth SG8......... 29 D6
Barron's Gn SG8...... 29 C4
Barrons Way 1 CB23 ..62 C5
Barrow Cl CB2........ 64 C5
Barrowcrofts CB24.... 104 B5
Barrowfield PE1...... 198 D6
Barrow La CB23...... 79 A4

Barrow Rd CB2 . . . . .64 E5
Barr's St PE7 . . . . .189 D7
Barry Lynham Dr CB8 . . .111 C2
Barry Wlk 3 PE2 . . . . . . .186 F7
Barsey Cl CB9 . . . . .38 C1
Barston Dro CB25 . . . . . .108 C7
Bartholomew's Wlk CB7. 240 C2
Bartholomew Cl CB10. . . .18 E2
BARTLOW 21 A7
Bartlow Hills (Tumuli)*
    CB21 . . . . .21 B6
Bartlow Pl CB9 . . . . .39 B1
Bartlow Rd
    Castle Camps CB21 . . . .22 D4
    Hadstock CB21 . . . . . . .20 D7
    Linton CB21 . . . . .35 E2
BARTON 63 B3
Barton CE Prim Sch CB23 .63 A4
Barton Cl
    Cambridge CB3 . . . . . . .64 B8
    Peterborough PE4 . . . . .204 F1
    Witchford CB6 . . . . . . .217 D1
Barton Holt PE13 . . . . . .237 F8
Barton La PE13 . . . . .237 F8
Barton Mews CB7 . . . . . .240 C4
BARTON MILLS 239 C2
Barton Rd
    Cambridge CB3 . . . . . . .64 B8
    Comberton CB23 . . . . . .62 D5
    Ely CB7 . . . . .240 C3
    Haslingfield CB23 . . . . . .47 A7
    Wisbech PE13 . . . . . . .245 A4
Bartons Cl CB21 . . . . .53 B2
Bartons Pl CB8 . . . . .110 E5
Barton Sq CB7 . . . . .240 C3
Bartram Gate PE4 . . . . . .204 E1
BARWAY 211 C6
Barway Rd CB7 . . . . .211 D6
Barway Rd CB7 . . . . .211 C6
Bascraft Way PE29 . . . . .142 A1
Basil Gn PE2 . . . . .186 D6
Basin Rd PE14 . . . . .236 E3
Bassenhally Ct PE7 . . . . .189 E7
Bassenhally Rd PE7. . . . .189 E8
Bassenthwaite PE29 . . . .141 B6
Basset Cl 3 CB4. . . . . . . .83 F8
Bassett Cl CB4. . . . . .83 F8
Bassingbourn Barracks
    SG8 . . . . .12 F8
BASSINGBOURN. 12 F4
Bassingbourn Prim Sch
    SG8 . . . . .12 D4
Bassingbourn Rd SG8. . . .12 B3
Bassingbourn Village Coll
    SG8 . . . . .12 E4
Bateman Mews CB2. . . . . .64 E7
Bateman St CB2 . . . . .64 E7
Bate's Dro CB6 . . . . .225 B3
Bateson Rd CB4 . . . . .83 D4
Bates's Dro CB6 . . . . . . .225 B5
Bath Cres PE28 . . . . .143 B8
Bath Rd PE13. . . . . .245 C7
Bath Row PE9 . . . . .244 B4
Bathurst PE2 . . . . .186 A4
Battle Gate CB23. . . . . . . .80 A8
Battle Gate Rd CB23 . . . . .80 A8
Battle Rd PE26. . . . . .171 E3
Baulkin's Dro PE12 . . . . .237 C8
Baulk La SG19 . . . . .43 A3
Baulks The CB22 . . . . .32 E7
Baulk The
    Thriplow SG8. . . . . .31 B2
    Whittlesey PE7 . . . . . . .189 E8
Bawtree Cres CB21 . . . . . .35 E3
Baxter Cl 3 PE13 . . . . . .245 E6
Baxter Dr 4 PE19 . . . . . . .74 E2
Baycliffe Cl 1 CB1 . . . . . .65 D5
Bayfield Dr CB25. . . . . . .130 C2
Bayford Pl 1 CB4 . . . . . . .83 F8
Bayliss PE29. . . . . .118 F7
Bayston Ct PE2 . . . . .186 E8
Beachampstead Rd 1
    PE19. . . . . .93 F6
Beach Rd CB24 . . . . .125 F3
Beacon Cl PE29 . . . . .141 A6
Beaconsfield Cl 4 CB9 . . .23 F7
Beaconsfield Terr CB4. . . .83 D4
Beald Way CB6 . . . . .240 B4
Beale Cl 2 PE29 . . . . . . .141 F8
Beales Way CB4 . . . . .84 A7
Bean Cl 3 PE19 . . . . .75 A6
Bear La SG7 . . . . .22 D6
Beatrice Rd PE13 . . . . . .245 D7
Beatty Rd PE19 . . . . .74 B2
Beauchamp Cl PE19. . . . . .74 B3
Beaufort St 3 CB9 . . . . . .23 F7
Beaufort Dr
    Chatteris PE16. . . . . . .241 B6
    St Neots PE19 . . . . . . .117 A5
Beaufort Gdns PE19. . . . . .75 C6
Beaulands Cl CB4. . . . . . .246 C4
Beaulieu Ct 1 CB6 . . . . .232 A1
Beaumaris Rd PE28 . . . . .168 C3
Beaumont Cl PE29. . . . . .141 F8
Beaumont Ct CB9 . . . . . . .24 B6
Beaumont Rd CB1 . . . . . . .65 D3
Beaumont Vale CB9 . . . . . .24 B6
Beaumont Way PE7 . . . . .186 C2
Beaupre Ave PE14 . . . . . .236 F3
Beaupre Com Prim Sch
    PE14. . . . . .236 F2
Beaupre Dro PE26 . . . . . .221 A2
Beauvale Gdns PE4 . . . . .204 E3
Beauvoir Pl PE7 . . . . . . .181 E5
Beaver Cl 8 PE19 . . . . . . .74 B5
Beccelm Dr 9 PE6 . . . . . .232 B8
Beche Rd CB5 . . . . .84 A2

Beche Way CB25. . . . . . .105 C7
Beck Cl PE15. . . . . .243 C4
Beckets Cl PE1 . . . . .197 F8
Beckett's Cl PE26. . . . . . .172 B8
Beckett Way 3 PE16. . . .241 C5
Beckingham PE2. . . . . . . .185 F3
Beck Rd CB7 . . . . .213 B4
BECK ROW. 213 F8
Beck Row Prim Sch
    IP28. . . . . .213 E8
Bec Rd PE19. . . . . .74 E5
Bede Pl PE1 . . . . .198 A6
Bedford Ave PE28. . . . . .143 B8
Bedford Cl
    Ely CB6 . . . . .240 A3
    2 Needingworth PE27. .208 A3
    St Ives PE27 . . . . .143 F7
Bedford Ct
    5 Haverhill CB9. . . . . . . .23 F7
    10 Thorney PE6. . . . . . .233 A3
Bedford Purlieus National
    Nature Reserve* PE8. .193 A4
Bedford Row PE13 . . . . .238 D8
Bedford St
    Peterborough PE1 . . . .198 B4
    St Neots PE19 . . . . .74 E6
    Wisbech PE13 . . . . . . .245 C6
Bedford Way PE28 . . . . .168 C3
Bedwell Hey La
    Little Thetford CB6 . . . .211 A8
    Witchford CB6. . . . . . . .217 E1
Beechams CE PE13 . . . . .235 C7
Beech Ave
    7 Doddington/Wimblington
    PE15 . . . . .223 A6
    Little Stukeley PE28. . . .152 A2
    Peterborough PE1 . . . . .197 F3
Beech Cl
    Great Shelford CB22 . . . .48 E3
    Huntingdon PE29. . . . . .141 E7
    Isleham CB7 . . . . .212 F5
    2 Thorney PE6 . . . . . . .233 A3
    Warboys PE28 . . . . . . .164 E4
Beech Croft CB8. . . . . . . .70 D2
Beech Dr PE27. . . . . .143 F5
Beech End PE28 . . . . . . .150 F4
Beeches Cl PE28 . . . . . . .213 D7
Beeches Prim Sch The
    PE1. . . . . .197 F3
Beeches Rd IP28 . . . . . . .213 D7
Beeches The
    Cambridge CB4 . . . . . . .83 F5
    Royston SG8 . . . . .5 D6
Beech Gr
    Haverhill CB9. . . . . .23 E8
    March PE15 . . . . .243 C5
    St Neots PE19 . . . . .74 F6
Beech La
    Ely CB7 . . . . .240 E5
    7 Eye PE6 . . . . .232 A1
    Pampisford CB2 . . . . . . .33 B5
Beech Rd PE6 . . . . .203 D8
Beechside SG19 . . . . .41 C6
Beech Tree Ct PE18 . . . . .230 B1
Beech Way CB21. . . . . . . .35 C2
Beechwood Ave
    Bottisham CB25. . . . . . .86 F6
    Melbourn SG8 . . . . .14 C5
Beechwood Cl
    Exning CB8. . . . . .110 C8
    Peterborough PE1 . . . . .198 C7
Beechwood Gdns PE16. . .241 C4
Beechwood Nature Reserve*
    CB1 . . . . .65 F2
Beechwood Rd 4 PE13 . .245 D7
Beehive Centre Ret Pk
    CB1 . . . . .84 B2
Bee's La PE13 . . . . .237 F6
Beeson Cl PE19. . . . . .95 F2
Beeston Dr PE7. . . . . . . .187 F5
Beeton Cl SG8 . . . . .14 C6
Beetons Cl PE7. . . . . . . .181 E5
Beevor Ct PE29 . . . . .152 E1
Beezling Cl 9 PE19. . . . . .74 C6
Beezling Fen Dro PE26. . .222 D3
BEGDALE. 237 F5
Begdale Rd PE14 . . . . . . .235 F5
Begwary Cl 7 PE19. . . . . .74 B5
Beild Dro PE26 . . . . .218 B7
Belbin Way CB22. . . . . . . .32 D8
Beldam Ave SG8. . . . . .5 E5
Beldams PE27 . . . . .208 A3
Beldam's Cl CB23. . . . . . .61 D4
Belgic Sq PE2 . . . . .198 E3
Belgrave Rd CB1. . . . . . . .65 C8
Belgrave Sq PE28. . . . . . .168 B4
Belham Rd PE1 . . . . .197 E7
Bellairs CB6. . . . . .216 E1
Bellamy Ct PE13 . . . . .74 E1
Bellamy's La PE14 . . . . . .238 D4
Bell Cl
    Ely CB6 . . . . .240 D5
    Meldreth SG8. . . . . .14 A8
    Stilton PE7 . . . . .176 A7
Bell Dro PE6. . . . . .232 F6
Belle Isle PE28 . . . . .140 B3
Belle Isle Cres PE28. . . . .140 B3
Bellerby Cl SG8 . . . . .14 C6
Bellfield PE28 . . . . .140 B3
Bellflower Dr PE7 . . . . . .182 A6
Bell Foundry Cl 1 SG19. .41 D5
Bell Gdns
    Haddenham CB6 . . . . . .210 A6
    Soham CB7 . . . . .212 B4
Bell Hill CB24. . . . . .141 B4
Bell Holt CB24. . . . . .240 E4
Bellings Rd CB9 . . . . .38 C2

Bell La
    Alconbury PE28 . . . . . .150 F4
    Barton Mills IP28 . . . . .239 D2
    Peterborough PE28. . . .121 B5
    4 Market Deeping PE6 . .231 F8
    Nuthampstead SG8 . . . . . .1 A2
    Southoe & Midloe PE19. . .95 E6
Bellman's Cl PE7 . . . . . . .189 D7
Bellmans Gr PE7. . . . . . .190 A7
Bellman's Rd PE7. . . . . . .189 F6
Bell Rd CB25 . . . . .86 E5
Bell's Dro
    Littleport CB6 . . . . .225 B6
    Sutton St James PE12. . .237 C8
Bells Mdw SG8 . . . . .11 A5
Bell's Pl PE1 . . . . .198 A2
Belmont Ct 8 CB9. . . . . . .23 F7
Belmont Gdns PE16 . . . . .241 C4
Belmont Pl PE15 . . . . . . .246 B3
Belmont Rd PE15 . . . . . . .243 D5
Belmore Cl 1 CB24. . . . . .209 A1
Belsars Cl 1 CB24. . . . . . .209 A1
Belsar's Hill (Fort)*
    CB24 . . . . .209 C1
Belsay Ct CB9 . . . . .23 D8
Belsay Dr PE2 . . . . .187 F5
Belsize Ave PE2. . . . . . . .186 E6
Belt Dro PE14 . . . . .235 F4
Belton Gdns 10 PE9 . . . . .244 C5
Belton Rd PE7 . . . . .187 F5
Belton's Hill PE28 . . . . . .137 F7
Belton St PE9 . . . . .244 C5
Belt The CB8 . . . . .73 D8
Belvedere PE26. . . . . . . .221 C2
Belvoir Cl 4 CB9 . . . . .23 E8
Belvoir Rd CB4 . . . . .246 C4
Belvoir Terr CB2 . . . . .64 E7
Belvoir Way PE1 . . . . . . .198 C8
Benacre CB9 . . . . .38 B1
Benams Ct PE5 . . . . .195 E2
Bencroft La PE28 . . . . . . .165 A4
Bendyshe Way
    Barrington CB22 . . . . . . .30 A8
    Harston CB22. . . . . .47 A1
Benedict Sq PE4 . . . . . . .204 A2
Benedict St CB6 . . . . . . .240 B5
Benefield Rd CB8 . . . . . . .112 F6
Benet Cl CB24 . . . . .105 C1
Bene't St CB2 . . . . .246 A2
Benians Ct CB3 . . . . .83 B3
Benland PE3. . . . . .197 A6
Bennett Rd
    13 Red Lodge IP28 . . . . .214 A1
    Wyton PE28 . . . . .154 A1
Benny's Way CB3 . . . . . . .82 E6
Benson St 5 CB4 . . . . .83 C4
Benson St 4 CB4 . . . . .83 C4
Benstead PE2 . . . . .185 E3
Bentinck St CB2 . . . . . . .246 B1
Bentley Ave PE7 . . . . . . .181 E6
Bentley Cl PE26. . . . . . . .171 B2
Bentley Rd CB2. . . . . .64 E6
Bentley St PE9 . . . . .244 C5
BENWICK 222 A5
Benwick Prim Sch PE15. .222 A5
Benwick Rd
    Doddington PE15. . . . . .222 D5
    Ramsey PE26 . . . . .221 E3
    Whittlesey PE7 . . . . . . .221 D7
Benyon Gr PE2 . . . . .186 B4
Berbers La PE28 . . . . . . .222 A3
Beresford Rd CB6 . . . . . .240 A5
Bergamont Cl 5 PE29 . . .118 F8
Bergamot Rd PE7 . . . . . . .23 C8
Bergholt Cl 4 CB5. . . . . . .84 E4
Berkeley Gn PE27 . . . . . .144 C4
Berkeley Rd PE13 . . . . . .197 C3
Berkley Ct 1 PE19. . . . . . .74 E4
Bermuda Rd CB4 . . . . .83 C4
Bernard Cl PE29 . . . . . . .141 D6
Bernard Rd PE28 . . . . . . .140 D3
Bernard St CB8 . . . . .240 B4
Berristead Cl CB6 . . . . . .210 C6
Berrybut Way PE9 . . . . . .244 D7
Berry Cl CB6 . . . . .210 F5
Berrycroft
    CB24. . . . . .212 B4
    Willingham CB24 . . . . . .124 A8
Berry Ct PE1 . . . . .197 E5
Berryfield PE15 . . . . .243 E7
Berry Gn CB21. . . . . .210 F5
Berry Green Pk NN14 . . .156 E5
Berry Leas PE6 . . . . .183 D1
Berry Rd CB8 . . . . .230 C6
Berry St 9 CB9 . . . . .23 E8
Betjamin Rd SG8 . . . . .5 C5
Betjaman Rd SG8 . . . . . . .11 B3
Betony Vale SG8 . . . . .5 E5
Betony Wlk CB9 . . . . .23 D8
Bettles Cl PE1 . . . . .198 A6
Betts Cl PE27 . . . . .144 B3
Between Close Dro
    CB24. . . . . .125 D2
Bevan Cl
    Huntingdon PE29 . . . . . .141 E6
    Warmington PE8 . . . . . .140 E7
Beverley Cl SG8 . . . . .5 B8
Beverley Ct PE6 . . . . .232 E6
Beverley Gdns PE9. . . . . .244 A6
Beverley Way 4 CB2. . . . . .5 D8
Beverstone PE2 . . . . .185 D5
Beville CB23. . . . . .161 F6
Bevills Cl PE15. . . . . .243 D3
Bevills Pasture PE15 . . . .220 D7
Bevills Pl PE15 . . . . .243 D3

Bevington Way PE19 . . . .74 E2
Bevishall PE4. . . . . .204 F1
Bevis La PE13 . . . . .235 C6
Bew Cl PE2 . . . . .187 D3
Bewick Pl PE7 . . . . .181 D8
Bewicks Mead CB25 . . . .130 C2
Bickerley Ct CB23. . . . . . .79 A3
Bickleigh Wlk PE3 . . . . . .197 A3
Bicton Ind Est PE28. . . . .114 B7
Bifield PE7 . . . . .185 F3
Biggen The CB22. . . . . . . .17 E8
Biggin Abbey* CB5. . . . . .84 F8
Biggin La
    Fen Ditton CB5. . . . . . . .84 F8
    Ramsey PE26. . . . . .171 E6
Big Gn PE8. . . . . .178 C3
Biggs Rd PE14 . . . . .236 D8
Bigram's La PE19 . . . . . . .114 C7
Bilberry Cl 1 PE19 . . . . . .74 C5
Bilberry End CB21 . . . . . .20 C7
Bill Hall Way PE28 . . . . . .168 D2
Billings Cl CB9 . . . . .38 F2
Bill Rickaby Dr CB8. . . . .111 A5
Binnimoor Rd PE15 . . . . .228 E4
Birch Ave PE16. . . . . .241 D5
Birch Cl
    Cambridge CB4 . . . . . . .83 F5
    Chatteris PE16. . . . . . . .241 D5
    Ely CB7 . . . . .240 D5
    Yaxley PE7. . . . . .182 A5
Birch Dr PE28 . . . . .151 E3
Birchen Cl PE7 . . . . .186 C3
Birches The
    January PE15. . . . . . . .243 B5
    Red Lodge IP28 . . . . . .134 A8
    3 Soham CB7 . . . . .212 A5
Birch Gr PE14 . . . . .236 B5
Birch Gr CB7 . . . . .186 C3
Birchtree Ave PE1 . . . . . .198 A7
Birch Trees Rd CB22 . . . . .49 A6
Birchwood PE2 . . . . .186 A3
Birchwood Ave PE15 . . . .243 B2
Bird Farm Rd CB21 . . . . . .66 E5
Bird La PE19. . . . . .95 A1
Birds Cl CB10. . . . . .18 A3
Bird's Dro
    Gorefield PE13. . . . . . . .237 D1
    Sutton St James PE12. . .237 B8
BIRD'S HUNDRED 189 C5
Birdwood Rd CB1 . . . . . . .65 D6
Birkdale Ave
    Mildenhall IP28 . . . . . . .239 B5
    Peterborough PE4 . . . . .204 B3
Birt La PE27 . . . . .144 A3
Biscay Cl CB9. . . . . .24 C7
Bishop Cl PE7 . . . . .175 F7
Bishop Creighton Prim Sch
    PE1. . . . . .198 B2
Bishop Laney Dr CB6. . . .240 E7
Bishops Cl
    Haverhill CB9. . . . . .23 E8
    Little Downham CB6 . . . .218 A7
    Peterborough PE1 . . . . .198 B3
Bishops Ct 8 CB9 . . . . . . .23 E8
Bishop's Ct CB2 . . . . .64 C1
Bishopsfield PE4 . . . . . . .204 D1
Bishops La
    10 Somersham PE28. . . .215 C1
    St Neots PE19 . . . . .74 F2
Bishop's Rd
    Cambridge CB2 . . . . . . .64 D1
    Peterborough PE1 . . . . .198 A1
Bishops Way
    Buckden PE19 . . . . .117 B4
    Great Paxton PE19 . . . . .96 E4
Bishops Wlk
    2 Barnack PE9. . . . . . .230 D3
    Ely CB7 . . . . .240 D4
Bishops Yd 12 PE28 . . . . .208 C8
Bishop Way CB7. . . . . . . .104 C3
Bishop Wynn Cl CB7 . . . .240 D3
Bittern Cl PE27 . . . . .143 F7
Bittern Gr CB7 . . . . .212 A5
Bittern Way PE15 . . . . . . .243 F5
Blaby's Dro PE15 . . . . . . .216 A4
Black Bank CB6. . . . . . . .218 B8
Black Bank Rd CB6 . . . . .218 B8
Black Bear La
    Leverington PE13 . . . . .245 F7
    Swaffham Bulbeck PE13 .110 F3
    Walsoken PE14 . . . . . . .238 C1
Blackberry Droveway
    CB25 . . . . .129 C1
Blackberry Way 6 IP28. .214 A1
Blackbird Way PE28. . . . .150 E4
Blackbush Dro PE7 . . . . .220 D8
Black Dike PE13 . . . . . . .237 E6
Blackdown Garth PE4. . . .204 D3
Black Dro
    March PE15. . . . . .223 E8
    Thorney PE6. . . . . .233 A5
    Wisbech St Mary PE13 . .234 B3
Black Dyke PE13 . . . . . . .237 F4
Blackfriars Rd 7 PE13 . . .245 C5
Blackfriars St 7 PE7 . . . .244 C5
Blackfriar St 12 PE9 . . . .244 C5
BLACKHALL. 227 A1
Blackhall Rd CB4 . . . . . . .83 C7
Black Ham Dro PE7 . . . . .182 E2
Black Hill Rd PE27 . . . . . .143 E6
Black Horse Dro CB6 . . . .226 B6
Black Horse La
    Chatteris PE16. . . . . . . .241 C6
    Swavesey CB24. . . . . . .122 C6

Blackmans Rd PE7. . . . . .175 D8
Blackmead PE2 . . . . .186 B4
Blackmill Rd PE16 . . . . . .241 B2
Blackmore Cl 4 CB9. . . . . .38 F1
Black Pit Dro CB4. . . . . . .124 B7
Blacksmith Cl SG19 . . . . .40 C3
Blacksmiths Cl
    Abbotsley PE19 . . . . . . .57 B5
    Ramsey Forty Foot PE26. .221 C2
Blacksmiths La
    Abbotsley PE19 . . . . . . .57 B5
    Ellington PE28. . . . . . . .139 A4
    Shudy Camps CB21 . . . . .22 C5
Blackstone Rd PE29. . . . .141 C7
Black Swan Cres PE7 . . . .186 B2
Black Swan Spinney
    PE8. . . . . .194 A4
Blackthorn Cl
    Cambridge CB4 . . . . . . .83 F6
    Chatteris PE16. . . . . . . .241 C3
Blackthorn Ct
    Coates/Eastrea PE7 . . . .190 F8
    2 Soham CB7. . . . . . . .212 A5
Blackwell Rd PE7 . . . . . . .186 C2
Blackwood Rd PE19. . . . . .39 B1
Bladon Way CB4 . . . . .83 B5
Blair Far CB9. . . . . .23 E8
Blair Way PE19 . . . . .74 E2
Blake Cl SG8. . . . . .13 D1
Blakeland Hill CB22. . . . . .17 D8
Blakes Way PE16. . . . . . .174 E2
Blandford Gdns PE1 . . . .198 E4
Blandford Wlk 1 CB4. . . . .83 C6
Blandford Wlk CB4. . . . . . .83 C7
Blashfield Cl 2 PE19 . . . .244 A6
Blaxhall Cl 8 CB9 . . . . . . .23 E7
Blaydon Pl CB6. . . . . . . .216 E2
Blea Wr PE29 . . . . .141 B6
Bledwick Dro PE13 . . . . .238 C3
Blench La CB23 . . . . .34 C1
Blencowe Terr 18 PE13. . .245 C5
Blenheim Cl
    2 Cambridge CB1 . . . . . .65 E5
    3 Eaton Socon PE19 . . . .74 C4
    Haverhill CB9 . . . . .39 B1
    Shepreth SG8. . . . . .29 E4
    Thistley Green IP28. . . . .213 D7
Blenheim Dr PE27 . . . . . .143 F7
Blenheim Gr PE19 . . . . . . .74 F8
Blenheim Rd
    Ramsey PE26. . . . . .172 A7
    Upwood PE26 . . . . .171 E3
Blenheim Way
    Emneth PE14 . . . . .245 E2
    Wyton PE28 . . . . .154 A1
    Yaxley PE7. . . . . .181 E5
Blethan Dr PE29 . . . . . . .141 A6
Blinco Gr CB1 . . . . .65 B5
Blind La
    8 Histon PE25. . . . . . . .231 C7
    Sawtry PE28 . . . . .168 C3
Bliss Way CB1 . . . . .66 C4
Block Fen Dro
    Chatteris PE16. . . . . . . .216 C6
    Wimblington PE15. . . . . .223 C5
Blockmoor Dro CB6. . . . .216 C4
Blockmoor Rd CB7 . . . . . .211 E6
Block Rd CB7. . . . . .212 C1
Bloie Rd CB9 . . . . .24 F1
Bloomfield Cl PE19 . . . . . .95 E1
Bloomfield Way PE28 . . . .168 C4
Blooms Ct IP28 . . . . .239 D4
Bloomsfield CB25. . . . . . .130 C1
Blossom Cl CB25. . . . . . .130 B4
Blossom Ct PE3. . . . . . . .197 B8
Blossom St 3 CB8. . . . . . .84 A1
Bluebell Ave PE1 . . . . . . .198 A8
Bluebell Cl PE26 . . . . . . .220 D3
Bluebell Ct CB23 . . . . .79 C5
Bluebell Wlk 1 CB6. . . . .218 D7
Blue Boar La PE28 . . . . . .218 D7
Bluecoat Prim Sch PE4 . .204 E3
Bluegate PE19. . . . . .118 F7
Blue La PE15. . . . . .223 A7
Blue Ridge Gdns PE15 . . .243 E5
Blue Water Rise PE7 . . . .186 C1
BLUNTISHAM 208 C5
Bluntisham Heath Rd
    PE28. . . . . .155 F3
Bluntisham Rd
    Bluntisham/Colne PE28. .208 D6
    1 Needingworth PE27 . . .208 A3
Blunt's La PE7 . . . . .189 E7
Blyth Dr PE28 . . . . .115 D2
Blythe Way
    Caldecote CB23 . . . . . . .80 C1
    Gamlingay SG19 . . . . . . .41 D5
Blyton Rd CB23 . . . . .49 A3
Boadicea Ct PE16 . . . . . .241 C5
Boardman Cl PE19 . . . . . . .95 F2
Boater's Way PE3 . . . . . .197 D1
Bodiam Way PE19. . . . . . .74 F2
Bodian Wlk 3 CB9 . . . . . .23 E8
Bodsey Toll Rd PE26. . . . .221 B3
Boeing Way IP28 . . . . . . .239 B5
Bogmoor Rd SG8 . . . . .7 C1
Bogs Gap La SG8 . . . . . . .11 B3
Bohemond St PE18 . . . . .141 C4
Boleness Rd PE13. . . . . . .245 C2
Boleyn Ave PE2 . . . . .186 C4
Boleyn Cl PE28 . . . . .23 D7
Boleyn Wlk CB8 . . . . .111 C3
Bolton Cl CB25 . . . . .130 A2

Bona La PE13 . . . . .235 B8
Boongate PE1 . . . . .198 C3
Booth Way PE19 . . . . .95 F1
Boot La CB22 . . . . .29 E8
Boot's Rd PE15 . . . . .223 F6
Boot The CB6 . . . . .209 D4
BORDEVILLE 244 D8
Boretree Way PE29 . . . . . . .141 A7
Borley Way CB1 . . . . .85 B1
Borough Cl PE13 . . . . .245 D3
Borough The CB6 . . . . .209 E4
Borrowdale CB4 . . . . .83 C6
Borrowdale Cl PE4 . . . . . . .204 E3
Borthwick Pk PE2 . . . . .185 D6
Bossert's Way CB23 . . . . . . .80 C2
Boswell Cl PE1 . . . . .197 E8
Bosworth Cl PE8 . . . . .178 B3
Bosworth Rd CB1 . . . . .65 D5
Bosworth Way **2** PE15. . .243 D2
Botolph Gn PE2 . . . . .186 C7
Botolph La CB2 . . . . .246 A2
Bottels Rd PE28 . . . . .164 E5
BOTTISHAM 86 F6
Bottisham Prim Sch CB25 86 F5
Bottisham Swimming Pool &
  Sports Ctr CB25 . . . . .86 E6
Bottisham Village Coll
  CB25 . . . . .86 E6
Bottle La PE13 . . . . .237 C7
Bough La PE28 . . . . .162 F1
Boulevard Ret Pk PE1 . . .197 D7
Boundary Dr PE15 . . . . . . .243 C3
Boundary Rd
  Haverhill CB9 . . . . .24 D5
  10 Red Lodge IP28 . . . . .214 A1
Boundary Road Ind Est
  CB9 .24 C5
Bourdillon Cl **1** PE28. . .121 B6
Bourges Bvd PE1 . . . . .197 D7
Bourges Ret Pk PE3 . . . . .197 F1
BOURN 60 C6
Bourn Bridge Rd CB21 . . . .34 A8
Bourn CE Prim Sch CB23. .60 C6
Bourne Rd
  Cambridge CB4 . . . . .84 C5
  Haverhill CB9 . . . . .24 B8
Bourneys Manor Cl **11**
  CB24 . . . . .209 A1
Bourn Rd CB23 . . . . .59 F8
Bourns The CB21 . . . . .67 A4
Bourn Windmill* CB23. . . . .79 A1
Bower Cl PE1 . . . . .198 C5
Bowers Croft CB1 . . . . .65 C3
Bower's La **1** CB7 . . . . . . .213 A5
Bowker Way PE7 . . . . .189 C8
Bowlings St PE27 . . . . .144 A3
Bowness Way **2** PE4 . . . .204 F2
Bowsers CB10 . . . . .20 D3
Bowsers La CB10 . . . . .20 B2
Bowthorpe Hall Gdns
  PE13 . . . . .245 D5
Bowthorpe Rd PE13. . . . . .245 D5
Boxer Rd PE8 . . . . .230 B1
Boxford Cl **20** CB9 . . . . . . .23 E7
Boxgrove Cl **14** PE6 . . . . .232 A1
BOXWORTH 101 B5
BOXWORTH END 123 E3
Boxworth Rd CB23 . . . . . .100 C4
Boyce Cl PE7 . . . . .189 D7
BOYCES BRIDGE 236 D4
Boyces Rd PE13 . . . . .245 E5
Boyton Cl CB9 . . . . .39 A2
Bozeat Way PE1 . . . . .197 C6
Brackenbury Cl CB24. . . . .104 C3
Brackenwood PE2 . . . . . . .185 D6
Brackhill Fen Dro PE28 . .208 E8
Brackley Cl
  3 Cambridge CB4 . . . . . . .83 D6
  Peterborough PE1 . . . . . .197 D3
Brackwood PE2 . . . . .185 D6
Brackyn Rd CB1 . . . . .65 B7
Bradbury Pl PE29 . . . . . . .141 E4
Bradden St PE3 . . . . .197 C6
Bradegate Dr PE1 . . . . . . .198 E7
Bradford's Cl CB25. . . . . . . .86 E6
Bradley Rd CB88 . . . . .72 F1
Bradmore St CB1 . . . . .246 C2
Bradrushe Fields CB1 . . . . .82 E3
Bradshaw Cl PE29 . . . . . . .141 E6
Bradshaw St PE15 . . . . . . .243 C2
Bradwell Rd PE3 . . . . .197 A2
Bradwells Ct CB1 . . . . .246 B2
Braeburn Ave PE13 . . . . . .245 C8
Braeburn Wlk SG8 . . . . .5 C7
Braefield
  Hemingford Abbots PE28 .142 F3
  1 Somersham PE28 . . . . .208 B8
Braemar Gdns PE7 . . . . . . .189 D6
Braggs La
  Hemingford Grey PE28 . .143 C1
  Wrestlingworth SG19 . . . .25 B4
Brailsford Cl PE3 . . . . .197 A4
Bramall Ct PE3 . . . . .197 C3
Bramble Cl
  Haverhill CB9 . . . . .38 D1
  Whittlesey PE7 . . . . .189 E6
  Yaxley PE7 . . . . .182 A6
Bramble Ct
  2 Brampton PE28 . . . . .140 C3
  6 Great Cambourne CB23. .79 C3
Bramble End
  Alconbury PE28 . . . . .150 F5
  Sawtry PE28 . . . . .168 B3
Bramble La PE14 . . . . .236 D3

Brambles The
  Balsham CB21 . . . . .53 C1
  Bar Hill CB23. . . . . .102 D3
  Cambridge CB2 . . . . .64 D2
  Girton CB3 . . . . .83 A6
  Hemingford Grey PE27 . .143 F1
  Littleport CB6 . . . . .242 D3
  3 Royston SG8 . . . . .5 E5
Bramble Wlk PE15 . . . . . .243 E7
Bramley Ave
  Melbourn SG8 . . . . .14 D6
  Needingworth PE27. . . . . .208 A2
Bramley Cl
  Cottenham CB24 . . . . . . .125 D3
  Offord Cluny PE19 . . . . . .118 A1
Bramley Ct
  Cambridge CB4 . . . . .84 B6
  Coldham PE14 . . . . .235 D1
Bramley Dr PE19. . . . . .118 A1
Bramley Gr PE28. . . . . .208 C5
Bramley Rd
  Haverhill CB9. . . . . .23 C7
  St Ives PE27 . . . . .144 B5
  Wisbech PE13 . . . . .245 C7
Bramleys The
  March PE15 . . . . .243 D1
  Shepreth SG8. . . . . .29 E4
Bramley Way CB23. . . . . . . .81 A4
BRAMPTON 140 C2
Brampton Cl PE13 . . . . . . .245 A4
Brampton Ct PE8 . . . . .187 D6
Brampton Gdns PE19 . . . . .75 A4
BRAMPTON LODGE 140 A1
BRAMPTON PARK 140 C1
Brampton Rd
  Buckden PE19 . . . . .117 C6
  Cambridge CB1 . . . . .84 B1
  Grafham PE28 . . . . .116 B7
  Huntingdon PE29. . . . . . . .141 B3
  Royston SG8 . . . . .4 B6
Brampton Village Prim Sch
  PE28. . . . . .140 C2
Brampton Wood Nature
  Reserve* PE19. . . . . .139 D1
Brancepeth Pl PE2. . . . . . .186 E7
Branch Bank
  Ely CB7 . . . . .218 F6
  Littleport CB7 . . . . .242 F2
Brand Rd CB23 . . . . .62 C7
BRANDON BANK 226 E3
BRANDON CREEK 226 D6
Brandon Cr CB1 . . . . .246 C2
Brandon Pl CB1. . . . . .246 C2
Brands Cl PE26 . . . . .172 A5
Brangehill La CB6 . . . . . . .216 D3
Branston Rise **6** PE1 . . . .198 C7
Brassey Cl PE1 . . . . .197 E6
Bravo La PE28 . . . . .151 E3
Brawn Way PE8. . . . . .183 D1
Bray **6** CB1 . . . . .84 A1
Braybrook PE2. . . . . .186 A3
Braybrooke Prim Sch PE2 186 B4
Braymere Rd PE7 . . . . .186 D2
Brays La CB7 . . . . .240 D4
Brazilian Terr CB8. . . . . . . .110 F3
Breach La CB6. . . . . .210 D6
Breach Rd PE28 . . . . .116 A7
Bream Cl PE28. . . . . .149 D6
Breamore Gdns PE3 . . . . .197 B3
Breckenwood Rd CB21. . . . .66 E6
Breckland Way IP28 . . . . .239 C5
Brecon Way PE29 . . . . .141 A4
Brenda Gautrey Way
  CB24. . . . . .125 E3
Brendon Garth PE4 . . . . . .204 E1
Brent Cl IP28 . . . . .239 D4
Brentwood Cl **6** CB5 . . . . .84 E4
Brentwood Ct CB5 . . . . .84 E4
Breton Ave PE15. . . . . .243 E2
BRETTON 197 A6
Bretton Cir PE1 . . . . .197 A6
Bretton Gate PE3 . . . . .197 A6
Bretton Gn **1** PE3 . . . . . .197 A5
Bretton Way
  Bretton PE3 . . . . .197 A7
  Peterborough PE3 . . . . . .196 F2
Brewerne PE2 . . . . .186 C4
Brewers Cl CB24. . . . . .123 F3
Brewers La PE13. . . . . .238 A4
Brewery Cl CB1 . . . . .234 D7
Brewery La SG8 . . . . .29 B2
Brewery Rd CB22 . . . . .33 A5
Brewhouse La CB7. . . . . . . .212 B4
Brewin Ave PE15. . . . . .243 B3
Brewin Chase The PE15. . .243 D4
Brewster Ave PE2. . . . . . . .186 F8
Brewster Avenue Inf Sch
  PE2. . . . . .186 F8
Briar Cl PE16 . . . . .241 D4
Briar Gr CB6. . . . . .240 A4
Briars End CB6 . . . . .217 E2
Briars The
  Isleham CB7 . . . . .212 F4
  Sawtry PE28 . . . . .168 B3
Briar Way PE1 . . . . .198 C5
Briary La SG8. . . . . .5 C5
Brickberry Cl PE7 . . . . . . .246 E4
Brickfields Ave CB88 . . . . .110 D7
Brickfields Dr CB6 . . . . .38 E2
Brickhills **6** CB24 . . . . . . .209 A1
Brickkiln La CB6. . . . . .218 B7
Brick Kiln Rd IP28 . . . . . . .239 D5
Brick Kilns PE29 . . . . .118 F8
Brick La CB6 . . . . .216 E3
Brickmaker's Arms La
  PE15. . . . . .223 B5

Brickmakers Way CB6. . .242 B1
Brick Row SG8 . . . . .8 D3
Brickstead Rd PE7 . . . . . . .186 D2
Bridewell Cl IP28. . . . . .239 B4
Bridewell Rd CB1. . . . . .66 A5
Bridgacre CB1. . . . . .246 C4
Bridge Cl CB22 . . . . .48 F6
Bridge Dro PE13 . . . . .234 B7
Bridge End
  Earith PE28 . . . . .208 E5
  Wansford PE8 . . . . .194 A3
Bridge End Rd IP28. . . . . . .213 E1
Bridgefoot
  Great & Little Chishill SG8. .15 B2
  St Ives PE27 . . . . .144 A3
Bridgehill Rd PE6. . . . . .205 A6
Bridge La
  Great Shelford CB22 . . . . .48 E4
  Wimblington PE15. . . . . . .223 B8
Bridge of Sighs* CB3. . . . .246 A3
Bridge Pl PE29 . . . . .141 E3
Bridge Rd
  Broughton PE28. . . . . .153 F8
  Ely CB7 . . . . .240 E2
  Histon CB24 . . . . .104 C2
  Impington CB24. . . . . .83 C8
  Mepal CB6. . . . . .216 E4
Bridge St
  Cambridge CB2 . . . . .246 A3
  Chatteris PE16. . . . . .241 B7
  Market Deeping PE6. . . . .231 E8
  Moulton CB8 . . . . .112 F5
  2 Peterborough PE1 . . . .198 A1
  St Ives PE27 . . . . .144 A3
  Whaddon SG8 . . . . .13 B8
  10 Wisbech PE13. . . . . . .245 C5
  Wistow PE28 . . . . .163 F7
  Wood Walton PE26 . . . . .161 E6
Bridle Cl
  Chatteris PE16. . . . . .241 D5
  The Cottons PE14 . . . . . .236 E2
Bridle End PE19 . . . . .98 B2
Bridle Way CB23 . . . . .63 F4
Brierley Wlk CB4 . . . . .83 C7
Briery Fields **2** CB6 . . . . .217 E1
BRIGGATE. 189 E6
Briggate Cres PE7 . . . . . . .189 C6
Briggate W PE7 . . . . .189 C6
Bright St PE1 . . . . .197 F3
Brigland Cl PE29. . . . . .141 B6
Brigstock Ct PE1 . . . . .197 C6
Brigstock Rd PE13 . . . . . . .245 B7
Brimbles Way PE7 . . . . . . .185 E5
Brimley Rd CB4 . . . . .83 D6
Bringhurst PE2 . . . . .186 A4
BRINGTON 147 D4
Brington CE Prim Sch
  PE28. . . . . .147 C4
Brington Rd PE28 . . . . .147 F7
BRINKLEY 70 E2
Brinkley Rd
  Brinkley CB8 . . . . .69 A6
  Carlton CB8. . . . . .54 F8
  Westley Waterless CB8 . . .70 D3
  Weston Colville CB21 . . . .54 C8
Brinkman Rd CB21. . . . . . . .35 D3
Bristol Ave PE4 . . . . .204 B3
Britannia Way PE13 . . . . . .245 C2
Britannic Way CB1. . . . . . . .67 F7
British Racing Sch CB8. .111 B8
Brittain Cl **5** PE19. . . . . . . .74 E2
Britten Pl CB1 . . . . .65 D7
Broadall's Dro PE26 . . . . . .221 D3
Broad Baulk CB6. . . . . .210 F6
Broad Cl PE1 . . . . .198 D5
Broadcroft Cres CB9 . . . . . .23 E8
Broad Dro
  Emneth PE14 . . . . .236 C5
  Upwell PE14. . . . . .229 D8
  Wisbech PE14. . . . . .235 F5
Broad Drove E PE13. . . . . .237 B4
Broad Drove W PE13 . . . . .237 B4
Broad End CB23 . . . . .100 A4
Broad End Rd PE14 . . . . . .245 F4
Broad Gate PE7 . . . . .237 A8
Broadgate La PE6. . . . . . . .231 F8
Broadgate Rd PE12 . . . . . .234 C8
Broadgate Way PE8 . . . . . .178 B3
BROAD GREEN
  Newmarket 91 D4
  Royston 8 C3
Broad Hill CB7 . . . . .212 B7
Broadhill Dro CB7 . . . . . . .212 B7
Broadhurst Rd **15** PE6. . . .230 B1
Broad La
  Cottenham CB24 . . . . . . .125 E5
  Haslingfield CB23 . . . . . . .47 A5
Broadlands CB6 . . . . .225 A5
Broadlands The PE1. . . . . .198 E5
Broad Leas PE27 . . . . .144 A4
Broadmeadow PE22. . . . . . .49 F1
Broad Piece CB7 . . . . .211 F5
Broads Rd CB25 . . . . .130 C6
Broad St
  Bourn CB23. . . . . .79 B4
  Cambridge CB1 . . . . .246 C2
  Ely CB7 . . . . .240 D3
  Haverhill CB9 . . . . .23 F8
  March PE15 . . . . .243 D4
  Stamford PE9. . . . . .244 B5
  Whittlesey PE7 . . . . .189 D7
Broadway
  Bourn CB23 . . . . .60 D8
  Chatteris PE16. . . . . .29 E3
  Crowland PE6 . . . . .232 B8

Broadway continued
  Farcet PE7. . . . . .187 C1
  Grantchester CB3 . . . . . . .64 A4
  Witchford CB6 . . . . .217 E1
  Yaxley PE7 . . . . .181 E5
Broad Way CB6. . . . . .210 C6
Broadway Gdns PE1 . . . . .198 B5
Broadway The
  Oakington/Longstanton
    CB24. . . . . .103 B5
  Romsey Town CB1 . . . . . .65 B8
  St Ives PE27 . . . . .144 A3
Broadway Theatre* PE1. 198 A3
Broadwater PE28. . . . . . . .138 C4
Broad Wheel Rd PE6. . . . .231 B4
Broad Wlk The PE19 . . . . . .74 E3
Brockholme Mews CB23 . .79 C5
Brockholt Rd CB23. . . . . . . .78 E2
Brocklesby Gdns PE3 . . . .197 C3
Brockley Rd CB23. . . . . . . .100 B4
Brocks Bsns Ctr CB9. . . . . .23 F5
Brockwood Cl **7** SG19 . . . .41 D6
Brodsworth Rd PE7. . . . . . .187 F5
Bromholme La PE28 . . . . . .141 A3
Bronze St PE15 . . . . .243 C7
Brook Cl
  Alconbury PE28 . . . . .150 F4
  Histon CB24. . . . . .104 B4
  March PE15 . . . . .243 C4
Brookdale CB23 . . . . .102 C3
Brook Dam La **14** CB7. . . .212 B4
Brooke Gr CB6. . . . . .240 A5
BROOK END. 136 B6
Brook End SG8 . . . . .11 C3
Brooke Rd SG8 . . . . .5 D8
Brookfield Cl CB22. . . . . . . .32 F5
Brookfield Dr CB24 . . . . . .123 F3
Brookfield Home Pk PE4 204 B2
Brookfield Rd
  Coton CB3. . . . . .82 B2
  Papworth Everard CB23 . .99 A4
  Sawston CB22 . . . . .32 F5
Brookfields CB1 . . . . .65 D7
Brookfields Cl CB8. . . . . . .111 B5
Brookfields Hospl CB1 . .65 C8
Brookfields Ind Pk PE4. . .204 B2
Brookfield Way
  Cambourne CB23. . . . . . . .79 A3
  Ramsey PE26. . . . . .172 A4
Brookfurlong PE3. . . . . . . .197 B6
Brookhampton St CB10 . .18 A5
Brook La
  Coton CB23 . . . . .82 C2
  Farcet PE7. . . . . .187 B2
  Stretham CB6 . . . . .210 F5
Brooklands Ave CB2 . . . . . .64 E6
Brook Rd
  Bassingbourn cum Kneesworth
    SG8. . . . . .12 D4
  Eaton Socon PE19 . . . . . .74 C4
  Kimbolton PE28 . . . . .114 B7
  Newton CB22. . . . . .31 B6
Brook Service Rd CB9. . . . .24 A8
Brookside
  Alconbury PE28 . . . . .150 F4
  Cambridge CB2 . . . . .246 B1
  Dalham CB8 . . . . .92 C8
  Exning CB8. . . . . .110 C8
  Great Paxton PE19 . . . . . .96 D4
  Huntingdon PE29. . . . . . . .141 D5
  Moulton CB8 . . . . .112 F5
  Oakington/Longstanton
    CB24. . . . . .123 F2
  Orwell SG8. . . . . .45 D1
  Peterborough PE4 . . . . . .204 D2
  Sawtry PE28 . . . . .143 B5
  St Ives PE27 . . . . .144 C4
Brookside Gr CB6. . . . . . . .242 C5
Brookside Ind Est PE28 . .168 B5
Brookside La **1** CB2. . . . . .64 E7
Brooks Rd CB1. . . . . .65 D8
Brook's Rd PE15 . . . . .243 D4
Brook St
  Elsworth CB23. . . . . .100 B3
  Peterborough PE1 . . . . . .198 A2
  Soham CB7 . . . . .212 C3
  St Neots PE19 . . . . .74 A6
Brook The CB6. . . . . .216 E1
Brookway PE27 . . . . .144 C4
Broom Cl
  7 Littleport CB7. . . . . . . .242 D4
  Peterborough PE1 . . . . . .198 E6
Broomfield Cl **4** IP28 . . . .214 A1
Broom Way PE27 . . . . .144 B5
Broom Wlk **5** PE8 . . . . . . .213 F8
Brotherhood Cl PE4 . . . . . .197 D6
Brotherhood Ret Pk PE4 197 D8
Brothers Pl CB1 . . . . .246 C3
BROUGHTON 153 F8
Broughton La PE28 . . . . . .154 B8
Brownes Rd PE28 . . . . . . .230 B1
Browning Dr PE19 . . . . .74 C6
Brownlow Dr **8** PE6 . . . . .230 B1
Brownlow Quay PE9 . . . . .244 C5
Brownlow Rd
  Cambridge CB4 . . . . .83 C6
  Peterborough PE1 . . . . . .198 A6
Brownlow St **6** PE6 . . . . .230 B1
Brownlow Terr PE9 . . . . . .244 C5
Brownshill Staunch
  PE27. . . . . .208 C3
Brown's Sq **6** PE19 . . . . . .74 F5
Broxbourne Cl CB1 . . . . . . .66 A7
Bruces Cl PE7 . . . . .233 C8
Brudenell PE2 . . . . .185 E2

Brunel Ct PE27 . . . . .144 B6
Brunel Dr PE7 . . . . .181 D6
Brunswick Cotts CB1. . . . .246 C3
Brunswick Ct CB21. . . . . . . .66 E5
Brunswick Gdns CB5 . . . .246 C3
Brunswick St CB5 . . . . . . .246 C3
Brunswick Wlk CB1 . . . . . .246 C3
Bryan Cl PE26 . . . . .172 B6
Brybank Rd CB9 . . . . .38 C1
Brynmore PE3 . . . . .204 A1
Bryony Cl
  Coates/Eastrea PE7 . . . .190 C7
  Haverhill CB9 . . . . .38 E1
Buchan St CB4 . . . . .83 E7
BUCKDEN 117 B4
Buckden CE Prim Sch
  PE19. . . . . .117 B4
Buckden Marina PE19. . . .117 E3
Buckden Rd
  Brampton PE28 . . . . .117 D7
  Grafham PE28 . . . . .116 A6
Buckingham Dr CB6 . . . . .240 D6
Buckingham Rd
  Cambridge CB3 . . . . .83 C3
  Haverhill CB9. . . . . .23 E7
Buckingham Way PE28. . .168 C2
Buckingham Wlk PE13 . . .245 D8
Buckingway Bsns Pk
  CB24. . . . . .101 E8
Bucking Way Rd CB3. . . . .101 D8
Buckland Cl PE3 . . . . .197 B4
Buckles Gdns PE7 . . . . . . .189 F7
Buckle St PE1 . . . . .198 C3
Buckley Rd PE19 . . . . .74 E4
Buck's Dro PE26 . . . . .220 D4
Bucksherd Cl CB23. . . . . . .79 B2
Buckshott Rd PE14. . . . . . .238 E3
Buck's La CB23 . . . . .45 F7
Buckthorn **2** CB7 . . . . . . .240 F6
Buckthorne Rd **4** PE7 . . .186 D3
Buckthorn Rd PE7 . . . . . . .186 D3
BUCKWORTH 149 E6
Buckworth Rd PE28 . . . . . .150 C5
Budge Cl PE28 . . . . .140 E2
Budleigh Cl CB1 . . . . .65 D7
Buffalo Way CB1 . . . . .66 A7
Buff La SG19 . . . . .43 A1
Building End SG8 . . . . .1 F8
Building End Rd SG8 . . . . . .1 F7
Bukehorn Rd PE6 . . . . . . .232 D4
Bulbeck Mill CB22 . . . . .29 F7
Bullard Laboratories CB3 83 A4
Bullen Cl
  Cambridge CB1 . . . . .65 D5
  Longstanton CB24 . . . . . .123 E2
Bullfinch Way
  Cottenham CB25 . . . . . . .125 D5
  Friday Bridge PE14 . . . . .236 A4
Bull La
  Broughton PE28 . . . . .164 A1
  Langley CB11 . . . . .1 F2
  Peakirk PE6 . . . . .206 B2
  West Wratting CB21 . . . . .53 F6
Bullock Rd
  Elton PE8 . . . . .184 B1
  Folksworth & Washingley
    PE7 . . . . .174 E7
  Great Gidding PE28 . . . . .167 B6
  Little Gidding PE28 . . . . .167 D2
Bullrush La CB23 . . . . .79 C3
Bulstrode Gdns CB3. . . . . . .83 A2
Bulteel Cl CB24 . . . . .105 C3
Bumpstead Rd CB9 . . . . . . .24 B5
Bunbury Ave PE28 . . . . . .239 C5
BUNKER'S HILL 235 A6
Buntings Cres CB25 . . . . .130 B3
Bunting's Dro PE7 . . . . . . .188 C4
Bunting's La PE7 . . . . .187 B5
Bunting's La PE8 . . . . .178 B3
Buntings Path CB25. . . . . .130 B3
Bunyan Cl **4** SG19 . . . . . . .41 D5
Burberry Rd PE19 . . . . . . .117 B3
Burcroft Rd PE13 . . . . .245 B6
Burdett Gr PE7 . . . . .189 F6
Burdett Rd PE13 . . . . .245 B4
Bure Cl PE27 . . . . .144 B6
Bures **14** CB9 . . . . .23 E7
Burford Way PE1 . . . . .198 D6
Burgess Rd CB25 . . . . .106 B7
Burgess's Dro CB25 . . . . .106 C7
Burghley Ave **9** PE8 . . . . .230 B1
Burghley Cl **9** PE6 . . . . . .230 B1
Burghley Ct PE9 . . . . .231 E8
Burghley House* PE9 . . . .244 F3
Burghley La PE9 . . . . .244 C3
Burghley Rd
  1 Peterborough PE1 . . . .198 A3
  4 Stamford PE9 . . . . . . .244 A7
Burghley Rise CB25 . . . . . .130 C2
Burghley Sq **2** PE1 . . . . . .198 A3
Burgoynes Farm Cl
  CB24. . . . . .104 D3
Burgoyne's Rd CB24 . . . . .104 D3
Buristead Rd CB22 . . . . . . .48 F5
Burkett Way CB24 . . . . . . .104 B5
Burleigh Pl CB1 . . . . .246 C3
Burleigh Rd PE27 . . . . . . .143 F8
Burleigh St CB1 . . . . .246 C3
Burleigh Terr PE27 . . . . . .144 A3
Burlife Cl CB1 . . . . .65 C6
Burlington Way PE28 . . . .168 C2
Burling Wlk CB24 . . . . . . .105 D3
Burma Rd CB22 . . . . .32 A1
Burmer Rd PE1 . . . . .197 E7
Burmoor Cl PE29 . . . . .141 B6
Burnaby Cl PE28 . . . . .140 C3
Burnet Gdns PE15 . . . . . . .243 C7
Burnett Way PE29 . . . . . . .141 B8

Burnham Cl CB1..........66 A6
Burns Cl PE1 ....197 F7
Burns Ct **3** PE19 ....74 D5
Burnsfield St PE16.......241 B5
Burnside CB1............65 D7
Burn Sq SG8 ....5 C8
Burn St PE15 ....243 D5
Burns Way PE2 ....143 F6
Burnt Chimney Dro CB6..225 B4
Burnt Cl
  Grantchester CB3 ....64 A4
  St Neots PE19 ....74 E3
Burnt House Cl CB9.......38 C1
Burnthouse Rd PE7 ......191 E1
Burnthouse Sidings PE7..191 F1
Burnt Up Dro PE7.......188 F2
Burntwood End CB10 .....19 E2
Burrell Cres PE28 ....239 C2
Burrell Way CB21.........53 B2
Burrel Rd PE27.........144 B6
Burrettgate Rd
  6 Leverington PE14....238 F1
  Walsoken PE13 ....245 F5
Burrett Gdns **8** PE14 ....238 F1
Burrett Rd PE14 ....238 F1
BURROUGH END 70 E4
Burrough Field CB4 .....104 C1
BURROUGH GREEN 70 F4
Burrowmoor Prim Sch
  PE15...................243 C3
Burrowmoor Rd PE15 ....243 C3
Burrows Dr PE29 ....141 C3
Burstellars PE27 ....144 A6
Burswood PE2...........185 F2
Burton Cl CB9............23 E7
Burton Ct PE1 ....198 C3
BURTON END 37 C8
Burton End
  Haverhill CB9...........23 E7
  West Wickham CB21......37 C8
Burton End CP Sch CB9...23 D7
Burton Hill 38 D5
Burtons SG8.............28 F1
Burton St PE1 ....198 C3
Burton Way PE28 ....137 F6
BURWELL 130 C2
Burwell Castle (site of)*
  CB25 ....130 E1
Burwell Mus* CB25......130 C1
Burwell Rd
  Eaton Socon PE19 ....74 C6
  Exning CB8.............110 A8
  Reach CB25.............129 E1
  Swaffham Prior CB25 ...108 E5
Burwell Reach PE2 .....186 C7
Burwell Village Prim Sch
  CB25..................130 B3
BURY 172 B4
Bury CE Prim Sch PE26..172 A4
Bury Cl
  Ramsey PE26...........171 F4
  St Ives PE27 ....143 F5
Buryfield PE26..........172 A4
Bury Gn CB6............218 A7
Bury La
  Chrishall SG8 ....8 D1
  Haddenham CB6 ....210 A5
  Lidgate CB8.............73 F8
  Meldreth SG8...........14 A5
  Moulton CB8............112 F6
  Sutton CB6.............216 D2
Bury Plantation SG8 ......5 F6
Bury Rd
  Great Shelford CB22 ....49 C4
  Kentford CB8...........134 B2
  Mildenhall IP28 ....239 E4
  Newmarket CB8.........111 C5
  Ramsey PE26...........172 A5
  Snailwell CB8..........111 E8
Burystead PE2..........187 B8
Bury The CB25..........86 C5
Bury Way PE27 ....143 F5
Bush Cl CB23 ....62 D5
Bushel La CB7 ....212 B4
Bushey Cl PE29 ....141 E5
Bushfield PE2 ....185 E3
Bushfield Com Coll PE2..185 E3
Bushfield Sports Ctr
  PE2...................185 E4
Bush La PE13............245 E5
Bushmead Gdns PE19 .....74 B3
Bushmead Prim Sch PE19 74 A3
Bushmead Rd PE19 ......74 A3
Bushy Cl PE7 ....186 D3
Bustard Hill PE28 ......113 D8
Bustler's Rise CB22 ......17 D8
Butcher Cl CB24 ....105 C3
Butchers Cl PE28 ....150 D6
Butcher's Hill CB10 .....18 A4
Butcher's La SG19 ......25 B4
Butcher's Row **8** CB7 ...240 D4
Bute Ct CB9 ....23 F6
Butlers Way CB22.........32 F7
Butler Way
  Cambridge CB4 ....83 D6
  Haslingfield CB23 ....47 A5
Butley Ct **2** CB9........23 E6
Butt Ave PE15 ....243 A3
Buttercup Rd CB4........83 D7
Buttermarket CB6.......240 D4
Buttermel Cl **1** PE29 ...118 F8
Buttermere PE2.........141 B6
Buttermere Pl **4** PE4...204 E3
Butt La
  Great Wilbraham CB21...68 A7
  Milton CB24............105 B3

Button End CB22.........47 D4
Butts Cl
  6 Soham CB7..........212 B3
  20 Somersham PE28.....215 C1
Butts Gn CB22 ....32 D5
Buttsgrove Way PE29 ...141 F7
Butt's La CB7...........211 F1
Butts The
  Fowlmere SG8...........15 D8
  Soham CB7 ....212 B3
Buxtons La SG8..........10 F3
Buzzard Cl PE28 ....142 B8
Byall Fen Dro PE15 .....223 E2
Bydand La PE19 ....95 F2
Byfield Rd CB23 ....99 B3
Byng Cl PE19 ....74 B2
Byres The PE7..........189 F7
Byron Cl
  Huntingdon PE29.......141 F6
  Peterborough PE2......187 D6
Byron Pl **10** PE19 ......74 C6
Byron Rd **2** SG8 ....5 E8
Byron Sq CB2............64 D2
BYTHORN 146 D4
Bythorne Bank PE13 ....237 C7
Bythorn Rd PE2.........187 C6
Bythorn Way PE2 ....187 C6

C

Cabbage Moor CB22 ......48 E8
Cadenham Rd CB25.......108 E3
Cadwin Field CB4.........83 F7
Caernarvon Rd PE19 .....74 F2
Caernarvon Wlk CB9......23 E8
Cage Hill CB25...........108 D5
Cage La
  Great Staughton PE19....94 B6
  Stretham CB6 ....210 F5
Cairns CB8 ....131 A3
Caithness Ct CB4 ....83 E8
Calcot St PE7...........186 D2
Caldbeck Cl PE4.........204 F2
CALDECOTE
  Highfields 61 B7
  Highfields 80 B1
  Stilton 175 D5
  St Neots................76 B1
Caldecote Cl PE2 ....187 E6
Caldecote Prim Sch CB23.80 C2
Caldecote Rd
  Stilton PE7............175 C7
  St Neots PE19 ....74 E3
Caldervale PE2 ....186 C6
Caledon Way **3** CB4.....83 E8
Calfe Fen Cl **2** CB7.....212 B5
Calfe Fen Dro CB7......212 B5
Calford Dr CB9 ....23 C8
CALFORD GREEN 24 F7
California PE28 ....151 F4
California Rd
  Huntingdon PE29.......141 E6
  St Ives PE27 ....143 E6
Callander Cl CB4 ....83 D7
Calvin Cl CB24..........125 F3
Camargue Dr PE15......243 D2
Camargue Pl **4** PE13 ...245 E3
Cambanks CB4 ....84 A4
Camber's New Dro PE7 ..220 D8
CAMBOURNE 79 D4
Cambourne Bsns Pk CB23 79 B5
Cambourne Rd CB23 ......79 B5
Cambrian Way PE4 .....204 E1
CAMBRIDGE 246 A2
Cambridge Airport CB1...84 F2
Cambridge Assessment
  CB1 ....246 C1
Cambridge Ave CB1....197 F5
Cambridge Bsns Pk CB4..84 C7
Cambridge Cl
  Haverhill CB9...........38 E1
  St Ives PE27 ....143 F8
Cambridge Cres SG8 .....13 A8
Cambridge Ct **10** PE19 ...74 F5
Cambridge Ctr for Sixth
  Form Studies CB1 .....246 C1
Cambridge & Cty Folk Mus*
  CB3 ....246 A4
Cambridge Dr
  St Ives PE27 ....143 F8
  Wisbech PE13 ....245 E4
Cambridge Gdns PE19 ...74 F5
Cambridge Leisure CB1...65 A6
Cambridge Pl CB1 ......246 C1
Cambridge Rd
  Babraham CB22 ....50 D4
  Balsham CB21............52 F2
  Barley SG8..............7 A3
  Barton CB23............62 E1
  Ely CB7 ....240 B3
  Eynesbury Hardwicke PE19 76 B4
  Fenstanton PE28 ....121 A6
  Foxton CB22............30 C7
  Fulbourn CB1............66 A5
  Girton CB3 ....48 E3
  Godmanchester PE29 ...141 F2
  Great Shelford CB22 ....48 F7
  Hardwick CB23 ....81 B3
  Hauxton CB22 ....48 A5
  Histon CB24............83 C8
  Madingley CB23.........81 F5
  Melbourn SG8 ....14 E7
  Milton CB24............105 C1
  Newton CB22............31 B8
  Oakington/Longstanton
  CB24 ....103 C4
  Orwell SG8..............45 C1

Cambridge Rd *continued*
  Sawston CB22 ....32 E8
  Stamford PE9............244 A6
  St Neots Rural PE19 .....75 C5
  Stretham CB6 ....210 E3
  Thetford CB6 ....211 A8
  Thriplow SG8 ....30 F3
  Waterbeach CB25 ....105 F7
  Wimpole SG8............27 F6
Cambridge Regional Coll
  (City Centre Campus)
  CB5 ....84 A2
Cambridge Regional Coll
  (Science Park Campus)
  CB4 ....83 F8
Cambridge Ret Pk CB5...84 B3
Cambridge Science Pk
  CB4 ....83 F8
Cambridgeshire Arts
  Theatre* CB1...........246 A2
Cambridgeshire Cl CB6 ..240 B4
Cambridge Sq PE28......143 B7
Cambridge St
  Godmanchester PE29 ...141 F2
  St Neots PE19 ....75 A5
Cambridge Sta CB1 ......65 A7
Cambridge Steiner Sch
  CB21..................66 D3
Cambridge Univ Botanic
  Gdn* CB2 ....64 F7
Cambridge Univ Ctr CB2 246 A1
Cambridge Univ Press
  CB2 ....64 F5
Cambridge Way CB1 ......38 E1
Cambridge Womens
  Resources Ctr CB1 .....84 A1
Cam Cl PE27.............144 A7
Cam Cswy CB4 ....84 B6
Camden Cl CB1..........246 B2
Cam Dro CB6.............240 C6
Camelia Cl PE4 ....204 D3
Camel Rd CB6...........242 C6
Cameron Rd CB4 ....83 E7
Camoys Cl PE28 ....151 F2
Campaign Ave PE2......186 D8
Campbell Cl IP28 ....239 B6
Campbell Dr PE4 ....204 E4
Campbell La CB2 ....64 C2
Campbell St PE1 ....181 C8
Campbell Way PE15....243 D7
Camping Cl CB6.........210 A6
Campion Cl **1** CB2......212 A5
Campion Rd PE1........198 B8
Campion Way SG8 ....5 F7
Campkin Ct CB4 ....83 F7
Campkin Rd CB4.........83 F7
Campole Dro PE16......241 E3
Camps Cl CB25..........106 B7
CAMPS END 22 A1
Camps Rd
  Bartlow CB21............21 B7
  Haverhill CB9...........23 F7
  Helions Bumpstead CB9 ..23 B1
Camside CB4 ....84 A4
Canal St **5** PE13........245 C5
Canberra Cl
  Bassingbourn SG8 ......13 B5
  Mildenhall IP28 ....213 E8
Canberra Ct PE26.......171 F7
Canberra Dr PE27.......143 F7
Canberra Rd PE26 ......171 E3
Canberra Way PE28 ....154 A1
Candidus Cl PE4........204 B5
Candy St PE2 ....186 E8
Cangle Junc CB9 ....24 A8
Canmore CB7...........208 C2
Canners Cl CB23..........61 E5
Cannon's Cl SG8.........10 F5
Cannon St
  Little Downham CB6 .....218 A6
  Wisbech PE13 ....245 C4
Cannon Terr **8** PE13 ...245 C4
Canon Cl CB3............39 A1
Canon Dr **4** PE29......230 D3
Canonsfield PE4........204 A4
Cantelupe Rd CB23 ......47 C7
Canterbury Ave CB6 ....240 A3
Canterbury Cl CB4.......83 C4
Canterbury Rd CB4.....204 B3
Canterbury St CB4.......83 C4
Cant's Dro PE13........234 C4
Canute Cres CB6.........91 C3
Canwell PE4............204 C4
Capio Fitzwilliam Hospl
  PE6...................196 E2
Capital Pk CB21 ....245 B4
Capper Rd CB25.........127 C1
Capstan Cl CB4 ....84 A3
Capthorne Cl PE7.......186 C2
Capuchin Ct CB1.........66 A7
Capulet Cl PE19 ....74 C3
Capulet Ct PE29 ....141 F7
Caravere Cl **2** CB4.......66 E5
Caraway Rd CB21.........66 E5
Cardiff Pl SG8 ....14 A3
Cardigan St CB8 ....111 A3
Cardinal Distribution Pk
  PE6...................196 E2
Cardinals Gate PE4 .....204 A5
CARDINAL'S GREEN 37 B1
Cardinals Way PE7 ....240 D4
Cardinal Way
  Godmanchester PE29 ...142 B1
  St Neots PE19 ....38 F1
Car Dyke Rd
  Landbeach CB25 ....105 A4
  Waterbeach CB25 ......106 A6

Carey Cl CB7 ....240 F1
Caribou Way CB1........66 A7
Carisbrook Ct PE3 .....186 B8
Carisbrooke Rd CB4......83 C5
Carisbrooke Way **8** PE19 .74 F2
Carleton Crest PE4 .....204 D1
Carlisle Terr PE27......144 B3
Carlow **9** CB1...........84 A2
CARLTON 55 A7
Carlton Cl
  Haverhill CB9...........38 F2
  10 Leverington PE13 ....238 B2
Carlton Ct PE5.........195 D2
CARLTON GREEN 55 A4
  Carlton Green Rd CB8....55 A6
CARLTON HILL 55 A8
Carlton Rd CB8 ....70 E1
Carlton Rise SG8 ....14 D5
Carlton Way CB4.........83 D5
Carlyle Rd CB4 ....246 A4
Carmel Ave PE2 ....186 E8
Carmel St CB10..........18 D2
Carmen St CB10 ....18 D3
Carnaby Cl PE29 ....142 A1
Carnation Way IP28.....133 F8
Carnegie Rd **16** PE28...230 B1
Caroline Pl CB1.........246 C2
Carpenters Cl PE15....224 B4
Carpenters Way **9** PE15 243 A6
Carpond La **3** CB6 .....210 C6
Carradale PE2 ....185 D5
Carrick Cl CB1...........65 E5
Carrier Cl PE2..........186 D8
Carrington Pl PE28 .....140 C3
Carrington's Dro PE6 ...232 B8
Carron Dr PE4 ....204 A3
Carrops The CB8........134 A6
Carr Rd PE1 ....198 D3
Carr's Lodge PE9 ......244 F8
Carsey Hill CB21.........22 B6
Carson Wlk CB8........110 F6
Carter Cl
  Brampton PE28 ....140 C3
  Duxford CB22 ....17 E8
Carter Rd CB25.........130 C3
Carters Cl PE3..........196 F3
Carters Croft CB10......21 B1
Carter St CB7...........212 E1
Carter's Way CB24......122 C5
Cartmel Way **12** PE6 ....232 A1
Cartwright Rd **5** SG8 ....5 D5
Caryer Cl PE2 ....186 D6
Carysfort Cl
  Over End PE6 ....178 D8
  Yaxley PE7 ....181 D4
Casburn's La CB25 ......130 A3
Casewick La **14** PE9....230 F7
Casewick Rd PE9 ....230 D2
Cassander Cl SG8 ....15 E8
Castelhythe CB7 ....240 D3
Castel Way PE7 ....175 D8
Casterton Rd PE9.......244 A6
Castle Ave CB9 ....23 E7
CASTLE CAMPS 22 F4
Castle Camps CE Prim Sch
  CB21..................22 E3
Castle Dr **7** PE6.......231 F7
Castle Dyke PE9 ....244 B5
CASTLE END 231 D7
Castle End Rd PE6......231 C7
Castle Gdns PE28 ......113 F4
Castle Hill CB29.........141 D3
Castle Hill Cl PE19......74 C2
Castle Hill Dr CB23 .....141 E4
Castle Hill Mid Sch CB9...23 E8
Castle La CB9 ....23 E8
Castle Manor Bus & Enter
  Coll CB9 ....23 E8
Castle Moat Rd PE29....141 D4
Castle Pk CB1...........246 A4
Castle Row **8** CB3.......83 C3
Castle Specl Sch CB4 ....83 E5
Castle St **11** PE13.......245 C5
Castle St
  Cambridge CB3 ....246 A4
  7 Stamford PE9 ....244 B5
Castle Wlk CB9 ....23 E8
CASTOR 195 D1
Castor CE Prim Sch PE5 .195 E2
Castor Hanglands National
  Nature Reserve* PE6...195 E7
Castor Mills PE5........184 F6
Castor Rd
  Castor PE6.............196 C6
  Marholm PE6...........203 D1
Casworth Way PE5......195 D2
Cat Field PE13..........237 E1
Catharine St CB1 ....65 B8
Cathedral Sq PE3.......198 A2
Cathedral View PE15 ...224 C4
Catherine Cl PE2 ....186 B7
Cathwaite PE4 ....204 F1
Catkin Cl CB9 ....38 E1
Catley PE4..............205 A1
Catley Pk CB1...........19 D6
Catling's La PE13 ......238 C2
Cats La PE13...........237 F7
Cattell's La CB25.......106 B8
Cattle Dike PE13 ....238 A2
Cattle Market Rd PE1 ...198 A2
Cattle Market Way **6**
  PE4...................198 A2
CATWORTH 136 D7
Causeway
  Godmanchester PE29 ...141 E1
  Great Staughton PE19....93 F6
  Pampisford CB22.........33 C5

Causeway Cl
  Great Staughton PE19....93 F6
  March PE15.............243 C2
Causeway Gdns PE15 ...243 D3
Causeway Pas CB1......246 C3
Causeway Rd PE28 .....154 A8
Causeway Sch The PE1...198 C3
Causeway Sh Ctr PE7 ...189 F7
Causewayside CB1......246 A1
Causeway The
  Bassingbourn SG8 ......13 A5
  Burwell CB25...........130 B2
  Elsworth CB23.........100 B4
  Haverhill CB9...........23 E8
  Isleham CB7 ....213 A5
  March PE15.............243 C2
  Soham CB7 ....212 B4
  Sutton CB6.............216 C2
  Thorney PE6............232 E2
  West Wratting CB21 .....53 E5
Cavalry Dr PE15 ....243 E2
Cavalry Pk PE15........243 D2
Cavalry Prim Sch PE15...243 E2
Cavell Cl PE3...........197 B4
Cavendish Ave CB1 ......65 B5
Cavendish Cl PE28 .....168 C3
Cavendish Ct **5** CB9 ....23 E6
Cavendish Rd CB1.......84 A4
Cavendish Way CB23.....80 C1
Cavenham Rd **12** PE28 ..214 E2
Caverstede Rd PE4 .....204 D1
Cavesson Ct CB4........83 C6
Cawdor Pl **6** PE2........74 F2
Cawood Cl PE15 ....243 E6
CAXTON 78 F1
Caxton Drift PE19.......77 F3
Caxton End
  Bourn CB23.............60 B7
  Eltisley PE19...........77 F3
  Caxton La CB22..........30 B5
Caxton Rd
  Bourn CB23.............60 C7
  Great Gransden SG19....58 E6
  St Ives PE27...........144 B6
Cecil Lodge Cl CB8 .....110 F3
Cecil Pacey Ct PE1......197 F7
Cecil Rd PE1 ....198 A6
Cedar Ave **5** PE15 .....223 A6
Cedar Cl
  Grafham PE28 ....115 F7
  March PE15.............243 E5
  Melbourn SG8 ....14 C5
Cedar Cres SG8..........5 B6
Cedar Ct CB7...........242 D4
Cedar Gr PE1 ....198 B8
Cedar Rd PE27..........143 F6
Cedar Wlk CB25 ....86 F6
Celta Rd PE2 ....187 D3
Celtic Cl PE2 ....187 D7
Cemetery Hill CB8 ......110 D7
Cemetery Rd
  St Neots PE19 ....74 F5
  1 Whittlesey PE7 .....189 E7
Cenacle The **1** CB3.....64 C7
Centenary Way PE28 ...140 C2
Central Ave
  Brampton PE28 ....140 D1
  Peterborough PE2......198 C2
Central Sq PE2 ....187 D5
Centre Dr CB8..........111 D2
Centre for Mathematical
  Sciences CB3...........83 B2
Centurion Way PE29 ...142 B1
Century Way PE15......243 C7
Cerris Rd PE1 ....198 B8
Chadburn PE4 ....205 A1
Chadley La PE29........141 F2
Chadwick Cl **3** CB4......83 E8
Chaffinch Way CB23 .....79 C4
CHAINBRIDGE 228 B7
Chainbridge La PE28....135 F8
Chain Cl PE1............198 B6
Chain Rd CB24..........208 C2
Chalfont Cl **2** CB1......65 F6
Chalk Cl CB8............35 C3
Chalkhill Barrow SG8 ...14 C4
Chalklands CB1..........35 C3
Chalk Rd PE13..........237 D1
Chalkstone Mid Sch CB9..24 A8
Chalkstone Way CB9 ....39 A1
Chalky La SG8...........8 D2
Chalky Rd CB1..........34 C3
Challis Cl CB22..........29 F8
Challis Ct CB2...........29 F8
Chalmers Rd CB1........65 C6
Chamberlain Way PE19...74 F7
Chambers Dr **10** CB4 ....83 E8
Chamois Cl CB22 ....32 F6
Champions Cl SG8 ......15 E8
Champneys Wlk CB3 .....64 C8
Chancellor Cl PE29 .....141 C7
Chancellors Wlk **2** CB4..83 E8
Chancery La **6** CB22 ....32 E7
Chandlers PE2 ....185 C5
Chandlers Ct CB25......130 B3
Chandler's Way PE15 ...243 A2
Chandler's Wharf **8** PE19 .74 E5
Chantry Cl
  Cambridge CB4 ....83 F4
  Chatteris PE16.........241 D6

Chantry Cl continued
Peterborough PE1 . . . . 198 A5
Swavesey CB24 . . . . .122 E6
Chantry The CB21 . . . . .67 A5
Chapel Ave 1 PE13 . . . . .235 B7
Chapel Cl
Hilton PE28 . . . . .120 B1
Litlington SG8 . . . . .12 A2
Needingworth PE27 . . . . . . 208 A3
Waterbeach CB25 . . . . . . .106 B7
Wrestlingworth SG19 . . . . . .25 B4
Chapel Ct PE8 . . . . .194 B2
CHAPEL END 174 D4
Chapel End
Great Gidding PE28 . . . . . .166 D2
Sawtry PE8 . . . . .168 C4
Chapel Field SG19 . . . . . . .41 D4
Chapel Field La PE28 . . . .215 B1
Chapelfield Rd PE13 . . . . .235 A2
Chapelfield Way CB22 . . . .32 F8
Chapel Gate PE12 . . . . . . .237 B7
Chapel Gdns
Benwick PE15 . . . . .222 A5
Coates/Eastrea PE7 . . . . . .190 C7
Chapel Hill CB23 . . . . .47 A3
Chapel La
Alwalton PE2 . . . . .185 F5
Chatteris PE16 . . . . .241 B6
Downham CB6 . . . . .218 A6
Easton PE28 . . . . .138 B4
Elm PE14 . . . . .236 B6
Elton PE8 . . . . .178 C8
Fowlmere SG8 . . . . .15 C8
Harston CB22 . . . . .47 F3
Houghton PE28 . . . . .143 A5
Kirtling CB8 . . . . .72 C5
Melbourn SG8 . . . . .14 E2
Newton PE13 . . . . .238 B5
2 Peterborough PE4 . . . .204 C3
Reach CB25 . . . . .129 D1
Soham CB7 . . . . .219 B2
St Ives PE27 . . . . .144 A3
Tydd St Giles PE13. . . . . . .237 F7
Whittlesey PE7 . . . . .227 A3
Wicken CB7 . . . . .211 E1
Willingham CB4 . . . . .208 E5
Wimblington PE15 . . . . . . .223 B6
Wisbech PE14 . . . . .235 D5
Chapel Rd
Beck Row, Holywell Row &
  Kenny Hill IP28. . . . . . . .213 D6
Earith PE28 . . . . .208 E3
Great Eversden CB23 . . . . .45 F8
Ramsey Heights PE26 . . . .170 F6
Weston Colville CB21 . . . . . .54 B5
Wisbech PE13 . . . . .245 B5
Chapel Row CB8 . . . . .91 F8
Chapel St
Alconbury PE28 . . . . .150 F4
Cambridge CB4 . . . . .84 A4
4 Crowland PE6. . . . . . . .232 B8
Duxford CB22 . . . . .32 D1
Ely CB6 . . . . .240 C4
Exning CB8 . . . . .110 B8
March PE15 . . . . .243 D3
Peterborough PE1 . . . . . . .198 B2
Stanground PE2 . . . . .187 C7
Stretham CB6 . . . . .210 F5
Warmington PE8 . . . . .178 B3
Waterbeach CB25 . . . . . . .106 B7
13 Wisbech PE13. . . . . . .245 C4
Yaxley PE7 . . . . .181 D5
Chapelwent Rd CB9. . . . . .38 E2
Chapel Yd
Kimbolton MK44 . . . . .113 E1
Stamford PE9. . . . . .244 C5
Chaplains Cl 6 CB9 . . . . .38 F1
Chaplins Cl PE7 . . . . .190 F8
Chaplin's Cl CB21. . . . . . . .66 F5
Chapman Ct CB4. . . . . .83 E7
Chapmans Cl CB25. . . . . .105 C7
Chapman's Cl SG8 . . . . . . .14 C6
Chapmans Dr 5 SG8 . . . . .79 C3
Chapman's Way CB24 . . .208 E1
Chapman Way PE19. . . . . .74 E1
Chapnall Cl PE13 . . . . . . .245 E4
Chapnall Rd PE13. . . . . . .245 D4
Chapple Dr CB9 . . . . .38 F1
Charcoal La PE28 . . . . . . .140 C3
Charding Cres SG8. . . . . . . .5 C7
Chariot Way CB4. . . . . .83 D8
Charlemont Dr PE15 . . . . .224 B5
Charles Babbage Rd CB3. .82 F2
Charles Cl
Newmarket CB8. . . . . .110 E3
Ramsey PE26 . . . . .172 A7
Charles Cope Rd PE2 . . . .185 F5
Charles Melrose Cl PE28 .239 B5
Charles Rd
Stamford PE9. . . . . .244 A7
Whittlesey PE7 . . . . .189 F6
Charles St
Cambridge CB1 . . . . .65 B7
Peterborough PE1 . . . . . . .198 B3
10 Wisbech PE13. . . . . . .245 C4
Charles' St PE19 . . . . .74 F5
Charlton Ct PE3 . . . . .197 B1
Charnocks Cl 3 SG19. . . . .41 D5
Charnwood Cl PE2 . . . . . .187 A7
Charrington Cl CB9 . . . . . .24 C6
Charters The 2 PE9 . . . . .230 C6
Chartfield Rd CB1. . . . . . . .65 F6
Chartwell Cl PE2. . . . . . . .187 A7
Chase Cl CB9. . . . . .39 A1

Chase Rd PE15 . . . . .221 F6
Chase St PE13 . . . . .245 C6
Chase The
Ely CB6 . . . . .240 B4
March PE15 . . . . .243 C4
Thorney PE6 . . . . .200 E7
Upwell PE14 . . . . .229 D7
Walton Dam PE14 . . . . . . .238 D4
Whittlesey PE7 . . . . .220 E7
Wimblington PE15 . . . . . . .224 A8
Wisbech PE13 . . . . .245 A7
Chaston Rd CB22 . . . . .49 A5
Chater Rd 3 PE8 . . . . . . .230 B1
Chatsfield PE4 . . . . .204 A6
Chatsworth Ave CB4 . . . . . .83 C5
Chatsworth Pl PE3 . . . . . .197 B2
CHATTERIS 241 D4
Chatteris Mus* PE16 . . . .241 C4
Chatteris Rd
Chatteris PE28 . . . . .215 D4
10 Somersham PE28. . . . .208 C8
Chaucer Cl
Cambridge CB2 . . . . .64 E6
11 Wisbech PE13. . . . . . .238 B2
Chaucer Pl PE19. . . . . .74 D6
Chaucer Rd
Cambridge CB2 . . . . .64 D7
Peterborough PE1 . . . . . . .197 E8
Royston SG8 . . . . .5 C8
Chaucer Way PE27. . . . . .143 F6
Chauntry Rd CB9 . . . . .23 F7
Chawston Cl 1 PE19. . . . .74 C5
Chedburgh Pl CB9 . . . . . . .39 B1
Cheddars La CB5 . . . . .84 B3
Chedworth St CB3 . . . . . . .64 C7
Cheere Way CB23 . . . . .99 B3
Chelmer Cl PE27. . . . . . . .144 B7
Chelmer Garth PE4 . . . . .204 F1
Chelmer Rd CB9 . . . . .24 B8
Chelmer Way CB6. . . . . . .240 D6
Cheltenham Cl PE1 . . . . .198 B6
Chelveston Way PE3 . . . . .197 C5
Chelwood Rd CB1. . . . . . . .65 F6
Cheney Ct PE2. . . . . .186 C4
Cheney Way CB4 . . . . .84 C5
Chequer La 1 CB7 . . . . .240 D4
Chequers Cl
Alconbury Weston PE28. . . .150 C6
Cambridge CB1 . . . . .65 B7
Fenstanton PE28 . . . . .121 B6
Orwell SG8. . . . . .45 E1
Chequers Cnr PE14 . . . . .236 E7
Chequers Croft PE28. . . . .120 B2
Chequers Ct
Church End CB24. . . . . . . .122 E7
1 Huntingdon PE29 . . . . .141 D4
Chequers La CB23 . . . . . . .99 B3
Chequers Rd CB24 . . . . . .104 C2
Chequer St PE28 . . . . .121 B6
Chequers Way PE29. . . . .141 D4
Cherry Bounds Rd CB3. . . .82 E8
Cherry Cl
Cambridge CB1 . . . . .65 E5
Linton CB21 . . . . .35 B3
Milton CB24 . . . . .105 D3
Cherry Ct CB23 . . . . .79 A4
Cherry Dr SG8 . . . . .5 C7
Cherryfields PE2 . . . . .185 E6
Cherry Hill IP28 . . . . .214 C3
CHERRY HINTON. 65 F5
Cherry Hinton CE Inf Sch
CB1 . . . . .65 F6
Cherry Hinton Close Limekiln
  Close Nature Reserve*
CB1 . . . . .65 F7
Cherry Hinton Com Jun Sch
CB1 . . . . .66 A6
Cherry Hinton Rd
Cambridge CB1 . . . . .65 B6
Great Shelford CB22 . . . . . .65 D1
Teversham CB1 . . . . .66 A6
Cherry Hinton West Pit
  Nature Reserve* CB1. . .65 E4
Cherryholt Ave PE15 . . . .243 C3
Cherry Holt La PE9 . . . . . .244 D5
Cherryholt Rd PE9 . . . . . .244 D5
Cherry Orch
Fulbourn CB21. . . . . .66 D5
Haddenham CB6 . . . . .210 A5
Oakington/Longstanton
  CB24. . . . . .103 C5
Cherry Orton Rd PE2. . . . .185 F5
Cherry Rd PE13 . . . . .245 C8
Cherry Rise CB6 . . . . .216 D1
Cherry Tree CB7 . . . . .128 C5
Cherry Tree Ave CB22 . . . .49 C4
Cherry Tree Cl
Huntingdon PE29 . . . . .141 C6
Litlington SG8 . . . . .12 A1
Cherrytree Gr PE7 . . . . . .198 C6
Cherrytree Gr PE7 . . . . . .189 F6
Cherrytree La CB7 . . . . . .212 B3
Cherry Tree La CB7 . . . . . .212 C3
Cherry Trees CB22 . . . . . . .48 F7
Cherry Tree Way PE28. . . .121 B6
Cherrywood Ave PE15. . . .243 B3
Cherrywood Gn PE15. . . . .243 B3
Chervil Cl PE7 . . . . .175 D8
Chervil Way 1 CB22 . . . . .79 C3
Cherwell Ct CB3 . . . . .64 C7
Chesham Rd PE28 . . . . . .168 C2
Chesnut Gr CB4. . . . . .83 F4
Chester Cl PE28 . . . . .143 B7
Chester Ct 8 CB9 . . . . . . .23 E6
Chesterfield Rd CB4 . . . . . .84 A6
Chesterfield Way 3 PE19 .74 E2
CHESTERFORD PARK 19 D1

Chesterford Research Pk
CB10. . . . . .19 D1
Chester Rd
Peterborough PE1 . . . . . . .198 C3
St Neots PE19 . . . . .74 C1
Wyton Airfield PE28. . . . . . .143 B7
CHESTERTON
Cambridge 84 A5
Peterborough. 184 E3
Chesterton Gr PE2 . . . . . .187 D6
Chesterton Hall Cres CB4 .83 F4
Chesterton La CB4 . . . . . .246 A4
Chesterton Rd CB4 . . . . . .246 A4
Chester Way PE29 . . . . . . .142 B1
Chestnut Ave PE1. . . . . . .198 C6
Chestnut Cl
Brampton PE28 . . . . .140 D2
Glinton PE6 . . . . .203 D8
Grafham PE28 . . . . .116 A7
Haslingfield CB23 . . . . .47 B4
Haverhill CB9 . . . . .23 F8
Huntingdon PE29 . . . . .141 E7
Mildenhall IP28 . . . . .239 E2
Peakirk PE6. . . . . .206 B2
Sawston CB22 . . . . .32 E7
Sawtry PE28 . . . . .168 B4
Chestnut Cres
March PE15. . . . . .243 B3
Whittlesey PE7 . . . . .189 C6
Chestnut Dr
5 Soham CB7 . . . . .212 B4
6 Thorney PE6 . . . . .233 A3
Chestnut Gr
Cambridge CB4 . . . . .83 F4
Little Stukeley PE28. . . . . .152 A2
St Neots PE19 . . . . .74 F4
Sutton La SG8. . . . . .13 B6
Chestnut Rd
St Ives PE27 . . . . .143 F6
7 Wisbech PE13. . . . . . .245 C4
Chestnut Rise
Bar Hill CB23 . . . . .102 D3
Burwell CB25. . . . . .130 B4
Chestnuts The
Elton PE8 . . . . .178 C8
Harston CB22 . . . . .48 A4
Chestnut Way CB6 . . . . . .216 E3
Chestnut Wlk 6 SG8. . . . . .5 C7
Chettisham CB6 . . . . .218 C5
CHEVELEY. 91 C6
Cheveley CE Prim Sch
CB8 . . . . .91 C7
Cheveley Rd
Newmarket CB8. . . . . .111 C3
Woodditton CB8. . . . . .91 C3
Cheviot Ave PE4 . . . . .204 E2
Chewells Cl CB6. . . . . .210 A6
Chewells La CB6 . . . . .210 A6
Cheyney Cl SG8. . . . . .11 B1
Cheyney St SG8. . . . . .11 B1
Chichester Way PE28 . . . .115 D2
Chiefs St CB6. . . . . .240 C4
Chieftan Way CB4. . . . . . . .83 D8
Chigwell Ct 7 CB5 . . . . . .84 E4
Chilcourt SG8 . . . . .5 C6
CHILDERLEY 80 C4
CHILDERLEY GATE. 80 C4
Childerley Hall* CB23. . . . .80 D8
Childers St PE7 . . . . .189 C8
Childs La 12 PE15. . . . . . .223 A5
Child's Pond Rd PE19 . . . . .75 A6
Chilford Hall Vineyard*
CB21 . . . . .35 D6
Chiltern Rise PE4 . . . . . . .204 D2
Chimswell Way CB9 . . . . . .23 C8
CHIPPENHAM 133 D8
Chippenham Fen National
  Nature Reserve* CB7 . .133 C2
Chippenham Mews PE2 . .186 C7
Chippenham Rd
Chippenham CB8 . . . . .133 C2
Fordham CB7 . . . . .213 A1
Snailwell CB8 . . . . .133 D1
Chisenhale PE2. . . . . .185 E6
Chishill Rd
Barley SG8. . . . . .7 A2
Great & Little Chishill SG8. . . .7 F3
Heydon SG8. . . . . .8 A4
Chishill St SG8 . . . . .7 F3
Chiswick Ave IP28 . . . . . .239 C6
Chiswick End SG8 . . . . .14 F8
CHITTERING. 127 B8
Chittering Dro CB25 . . . . .127 C8
Chivers Rd CB9 . . . . .23 D7
Chivers Way CB24. . . . . . .104 B2
CHRISHALL 8 C4
Chrishall Holy Trinity CE
  Prim Sch SG8 . . . . .8 C4
Chrishall Rd SG8 . . . . .15 F6
CHRISTCHURCH 229 D3
Christ Church Cl PE9 . . . .244 B6
Christchurch St CB1 . . . . .246 C3
Christie Dr PE29 . . . . .141 A5
Christopher Cl PE1 . . . . . .197 F8
Christopher Dr PE13 . . . . .245 D4
Christopher Tye Cl 3
CB21 . . . . .34 B7
Christs Coll Cl CB21 . . . . .246 B3
Christ's Cl
Bassingbourn SG8 . . . . . . .12 E5
Cottenham CB24 . . . . .125 F6
Coveney CB6. . . . . .217 C5
Dullingham CB8 . . . . .70 E8
Exning CB8. . . . . .110 C8
Great & Little Abington
CB21 . . . . .34 C7
Great Wilbraham CB21 . . . .67 F7

Church Cl continued
Newborough PE6. . . . . . . .205 C8
Ramsey PE26. . . . . .221 C2
Stilton PE7 . . . . .176 A7
The Stukeleys PE28. . . . . . .151 F2
Whittlesford CB22 . . . . .32 C5
Church Cswy PE28 . . . . . .168 C4
Church Dr PE2 . . . . .185 F5
Church Dro PE14 . . . . .236 F2
Church End
Arrington SG8 . . . . .44 D1
Barley SG8. . . . . .7 A1
Cambridge CB1 . . . . .65 F8
CHURCH END. 136 E7
Church End CB3 . . . . .82 B2
CHURCH END. 77 D4
Church End
Everton SG19. . . . . .40 C3
Gamlingay SG19 . . . . .41 E5
CHURCH END. 151 F2
Church End
Hilton PE28 . . . . .99 B8
Horningsea CB25. . . . . . . .106 A2
8 Leverington PE13 . . . .238 B2
CHURCH END. 208 C1
Church End
Over CB24. . . . . .208 D1
Parson Drove PE13 . . . . . .234 E8
Church End CB24 . . . . . . .165 D1
Church End CB24 . . . . . . .124 F4
CHURCH END. 122 E7
Church End
Weston Colville CB21 . . . . . .54 A7
Whaddon SG8 . . . . .28 B2
CHURCH END. 169 D2
Church Farm Cl
Church End PE28. . . . . . . .165 D1
Wentworth CB6. . . . . .217 B1
Church Farm La SG8. . . . . .11 B1
Church Fen Dro CB6 . . . . .209 E3
Churchfield SG8 . . . . .7 A3
CHURCH FIELD. 189 B7
Churchfield Ave CB22 . . . .32 F8
CHURCH FIELD. 189 B7
Churchfield Ct
Girton CB3 . . . . .103 E2
Peterborough PE4 . . . . . . .197 E8
Churchfield Rd
Peterborough PE4 . . . . . . .197 D8
Upwell PE14 . . . . .236 F2
Churchfields PE13 . . . . . . .235 B7
Churchfield Way
Whittlesey PE7 . . . . .189 C7
5 Wisbech St Mary PE13. .235 B7
Church Gate 18 PE6. . . . .231 F8
Churchgate St 9 CB7. . . .212 B4
Church Gdns
Beck Row, Holywell Row &
  Kenny Hill IP28. . . . . . . .213 D6
North Green PE7. . . . . .190 F8
Church Gn CB10 . . . . .18 B7
Church Gr PE14. . . . . .236 A6
Church Hill
Castor PE5. . . . . .195 E2
Grafham PE28 . . . . .115 F6
Churchhill Cl CB6 . . . . . . .216 E2
Churchill Cl CB6 . . . . .240 A4
Churchill Cl PE7 . . . . .187 C1
Churchill Ave
Haverhill CB9 . . . . .39 B1
Houghton & Wyton PE28 . . .143 B7
Newmarket CB8. . . . . .110 D5
Churchill Cl CB6 . . . . .240 A4
Churchill Coll CB3 . . . . . . .83 B3
Churchill Cl
Little Downham CB6 . . . . . .218 A6
Newmarket CB8. . . . . .110 F3
Churchill Dr IP28 . . . . . . .239 B5
Churchill Rd
Cambridge CB3 . . . . .83 B3
Gorefield PE13. . . . . .237 F3
Stamford PE9. . . . . .244 B7
Wisbech PE13 . . . . .245 D4
Church La
Abington Pigotts SG8 . . . . . .11 F5
Alwalton PE2 . . . . .185 F5
Arrington SG8 . . . . .44 D1
Ashwell SG7. . . . . .2 D4
Balsham CB21 . . . . .53 B2
Barton CB23 . . . . .63 B4
Barton Mills IP28 . . . . .239 D1
Beck Row, Holywell Row & Kenny
  Hill IP28. . . . . .213 D6
Brington & Molesworth
PE28 . . . . .147 C4
Burwell CB25. . . . . .130 B1
Cambridge CB2 . . . . .64 C2
Castle Camps CB21. . . . . . .22 E3
Chatteris PE16. . . . . .241 C6
Cheveley CB8 . . . . .91 C6
Comberton CB23 . . . . .62 C3
Conington PE7 . . . . .168 E8
Cottenham CB24 . . . . .125 F6
Covington PE28 . . . . .135 C2
Croydon SG8 . . . . .27 A8
Doddington/Wimblington
PE15 . . . . .222 F5
Ellington PE28 . . . . .138 F4
Elsworth CB23. . . . . .100 B4
Ely CB7 . . . . .240 C4
Exning CB8. . . . . .110 C8
Fenstanton PE28 . . . . .121 B6
Fulbourn CB21. . . . . .67 A5
Gamlingay SG19 . . . . .41 D5
Girton CB3 . . . . .82 E8
Graveley PE19 . . . . .97 F5
Great & Little Abington
CB21 . . . . .34 B7
Great Paxton PE19 . . . . . . .96 D5
Guilden Morden SG8 . . . . . .10 F5

Church La continued
Haddenham CB6 . . . . .210 A6
Helpston PE6. . . . . .231 B4
Hemingford Abbots PE28 . .143 A3
Hemingford Grey PE28 . . .143 C2
Histon CB24 . . . . .120 B1
Huntingdon PE29 . . . . .142 A5
Isleham CB7 . . . . .213 A5
Kennett CB8. . . . . .133 F5
Kingston CB23 . . . . .61 B3
Leighton PE28 . . . . .148 D3
Linton CB21 . . . . .35 C2
Little Eversden CB23. . . . . .46 A7
1 Littleport CB6. . . . . . . .242 D4
Little Staughton MK44. . . . .93 B2
Madingley CB23. . . . . .81 E4
Milton CB24 . . . . .105 D2
Newmarket CB8. . . . . .111 A3
Newton PE13. . . . . .238 A5
Pampisford CB22. . . . . .33 B5
Papworth Everard CB23 . . . .99 A2
Peterborough PE2 . . . . . . .187 B7
Ramsey PE26. . . . . .171 B2
Royston SG8 . . . . .5 D6
Sawston CB22 . . . . .32 F7
Sibson cum Stibbington
PE8 . . . . .194 C2
Snailwell CB8. . . . . .132 A3
Spaldwick PE28 . . . . .137 F6
Stamford PE9. . . . . .244 C4
Stetchworth CB8 . . . . .90 A2
Stow Longa PE28. . . . . . . .137 B3
Sutton CB6. . . . . .216 E2
Tallington PE9 . . . . .230 F6
Tilbrook PE28. . . . . .113 B7
Tydd St Giles PE13. . . . . . .237 F6
Warmington PE8 . . . . .178 B2
Westley Waterless CB8 . . . .70 B5
Whittlesford CB22 . . . . .32 C5
Wilburton CB6 . . . . .210 B6
4 Willingham CB24 . . . . .209 A1
Worlington IP28 . . . . .213 F4
Wrestlingworth SG19 . . . . . .25 C5
Church Lane Cl IP28. . . . .239 D2
Church Leys PE28. . . . . . .121 C6
Church Mdw IP28 . . . . . . .239 D2
Church Mdws PE19 . . . . . .74 F5
Church Mews 20 PE13. . .245 C5
Church Path CB21 . . . . . . .20 B6
Church Pl PE29 . . . . .141 E2
Church Rate Wlk CB3 . . . . .64 E8
Church Rd
Brampton PE28 . . . . .140 C2
Buckworth PE28 . . . . .149 D6
Carlton CB8. . . . . .55 A6
Catworth PE28 . . . . .136 D7
Chrishall SG8 . . . . .8 D3
Christchurch PE14. . . . . . .229 D3
Conington PE7 . . . . .168 D8
Easton PE28 . . . . .138 B4
Everton SG19. . . . . .40 C3
Friday Bridge PE14 . . . . . .236 A3
Glatton PE28 . . . . .175 E1
Grafham PE28 . . . . .115 E7
Great Wilbraham CB21 . . . .67 F8
Haunton CB22 . . . . .48 A5
Huntingdon PE29 . . . . .245 F7
Little Stukeley PE28. . . . . .151 F2
Little Wilbraham CB1. . . . . .86 F2
Moulton CB8 . . . . .112 F5
Shepreth SG8. . . . . .29 E4
Shudy Camps CB21. . . . . . .22 C5
Stow cum Quy CB25. . . . . . .85 F4
Teversham CB1 . . . . .85 B2
Thistley Green IP28. . . . . . .213 D6
Toft CB23 . . . . .61 C4
Warboys PE28 . . . . .164 E4
Wentworth CB6 . . . . .217 C1
Wicken CB7 . . . . .211 F1
Wisbech PE13 . . . . .238 B1
Wisbech St Mary PE13 . . . .235 B7
Wittering PE8 . . . . .230 B1
Church St
Abington CB21. . . . . .34 C7
Ashley CB8. . . . . .91 F8
Bourn CB23 . . . . .60 C5
Buckden PE19 . . . . .117 A4
Cambridge CB4 . . . . .84 A4
12 Doddington/Wimblington
PE15 . . . . .223 B7
Exning CB8. . . . . .110 C8
Fen Ditton CB5. . . . . .84 E6
Fen Drayton CB24 . . . . . . .121 F5
Fenstanton PE28 . . . . .121 B6
Fordham CB7 . . . . .212 F1
Gamlingay SG19 . . . . .41 D5
Great Chesterford CB10 . . . .18 D2
Great Eversden CB23 . . . . .45 E7
Great Gransden SG19. . . . . .58 E4
Great Shelford CB22 . . . . . .67 F8
Great Wilbraham CB21 . . . .67 F8
Guilden Morden SG8 . . . . . .10 E4
Harston CB22 . . . . .47 D2
Haslingfield CB23 . . . . .46 F5
Hemingford Grey PE28 . . .143 C2
Histon CB24. . . . . .104 B5
Holme PE7 . . . . .176 F4
Ickleton CB10 . . . . .18 A4
6 Isleham CB7 . . . . .213 A5
Litlington SG8 . . . . .12 A2
Little Gransden SG19. . . . . .58 E3
March PE15 . . . . .243 C1
Market Deeping PE6. . . . . .231 F8
Needingworth PE27. . . . . . .208 A2
Northborough PE6 . . . . . . .231 N1
Old Hurst PE28 . . . . .154 D7
Peterborough PE1 . . . . . . .198 A2
Sawtry PE28 . . . . .168 B4

Church St continued
[1] Somersham PE28. . . . . . 208 C8
Stamford PE9. . . . . 244 B4
Stanground PE2. . . . . 187 C7
Stapleford CB22. . . . . 49 C4
Steeple Morden SG8. . . . . . 11 B1
Stilton PE7. . . . . 175 F7
St Ives PE27. . . . . 143 F4
St Neots PE19. . . . . 74 F5
[5] Thorney PE6. . . . . 233 A3
Thriplow SG8. . . . . 31 C1
Warmington PE8. . . . . 178 A3
Werrington PE4. . . . . 204 C3
Whaddon SG8. . . . . 28 B2
Whittlesey PE7. . . . . 189 D6
Willingham CB24. . . . . 209 A1
Wistow PE28. . . . . 163 F7
Withersfield CB9. . . . . 38 C4
Woodhurst PE28. . . . . 155 B5
Yaxley PE7. . . . . 181 D4
Church Terr [16] PE13. . . . 245 C5
Church View
Keyston PE28. . . . . 146 A3
[9] Northborough PE6. . . . . 231 F7
Oakington/Longstanton
CB24. . . . . 103 C6
[4] St Neots PE19. . . . . 74 F5
[3] Witchford CB6. . . . . 217 E1
Church View Cl PE2. . . . . . 187 B7
Church Way
Alconbury PE28. . . . . 150 E5
Downham CB6. . . . . 218 A7
Haslingfield CB23. . . . . 47 A5
Little Stukeley PE28. . . . . . . 151 D4
Church Wlk
Chatteris PE16. . . . . 241 D5
Little Gransden SG19. . . . . . 58 E3
Mildenhall IP28. . . . . 239 B4
Peterborough PE1. . . . . 198 A3
[2] St Neots PE19. . . . . 74 E5
Stow Longa PE28. . . . . 137 B3
Sturmer CB9. . . . . 24 E4
Upton PE6. . . . . 195 B5
Churchyard The IP28. . . . 239 B4
Cinders Cl [3] PE27. . . . . . 208 A2
Cinques Rd SG19. . . . . 41 C6
Cinques The SG19. . . . . . . 41 B6
Cirrus Ct PE29. . . . . 141 D7
Cissbury Ring PE4. . . . . . . 204 C2
City of Ely Com Coll CB6 240 C6
City Rd
Cambridge CB1. . . . . 246 C2
Littleport CB6. . . . . 242 E4
March PE15. . . . . 199 B2
Peterborough PE3. . . . . 198 A2
Civic Ind Est CB9. . . . . 23 F5
Clack La PE28. . . . . 135 D8
Clare Cl
Mildenhall IP28. . . . . 239 D5
Stamford PE9. . . . . 244 A5
Waterbeach CB25. . . . . 106 A8
Clare Coll CB2. . . . . 246 A2
Clare Coll Pavilion CB2. . 64 F5
Clare Coll (The Colony)
CB4. . . . . 246 A4
Clare Ct PE27. . . . . 144 A4
Clare Dr CB23. . . . . 80 C2
Claremont [1] CB1. . . . . . . 64 F7
Claremont Rd PE13. . . . . . 245 E5
Clarence Rd
Peterborough PE1. . . . . 197 E5
Wisbech PE13. . . . . 245 D6
Clarendale Est CB88. . . . . 55 F6
Clarendon Rd
Cambridge CB2. . . . . 64 F6
Haverhill CB9. . . . . 23 F7
Clarendon St CB1. . . . . . . 246 B2
Clarendon Way PE6. . . . . 203 F8
Clare Pl CB88. . . . . 111 B2
Clare Rd
Cambridge CB3. . . . . 64 C8
Huntingdon PE29. . . . . 142 A7
[3] Northborough PE6. . . . . 231 F7
Peterborough PE1. . . . . 197 F6
Clare St
Cambridge CB4. . . . . 246 A4
Chatteris PE16. . . . . 241 B4
Clarke's La CB6. . . . . 210 C5
Clarkes Way SG8. . . . . 12 F5
Clark Rd SG8. . . . . 5 D7
Clark's Dro CB7. . . . . 212 A4
Clarkson Ave PE13. . . . . . 245 D5
Clarkson Cl CB3. . . . . 83 B2
Clarkson Ct PE13. . . . . 245 D6
Clarkson Inf Sch The
PE13. . . . . 245 E6
Clarkson Rd CB3. . . . . 83 B2
Claudian Cl CB9. . . . . 24 D7
Claybush Rd PE13. . . . . . . 186 C1
Claybush Rd SG7. . . . . 2 D3
Clay Cl La CB24. . . . . 104 D3
Claydon Cl CB21. . . . . 22 E4
Claygate PE7. . . . . 189 D7
Claygate Rd CB11. . . . . 65 F6
CLAYHITHE. 106 D5
Clayhithe Rd CB25. . . . . . 106 C5
Clayhive Dr [6] CB9. . . . . . 23 F7
Clay La
Abbots Ripton PE28. . . . . . 162 A1
Castor PE5. . . . . 195 E2
Little Stukeley PE28. . . . . . . 151 F7
CLAYPIT HILL. 61 D2
Claypole Dr [3] PE6. . . . . . 231 F7
Clay St
Histon CB24. . . . . 104 B5
Soham CB7. . . . . 212 B4
Clayton CI PE28. . . . . 186 A4
Clayton Cl PE13. . . . . 245 F6

Claytons Way PE29. . . . . . 141 F5
Clayway CB7. . . . . 240 E6
Clear Cres SG8. . . . . 14 D5
Cleatham PE3. . . . . 197 A4
Clematis Cl IP28. . . . . 213 F1
Clement Dr PE2. . . . . 186 D8
Clements Cl CB9. . . . . 23 F7
Clements Dr CB9. . . . . 23 F7
Clement's La CB9. . . . . 23 F7
Clements Prim Sch CB9. . . 23 F7
Clement's Way [1] IP28. . 213 F8
Clerk Maxwell Rd CB3. . . . 83 A2
Cleveland Bay PE15. . . . . 243 E2
Cleveland Ct PE4. . . . . 204 E2
Cleve Pl PE6. . . . . 232 A1
Cleves Rd CB9. . . . . 23 D6
Cley Ct CB9. . . . . 38 C1
Clifden Cl SG8. . . . . 44 D1
Cliff Cres PE9. . . . . 244 B5
Cliff Rd PE9. . . . . 244 B5
Clifton Ave PE3. . . . . 197 E3
Clifton Ct CB1. . . . . 65 A6
Clifton Rd
Cambridge CB1. . . . . 65 A6
Huntingdon PE29. . . . . 141 D7
Clifton Way CB1. . . . . 65 A7
Clipston Wlk PE3. . . . . 197 C5
Cliveden Cl CB4. . . . . 83 C5
Clive Hall Dr CB24. . . . . . . 124 A1
Cloisters Sh Ctr CB7. . . . . 240 D4
Cloisters The
[6] Ely CB7. . . . . 240 D4
Eye PE6. . . . . 232 A1
CLOPTON. 156 E5
Close The
Babraham CB22. . . . . 50 E2
Godmanchester PE29. . . . . 142 A1
Kennett CB8. . . . . 133 F5
Papworth Everard CB23. . . 99 B3
Royston SG8. . . . . 5 F7
St Neots PE19. . . . . 74 E6
Sutton CB6. . . . . 216 E1
Close Victoria SG19. . . . . . 25 B4
Cloughs Cross PE13. . . . . 234 D8
Clover Cl PE26. . . . . 220 D3
Clover Ct
Cambridge CB1. . . . . 66 A5
Linton CB21. . . . . 35 D2
Clover End [2] CB6. . . . . . 217 D1
Clover Field CB9. . . . . 23 D8
Cloverfield Dr [4] CB7. . . . 212 A5
Clover Rd PE19. . . . . 74 C3
Clover Way [1] IP28. . . . . . 214 A1
Club Way PE7. . . . . 186 E4
Clydesdale Cl PE15. . . . . . 243 E2
Clydesdale Rd [6] SG8. . . . . 5 E6
Coach Dr CB23. . . . . 46 D5
Coach House La CB22. . . . . 31 B7
Coach La CB8. . . . . 91 D5
Coach Mews [22] PE28. . . 215 C1
Coalwharf Rd PE13. . . . . . 245 B4
COATES. 190 F8
Coates Ct PE14. . . . . 236 D6
Coates Dro CB7. . . . . 213 A5
Coates Prim Sch PE7. . . . . 190 F8
Coates Rd PE7. . . . . 190 D7
Cobbet Pl PE1. . . . . 198 B3
Cobble Yd CB1. . . . . 246 C3
Cobden Ave PE1. . . . . 197 F4
Cobden St PE1. . . . . 197 F4
Cobholm Pl [4] CB4. . . . . . 83 F8
Cob Pl PE29. . . . . 118 F7
Cobwebs PE28. . . . . 142 D8
COCKAYNE HATLEY. 25 C8
Cock Bank PE7. . . . . 191 C2
Cockbrook La
Brington & Molesworth
PE28. . . . . 147 C8
Old Weston PE28. . . . . 157 C2
Cockburn St CB1. . . . . 65 B8
Cockcroft PE13. . . . . 83 B2
Cockerell Rd CB4. . . . . 83 D5
Cockerton Rd CB3. . . . . . . 103 E1
Cocketts Dr PE13. . . . . 245 E5
Cockfen La CB25. . . . . 105 C7
Cock Fen Rd PE14. . . . . . . 229 F3
Cockhall Cl SG8. . . . . 12 A1
Cockhall La SG8. . . . . 12 A1
Cockle Cl CB22. . . . . 31 C7
Cockpen Rd CB7. . . . . 131 A8
Cockrells PE19. . . . . 75 C7
Codling Wlk CB23. . . . . 78 F4
Codrington Ct [2] PE19. . . 74 B3
Cody Rd CB25. . . . . 127 B1
Coggeshall Cl [5] CB5. . . . 84 E4
Cohort Way PE7. . . . . 142 B1
Colbeck Rd CB7. . . . . 38 E2
Colbron Cl SG7. . . . . 2 C4
Colburn Rd CB9. . . . . 24 D7
Cold Arbour SG19. . . . . 56 A1
COLDHAM. 235 D1
Coldham Bank PE15. . . . . 228 D8
COLDHAM HALL. 228 E8
Coldham Hall Chase
PE14. . . . . 235 E1
Coldham La Bus Pk CB1. . . 65 E8
COLDHAM'S COMMON. . . . 84 D2
Coldhams Cres PE29. . . . . 141 H6
Coldham's Dr CB1. . . . . 84 C1
Coldham's La CB1. . . . . 84 C2
Coldhams N PE29. . . . . 141 H6
Coldham's Rd CB1. . . . . 84 B2
Coldhams S PE29. . . . . 141 H5
Cold Harbour SG7. . . . . 2 E7
Cold Harbour Cnr PE13. . . 235 C5
Coldhorn Cres PE13. . . . . . 245 D1
Cole Cl [1] CB6. . . . . 217 D1
Coleridge Com Coll CB1. . . 65 C7

Coleridge Ct [1] PE19. . . . . 74 C6
Coleridge Pl PE1. . . . . 197 E8
Coleridge Rd CB1. . . . . 65 B6
COLESEED HOUSE. 228 D2
Coleseed Rd PE15. . . . . . . 228 D2
Colesfield CB24. . . . . 123 E2
Coles La
Brinkley CB8. . . . . 70 D2
Linton CB21. . . . . 35 C2
Oakington/Longstanton
CB24. . . . . 103 C6
Coles Rd CB24. . . . . 105 D2
College Bus Pk CB1. . . . . . . 65 F7
College Cl CB25. . . . . 86 E6
College Cres CB23. . . . . 47 B5
College Ct PE28. . . . . 168 C3
College Fields CB4. . . . . 83 F6
College Gdns PE15. . . . . . . 243 E7
College Heath Mid Sch
IP28. . . . . 239 C6
College Heath Rd IP28. . . . 239 D6
College Pk PE1. . . . . 198 C5
College Rd
Histon CB24. . . . . 104 B1
Soham CB7. . . . . 212 B3
College The CB7. . . . . 240 D4
Collett's Bridge La PE14 236 C5
Collier Rd CB1. . . . . 246 C2
Colliers La CB25. . . . . 86 A6
Collier Way CB22. . . . . 49 C4
Collingham PE2. . . . . 185 F3
Collings Pl CB8. . . . . 110 E5
Collingwood Ave PE15. . . 243 E3
Collingwood Dr CB24. . . . 123 E2
Collingwood Rd PE19. . . . . 74 B2
Collin's Hill CB7. . . . . 212 F1
Collinson Cres PE28. . . . . 152 E1
Coll of Animal Welfare The
PE29. . . . . 119 C5
Coll of West Anglia - Isle
Coll The PE16. . . . . 241 C5
Coll of West Anglia - Milton
Coll The CB24. . . . . 105 D3
Collyweston Great Wood &
Easton Hornstocks National
Nature Reserve* PE8. . . . 192 A6
Collyweston Rd PE9. . . . . . 230 B2
Colmworth Bsns Pk PE19. . 74 C1
Colmworth Gdns [5] PE19. 74 C2
Colmworth Rd MK44. . . . . . 93 B1
COLNE. 208 D6
COLNEFIELDS. 208 D8
Colne Fields
Colne PE28. . . . . 215 D1
Somersham PE28. . . . . 208 D8
Colne Rd
Bluntisham PE28. . . . . 208 C6
Colne PE28. . . . . 208 C8
Earith PE28. . . . . 208 D6
Colne Valley Rd CB9. . . . . . 24 A7
Colorado PE28. . . . . 151 F3
Colts Croft SG8. . . . . 7 E2
Coltsfoot Cl CB1. . . . . 66 A5
Coltsfoot Dr
Peterborough PE2. . . . . 186 E7
Royston SG8. . . . . 5 E6
Columbine Rd CB6. . . . . . . 240 B6
Colville Rd
Newton CB1. . . . . 238 A5
Wisbech PE13. . . . . 245 E5
Colville Cty Prim Sch CB1 65 F5
Colville Rd CB1. . . . . 65 F5
Colwyn Ave PE1. . . . . 198 E6
Colwyn Cl CB4. . . . . 83 D5
COMBERTON. 85 D2
Comberton Rd
Barton CB23. . . . . 62 F5
Little Eversden CB23. . . . . . 46 C8
Toft CB23. . . . . 61 B6
Comberton Village Coll
CB23. . . . . 62 A4
Comet Rd PE13. . . . . 143 A8
Comet Way
Mildenhall IP28. . . . . 239 B5
St Ives PE27. . . . . 144 A7
Comfrey Ct CB1. . . . . 66 A5
Commerce Rd PE2. . . . . . . 185 C5
COMMERCIAL END. 108 E3
Commercial End CB25. . . . 108 B3
Commercial Rd PE15. . . . . 243 C7
Common Acre La CB6. . . . 225 D6
Common Dro
Southery PE38. . . . . 226 E8
[2] Whittlesey PE7. . . . . 189 C8
Wimblington PE15. . . . . . . 223 C6
Common Gate Dro CB7. . . 212 E5
Common La
Ashwell SG7. . . . . 2 B6
Babraham CB22. . . . . 50 D8
Hemingford Abbots PE28. . 142 F3
Sawston CB22. . . . . 32 D7
Common Rd
Parson Drove PE12. . . . . . . 233 F7
Weston Colville CB21. . . . . 54 E4
West Wratting CB21. . . . . . 54 E2
Whittlesey PE7. . . . . 189 C8
Witchford CB6. . . . . 217 B8
Commons Dr PE7. . . . . 181 D8
Commons Rd PE7. . . . . 189 C8
Common The CB21. . . . . . . 53 F4
Compton Fields CB7. . . . . 240 E7
Conder Cl CB24. . . . . 105 C3
Coneygear Ct PE29. . . . . . 141 C7
Coneygear Rd PE29. . . . . . 141 E8
Coneygree Rd PE2. . . . . . . 187 D6
Coneywood Rd PE15. . . . . 223 A7

Conference Way PE13. . . . 245 C8
Conifers The PE2. . . . . 185 F6
Coningsby Rd PE3. . . . . . . 204 A2
CONINGTON
Fenstanton. 121 C1
Sawtry. 168 C8
Conington La PE7. . . . . 168 C8
Conington Rd CB3. . . . . . . 121 B3
Coniston Cl PE29. . . . . 141 B6
Coniston Rd
Cambridge CB1. . . . . 65 B6
Peterborough PE4. . . . . 204 E3
Conley Cl PE26. . . . . 172 B7
Connaught Rd CB9. . . . . 23 E7
Connor's Cl SG8. . . . . 10 F4
Conquest Dro PE7. . . . . . . 187 D1
Constable Ave [4] PE19. . . 74 D5
Constable Cl PE7. . . . . 190 A8
Constable Cres PE7. . . . . . 190 A8
Constable Rd
[1] Haverhill CB9. . . . . 38 D1
St Ives PE27. . . . . 144 A7
Constables Leys PE28. . . . 113 F5
Consul Ct [8] CB4. . . . . 83 E7
Control Tower Mus* SG8. . 12 B8
Convent Dr CB25. . . . . 105 F8
Conway Ave PE4. . . . . 204 C2
Conway Cl
[3] Cambridge CB1. . . . . . . 65 F6
Haverhill CB9. . . . . 23 D8
March PE15. . . . . 243 B3
Conway Pl [4] PE19. . . . . . . 74 F2
Conworth CF PE1. . . . . 198 D5
Cook Cl CB4. . . . . 84 B6
Cook Close Rd PE7. . . . . . . 181 D6
Cook Dr PE19. . . . . 74 E2
Cook's Dro
Beck Row, Holywell Row &
Kenny Hill IP28. . . . . . . 213 B8
Earith PE28. . . . . 208 E6
Cook's Gn PE15. . . . . 222 F5
Cook's Hole PE6. . . . . 193 C4
Cooks La PE28. . . . . 168 D5
Cookson Cl PE7. . . . . 181 D4
Coolidge Gdns CB24. . . . . 125 F4
Coombelands SG8. . . . . 13 E1
Coombelands Rd [8] SG8. . . 5 E8
Coombe Rd SG8. . . . . 4 A1
Cooper Rd CB23. . . . . 79 B2
Cooper's Cl CB8. . . . . 93 A6
Cooper's Cl CB8. . . . . 90 A1
Cooper Thornhill Rd [1]
PE7. . . . . 175 F7
Cootes La CB24. . . . . 121 E5
Cootes Mdw PE27. . . . . . . 144 B3
Copalder Cnr PE15. . . . . . . 222 B6
Copeland
Longthorpe PE3. . . . . 196 F2
Peterborough PE3. . . . . 197 A3
Copel Cl CB23. . . . . 80 B1
Copellis Cl CB9. . . . . 39 A2
Copes Cl PE19. . . . . 117 B4
Cophall Dro CB6. . . . . 217 E7
Copland Rd CB10. . . . . 17 F3
Coploe Rise CB10. . . . . 18 A3
Copperbeech Cl PE27. . . . 144 A5
Copper Beech Way PE7. . . 187 B7
Copperfields SG8. . . . . 5 B6
Copperfield Way CB25. . . . 130 C1
Coppice Ave CB22. . . . . 49 B6
Coppice Dr CB23. . . . . 79 A4
Coppice The
Histon CB24. . . . . 104 C1
Littleport CB6. . . . . 242 C1
Coppingford Cl PE12. . . . . 187 D6
Coppins Cl PE28. . . . . 168 A4
Coppins Ct PE14. . . . . 245 E2
Copse The PE29. . . . . 140 F5
Copsewood PE4. . . . . 204 C4
Copy Hill CB9. . . . . 23 E3
Coral Park Trading Est
CB8. 84 B2
Corbett St CB24. . . . . 125 E4
Cordell Cl PE27. . . . . 143 E6
Cordon St PE11. . . . . 245 C4
Coree Cl CB2. . . . . 65 A5
Corfe Ave PE4. . . . . 204 C2
Corfe Cl [1] PE19. . . . . 74 F2
Cormas Cl [5] SG8. . . . . 5 E8
Corner Cl CB7. . . . . 219 B5
CORNER LODGE. 227 F2
Corn Exchange St CB2. . . . 246 A2
Cornfield La CB24. . . . . 242 C4
Cornfields [1] PE15. . . . . . . 222 F5
Cornish Cl CB21. . . . . 37 A3
Corn Mill PE15. . . . . 243 C3
Cornmills Rd CB7. . . . . 212 D2
Cornstall Bldgs [3] PE9. . . 247 F6
Cornwall Cl PE19. . . . . 74 B4
Cornwallis Dr PE19. . . . . . . 74 A3
Cornwallis Rd CB9. . . . . 23 F6
Cornwall Rd
[8] Stamford PE9. . . . . 244 B6
Wyton Airfield PE28. . . . . . 143 A8
Corona Rd CB4. . . . . 83 E4
Coronation Ave
[3] Crowland PE6. . . . . 232 B8
Huntingdon PE29. . . . . 141 E5
Parson Drove PE12. . . . . . . 234 A7
Royston SG8. . . . . 5 C5
[9] Somersham PE28. . . . . 215 C1
Warboys PE28. . . . . 164 F6
Whittlesey PE7. . . . . 189 F7
Coronation Cl
March PE15. . . . . 243 C2
Waterbeach CB25. . . . . 106 A7
Coronation Mews [2] CB2. 64 F2
Coronation St CB2. . . . . . . 246 B1

Corporation Bank PE6. . . . 207 F7
Corporation Rd PE13. . . . . 245 D3
Corpus Christi Coll CB2. . . 246 A2
Corpus Christi La PE29. . . 141 E1
Corrie Rd CB1. . . . . 65 B7
Corsican Pine Cl CB8. . . . . 110 F5
Corunna Cl [7] PE19. . . . . . 74 C5
Corvus Cl SG8. . . . . 13 E6
Cosgrove Cl PE3. . . . . 197 C6
Cosin Ct CB1. . . . . 246 A1
Cossington Cl CB24. . . . . . 125 D2
Cotes The CB7. . . . . 211 F6
COTON. 82 B2
Coton CE Prim Sch CB23. . 82 B2
Coton Rd CB3. . . . . 63 E5
Cotswold Cl
March PE15. . . . . 243 E4
Peterborough PE4. . . . . 204 E1
COTTENHAM. 125 C4
Cottenham Cl [6] CB24. . . 208 D1
Cottenham Prim Sch
CB24. . . . . 125 D4
Cottenham Rd
Histon CB24. . . . . 104 B5
Landbeach CB24. . . . . 126 B1
Cottenham Village Coll
CB24. . . . . 125 E3
Cottesmore Cl PE3. . . . . . . 197 C4
Cotton Cl
Conington PE7. . . . . 168 C8
[5] March PE15. . . . . 168 C2
Cotton Ct [1] PE29. . . . . . . 141 F7
Cotton End PE3. . . . . 197 A4
Cotton End Rd CB8. . . . . . . 110 C8
Cotton La PE19. . . . . 97 C7
Cottons Cnr PE14. . . . . 229 D6
Cotton's Field CB23. . . . . . 102 B1
Cottons Head PE14. . . . . . 236 E3
COTTONS THE. 236 E3
Cottons The PE14. . . . . 110 F5
Cottrell's La CB23. . . . . 100 B4
Coulson Cl CB24. . . . . 105 C2
Coulson Way PE28. . . . . . . 150 F4
Council Rd [4] PE13. . . . . . 245 E6
Council St PE1. . . . . 197 D8
Countess Cl PE19. . . . . 74 B3
County Rd
Hampton Vale PE7. . . . . . . 181 C8
March PE15. . . . . 243 D6
Coupals Cl CB9. . . . . 24 D7
Coupals Prim Sch CB9. . . . 24 D7
Coupals Rd CB9. . . . . 24 E6
Courier Cl IP28. . . . . 239 B6
Courtland Ave CB1. . . . . . . 65 C5
Courtney Way CB4. . . . . 83 E4
Courtyards CB22. . . . . 48 F3
Courtyard Way CB24. . . . . 125 E5
Cousins Cl PE15. . . . . 243 C4
Covehite Ct [6] CB9. . . . . . 23 E6
COVENEY. 217 C5
Covent Gdn
Cambridge CB1. . . . . 246 C1
[12] Huntingdon PE29. . . . 209 A1
Covent Gdns CB24. . . . . . . 209 A1
Coventry Cl PE4. . . . . 204 B3
Covert Cl CB22. . . . . 39 A1
Covert The
[1] Comberton CB23. . . . . 62 D6
Peterborough PE3. . . . . 197 B1
COVINGTON. 135 D2
Cowbridge Hall Dro CB6. 218 B6
Cow Brook La CB23. . . . . . . 99 A3
Cow Brook Pl [2] CB23. . . . 99 A3
Cowdell End PE28. . . . . . . 100 B4
Cowgate PE1. . . . . 197 F2
Cow & Hare Pas PE27. . . . 144 A3
Cow La
Fulbourn CB21. . . . . 66 E5
Godmanchester PE29. . . . . 142 C2
Great Chesterford CB10. . . 19 A4
Rampton CB24. . . . . 124 F6
Cowley Cl PE28. . . . . 115 D3
Cowley Pk CB4. . . . . 84 B7
Cowley Rd CB4. . . . . 84 C7
COWLINGE. 73 D1
Cowlinge Cnr CB88. . . . . . . 73 D8
Cowper Rd
Cambridge CB1. . . . . 65 B6
Huntingdon PE29. . . . . 141 D5
Peterborough PE1. . . . . 197 E8
Cowpers Ct [4] PE19. . . . . . 74 D6
Cow & Sheep Dro IP28. . . 213 C2
Cowslip Cl SG8. . . . . 5 F5
Cowslip Dr CB6. . . . . 211 A7
Cowslip Pl PE15. . . . . 243 E5
Cow Way PE7. . . . . 190 D8
Coxons Cl PE29. . . . . 141 E5
Coxs Cl CB21. . . . . 23 C7
Cox's Cl CB22. . . . . 49 C4
Cox's Dro CB21. . . . . 66 F6
Cox's End [15] CB24. . . . . 208 D1
Cox's La
Chatteris PE16. . . . . 241 E6
Wisbech PE13. . . . . 245 A3
Crabapple Cl PE28. . . . . . . 168 B3
Crabapple Gdns PE13. . . . 185 D6
Crab Apple Way SG19. . . . . 41 C5
Crabbe Field CB23. . . . . . . 102 C3
Crabtree PE4. . . . . 205 B1
Crabtree Croft CB21. . . . . . 35 B3
Crafts Way CB23. . . . . 102 C3
Craft Way SG8. . . . . 11 B2
Craig St PE1. . . . . 197 F3
Craister Ct CB4. . . . . 83 E7
Cramswell Cl CB21. . . . . . . 23 E6

Cra

Crandal Way CB22 . . . . .49 A4
Crane Ave PE7 . . . . .181 F6
Crane Cl **3** PE28 . . . . 208 C8
Cranemore PE4 . . . . .204 A4
Crane's La CB23 . . . . .61 A2
Crane St PE28 . . . . .140 C3
Cranfield Pl **2** PE28 . . . 208 C8
Cranfield Way
  Brampton PE28 . . . . .140 D2
  Buckden PE19 . . . . .117 A3
Cranford Dr PE3 . . . . .197 C4
Cranleigh Cl CB2 . . . . .64 D1
Cranmer Rd CB3 . . . . .83 B1
Cranmore Dro PE6 . . . . .206 D8
Cranny The PE19 . . . . .117 F2
Cranwells Way **4** CB4 . . . .83 B7
Cratherne Way CB4 . . . . .83 F7
Crathern Way CB4 . . . . .83 F7
Crauden Gdns CB7 . . . . .240 E5
Craven Cl CB2 . . . . .64 D2
Craven Ct CB8 . . . . .110 F7
Craven Way CB8 . . . . .110 E6
Crawford Cl **11** CB4 . . . . . .83 E8
Crawford Gdns **2** PE6 . . . 232 C8
CRAWLEY END 8 D5
Crawley End SG8 . . . . .8 D4
Crawthorne Rd PE1 . . . . .198 A3
Crawthorne St **11** PE1 . . . .198 B3
Crease Dro PE6 . . . . .232 B8
Crease Rd
  Conington PE28 . . . . .168 F5
  Sawtry PE28 . . . . .169 B6
Crecy Ct PE19 . . . . .74 C5
Creek Fen PE15 . . . . .228 D5
Creek Rd PE15 . . . . .243 D4
Crescent Cl PE7 . . . . .190 A7
Crescent Rd
  Histon CB24 . . . . .104 C1
  Whittlesey PE7 . . . . .189 F7
Crescent The
  Cambridge CB3 . . . . .83 B3
  Dullingham CB8 . . . . .89 C1
  Eaton Socon PE19 . . . . .74 C3
  Eye PE6 . . . . .232 A1
  Impington CB24 . . . . .104 C1
  Littleport CB6 . . . . .242 C3
  Peterborough PE2 . . . . .186 E7
  4 Soham CB7 . . . . .212 B3
  St Ives PE27 . . . . .144 A5
  St Neots PE19 . . . . .74 F6
  Wicken CB7 . . . . .211 E1
  Wisbech PE13 . . . . .245 C4
Cressbrook Dr CB23 . . . . .79 C3
Cressener Terr **3** PE19 . . . .74 F5
Cresset The* PE3 . . . . .197 A6
Cresswells La CB7 . . . . .240 E4
Crester Dr **3** PE4 . . . . .204 C3
Criccieth Way PE19 . . . . .74 F1
Cricketers Cl PE15 . . . . .243 C3
Cricketers Way
  3 Benwick PE15 . . . . .222 A5
  Chatteris PE16 . . . . .241 D3
  Wisbech PE13 . . . . .245 A6
Cricketfield La PE26 . . . . . . .172 A6
Cricket Field Rd CB8 . . . . . . .111 B2
Cricket Sch CB1 . . . . .246 C1
Crick's Rd IP20 . . . . .213 D6
Cripple Sidings La PE2 . . .187 A8
Crispin Cl
  Haverhill CB9 . . . . .23 D7
  11 Impington CB4 . . . . . . .83 D7
Crispin Pl CB1 . . . . .246 C3
Crockfords Rd CB8 . . . . .111 A2
Crocus Gr PE1 . . . . .198 A8
Crocus Way PE7 . . . . .181 F6
Croft Cl
  Brampton PE28 . . . . .140 D2
  Histon CB24 . . . . .104 B5
Crofters The CB8 . . . . .210 F6
Croftfield Rd PE29 . . . . .141 F1
Croftgate CB3 . . . . .64 A7
Croft Gdns CB3 . . . . .64 C7
Croft La
  Haverhill CB9 . . . . .24 B6
  Oakington/Longstanton
   CB24 . . . . .103 B6
Croft Park Rd CB6 . . . . .242 D3
Croft Pl IP28 . . . . .239 C4
Croft Rd
  Isleham CB7 . . . . .213 A5
  Newmarket CB8 . . . . .110 E5
  Outwell PE14 . . . . .229 D7
Crofts The PE19 . . . . .95 F1
Croft The
  Christchurch PE14 . . . . . . .229 D3
  Fulbourn CB21 . . . . .66 E5
  Stamford PE9 . . . . .244 D5
Croft Way PE7 . . . . .186 C2
Croftwood CB6 . . . . .216 D1
Crome Ditch Cl CB3 . . . . .64 A4
Cromwell Cl
  2 Northborough PE6 . . . .231 F7
  Ramsey PE26 . . . . .171 F6
Cromwell Com Coll
  PE16 . . . . .241 C4
Cromwell Ct **4** PE19 . . . . . .74 F3
Cromwell House* PE29 . . .141 D5
Cromwell Mews PE6 . . . . . . .231 C4
Cromwell Mus* PE29 . . . .141 D4
Cromwell Park Prim Sch
  PE29 . . . . .141 A5
Cromwell Pk CB24 . . . . .208 E1
Cromwell Pl PE27 . . . . .144 B3
Cromwell Rd
  Cambridge CB1 . . . . .84 B1

Cromwell Rd continued
  Ely CB6 . . . . .240 C4
  March PE15 . . . . .243 D6
  Peterborough PE1 . . . . .197 F4
  St Neots PE19 . . . . .74 F3
  11 Sutton CB6 . . . . .216 E1
  Wisbech PE13 . . . . .245 B3
Cromwell Sq PE29 . . . . .141 D5
Cromwell Terr PE27 . . . . . . .144 B3
Cromwell Way PE28 . . . . . . .168 B3
Cromwell Wlk PE29 . . . . . . .141 D5
Crooked Bank
  Begdale PE14 . . . . .235 F5
  Wisbech PE14 . . . . .235 D5
Croot Cl PE28 . . . . .140 B2
CROPLEY GROVE 92 D3
Cropston Rd PE1 . . . . .198 E7
Crosfield Ct CB4 . . . . .83 E7
Cross Bank CB7 . . . . .219 F8
Cross Bank Dro CB7 . . . . . . .211 C5
Crossberry Way PE6 . . . . . . .231 B4
Cross Cl CB9 . . . . .39 A1
Cross Dro
  Haddenham CB6 . . . . .209 E3
  Littleport CB7 . . . . .226 A1
  Southery PE38 . . . . .226 E7
  Stretham CB6 . . . . .210 F3
  Tydd St Giles PE13 . . . . . . .237 C5
  Warboys PE28 . . . . .215 C6
  Waterbeach CB25 . . . . .127 D4
  Whittlesey PE7 . . . . .190 F6
  Wilburton CB6 . . . . .210 C3
  Wistow PE28 . . . . .172 E1
Cross Farm Cl PE28 . . . . . . .120 C2
Cross Gn CB8 . . . . .70 F8
Crosshall Inf Sch PE19 . . . .74 C6
Crosshall Jun Sch PE19 . . .74 C6
Crosshall Rd PE19 . . . . .74 D6
Cross Hall Rd PE19 . . . . .74 D6
Cross Keys Ct CB24 . . . . . . .125 D3
Cross La
  Little Downham CB6 . . . . . .218 A6
  Melbourn SG8 . . . . .14 C6
  Wisbech PE13 . . . . .235 D6
Cross Lane Cl SG8 . . . . .45 E1
Cross Rd
  March PE15 . . . . .227 F2
  Sutton St Edmund PE12 . . . .237 A4
  Whittlesey PE7 . . . . .189 C7
Crossroad Cotts CB10 . . . . .17 E2
Cross St
  Cambridge CB1 . . . . .246 C1
  Covington PE28 . . . . .135 D2
  Farcet PE7 . . . . .187 D1
  Huntingdon PE29 . . . . .141 E5
  Peterborough PE1 . . . . .198 A2
Cross The PE28 . . . . .161 F6
Crossway Hand PE7 . . . . . . .189 B8
Crossways
  Barley SG8 . . . . .6 F1
  Linton CB21 . . . . .35 D2
Crossways Gdns CB2 . . . . . . .64 D2
Crow Dean CB23 . . . . .79 A3
CROW END 60 D7
Crowhill **6** PE29 . . . . .118 F8
Crow Hill La CB23 . . . . .79 B3
Crowhurst PE4 . . . . .204 C5
CROWLAND 207 A8
Crowland Rd
  Deeping St James PE6 . . . .207 A6
  Eye PE6 . . . . .232 A3
  Haverhill CB9 . . . . .23 F8
  Newborough PE6 . . . . .232 A2
  Thorney PE6 . . . . .232 E5
Crowlands CB24 . . . . .125 D4
Crowland Way CB4 . . . . .83 F7
Crown Ave PE14 . . . . .229 D3
Crown Cl
  Hail Weston PE19 . . . . .95 A1
  March PE15 . . . . .243 C2
  Margery's Croft PE13 . . . . .238 B1
  St Ives PE27 . . . . .144 A4
  Warboys PE28 . . . . .164 F6
Crown Gdns
  Alconbury PE28 . . . . .150 E4
  Little Downham CB6 . . . . . .218 A6
Crown La **2** CB6 . . . . .242 D4
Crown Lakes Ctry Pk*
  PE7 . . . . .187 B2
Crown Mews PE26 . . . . .172 B7
Crown Pl PE27 . . . . .144 A3
Crown Rd PE14 . . . . .229 D3
Crown St
  Peterborough PE1 . . . . .197 E7
  Stamford PE9 . . . . .244 B5
  St Ives PE27 . . . . .144 A3
Crown Wlk
  Newmarket CB8 . . . . .111 A4
  St Ives PE27 . . . . .144 A3
Crowson Cres **6** PE6 . . . .231 F7
Crow Spinney La PE28 . . .115 D2
Crowthorne Cl CB1 . . . . .65 F6
Crow Tree St SG19 . . . . .58 D4
CROXTON 76 F4
Croxton Gdns PE28 . . . . . . .136 D6
CROYDON 26 E4
Croydon Hill SG8 . . . . .26 E8
Croydon Rd
  Arrington SG8 . . . . .44 C1
  Croydon SG8 . . . . .27 B8
Croyland Rd PE4 . . . . .204 D1
Crummock Wr PE29 . . . . . . .141 C5
Crunch Croft CB9 . . . . .24 E5
Crystal Dr PE2 . . . . .186 D8
Cubitt Way PE2 . . . . .187 A8
Cuckoo La
  Lolworth CB23 . . . . .101 F5
  Rampton CB24 . . . . .124 E5

Culley Ct PE2 . . . . .185 B2
Culloden Cl PE19 . . . . .74 C5
Cumberland Cl PE28 . . . . . .143 A8
Cumberland Way **3** PE19 . .74 F1
Cundell Dr CB23 . . . . .125 E4
Cunningham Cl CB4 . . . . .83 E6
Cunningham Rd PE2 . . . . . . .186 E8
Cunningham Way PE19 . . . .74 A2
Curf PE16 . . . . .222 F3
Curf Fen Dro PE16 . . . . .222 E4
Curlew Ave PE16 . . . . .241 C5
Curlew Cl PE7 . . . . .189 F8
Curlew Cres **6** SG6 . . . . . . .5 E8
Curlew Gr PE2 . . . . .187 D2
Curlew Pl **2** PE19 . . . . .75 B6
Curringtons Cl CB24 . . . . . .125 E4
Cutter Ferry Cl CB4 . . . . .84 A3
Cutter Ferry La CB4 . . . . . . .246 C4
Cygnet Dr PE16 . . . . .241 C6
Cygnet Pk PE7 . . . . .186 E3
Cygnet Rd PE7 . . . . .186 E3
Cypress Cl
  6 Doddington PE15 . . . . .223 A6
  Peterborough PE3 . . . . .197 A2
Cyprus Rd CB1 . . . . .65 C7

D

Dacre Gn SG8 . . . . .5 F6
Daffodil Gr PE2 . . . . .187 C7
Dagless Way PE15 . . . . .243 D7
Daimler Ave PE7 . . . . .181 E6
Daintree Ct PE27 . . . . .208 A3
Daintree Rd PE26 . . . . .220 D4
Daintrees Rd CB24 . . . . .121 F6
Daintree Way PE28 . . . . . . .143 D1
Dairy Dro
  Littleport CB6 . . . . .225 C6
  Thorney PE6 . . . . .233 E2
Daisy Cl CB4 . . . . .83 D7
Dakota Rd IP28 . . . . .213 E8
Dalby Ct PE1 . . . . .198 C8
Dale Cl PE2 . . . . .185 F5
Dalegarth CB4 . . . . .83 F4
Dales Way PE27 . . . . .208 A3
Dale The CB24 . . . . .142 A4
Dale Way CB22 . . . . .32 F8
DALHAM 92 E8
Dalham Rd
  Ashley CB8 . . . . .92 B7
  Moulton CB8 . . . . .112 F4
Dalton Sq CB4 . . . . .84 B5
Dalton Way CB6 . . . . .240 D6
Dam Bank Dro CB6 . . . . .209 C4
Damms Pastures CB23 . . . .80 D2
Damson Way CB23 . . . . .79 A3
Dane Dr CB3 . . . . .83 A1
Dane Hill CB8 . . . . .133 E5
Dane Hill Rd CB8 . . . . .133 D5
Danesbury Cl CB1 . . . . .84 C1
Danes Cl PE1 . . . . .198 C4
Daniel Ct PE9 . . . . .244 C4
Danish Ct PE4 . . . . .204 A4
Daphmoir Cl CB22 . . . . .29 F8
Dapple Gdns PE7 . . . . .189 D8
Darford PE28 . . . . .208 E6
Darley Cl PE8 . . . . .230 C1
Darrington Cl **11** PE19 . . . .74 B3
Dart Cl PE27 . . . . .144 B6
Dartford Rd PE15 . . . . .243 C4
Darthill Rd PE15 . . . . .243 D5
Dartmoor Dr PE29 . . . . .141 A4
Darwin Cl
  Ely CB6 . . . . .240 A4
  Mildenhall IP28 . . . . .239 C6
  3 Stamford PE9 . . . . .244 A7
Darwin Coll CB3 . . . . .246 A1
Darwin Dr CB4 . . . . .83 D5
Darwin Pl CB8 . . . . .111 B1
Darwood Ct PE27 . . . . .144 B3
Daules Rd PE28 . . . . .140 E1
Davey Cl CB24 . . . . .104 C3
Davey Cres CB22 . . . . .49 A6
David Bull Way CB24 . . . . . .105 D3
David Chalmers Cl PE2 . .186 F8
David's Cl PE14 . . . . .204 B6
David's La PE4 . . . . .204 B6
David St **5** CB1 . . . . .65 A8
Davie La PE7 . . . . .201 A1
Da Vinci Cl PE7 . . . . .144 A7
Davis Rd CB1 . . . . .96 A2
Davison Rd CB6 . . . . .240 E8
Davy Rd CB1 . . . . .65 B7
Daw's Cl **5** CB1 . . . . .65 F6
Daw's Dro PE7 . . . . .220 D8
Dawson Cl PE4 . . . . .205 C8
Daymond St PE1 . . . . .186 D7
Days Cl SG8 . . . . .5 C5
Day's Lode Rd PE15 . . . . . . .224 C7
Days Mdw CB24 . . . . .103 C6
Deaconscroft PE3 . . . . .197 B5
Deacons La CB7 . . . . .240 D5
Deacon St PE1 . . . . .197 F3
Deal Cl PE29 . . . . .141 B8
Deal Gr CB22 . . . . .32 F8
Dean Dr CB1 . . . . .65 B4
Dean Dro PE16 . . . . .215 F6
Dean Peacock Ct CB6 . . .240 F6
Dean Rd CB21 . . . . .21 B8
Deans Cl CB9 . . . . .39 A1
Dean's Ct PE1 . . . . .198 A2
Debden CB6 . . . . .185 E4
Debdale Ct PE7 . . . . .189 F5
Debden Gn CB25 . . . . .240 B4
De Bec Cl PE1 . . . . .198 C3

De Beche Cl CB23 . . . . .99 B3
Deben Ave PE27 . . . . .144 A7
Deben Cl PE15 . . . . .243 B5
Deben Rd CB9 . . . . .24 B8
Decoy Rd
  Borough Fen PE6 . . . . .207 A3
  Gorefield PE13 . . . . .237 D2
Deene Ct PE3 . . . . .197 C5
DEEPING GATE 231 E8
Deeping Lakes Nature
  Reserve* PE6 . . . . .206 D5
Deeping Rd PE6 . . . . .206 B3
DEEPING ST JAMES 206 A7
Deeping St James Com Prim
  Sch **10** PE6 . . . . .231 F8
Deeping St James Rd
  PE6 . . . . .231 E7
Deepings Sch The **17**
  PE6 . . . . .231 C7
Deerfield Rd PE15 . . . . .243 E4
Deerhurst Way **13** PE6 . .232 A1
Deerleap PE3 . . . . .197 A5
Deerpark Rd PE28 . . . . .168 A4
Deer Valley Rd **11** PE2 . .186 E8
De Freville Ave CB4 . . . . . . .246 C4
De Freville Rd CB22 . . . . .49 A6
Degas Dr PE27 . . . . .144 A7
De Havilland Ct **4** IP28 . .239 B5
De Havilland Rd PE13 . . . . .245 C6
De-Havilland Rd PE13 . . . . .245 C6
Deighton Cl PE27 . . . . .144 B5
De La Haye Cl CB23 . . . . .99 B3
Delamere Cl
  Little Wilbraham CB8 . . . . . .68 F6
  Peterborough PE1 . . . . .198 C5
Delapre Ct **9** PE6 . . . . . . .232 A1
De La Warre Way CB23 . . . . .79 B4
Delbrig Dro CB7 . . . . .212 C5
De Lisle Cl CB23 . . . . .99 B3
Dells Cl PE28 . . . . .166 D2
Dell The
  Peterborough PE2 . . . . .186 E7
  Royston SG8 . . . . .5 C5
Delph PE7 . . . . .189 D7
Delph Ct PE2 . . . . .187 F6
Delph Dro IP28 . . . . .212 F8
Delph St PE7 . . . . .189 D7
Delta La PE28 . . . . .151 E3
Delves Way PE7 . . . . .186 D2
Delve Terr PE16 . . . . .241 E5
Dendys PE28 . . . . .143 D1
Dengaine Cl CB23 . . . . .99 B2
Denham Rd CB8 . . . . .92 E8
Denham Wlk **11** PE3 . . . .197 C4
Denis Dr PE2 . . . . .186 A4
Denmark Dr PE2 . . . . .186 A4
Denmark Rd CB24 . . . . .125 E3
Dennis Gn SG19 . . . . .41 C4
Dennis Rd CB5 . . . . .84 F4
Dennis Wilson Ct CB2 . . . . .64 D4
Denny Cl **9** CB24 . . . . .208 D1
DENNY END 105 F8
Denny End Rd CB25 . . . . . . .105 F8
Denson Cl CB25 . . . . .106 A8
DENTON 175 E4
Denton Rd
  Glatton PE28 . . . . .175 E1
  Peterborough PE2 . . . . .187 C6
Dentons Chase PE26 . . . . .220 E4
Depot Rd CB8 . . . . .110 E6
Deptford Cl PE15 . . . . .243 B5
Derby Dr PE1 . . . . .198 C6
Derby Rd CB1 . . . . .65 B6
Derby St CB3 . . . . .64 C7
Derby Way CB8 . . . . .110 D5
Derwent Cl
  Cambridge CB1 . . . . .65 D5
  Huntingdon PE29 . . . . .141 B5
  St Ives PE27 . . . . .144 B6
Derwent Dr PE4 . . . . .204 B8
Derwood Gr PE4 . . . . .204 B5
Desborough Ave PE2 . . . . .187 D5
Desborough Rd PE29 . . . . .142 A6
Desmond Ave CB1 . . . . .65 F6
Devana Cl PE29 . . . . .118 F8
De Vere Cl PE28 . . . . .143 B1
Devils Pl PE16 . . . . .243 D4
Devil's Dyke Nature
  Reserve* CB25 . . . . .109 B5
Devoke Cl PE29 . . . . .141 B6
Devon Cl PE27 . . . . .144 A8
Devonshire Cl PE28 . . . . . . .168 B3
Devonshire Rd CB1 . . . . .65 A8
Dewpond Cl **4** PE19 . . . . . .75 A6
Dexter Cl **10** PE15 . . . . . . .223 A5
Dexter La CB6 . . . . .242 C3
Dexter Way PE28 . . . . .178 B3
Dial Cl PE19 . . . . .95 F2
Diamond Cl CB24 . . . . .64 E5
Diana Cl PE7 . . . . .190 A6
Dickasons SG8 . . . . .14 D7
Dickens St PE1 . . . . .198 B3
Dickerson Cl **1** SG19 . . . . .41 D6
DIDDINGTON 96 A8
Digby Ct **8** PE19 . . . . .74 A1
Dillestone Ct CB9 . . . . .24 E5
DILLINGTON 94 C7
Dimmock's Cote CB6 . . . .211 B3
Dimmock's Cote Rd CB7 . .211 B3
Dingley Ct PE3 . . . . .197 C5
Dip The CB8 . . . . .111 D2
Discovery Way CB4 . . . . .84 C6
Ditchburn Pl
  8 Cambridge CB1 . . . . . . .65 A8
  Cambridge CB1 . . . . .84 A1
Ditchfield CB25 . . . . .108 D8

Ditchfields **2** PE28 . . . . . .215 C1
Ditton Cl CB8 . . . . .111 A1
Ditton Fields CB5 . . . . .84 C3
Ditton Gn CB8 . . . . .90 D1
DITTON GREEN 90 E1
Ditton La CB5 . . . . .84 E4
Ditton Lodge Fst Sch
  CB8 . . . . .111 B2
Ditton Wlk CB5 . . . . .84 C4
Dixies Cl SG7 . . . . .2 D3
Dixon's Dro PE14 . . . . .238 F5
Dixons Rd **11** PE2 . . . . . . .231 E8
Dobson Wlk **11** PE15 . . . .223 B7
Dock Bsns Pk The CB7 . . .240 D2
Dockings La CB7 . . . . .213 A5
Dock La CB25 . . . . .106 A2
Dock Rd PE16 . . . . .241 C6
Dock The CB7 . . . . .240 D2
Doctor's Cl CB24 . . . . .104 D3
Docwra Rd CB23 . . . . .99 A3
Docwra's Cl SG8 . . . . .29 D5
DODDINGTON 223 A6
Doddington Com Hospl
  PE15 . . . . .222 F6
Doddington Dr PE3 . . . . . . .197 B2
Doddington Rd
  Benwick PE15 . . . . .222 A5
  Chatteris PE16 . . . . .241 A8
  Doddington/Wimblington
   PE15 . . . . .223 B6
Dodds Mead CB23 . . . . .47 A5
Dodford La CB3 . . . . .103 E2
Dogget La CB21 . . . . .66 F4
Doggett Rd CB1 . . . . .65 E6
Dog Kennel La SG8 . . . . .5 D6
DOGSTHORPE 198 C7
Dogsthorpe Gr PE1 . . . . . . .198 A5
Dogsthorpe Jun & Inf Sch
  PE1 . . . . .198 B7
Dogsthorpe Rd PE1 . . . . . . .198 A5
Dogsthorpe Star Pit & Little
  Wood Nature Reserve*
  PE6 . . . . .205 E2
Doles The **3** CB24 . . . . . . .208 D1
Dole The CB24 . . . . .104 C3
Dolls Cl CB21 . . . . .53 C1
Dolphin Cl
  Cambridge CB1 . . . . .66 A7
  Linton CB21 . . . . .35 D2
Dolphin La
  11 Ely CB7 . . . . .240 D4
  Melbourn SG8 . . . . .14 B6
Dolphins Way SG19 . . . . .41 D6
Dolphin Way CB22 . . . . .49 B4
Dome Leisure Ctr IP28 . . .239 E4
Donaldson Dr PE4 . . . . .204 F2
Donegal **7** CB1 . . . . .84 A2
Donegal Cl PE4 . . . . .204 D2
Donne Cl SG8 . . . . .5 C8
Donnington Pk PE13 . . . . . .238 A1
Dorchester Cres **3** PE1 . .198 D7
Dorchester Way PE13 . . . . .143 B7
Doris St CB8 . . . . .110 F3
Dorling Way PE28 . . . . .140 B3
Dorral Dean CB23 . . . . .80 B1
Dorvis La CB10 . . . . .21 B1
Double Bank La PE28 . . . . .161 B7
Doughty St PE1 . . . . .198 B2
Douglas House Hospl CB2 .64 E5
Douglas Rd **3** PE6 . . . . . . .231 E8
Douglas Way PE29 . . . . .79 B3
Doug Smith Cl CB8 . . . . .110 F6
Dove Cl PE28 . . . . .121 C5
Dovecote Cl
  Peterborough PE1 . . . . .198 A2
  Yarwell PE8 . . . . .183 A8
Dove Cote Cl CB24 . . . . .99 A5
Dovecote La PE7 . . . . .181 C5
Dovecote Rd
  Great Paxton PE19 . . . . . . .96 D3
  Upwell PE14 . . . . .229 D7
Dovehouse Cl
  Ely CB7 . . . . .240 D3
  Fowlmere SG8 . . . . .15 E8
  Godmanchester PE29 . . . . .142 A1
  St Neots PE19 . . . . .74 F6
Dove House Rd CB9 . . . . . . .24 A8
Dovehouse Wood PE28 . .162 B1
Dover Cl PE29 . . . . .141 E8
Dover Rd PE4 . . . . .204 C2
Dover St **2** CB1 . . . . .246 C2
Dove Willow PE6 . . . . .207 D6
Dovey Cl PE27 . . . . .144 B6
Dowding Way CB4 . . . . .83 D6
Dowgate Rd **3** PE13 . . . . .245 A7
Downe Cl CB23 . . . . .99 A2
DOWN END 212 D2
Down Gate PE3 . . . . .197 A1
Downham Feoffees Prim Sch
  CB6 . . . . .218 A7
DOWNHAM HYTHE 217 D6
Downham Dro
  CB6 . . . . .217 D6
Downham Rd
  Ely CB6 . . . . .240 B7
  Outwell PE14 . . . . .236 F2
Downham's La CB4 . . . . . . .84 A6
Downing Cl
  Bottisham CB25 . . . . .86 E6
  Mildenhall IP28 . . . . .239 D5
  Newmarket CB8 . . . . .111 A1
Downing Coll CB2 . . . . .246 B1
Downing Cres PE9 . . . . .244 B3
Downing Cl CB25 . . . . .108 A1
Downing Pl CB22 . . . . .246 B2
Downing St CB23 . . . . .246 B2
Downlands SG8 . . . . .5 D8
Downs Cres CB9 . . . . .23 F8

Downs Pl CB9 . . . . 23 F8
Downton Dr CB9 . . . . . . 23 E8
Dowsdale Bank PE6 . . . . 233 A8
Dragon Fly Cl PE7 . . . . 186 C2
Dragoon Dr **4** PE15 . . . 243 D2
Drain Rd PE6 . . . . 205 A7
Drake Ave PE16 . . . . . . 241 C6
Drake Cl PE29 . . . . 141 F6
Drake Rd PE19 . . . . 74 B2
Drake Way CB24 . . . . . 104 C5
Draper's Cl PE18 . . . . . 178 C3
DRAPERS GREEN 23 B2
Drapers La CB9 . . . . . . 23 B2
Drapery Row **1** CB8 . . . 111 A3
Drayhorse Rd PE26 . . . . 172 A5
Drayton Cl CB1 . . . . . . 66 A5
Drayton Rd CB1 . . . . . . 66 A5
Drewels La PE19 . . . . . 56 D4
Driffield Way PE2 . . . . . 186 D8
Drift Ave PE9 . . . . 244 D7
Drift Gdns PE9 . . . . . . 244 D7
Drift Rd PE9 . . . . 244 C6
Drift The
  Elsworth CB23 . . . . . 100 B4
  Exning CB8 . . . . 110 A8
  Newmarket CB8 . . . . 111 B2
  Oakington/Longstanton
  CB24 . . . . 103 B5
  Sutton PE5 . . . . 194 F3
Drings Cl **2** CB24 . . . . 208 D1
Drinkwater Cl CB8 . . . . 110 E4
Drivers Ave PE29 . . . . . 141 E5
Drivers Cl **8** PE15 . . . 223 A6
Drive The
  Perry PE28 . . . . 115 D1
  Peterborough PE3 . . . 197 E2
  St Ives PE27 . . . . . . 143 E4
Drosier Rd CB1 . . . . . . 246 C1
Drove Gdns CB23 . . . . . 79 C3
Drove Rd SG19 . . . . . . 41 A6
Drovers Cl PE26 . . . . . 221 A4
Drove The
  Farcet PE26 . . . . . . 220 D7
  Witchford CB6 . . . . . 217 E1
Droveway The PE6 . . . . 199 B3
Druce Ave PE26 . . . . . 154 A1
Drummer St CB1 . . . . . 246 B2
Drury La
  Bluntisham/Colne PE28 208 D7
  Melbourn SG8 . . . . . 14 C6
  Wicken CB7 . . . . 211 F2
Drybread Rd PE7 . . . . . 189 F8
Dryden Cl PE27 . . . . . . 143 E6
Dryden Ct **7** PE19 . . . 75 A5
Dryden Rd PE1 . . . . . . 197 E7
DRY DRAYTON 102 C1
Dry Drayton CE Prim Sch
  CB23 . . . . 102 C1
Dry Drayton Rd
  Madingley CB23 . . . . 81 D7
  Oakington & Westwick
  CB24 . . . . 103 A4
Dry Leys PE2 . . . . 186 C6
Dubbs Knoll Rd SG8 . . . 10 F5
Duberly Cl PE28 . . . . . . 115 E2
Duchess Cl PE19 . . . . . 74 A3
Duchess Dr
  Newmarket CB8 . . . . 111 D2
  Woodditton CB8 . . . . 90 E8
Duck Dro CB7 . . . . 219 D5
DUCK END 97 F5
Duck End
  Girton CB3 . . . . 82 D8
  Godmanchester PE29 . 141 F1
Duck La
  Haddenham CB6 . . . . 210 A6
  St Neots PE19 . . . . . 74 F4
DUCKPUDDLE BUSH . . . 4 F2
Ducks La CB8 . . . . 110 C7
Duck St PE8 . . . . 178 D8
Duckworth Cl **2** PE7 . . 189 E7
Duddery Hill CB9 . . . . . 79 B1
Duddery Rd CB9 . . . . . . 24 A7
Duddington Gdns PE7 . . 189 D7
Duddle Dr CB24 . . . . . . 123 E3
Dudley Ave PE4 . . . . . . 204 C2
Dudley Rd CB5 . . . . . . 84 F4
Duke of Bedford Prim Sch
  PE6 . . . . 233 B3
Dukes Dr PE26 . . . . . . 221 C2
Dukes Mdw CB22 . . . . . 49 C5
Dukesmead PE4 . . . . . . 204 B2
Dukesmead Mobile Home Pk
  PE4 . . . . 204 B2
Dukes Rd PE19 . . . . . . 74 B4
Duke St
  Peterborough PE2 . . . 187 A7
  Wisbech PE13 . . . . . 245 D4
DULLINGHAM 70 D8
DULLINGHAM LEY 71 A5
Dullingham Rd
  Newmarket CB8 . . . . 110 F1
  Stetchworth CB8 . . . . 89 D3
  Woodditton CB8 . . . . 89 F7
Dullingham Sta CB8 . . . 89 B2
DULOE 73 C6
Duloe Rd PE19 . . . . . . 74 B5
Dunblane Dr PE2 . . . . . 185 D4
Duncan Way PE29 . . . . 141 F7
Duncock La CB23 . . . . . 100 B4
Duncombe's Rd PE7 . . . 191 F8
Dundee Cl CB4 . . . . . . 84 A5
Dundee Ct PE2 . . . . . . 185 C5
Dungate La CB21 . . . . . 52 B6
Dunholt Way PE28 . . . . 208 D6
DUNKIRK 224 F1
Dunkirk Dro PE28 . . . . 215 C4

Dunmowe Way CB21 . . . 66 E5
Dunnocks The CB24 . . . 125 D4
Dunsberry
  Marholm PE3 . . . . . . 203 F1
  Peterborough PE3 . . . 196 F8
Dunsbridge Turnpike SG8 29 F2
Dunsey Wood Cl CB9 . . . 38 E1
Dunsmore Cl CB5 . . . . . 84 E4
Dunstal Field CB24 . . . . 125 D2
Dunstall's Dro CB7 . . . . 218 E1
Dunstan St CB6 . . . . . . 240 B5
Dunster Dr CB9 . . . . . . 23 E8
Durham Cl PE28 . . . . . . 168 C2
Durham Rd PE1 . . . . . . 198 C3
Durham Way
  Newmarket CB8 . . . . 110 E5
  Wyton Airfield PE28 . . 143 B8
Durnford Way CB4 . . . . 83 E5
DUXFORD 17 D8
Duxford Aircraft Mus
  (Imperial War Mus at
  Duxford)* CB22 . . . . 31 F1
Duxford Airfield CB22 . . 17 A8
Duxford Camp CB22 . . . 31 F1
Duxford CE Com Prim Sch
  CB22 . . . . 32 D1
Duxford Rd
  Hinxton CB10 . . . . . . 18 A7
  Ickleton CB10 . . . . . 17 F5
  Whittlesford CB22 . . . 32 D4
Dwyer-Joyce Cl CB24 . . 104 B4
DYER'S GREEN 13 C8
Dykemoor Dro PE15 . . . 222 C4
Dykemoor Drove N PE15 222 E5
Dyson Cl
  Peterborough PE1 . . . 197 F3
  The Stukeleys PE29 . . 141 A5
Dyson's Dro CB25 . . . . 130 B5

E

Eachard Rd CB3 . . . . . . 83 B5
Eagle Ct PE19 . . . . 75 B7
Eagle La CB8 . . . . 89 D1
Eagle's La CB6 . . . . . . 218 A7
Eaglesthorpe PE1 . . . . . 197 E7
EAGLETHORPE 178 A4
Eagle Way PE19 . . . . . . 142 A8
Eames Gdns PE1 . . . . . 198 E6
Eardley Grange PE6 . . . 207 F6
EARITH 208 E6
Earith Fen Dro PE28 . . . 208 F7
Earith Prim Sch PE28 . . 208 E5
Earith Rd
  Bluntisham/Colne PE28 208 D7
  Willingham CB24 . . . . 209 A2
Earl Cl **1** PE14 . . . . . . 74 B4
Earle St **4** PE13 . . . . . 245 D4
Earls Cl PE2 . . . . 187 B6
Earls Hill Gdns SG8 . . . . 5 C6
Earl Spencer Ct PE2 . . . 186 B8
Earl St CB1 . . . . 246 B2
Earlswood PE2 . . . . 185 E5
Earning St PE29 . . . . . . 141 F1
Earth Cl PE2 . . . . 187 E5
Easby Rise PE6 . . . . . . 232 B2
Eastalls Cl **15** PE15 . . . 223 A5
Eastbourne Cl **2** PE16 . 241 C3
Eastbourne Rd PE16 . . . 241 C3
East Chadley La PE29 . . 141 F2
East Cl PE15 . . . . 243 B6
East Delph PE7 . . . . . . 189 E8
East Dr
  Caldecote CB23 . . . . 80 C1
  March PE15 . . . . 243 F4
Eastern Ave
  Haverhill CB9 . . . . . . 23 E8
  Peterborough PE1 . . . 198 C8
  1 Soham CB7 . . . . . 212 B4
Eastern Cl PE11 . . . . . . 198 D7
Eastern Ind Est PE1 . . . 198 E3
East Fen Comm CB7 . . . 212 C4
East Fen Dro PE7 . . . . . 212 D4
East Fen Rd CB7 . . . . . 213 B5
EASTFIELD 198 D4
Eastfield CB4 . . . . 84 A5
Eastfield Cty Inf Sch
  PE27 . . . . 144 A4
Eastfield Dr PE7 . . . . . . 189 F6
Eastfield Gr PE1 . . . . . . 198 B4
Eastfield Rd
  Peterborough PE1 . . . 198 C4
  Royston SG8 . . . . 5 E6
  1 Wisbech PE13 . . . 245 E7
Eastfields CB6 . . . . 242 C3
Eastfield Way PE14 . . . . 245 C6
EASTGATE 198 B2
Eastgate
  Great Chesterford CB10 18 D2
  15 Market Deeping PE6 231 F8
  Peterborough PE1 . . . 198 B2
  Whittlesey PE7 . . . . . 189 E7
Eastgate Mews PE7 . . . 189 E7
EAST HATLEY 43 A1
East Hatley SG19 . . . . . 43 A1
East Hertford St CB4 . . . 246 A4
Eastholm Cl PE1 . . . . . 198 C3
East La SG19 . . . . 41 C6
Eastleigh Rd PE1 . . . . . 198 C3
East Meadowgate PE14 . 236 C7
Eastmoor La PE15 . . . . 223 A5
East of England
  Showground* PE2 . . . 185 C4
East of England Way
  PE2 . . . . 185 B4
EASTON 138 C4

Easton Rd PE19 . . . . . . 114 C3
East Park St PE16 . . . . 241 C4
EAST PERRY 116 E3
East Perry PE28 . . . . . . 115 E2
East Rd
  Cambridge CB1 . . . . . 246 C2
  Isleham CB7 . . . . 213 A5
  8 Northborough PE6 . 231 F7
  Tydd St Mary PE13 . . 238 C8
EASTREA 190 D7
Eastrea Ct PE2 . . . . . . 187 E6
Eastrea Rd PE7 . . . . . . 189 F7
East St
  Bluntisham/Colne PE28 208 C5
  Great Gransden SG19 . 58 E4
  Huntingdon PE29 . . . 141 F5
  1 Kimbolton PE28 . . 113 F4
  Manea PE15 . . . . 224 C4
  Stamford PE9 . . . . . 244 C5
  St Ives PE27 . . . . . . 144 A3
  St Neots PE19 . . . . . 74 F5
East Sta Rd PE2 . . . . . . 187 A8
East View IP28 . . . . 213 C3
East Villa PE15 . . . . . . 224 B3
East Water Cres PE7 . . . 186 C1
East Way CB22 . . . . . . 50 A1
Eastwood PE16 . . . . . . 241 C3
Eastwood Ave PE15 . . . 243 E7
Eastwood Cl CB6 . . . . . 216 E2
Eastwood End PE15 . . . 223 C7
Eaton Cl
  Cambridge CB4 . . . . . 84 A6
  Huntingdon PE29 . . . 142 A7
Eaton Ct PE19 . . . . 74 C1
Eaton Est PE15 . . . . . . 223 B7
EATON FORD 74 C4
EATON SOCON 74 B3
Eaudyke Bank PE13 . . . 237 F7
Eayre Ct PE19 . . . . 75 A5
Eccles Cl CB22 . . . . 32 F8
Eccles Rd PE8 . . . . 193 D8
Echo Hill SG8 . . . . 5 C5
Echo La PE28 . . . . 151 E3
Ecton Gr **7** PE14 . . . . . 236 A5
Eden Cres PE16 . . . . . . 241 C4
Edendale Cl CB1 . . . . . . 65 C5
Edenfield PE2 . . . . 186 C6
Eden Rd CB9 . . . . 24 A8
Eden St Backway CB1 . . 246 C2
Eden St CB1 . . . . 246 C3
Edgcote Cl PE3 . . . . . . 197 C5
Edge Bank PE14 . . . . . . 236 F6
Edgeborough Cl CB8 . . . 134 A1
Edgecombe CB4 . . . . . . 83 F7
Edgerley Drain Rd PE1 . 198 F5
Edgerley Dro PE6 . . . . . 205 F8
Edinburgh Ave
  Peterborough PE4 . . . 204 B3
  Sawston CB22 . . . . . 32 F8
Edinburgh Dr
  Eaton Socon PE19 . . . 74 B4
  St Ives PE27 . . . . . . 143 F7
  Wisbech PE13 . . . . . 245 C8
Edinburgh Rd
  Cambridge CB4 . . . . . 84 A5
  Newmarket CB8 . . . . 110 E4
  Stamford PE9 . . . . . 244 B7
Edis Ct PE2 . . . . 187 B6
Edison Dr PE7 . . . . 181 D6
Edison Rd PE27 . . . . . . 144 C6
Edis Way CB22 . . . . 30 C5
Edith Cavell Hospl PE3 . 197 B4
Edmonds Cl PE19 . . . . . 244 D6
Edmund Cl
  Haverhill CB9 . . . . . . 23 F7
  Milton CB24 . . . . 105 C2
Edwalton Ave PE3 . . . . 197 E3
Edward Rd
  Stamford PE9 . . . . . 244 B7
  St Neots PE19 . . . . . 74 F2
Edward St CB1 . . . . 84 A1
Edwards Way PE15 . . . . 224 B4
Edwards Wlk PE28 . . . . 208 E6
Edwinstowe Cl PE2 . . . 186 A6
Egar Way PE3 . . . . 196 F2
Egerton Cl CB5 . . . . . . 84 D4
Egerton Rd CB5 . . . . . . 84 E4
Egremont Rd CB23 . . . . 81 A3
Egremont St CB6 . . . . . 240 C5
Ehringshausen Way CB9 . 24 B6
Eight Acres PE9 . . . . . . 244 A5
Eighth Ave PE13 . . . . . 245 E4
Ekin Rd CB5 . . . . 84 D3
Ekin Wlk CB5 . . . . 84 D3
Eland Way CB1 . . . . . . 66 A7
Elbourn Way SG8 . . . . . 12 F5
Eldith Ave CB7 . . . . 233 F8
Elder Cl
  Cambridge CB4 . . . . . 83 F6
  Sawston CB22 . . . . . 32 D8
Eldern PE2 . . . . 186 C4
ELDERNELL 202 B2
Eldernell La PE7 . . . . . . 191 B8
Elder Pl PE16 . . . . 241 D4
Elder's Gate PE12 . . . . 237 E8
Eldith Ave CB7 . . . . 213 A1
Eldo Gdns PE29 . . . . . . 213 D6
Eldon La IP28 . . . . 214 B8
Eldo Rd PE27 . . . . 143 D6
Elean Bsns Pk CB6 . . . . 216 F2
Eleanor Cl PE9 . . . . 244 A6
Elecks La SG19 . . . . 11 D8
Elfleda Rd CB5 . . . . 84 C3
Elford Closes CB5 . . . . 153 D7
Elgar Rd PE9 . . . . 244 A6
Eigpod's Brewery Tours, Gdn
  & Visitors Ctr* PE13 . 245 A4
Elin Way SG8 . . . . 14 B8

Eliot Rd SG8 . . . . 5 D8
Elizabethan Way PE28 . 140 B2
Elizabeth Ave CB8 . . . . 110 E5
Elizabeth Ct
  5 Eaton Socon PE19 . 74 C4
  Hemingford Grey PE27 143 F1
  Peterborough PE1 . . . 198 A5
  2 Sutton CB6 . . . . . 216 E2
Elizabeth Dr PE29 . . . . 142 B6
Elizabeth Par CB8 . . . . 110 E5
Elizabeth Rd PE19 . . . . 244 A6
Elizabeth Terr PE13 . . . 245 D4
Elizabeth Way
  Bluntisham/Colne PE28 208 D7
  Burrough Green CB8 . . 70 F4
  Cambridge CB4 . . . . . 83 F4
  Gamlingay SG19 . . . . 41 C6
  Haddenham CB6 . . . . 210 A6
  Littleport CB6 . . . . . . 239 F3
Elliedene Rd CB4 . . . . . 83 D6
Ellindon PE3 . . . . 197 B7
Ellingham Ave PE15 . . . 243 C3
ELLINGTON 139 A4
Ellington Rd PE28 . . . . 149 E1
ELLINGTON THORPE . . . 139 A2
Elliot Ave PE3 . . . . 196 F2
Elliott Cl CB8 . . . . 111 A6
Elliott Rd PE15 . . . . . . 243 B5
Ellis Cl CB24 . . . . 125 D3
Ellison Cl CB4 . . . . 83 D7
Ellison La CB23 . . . . . . 81 A4
Elloe Bank
  Newton PE13 . . . . . . 237 B2
  Tydd St Giles PE13 . . 237 B5
Ellwood Ave PE2 . . . . . 187 E5
Ellwoods Cl CB4 . . . . . . 213 A5
ELM 236 B5
Elm CE Prim Sch PE14 . 236 B5
Elm Cl
  Dullingham CB8 . . . . 70 D8
  Haverhill CB9 . . . . . . 23 F8
  Huntingdon PE29 . . . 141 E7
  March PE15 . . . . 243 D7
  5 Market Deeping PE6 231 E8
  Stilton PE7 . . . . 175 F7
  Witchford CB6 . . . . . 217 E2
  Yaxley PE7 . . . . 181 F7
Elm Cres PE16 . . . . 203 D8
Elm Croft PE19 . . . . . . 95 F3
Elmcroft Cl **6** IP28 . . . 213 F8
Elm Ct
  Elmdon CB11 . . . . . . 9 B4
  5 Sturmer CB9 . . . . 24 E5
ELMDON 9 A4
Elmdon Lee CB11 . . . . . 9 E1
Elmdon Rd CB23 . . . . . 29 B8
Elm Dr
  Little Stukeley PE28 . . 151 E3
  Offord Cluny PE19 . . . 118 A2
  St Ives PE27 . . . . . . 143 F6
Elm End PE28 . . . . 150 F4
Elmfield CB6 . . . . 240 C5
Elmfield Dr PE14 . . . . . 245 E1
Elmfield Rd
  Cambridge CB4 . . . . . 84 A5
  Peterborough PE1 . . . 198 A7
Elm High Rd PE14 . . . . 245 E1
Elmhurst Cl CB7 . . . . . . 24 B7
Elm Low Rd PE14 . . . . 245 D2
Elmondbury CB11 . . . . . 9 A4
Elmore Rd PE3 . . . . 197 A3
Elm Pk PE7 . . . . 189 E7
Elm Rd
  Folksworth PE7 . . . . . 175 D8
  Little Stukeley PE28 . . 152 A2
  March PE15 . . . . 243 D8
  Wisbech PE13 . . . . . 245 D3
Elm Rd Prim Sch PE13 . 245 D4
Elm's Ave CB22 . . . . . . 49 A5
Elms Cl CB22 . . . . 32 D2
Elmside PE14 . . . . 236 D5
Elm Side CB6 . . . . 242 B5
Elms Rd
  Freckenham IP28 . . . 213 E2
  Isleham IP28 . . . . . . 213 F1
Elm St
  Cambridge CB1 . . . . . 246 B3
  Peterborough PE2 . . . 186 F7
  Stamford PE9 . . . . . 244 C5
Elms The
  Chatteris PE16 . . . . . 241 E4
  Great Chesterford CB10 18 E3
  Haslingfield CB23 . . . 47 C5
  Milton CB24 . . . . 105 C2
Elm Tree Cl CB23 . . . . . 79 C3
Elm Tree Dr SG8 . . . . . 12 F4
Elm Way
  Melbourn SG8 . . . . . 14 C5
  Papworth Everard CB23 99 A3
  Sawtry PE28 . . . . . . 168 B3
  Willingham CB24 . . . . 209 A1
Elm Wlk SG8 . . . . 5 F7
Elsie's Way PE29 . . . . . 141 F6
Elstone PE2 . . . . 186 A4
Elstow Cl **7** CB24 . . . . 208 D1
ELSWORTH 100 C4
Elsworth CE Prim Sch
  CB23 . . . . 100 A4
Elsworth Cl PE27 . . . . . 144 C5
Elsworth Pl CB1 . . . . . . 65 A6
Elsworth Rd
  Boxworth CB23 . . . . . 101 A5
  Conington CB23 . . . . 100 C8
Elter Wlk PE4 . . . . 204 E3
Elter Wy PE29 . . . . 141 A5
ELTISLEY 77 E4
Eltisley Ave CB3 . . . . . . 64 C7
Eltisley Rd SG19 . . . . . . 58 E6
ELTON 178 D8

Elton CE Prim Sch PE8 . 178 D8
Elton Hall & Gdns* PE8 . 178 D6
Elton Rd
  Sibson cum Stibbington
  PE8 . . . . 183 C8
  Water Newton PE8 . . 184 B7
Elvedon Way
  Haverhill CB9 . . . . . . 38 B1
  Newmarket CB8 . . . . 110 E5
Elwyn Ct PE15 . . . . 243 D3
Elwyndene Rd PE15 . . . 243 D3
Elwyn Rd PE15 . . . . 243 D4
ELY 240 C3
Ely Cath CB7 . . . . 240 D4
Ely Cl PE4 . . . . 204 B3
Ely Mus* CB7 . . . . 240 D4
Ely Pl **16** PE13 . . . . . . 245 C5
Ely Rd
  Downham CB6 . . . . . 218 B6
  Ely CB7 . . . . 218 D4
  Landbeach CB25 . . . . 105 F8
  Littleport CB6 . . . . . . 242 C2
  Milton CB24 . . . . 105 E3
  Soham CB7 . . . . 211 F7
  Stretham CB6 . . . . . 210 F5
  Sutton CB6 . . . . 216 F2
  Waterbeach CB25 . . . 126 E3
  Wentworth CB6 . . . . 217 A2
Ely St John's Prim Sch
  CB6 . . . . 240 A4
Ely St Marys CE Jun Sch
  CB7 . . . . 240 F6
Ely Way CB6 . . . . 210 A7
Embankment Rd **4** PE1 . 198 A1
Embry Rd **19** PE8 . . . . 230 B1
Emery Cl PE28 . . . . 140 C3
Emery Pl PE19 . . . . 74 F7
Emery Rd CB1 . . . . 84 A1
Emery St CB1 . . . . 246 B2
Emlyns Gdns PE9 . . . . . 244 C6
Emlyns St PE9 . . . . 244 C6
Emmanuel Cl IP28 . . . . 239 D5
Emmanuel Coll CB1 . . . 246 B2
Emmanuel Rd
  Cambridge CB1 . . . . . 246 B2
  Stamford PE9 . . . . . 244 B7
Emmanuel St CB1 . . . . 246 B2
EMMAUS 127 E2
EMNETH 236 E6
EMNETH HUNGATE 236 E6
Emperor Ct **3** CB4 . . . . 83 E8
Empingham Rd PE9 . . . 244 A5
Empire Theatre* PE13 . . 245 C5
Empson Rd PE1 . . . . . . 198 F5
Emson's Cl CB21 . . . . . 35 D2
Enderbys Wharf PE27 . . 144 A3
Enfield Cl **8** CB1 . . . . . 84 A2
Enfield Cl PE6 . . . . 232 B1
Enfield Gdns PE3 . . . . . 197 C4
Engaine PE2 . . . . 186 B5
Engine Rd CB7 . . . . 211 F5
Engine Yd CB6 . . . . 240 B4
Engleric SG8 . . . . 8 D4
English Rd PE6 . . . . 233 B4
English St PE1 . . . . 197 E5
Ennerdale Cl PE7 . . . . . 226 B6
Ennerdale Rise PE4 . . . 204 D2
Ennion Cl CB7 . . . . 212 B3
Ennisdale Cl **9** CB4 . . . 83 E7
Enniskillen Rd CB4 . . . . 84 B5
Enterprise Way
  Bretton PE3 . . . . 197 B8
  Wisbech PE13 . . . . . 245 A2
Erasmus Cl CB4 . . . . . . 83 D5
Erica Rd PE27 . . . . 144 A6
Eriswell Rd
  Beck Row, Holywell Row &
  Kenny Hill IP28 . . . . 214 B8
  Haverhill CB9 . . . . . . 24 B8
Ermine Bsns Ctr PE29 . . 141 B8
Ermine Bsns Pk PE29 . . 141 B8
Ermine Cl
  March PE15 . . . . 243 C2
  Royston SG8 . . . . 5 D8
Ermine Cres PE7 . . . . . 176 A7
Ermine Ct PE29 . . . . . . 141 C5
Ermine St
  Caxton CB23 . . . . . . 78 E2
  Huntingdon PE29 . . . 141 C5
  Little Stukeley PE28 . . 151 F2
  The Stukeleys PE28 . . 141 A8
Ermine Street N CB23 . . 99 A4
Ermine Street S CB23 . . 78 C8
Ermine Way
  Arrington SG8 . . . . . 44 C4
  Sawtry PE28 . . . . . . 168 C3
Erratts Hill CB8 . . . . . . 73 D1
Eskdale Cl **1** PE4 . . . . 204 E3
Essendyke PE3 . . . . 197 A7
Essex Cl CB4 . . . . 83 E5
Essex Hill CB11 . . . . . . 9 B2
Essex Rd
  Huntingdon PE29 . . . 141 E8
  5 Stamford PE9 . . . 244 B6
Estelle Cl PE26 . . . . . . 220 D2
Estover Rd PE15 . . . . . 243 E6
Etheldreda St CB6 . . . . 240 B4
Ethelred Cl PE26 . . . . . 172 B8
ETTON 231 C5
Eurocentre Sch CB2 . . . 64 F7
Europa Way **1** PE13 . . 245 B2
Euston St PE29 . . . . . . 141 E4
Euximoor Dro PE14 . . . 229 B5

Evans Cl
Brampton PE28 . . . . **140** D3
Royston SG8 . . . .**5** D7
Evans Way CB22 . . . .**32** E8
Everdon Way PE3 . . . . **197** C5
Ever Gn CB8 . . . .**55** F6
Evergreen Dr PE7 . . . . **186** B2
Evergreen La CB8 . . . .**55** F7
Evergreens CB4 . . . .**84** B5
Everingham PE2 . . . . **185** D5
Eversden Cl CB23 . . . .**61** D5
Eversden Rd CB23 . . . .**46** C5
Eversley Cl CB24. . . . . **125** D4
EVERTON **40** C3
Everton Hill SG19 . . . .**40** B3
Everton Lower Sch SG19 . . .**40** D3
Everton Rd
Gamlingay Great Heath
SG19 . . . .**40** E3
Sandy SG19 . . . .**40** B1
Eves Cl PE6 . . . . **207** D1
Ewingswood 1 PE28. . . . . **168** C2
Exchange Sq PE13 . . . . **245** B5
Exchange St PE1. . . . . **198** A2
Exeter Cl
Cambridge CB2 . . . .**64** D1
2 Market Deeping PE6 . . **231** F8
Exeter Ct 10 CB9. . . . .**23** E6
Exeter Rd
Newmarket CB8. . . . . **111** A4
Peterborough PE1 . . . . **197** F6
7 Wittering PE8. . . . . **230** B1
Exmoor Cl PE29 . . . . **141** A4
EXMOOR GRANGE **229** B4
EXNING **110** B8
Exning Prim Sch CB8 . . . . . **110** B8
Exning Rd CB88. . . . . **110** D6
EYE **232** B1
Eyebury Rd PE6. . . . . **199** A6
Eye CE Prim Sch PE6 . . . . . **232** B1
EYE GREEN **232** B2
Eye Green Ind Est PE6 . . . **232** A2
Eye Green Nature Reserve*
PE6 . . . . **232** B2
Eye Hill Dro CB7. . . . . **211** F7
Eye Rd PE1. . . . . **198** E7
Eyeworth Rd SG19 . . . .**25** B2
EYNESBURY **74** F3
Eynesbury CE Prim Sch
PE19. . . . .**74** E4
Eynesbury Gn PE19 . . . .**74** F4
Eynesford Cl PE7 . . . . **188** A5
Eyrescroft PE3. . . . . **197** A7
Eyrescroft Prim Sch PE3 **197** A7
Eyresford Cl PE7. . . . . **188** A5

F

Faber La PE8 . . . . **183** D1
Fairacre CB10 . . . .**18** C3
Fairbairn Rd CB4 . . . .**84** C5
Fairchild Way PE11 . . . . **198** A7
Fair Ct CB1. . . . . **246** C3
Fairey Ave PE29. . . . . **141** F1
Fairey Fox Dr 1 IP28 . . . **239** B5
Fairfax Ct
Ely CB6 . . . . **240** C4
St Neots PE19 . . . .**74** F3
Fairfax Rd CB1 . . . .**84** B1
Fairfax Way
March PE15 . . . . **243** E1
10 Market Deeping PE6 . . **231** F8
Fairfield
Gamlingay SG19 . . . .**41** C5
5 Sutton CB6. . . . . **216** E1
Fairfield Dr PE26 . . . . **172** A6
Fairfield Rd PE2 . . . . **187** A8
Fairfields
Sawston CB22 . . . .**50** A1
St Ives PE27 . . . . **144** B4
Fairfields Cres PE27 . . . . . **144** B4
Fairfield Way CB21. . . . .**35** D3
Fair Green The CB25 . . . . . **129** D1
Fairhaven Cl
Duxford CB22 . . . .**32** D1
Lode CB25 . . . . **107** C2
Fairhaven Way CB8 . . . . . . **110** E5
Fairlawns CB8. . . . . **110** E5
Fairlawns Rd CB88. . . . . . . **110** F2
Fairmead Way PE3. . . . . . . **197** E2
Fairsford Pl CB1. . . . .**84** A2
Fair St CB1. . . . . **246** C3
Fairstead House Sch
CB8 . . . . **111** B4
Fairview Ave PE16 . . . . **241** B2
Fairview Dr PE16 . . . . **241** B2
Fairview Gr CB25 . . . . **108** E5
Fairway
Chatteris PE16. . . . . **241** B3
Girton CB3 . . . . **103** E2
Fairway The
Bar Hill CB23 . . . . **102** D3
Bluntisham/Colne PE28. . **208** C6
Falcon Cl
Haverhill CB9. . . . .**24** C8
5 St Neots PE19 . . . .**75** B7
Falcon Dr PE29 . . . . **142** B7
Falconer Rd CB9. . . . .**24** C5
Falcon La
4 Whittlesey PE7. . . . . . **189** D6
10 Wisbech PE13. . . . . . . **245** C5
Falcon Mews CB6. . . . . **240** B5
Falcon Rd
Stukeley PE29 . . . . **141** A6

Falcon Rd continued
6 Wisbech PE13. . . . . **245** C5
Falcon Way
Bexnders Lane PE9 . . . . . . **117** B3
Peterborough PE7 . . . . **186** C1
Falklands Dr PE13 . . . . **245** E3
Falklands Rd CB9. . . . .**39** A1
Falkner Rd CB22. . . . .**33** A8
Fallodan Rd PE7 . . . . **185** C3
Fallow Corner Dro PE15. **224** A3
Fallow Dr PE19 . . . .**74** B5
Fallowfield
Cambridge CB4 . . . .**84** B5
Littleport CB6 . . . . **242** C3
Peterborough PE2 . . . . **185** D5
Fallowfield Ct 8 CB9 . . . . .**23** E7
Fall's Dro PE6. . . . . **232** F7
Falmouth Ave CB8 . . . . **110** F3
Falmouth Gdns CB8. . . . . . **111** A6
Falmouth St 1 CB8. . . . . . **110** F3
Falstaff Rd PE19 . . . .**74** C3
Fane Cl PE9 . . . . **244** B7
Fane Rd PE4. . . . . **197** E8
Fanshawe Rd CB1 . . . .**65** A6
Faraday Cl PE7 . . . . **181** D6
FARCET. **187** C2
Farcet CE Prim Sch PE7. **187** C2
Farcet Cl 5 PE19 . . . .**74** C6
Fardell Rd 6 PE13. . . . . . . **245** C4
Fardell's La CB23. . . . . **100** A4
Farendon Rd PE28 . . . . **140** E1
Farfield Cl PE28 . . . . **168** A5
Farleigh Fields PE2 . . . . . . **185** D7
Farm Cl
Ramsey PE26. . . . . **171** C3
Sawtry PE28 . . . . **168** B4
Farmer's End CB23 . . . .**61** E5
Farmer's Row CB21. . . . .**66** E4
Farm La
Papworth Everard CB23 . . . .**99** C2
Thriplow SG8 . . . .**31** B1
**Farmland Mus & Denny
Abbey The*** CB25 . . . . . **127** A5
Farm Rise CB22. . . . .**32** C5
Farmstead Cl CB24. . . . . . . **104** B5
Farm View PE5 . . . . **195** E2
Far Pasture PE4 . . . . **204** B5
Farrier Ct SG8 . . . .**5** C7
Farriers Ct PE2 . . . . **186** D7
Farriers Gate PE26 . . . . **241** D5
Farriers Way PE28 . . . . **164** F5
Farringdon Cl PE1. . . . . **198** A1
Farringford Cl 4 CB4. . . . . .**83** C6
Farthing Dro PE38 . . . . **226** D6
Farthing La PE27 . . . . **144** B4
Fassage Cl CB25 . . . . **107** C2
Fastnet Cl CB9. . . . .**24** D8
Faulkner Cl CB24. . . . . **105** C2
Fawcett Prim Sch CB2. . . . .**64** D3
Fawsley Garth PE3. . . . . . . **197** C6
Fayway NN14 . . . . **156** F2
Fazeley CB1. . . . . **246** C2
Feast Cl CB7 . . . . **212** E1
Feilden Way CB8 . . . . **110** E5
Felbrigg Wlk PE2. . . . . **187** F6
Feldale Pl PE7. . . . . **189** F8
Fellowes Dr PE26 . . . . **172** A6
Fellowes Gdns PE2 . . . . **187** A7
Fellowes Rd PE2. . . . . **187** A7
Felsham Chase CB25. . . . . . **130** C2
Felsted Ave PE13 . . . . **245** E5
Feltham Cl CB5 . . . . **212** E1
Felton St CB1. . . . .**65** A8
Felton Way CB7. . . . . **240** E6
Feltwell Pl 1 CB9 . . . .**24** B8
Fen Bank Rd CB7. . . . . **213** A6
Fenbridge Rd PE4. . . . . **204** C4
Fen Cl PE13 . . . . **245** E6
Fen Cswy* PE7. . . . . **189** A8
Fen Cswy The CB3 . . . . **246** A1
FEN DITTON **84** F5
Fen Ditton Prim Sch CB5. .**84** F5
Fendon Cl CB1. . . . .**65** B3
Fendon Rd CB1. . . . .**65** B3
FEN DRAYTON **122** F6
**Fen Drayton Nature
Reserve*** CB24. . . . . **121** F7
Fen Drayton Prim Sch
CB24. . . . . **121** F6
Fen Drayton Rd CB24 . . . . **122** C5
Fen Dro PE7. . . . . **176** C8
Fendyke La PE13 . . . . **237** F1
FEN END. **57** D6
Fen End
Over CB24 . . . . **208** D1
Willingham CB24. . . . . **209** A1
FENGATE **198** D2
Fengate PE1. . . . . **198** D1
Fengate Cl 1 PE1 . . . . **198** D2
Fengate Mobile Home Pk
PE1. **198** D1
Fengate Rd PE14 . . . . **238** F1
Fengate Trad Est PE1 . . . . **198** D2
Fenhall Field PE13 . . . . **237** C1
Fen La
Sawtry PE28 . . . . **168** C3
Stilton PE7. . . . . **176** C8
Swaffham Bulbeck CB25 . . **108** A4
Tydd St Giles PE13. . . . . . . **237** B5
Fenland Cl 3 PE15 . . . . **223** B7
Fenland & District Ind Est
PE7. **189** F5
Fenland Rd PE13 . . . . **245** E6
Fenland St PE15 . . . . **243** D4
**Fenland & West Norfolk
Aviation Mus*** PE14 . . . **238** F3
Fenland Wlk PE15 . . . . **243** D4

Fenleigh Cl CB25 . . . . **106** B8
Fennec Cl CB1. . . . .**66** B6
Fennels Cl CB9 . . . .**24** A7
Fenners Lawn CB1. . . . . . . **246** C1
Fenny La SG8. . . . .**29** A1
Fen Rd
Bassingbourn cum Kneesworth
SG8. . . . .**12** B7
Little Wilbraham CB1. . . . . .**86** D2
Lode CB25 . . . . **107** B4
Milton CB4 . . . .**84** D6
Newton PE13. . . . . **237** E4
Parson Drove PE12 . . . . . . **234** C7
Pidley cum Fenton PE28 . . **165** E1
Shingay cum Wendy SG8 . . .**26** F1
Wisbech St Mary PE13 . . . **234** E2
Fen Side
Haddenham CB6 . . . . **209** L4
Wicken CB7. . . . . **211** D3
Fenside Dr PE6 . . . . **207** C1
Fenside Rd PE28. . . . . **165** D8
Fen St PE7. . . . . **176** A2
FENSTANTON **122** C5
**Fenstanton & Hilton Prim
Sch** PE28. . . . . **121** C6
Fen The PE28 . . . . **121** B6
FENTON **165** B4
Fenton Hill CB23. . . . . **165** C3
Fenton Rd
Haverhill CB9. . . . .**24** B8
Warboys PE28 . . . . **165** A4
Fen View
Chatteris PE16. . . . . **241** B3
Christchurch PE14. . . . . . . **229** D3
6 Doddington/Wimblington
PE15. . . . . **222** F5
Peterborough PE2 . . . . **187** F6
Fen View Ct CB4 . . . .**84** D5
Fen Way 8 PE14 . . . . **236** A5
Feoffees Rd 5 PE28 . . . . . **208** C8
Ferndale
Teversham CB1. . . . .**66** C8
Yaxley PE7 . . . . **181** D6
Ferndale Cl CB88 . . . . **111** B5
Ferndale Rise CB5. . . . .**84** C4
Ferndale Way PE1 . . . . **205** B1
Ferndown Dr PE28 . . . . **137** F6
Ferneley Cres 8 CB8 . . . . **111** A4
Fern Gr CB9 . . . .**23** E8
Fernie Cl PE6. . . . . **205** D8
Fernlea Cl CB1 . . . .**65** F7
Ferrars Ave PE19 . . . .**74** E4
Ferrars Ct 4 PE29 . . . . **141** D4
Ferrars Rd PE29 . . . . **141** D5
Ferrars Way CB4. . . . .**83** D6
Ferriman Rd PE28 . . . . **137** C6
Ferry Bank PE38 . . . . **226** D8
Ferry Cutter La CB4. . . . . . **246** C4
Ferry Dr PE6 . . . . **196** D3
Ferry Hill
Castor PE5 . . . . **196** B1
Chatteris PE16. . . . . **215** E6
Ferry La
Beck Row, Holywell Row &
Kenny Hill IP28 . . . . **213** D5
Cambridge CB4 . . . .**84** B4
Newton PE13. . . . . **238** B5
Ferry Mdw PE27 . . . . **208** A1
Ferry Meadows Ctry Pk*
PE2 . . . . **185** D8
Ferry Path CB1 . . . . **246** B4
Ferryview PE2. . . . . **185** E6
Ferry Way CB6. . . . . **242** D6
Festival Cl PE15 . . . . **224** C4
Festival Ct PE13 . . . . **197** B5
Festival Rd CB7. . . . . **213** A5
Festival Way CB6 . . . . **226** B6
Fews Cl 4 PE27 . . . . **208** A3
Field Ave PE13. . . . . **237** F7
Field Baulk PE15. . . . . **243** D2
Field Cl
Abbotsley PE19 . . . .**57** A6
Alconbury PE28 . . . . **150** F5
Buckden PE19 . . . . **117** B4
Grafham PE28 . . . . **116** A7
Linton CB21. . . . .**35** B2
Little Paxton PE19 . . . .**95** F2
Warboys PE28 . . . . **164** F5
Field Cottage Rd PE19 . . . .**74** C3
Field End
Balsham CB21. . . . .**53** B2
Witchford CB6 . . . . **217** D2
Fielden Way CB8 . . . . **110** E5
Fielder Dr PE2 . . . . **187** E6
Fieldfare Way 10 SG8 . . . . .**5** E8
Field Farm Cotts CB10 . . . .**18** F7
Field Gate CB6 . . . . **216** D2
Fielding Cl 2 PE19 . . . .**74** C6
Fielding Pl PE19 . . . .**97** F4
Field La CB5. . . . .**84** E6
Field Rd
Kingston CB23. . . . .**61** B3
Mildenhall IP28 . . . . **239** C5
Ramsey PE26. . . . . **172** A7
Field Rise PE7 . . . . **181** D5
Field Row CB23. . . . .**61** B3
Fields End Cl PE7. . . . . **186** D3
Fieldside
Ely CB6 . . . . **240** B4
Stretham CB6 . . . . **210** E5
Whittlesey PE7 . . . . **190** F8
Fieldside View PE13. . . . . . **237** F7
Field Terr PE7 . . . . **187** C2
Field Terr Rd CB8 . . . . **110** F5
Field View
Bar Hill CB23 . . . . **102** B2
Harston CB22 . . . .**48** A4

Field View continued
Haverhill CB9. . . . .**38** C1
Field Way CB1. . . . .**65** C3
Field Wlk
Mildenhall IP28 . . . . **239** C5
Peterborough PE1 . . . . **198** B2
Fifth Ave PE13. . . . . **245** E4
Fifty Dro CB6. . . . . **225** C7
Fifty Rd
Christchurch PE14. . . . . . . **229** D1
Manea PE14. . . . . **224** D7
Figtree Wlk PE1. . . . . **198** B8
Fillance The SG8. . . . .**12** D5
Fincham Rd IP28 . . . . **239** B5
Fincham's Cl CB21. . . . .**35** D2
Finchfield PE1. . . . . **198** F7
Finchley Ave IP28 . . . . **239** B6
Finchley Gn PE3 . . . . **197** E4
Finch Rd CB4. . . . .**83** D5
Finch's Cl CB22. . . . .**49** B5
Finch's Field CB23. . . . .**46** A7
Finch's Rd CB23 . . . .**46** A7
Firdale Cl PE6 . . . . **206** C2
Firelots Dro PE15 . . . . **223** C8
First Ave
Warboys PE28 . . . . **164** E6
Wisbech PE13 . . . . **245** D5
First Broadpool Dro
PE28. . . . . **165** E8
First Drift PE9 . . . . **244** B2
First Dro
Burwell CB25. . . . . **130** C7
Peterborough PE2 . . . . **198** D1
First Furlong Dro PE16. . . **241** A3
Firs The CB22. . . . .**32** D2
First Marsh Rd PE14 . . . . . **238** D2
First Turf Fen Dro PE28 . . **165** B8
Fisher Cl
Duxford CB22 . . . .**17** E8
Haverhill CB9. . . . .**24** D7
Ramsey St Mary's PE26. . . **220** D2
Fishermans Cl PE26. . . . . . **171** B1
Fishermans Dr PE15 . . . . . **243** A5
Fishers Bank CB6. . . . . **242** E3
Fishers Cl PE7. . . . . **175** F7
Fisher's La
Cambridge CB1 . . . .**65** F6
Orwell SG8. . . . .**45** D2
Fisher St CB4. . . . . **246** A4
Fishers Way PE29 . . . . **118** F8
Fishers Yd 4 PE19. . . . .**74** E5
Fish Hill SG8 . . . .**5** D6
Fison Rd CB5. . . . .**84** E4
FITTON END **238** A3
Fitton End Rd PE13 . . . . . . **237** F3
Fitzgerald Cl CB6. . . . . **240** E8
Fitzroy Cl CB1. . . . . **246** C3
Fitzroy La CB5 . . . . **246** C3
Fitzroy St
Cambridge CB1 . . . . **246** C3
Newmarket CB8. . . . . **111** A3
Fitzwilliam Coll CB3 . . . .**83** B4
Fitzwilliam Mus The*
CB2 . . . . **246** A1
Fitzwilliam Rd
Cambridge CB2 . . . .**64** F6
Stamford PE9 . . . . **244** A7
Fitzwilliam St
Cambridge CB2 . . . . **246** B1
Peterborough PE1 . . . . **198** A3
Five Acres SG8 . . . .**28** F1
Five Arches PE2 . . . . **185** C6
**Five Arches Pit Nature
Reserve*** PE28. . . . . **169** C2
Five Hundred Dro PE15 . . **224** A4
Fiveways IP28. . . . . **239** F2
Flackdale Rd PE28 . . . . **120** B1
Flag Bsns Exchange PE1 **198** E3
Flag Fen* PE6. . . . . **199** B2
Flag Fen Rd PE1. . . . . **198** C4
Flaggrass Hill Rd PE15 . . . **243** E8
Flambards Cl SG8. . . . .**14** B8
Flamborough Cl PE2 . . . . . **197** E1
Flamsteed Dr PE2 . . . . **140** F5
Flamsteed Rd CB1. . . . . **165** A6
Flatford Rd CB9 . . . .**23** C8
Flat Rd CB24 . . . . **209** B3
Flat The CB8. . . . . **111** F7
Flavian Cl CB9. . . . .**24** D7
Flawn Way PE19 . . . .**74** D2
Flaxfields CB21 . . . .**35** C3
Flaxland PE3 . . . . **197** A6
Fleam Dyke Cotts CB21 . . .**67** C2
Flecks La
Shingay cum Wendy SG8. . .**26** D1
Steeple Morden SG8. . . . . . .**11** D8
Fleet Cl CB6. . . . . **242** D4
Fleet The SG8 . . . .**5** C6
Fleet Way PE2 . . . . **187** B6
Fleetwood CB4 . . . . **240** C5
Fleetwood Cl PE15. . . . . . . **243** D2
Flegcroft PE7. . . . . **189** F1
Fleming Ave IP28. . . . . **239** C5
Fleming Cl PE7 . . . . **181** D6
Fleming Ct
March PE15 . . . . **243** F3
Woodston PE2. . . . . **185** D8
Flemington IP28 . . . . **239** B6
Fletcher Ave CB25. . . . . **107** E6
Fletchers Cl PE26. . . . . **172** A7
Fletcher's Terr 3 CB1. . . . .**65** A8
Fletton Ave PE2. . . . . **187** A8
Fletton Fields PE2 . . . . **187** A7
Fletton Parkway PE2. . . . . **185** F2
Flint Cl PE28 . . . . **140** C2
FLINT CROSS **15** B2
Flint Ct CB21. . . . .**35** B2
Flint House Rd PE14 . . . . . **229** F5

Flint La CB25 . . . . **126** E3
Flint Way
Elm PE14. . . . . **236** A4
St Neots PE19 . . . .**74** E2
Flood's Ferry PE15. . . . . . . **222** A8
Flood's Ferry Rd PE15 . . . **222** B7
Flore Cl PE3 . . . . **197** C5
Florence Cl PE7 . . . . **189** F6
Florida Ave PE29. . . . . **141** F8
Flowers Cl PE26 . . . . **172** A7
Flower St 2 CB1. . . . .**84** A1
Flowmere Rd SG8. . . . .**8** A5
Fodderfen Dro
Beck Row, Holywell Row &
Kenny Hill IP28. . . . . **219** F1
Wicken CB7 . . . . **211** C3
Fodder Fen Dro CB7. . . . . **219** B3
Fodder Fen Rd PE15 . . . . . **224** C6
Foder Way PE7 . . . . **186** E3
Fold La PE13 . . . . **237** F7
Fold The PE7 . . . . **190** F8
Folgate La PE14 . . . . **238** F6
FOLKSWORTH **175** D8
Yaxley **180** D1
Folksworth CE Prim Sch
PE7. **175** D8
Folksworth Rd PE7 . . . . . . **180** L1
Folly Cl PE7 . . . . **181** C5
Folly Dro CB7. . . . . **239** B6
Folly Rd IP28. . . . . **239** B6
Folly's Dro PE13 . . . . **234** F3
Fontwell Ave CB4. . . . .**83** C5
Fontwell Gdns 2 PE9 . . . **244** B5
Foot Dro PE26 . . . . **172** A8
Footpath The CB23. . . . .**82** C2
Ford Cl
Beck Row, Holywell Row &
Kenny Hill IP28. . . . . **213** D7
Eaton Socon PE19 . . . .**74** D5
Yaxley PE7 . . . . **181** C6
Ford End
Alconbury PE28 . . . . **150** F4
Hail Weston PE19 . . . .**95** B1
FORDHAM **212** F1
Fordham Abbey* CB7. . . . **131** E8
Fordham CE Prim Sch
CB7. **212** F1
Fordham Cl SG7. . . . .**2** D5
Fordham Moor CB7. . . . . . **212** E3
Fordham Rd
Exning CB8. . . . . **131** E3
Freckenham IP28 . . . . **213** B2
Isleham CB7 . . . . **213** A4
Newmarket CB8. . . . . **110** F8
5 Royston SG8 . . . .**5** E5
Snailwell CB8. . . . . **212** A3
5 Soham CB7. . . . . **112** B3
Fordham Way SG8 . . . .**14** D5
Fordwich Cl 1 CB4. . . . .**83** D6
Fore Hill CB7 . . . . **240** D4
Foreman's Rd SG8. . . . .**31** B2
Forest End CB8. . . . . **134** A6
Forest Glade CB9. . . . .**38** F2
Forest Rd CB1 . . . .**65** C5
Forest Way IP28. . . . . **239** E4
Forge Cl PE19 . . . .**74** B2
Forge End
Great Shelford CB22. . . . . . .**49** C4
Peterborough PE7 . . . . **185** A4
Forge Way PE26. . . . . **164** F5
Forster Rd PE28 . . . . **140** E1
Forsythia Rd PE27. . . . . **144** A6
Fortescue Rd CB4. . . . .**83** E6
Forties Cl CB9 . . . .**24** D8
Fortune Way SG8 . . . .**12** E5
Forty Acre Rd PE1. . . . . **198** D2
Forty Foot Bank
Doddington PE26 . . . . **222** C3
Ramsey Forty Foot PE26 . . **221** C3
Ramsey PE26. . . . . **221** E2
Forum Ct 7 CB4. . . . .**83** E7
Foster Ct PE29. . . . . **141** F7
Foster Rd
Cambridge CB2 . . . .**64** D2
Peterborough PE2 . . . . **186** D8
Foster Way CB23. . . . .**79** B3
Foul Anchor PE13. . . . . **238** D8
Foundry Cl CB24. . . . . **125** D3
Foundry Rd PE9 . . . . **244** A5
Foundry Way
Eaton Socon PE19 . . . .**74** B1
March PE15. . . . . **228** B6
Ramsey PE26. . . . . **172** A5
Foundry Wlk PE27 . . . . **144** A3
Fountain La
Haslingfield CB23 . . . .**47** B5
Soham CB7 . . . . **212** B4
Fountains Pl PE6 . . . . **232** B1
Four Acres
Fenstanton PE28 . . . . **121** C2
Great Chesterford CB10 . . . .**18** D3
Four Chimneys Cres
PE7. **186** C2
Fourfields Prim Sch PE1 **181** E6
Four Gotes PE13 . . . . **238** C7
Four Hundred Dro PE15. . **221** E5
Four Oaks PE13 . . . . **245** E4
Fourth Dro
Downham CB6. . . . . **225** A1
Peterborough PE1 . . . . **198** F3
Four Went Ways CB21. . . . .**51** A1
FOWLMERE **15** D8
Fowlmere Nature Reserve*
SG8 . . . .**15** D8
Fowlmere Prim Sch SG8 . .**15** D8
Fowlmere Rd
Foxton SG8. . . . .**30** D3

Fowlmere Rd *continued*
Heydon SG8. . . . . .7 F8
Newton CB22. . . . . .31 B6
Shepreth SG8. . . . . .29 F4
Thriplow SG8. . . . . .31 A2
Fox Brook PE19. . . . . .75 C5
Foxburrow Cl CB9 . . . . .38 F1
Fox Cl PE19 . . . . .75 A5
Fox Cnr SG8. . . . . .10 F5
Fox Covert
Stilton PE7. . . . . .175 F7
St Neots PE19 . . . . .75 C5
Foxcovert Rd
Peakirk PE6. . . . . .204 A8
Werrington PE4. . . . . .204 B4
Foxdale PE1. . . . . .197 F7
Fox Dale PE9 . . . . .244 A6
Foxenfields PE28 . . . . .162 C1
Foxglove Bank SG8 . . . . .5 F5
Foxglove Cl
3 Eaton Socon PE19 . . . . . .74 C5
Yaxley PE7. . . . . .182 A7
Foxglove Way
January PE15. . . . . .243 E6
Ramsey St Mary's PE26. . . .220 D3
Fox Gn CB8. . . . . .55 F7
Fox Gr PE29 . . . . .141 F2
Fox Hill SG8. . . . . .11 A5
Fox Hill Rd SG8. . . . . .10 F5
Foxhollow CB23. . . . . .79 B2
Fox Hollow CB23. . . . . .102 A6
Foxley Cl PE4. . . . . .204 C4
Fox Rd
Balsham CB21. . . . . .52 F3
Bourn CB23. . . . . .60 D5
Catworth PE28. . . . . .136 D8
Fox's Cl CB24. . . . . .105 D2
Fox St SG19 . . . . .58 E5
Fox's Way CB23. . . . . .62 D6
FOXTON 30 D5
Foxton Prim Sch CB22 . . . .30 C5
Foxton Rd
Barrington CB22 . . . . .29 F8
Foxton CB22. . . . . .30 A7
Foxton Sta CB22 . . . . .30 C6
Foxtrot La PE28. . . . . .151 F3
Fox Wood N CB7. . . . . .212 B5
Fox Wood S CB7 . . . . .212 B4
Framlingham Rd PE7 . . . . .187 F5
Francis Cl CB3 . . . . .23 F8
Francis Darwin Ct CB4 . . .83 C5
Francis Gdns PE1. . . . . . . .197 F8
Francis Pas 3 CB2 . . . . .64 E7
Frank Bridges Cl 2 CB7 212 B3
Frankland Wlk CB23 . . . . .240 F6
Franklin Cres PE1. . . . . . . .198 E6
Franklin Gdns CB24 . . . . .125 D4
Frank Perkins Parkway
PE2. .187 B8
Frank Perkins Way PE1 . .198 D4
Franks La PE13 . . . . .237 F5
Frank's La CB4 . . . . .84 B5
Fraserburgh Way 2 PE2 185 C4
Fraser Dr PE27 . . . . .84 A6
Fraser Rd CB4. . . . . .84 A6
FRECKENHAM 213 C3
Freckenham Rd IP28. . . . .213 E3
Fred Archer Way CB8 . . . .111 A3
Fred Dannatt Rd IP28. . . .239 A6
Frederick Talbot Cl 5
CB7. .212 B4
Free Church Pas PE27 . . . .144 A3
Freedom Bridge PE13. . . .248 B6
Freeman Cl 1 PE6. . . . . . . .230 B1
Freemantle Ct 1 PE19 . . .74 B3
Free Sch La CB2. . . . . .246 A2
Freesia Way PE7. . . . . .181 F6
Freewood La CB11. . . . . .9 B3
French Dro PE6. . . . . .232 E7
French's Rd
Cambridge CB4 . . . . .83 D4
Walpole PE14. . . . . .238 F8
Freshfields CB8. . . . . .110 F4
Freston PE4. . . . . .204 F2
Friar Cl CB9 . . . . .38 F1
Friar's Cl CB1 . . . . .65 F5
Friars Nine CB6. . . . . .242 C4
Friar's Pl CB6 . . . . .242 C5
Friar's Way CB23 . . . . .242 C5
Friar Way CB23. . . . . .79 B2
FRIDAY BRIDGE 236 A4
Fridaybridge Prim Sch
PE14. . . . . .236 A3
Fridaybridge Rd PE14. . . .236 A4
Friday St PE28. . . . . .213 D6
Friends Cl PE19. . . . . .98 C2
Frinton Way 4 PE13 . . . . .245 E5
Fritton Ct 7 PE13. . . . . .23 E6
Frobisher Cl PE29. . . . . . . .141 F6
Frog End
Great Wilbraham CB21 . . . .67 F7
Haslingfield CB23 . . . . .47 A6
Little Wilbraham CB1. . . . . .86 C2
Shepreth SG8. . . . . .29 F2
Frogge St CB10. . . . . .18 B3
Frogmore CB8. . . . . .110 B7
Frogs Abbey CB6 . . . . .217 F4
Frogs Abbey La PE15. . . . .223 B7
Frogs Hall PE28. . . . . .208 C5
Froize End PE28. . . . . .210 A5
Fromont Way CB24. . . . . . .105 C3
Fromont Cl CB21. . . . . .66 E4
Front Rd
Murrow PE13. . . . . .234 D6
Tydd St Giles PE13. . . . . . .238 D8
Front St CB8 . . . . .92 F4
Frowd Cl PE7. . . . . .212 E1
Frumetty La PE28. . . . . . . .150 F4

Fryers Callis PE9 . . . . . . .244 C3
Fryth Cl CB9. . . . . .39 A1
FULBOURN. 66 F4
Fulbourn Hospl CB1 . . . . . .66 B5
Fulbourn Nature Reserve ✱
CB21 .67 B4
Fulbourn Old Drift CB1. . . .66 A6
Fulbourn Prim Sch CB21 . .66 F5
Fulbourn Rd
Cambridge CB1 . . . . .65 F5
Fulbourn CB1. . . . . .66 D7
Fulbridge Rd PE1. . . . . . . .197 F8
Fulbridge Sch PE1. . . . . . . .197 F7
Fulbrooke Rd CB3 . . . . .64 A7
Fulham Rd PE3 . . . . .197 E4
Fullards Cl PE29 . . . . .155 B4
Fuller Cl PE28 . . . . .137 F6
Fuller's Hill SG19 . . . . .42 D7
Fuller's La 5 PE15 . . . . . . .223 B7
Fuller Way CB3 . . . . .83 B3
Fundrey Rd PE13 . . . . .245 E5
Funtham's La PE7 . . . . . . .188 D7
Furlongs The PE27 . . . . . . .208 A2
Furlong Way CB23 . . . . .80 B1
Furrells The CB21. . . . . .35 C3
Furrowfields Rd PE16 . . . .241 C5
Furrows The PE27. . . . . . . .144 A4
Furrow The CB6 . . . . .242 C3
Furtherford CB24 . . . . .208 E1
Furze Gr SG8. . . . . .5 E5
Furze Ride PE1. . . . . .198 B8
Fydell Ct PE19. . . . . .75 B7

G

Gables Cl SG8. . . . . .29 A1
Gables Dr PE3. . . . . .197 D2
Gables The PE28. . . . . .121 A5
Gadd's La PE13 . . . . .235 D8
Gadwall Way 5 CB7 . . . . .212 A5
Gage Cl SG8. . . . . .5 D8
Gainsborough Ave 6
PE19. .74 C5
Gainsborough Cl CB4 . . . .84 B6
Gainsborough Dr PE27. . .144 A7
Gainsborough Rd CB9. . . . .38 D1
Gains La PE26 . . . . .189 C4
Gala Cl PE7. . . . . .176 A8
Galfrid Rd CB5 . . . . .84 D2
Gallery The CB7 . . . . .240 D4
Gallions Cl PE4 . . . . .204 C4
Gallows Hill (Tumulus)✱
SG7. . . . . .3 E1
Gall's Dro PE13 . . . . .235 A4
Galloway 41 D5
GAMLINGAY 41 B6
Gamlingay Cinques Nature
Reserve✱ SG19. . . . . . . .41 A7
Gamlingay Fst Sch SG19 41 D5
GAMLINGAY GREAT
HEATH 40 E3
Gamlingay Meadows Nature
Reserve✱ SG19. . . . . . . .41 A4
Gamlingay Rd
Gamlingay SG19 . . . . .41 D8
Potton SG19. . . . . .41 C1
Waresley SG19 . . . . .57 E1
Gamlingay Village Coll
SG19 .41 C8
Gamlingay Wood Nature
Reserve✱ SG19. . . . . . . .41 E8
Gamsey Wood Nature
Reserve✱ PE28. . . . . . . .162 A8
Gannet Cl CB9. . . . . .24 C8
Gannocks Cl PE2. . . . . .185 F5
Ganwick Cl CB9. . . . . .38 F2
Gaol St 12 PE13. . . . . .245 C4
Garden Cl
Royston SG8 . . . . .5 E7
St Ives PE27 . . . . .144 A6
Sutton CB6. . . . . .216 E1
GARDEN COTTAGE. 93 D5
Garden Ct
Burwell CB25. . . . . .130 C4
Ramsey PE26. . . . . .172 A4
Garden End CB6 . . . . .14 D5
Garden End Rd PE1. . . . . .198 B6
Gardeners La 7 CB22. . . .212 B4
Gardens Fields CB22. . . . . .48 E3
Garden Gr PE7. . . . . .198 B6
Garden La
Royston SG8 . . . . .5 D5
Wisbech St Mary PE13 . . .235 A7
Garden Rd PE1 . . . . .198 A6
Gardens The PE15. . . . . . . .243 A6
Garden Wlk
Cambridge CB4 . . . . .83 D4
Histon CB24. . . . . .104 C5
Royston SG8 . . . . .5 E7
Gardiners La SG7. . . . . .2 D4
Garlic Row CB5. . . . . .84 B3
Garner Ave PE28. . . . . .164 E5
Garner Cl CB24. . . . . .105 C3
Garner Ct PE29 . . . . .141 F7
Garrett Rd CB4 PE9 . . . . .244 B4
Garret Hostel La CB2 . . . .246 A3
Garrick Wlk PE7 . . . . .187 B7
Garry Dr CB4. . . . . .84 A7
Garton St PE1 . . . . .198 A5
Gascoigne PE6. . . . . .203 F5
Gas La
Ely CB7. . . . . .240 D3
Stamford PE9. . . . . .244 C5
Thorney PE6. . . . . .233 A3
Gas Rd PE15. . . . . .243 D3
Gas St SG19 . . . . .244 C5

Gatenby PE4. . . . . .204 C4
Gateway Gdns CB6. . . . . . .240 B3
Gateways CB8 . . . . .90 F6
GATLEY END. 3 C7
Gaul Rd PE15. . . . . .243 B4
Gault Bank PE15. . . . . .227 D1
GAULTREE 236 D6
Gaultree Sq PE14 . . . . . . .236 D6
Gavel St PE7 . . . . .181 C8
Gayton Cl 3 CB2. . . . . .64 D3
Gayton Ct PE3 . . . . .197 C5
Gazeley Gdns PE7. . . . . . . .187 B2
Gazeley Rd
Ashley CB8. . . . . .92 A8
Cambridge CB2 . . . . .64 D4
Kentford CB8. . . . . .134 C1
Moulton CB8. . . . . .112 F6
Gazelle Cl 4 PE19. . . . . . . .74 B5
Gazelle Way CB1. . . . . .66 B7
Geddington Rd PE2. . . . . .186 E8
Geneva St PE1. . . . . .198 A3
Geoffrey Bishop Ave
CB21. .67 A4
George Alcock Way PE7. .187 D2
George Campbell Leisure Ctr
PE15. . . . . .243 C4
George Gdns PE7. . . . . . . .189 D8
George Gibson Cl CB8 . . .110 C8
George IV St CB2 . . . . . . .246 C1
George La
Buckden PE19 . . . . .117 A4
Royston SG8 . . . . .5 D5
Warboys PE28 . . . . .164 E5
George Lambton Ave
CB8 . . . . .110 F6
George Nuttall Cl CB4 . . . .84 A6
George Pateman Ct 2
CB1. . . . . .64 F7
George Pl 7 PE19 . . . . .74 F2
George St
Cambridge CB4 . . . . .83 F4
Huntingdon PE29. . . . . .141 D4
March PE15. . . . . .243 D4
Peterborough PE2 . . . . .186 F8
Stilton PE7. . . . . .175 F8
7 Willingham CB24 . . . . .209 A1
Georgia PE28 . . . . .151 E4
Georgian Cl PE3. . . . . .197 E2
Georgina Cl PE15 . . . . .224 B4
Gerard Cl CB5 . . . . .84 C2
Gerard Rd CB5 . . . . .84 D3
Gery Ct PE19 . . . . .74 C5
Giant's Hill ✱ CB24 . . . . . .125 A5
Gibralter La CB24. . . . . . . .122 E5
Gibson Ave PE16 . . . . .241 B3
Gibson Cl CB25. . . . . .106 A7
Gidding Gr PE28. . . . . .166 B1
Gidding Rd PE28. . . . . .167 D3
Giddings Cl PE2 . . . . .185 F4
Gidney La 8 CB7 . . . . .212 B3
Gifford Pl CB2 . . . . .246 A3
Gifford's Cl CB3 . . . . .82 E8
Giffords Way 4 CB24 . . . .208 D1
Gilbert Cl CB14 . . . . .83 C5
Gilbert Rd
Cambridge CB4 . . . . .83 D5
Littleport CB6 . . . . .242 B5
Gilbert Scott Dr CB6 . . . .240 E7
Gildale PE4. . . . . .204 D4
Gilmerton Cl CB22. . . . . . . .99 B3
Gilmerton Dr PE1. . . . . . . .198 D7
Gilmour Rd CB2 . . . . .64 F6
Gilpin Pl CB2 . . . . .64 F6
Gilpin Rd CB23 . . . . .64 F6
Gilpin St PE1. . . . . .197 E6
Gimber Ct 5 PE29. . . . . . .141 F7
GIMBERS END. 115 B2
Gimbert Rd CB7 . . . . .212 B4
Gimbert Sq PE15. . . . . . . .243 C4
Gipping Cl 1 CB9 . . . . .27 B8
Gipsey Cnr PE19 . . . . .56 C5
Gipsy Cl PE16 . . . . .241 B5
Gipsy Dro PE16 . . . . .215 F6
Gipsy La PE15 . . . . .243 A7
GIRTON 82 F8
Girton Cl
Mildenhall IP28 . . . . .239 C6
Peterborough PE29. . . . . . .111 B1
Girton Coll
Cambridge CB3 . . . . .83 B2
Girton CB3. . . . . .82 F6
Girton Cres PE29 . . . . .142 A7
Girton Glebe Prim Sch
CB3. .103 C1
Girton Rd
Girton CB3. . . . . .82 F7
Haverhill CB9. . . . . .24 B7
Girton Way PE19 . . . . .74 B4
Gisborne Rd CB1 . . . . .65 C6
Gladeside CB23. . . . . .102 C4
Gladstone Park Com Recn
Ctr PE1. . . . . .197 E5
Gladstone Prim Sch PE1 .197 F5
Gladstone St PE1 . . . . .197 F3
Gladstone Way CB1. . . . . . .65 F5
Glamis Cl CB9 . . . . .23 D8
Glamis Gdns PE13 . . . . . . .197 B2
Glanely Gdns CB8 . . . . . . .110 C8
Glassmoor Bank PE27 . . .208 C7
Glastonbury Cl 11 PE6 . .232 A1
GLATTON 175 F1
Glatton Dr PE2 . . . . .187 D6
Glatton La PE28 . . . . .175 B2
Glatton Rd PE28 . . . . .168 A6
Glatton Ways PE28. . . . . . .175 F1
Glebe Ave PE28. . . . . .185 C4

Glebe Cl
Chatteris PE16. . . . . .241 D5
Gorefield PE13. . . . . .237 E3
Great Paxton PE19 . . . . .96 E4
Toft CB23. . . . . .61 E5
Wimblington PE15 . . . . .224 B4
Glebe Cres CB22. . . . . .33 B4
Glebe Ct PE2 . . . . .187 A8
Glebe Gdns 2 PE6. . . . . . .232 B8
Glebe La
Buckden PE19 . . . . .117 A3
Cambourne CB23. . . . . .79 C4
Great Shelford CB22 . . . . . .49 B5
Glebelands Cty Prim Sch
PE16. . . . . .241 D5
Glebe Rd
Barrington CB22 . . . . .29 F8
Brampton PE28 . . . . .140 E2
Cambridge CB1 . . . . .65 B4
Hemingford Grey PE28 . . .143 D1
Huntingdon PE29. . . . . .141 D7
Perry PE28. . . . . .115 D3
Peterborough PE2 . . . . .187 A8
Sawtry PE28 . . . . .168 A4
Stilton PE7. . . . . .176 A7
Waterbeach CB25 . . . . .106 A7
Glebe The
Haverhill CB9. . . . . .39 A1
Ramsey PE26. . . . . .172 B4
Glebe Way
Haddenham CB6 . . . . .209 F6
Histon CB24. . . . . .104 C4
Glemsford Pl 2 CB9 . . . . . .24 B8
Glemsford Rise PE2. . . . . .186 C7
Glenacre Cl 3 CB1. . . . . . . .65 E5
Glenariff Cl 7 PE19. . . . . . .74 E4
Glencoe Way PE2. . . . . . . .185 D3
Glen Cres PE9. . . . . .244 C7
Glendale PE2 . . . . .185 D6
Glendon Gdns PE13. . . . . .245 A7
Gleneagles PE2. . . . . .185 F6
Glenfields PE2. . . . . .189 C8
Glenmere Cl CB1 . . . . .65 D5
Glen Rd 1 PE8. . . . . .230 B1
Glen The PE2 . . . . .187 B7
GLENTHORN 227 F3
Glenton St PE1 . . . . .198 C2
Glenville Cl CB1. . . . . .85 B1
GLINTON 203 E8
Glinton Rd
Helpston PE6. . . . . .203 A8
Newborough PE6 . . . . .204 E8
Glisson Rd CB1 . . . . .246 C1
Global Centre Ind Est
PE1. .198 E4
Globe La
Alconbury PE28 . . . . .150 E3
3 Littleport CB6. . . . . . . .242 D4
Gloucester Ct CB13 . . . . . .245 D7
Gloucester Pl 4 PE1. . . . .198 B3
Gloucester Rd
Brampton PE28 . . . . .140 D1
Haverhill CB9. . . . . .23 F7
Peterborough PE2 . . . . .187 B7
Sawtry PE28 . . . . .168 C3
Glover Ct 7 Stamford . . .244 B6
Wyton Airfield PE28. . . . . .143 B8
Glover Cl CB22 . . . . .32 F6
Glover St CB24 . . . . .208 D1
Goddard Cres 1 PE13 . . .245 D7
Godby Cr 4 PE29. . . . . . . .141 F6
Godesdone Rd CB5 . . . . . . .84 A3
Godfrey Cl PE6 . . . . .207 D1
Goding Way CB24 . . . . . . .105 E2
GODMANCHESTER 141 E2
Godmanchester Com
Swimming Pool PE29. . .141 F2
Godmanchester Prim Sch
PE29. . . . . .141 F2
Godric Sq PE2 . . . . .186 D6
Godsey La 2 PE6. . . . . . . .231 E8
Godwin Cl CB1. . . . . .65 C4
Godwin Rd PE13. . . . . .245 D7
Godwit Cl PE7. . . . . .201 A1
Goffers Knoll (Tumulus)✱
SG8 . . . . .14 E1
Goffsmill PE3. . . . . .197 A4
Gog Magog Way CB22. . . . .49 C5
Goldcrest Cl 3 CB23. . . . . .79 C3
Golden Drop PE6 . . . . .231 C4
Golden Miller Cl CB8 . . . .110 D7
Golden Rod 3 PE29 . . . . .118 F8
Goldfinch Dr CB24 . . . . . .125 D4
Goldhay Way PE2 . . . . .185 F2
Goldie La PE2 . . . . .185 F6
Golding Pl 13 PE13 . . . . . .248 C8
Golding Rd CB1. . . . . .65 B6
Goldings Cl CB9 . . . . .39 A2
Goldpits PE28 . . . . .164 F5
Gold St PE15 . . . . .243 C7
Golf La PE28. . . . . .151 F3
Golf Links Rd
Barton Mills IP28 . . . . .214 A3
Worlington IP28 . . . . .239 A1
Gonville Cl IP28 . . . . .239 D6
Gonville Pl CB1. . . . . .246 C1
Goochgate PE12. . . . . .237 A7
Goodacre PE2 . . . . .186 A4
Goodchilds Gdns 5 CB7 213 A5
Goode Cl CB24 . . . . .125 D4
Goodens La PE13 . . . . .238 A5
Goodhall Cl PE29 . . . . .141 C6
Goodwin Ave CB21. . . . . . . .53 C2
Goodwin Gr CB7. . . . . .240 F7
Goodwin Wlk PE4. . . . . . . .204 C4

Goodwood Rd
Peterborough PE3 . . . . .196 F3
Royston SG8 . . . . .5 F6
Goose Cross CB23 . . . . .80 B1
Goose Fen Dro CB7. . . . . .211 C6
Gordon Ave
March PE15. . . . . .243 D4
Peterborough PE2 . . . . .186 E7
Gordon Cl PE19. . . . . .95 F1
Gordon Ct PE13. . . . . .245 C3
Gordon Rd PE19 . . . . .95 F1
Gordon Way PE2. . . . . .186 C7
Goredike Bank PE13 . . . . .237 E3
GOREFIELD. 237 E2
Gorefield Prim Sch PE13 .237 E2
Gorefield Rd PE13 . . . . . . .237 F2
Gore Tree Rd PE28 . . . . . .120 C7
Gorse Cl 8 IP28. . . . . .214 A1
Gorse Gn PE1 . . . . .198 B8
Gorse Way PE27 . . . . .144 B5
Goshawk Cl PE29 . . . . .142 A8
Gosling's Dro PE7 . . . . . . .220 A8
Gosling Way CB22. . . . . .33 A8
Gosmoor La PE14. . . . . . . .236 B5
Gossian Cl PE27. . . . . .144 A6
Gostwick PE2. . . . . .185 D5
Gote La PE13. . . . . .237 E3
Gough Way CB3 . . . . .82 F6
Governess Cl 8 PE15. . . . .223 B7
Gower Rd SG8. . . . . .5 C7
Gowers The CB3 . . . . .103 C1
Grace Sch of Medicine
CB1. . . . . .65 D5
Gracious St PE7 . . . . .189 D7
Graeme Rd PE5. . . . . .194 F2
GRAFHAM 116 A7
Grafham Cl PE2. . . . . .187 E4
Grafham Rd PE28. . . . . . . .138 F4
Grafham Water Ctr ✱
PE28. . . . . .116 B5
Grafham Water Nature
Reserve✱ PE28. . . . . . . .115 C3
Grafton Ave PE2. . . . . .197 C3
Grafton Cl PE27. . . . . .143 F8
Grafton Ctr The CB1 . . . . .246 C3
Grafton Dr CB23 . . . . .80 B2
Grafton St CB1 . . . . .246 C2
Graham Rd CB4. . . . . .83 E8
Grain Cl CB22 . . . . .49 A5
Grainger Ave PE29 . . . . . . .118 F8
Grammar Sch Wlk PE29. .141 D4
Granary Cl PE29. . . . . .141 E1
Granary Ct CB23. . . . . .81 F5
Granary End 4 CB6. . . . . .217 E1
Granary La 5 CB6. . . . . . . .242 D4
Granary Rd CB8. . . . . .111 B2
Granary The
Old Hurst PE28 . . . . .154 D7
Swavesey CB24 . . . . .168 B4
Granary Way CB23 . . . . .79 B3
Granby St
Littleport CB6 . . . . .242 D4
Newmarket CB8. . . . . .111 B3
Peterborough PE1. . . . . . . .198 B2
Grand Arc CB2. . . . . .246 B2
GRANDFORD HOUSE. . . .227 F6
Grandridge Cl CB21. . . . . . .66 F4
Grange Ave PE1. . . . . .198 A6
Grange Cl PE28. . . . . .168 C2
Grange Cres PE2 . . . . .186 A5
Grange Ct CB3. . . . . .64 B8
Grange Dr CB3 . . . . .82 E7
Grange Farm Cl PE19 . . . . .57 B5
Grange Farm The IP28 . . .239 C1
Grangehill Rd PE13 . . . . . .237 B6
Grange La
Barton Mills IP28 . . . . .239 C2
Littleport CB6 . . . . .242 B2
Grange Rd
Cambridge CB3 . . . . .64 B8
Duxford CB22 . . . . .17 A6
Ickleton CB10 . . . . .9 A8
March PE15. . . . . .228 A1
Peterborough PE3 . . . . .197 D4
6 Somersham PE28 . . . .228 C8
Wisbech PE13 . . . . .245 A7
Grange The
Meldreth SG8. . . . . .14 B8
8 Somersham PE28 . . . .208 C8
Granhams Cl CB22. . . . . . . .49 A6
Granham's Rd
Cambridge CB2. . . . . .65 C1
Great Shelford CB22 . . . . . .49 C1
Gransden Rd
Abbotsley PE19 . . . . .57 E6
Caxton CB23 . . . . .59 D8
Gransley Rise PE3 . . . . . . .197 C3
Granta Cl
Great Chesterford CB10 . . .18 B7
St Ives PE27 . . . . .144 B7
Witchford CB6 . . . . .217 D1
Granta Cotts CB10 . . . . . . .18 C2
Granta Leys CB21. . . . . .35 A6
Granta Pk CB21. . . . . .34 A6
Granta Pl CB2 . . . . .246 A2
Granta Rd CB22. . . . . .32 E5
Granta Terr CB22. . . . . .49 B4
Granta Vale CB21. . . . . .35 D2
GRANTCHESTER 64 A4
Grantchester Mdws CB3 . .64 C7

Grantchester Rd
Barton CB23 . . . . .63 D7
Cambridge CB2 . . . . .64 B2
Coton CB23 . . . . .82 C1
Grantchester CB3 . . . . .64 B6
Grantchester Rise CB25 . .130 B5
Grantchester 3 CB3 . .64 C7
Grantham Cl SG8 . . . . .5 B8
Granville Ave PE6 . . . . . . .231 F7
Granville Gdns IP28 . . . . . .239 A4
Granville St PE1 . . . . .198 A4
Grasmere PE29 . . . . .141 B6
Grasmere Gdns
Cambridge CB1 . . . . .246 A4
Peterborough PE4 . . . . .204 D3
Grassgate La PE14 . . . . . . .238 E3
Grass Plant Cotts CB8. . .131 B4
Grass Yd 3 PE28 . . . . . . .113 F4
Gravel Bridge Rd CB24. .123 C6
Gravel Dro
Beck Row, Holywell Row &
Kenny Hill IP28. . . . . .213 C6
Witcham CB6. . . . . .216 F4
Gravel End CB6. . . . . .217 C5
Gravel End La
Coveney CB6 . . . . .217 D5
Witchford CB6. . . . . .217 E1
GRAVELEY 97 F4
Graveley Rd PE19 . . . . .97 A8
Graveley Way PE28 . . . . . .98 E8
GRAVEL HOUSE 228 C6
Gravel Pit Hill SG8 . . . . . . .16 C8
Gravel Wlk PE1 . . . . .198 A2
Gray Ct PE1 . . . . .197 A8
Grayling Cl CB4 . . . . .84 A4
Gray Rd CB1 . . . . .65 D6
Grays Cl SG8 . . . . .5 C8
Grays Gr MK44 . . . . .93 B2
Grays La
Emneth PE14 . . . . .236 C6
March PE15 . . . . .243 D4
Graysmoor Dro PE14. . . . .228 B8
Gray's Rd SG19 . . . . .41 D6
GREAT ABINGTON 34 C5
Great Abington Prim Sch
CB21. .34 C5
GREAT BRADLEY 55 F7
GREAT CAMBOURNE 79 B2
Great Chesterford Prim Sch
CB10. . . . . .18 D2
GREAT CHESTERFORD . .18 D2
Great Chesterford Sta
CB10. . . . . .18 C1
GREAT CHISHILL 7 F2
Great Cl CB23 . . . . .63 B4
Great Dro
Soham CB7 . . . . .211 F3
Swaffham Prior CB7 . . . . . .128 C6
Yaxley PE7 . . . . .182 A5
Great Eastern Rd
March PE15 . . . . .243 D7
Wisbech PE13 . . . . .245 B4
Great Eastern St CB1 . . . .65 B8
Greater Foxes CB21 . . . . . .66 F5
GREAT EVERSDEN 45 E8
Great Farthing Cl PE27. .144 B4
Great Fen Rd CB7. . . . . . . .212 B8
Greatford Rd PE9. . . . . . . .230 C6
GREAT GIDDING 166 D3
Great Gidding CE Prim Sch
PE28. . . . . .166 D3
Great Gn SG8 . . . . .11 A5
GREAT GRANSDEN 58 D5
Great Heath Prim Sch
IP28. . . . . .239 D6
Great How PE27 . . . . .143 F7
Great La CB25 . . . . .129 C1
Greatlands PE28 . . . . .39 A4
Great & Little Shelford CE
Prim Sch CB22 . . . . .48 F4
Great Northern St PE29 .141 D5
Great North Fen Dro
CB24. . . . . .125 C6
Great North Rd
Buckden PE19 . . . . .150 E4
Alconbury PE19 . . . . .117 A5
Eaton Socon PE19 . . . . .74 B2
Peterborough PE2 . . . . .185 A4
Sibson cum Stibbington
PE8 . . . . .183 E8
Southoe & Midloe PE19. . . . .95 F4
St Neots PE19 . . . . .74 C7
Wothorpe PE9 . . . . .244 A2
Great Parlow Cl PE19 . . . . .97 E7
GREAT PAXTON 96 E4
Great Paxton CE Prim Sch
PE19. . . . . .96 E5
GREAT RAVELEY 163 B7
GREAT SHELFORD 48 F5
GREAT STAUGHTON 94 B6
Great Staughton Prim Sch
PE19. . . . . .93 F6
GREAT STUKELEY 152 A2
Great Whyte PE26 . . . . . . .172 A8
GREAT WILBRAHAM 68 A7
Great Wilbraham CE Prim
Sch CB21 . . . . .67 F8
Great Wilbraham Rd CB1. .86 F1
GREAT WRATTING 39 D5
Grebe Cl
Mildenhall IP28 . . . . .239 D3
Whittlesey PE7 . . . . .190 A8
Grebe Ct PE7 . . . . .190 A8
Grebe Way 3 PE19 . . . . . .75 B7

Greenacres
Duxford CB22 . . . . .32 D1
Peterborough PE4 . . . . .204 A4
Green Acres SG19 . . . . .41 C5
Green Bank Rd CB25 . . . . .108 B2
Greenbanks SG8 . . . . .14 C5
Greenbury Cl SG8. . . . . .6 F1
Green Cl PE19 . . . . .94 A6
Greendale PE29. . . . . .141 A6
Green Drift SG8 . . . . .5 B6
Green Drift The PE9. . . . . .230 B3
Green Dro
Coveney CB6 . . . . .217 D4
Crowland PE6 . . . . .232 D8
Elm PE14 . . . . .236 D2
Northside PE6 . . . . .200 F4
Thorney PE6 . . . . .233 A6
GREEN END 62 C6
Green End
Comberton CB23 . . . . .62 C6
Fen Ditton CB5. . . . . .84 E6
Gamlingay SG19 . . . . .41 C5
GREEN END 152 A1
Green End CB25 . . . . .105 D8
GREEN END 93 A3
Green End
Little Staughton MK44. . . . . .93 A3
Little Stukeley PE28. . . . . . .152 A1
Stretham CB6 . . . . .210 F4
Green End Ind Est SG19. . .41 C5
Green End Rd
Cambridge CB4 . . . . .84 B6
Sawtry PE28 . . . . .168 B2
St Neots PE19 . . . . .75 A5
Green Farm Cl PE5 . . . . . .195 E2
Greenfield SG8 . . . . .5 B7
Greenfield Cl CB22. . . . . . . .49 D4
Greenfields
Earith PE28 . . . . .208 E6
Eltisley PE19 . . . . .77 E4
Hemingford Grey PE27 . . . .143 F1
Newmarket CB8. . . . . .111 C3
1 St Neots PE19 . . . . .75 A6
Greenfields Way CB9. . . . . .23 F6
Greenford Cl SG8 . . . . .28 D8
Greengage Cl SG8 . . . . .14 C4
Greengage Rise SG8 . . . . .14 C5
Greengarth PE27. . . . . .144 A5
Greengate Ct PE1. . . . . . . .198 C4
Greenham PE3. . . . . .197 A4
Greenhaze La CB23 . . . . . . .79 B3
Green Head Rd CB25. . . . .108 D4
Green Hill 4 CB6. . . . . . . .211 B7
Greenhill Rd PE8 . . . . .178 F8
Greenhills CB7 . . . . .212 C3
Green How PE27 . . . . .143 E6
Green La
Ashwell SG7 . . . . .2 E5
6 Benwick PE15 . . . . .222 A5
Brampton PE28 . . . . .140 D2
Christchurch PE14 . . . . .229 D3
Ellington PE28 . . . . .138 F4
Everton SG19 . . . . .40 C3
Great Staughton PE19 . . . . .93 F6
Hail Weston PE19 . . . . .95 A1
Leverington PE13. . . . . .237 F2
Linton CB21 . . . . .35 C2
Peterborough PE1 . . . . .198 A4
Red Lodge IP28 . . . . .133 F8
Stamford PE9 . . . . .244 B7
St Ives PE28 . . . . .145 F6
Yaxley PE7 . . . . .181 D6
Greenlands CB2 . . . . .65 B3
Green Lanes CB25 . . . . . . .130 C1
Greenleas CB24. . . . . .104 B5
Green Leys PE27. . . . . .143 F5
Greenlow SG8 . . . . .14 A4
Green Man La CB22. . . . . . .47 F2
Green Pk
Brinkley CB8 . . . . .70 D2
Cambridge CB4 . . . . .84 B6
Chatteris PE16. . . . . .241 E5
Green Rd
Newborough PE6 . . . . .205 F3
Newmarket CB8. . . . . .111 B2
Upwell PE14. . . . . .229 E8
Green Rd The CB22 . . . . . . .33 A8
Green Side CB25 . . . . .106 B7
Greenside Cl CB24 . . . . . . .122 C6
Green's Rd CB4 . . . . .83 E4
Green St
Cambridge CB2 . . . . .246 A3
Duxford CB22 . . . . .32 D1
Haverhill CB9. . . . . .24 C8
March PE15 . . . . .243 E3
Royston SG8 . . . . .5 D8
Willingham CB24 . . . . .209 A1
Greenstock La PE13. . . . . .238 A6
Green The
Ashley CB8. . . . . .91 F8
Beck Row, Holywell Row & Kenny
Hill IP28 . . . . .213 C7
Brampton PE28 . . . . .140 D2
Cambridge CB4 . . . . .84 B5
Castor PE5. . . . . .195 E2
Foxton CB22. . . . . .30 B5
Glinton PE6 . . . . .203 E8
Great Staughton PE19 . . . . .93 F7
Haddenham CB6 . . . . .210 A6
Histon CB24. . . . . .104 B4
Kingston CB23 . . . . .61 B3
Kirtling CB8 . . . . .72 C5
Lolworth CB23 . . . . .101 F5
Peterborough PE4 . . . . .204 C3
Royston SG8 . . . . .5 D6

Green The continued
Snailwell CB8. . . . . .132 A3
Somersham PE28. . . . . .215 C1
Steeple Morden SG8 . . . . . . .11 C1
6 Thorney PE6 . . . . .233 A3
Winwick PE28 . . . . .158 A6
Yaxley PE7 . . . . .181 E5
Green Tiles Cl PE29 . . . . . .152 E1
Greenway PE19 . . . . .117 B4
Greenwood Cl
1 Haverhill CB9 . . . . .23 E7
Ramsey PE26. . . . . .172 A5
Greenwood Way 10
PE15. . . . . .223 B7
Gregory Rd IP28. . . . . .239 A6
Grenadier Dr PE16 . . . . . .241 C6
Grenadier Rd CB9 . . . . .23 C8
Greneway Mid Sch SG8 . . . .5 F7
Grenfell Rd PE26. . . . . .172 A5
Grenville Way PE19 . . . . . .74 B2
Gresham Pl CB1 . . . . .246 C1
Gresham Rd CB1. . . . . .246 C1
Gresley Dr PE9 . . . . .244 B4
Gresley Way
March PE15 . . . . .243 B6
Peterborough PE3 . . . . .197 C6
Gretton Cl PE2 . . . . .186 C7
Greville Rd CB1. . . . . .65 B7
Greville Starkey Ave CB8 .110 F5
Greys SG8. . . . . .5 A4
Greys The PE15 . . . . .243 E2
Greystoke Ct 1 CB1 . . . . .65 E5
Greystoke Rd CB1. . . . . .65 E5
Grieve Ct CB4 . . . . .84 C5
Griffins Cl PE6. . . . . .207 D1
Griffiths Ct PE2. . . . . .185 E5
Grimshaw Wood Nature
Reserve * PE5. . . . . .196 F6
Grimmer's Rd 6 PE13 . . .245 F7
Grimshaw Rd PE1. . . . . . . .198 B6
Grip The CB21 . . . . .35 B1
Groat La SG19. . . . . .41 D8
Grosvenor Gdns PE19 . . . . .74 E6
Grosvenor House Ct 6
IP28 . . . . .239 B5
Grosvenor Rd PE13 . . . . . .245 D7
Grosvenor Yd CB8 . . . . . . .111 A3
Grounds Ave PE15 . . . . . . .243 F4
Grounds Way PE7. . . . . . . .191 A8
Grove Cl CB23 . . . . .80 B1
Grove Ct
Little Paxton PE19 . . . . .95 F2
St Ives PE27 . . . . .144 A4
Grove End PE28. . . . . .120 C1
Grove Gdns
14 Elm PE14 . . . . .236 A5
Fordham CB7. . . . . .212 E2
Grove La
Brampton PE28 . . . . .140 D3
Cambridge CB1 . . . . .246 B1
Hilton PE28 . . . . .120 C7
Peterborough PE3 . . . . .197 A2
Rivenhall SG19. . . . . .197 E2
Grovemere Ct PE28 . . . . . . .114 B7
Grove Pk
Fordham CB7. . . . . .212 E2
Wisbech PE13 . . . . .245 A4
Grove Prim Sch The CB4 . .83 F6
Grove Rd
Little Paxton PE19 . . . . .95 F2
Sawston CB22 . . . . .33 A8
Grove St PE2 . . . . .186 F8
Grove The
Cambourne CB23 . . . . .79 C5
Cambridge CB4 . . . . .84 B6
Chatteris PE16. . . . . .241 C5
Huntingdon PE29 . . . . .142 B6
Linton CB21 . . . . .35 B3
Mildenhall IP28 . . . . .213 D8
Orwell SG8. . . . . .28 D8
St Neots PE19 . . . . .74 E6
1 Stretham CB6. . . . . .210 F5
Whittlesey PE7 . . . . .189 F6
Wistow PE28 . . . . .163 F6
Grove Way PE26 . . . . .172 A4
Grunty Fen Rd CB6 . . . . . .210 F8
Guanockgate Rd PE12. . . .234 C8
Guash Way PE9. . . . . .244 D7
Guelder Rd 2 PE7. . . . . . .186 D3
Guelder Rose 6 CB7 . . . . .240 F5
Guernsey Way CB6 . . . . . .242 C3
Guest Rd CB1. . . . . .246 C2
Guildenburgh Cres PE7 . .190 E4
GUILDEN MORDEN 10 E4
Guilden Morden CE Prim Sch
SG8 . . . . .10 F5
Guildhall Pl 5 CB1 . . . . . .246 A2
Guildhall St 4 CB1 . . . . . .246 A2
Guild Rd PE13 . . . . .245 E6
Guilsborough Rd PE6 . . . . .232 B2
Guineas Cl CB8 . . . . .110 E6
Guineas The CB8. . . . . .110 A4
Guise La SG8 . . . . .12 D6
Gull Bank PE13 . . . . .234 E3
Gull Dro PE13 . . . . .234 D3
Gull La PE13 . . . . .238 A3
Gull Rd PE13 . . . . .234 F3
Gull Way
Chatteris PE16. . . . . .241 C6
Whittlesey PE7 . . . . .190 A8
Gullymore PE3. . . . . .196 F8
Gunhild Cl CB1. . . . . .65 D5
Gunhild Ct CB1 . . . . .65 C5
Gunhild Way CB1 . . . . .65 C5
Gunnell Cl CB24 . . . . .105 D2
Gunning Rd CB6. . . . . .240 E8
Gunnings Way PE28 . . . . . .143 C1
Gunning Way CB4. . . . . .83 C6

GUNTHORPE 204 D2
Gunthorpe Prim Sch
PE4. . . . . .204 E2
Gunthorpe Rd
Newborough PE6 . . . . .204 F4
Peterborough PE4 . . . . .204 E2
Gunthorpe Ridings PE4 . .205 A2
Guntons Cl CB21 . . . . .212 B4
Gunton's Rd PE6. . . . . .205 C6
Gurlings Cl CB9. . . . . .39 A2
Gurnard Leys PE3. . . . . . . .204 A1
Gurney Way CB4 . . . . .83 E4
Guthlac Ave PE4 . . . . .204 D1
Guyatt Ct CB25 . . . . .130 B2
GUYHIRN 234 F2
Guyhirn CE Prim Sch
PE13. . . . . .235 A2
Guyhirn Gull PE13 . . . . . . .234 E3
Gwydir St CB1. . . . . .65 A8
Gypsy Cnr PE28. . . . . .150 B6
Gypsy La PE13 . . . . .238 C4
Gypsy's Wlk CB8. . . . . .91 A8

H

Hacke Rd PE3 . . . . .197 D3
HADDENHAM 210 B6
Haddenham End Field
CB6. . . . . .210 A7
Haddenham Rd CB6. . . . . .217 A1
HADDON. 180 B6
Haddon Cl PE2 . . . . .187 E5
Haddon Rd
Haddon PE7. . . . . .180 C6
Peterborough PE3 . . . . .197 E3
Haddon Way PE7 . . . . .187 B2
Haddow's Cl CB24 . . . . . . .123 F2
Haden Way
Over CB24. . . . . .208 F1
Willingham CB24 . . . . .123 F8
Hadleigh Cl CB5 . . . . .84 E4
Hadley Rd PE4. . . . . .204 D1
Hadrian Cl CB9 . . . . .24 D7
Hadrians Ct PE2. . . . . .187 B8
HADSTOCK 20 C6
Hadstock Rd CB21. . . . . . . .35 B1
Hagbech Hall Cl PE14. . . .236 D6
Haggers Cl CB24 . . . . .105 D2
Hagger's Cl SG8. . . . . .14 D6
Haggis Gap CB21 . . . . .66 F5
Haig Ct CB4 . . . . .84 A4
Haigh's Cl PE16. . . . . .241 B4
HAIL WESTON. 95 B1
Hake's Dro PE15. . . . . .227 C2
Halcyon Ct PE29 . . . . .141 C6
Hale Ave CB4 . . . . .83 D4
Hale Cl SG8 . . . . .14 C6
Hale Dro CB6. . . . . .225 E6
Hale Fen CB6. . . . . .242 C8
Hale Fen La CB6 . . . . .217 A4
Hale Fen Rd CB6 . . . . .225 E4
Hales Barn Rd CB9. . . . . . . .38 E2
Haley Cl
Hemingford Grey PE28 . . . .143 B1
Wisbech PE13 . . . . .245 C8
Half Acre Dro CB7. . . . . . . .211 C7
Half Acre La CB7 . . . . .211 D8
Halfpenny La PE14 . . . . . . .245 D1
Halfpenny Toll Rd PE14. .229 E4
Halifax Rd
Cambridge CB4 . . . . .83 B4
Mildenhall IP28 . . . . .213 E8
Halifax Way CB8. . . . . .110 E5
Hallards The 6 PE19. . . . . .74 C6
Hallaton Rd PE1 . . . . .198 D8
Hall Bank PE13 . . . . .237 E7
Hall Barn Rd CB7 . . . . .212 F4
Hall Bridge Rd PE14 . . . . .236 D1
Hall Cl
Bourn CB23 . . . . .60 C5
Foxton CB22. . . . . .30 B6
Huntingdon PE29 . . . . .142 A6
Little Paxton PE19 . . . . .95 F2
Hall Cres CB22. . . . . .33 A7
Hallcroft Rd PE7. . . . . .189 C8
Hall Dike PE14. . . . . .236 F4
Hall Dr
Hardwick CB23 . . . . .80 F3
Highfields CB23 . . . . .80 C2
Hall End CB24 . . . . .105 D2
Halley Cl PE20 . . . . .141 A5
Hall Farm La SG19. . . . . . . .58 D4
Hall Farm Rd 2 CB4. . . . .83 D5
Hallfields La PE4 . . . . .204 E1
Hall Gate Rd PE12 . . . . . . .234 B8
Hall Green La PE28 . . . . . .121 B6
Hall La
Abbots Ripton PE28. . . . . . .152 D8
Brinkley CB8 . . . . .70 E2
Burwell CB25 . . . . .130 B1
Great & Little Chishill SG8. . . .7 F2
Peterborough PE4 . . . . .204 C4
Tilbrook PE28 . . . . .113 C8
20 Wittering PE8 . . . . .230 B1
Hall Rd
Outwell PE14. . . . . .236 F3
St Neots PE19 . . . . .74 E3
Hall St CB7. . . . . .212 B5
Hallwyck Gdns CB8 . . . . . .110 F2
Halstead Cl 2 PE13. . . . . .245 E5
Hamden Way CB23. . . . . . . .99 B3
HAMERTON 159 B4
Hamerton Rd
Alconbury Weston PE28. . . .150 F7
Buckworth PE28 . . . . .149 D6
Winwick PE28 . . . . .158 C5

Hamerton Zoological Pk★
PE28. . . . . .159 B5
Hamilton Ct CB8. . . . . .110 E2
Hamilton Rd
Cambridge CB4 . . . . .246 B4
Ely CB6 . . . . .240 B4
Newmarket CB8. . . . . .110 E3
Hamiltons The CB8. . . . . . .110 E2
Ham La PE2 . . . . .185 E7
Hamlet Cl PE29 . . . . .141 F6
Hamlet Rd CB9 . . . . .24 B7
Hamlet The CB6 . . . . .218 C6
Hammond Cl
Cowlinge CB8. . . . . .73 D1
Newmarket CB8. . . . . .110 E6
Pampisford CB22. . . . . .33 B5
Wittering PE8 . . . . .230 C1
Hammond Way PE28 . . . . .208 C8
Hampden Gdns CB1. . . . . . .84 B1
Hampden Rd 2 CB1 . . . . .245 D5
Hampden Rise SG8 . . . . .5 D4
Hampden Way PE26 . . . . . .75 A3
Hampshire Rd PE28 . . . . . .143 B8
Hampstead Ave IP28. . . . . .239 B6
Hampton Cl PE28 . . . . .121 C6
Hampton Coll PE7 . . . . .186 D1
Hampton Ct PE3 . . . . .197 C6
HAMPTON HARGATE 186 D2
Hampton Hargate Prim Sch
PE7. . . . . .186 C2
Hampton Vale Prim Sch
PE7. . . . . .186 C1
Hanaper Dr SG8 . . . . .6 F1
Hanbury PE2 . . . . .185 F3
HANCHET END 38 C1
Hanchet End CB9 . . . . .38 B1
HANCHETT VILLAGE 23 B8
Hankey St PE1. . . . . .197 F4
Hanmer Ave IP28 . . . . .239 C5
Hannath Rd PE14 . . . . .238 E8
Hannington Cl PE7. . . . . . . .190 A7
Hanover Cl
Bar Hill CB23 . . . . .102 B3
Eaton Socon PE19 . . . . .74 D5
Hanover Ct
Brampton PE28 . . . . .140 D3
Cambridge CB1 . . . . .246 B1
Peterborough PE3 . . . . .197 A8
Hansel Cl PE2 . . . . .186 E8
Hansell Rd PE28 . . . . .140 B3
Hanson Ct CB4 . . . . .83 E7
Harbins La PE19 . . . . .57 C6
Harbour Ave CB23. . . . . . . .62 D6
Harbour Ct PE16. . . . . .241 C6
Harbour Sch CB6 . . . . .210 C6
Harcombe Rd CB1 . . . . .65 E6
Harcourt PE29 . . . . .142 A2
Hardfields Ct CB7. . . . . . . .212 C3
Harding Cl 1 CB25 . . . . . .106 A7
Harding Way
Cambridge CB4 . . . . .83 C5
Histon CB24. . . . . .104 B4
St Ives PE27 . . . . .144 B5
Hardman Rd CB22 . . . . .30 C5
HARDWICK
Buckden. 117 A5
Cambridge 81 B3
Hardwick Com Prim Sch
CB23. . . . . .81 A3
Hardwick Ct PE3. . . . . .197 B2
Hardwicke Cl CB6. . . . . . . .242 C5
Hardwicke Fields CB6. . . .210 A6
Hardwicke La PE19 . . . . . . .57 B6
Hardwicke Rd SG19. . . . . . .58 F6
Hardwick Road Ind Est
SG19 .58 F6
Hardwick La PE19. . . . . . . .117 A5
Hardwick Rd
Haverhill CB9. . . . . .24 B8
St Neots PE19 . . . . .74 E3
Toft CB23. . . . . .61 E6
Hardwick St CB3. . . . . .64 C7
Hardy Cl
Huntingdon PE29 . . . . .141 F6
Longstanton CB24 . . . . .123 E2
Hardy Dr SG8. . . . . .5 D8
Hardy Pl 1 PE19 . . . . .74 D6
Hardy's La PE7 . . . . .189 E6
Harebell Cl
Cambridge CB1 . . . . .66 A5
Huntingdon PE29 . . . . .141 D5
January PE15. . . . . .243 E6
Peterborough PE1 . . . . .206 B1
Ramsey St Mary's PE26 . . . .220 D3
Harebell Dr PE7 . . . . .182 A7
Harefield Rise CB21. . . . . . .35 E2
HARE PARK 88 A3
Harewood Gdns PE3 . . . . .197 B2
Hargate Way
Hampton Hargate PE7. . . . .186 B2
Peterborough PE7. . . . . .186 D3
Hargood Ct 8 PE19 . . . . . .74 B3
Hargreaves Rd 6 SG8 . . . . .5 D5
Harland Rd PE19. . . . . .74 E6
Harlech St 5 PE19 . . . . . . .74 F2
Harlech Grange PE3 . . . . .197 B1
Harlestones Rd CB24. . . . .125 D4
Harley Ind Pk PE19 . . . . . . .96 D2
HARLTON 46 C5
Harlton Cl PE2 . . . . .186 D8
Harlton Rd
Great Eversden CB23 . . . . . .45 F7
Haslingfield CB23 . . . . .46 F5
Harn Rd PE7. . . . . .186 C2
Harold Heading Cl PE16. .241 B3
Harold's Bank PE13. . . . . .237 B1
HAROLDSBRIDGE 237 C2
Harper's Dro PE26 . . . . . . .170 F7

Harradine Cl PE29 .... 155 B5
Harrier Cl PE29 .... 142 A8
Harrington Dr PE6 .... 232 C8
Harrington Sq 10 PE6 .. 232 B8
Harris Cres PE27 .... 208 A2
Harris La PE28 .... 163 E6
Harrison Cl PE3 .... 196 F3
Harrison Pl PE1 .... 144 A5
Harrison's Dro
　Burwell CB25 .... 129 A8
　Swaffham Prior CB7 ...... 128 D7
Harrison Way PE27 ...... 144 B3
Harris Rd CB4 .... 83 D6
Harris La PE28 .... 163 E7
Harris St PE1 .... 197 F6
Harris Way PE28 .... 154 A1
Harrold Dro PE12 .... 234 C8
Harrolds Cl 5 PE14 .. 238 F1
Harrow Rd CB9 .... 23 E7
Harry Palmer Cl CB2 .. 212 E1
Harry Scott Ct CB4 ...... 83 E7
Harrys Way PE13 .... 245 C2
HARSTON 48 A3
Harston Mill CB22 ...... 47 D2
Harston & Newton Sch
　CB22 .... 47 F2
Harston Rd CB22 .... 31 B8
Hart Cl CB9 .... 38 F1
Hartfield Rd CB8 .... 70 E4
HARTFORD 142 A6
Hartford Ct PE2 .... 187 D6
Hartford Jun & Inf Sch
　PE29 .... 141 F5
Hartford Rd PE29 .... 141 E4
Hartington Gr CB1 ...... 65 A5
Hartlands PE7 .... 190 E8
Hartley Cl CB25 .... 106 B8
Hart Rd PE26 .... 171 E3
Hartwell Ct PE3 .... 197 C5
Hartwell Way
　Peterborough PE3 ...... 197 B5
　Ravensthorpe PE3 ...... 197 C6
Harvest Cl
　11 Doddington PE15 .. 223 A5
　Stilton PE7 .... 175 F8
Harvest Ct PE27 .... 144 A4
Harvester Way
　Crowland PE6 .... 232 B8
　Peterborough PE1 ...... 198 C1
Harvest Way CB1 ...... 84 A2
Harvey Cl 4 PE8 .... 230 B1
Harvey Dr 5 PE28 .. 215 C1
Harvey Goodwin Ave CB4 .83 D4
Harvey Goodwin Gdns
　CB4 .... 83 D4
Harvey Rd CB1 .... 246 C1
Harvey St 8 PE19 ...... 74 E4
Haselhurst Cl PE15 .. 243 F4
HASLINGFIELD 47 B6
Haslingfield Endowed Prim
　Sch CB3 .... 47 A5
Haslingfield Rd
　Barrington CB22 .... 29 F8
　Barton CB23 .... 63 B2
　Harlton CB23 .... 46 E6
　Haslingfield CB23 ...... 47 C3
Hasse Rd CB7 .... 212 C8
Hassock Hill Dro CB22 . 237 D3
Hassock Way 1 PE15 . 223 B7
Hastings Rd PE14 .... 204 C2
Hatchet La PE19 .... 114 B2
Hatfield Rd PE28 .... 168 A4
Hathaway Cl PE19 ...... 74 C3
Hatherdene Cl CB1 ...... 65 E8
Hatley Cl PE19 .... 75 A7
Hatley Dr CB23 .... 130 B3
HATLEY END 25 B5
Hatley Rd
　Gamlingay SG19 .... 41 F4
　Wrestlingworth & Cockayne
　　Hatley SG19 .... 25 A7
HATLEY ST GEORGE 43 A3
Hatton Park Prim Sch
　CB24 .... 123 F2
Hatton's Pk CB24 .... 123 F2
Hatton's Rd CB23 .... 102 C7
Hautboy La PE8 .... 178 B3
HAUXTON 48 B4
Hauxton Prim Sch CB22..48 C4
Hauxton Rd
　Cambridge CB2 .... 48 C8
　Great Shelford CB22 ...... 48 D4
Havelock Cl SG19 .... 11 C5
Havelock Dr PE2 .... 187 E6
Haven The CB21 .... 66 F5
HAVERHILL 24 C8
Haverhill Bsns Pk CB9 .. 24 B4
Haverhill Leisure Ctr CB9 .24 B7
Haverhill Rd
　Castle Camps CB21 ...... 22 E4
　Horseheath CB21 .... 37 A3
　Little Wratting CB9 ...... 39 F3
　Stapleford CB22 .... 49 E5
　Steeple Bumpstead CB9 .. 24 A1
Haveswater Cl 1 PE4.. 204 E2
Haviland Way CB4 ...... 83 F6
Hawcrofts La CB24 .... 208 D2
Hawe's La CB7 .... 211 E2
Hawkenbury PE29 ...... 141 C5
Hawk Dr
　Huntingdon PE29 ...... 142 B7
　Wyton PE28 .... 154 A1
Hawkesden Rd PE19 .. 75 B6
Hawkes End PE28 .... 140 E2
Hawkesford Way PE19 .. 74 F7
Hawkes La PE27 .... 208 A4
Hawkins Dr CB23 .... 115 D3
Hawkins Dr 1 PE13...245 E5

Hawkins Rd CB4 .... 83 F7
Hawkins's Dro CB7 ...... 242 F3
Hawkshead Way 2 PE4..204 E3
Hawthorn Ave
　Hauxton CB22 .... 48 B4
　Sawston CB22 .... 32 F6
Hawthorn Cl
　Little Paxton PE19 ...... 95 F2
　Littleport CB6 .... 242 E3
　Newborough PE6 .... 207 C1
　Royston SG8 .... 5 F7
Hawthorn Dr PE29 .... 141 D5
Hawthorne Ave PE13 .. 245 C8
Hawthorne Dr PE7 ...... 189 F6
Hawthorne Gr PE15 .. 243 C5
Hawthorn End 1 PE28 . 150 F5
Hawthorne Rd CB22 .... 49 B4
HAWTHORN LODGE 93 D5
Hawthorn Rd
　Emneth PE14 .... 236 D5
　Folksworth PE7 .... 175 D8
　Haverhill CB9 .... 38 D1
　Peterborough PE1 ...... 198 C6
　Ramsey PE26 .... 171 F7
　St Neots PE19 .... 74 E6
　Yaxley PE7 .... 181 F5
Hawthorn Way
　Burwell CB25 .... 130 C3
　Cambridge CB4 .... 83 F4
　Royston SG8 .... 5 F7
　Sawtry PE28 .... 168 B3
　St Ives PE27 .... 144 A5
Hawthorn Wlk 4 IP28 ..213 F8
Hawtreys The CB23 ...... 62 D5
Hay Cl CB21 .... 53 B1
Haycocks Rd CB9 .... 23 C8
Haycraft Cl PE28 .... 116 A7
Haycroft The PE19 .... 117 F2
Haydock Rd SG8 .... 5 F6
Hayes Wlk PE8 .... 178 D8
Hay Fen Cl 6 CB6 .. 210 F5
Hayfield Ave CB22 ...... 32 F7
Hayland Dro IP28 .... 213 B7
Hayle Cl PE19 .... 95 A1
Hayley Wood Nature
　Reserve* CB23 .... 43 C6
Hayling Ave PE19 .... 96 A2
Hayling Cl 4 PE29...118 F7
Hayman's Way CB23 .. 239 A1
Haymarket Rd 7 CB3 ...83 C3
Hay St SG8 .... 11 B2
Hayster Dr CB1 .... 65 E6
Hayter Cl CB21 .... 53 F4
Haywardsfield PE3 .... 197 A1
Haywoods La SG8........ 5 E7
Hazen Cl CB23 .... 29 F8
Hazel Cl
　Chatteris PE16 .... 241 D4
　Haverhill CB9 .... 23 E7
　Mildenhall IP28 .... 239 E4
Hazel Croft PE4 .... 204 A4
Hazel Ct 7 CB6 .... 210 F5
Hazel Gdns 1 PE13...245 D4
Hazel La CB23 .... 79 C5
HAZEL STUB 23 C7
Hazel Way PE27 .... 144 B4
Hazelwood Cl CB4 ...... 83 B6
Hazelwood Wlk PE29..141 F7
Head Fen Dro CB6 .... 224 F3
Headford Cl CB5 .... 84 D4
Headington Cl CB1 ...... 65 F5
Headington Dr CB1 ...... 65 F5
Headlake Dro CB22 .. 128 E1
Headland Ave CB9 ...... 23 E7
Headlands
　Fenstanton PE28 .... 121 C5
　Huntingdon PE29 .... 141 C3
Headlands Way PE7 .. 189 D8
Headley Gdns CB22 ...... 49 B4
Headley's La CB22 ...... 217 A2
Heasman Cl CB8 .... 110 F5
Heath Ave SG8 .... 5 C6
Heathball Rd CB8 .... 111 C3
Heathcote Cl PE15 .. 243 F4
Heather Ave PE11 .... 198 A8
Heatherdale Cl PE7 .. 187 C5
Heathersett Cl CB8 .. 110 E3
Heatherset Way 1 IP28.. 213 F1
Heath Farm Rd IP28 .. 213 F1
Heathfield
　Royston SG8 .... 5 B6
　Thriplow CB22 .... 31 E1
Heath House CB4 .... 84 A5
Heath La PE28 .... 163 A7
Heath Rd
　Barnack PE9 .... 230 C3
　Bottisham CB25 .... 87 B4
　Burwell CB25 .... 109 D5
　Exning CB8 .... 110 A8
　Gamlingay SG19 .... 41 A4
　Helpston PE6 .... 231 C2
　Mildenhall IP28 .... 239 E5
　Newmarket CB8 .... 111 C3
　Swaffham Bulbeck CB25 ..108 B2
　Swaffham Prior CB25 ..109 A3
　Warboys PE28 .... 165 C6
Heath Row PE1 .... 205 B1
Heath View PE1 .... 208 B8
Heaton Cl
　Ely CB6 .... 240 F7
　Peterborough PE3 ...... 197 B3
Heaton Dr CB4 .... 240 F7
Hectare The CB22 ...... 48 F7
Hedda Dr PE7 .... 186 A4
Heddon Way PE27 .... 144 B6
Hedgelands
　Peterborough PE4 .... 204 C5

Hedgelands continued
　Wisbech PE13 .... 245 C6
Hedgerley Cl CB3 .... 83 A2
Heffer Cl CB22 .... 49 C4
Heights Dro Rd PE26 .. 170 D6
Helen Cl 8 CB5 .... 84 D4
Helens Cl PE26 .... 171 B1
Helions Bumpstead Rd
　CB9 .... 23 F5
Helions Park Ave CB9 .. 24 A7
Helions Park Gdns CB9 ..24 A7
Helions Park Gr CB9 .. 24 A7
Helions Service Rd CB9 ..24 A7
Helions Wlk CB9 .... 24 A7
Helmsdale Gdns PE4...200 B2
Helmsley Ct PE7 .... 187 F5
HELPSTON 231 C4
Helpston Rd
　Castor PE5 .... 195 D2
　Etton PE6 .... 203 C8
Heltwate PE3 .... 197 C7
Heltwate CB4 .... 81 C8
Heltwate Sch PE3 ...... 197 B7
HEMINGFORD ABBOTS . 142 E3
Hemingford Cres PE27 . 187 E6
HEMINGFORD GREY ..143 E1
Hemingford Grey Prim Sch
　PE28 .... 143 D2
Hemingford Rd
　Cambridge CB1 .... 65 B8
　Hemingford Grey PE27 ..143 F2
Hemington Cl 10 CB24 . 208 D1
Hemlocks The CB23 ...... 47 B5
Hemmerley Dr PE7 .. 189 E8
Hempfield Pl CB6 .... 242 D4
Hempfield Rd CB6 ...... 242 D4
Hempsals 12 PE19 .... 74 C6
Hempsals Rd or Meadow Dro
　CB24 .... 209 C1
Hempstead Rd
　2 Haverhill CB9 .... 38 C1
　Peterborough PE7 ...... 186 C1
Hen Brook PE19 .... 74 F4
Henderson Cl CB9 ...... 38 C1
Henford Gdns PE15 .. 243 D5
Henley Rd CB1 .... 84 B2
Henley Way CB7 .... 240 F6
Henry Cl CB9 .... 23 D6
Henry Crabb Rd CB6 .. 242 A6
Henry Morris Rd
　Bassingbourn CB23 .... 104 C3
　Sawston CB22 .... 32 C6
Henry Orbell Cl 3 PE15..243 E4
Henry St
　Peterborough PE1 ...... 198 A4
　Wisbech PE13 .... 245 C5
Henry Warby Ave 8
　PE14 .... 236 A5
Henshaw PE1 .... 198 E6
Henson Cl PE13 .... 245 C8
Henson Rd PE13 .... 243 C5
Herbert Human Cl 3
　CB7 .... 212 B4
Herbert St CB4 .... 83 E4
Herbert Twinn Ct CB5 .. 84 D4
Hercules Cl 3 CB4 ...... 83 B8
Hereford Cl 7 PE28 .. 208 C8
Hereward PE28 .... 208 E6
Hereward Ave IP28 .. 239 C5
Hereward Cl
　Haddenham CB6 .... 209 E4
　Histon CB24 .... 104 C3
　2 Peterborough PE1 .. 198 B2
Hereward Com Coll PE1. 198 D5
Hereward Rd
　Peterborough PE1 ...... 198 B2
　1 Wisbech PE13 .... 245 D5
Hereward St
　Ely CB6 .... 240 B4
　March PE15 .... 243 D5
Hereward Way PE14 .. 231 F8
Herewood Cross Sh Ctr
　PE1 .... 198 A2
Heritage Park Prim Sch
　PE7 .... 187 F5
Hermitage Rd PE28 .. 208 E6
Herne Rd PE26 .... 220 D4
Heron Cl PE7 .... 189 F8
Heron Ct
　Peterborough PE2 ...... 187 D6
　1 Soham CB7 .... 212 A5
Heron Pk PE1 .... 75 B6
Heron Rd PE13 .... 245 D2
Heronry Dr PE6 .... 196 E2
Herons Cl
　6 Ely CB6 .... 240 B5
　Tallington PE9 .... 230 F6
Heron's Cl CB1 .... 65 D4
Heronshaw PE16 .... 241 D4
Herons The CB24 .... 125 D4
Heron Way PE27 .... 143 F7
Heron Wlk PE15 .... 243 F5
Herrick Cl PE1 .... 197 E8
Herring's Cl CB25 .... 85 F5
HERRINGSWELL 113 E8
Herringswell Rd
　Herringswell IP28 .... 214 B2
　Kentford CB8 .... 134 B4
Herschel Rd CB3 .... 83 B1
Hertford Cl CB6 .... 240 A3
Hertford La SG8 .... 8 E5
Hertford St CB4 .... 246 A4
Hervey Cl 3 CB6 .... 240 B3
Herv&tt Cl CB8 .... 110 E8
Hetley PE2 .... 186 A4
Hexham Ct 3 PE1 .. 198 D3
HEYDON 8 A5

Heydon La
　Elmdon CB11 .... 8 F4
　Heydon SG8 .... 8 B5
Heydon Rd SG8 .... 7 E2
Heyford Cl PE4 .... 204 F2
Heyford Ct 8 IP28 .. 239 B5
Hiblings Row PE15 .. 224 B4
Hickling Wlk PE4 .... 204 E3
Hicks La
　Girton CB3 .... 82 E8
　Peterborough PE7 ...... 186 F5
Hicks Way 4 CB4 ...... 24 E5
Hide Cl CB22 .... 32 F6
Higham Rd IP28 .... 214 E1
High Barns CB7 .... 240 E6
High Broadgate PE13 .. 237 F7
Highbury St PE1 .... 198 A5
High Cl SG8 .... 6 F4
Highclere Cl CB8 ...... 110 D8
Highclere Rd 1 PE1 .. 198 A1
High Court Way PE7 .. 181 D8
HIGH CROSS 82 E2
High Cswy PE7 .... 189 E7
Highdene Rd CB1 ...... 66 A6
High Ditch Rd CB5 ...... 85 A4
High Fen Crooked Dro
　PE28 .... 215 B5
High Fen Straight Dro
　PE28 .... 215 B6
Highfield Ave
　Alconbury Weston PE28.. 150 D6
　Cambridge CB4 .... 83 E5
Highfield Cl CB22 .... 17 D8
Highfield Cotts SG8 ...... 4 B7
Highfield Dr CB6 .... 242 C3
Highfield Gate CB21 .. 66 F6
Highfield Rd
　Helpston PE6 .... 231 A3
　Histon CB24 .... 104 C1
　March PE15 .... 243 D7
HIGHFIELDS 80 D2
Highfields PE14 .... 236 D5
Highfield Sch CB6 .... 240 C5
Highfields Rd CB23 .. 80 C2
High Flyer Cotts CB7.. 240 F7
Highgate Gn PE8 .... 178 D8
High Gn
　Abbotsley PE19 .... 57 B6
　Great Shelford CB22 .. 49 A6
High Haden Rd PE28 .. 175 B1
HIGH HARTHAY 139 E3
Highlands SG8 .... 5 E6
Highlands The CB8 .. 110 D8
Highlees Prim Sch PE3 . 197 C6
High Leys PE27 .... 143 F5
Highw
　Harston CB22 .... 47 F3
　Ramsey PE26 .... 172 A3
High Park Cnr CB7 ...... 132 D5
High Piece Cres CB24 .. 208 C1
High Rd
　Downham CB6 .... 217 F6
　Gorefield PE13 .... 237 E3
　Newton PE13 .... 238 A5
　Tydd St Giles PE13 ...... 233 B8
　Wisbech St Mary PE13 . 235 A6
High Sch Cl PE15 .... 243 D6
Highsett CB1 .... 84 D4
High Side PE13 .... 235 A8
High St
　Abbotsley PE19 .... 57 B6
　Abington Pigotts SG8.... 11 F5
　Alconbury PE28 .... 150 F4
　Alconbury Weston PE28.. 150 D6
　Ashley CB8 .... 91 F8
　Ashwell SG2 .... 2 D4
　Babraham CB22 .... 33 D8
　Balsham CB21 .... 53 A2
　Barley SG8 .... 6 F2
　Barrington CB22 .... 29 E8
　Barton CB23 .... 63 B4
　Bassingbourn SG8 ...... 12 F4
　Benwick PE15 .... 237 A6
　Bluntisham/Colne PE28.. 208 C5
　Bottisham CB25 .... 86 F5
　Bourn CB23 .... 80 A4
　Boxworth CB23 .... 101 B5
　Brampton PE28 .... 144 C8
　Brinkley CB8 .... 70 D2
　Buckden PE19 .... 117 A4
　Burwell CB25 .... 109 B8
　Cambourne CB23 .... 79 B3
　Castle Camps CB21 ...... 22 E3
　Castor PE5 .... 195 F2
　Catworth PE28 .... 136 D7
　Chatteris PE16 .... 241 C5
　Cherry Hinton CB1 ...... 66 A7
　Cheveley CB8 .... 91 C7
　Chippenham CB7 .... 132 E8
　Chrishall SG8 .... 8 D3
　Conington CB23 .... 101 C1
　Coton CB23 .... 82 B2
　Cottenham CB24 .... 125 E4
　Croxton PE19 .... 76 F4
　Croydon SG8 .... 27 A7
　Doddington/Wimblington
　　PE15 .... 223 A5
　Dry Drayton CB23 .... 108 B1
　Earith PE28 .... 208 E5
　Ellington PE28 .... 139 A4
　Ely CB7 .... 244 B3
　Eye PE6 .... 232 A1
　Eyeworth SG19 .... 10 A8
　Fen Ditton CB5 .... 84 E5
　Fen Drayton CB24 .... 123 C3
　Fenstanton PE28 .... 121 A6
　Fowlmere SG8 .... 15 E8
　Foxton CB22 .... 30 B5

High St continued
　Fulbourn CB21 .... 66 F5
　Girton CB3 .... 103 E1
　Glinton PE6 .... 203 E8
　Grantchester CB3 ...... 64 A4
　Graveley PE19 .... 97 F5
　Great Chesterford CB10 .. 18 E2
　Great Eversden CB23 .. 45 E8
　Great & Little Abington
　　CB21 .... 34 C6
　Great Paxton PE19 ...... 96 D4
　Great Shelford CB22 .. 48 E3
　Great Wilbraham CB21 .. 67 F7
　Guilden Morden SG8 .. 10 F4
　Haddenham CB6 .... 209 E4
　Hail Weston PE19 .... 74 B8
　Harlton CB23 .... 45 D5
　Harston CB22 .... 47 B5
　Haslingfield CB23 .... 47 B5
　Hauxton CB22 .... 48 C5
　Haverhill CB9 .... 24 A7
　Hemingford Abbots PE28 . 143 A3
　Hemingford Grey PE28 .. 143 C2
　Hildersham CB21 .... 34 E5
　Hilton PE28 .... 120 B1
　Hinxton CB10 .... 18 B7
　Histon CB24 .... 104 B4
　Holywell-cum-Needingworth
　　PE27 .... 144 F5
　Horningsea CB25 .... 106 A1
　Huntingdon PE29 .... 141 D4
　Kimbolton PE28 .... 113 F4
　Knapwell CB23 .... 100 E3
　Landbeach CB25 .... 105 D6
　Linton CB21 .... 35 C2
　Little Paxton PE19 ...... 95 F2
　Littleport CB6 .... 242 D4
　Little Staughton MK44.... 93 B1
　Little Wilbraham CB1 .. 86 E1
　Lode CB25 .... 107 C2
　Longstanton CB24 .... 123 F3
　Longstowe CB23 .... 59 F2
　Madingley CB23 .... 81 F5
　Manea PE15 .... 224 C4
　March PE15 .... 243 D3
　Market Deeping PE6 ...... 231 D8
　Maxey PE6 .... 231 C2
　Melbourn SG8 .... 14 C5
　Meldreth SG8 .... 13 B8
　Mepal CB6 .... 216 E3
　Mildenhall IP28 .... 239 C4
　Milton CB24 .... 105 D2
　Needingworth PE27 ...... 208 A3
　Newmarket CB8 .... 110 F3
　Oakington CB24 .... 103 C6
　Offord Cluny PE19 ...... 96 F8
　Orwell SG8 .... 45 E1
　Over CB24 .... 208 D1
　Pampisford CB22 .... 33 B5
　Peterborough PE7 ...... 187 A6
　Pidley cum Fenton PE28 .. 155 E8
　Rampton CB24 .... 124 E5
　Ramsey PE26 .... 172 A6
　Royston SG8 .... 5 D6
　Sawston PE28 .... 32 F6
　Sawtry PE28 .... 168 B4
　Shepreth SG8 .... 29 E4
　Soham CB7 .... 212 B4
　Somersham PE28 .... 208 C8
　Spaldwick PE28 .... 127 A4
　Stamford PE9 .... 244 B5
　Stretchworth CB8 ...... 90 A2
　Whittlesford CB22 .... 32 C5
　Wicken CB7 .... 211 E1
　Wilburton CB6 .... 210 C5
　8 Willingham CB24 .. 209 A1
　Wisbech CB13 .... 245 C5
　Witcham CB6 .... 217 A3
　Wrestlingworth SG19 .. 25 B4
　Yelling PE19 .... 98 C1
High Street Back 2 CB7 .240 D4
High Street Pas CB7 .. 240 D4
High Street St Martin's
　PE9 .... 244 C4
Hightown Dro CB23 .... 81 A4
Highway The PE19 .... 94 A6
Hilda Cl PE14 .... 77 D5
Higney Rd PE7 .... 186 C1
Hilda Clarke Cl 1 PE16 .241 C3
Hilda St CB4 .... 246 A4
HILDERSHAM 34 F5
Hildersham Mill CB21..34 E5
Hildersham Rd CB21 .. 34 D7
Hillary Cl PE29 .... 244 D6
Hilburn Rd PE13 .... 245 B4

Hill Cl
Brington & Molesworth
PE28 . . . . 147 C5
Little Stukeley PE28 . . . . . . 151 F1
Newmarket CB8 . . . . 110 E3
Peterborough PE1 . . . . . . 198 D5
Sawtry PE28 . . . . 168 B3
Hill Cres CB9 . . . . 39 A1
Hillcrest CB23 . . . . 102 C3
Hillcrest Ave PE7 . . . . 181 E5
Hillcrest Dr PE13 . . . . 235 A2
Hill Est
Ramsey PE26 . . . . 172 B4
St Ives PE28 . . . . 143 B5
Hill Farm Rd CB22 . . . . 32 B3
Hill Farms CB1 . . . . 66 C2
Hillfield
Alconbury PE28 . . . . 150 F5
Foxton CB22 . . . . 30 C5
Hillfield Rd CB23 . . . . 62 D6
Hill La CB9 . . . . 24 F3
Hill Rd
Over CB24 . . . . 208 E1
Wistow PE26 . . . . 164 A8
Hill Rise
St Ives PE27 . . . . 143 E7
St Neots PE19 . . . . 75 A5
Hill Row CB6 . . . . 209 E6
Hill Row Cswy CB6 . . . . 209 A6
Hills Ave CB1 . . . . 65 B5
Hillside
Orwell SG8 . . . . 45 E2
Royston SG8 . . . . 5 D5
Sawston CB22 . . . . 32 F8
Sutton CB6 . . . . 216 D1
Hillside Cl
Ellington PE28 . . . . 138 F4
Ufford PE9 . . . . 230 F2
Hillside Cotts PE28 . . . . . . 146 A4
Hillside Gdns PE9 . . . . 230 B1
Hillside La SG8 . . . . 44 C4
Hillside Mdw CB7 . . . . 212 F1
Hillside Rd PE15 . . . . 243 B5
Hills La CB6 . . . . 240 B4
Hills Rd CB2 . . . . 246 C1
Hills Rd Sixth Form Coll
CB1 . . . . 65 A6
Hillstead CB22 . . . . 49 D7
Hills View CB22 . . . . 49 B6
Hill View
Dry Drayton CB23 . . . . . . 102 D1
Lidgate CB8 . . . . 73 F8
Hillward Cl PE2 . . . . 186 C6
Hillway CB21 . . . . 35 C2
Hilsdens Dr PE29 . . . . 142 A1
HILTON 121 B1
Hilton Rd PE28 . . . . 120 E3
Hilton St CB24 . . . . 208 D1
Hinchcliffe PE2 . . . . 185 E2
Hinchinbrooke Rd PE28 . . 117 D8
Hinchingbrooke Ctry Pk★
PE29 . . . . 140 F4
Hinchingbrooke Dr PE16 . 241 B4
Hinchingbrooke Hospl
PE29 . . . . 141 B5
Hinchingbrooke House★
PE29 . . . . 141 B3
HINCHINGBROOKE
PARK 206 D5
Hinchingbrooke Sch
PE29 . . . . 141 A4
Hines Cl CB23 . . . . 63 A4
Hines La CB23 . . . . 62 C5
Hinkins Cl SG8 . . . . 14 D6
Hinton Ave CB1 . . . . 65 C5
Hinton Cl PE7 . . . . 189 D8
Hinton Rd CB21 . . . . 66 D5
Hinton View CB6 . . . . 210 A6
Hinton Way
Great Shelford CB22 . . . . . 49 C6
Wilburton CB6 . . . . 210 C6
HINXTON 18 A7
Hinxton Rd CB22 . . . . 17 E8
Hinxworth Rd SG7 . . . . 2 B4
HISTON 104 B3
Histon & Impington Inf Sch
CB24 . . . . 104 B3
Histon & Impington Jun Sch
CB24 . . . . 104 C4
Histon Rd
Cambridge CB4 . . . . 83 C4
Cottenham CB24 . . . . . . 104 C8
Hitches St 4 CB6 . . . . 242 D4
Hitherford CB24 . . . . 208 E1
Hive Rd CB6 . . . . 217 A4
Hives The PE19 . . . . 74 D4
Hoadly Rd CB3 . . . . 83 B5
Hobart Ct PE15 . . . . 243 C5
Hobart Rd CB1 . . . . 65 C7
Hod Fen Dro
Denton & Caldecote PE7 . 177 A7
Yaxley PE7 . . . . 181 F2
Hodgson Ave PE4 . . . . 204 B6
Hod Hall La CB6 . . . . 210 A5
Hodley Pl CB23 . . . . 99 B1
Hodney Rd 5 PE6 . . . . 232 A1
Hodson's Dr PE29 . . . . 141 E5
Hodwell SG7 . . . . 2 D4
Hogarth Cl PE27 . . . . 144 A7

Hogarth Pl 2 PE19 . . . . . . 74 D5
Hogens La PE13 . . . . 238 A5
Hog Fen Dro PE7 . . . . 182 A5
Hogherd's La 8 PE13 . . . . 245 C5
Hoghill Dro CB6 . . . . 209 F3
Hogsden Leys PE19 . . . . . . 75 C7
Hog's La SG8 . . . . 8 A3
Holbein Rd PE27 . . . . 144 A7
Holben Cl CB23 . . . . 63 B3
Holborn Ave IP28 . . . . 239 B6
Holbrook Rd
Cambridge CB1 . . . . 65 B4
Haverhill CB9 . . . . 23 E6
Holburn View PE28 . . . . . . 168 B2
Holcroft PE2 . . . . 186 B3
Holden End CB10 . . . . 21 B2
Holdfield PE3 . . . . 197 B6
Holdich St PE3 . . . . 197 E2
Holdsworth Valley Prim Sch
CB8 . . . . 110 F3
Holgate La PE4 . . . . 204 B7
Holkham Mead CB25 . . . . . 130 C2
Holkham Rd PE2 . . . . 185 D3
Holland Ave PE4 . . . . 204 D1
Holland Pk CB8 . . . . 91 C7
Holland Rd PE9 . . . . 244 C6
Hollands Bsns Ctr CB9 . . . . 24 B6
Hollands Rd CB9 . . . . 24 A6
Hollands Road Ind Est
CB9 . . . . 24 A6
Hollans Ctr The CB9 . . . . . . 24 A6
Hollendale Wlk 6 CB6 . . . 240 A3
Hollesley Ave CB9 . . . . 23 C8
Holliday's Rd PE28 . . . . . . 208 D5
Hollies Cl SG8 . . . . 5 E6
Hollies The PE15 . . . . 243 E7
Hollmans Cl CB21 . . . . 66 F4
Hollow Hill CB9 . . . . 38 B4
Hollow La PE26 . . . . 172 E6
Hollow Rd
Chrishall SG8 . . . . 8 D1
Elmdon CB11 . . . . 9 C4
Ramsey Forty Foot PE26 . . 221 C2
Hollow The PE29 . . . . 142 B6
Holly Ave PE14 . . . . 236 A5
Hollybush Way CB21 . . . . . 35 D3
Holly Cl
Newborough PE6 . . . . 207 C1
Red Lodge IP28 . . . . 213 F1
Hollycroft CB PE14 . . . . . . 236 D5
Hollycroft Rd PE14 . . . . . . 236 D5
Holly Dr 4 PE15 . . . . 223 A6
HOLLY END 236 E5
Hollymount 6 CB1 . . . . . . 84 A2
Hollytrees CB23 . . . . 102 C3
Holly Way 7 PE6 . . . . 231 E8
Holly Wlk
Ely CB7 . . . . 240 F5
3 Mildenhall IP28 . . . . . . 213 F8
Peterborough PE7 . . . . . . 186 D3
HOLME 177 A4
Holme CE Prim Sch PE7 . . 177 A4
Holme Cl
Castor PE5 . . . . 195 D2
Oakington/Longstanton
CB24 . . . . 103 C5
Holme Dro PE28 . . . . 208 E7
Holme Fen Dro PE28 . . . . . 208 D7
Holme Fen National Nature
Reserve★ PE7 . . . . 177 C7
Holmehill PE29 . . . . 118 F8
Holme La CB6 . . . . 218 A6
Holme Rd
Ramsey PE26 . . . . 220 C3
Yaxley PE7 . . . . 181 E4
Holmes Dr PE13 . . . . 245 E5
Holmes La CB7 . . . . 212 B5
Holmes Rd PE6 . . . . 203 F7
Holmes The CB6 . . . . 242 E4
Holmes Way PE4 . . . . 204 E2
Holme Way CB22 . . . . 32 F8
Holmewood PE7 . . . . 176 F4
Holmewood Cres PE7 . . . . 176 F4
Holmsey Gn IP28 . . . . 176 F4
Holmsey Green Gdns 2
IP28 . . . . 213 F8
Holt Cl 8 PE8 . . . . 230 B1
Holt Fen CB6 . . . . 211 B7
Holyrood Cl CB4 . . . . 83 C6
HOLYWELL 144 F2
Holywell CE (C) Prim Sch
PE27 . . . . 208 A2
Holywell Cl PE3 . . . . 197 A1
Holywell Ferry Rd CB24 . . 121 F6
Holywell Front PE27 . . . . 144 F2
HOLYWELL ROW 214 A8
Home Cl
Burton End CB21 . . . . 37 B8
Grafham PE28 . . . . 116 A6
Histon CB24 . . . . 104 B4
Home End CB21 . . . . 37 B8
Home Farm Cl
Abbotsley PE19 . . . . 57 B6
Colne PE28 . . . . 208 D6
Hilton PE28 . . . . 120 B1
Rampton CB24 . . . . 124 F4
Home Farm Rd PE28 . . . . . 143 B5
Homefield Cl CB24 . . . . . . 104 C3
Homefield Rd CB9 . . . . 23 F5
Homefield Rd Units CB9 . . 23 F5
Home Pasture PE4 . . . . . . 204 B5
Homerton Coll CB2 . . . . . . 65 A5
Homerton St CB2 . . . . 65 A6
Homestall Cres CB9 . . . . . . 38 B4
Homestead 12 PE28 . . . . . 215 C1
Homing The CB5 . . . . 84 E3
Honeydon Ave PE19 . . . . . . 74 B5
Honey Dro PE15 . . . . 223 E4

Honeyhill PE4 . . . . 205 A1
Honey Hill
9 Cambridge CB3 . . . . . . 83 C3
Fen Drayton CB24 . . . . . . 122 A4
Fenstanton PE28 . . . . . . 121 B6
Gamlingay SG19 . . . . 41 D4
West Wratting CB21 . . . . . 53 E5
Honey Hill Mews CB3 . . . . . 83 C3
Honeyhill Rd PE13 . . . . . . 237 C2
Honey La PE16 . . . . 241 C2
Honeymead Rd PE15 . . . . . 223 B7
Honeysome Rd PE16 . . . . . 241 A5
Honeysuckle Cl
Haverhill CB9 . . . . 38 E1
Red Lodge IP28 . . . . 134 A8
2 Soham CB7 . . . . 212 B4
Honeysuckle Ct PE2 . . . . . 186 D7
Honeyway SG8 . . . . 5 E6
Hoo Cl PE19 . . . . 117 B4
Hoof Cl CB6 . . . . 242 D3
HOOK 223 D8
Hook Dro PE15 . . . . 228 B1
Hook La PE15 . . . . 223 C7
Hook Rd PE15 . . . . 223 C7
Hook's Dro PE13 . . . . 234 C4
Hook's Mill SG8 . . . . 10 E7
Hooper St CB1 . . . . 84 A1
Hopbine Ct PE26 . . . . 171 F5
Hope St CB1 . . . . 65 B8
Hop Gdns CB23 . . . . 78 F3
Hopkins Cl CB4 . . . . 84 A6
Hop Row CB6 . . . . 210 A6
Hopton Rise CB9 . . . . 38 B1
Hornbeam Rd
Hampton Hargate PE7 . . . 186 B2
Mildenhall IP28 . . . . 239 D5
HORNINGSEA 106 A1
Horningsea Rd
Fen Ditton CB5 . . . . 84 F6
Horningsea CB5 . . . . 85 A8
Horn La
Kirtling CB8 . . . . 72 B5
Linton CB21 . . . . 35 B2
Horse Comm Cl PE29 . . . . 141 E5
Horse Comm La PE29 . . . . 141 E5
Horse Dro PE26 . . . . 221 A1
Horse Fair Sh Ctr PE13 . . . 245 C5
Horsegate
Market Deeping PE6 . . . . . 231 E8
Whittlesey PE7 . . . . 199 D7
Horsegate Gdns PE16 . . . . 241 C5
Horsegate La PE7 . . . . 189 C7
Horse & Gate St CB24 . . . . 121 F5
Horsehead Dro PE14 . . . . . 229 F4
HORSEHEATH 37 A3
Horseheath Gn CB21 . . . . . 37 C1
Horseheath Pk CB21 . . . . . 37 D3
Horseheath Rd
Linton CB21 . . . . 35 D2
Withersfield CB9 . . . . 38 A4
Horseley Fen Dro PE16 . . . 241 E1
HORSE MOOR 228 D1
Horsemoor Rd PE15 . . . . . 223 D8
Horseshoe Cl
Balsham CB21 . . . . 53 C2
Barley SG8 . . . . 6 F1
Elmdon CB11 . . . . 9 B4
Horseshoe Ct PE14 . . . . . 236 E2
Horseshoe La
4 Haverhill CB9 . . . . 23 E7
8 Stamford PE9 . . . . 244 B5
Horseshoes La CB21 . . . . . 54 D5
Horseshoes Way PE28 . . . . 140 D2
Horseshoe Terr PE13 . . . . 245 B7
Horse-Shoe Terr PE13 . . . 245 A7
Horseshoe Way PE7 . . . . . 186 D2
Horse Ware CB24 . . . . 208 D2
Horseway PE16 . . . . 223 C1
Horsey Hill (Civil War Fort)★
PE7 . . . . 188 A4
Horsham Cl 3 CB9 . . . . . . 38 C1
Horsley Hale CB6 . . . . 242 D8
Horton Wlk PE3 . . . . 197 D5
Hospital Rd PE15 . . . . 222 E6
Hostmoor Ave PE15 . . . . . 243 A7
Hotel La PE28 . . . . 151 F3
HOUGHTON 143 A5
Houghton Ave PE2 . . . . . . 187 F5
Houghton Gdns CB6 . . . . . 240 B4
Houghton Grange PE28 . . 143 C6
Houghton Hill Rd PE28 . . . 143 B5
Houghton Meadows Nature
Reserve★ PE28 . . . . 143 A4
Houghton Mill★ PE28 . . . . 143 A4
Houghton Prim Sch
PE28 . . . . 143 A5
Houghton Rd
Huntingdon PE29 . . . . 142 C6
St Ives PE27 . . . . 143 E5
Houghtons La CB7 . . . . . . 212 D1
Houldsworth Terr CB8 . . . 110 F3
Housman Ave SG8 . . . . 5 C8
Howard Cl CB5 . . . . 84 D4
Howard Ct CB5 . . . . 84 E4
Howard De Walden Way
CB8 . . . . 111 A4
Howard Rd
Cambridge CB5 . . . . 84 E4
Eaton Socon PE19 . . . . . . 74 C1
Meldreth SG8 . . . . 14 A8
Howard Road Ind Est
PE19 . . . . 74 C1
Howard's La CB21 . . . . 37 A2
Howell Dr PE28 . . . . 152 E1
Howe Rd CB9 . . . . 190 F5
Howes Pl CB3 . . . . 83 A5
Howgate Rd CB4 . . . . 83 D7

How Hill (Tumulus)★
IP27 . . . . 214 F7
Howitt's Gdns PE19 . . . . . . 75 A2
Howitts La PE19 . . . . 74 F4
Howitt's La 8 PE19 . . . . . . 74 F3
Howland PE7 . . . . 186 A3
Howletts Hill PE13 . . . . . . 245 C4
Howlett Way CB25 . . . . 86 E6
Hoylake Dr PE7 . . . . 187 C5
Huddleston Way CB22 . . . . 33 A7
Hudpool PE29 . . . . 118 F7
Hudson Cl 1 CB9 . . . . 24 C6
Hudson Leisure Ctr
CB23 . . . . 23 A8
Hudson's Cl PE13 . . . . 245 A5
Hughes Hall CB1 . . . . 246 C1
Hulatt Rd CB1 . . . . 65 C4
Humberdale Way PE28 . . . 164 F5
Humber Dr PE7 . . . . 181 E6
Humberley Cl 1 PE19 . . . . 74 F3
Humber Rd PE29 . . . . 142 F7
Humberstone Rd CB4 . . . . 246 C4
Humphreys Rd CB4 . . . . . . 83 E6
Humphreys Way CB24 . . . 105 D3
Humphrys St PE2 . . . . 186 D8
Hunchback La PE14 . . . . . . 238 E2
Hundon Pl CB9 . . . . 24 B8
Hundred Acre Way 12
IP28 . . . . 214 A1
Hundred Rd PE15 . . . . 243 C8
Hundreds Rd PE6 . . . . 232 C6
Hungarton Cl PE2 . . . . 198 D7
Hungate Rd PE14 . . . . 236 E6
Hunsbury Cl PE7 . . . . 189 F6
Hunters Chase PE15 . . . . . 243 E2
Hunters Cl PE16 . . . . 241 D5
Hunters Rowe PE14 . . . . . . 245 D2
Hunters Way
Kimbolton PE28 . . . . 113 F5
Royston SG8 . . . . 5 E6
Hunting Ave PE2 . . . . 186 F7
HUNTINGDON 141 F4
Huntingdon Jun & Inf Sch
PE29 . . . . 141 E6
Huntingdon Leisure Ctr
PE29 . . . . 141 D6
Huntingdon Racecourse
CB28 . . . . 140 C5
Huntingdon Rd
Boxworth CB23 . . . . 101 E7
Brampton PE28 . . . . 141 A2
Cambridge CB3 . . . . 83 A5
Chatteris PE16 . . . . 241 B4
Fen Drayton CB24 . . . . . . 121 D4
Houghton & Wyton PE28 . 142 F5
Lolworth CB23 . . . . 102 B5
Ramsey PE26 . . . . 172 B6
Sawston CB22 . . . . 33 A8
St Neots PE19 . . . . 75 A8
Huntingdonshire Regional
Coll
Huntingdon PE29 . . . . 141 E6
St Neots PE19 . . . . 74 F6
Huntingdon St PE19 . . . . . 74 F6
Huntingdon Sta PE29 . . . . 141 C4
Hunting Gr CB23 . . . . 101 B5
Huntings Dr PE28 . . . . 168 B4
Huntley Cl CB5 . . . . 84 E4
Huntly Gr PE1 . . . . 198 B4
Huntly Rd PE2 . . . . 186 E7
Hunts Cl 4 PE15 . . . . 222 F5
Hunts End PE19 . . . . 117 B4
Hunts End Ct PE19 . . . . . . 117 B4
Hunts Gate PE12 . . . . 237 F8
Hunts La CB10 . . . . 18 B7
Huntsmans Gate PE1 . . . . 196 F3
Huntsmill CB21 . . . . 66 E4
Hunts Rd CB22 . . . . 17 D8
Hurdleditch Rd SG8 . . . . . . 28 D8
Hurdle Dro IP28 . . . . 213 D8
Hurdles The PE28 . . . . . . 140 E2
Hurdles Way CB22 . . . . 31 E1
Hurrell Rd CB4 . . . . 83 C6
Hurrell's Row CB22 . . . . . . 47 E2
Hurricane Cl PE29 . . . . . . 141 B8
Hurrys Cl CB22 . . . . 32 E7
Hurst Ave 1 PE15 . . . . . . 243 E4
Hurstingstone PE27 . . . . . 144 A5
Hurst La CB6 . . . . 240 A6
Hurst Park Ave CB4 . . . . . . 83 C5
Hurts Croft CB7 . . . . 212 E1
Hutchinson Cl PE15 . . . . . 224 A4
Hut Field La CB23 . . . . 99 A3
Huttles Gn SG8 . . . . 29 E4
Hyholmes PE3 . . . . 196 F7
Hyll Cl CB10 . . . . 18 D3
Hyperion Way CB8 . . . . . . 110 D8
Hythe Cl CB25 . . . . 130 A3
Hythegate PE4 . . . . 204 D4
Hythe La
Burwell CB25 . . . . 130 A3
Ely CB7 . . . . 240 D4
Hythe The
Littleport CB6 . . . . 242 D5
Reach CB25 . . . . 129 D1

I

Ibberson's Dro PE15 . . . . . 221 F4
Ibbott Cl PE2 . . . . 187 E5
Ibbott Cres 7 PE28 . . . . . 215 C1
Iceni Way
Exning CB8 . . . . 110 B8
Kings Hedges CB4 . . . . . . 83 D7
Icewell Hill CB8 . . . . 111 A4
ICKLETON 18 A4

Ickleton Grange CB10 . . . . . 17 A1
Ickleton Pl CB9 . . . . 24 B8
Ickleton Rd
Duxford CB22 . . . . 17 E7
Elmdon CB11 . . . . 9 A4
Great Chesterford CB10 . . 18 C2
Hinxton CB10 . . . . 18 B6
Icknield Cl
Cheveley CB8 . . . . 91 C5
Ickleton CB10 . . . . 18 A3
Icknield Fst Sch SG8 . . . . . . 5 F7
Icknield Prim Sch The
CB22 . . . . 33 A8
Icknield Wlk SG8 . . . . 5 F6
Ida Darwin Hospl CB21 . . . 66 D5
Ihlec Cl PE4 . . . . 204 E1
Ilex Cl PE7 . . . . 186 C3
Ilex Rd PE27 . . . . 144 B6
Illing's La PE28 . . . . 164 A1
Illingworth Way CB22 . . . . 30 C5
Illston Pl PE1 . . . . 198 D7
Impala Dr CB1 . . . . 66 A7
Impett's La CB21 . . . . 67 A4
IMPINGTON 104 C2
Impington La CB24 . . . . . . 104 C3
Impington Village Coll
CB24 . . . . 104 D3
India La PE28 . . . . 151 F2
Infield Rd PE28 . . . . 167 C7
Ingham Hall Gdns PE13 . . 234 D7
Ingham Rd CB9 . . . . 24 A8
INGLEBOROUGH 238 E5
Ingleborough PE1 . . . . . . 198 A5
Ingleborough Mill PE14 . . 238 E5
Ingle Rd PE14 . . . . 236 B5
Ingle's La 14 PE15 . . . . . . 223 A5
Ingoldsby Cl 3 PE15 . . . . 243 D2
Ingram St PE19 . . . . 141 E4
Inhams Cf PE13 . . . . 234 D5
Inhams Ct PE7 . . . . 189 E6
INHAM'S END 189 F6
Inham's Rd PE7 . . . . 189 E6
Inhams Way PE28 . . . . . . 116 A7
Inkerman Rise PE19 . . . . . 74 C5
Inley Dro PE12 . . . . 237 A8
Innovation Way PE2 . . . . . 185 B5
Interchange Ind Est The
PE29 . . . . 141 C8
Inverness Cl CB4 . . . . 84 A5
Iowa PE28 . . . . 151 E4
Iram Dro CB24 . . . . 209 B1
Irchester Pl PE3 . . . . 197 D4
Ireton Cl PE19 . . . . 74 F3
Ireton's Way
Chatteris PE16 . . . . 241 F2
Mepal PE16 . . . . 216 C6
Ireton Way PE15 . . . . 243 D2
Iris Dr PE2 . . . . 186 E8
Irnham Rd PE9 . . . . 244 C7
Ironmonger St 2 PE9 . . . . 244 C5
Irving Burgess Cl PE7 . . . 189 C8
Isaacson Rd CB25 . . . . . . 109 C8
Isham Rd PE1 . . . . 197 D4
Isherwood Cl
Dogsthorpe PE1 . . . . 198 A6
Royston SG8 . . . . 5 C8
Isinglass Cl CB8 . . . . 111 E2
Isis Way PE2 . . . . 185 B5
ISLANDS COMMON 74 E7
Isle Bridge Rd PE14 . . . . . 236 F2
ISLEHAM 213 A5
Isleham CE Prim Sch
CB7 . . . . 213 A5
Isleham Marina IP28 . . . . 213 B6
Isleham Rd CB7 . . . . 212 F2
Isle of Ely Way
Chatteris PE16 . . . . 241 C7
March PE15 . . . . 243 A4
Isons Cl SG8 . . . . 15 E8
Itter Cres PE4 . . . . 197 E8
Ivan Clark's Cnr CB21 . . . . 34 C7
Ivatt St CB24 . . . . 125 E5
Ivatt Way PE3 . . . . 197 C2
Ivelbury Ct PE29 . . . . 117 A3
Ivel Cl PE19 . . . . 74 C4
Iver Cl CB1 . . . . 65 F7
Ives Dro PE7 . . . . 189 A4
Ivesdyke Cl 4 PE13 . . . . . 238 B2
Ivett's Cl CB23 . . . . 45 E7
Ivydene CB25 . . . . 128 A2
Ivy Field CB23 . . . . 63 B4
Ivy Dro PE26 . . . . 192 A6
Ivy Way PE28 . . . . 138 A6
Ixworth Cl 8 PE6 . . . . . . 232 A1
Ixworth Rd 3 CB9 . . . . . . 23 E6
Izaak Walton Way CB4 . . . 84 C5
Izzard Rise PE19 . . . . 96 E4

J

Jack Haws La 4 PE9 . . . . 230 D4
Jack Hunt Sch PE3 . . . . . . 197 B3
Jack Hunt Swimming Pool
PE3 . . . . 197 B3
Jack Jarvis Cl 3 CB8 . . . . 111 A3
Jackson Cl PE2 . . . . 48 C5
Jackson's La CB10 . . . . 18 D3
Jackson's Sq CB10 . . . . 18 D3
Jackson's Way SG8 . . . . . . 15 E8
Jack Warren Gn CB5 . . . . . 84 F3
James Carter Rd IP28 . . . . 239 A6
James Ct PE19 . . . . 74 F2
James Essex Dr CB4 . . . . . 240 E7
James Gage Cl PE16 . . . . . 241 B3
James Gdns PE7 . . . . 189 E7
James Nurse Cl CB1 . . . . . 66 A6

James St CB5 .... 246 C3
Janus Cl CB9 .... 24 D6
Jarman's La IP28 .... 213 D7
Jarman Way SG8 .... 5 B7
Jarvis Way CB8 .... 110 E5
Jasmin Cl PE13 .... 245 F7
Jasmine Ct
  Cambridge CB1 .... 65 C5
  Peterborough PE2 ...... 185 E2
Jasmine Way PE7 .... 181 F6
Jay Cl CB9 .... 24 C7
Jaywick Rd CB9 .... 24 A8
Jeavons La **6** CB23 .... 79 C3
Jedburgh Cl CB4 .... 83 E7
Jefferson Cl **22** PE8 . 230 B1
Jeffery Ave **4** PE13 .. 245 E7
Jeffrey Cl SG8 .... 5 C8
Jeffrey Dr PE28 .... 152 E1
Jellicoe Pl PE19 .... 74 A2
Jenkins Cl PE19 .... 74 B2
Jennings Ave PE19 .... 74 E2
Jenyns Cl CB25 .... 86 E7
Jepps La SG8 .... 5 D6
Jermyn Cl CB4 .... 83 D6
Jersey Way CB4 .... 242 C3
Jerusalem Dro CB6 ...... 217 A5
Jesus Coll CB5 .... 246 B3
Jesus La CB1 .... 246 B3
Jesus Terr CB1 .... 246 C3
Jetty The PE13 .... 235 C7
Jew House Dro PE14 ..... 235 E3
Jim Mollison Ct **2** IP28 239 B5
J J Thompson Ave CB3 .... 82 F2
Job's La PE15 .... 243 C1
John Amner Cl CB6 ...... 240 D6
John Bends Way PE13 .... 234 D7
John Breay Cl SG8 .... 29 D4
John Clare Prim Sch
  PE6 .... 231 B4
John Clare Theatre*
  PE1 .... 198 A2
John Clarke Ct CB4 ...... 84 A6
John Conder Ct CB1 ...... 65 C7
John Falkner Inf Sch
  CB22 .... 32 E7
John F Kennedy Ct **2**
  PE13 .... 245 D4
John Impey Way SG8 ...... 14 D6
John King Gdns PE2 ..... 187 C7
John Mansfield Sch PE1 . 198 B8
John Paxton Jun Sch
  CB22 .... 32 F8
John's Acre CB22 .... 32 F6
John Sale Cl SG7 .... 2 C4
John's Cl SG8 .... 15 E8
Johnson's Dro PE13 ..... 234 B7
Johnson Way PE16 .... 241 C6
Johnson Wlk PE1 .... 197 F7
John St
  Cambridge CB1 .... 246 C2
  Royston SG8 .... 5 D6
John Thompson Rd **3**
  PE13 .... 245 D4
John Wesley Rd PE4 ..... 204 A2
Joiner's Cl CB21 .... 35 B2
Joiner's Rd CB21 .... 35 B2
Jolley Cl PE15 .... 224 B4
Jolley Way CB4 .... 83 F6
Jones Cl PE15 .... 243 B3
Jones Ct PE26 .... 172 B7
Jones Dr CB23 .... 99 A3
Jones La PE7 .... 190 C7
Jones's Dro PE7 .... 221 F8
Jopling Way CB22 .... 48 C4
Jordan Mews **2** PE1 .. 198 B3
Jordans Yd CB1 .... 246 A3
Jorose St PE3 .... 197 A3
Jorose Way PE3 .... 197 F3
Joscelynes CB22 .... 49 C4
Joshua Cl **2** PE16 ... 241 C5
Josiah Ct CB25 .... 106 C8
Joyce's Cl CB22 .... 32 F6
Jubilee Ave PE28 .... 164 D6
Jubilee Cl
  Brampton PE28 .... 140 B3
  Isleham CB7 .... 213 A5
  Little Paxton PE19 .... 95 F2
  Waterbeach CB25 ...... 106 A8
Jubilee Cl CB8 .... 90 A1
Jubilee End SG8 .... 11 B2
Jubilee St PE2 .... 186 F8
Jubilee Terr CB7 .... 240 D3
Jubilee Way
  Mildenhall IP28 ...... 239 C4
  Steeple Morden SG8 .... 11 B2
Jubilee Wlk
  Haverhill CB9 .... 24 A7
  Wisbech PE13 .... 245 D8
Judson Ct **3** PE29 ... 141 F8
Julian Cl CB9 .... 24 D7
Julius Martin La CB1 ... 212 A4
Junction Rd IP28 .... 239 B5
Junction The* CB1 ...... 246 C1
Junction The **2** PE15 243 D7
Juniper Cl IP28 .... 239 E5
Juniper Cres PE3 .... 197 A2
Juniper Dr
  Chatteris PE16 .... 241 D5
  .... CB7 .... 240 F5
Juniper Rd **11** IP28 . 214 A1
Jupiter Cl **2** CB9 .... 24 C6
Jury Rd PE7 .... 181 C8
Justinian Cl CB9 .... 24 D6
Jutland Rise PE19 ...... 74 C5

K

Kaldor Ct CB4 .... 83 E7
Kansas PE28 .... 151 E4
Katharine Way PE3 ...... 197 A5
Kathleen Elliot Way CB1 65 F7
Kay Hitch Way CB24 ..... 104 B2
Keates Rd CB22 .... 66 A5
Keates Cl **5** 5 C8
Keats Ct PE19 .... 74 C6
Keats Way PE1 .... 197 D7
Keble Cl PE8 .... 244 A7
Keble Ct PE9 .... 244 A7
Kedleston Rd PE7 .... 187 E6
Keep The CB9 .... 23 E7
Keeton Rd PE1 .... 197 E7
Kefford Cl SG8 .... 12 F5
Keillers Cl PE13 .... 245 A7
Keith Day Rd CB2 .... 65 A3
Kelful Ct PE7 .... 190 D7
Kelsey Cres CB1 .... 66 A7
Kelsey Kerridge Sports Ctr
  CB1 .... 246 C1
Kelsey Way PE15 .... 243 D2
Kelso Ct PE14 .... 204 C1
Kelvin Cl CB1 .... 65 D5
Kemmann La CB23 .... 79 B3
Kendal Cl PE14 .... 204 F2
Kendall Croft PE7 ...... 189 E6
Kendal Way PE28 .... 154 A1
Kendal Way CB4 .... 83 A6
Kendrick Cl PE2 .... 187 D6
Kenilworth Ave PE1 ..... 188 A5
Kenilworth Cl **3** PE19 74 C3
Kenlan Rd PE13 .... 245 D6
Kennedy Croft CB24 ..... 126 A7
Kennedy Rd CB7 .... 213 A5
Kennels Rd PE6 .... 196 E1
Kennet Gdns PE4 .... 204 E1
Kennetside CB8 .... 73 D1
KENNETT 134 F5
KENNETT END 111 E8
Kennett Prim Sch CB8 ... 133 F5
Kennett Rd or Moulton Rd
  CB8 .... 112 F7
Kennett Sta CB8 .... 133 F3
Kennulphs Cl **3** PE6 . 232 C8
Ken Simpson Com Sch
  PE4 .... 204 B4
Ken's Cl CB24 .... 105 D2
Kent Cl
  Ely CB6 .... 240 B5
  St Ives PE27 .... 143 F7
KENTFORD 113 B2
Kentings CB23 .... 62 B5
Kenterne Pl **1** PE14 . 204 F2
Kentra Cl PE13 .... 245 A8
Kent Rd
  Huntingdon PE29 ...... 141 E8
  Peterborough PE3 .... 197 E2
Kents La PE7 .... 212 B4
Kent Way
  Cambridge CB4 .... 83 F7
  January PE15 .... 243 C4
Kentwell Pl CB25 .... 130 C2
Kenwood Gdns CB21 ...... 35 E2
Kerridge Cl CB1 .... 66 A4
Kespar CB8 .... 73 D6
Kesters Cl CB23 .... 81 B2
Kesteven Cl **6** PE6 .. 231 E8
Kesteven Rd PE6 .... 244 B7
Kesteven Wlk PE1 .... 198 B2
Kestrel Cl
  Cottenham CB24 .... 125 E5
  Huntingdon PE29 ...... 142 A7
Kestrel Dr **2** PE14 .. 245 D2
Kestrel Pl **4** PE19 ... 75 B7
Kestrel Rd CB9 .... 24 C7
Kestrel Way **3** SG8 .... 5 E8
Keswick Cl PE4 .... 204 F3
Kettering Rd PE7 .... 187 A6
Kettlefields CB8 .... 89 F1
Kettlefields CP Sch CB8 89 F1
Kettles Cl CB22 .... 103 C5
Kettle's Yd* CB1 .... 246 A4
Keynes Rd CB5 .... 84 D4
KEYSTON 146 B3
Keyston Rd PE28 .... 135 D2
Key Theatre* PE1 .... 198 A1
Kidmans Cl
  Hilton PE28 .... 120 B1
  Newton CB22 .... 31 B7
Kildare Dr PE3 .... 197 C4
Kilderkin Cl PE14 ...... 236 A3
Kilham PE2 .... 185 E2
Kilkenny Ave CB6 .... 240 E7
Killem's Gn CB11 .... 1 E4
Kilmaine Cl CB4 .... 83 F8
Kiln Cl
  2 Little Downham CB6 218 B7
  St Ives PE27 .... 143 E6
Kiln House Yd SG8 .... 5 C6
Kiln La CB7 .... 240 F5
Kilverstone PE4 .... 204 B6
Kimberley Rd CB4 .... 246 C4
KIMBOLTON 113 F6
Kimbolton Ct PE1 .... 197 F3
Kimbolton Prep Sch
  PE28 .... 113 C5
Kimbolton Rd
  Hail Weston PE19 ...... 74 A8
  Pertenhall MK44 ...... 113 D1
  Kimbolton Sch PE28 ... 113 F4
Kim Rd PE28 .... 114 A7
Kinderley Cty Prim Sch
  PE13 .... 237 F6

Kinderley Rd PE13 ...... 245 C8
King Cob CB6 .... 210 F5
Kingdon Ave CB7 .... 219 B5
King Edgar Cl CB6 ...... 240 D7
King Edward Ctr (Cromwell
  Com Coll) PE16 ...... 241 C5
King Edward Rd PE16 .... 241 C5
King Edward VII Rd CB8 . 110 E5
Kingfisher Cl
  Bourn CB23 .... 60 C6
  Chatteris PE16 .... 241 C6
  Haverhill CB9 .... 24 C8
  Little Paxton PE19 .... 96 A2
  March PE15 .... 243 A8
  Sawston CB22 .... 32 E6
  Yaxley PE7 .... 181 D5
Kingfisher Dr
  Burwell CB25 .... 130 B4
  Soham CB7 .... 212 A5
  6 Wisbech PE14 ... 245 D2
Kingfisher Gn PE27 ..... 143 F7
Kingfisher Rd PE27 ..... 189 F8
Kingfishers PE2 .... 185 D6
Kingfisher Way
  Cambridge CB2 .... 64 F6
  Cottenham CB24 .... 125 D5
  Mildenhall IP28 ...... 239 D4
  The Stukeleys PE29 ... 141 A6
King George Ave CB8 .... 110 E4
King Henry Chase **2**
  PE3 .... 197 A5
King James Way SG8 ...... 5 D6
King's Ave CB7 .... 240 E7
Kingsbridge Ct PE4 ..... 204 A5
Kingsbrook PE27 .... 144 A5
Kings Cl
  Huntingdon PE29 ...... 142 A7
  Mildenhall IP28 ...... 239 D5
  North Green PE7 ...... 190 F8
Kings Coll CB2 .... 246 A2
Kings Coll Sch CB3 ...... 83 C1
Kings Ct
  Exning CB8 .... 110 B8
  Newmarket CB8 .... 110 F7
King's Delph PE7 .... 180 B8
King's Delph Dro PE7 ... 187 E2
King's Dr CB8 .... 111 B1
KING'S DYKE 188 E6
King's Dyke PE7 .... 188 E6
Kings Dyke Cl PE2 ...... 187 E6
Kingsfield Prim Sch
  PE3 .... 241 B5
King's Gate CB23 .... 78 E1
King's Gdns
  Huntingdon PE29 ...... 141 D5
  Peterborough PE1 .... 198 A5
Kings Gr CB23 .... 90 A4
KINGS HEDGES 83 E7
Kings Hedges Pct 2 ..... 144 A6
Kings Hedges Prim Sch
  CB4 .... 83 E7
King's Hedges Rd CB4 .... 83 D7
Kings Jun Sch The CB7 .. 240 C5
King's Jun Sch The CB8 . 240 C5
King's La
  Cambridge CB1 .... 246 A2
  Elmdon CB11 .... 9 A3
  St Neots PE19 .... 74 B5
Kingsland Way SG7 .... 2 D4
Kingsley Ave PE13 ...... 245 A4
Kingsley Cl **1** PE9 .. 230 D3
Kingsley Rd PE1 .... 198 C4
Kingsley St PE15 .... 243 D5
Kings Mead CB8 .... 91 C7
Kings Mill La
  Great Shelford CB22 ... 48 F4
  2 Stamford PE9 ... 244 B4
Kings Par CB7 .... 212 B3
King's Par CB2 .... 246 A2
Kings Rd
  Eaton Socon PE19 ...... 74 B3
  Hardwick CB23 .... 81 A2
  Peterborough PE2 .... 187 B6
  Stamford PE9 .... 244 B6
  St Ives PE27 .... 144 A4
  St Neots PE19 .... 74 F6
  Wisbech PE13 .... 245 C4
King's Rd CB3 .... 64 B7
Kings Ride SG8 .... 4 C3
KINGS RIPTON 153 C5
Kings Ripton Rd PE29 ... 152 D1
Kings Sch PE1 .... 198 C4
King St
  Cambridge CB1 .... 246 B3
  Doddington/Wimblington
  PE15 .... 223 B7
  Mildenhall IP28 ...... 239 C4
  14 Over CB24 ..... 208 D1
  1 Peterborough PE1 198 A2
  Rampton CB24 .... 124 C4
  Royston SG8 .... 5 D6
  Somersham PE28 .... 215 B1
  West Deeping PE6 ..... 231 A8
  Wisbech PE13 .... 245 C5
Kings Theatre* **3** CB8 110 F3
KINGSTON 80 B7
Kingston Cl PE19 .... 141 E8
Kingston Dr PE2 .... 187 E5
Kingston Pas **2** CB5 . 111 A3
Kingston Rd CB23 .... 61 D1
Kingston St CB1 .... 65 A8
Kingston Way PE28 ...... 163 F6
Kingsway
  Arbury CB4 .... 83 D6

Kingsway continued
  Duxford Airfield CB22 . 31 F1
  Leverington CB22 ..... 245 F7
  Mildenhall IP28 ...... 239 C4
  Newmarket CB8 .... 110 F4
  Royston SG8 .... 5 D8
King's Wlk **3** PE13 .. 245 C4
KINGSWOOD PARK 243 B2
Kingswood Rd PE15 ...... 243 C3
Kinnaird Way PE13 .... 65 C4
Kinnears Wlk PE2 .... 185 F2
Kinross Rd CB4 .... 84 A5
Kintbury CB22 .... 17 D8
Kintbury Cl PE1 .... 197 E8
Kipling Cl PE19 .... 74 D5
Kipling Rd **1** SG8 .... 5 E8
Kirby Cl CB4 .... 83 F5
Kirby Cross Ave CB6 .... 242 B5
Kirby Rd CB25 .... 127 C1
Kirby's Cl **12** CB24 . 208 D1
Kirby Terr CB25 .... 127 B1
Kirby Wlk PE3 .... 197 C5
Kirkgate PE13 .... 237 F7
Kirkgate St PE13 .... 245 E7
Kirkham's La PE14 ...... 236 C4
Kirkmeadow PE3 .... 197 A8
Kirk Ogden Cl PE15 ..... 243 D3
Kirk's La PE14 .... 235 E5
Kirkstall PE2 .... 186 B3
Kirkton Gate PE3 .... 197 A1
Kirkwood Cl PE3 .... 197 A2
Kirkwood Rd CB4 .... 83 F7
KIRTLING 72 C6
KIRTLING GREEN 72 C4
Kirtling Pl **5** CB9 ... 24 B8
Kirtling Rd
  Kirtling CB8 .... 72 D7
  Woodditton CB8 .... 90 E1
KIRTLING TOWERS 72 A9
Kisby Ave PE20 .... 142 A1
Kite Cl PE29 .... 142 A7
Kitson Gdns CB6 .... 210 F5
Knapp Rise CB23 .... 47 A5
Knapp The CB23 .... 47 A5
KNAPWELL 100 E2
Knaresborough Ct **10**
  PE19 .... 74 F1
Knarr Fen Rd PE6 .... 202 D8
Knaves Acre Dro CB7 .... 212 E5
KNEESWORTH 13 A6
Kneesworth House (Hospital)
  SG8 .... 13 C5
Kneesworth Rd SG8 ...... 13 F8
Kneesworth St SG8 .... 5 C7
Knight Mews PE2 .... 187 A6
Knighton Cl PE7 .... 186 D1
Knights Cl
  Eaton Socon PE19 ...... 74 B4
  13 Leverington PE13 238 B2
Knight's Cl **11** PE15 223 A5
KNIGHTS END 228 A1
Knight's End Rd PE15 ... 243 C1
Knights Way CB24 .... 105 D3
Knipe Dr PE29 .... 141 B7
Knole Wlk PE3 .... 197 B3
Knowle Ct CB8 .... 242 B5
Knowles Ave PE28 .... 164 E5
Knowles Cl PE28 .... 140 E2
Knox End CB10 .... 21 A2
Knutsford Rd SG8 .... 12 E5
Kooreman Ave PE13 ...... 245 D7
Kyle Cres PE28 .... 140 D2
Kym Rd PE19 .... 74 C4

L

Laburnham Gr PE1 .... 198 B8
Laburnum Ave
  Mildenhall IP28 ...... 239 E5
  Yaxley PE7 .... 181 F6
Laburnum Cl
  Cambridge CB4 .... 83 F4
  Red Lodge IP28 .... 213 F1
  5 Wisbech PE13 ... 245 E7
Laburnum Gr PE15 .... 243 C6
Laburnum La CB25 .... 130 A3
Laburnum Way PE27 ...... 144 A5
Lacey's La CB8 .... 110 B7
Lacey's Way CB22 .... 32 D1
Lacks Cl CB24 .... 125 D3
Laddus Bank PE14 .... 236 C1
Laddus Dro PE14 .... 229 B8
LADDUS FENS 236 B1
Ladies Hill SG19 .... 58 D4
Ladybower Way PE4 ...... 204 E3
Lady Charlotte Rd PE7 . 186 C3
Ladygate **1** PE2 ..... 186 C4
Lady Jermy Way CB1 ..... 85 B1
Lady Lodge Dr PE2 ...... 186 A5
Lady Margaret Rd CB3 ... 83 C3
Lady Romayne Cl PE9 .... 244 C4
Lady's Dro PE14 .... 236 D6
Lady Smith Ave PE19 ... 189 F8
Lady's Wood Nature
  Reserve* PE26 .... 170 C2
Ladywalk CB24 .... 123 F3
Ladywell CB6 .... 74 B4
Laith Rd CB23 .... 79 B2
Lake Ave PE13 .... 229 F3
Lake Cl PE13 .... 245 D4
Lake Dro PE14 .... 190 E6
Lakefield Ave PE19 ..... 96 A2
Lakes Dro CB6 .... 209 F3
LAKES END 229 F3
Lakeside
  Hamrton Hargate PE7 .. 186 C2

Lakeside continued
  Peterborough PE4 .... 204 D4
Lakeside Cl
  Little Paxton PE19 .... 96 A2
  Perry PE28 .... 115 D3
Lakeview Ct PE29 .... 141 B7
Lakeview Way PE7 .... 186 D2
Lakeway **8** PE28 ..... 215 C1
Lake Way PE29 .... 141 C5
Lamb Dro CB23 .... 79 C3
Lambert Mews PE9 ...... 244 C4
Lambes Ct PE4 .... 204 A4
Lambeth Wlk PE25 ...... 244 A6
Lamb Fair Ct CB21 ...... 35 D2
Lamble Cl IP28 .... 213 F8
Lambourn Cl **1** CB2 .. 64 D3
Lambourne Rd CB23 ...... 81 A3
Lambs' Cross CB24 ..... 103 F8
Lambs Dro PE15 .... 228 B1
Lamb's La
  Cottenham CB24 .... 125 D3
  Glatton PE28 .... 175 D2
Lamb's Pl PE15 .... 243 D4
Lammas Field **4** CB3 . 64 C7
Lammas Gdns PE29 ...... 141 D5
Lammas Rd PE1 .... 198 A7
Lammas Way
  St Ives PE27 .... 143 F4
  St Neots PE19 .... 74 E6
Lamport Dr PE29 .... 141 F8
Lancaster Cl
  Old Hurst PE28 ...... 154 D6
  Warboys PE28 .... 164 F4
Lancaster Ct PE7 ...... 181 F6
Lancaster Dr PE27 ..... 144 A6
Lancaster Rd
  Mildenhall IP28 ...... 213 E8
  Ramsey PE26 .... 171 E3
  10 Stamford PE9 .. 244 B6
Lancaster Way
  Ely CB6 .... 217 F1
  Godmanchester PE29 ... 141 F8
  Huntingdon PE29 ..... 141 B8
  Wyton PE28 .... 155 A1
  Yaxley PE7 .... 181 F6
Lancaster Way Bsns Pk
  CB6 .... 217 F1
Lancelot Way PE28 ..... 121 C5
Lancing Cl PE14 .... 204 C3
Landau Way PE15 .... 243 E6
LANDBEACH 105 D3
Landbeach Rd CB24 ..... 105 D3
Lander Cl PE27 .... 144 B5
Landcliffe Cl PE27 .... 144 B5
Landcr Cl PE27 .... 105 C3
Landseer Ct CB24 .... 23 F6
LANDWADE 132 C4
Landwade Rd
  Exning CB8 .... 131 B4
  Fordham CB25 .... 131 D5
Lane End PE9 .... 38 B1
Lanes The
  Great Wilbraham CB21 . 67 F8
  Over CB24 .... 208 D1
  St Ives PE28 .... 143 A5
Lane The
  Easton PE28 .... 138 B4
  Hauxton CB22 .... 48 B4
  Old Hurst PE28 ...... 154 E6
  St Neots PE19 .... 75 A5
  Stow Longa PE28 ..... 137 B2
  West Deeping PE6 .... 231 B7
Langdale Cl PE1 .... 166 A7
Langdyke PE1 .... 198 F6
Langford Rd PE2 .... 187 A7
Langham Rd CB1 .... 65 C6
Langham Way
  Ely CB7 .... 240 E7
  Haverhill CB9 .... 38 B1
Langley Cl PE3 .... 197 B8
Langley Ct PE27 .... 144 A4
Langley Gr PE27 .... 144 A4
Langley Lawn CB11 .... 1 D2
Langley Way PE28 ...... 143 B1
Langton Cl PE1 .... 198 C4
Langwood Cl **7** PE13 . 243 B1
Langwood Fen Dro PE16 . 216 D8
Langwood Hill Dro PE16 216 B7
Lankester Rd SG8 .... 11 B2
Lannesbury Cres PE19 ... 75 C7
Lansbury Cl **4** PE19 . 74 E6
Lansdowne Cl CB6 ...... 240 B3
Lansdowne Rd
  Cambridge CB3 .... 82 F3
  Yaxley PE7 .... 181 D6
Lansdowne Way PE2 ..... 186 D7
Lansdowne Wlk PE2 ..... 186 D7
Lanstone Stile CB21 .... 67 A5
Lantree Cres CB22 ...... 64 D1
Lanwades Pk CB8 .... 133 F1
Lapwing Cl IP28 .... 239 D4
Lapwing Dr PE7 .... 190 A8
Lapwings Cl CB1 .... 85 B1
Lapwing Way **11** CB22 212 A5
Larch Cl PE7 .... 181 E6
Larches The **2** PE15 . 243 A5
Larch Gr PE1 .... 198 C6
Larham Way PE16 .... 241 B5
Lark Cl IP28 .... 213 F4
Lark Cres PE29 .... 142 A6
Lark End PE19 .... 74 E4
Larkfield Rd CB7 ...... 240 E6
Lark Grange CB7 .... 219 D4
LARK HALL CORNER 69 B1
Larkhall Rd CB7 .... 212 D1
Lark Hill CB8 .... 112 E5

Larkin Cl CB4. . . . . .84 A6
Larkin Pl SG8. . . . . .13 D1
Larkins Rd SG8 . . . . .26 F6
Larklands PE3 . . . . .197 B1
Lark Rd IP28 . . . . .239 D4
Lark Rise CB23 . . . . .80 F3
Larks Cl CB9. . . . . .24 C7
Larksfield PE13 . . . . .245 C3
Larkspur Cl **4** IP28. . . . . .213 F1
Larkspur Wlk PE4. . . . . .204 D3
Lark Way PE28. . . . . .150 E4
Larmor Dr CB3 . . . . .83 B3
Laroc Cl PE29 . . . . .141 F1
Latham Ave PE2 . . . . .186 C6
Latham Cl CB2. . . . . .64 D6
Latham Rd
  Cambridge CB2 . . . . .64 D6
  Huntingdon PE29. . . . . .141 C8
Latimer Cl CB5 . . . . .84 E3
Latin Cl PE19 . . . . .118 A2
LATTERSEA FIELD 190 B6
Lattersey Cl PE7 . . . . .189 F7
*Lattersey Nature Reserve**
  PE7 .190 A5
Lattimers Paddock PE9 . . . .230 C4
Laughton's La PE28. . . . . .143 A5
Laundress La CB3. . . . . .246 A2
Laundry La CB1. . . . . .65 D5
  Laureate CP Sch CB8 . . . . . . .110 E6
Laureate Gdns CB8 . . . . .110 E6
Laureate Paddocks CB8 . . . .110 E6
Laureate Sch Rd CB8 . . . . . . .110 E6
Laurel Cl
  Haverhill CB9. . . . . .38 D2
  Mepal CB6. . . . . .216 E3
  3 Red Lodge IP28 . . . . . . .214 A1
  Sawtry PE28 . . . . .168 A3
  Yaxley PE7 . . . . .181 D4
Laurel Dr
  Elm PE14 . . . . .236 A5
  Thorney PE6. . . . . .232 F3
Laurels Cl PE19. . . . . .74 F4
Lauriston Pl **1** CB4. . . . . .83 E8
Lavender Cl
  8 Red Lodge IP28 . . . . . . .213 F1
  Yaxley PE7 . . . . .181 F6
Lavender Cres PE1. . . . . .198 B8
Lavender Ct **4** PE29 . . . . . . .141 F7
Lavender Field CB9 . . . . .23 D8
Lavender Rd CB4. . . . . .84 A7
Lavender Way PE27 . . . . .144 A6
Lavington Grange PE1. . . . . . .198 E6
Law Cl CB6. . . . . .242 D3
Lawn Ave PE1 . . . . .198 A7
Lawn La
  Little Downham CB6 . . . . . . .218 A7
  Sutton CB6. . . . . .216 E1
Lawns Cres CB6 . . . . .218 A7
Lawns Cl SG8. . . . . .5 D6
Lawns The
  Cambridge CB3 . . . . .83 A2
  Everton SG19. . . . . .40 C3
  Melbourn SG8 . . . . .14 C5
  Walton PE4 . . . . .204 E1
  Wisbech PE13 . . . . .245 B6
Lawn The CB22 . . . . .32 C5
Lawrance Lea CB22 . . . . .47 F2
Lawrence Ave PE7 . . . . .187 C2
Lawrence Cl CB3 . . . . .82 D8
Lawrence Rd
  Eaton Socon PE19 . . . . .74 C5
  Ramsey PE26. . . . . .172 C7
  Wittering PE8 . . . . .230 B1
Lawrence Way CB4 . . . . .83 F7
Law's Cl PE6 . . . . .206 F1
Laws Cres PE28 . . . . .140 C4
Law's Lawn PE8 . . . . .192 C2
Lawson Ave PE2 . . . . .187 D6
Lawson Cl CB24 . . . . .104 B4
Laxton Cl PE19 . . . . .74 C4
Laxton Grange PE28 . . . . .208 C5
Laxton Way CB4 . . . . .84 C6
Layer Rd CB9. . . . . .23 E7
Layston Pk SG8 . . . . .5 E5
Layton Cres PE28 . . . . .140 D2
Lea Brooks Cl PE28 . . . . .164 F4
Leach Cl PE13 . . . . .245 C2
Leaden Hill SG8 . . . . .28 D8
Leaden's La PE19 . . . . .117 C3
Leader's Way CB8 . . . . .110 E4
Leading Dro PE7. . . . . .181 E4
Leaf Ave PE7 . . . . .186 D3
Leafere Way **1** PE13. . . . . . .238 E7
Leaford Dr CB6. . . . . .218 B6
Lea Gdns PE3 . . . . .197 F1
Leam The PE14 . . . . .236 A4
Lea Rd PE28. . . . . .143 C1
Leas Cl PE27 . . . . .144 A4
Leather La CB9 . . . . .23 E7
Lebanon Dr PE13 . . . . .245 F7
Ledbury Rd PE3 . . . . .197 C3
Ledham Rd PE2 . . . . .185 D4
Ledo Rd CB22 . . . . .31 F2
Leechcroft PE28 . . . . .121 C6
Lee Cl
  Cottenham CB24 . . . . .125 D3
  Hanchet End CB9. . . . . .38 F2
Lee Rd PE7. . . . . .181 E4
Lees La PE19 . . . . .95 E5
Lees Way CB3 . . . . .103 E1
Leete Pl SG8. . . . . .5 C7
Leete Rd CB1. . . . . .65 F5

Leete's La CB23. . . . . .46 A8
Leeway Ave CB22 . . . . .49 B5
Leger Cl PE27 . . . . .144 A6
Legge–Bourke Ct PE13. . . . .245 F6
Legg Rd **2** PE8. . . . . .230 B1
Legion Ct CB4. . . . . .83 E7
Legion Way PE29 . . . . .142 B1
Leicester Cl CB6. . . . . .240 A3
Leicester Terr **3** PE1. . . . . .198 B3
Leighton PE2 . . . . .186 C4
LEIGHTON
  BROMSWOLD 148 D3
  Leighton Prim Sch PE2 . . . . . .186 C4
Leinsters Cl PE13 . . . . .197 D3
Leiston Ct PE6. . . . . .232 A1
Leiston Rd CB9. . . . . .23 E7
Lemur Dr CB1. . . . . .66 B7
Lensfield Rd CB2 . . . . .246 B1
Lenton Cl PE28 . . . . .140 D2
Lents Way CB4 . . . . .84 C5
Leofric Sq PE1. . . . . .198 E3
Leonard Cl **2** CB5. . . . . .84 E4
Leopold Wlk CB24 . . . . .125 E3
Lerowe Rd PE13 . . . . .245 E7
Les Baux Pl **5** PE13. . . . . . .245 E3
Leslie Green Rd PE28 . . . . . . .143 B5
Lessingham PE2 . . . . .185 D4
Lester Dr CB6. . . . . .210 A6
Lester Piggott Way CB8. . . . .110 F6
Lethbridge Rd PE4. . . . . .204 E2
Lettice Martin Croft CB22 . . .32 D5
Levellers La PE19. . . . . .74 F3
Leveret Way PE19. . . . . .75 C5
LEVERINGTON. 238 B2
  Leverington Comm PE13 . . . .235 B8
  Leverington Prim Sch
    PE13. . . . . .238 B2
  Leverington Rd PE13 . . . . . . .245 A6
  Leverington Road Ind Est
    PE13 . . . . .245 B7
Levers Wr PE29 . . . . .141 C5
Levitt's Dro PE6 . . . . .200 C4
Lewes Gdns PE4 . . . . .204 C3
Lewis Cl
  Great & Little Abington
    CB21. . . . . .34 C5
  March PE15. . . . . .243 B3
Lewis Cres CB21. . . . . .34 C5
Lexington Cl **3** CB4. . . . . .83 C5
Leyburn Cl CB1 . . . . .66 A7
Ley Rd CB88. . . . . .90 A1
Leys Ave CB4 . . . . .83 F5
Leys Rd
  Cambridge CB4 . . . . .83 F5
  St Neots PE19 . . . . .74 E6
  Leys Sch The CB2. . . . . .246 B1
Leys The
  Alconbury PE28. . . . . .150 F4
  Little Gransden SG19. . . . . . . .58 E3
  Peterborough PE3. . . . . .197 A1
  Sawtry PE28 . . . . .168 C3
Leys Wlk CB22. . . . . .48 C4
Leyton Ave IP28 . . . . .239 B6
Liberator Rd PE26 . . . . .171 E3
Lichfield Ave PE4 . . . . .204 B3
Lichfield Rd CB1. . . . . .65 B6
Licking's Dro PE13. . . . . .245 A2
LIDGATE 73 E8
Lidgate Cl PE2. . . . . .186 C7
Lidgate Rd CB88 . . . . .92 E7

Lincoln Rd *continued*
  Mildenhall IP28 . . . . .213 E8
  Peterborough PE4 . . . . .197 C8
Ramsey PE26. . . . . .171 E3
Stamford PE9 . . . . .244 D7
Wyton Airfield PE28. . . . . . . .143 A8
Linden Cl
  Barnack PE9 . . . . .230 D4
  Cambridge CB4 . . . . .83 C4
  Haddenham CB6 . . . . .210 A5
Linden Dr PE16. . . . . .241 C4
Linden End CB6 . . . . .210 A5
Linden Gr PE2. . . . . .185 C5
Linden Gr PE29 . . . . .141 F2
Lindens Cl PE13 . . . . .234 A2
Linden Way CB6 . . . . .210 A5
Lindeth Cl PE29. . . . . .141 A7
Lindisfarne Cl **9** PE19 . . . . . .74 F1
Lindisfarne Rd PE6. . . . . .232 A1
Lindridge Wlk PE13. . . . . .197 A2
Lindsay Cl
  Huntingdon SG8. . . . . .13 C1
  Wyton PE28 . . . . .143 A8
Lindsells Wlk PE16. . . . . .241 C5
Lindsey Cl PE4. . . . . .204 D1
Lindsey Rd
  Stamford PE9. . . . . .244 C6
  5 Uffington PE9. . . . . .230 C6
Lingfield Rd **7** SG8. . . . . .5 E6
Ling Garth PE1. . . . . .198 B8
Lingholme Cl **2** CB4. . . . . .83 C5
Lingmoor PE29 . . . . .141 A6
Lingrey Ct CB2 . . . . .64 D2
Lingwood Pk PE3. . . . . .197 A1
Link Dr PE28 . . . . .140 C3
Link La CB6. . . . . .216 E1
Link Rd
  Peterborough PE1. . . . . .197 F3
  Sawston CB22. . . . . .32 F8
Links Cl IP28 . . . . .213 F4
Linkside PE2. . . . . .204 B1
Links The CB8 . . . . .89 D8
Links Way PE27. . . . . .143 F4
Linley Rd
  St Neots PE19 . . . . .74 E3
  Whittlesey PE7 . . . . .189 E6
Linlithgow Cl CB23. . . . . .99 A3
Linnet PE2 . . . . .185 A6
LINTON. 35 E3
Linton CE Inf Sch CB21. . . . . .35 C2
Linton Cl CB8. . . . . .110 F5
Linton Hts Jun Sch CB21. . .35 D2
Linton Pl CB9. . . . . .24 B8
Linton Rd
  Balsham CB21. . . . . .52 F2
  Great Abington CB21. . . . . . . .34 D6
  Hadstock CB21. . . . . .20 B8
  Horseheath CB21. . . . . .36 F3
  Linton Village Coll CB21. . . .35 B2
Linton Zoological Gdns*
  CB21 .35 B1
Linwood La PE15 . . . . .223 A8
Lion Cl PE26. . . . . .220 D3
Lionel Walden Prim Sch
  PE15. . . . . .223 A5
Lion Farm Ct PE19 . . . . .57 C6
Lions Cross PE29 . . . . .119 A8
Lion Cl CB6. . . . . .210 A6
Lion Wlk PE26. . . . . .172 A5
Lion Yard Sh Ctr CB1. . . . . . . .246 B2
Lion Yd
  Cambridge CB1 . . . . .246 B2
  Ramsey PE26. . . . . .172 B6
LIPREAS THE. 202 B1
Lisburn Rd CB1. . . . . .111 B3
Lisle Cl CB7 . . . . .240 E5
Lisle La CB7 . . . . .240 E4
Lisle Wlk CB1. . . . . .66 A6
Lister Hospl PE1. . . . . .197 F7
Lister's Rd PE14 . . . . .236 E1
Litchfield Cl PE7. . . . . .181 F5
LITTLINGTON. 12 B2
Litlington Rd SG8. . . . . .11 E1
LITTLE ABINGTON 34 B7
Little Back La CB25. . . . . .129 D1
Little Bowsers CB10. . . . . .20 D3
LITTLEBURY GREEN 9 F2
Little Casterton Rd PE9 . . . .244 A6
LITTLE CATWORTH 137 A6
Little Catworth PE28 . . . . . . .137 B6
LITTLE CHISHILL. 1 C7
Little Chishill Rd SG8 . . . . . . .1 D6
Little Church St **21** PE13 . .245 C5
LITTLE CI PE6. . . . . .232 A1
Littlecotes Cl PE28. . . . . .137 F7
LITTLE DITTON 90 F2
Little Ditton CB8. . . . . .90 F2
LITTLE DOWNHAM 218 A5
LITTLE DOWNHAM 218 A4
LITTLE END. 74 C1
Little End Rd PE19 . . . . .74 B1
Little End Road Ind Est
  PE19. . . . . .74 B2
LITTLE EVERSDEN. 46 A7
Little Farthing Cl PE27 . . . . .144 B4
Little Fen Dro
  Burwell CB25. . . . . .129 E6
  Swaffham Prior CB25. . . . . . .129 A1
Little Fendyke La PE14. . . . . .236 E5
Littlefield Cl
  Godmanchester PE29 . . . . . .118 F8
  Wilburton CB6. . . . . .210 C6
LITTLE GIDDING. 158 F8
Little Gn
  Cheveley CB8. . . . . .91 C5
  Guilden Morden SG8 . . . . .11 A7
  Warmington PE8 . . . . .178 B3

LITTLE GRANSDEN 58 D3
Little Gransden La SG19. .58 D4
LITTLE GREEN. 178 C3
Little Hasse Dro CB7. . . . . . .212 C6
LITTLE HEATH. 41 C4
Little Heath SG19 . . . . .41 C4
Little How PE27. . . . . .143 E6
Little Johns Cl PE3 . . . . .196 F3
Little La
  Ely CB6 . . . . .240 B4
  Great Gransden SG19 . . . . . . .58 E4
  Melbourn SG8 . . . . .14 C6
LITTLE LINTON. 35 B3
LITTLE LONDON. 243 C4
Little London CB7 . . . . .212 F5
Little London Dro CB7 . . . . . .212 F5
Little London La CB7. . . . . . . .212 F5
Little Marefen Dro CB4. . . . . .242 A7
Little Mdw CB2. . . . . .102 B2
Littlemeer PE2 . . . . .185 F4
Little Moor PE28. . . . . .121 C5
Little Northfields **3** PE29 . .118 D7
LITTLE OUSE. 226 D4
Little Paddocks CB10 . . . . . . .19 A4
LITTLE PAXTON 95 E2
Little Paxton La PE19 . . . . .95 F2
Little Paxton Prim Sch
  PE19. .95 F1
LITTLEPORT. 242 C4
Littleport Com Prim Sch
  CB6 . . . . .242 B4
Littleport Sta CB6. . . . . .242 E6
Little Ramper PE13 . . . . .238 B4
LITTLE RAVELEY. 163 B4
Little St Mary's La CB2. . . . . .246 A1
Little Setchel Dro CB24 . . . .209 F2
LITTLE SHELFORD. 48 E3
Little St CB6. . . . . .218 B6
LITTLE STAUGHTON 93 B2
LITTLE STUKELEY 151 C4
LITTLE THETFORD. 211 B7
Little Thetford CE Prim Sch
  CB6 . . . . .211 B7
Little Whyte PE26. . . . . .172 B7
LITTLE WILBRAHAM 86 E1
Little Wilbraham Rd CB1. .86 D4
Littleworth Dro PE12. . . . . . .233 F8
Littleworth End PE19. . . . . . .118 A1
LITTLE WRATTING. 39 D3
Livermore Gn PE4 . . . . .204 A6
Loch Fyne Cl PE2. . . . . .185 C4
Lock Lomond Way PE2. . . . . .185 C4
Locks Cl PE6 . . . . .206 B7
Locksgate **1** PE28. . . . . .215 C1
Locks Gn PE26. . . . . .183 A8
Lockspit Hall Dro
  Cottenham CB24 . . . . .125 F8
  Ottenham CB24 . . . . .209 F1
LODE. .107 C2
Lode Ave
  Outwell PE14 . . . . .236 F1
  Waterbeach CB25 . . . . .106 B7
Lode Cl CB7 . . . . .212 B3
Lode La CB7 . . . . .211 E1
Lode Ave PE3 . . . . .196 F2
Lode Rd
  Bottisham CB25. . . . . .86 D7
  Lode CB25 . . . . .107 D1
Lodes End Dro PE26 . . . . .220 F2
Lode Way
  Chatteris PE16. . . . . .241 C6
  Haddenham CB6 . . . . .210 A5
Lodge Cl PE29 . . . . .141 C4
Lodge Dro SG8. . . . . .13 C6
Lodge Rd SG8 . . . . .31 A1
Loftsteads **3** PE28. . . . . . . .215 C1
Logan's Way CB4 . . . . .84 A3
Loire Ct PE1. . . . . .197 E4
Lomax Dr PE28 . . . . .140 C3
Lombardy Dr PE1. . . . . .198 B8
London La PE19 . . . . .96 E4
London Rd
  Barley SG8. . . . . .6 F1
  Chatteris PE16. . . . . .241 C2
  Fenstanton PE28 . . . . .120 E7
  Fowlmere SG8. . . . . .15 D5
  Godmanchester PE29 . . . . . .141 F1
  Great Chesterford CB10 . . . . .18 C2
  Great Shelford CB22 . . . . .49 B4
  Harston CB22 . . . . .48 F3
  Hemingford Grey PE27 . . . . .143 F1
  Kimbolton PE28. . . . . .114 A4
  Peterborough PE7. . . . . .186 F3
  Royston SG8 . . . . .5 D4
  Sawston CB22. . . . . .32 F5
  Stamford PE9. . . . . .244 C2
  Wansford PE8 . . . . .194 B2
  Yaxley PE7 . . . . .181 C5
London Sn
  Godmanchester PE29 . . . . . .141 F1
  Whittlesey PE7 . . . . .189 D6
Lone Tree Ave CB24 . . . . .83 C8
Lone Tree Gr CB24 . . . . .83 C8
Longchamp Dr CB7 . . . . .240 F6
Long Cswy
  Peterborough PE1. . . . . .198 A2
  Whittlesey PE7 . . . . .189 E6
Long Dolver Dro CB7 . . . . . . .212 B6
Long Dro
  Bury PE26 . . . . .172 F5
  Cottenham CB24 . . . . .125 F3
  Downham CB6. . . . . .224 F3
  Elm PE14 . . . . .235 B1
  Feltwell PE38. . . . . .226 F6
  Haddenham CB6 . . . . .209 C5
  Holme PE7. . . . . .177 D5
  Over CB24 . . . . .208 D3

Long Dro *continued*
  Parson Drove PE13 . . . . .234 B5
Ramsey PE26. . . . . .221 D2
Somersham PE28. . . . . .215 D2
Waterbeach CB25 . . . . .106 D8
Whittlesey PE7 . . . . .200 C3
Longfellow Pl **5** PE19 . . . . .74 D5
Longfield Gate PE2 . . . . .186 A6
Longfield Rd CB6. . . . . .242 B5
Longfields CB6 . . . . .240 A3
Long Furlong CB24 . . . . .208 D1
Longhead La PE14 . . . . .238 D3
Longhill Rd PE15 . . . . .228 B6
Long Holme Dro CB24 . . . . . .208 E3
Longholme Rd PE26 . . . . .171 A4
Long La
  Coveney CB6. . . . . .217 C4
  Fowlmere SG8. . . . . .15 D8
  Gamlingay SG19 . . . . .41 F6
  Hemingford Grey PE28 . . . . .120 C8
  Linton CB21. . . . . .35 C1
  Over CB24 . . . . .208 C2
  Spaldwick PE28 . . . . .137 C5
  Willingham CB24 . . . . .124 A8
Long Lots PE14 . . . . .236 F8
LONG MEADOW 107 F2
Long Meadow Field
  PE13. . . . . .237 F2
Long Meadow Rd CB25. .107 F2
Longmere La CB7. . . . . .212 A5
Long Nightlayer's Dro
  PE16. . . . . .241 E8
Long North Fen Dro CB6 . .216 A4
Long Pasture PE4. . . . . .204 B5
Long Rd
  Cambridge CB2 . . . . .64 F4
  Comberton CB23. . . . . .81 D2
Long Reach Rd CB4 . . . . .84 F4
Long Road Sixth Form Coll
  CB2 .64 F3
Longsands Coll PE19 . . . . .75 A6
Longsands Rd **3** PE19 . . . . .75 A6
Longsands Rd PE19 . . . . .75 A5
Longstaff Way PE29. . . . . .142 A6
LONGSTANTON. 124 E2
Longstanton Rd
  Oakington/Longstanton
    CB24 . . . . .103 B6
  Over CB24 . . . . .123 B7
LONGSTOWE. 59 F3
LONGTHORPE 197 A1
Longthorpe Ct PE3 . . . . .197 A2
Longthorpe Gn PE3 . . . . .197 B1
Longthorpe House Mews
  PE3. .196 F2
Longthorpe Parkway
  PE3. .186 A3
Longthorpe Prim Sch
  PE3. .197 A2
Longueville Ct PE2. . . . . .186 B5
Longview PE2 . . . . .185 D1
Longwater PE2 . . . . .186 B6
Longwood CB23 . . . . .81 B8
Longworth Ave CB4. . . . . .84 A3
Lonsdale CB22. . . . . .35 E2
Lonsdale Terr PE13 . . . . .245 C3
Loop Rd PE28. . . . . .146 A4
Lophams Cl CB9 . . . . .38 F2
Lord's Croft La CB9. . . . . .24 A7
Lord's Gd Dro CB25. . . . . .128 D2
Lordship Cl
  Orwell SG8. . . . . .45 E1
  Willingham CB24 . . . . .209 A1
Lordship Dr SG8. . . . . .5 E1
Lordship End PE12 . . . . .233 E8
Lords La PE13. . . . . .235 D7
Lord's La PE13. . . . . .235 D6
Loris Ct CB1. . . . . .66 A7
Lorna Ct PE27 . . . . .143 F6
Lornas Field PE7 . . . . .186 D2
Losecoat Cl PE9 . . . . .244 D7
Lotfield St SG8 . . . . .45 E1
Lottings Way PE19 . . . . .74 C6
Loughborough Univ of
  Peterborough PE1. . . . . .198 A3
Loughrigg Cl PE29 . . . . .141 B7
Loughton Ct CB5 . . . . .84 E4
Louthe Way PE28 . . . . .168 C3
Loveday Cl SG8. . . . . .8 D3
Love La
  Ashwell SG7. . . . . .2 A5
  Houghton & Wyton PE28. . . .143 A5
  Whittlesey PE7 . . . . .189 D6
  Wisbech PE13 . . . . .245 C4
Lovell Rd CB4 . . . . .84 B7
Lovells The PE14. . . . . .236 D6
Lovers La PE5 . . . . .194 F2
Love's Cl CB24. . . . . .104 C2
Love's Hill PE5 . . . . .195 F1
Love's La **1** CB24. . . . . .209 A1
Lowbury Cres CB24 . . . . .103 B6
Lowburyholme Rd CB24. .208 C1
Low Cross PE7. . . . . .189 D8
LOWER CAMBOURNE 78 F4
Lower Downs Slade CB9 . .24 A8
Lower Dro CB7 . . . . .211 D3
Lower End CB25. . . . . .108 E5
Lower End PE26 . . . . .217 C2
Lower Field CB11 . . . . .6 F5
Lower Gower Rd SG8 . . . . .5 D8
Lower King St SG8. . . . . .5 D6
Lower Park St CB5. . . . . .246 A3
Lower Rd
  Croydon SG8 . . . . .26 D5
  Ely CB7 . . . . .218 D1
  Wicken CB7 . . . . .211 E2
Lower St SG8 . . . . .31 B1

Lower Wood Nature
Reserve* CB8............54 C6
Lower Yd CB8.............132 A2
Loweswater PE29.........141 C5
Low Fen Dro Way CB5....85 B4
Lowfields CB23............46 B8
Low Gate PE13............237 F8
Low Harthay PE28.........139 D3
Lowick Gdns PE3.........197 C5
Lowndes Dro PE27........144 F7
Low Park Cnr CB7.........133 A6
Low Rd
  Burwell CB25............130 B2
  Crowland PE6............207 F7
  Fenstanton PE28........121 A7
  Hemingford Grey PE27..144 A1
  Little Stukeley PE28....151 D3
  Queen Adelaide CB7....218 F4
  The Stukeleys PE28.....140 C7
  Wisbech PE14...........245 E1
Lowry Cl
  Haverhill CB9............38 D1
  St Ives PE27.............144 A7
Lowry Rd PE19............74 C6
Low Side PE14............236 E2
Lowther Gdns PE4........204 D2
Lowther St CB8...........110 F3
Loxley PE4................204 A4
Loxley Gdns PE8.........142 F5
Luard Cl CB2.............65 A4
Luard Rd CB2.............65 A5
Lucas Ct PE29...........141 F7
Lucas La SG7.............2 E4
Lucerne Cl
  Cambridge CB1..........66 A6
  Red Lodge IP28.........213 F1
Lucketts Cl CB24.........104 B5
Luck's La PE19............117 A4
Lucombe Dr PE13.........245 F7
Lucy Cavendish Coll CB3.83 C3
Luddington Cl PE19.......96 E4
LUDDINGTON IN THE
  BROOK..................166 B4
Luddington Rd
  Great Gidding PE28......166 C3
  Peterborough PE4........204 D1
Ludlow La CB21...........67 A5
Lug Fen Droveway CB25..107 A5
Luke St PE19..............74 E4
Lulworth Dr CB8..........23 E8
Lumen Rd SG8.............5 D7
Lumley Cl CB6............240 E8
Lundy Cl CB9.............24 D7
LUTTON.................174 C4
Lutton Gate Rd PE12.....234 A8
Lutton Gr PE3............197 C6
Lye Cl PE19...............94 A6
Lyles Rd CB24............125 D4
Lymage Rd PE28..........115 D3
Lyme Wlk PE3............197 C6
Lynch La SG8.............15 E8
Lynchwood PE2...........185 C5
Lyndale Pk PE2...........185 C6
Lyndewode Rd CB1.......246 C1
Lyndhurst Cl CB24.......105 C2
Lynfield La CB4...........84 A4
Lynn Rd
  Ely CB7.................240 D6
  Littleport CB6...........242 F6
  Wisbech PE13...........245 C6
Lynton CB4...............240 D6
Lynton Dr CB6............240 D6
Lynton Way PE1..........197 F6
Lynton Way CB22.........33 A8
Lynx The CB1.............66 A7
Lyons Ct PE16............241 C4
Lyon's Dro PE15..........223 F4
Lysander Cl PE27.........143 F7
Lythemere PE2............186 C4
Lyvelly Gdns PE1........198 E6

M

Maarnford Cl CB22........17 D8
MacAulay Ave CB22.......49 B6
Macbeth Cl PE29.........141 F6
McCalmont Way CB8......111 E2
Mace Rd PE2..............187 D5
Macfarlane Cl CB24.......104 C2
Mackenzie Rd [**8**] CB1....84 A1
MacKerel Hall SG6........5 B6
Macpherson Robertson Way
  IP28...................239 A5
Maddingley Way CB6......210 A7
Madecroft PE28...........165 A5
Madeley Ct PE28.........143 C2
MADINGLEY..............81 E5
Madingley Hall* CB23....81 E5
Madingley Rd
  Cambridge CB3..........83 B3
  Dry Drayton CB23.......102 B1
Madingley Sch CB23......81 F5
Madingley Wood CB23....82 A4
Madras Rd CB1...........65 C7
Maffit Rd PE5............195 D3
Magazine Cl PE13........245 A4
Magdalene CB21..........245 A4
Magdalene Cl CB24.......123 F2
Magdalene Coll CB4......246 A4
Magdalene St CB2........246 A3
Magee Rd PE4............204 D1
Magistrates Rd PE7......181 D8
Magna Cl CB21...........34 C6
Magnolia Ave PE3.........197 A2
Magnolia Cl
  Cambridge CB1..........65 B5
  [**2**] Red Lodge IP28....213 F1

Magrath Ave CB4........246 A4
Maiden La PE9...........244 C5
Maids' Cswy CB5........246 C3
Mailes Cl CB23............63 B4
Main Dro CB6............225 A2
Main Rd
  Etton PE6..............203 B8
  Little Gransden SG19....58 D3
  Parson Drove PE13......234 E7
  Uffington PE9..........230 D6
  Upwell PE14............229 E7
  Wisbech PE14...........236 A3
Main St
  Ailsworth PE5..........195 D2
  Barnack PE9............230 D3
  Bythorn & Keyston PE28..146 D4
  Caldecote CB23..........61 B6
  Castor PE5.............195 D3
  Coveney CB6............217 B5
  Downham CB6...........217 D8
  Ely CB7................219 B5
  Farcet PE7.............187 C2
  Great Gidding PE28......166 D3
  Hardwick CB23...........81 A1
  Hatley SG19..............43 A3
  Huntingdon PE29........142 A6
  Little Downham CB6.....218 A6
  Littleport CB6..........242 D4
  Old Weston PE28........145 F7
  Shudy Camps CB21......21 F6
  Southorpe PE9..........230 E1
  Stow cum Quy CB25......85 F5
  Thetford CB8...........211 B7
  Ufford PE9.............230 F3
  Upton PE28.............160 D1
  Welney PE14............225 A8
  Wentworth CB6..........217 B1
  Witchford CB6..........217 E1
  Yarwell PE8............183 A8
  Yaxley PE7.............181 E5
Main Street PE28.........166 A3
Maio Rd CB4..............83 F5
Maitland Ave CB4.........84 B6
Major Haddock Cl SG8.....5 C7
Malborne Way PE2........186 B4
Malcolm St CB1..........246 B3
Malcolm Way CB8.........111 B5
Malden Cl CB5............84 D3
Malden Way PE19.........74 D2
Maldon Rd PE13..........245 E5
Malecoff PE29............118 F7
Males Cl CB24............125 E5
Malin Cl CB9.............24 D7
Mallard Cl
  Chatteris PE16..........241 C5
  Whittlesey PE7.........189 F8
Mallard Ct PE19...........75 A5
Mallard La PE19...........75 A4
Mallard Rd
  Peterborough PE3.......204 A1
  Royston SG8..............5 C6
Mallard Rise CB6.........210 A6
Mallards The
  Peakirk PE6............206 B1
  St Ives PE27...........143 F7
Mallard Way PE15........243 F5
Mallett Cl PE15..........243 F4
Malletts Rd CB1...........66 A5
Mallory La [**11**] PE9......244 B5
Mallory Rd PE1...........198 C2
Mallow La PE7............175 D8
Mallows Cl [**2**] CB23......62 D6
Mallow Wlk
  Haverhill CB9.............23 C8
  [**1**] Royston SG8.........5 E5
Malmesbury Dr PE6......232 A1
Malory Pl CB23............99 A3
Malta Rd CB1.............65 B7
Maltby Cl [**17**] PE8........230 B1
Malt Cl [**3**] CB8..........111 B3
Malt Dr PE13.............245 B3
Malthouse La PE14.......141 D4
Malthouse La PE26.......171 F5
Malthouse Way CB22......29 F8
Malting End CB8...........72 D4
Malting La
  Cambridge CB3...........64 C8
  Ellington PE28..........139 A4
  Foxton CB22..............30 C5
  Islesham CB7...........213 A5
  Litlington SG8...........12 A2
Maltings Cl
  Moulton CB8............112 E5
  Royston SG8..............5 C7
Maltings La SG8...........5 C7
Maltings Pl SG19.........41 D5
Maltings The
  Alconbury PE28.........150 E5
  Cambourne CB23.........80 B2
  Eaton Socon PE19.......74 C5
  Gamlingay SG19.........41 D6
  Sawtry PE28............168 B4
  St Martin's Without PE9..244 C2
  [**3**] Thorney PE6.........233 A3
Malting The PE26.........171 F5
Maltmas Dro PE14........235 F2
Malton La SG8.............29 B4
Malton Rd
  Meldreth SG8............29 C3
  Orwell SG8..............45 F1
Maltsters Way CB4........84 A4
Malus Ct PE7.............186 C3
Malvern Cl CB8...........111 B2
Malvern Rd
  Cambridge CB1...........65 E6
  Peterborough PE4.......204 E2
Manasty Rd PE2..........185 D2
Mancetter Sq PE4........204 B1

Manchester Rd PE28.....117 D8
Manchester Way PE27....144 A8
Mandene Gdns SG19......58 E4
Manderston Rd CB8......110 E4
Mander Way CB1..........65 C5
Mandeville
  Burwell CB25...........109 B8
  Peterborough PE2.......185 F4
Mandeville Rd PE28......140 C3
Mandrill Cl CB21..........66 A7
MANEA.................224 B4
Manea Prim Sch PE15....224 C4
Manea Rd PE15...........223 D6
Manea Sta PE15..........224 B6
Maners Way CB1...........65 C4
Mangers La CB22..........32 D1
Manhattan Dr CB4........246 C4
Manners Ct [**4**] PE9......230 C6
Manor at Hemingford Grey
  The* PE28..............143 B2
Manor Cl
  Brampton PE28..........140 E2
  Buckden PE19...........117 A3
  Farcet PE7.............187 C2
  Graveley PE19............98 A5
  [**2**] Great Staughton PE19..93 F6
  Harston CB22.............47 F3
  Little Paxton PE19.......95 F2
  Little Wilbraham CB1.....86 D1
  Ramsey Forty Foot PE26.221 A3
  [**18**] Somersham PE28....215 C1
  St Ives PE27...........142 F5
  Witchford CB6..........217 E1
  [**11**] Wittering PE8.......230 B1
  Yaxley PE7.............181 D5
Manor Com Coll CB4.....83 F6
Manor Cres CB23..........81 A1
Manor Ct CB21............64 B8
Manor Ct Rd CB8.........217 E1
Manor Dr
  Fenstanton PE28.......121 B6
  Peterborough PE6.......205 A3
  Sawtry PE28............168 C4
Manor Est [**1**] PE5.......223 A5
Manor Farm Cl
  Haverhill CB9............24 B7
  Oakington & Westwick
    CB24.................103 C6
Manor Farm Ct
  Cottenham CB24.........125 D3
  Perry PE28.............115 D2
Manor Farm La PE5.......195 E2
Manor Farm Rd
  Beck Row, Holywell Row &
    Kenny Hill IP28........213 D7
  Girton CB23............103 E2
  St Neots PE19...........75 A5
  Waresley SG19...........57 D2
Manor Gdns
  Buckden PE19...........117 A4
  Peterborough PE2.......187 C7
  Wisbech PE13...........245 B5
Manor Gr PE19.............75 A5
Manor House Cl [**1**] PE19..74 C2
Manor House St PE1......198 A3
Manor La
  Alconbury PE28.........150 F5
  Boxworth CB23..........101 C6
  Great Chesterford CB10.18 D2
  Great Gransden SG19....58 D4
  Manor Leisure Ctr PE7..189 E6
  Peterborough PE4.......204 A4
Manor Pl CB1.............246 B3
Manor Rd
  Folksworth PE7.........180 D1
  Gamlingay SG19..........41 D6
  Haverhill CB9............24 B7
  Hemingford Grey PE28..143 B1
  Little Shelford CB22.....48 E4
  Meldreth SG8............29 A1
  Mildenhall IP28.........239 B4
  Sutton PE5.............194 F2
  Witchford CB6..........217 E2
Manor St
  Cambridge CB1..........246 B3
  Wistow PE28............164 A7
Manor View
  Barton Mills IP28.......239 D2
  Whittlesey PE7.........189 D6
Manor Way
  Hail Weston PE19........95 A1
  Market Deeping PE6.....231 F8
Manor Wlk CB21...........67 A5
Manse Dr CB24...........125 C3
Mansel Ct CB4............83 E6
Mansel Rd PE13..........245 D3
Mansel Way CB4...........83 E6
Mansfield Cl CB24........105 C2
Mansfield Ct PE1.........198 C5
Manton PE3..............197 A3
Maple Ave
  Sawston CB22............32 F5
  Wisbech PE13...........245 C7
Maple Cl
  Bluntisham/Colne PE28..208 C6
  Bottisham CB25..........86 F5
  [**4**] Bourn CB23..........79 C3
  Cambridge CB4...........83 F8
  Linton CB21..............35 B3
  Sawtry PE28............168 A3
Maple Ct
  Gamlingay SG19.........41 C5
  Yaxley PE7.............181 F6
Maple Dr
  Huntingdon PE29........141 E8
  Little Stukeley PE28....151 E3
  Stilton PE7.............176 A7

Maple End PE28..........150 F4
Maple Gr
  March PE15.............243 C5
  Peterborough PE1.......198 C7
Maple Grove Inf Sch
  PE15..................243 C5
Maple Rd PE14...........236 A5
Maples The
  Fulbourn CB21...........66 E5
  Peterborough PE1.......198 F5
Maple Way
  Melbourn SG8............14 C5
  Royston SG8..............5 E8
Maple Wlk PE7...........186 C2
MARCH.................243 B4
March & District Mus*
  PE15..................243 D4
Marchioness Way [**3**]
  PE15...................74 B2
March La CB1.............65 F8
March Rd
  Coates/Eastrea PE7.....191 A8
  Coldham PE14...........235 F2
  Elm PE13...............227 F8
  Guyhirn PE13...........235 A2
  Welney PE14............229 F1
  Whittlesey PE7.........189 F1
  Wimblington PE15.......223 B7
March Riverside PE14....229 C8
March's Cl CB21...........66 E5
March Sta PE15...........243 D6
March Trad Est PE15.....243 B7
Marconi Dr PE7..........181 D6
Marcus Cl CB9............24 D7
Mardale Gdns PE4........204 F2
Marefen Dro CB6.........225 C3
Manor Fen Nature Reserve*
  CB24..................122 F8
Marfleet Cl CB22..........48 F7
MARGERY'S CROFT......238 B1
Margetts PE23...........143 D1
Margett St CB24..........125 E4
MARHOLM................203 E1
Marholm Rd
  Castor PE6.............196 B3
  Peterborough PE3.......204 B1
  Ufford PE9.............231 A2
Marian Way PE14........241 C2
Marigold Dr IP28.........133 F8
Marina Dr PE15..........243 A5
Mariner's Way CB4........84 A3
Marino Ct CB8...........110 F3
Marion Cl CB3............83 B8
Marion Sq CB22...........49 A6
Maris La CB2.............64 C2
Marius Cres PE7.........186 C3
Markby Cl CB22...........17 D8
MARKET DEEPING.......231 D8
Market Hill
  Cambridge CB2..........246 A2
  Chatteris PE16.........241 C5
  [**2**] Huntingdon PE29....5 D6
  St Ives PE27...........144 A3
Market La
  Linton CB21.............35 B2
  St Ives PE27...........144 A3
Market Mews PE13.......245 C5
Market Pas CB1..........246 A3
Market Pl
  [**5**] Ely CB7............240 D4
  Little London PE15......243 D4
  Mildenhall IP28.........239 C4
  St Neots PE19...........74 E7
  Whittlesey PE7.........189 E7
  Wisbech PE13...........245 C5
Market Rd PE27..........144 B3
Market Sq
  Cambridge CB2..........246 A2
  [**8**] Ely CB7.............240 D4
  Royston SG8..............5 D5
  St Neots PE19...........74 E7
Market St
  Cambridge CB2..........246 A3
  Ely CB7................240 D4
  Fordham CB7............212 E1
  Mildenhall IP28.........239 C4
  Newmarket CB8..........111 A3
  Swavesey CB24..........122 E6
  Whittlesey PE7.........189 D7
  [**13**] Wisbech PE13......245 C5
Market Way CB4..........217 A2
Markfield Rise CB6.......216 D1
Markham Cl PE14........237 D8
Markham Ret Pk PE9....244 D7
Markhams Cl [**3**] PE8.....38 F1
Mark's Way CB3..........103 E1
Marlborough Cl
  St Ives PE27...........143 F7
  Yaxley PE7.............181 E5
Marlborough Ct
  [**10**] Haverhill CB9......23 E7
  Newnham CB3............83 B8
Marlborough Rd CB1......245 A4
Marley Rd PE27..........143 F8
Marlowe Ct [**2**] PE19.....74 D6
Marlowe Gr PE4..........197 E8
Marmora Rd CB1.........64 C7
Marne Ave PE4...........204 C1
Marne Rd PE7............189 F5
Marquis Cl [**4**] PE19......74 D8
Marriott Cl PE15.........198 E5
Marriott Cl PE26.........240 C4
Marriotts Cl PE26........221 A4
Marriott's Dro PE26.....221 A4

Marritt Cl PE16...........241 B6
Marroway La [**4**] CB6....217 D1
Marshall Rd CB1...........65 A5
Marshall's Bank PE13....234 D8
Marshall's Cl CB1..........85 A1
Marshall's La CB6........218 B6
Marshall's Way PE7......187 C2
Marsham PE2.............185 F3
Marsh Cl PE15............243 F6
Marshfields Sch CB1......198 D7
Marsh La PE26............143 D1
Marshland High Sch
  PE14..................238 E4
MARSHLAND ST JAMES..236 F8
Marsh Rd
  Outwell PE14...........236 F4
  Walpole PE14...........238 F8
Marsh The PE14..........238 F8
Marsh Wlk [**5**] PE13......245 D5
Marston Rd PE19..........75 A3
Martin Ave PE15.........243 A7
Martin Cl
  Godmanchester PE29....119 A8
  Mildenhall IP28.........239 D3
  Soham CB7..............212 A5
Martin Ct
  Peterborough PE4.......204 C4
  Whittlesey PE7.........189 E7
Martindale Way CB22.....32 E8
Martingale Cl [**3**] CB4....83 C6
Martingale Rd [**4**] CB4....5 E6
Martin Luther King Cl
  PE29..................141 F6
Martin Rd CB25..........130 B3
Martinsbridge PE1........198 F7
Martins La
  Linton CB21.............35 E2
  Witcham CB6............217 A3
Martin's La CB6..........218 A6
Martins Mews CB9........38 C1
Martins Way PE2.........185 F5
Marwick Rd PE15........243 D7
Mary Armyne Rd PE2....186 B5
Maryland Ave
  Huntingdon PE29........141 F8
  Swaffham Bulbeck CB25.108 B2
Marylebone Rd PE15.....243 C4
Mary Walsham Cl PE2....187 E5
Masefield Ave PE19......74 C6
Masefield Way SG8.......13 D1
Maskew Ave PE1.........197 E6
Mason Cl CB9.............38 F2
Mason Gdns IP28........213 D6
Mason Rd CB25...........130 A3
Master Dike PE12........237 D8
Masterton Cl PE4........204 D7
Masterton Rd PE9.......244 C7
Matley PE2...............185 E5
Matley Prim Sch PE2....185 E5
Matt Dawson Cl CB8......110 F6
Matthew Parker Cl CB25.105 D7
Matthews La CB8.........55 F6
Matthew Wren Cl CB6....218 A6
Maule Cl
  Huntingdon PE29........141 E6
  St Neots PE19...........74 E1
Maurice Cl PE28.........113 F5
Mawson Cl CB6...........240 B3
Mawson Rd CB1..........246 C1
MAXEY.................231 C7
Maxey Rd
  Helpston PE6...........231 C5
  Northborough PE6.......231 D7
Maxey View [**10**] PE6.....231 C5
Maxham's Green Rd PE6.203 B6
Maxwell Rd PE7..........186 C3
Mayes Mdw CB8..........112 E5
Mayfair Gdns PE1........133 C3
Mayfield PE1.............117 A3
Mayfield Cl [**2**] CB6.......240 B5
Mayfield Cres PE29......141 F6
Mayfield Prim Sch CB4...83 C5
Mayfield Rd
  Coates/Eastrea PE7.....190 D7
  Girton CB3..............82 F8
  Huntingdon PE29........141 F6
  Peterborough PE1.......198 A6
Mayfield Way CB23.......79 C2
Mayflower Rd [**1**] PE13...245 E3
Mayfly Cl PE16...........245 B3
Maynards CB22...........32 C5
Mayner's Dike PE12......237 E8
Mayor's Cl PE15.........243 D7
Mayor's Wlk PE3.........197 E3
Maypole Croft CB21......37 C8
Maypole La CB8..........90 E3
May's Ave CB25..........53 A2
Maysfield Dr [**8**] PE13....238 B2
May's La PE13............238 A2
May St SG8...............7 E2
Mays Way CB4............84 B6
Maytrees PE27...........143 F1
Maze Rd PE28............120 C1
Mead Cl PE3.............204 B1
Meadenvale PE1.........198 F5
Meadlands Main Dro
  CB6...................215 F1
Meadowbrook CB6.......209 E4
Meadow Bsns Ctr The
  PE27..................144 B2
Meadow Cl
  Chatteris PE16.........241 C3
  Little Paxton PE19......95 F2
  [**7**] Soham CB7...........212 B3
  Stilton PE7.............175 F8

Meadow Cl continued
St Ives PE27 . . . . .144 B3
Witchford CB6 . . . . .217 E2
Meadowcroft CB6 . . . . . . .210 F5
Meadowcroft Way SG8 . . .28 E8
Meadow Ct CB6 . . . . .242 B5
Meadow Dr PE15 . . . . . . .243 F3
Meadow Drift CB23 . . . . . .100 B5
Meadow Dro PE28 . . . . . . .208 E6
Meadow Farm CB CB24 . .103 D6
Meadowfield Rd CB22 . . . .32 E6
Meadowgate PE9 . . . . . . .230 F5
Meadowgate La PE14 . . . .245 E2
Meadowgate Sch PE13 . . . .245 E3
Meadow Gr PE1 . . . . .205 B1
Meadow How PE27 . . . . . .143 F6
Meadow La
Earith PE28 . . . . .208 E6
Haddenham CB6 . . . . .209 F6
Hemingford Abbots PE28 . . .142 F3
Hemingford Grey PE28 . . . .143 D3
Houghton & Wyton PE28 . . .143 B4
Linton CB21 . . . . .35 B2
Little Heath SG19 . . . . .41 D3
Offord Darcy PE19 . . . . . . .117 F2
Over CB24 . . . . .200 D6
Ramsey PE26 . . . . .172 B4
St Ives PE27 . . . . .144 C3
Thornhaugh PE8 . . . . .193 F5
Meadowlands
Burwell CB25 . . . . .130 B1
March PE15 . . . . .243 A6
Meadowlands Rd CB5 . . . .84 E3
Meadow Prim Sch The
CB21 . . . . .53 B2
Meadow Rd
Great Chesterford CB10 . . . .18 D3
Great Gransden SG19 . . . . .58 B5
Newborough PE6 . . . . .204 D8
Peakirk PE6 . . . . .206 C1
Ramsey PE26 . . . . .171 B1
Willingham CB24 . . . . .209 B1
Meadow Rise
Bourn CB23 . . . . .60 C6
Stukeley PE29 . . . . .140 F5
Meadows Cl 5 PE19 . . . . .74 F5
Meadows The
Haslingfield CB23 . . . . .47 B5
Worlington IP28 . . . . .213 F4
Meadowsweet PE19 . . . . .74 B6
Meadowsweet Cl
2 Cambourne CB23 . . . . . .79 A4
Haverhill CB9 . . . . .38 E1
MEADOW THE 215 C2
Meadow View PE19 . . . . . .77 E4
Meadow Way
Doddington/Wimblington
PE15 . . . . .223 B7
Earith PE28 . . . . .208 E6
Ely CB6 . . . . .240 A3
Godmanchester PE29 . . . . .142 A2
Great Paxton PE19 . . . . . . .96 E4
Harston CB22 . . . . .48 A3
Melbourn SG8 . . . . .14 C6
Mepal CB6 . . . . .216 E3
Warboys PE28 . . . . .164 F5
Meadow Way S 7 PE15 . .223 B7
Meadow Wlk CB21 . . . . . .34 C6
Mead The PE4 . . . . .204 B1
Mead View CB24 . . . . . . .103 B5
Mealsgate PE4 . . . . .204 F2
Medallion Ct 1 PE19 . . . .74 F5
Medbourne Gdns PE1 . . . .198 C8
Medcalfe Way SG8 . . . . . .14 D6
Medeswell PE2 . . . . .186 C4
Medieval Village of Clopton
(site of)* SG8 . . . . .26 E6
Medieval Village of Croydon
(site of)* SG8 . . . . .27 B8
Medieval Village of Great
Childerley (site of)*
CB23 . . . . .80 D8
Medieval Village of
Landbeach (site of)*
CB25 . . . . .105 C7
Medieval Village of Papley
(site of)* PE8 . . . . .174 B7
Medieval Village of
Sibberton (site of)*
PE8 . . . . .193 E5
Medieval Village of
Wintringham (site of)*
PE19 . . . . .75 F4
Midland Gr 6 PE19 . . . . . .75 A5
Medlar Way CB23 . . . . . . .79 A4
Medway Cl PE13 . . . . .245 E4
Medway Rd PE29 . . . . . . .141 E7
Medway The CB6 . . . . . . .240 D6
Medworth PE2 . . . . .185 F3
Meeting La
Litlington SG8 . . . . .12 A2
Melbourn SG8 . . . . .14 C6
Meeting Wlk CB9 . . . . . . .24 B8
Megans Way 4 PE16 . . . .241 C5
Meggan Gate PE21 . . . . . .197 A1
Megg's Dro PE26 . . . . . . .221 D2
Megs Cl PE28 . . . . .208 D5
MELBOURN 14 D5
Melbourn Bury SG8 . . . . . .14 B5
Melbourne Ave PE15 . . . .243 B7
Melbourne Dr IP28 . . . . . .239 B5
Melbourne Rd PE9 . . . . . .244 D6
Melbourn Prim Sch SG8 . . .14 C6

Melbourn Rd SG8 . . . . . . .5 D7
Melbourn Science Pk
SG8 . . . . .14 D7
Melbourn St SG8 . . . . .5 D6
Melbourn Village Coll
SG8 . . . . .14 C7
Meldon Pl CB6 . . . . .240 D5
MELDRETH 29 A2
Meldreth Manor Sch SG8 . .29 A1
Meldreth Rd
Shepreth SG8 . . . . .29 D4
Whaddon SG8 . . . . .28 C1
Meldreth Sta SG8 . . . . .14 B7
Meldreth Prim Sch SG8 . . . .14 B8
Melford Cl
Burwell CB25 . . . . .130 C2
Peterborough PE3 . . . . .197 A2
Mellis Cl CB9 . . . . .38 B1
Mellows Cl PE1 . . . . .198 C3
Melrose Dr PE2 . . . . .187 A7
Melrose Gdns CB8 . . . . . .110 E4
Melton Cl 1 CB8 . . . . .111 B2
Melvin Way CB24 . . . . . . .104 A4
Memorial Ct CB3 . . . . .83 C1
Mendip Gr PE4 . . . . .204 E2
MEPAL 216 E4
Mepal Long Highway
CB6 . . . . .216 C4
Mepal Outdoor Ctr PE16 . .216 C6
Mepal Rd CB6 . . . . .216 E2
Mepal Short Highway
CB6 . . . . .216 C5
Mepal & Witcham CE Prim
Sch CB6 . . . . .216 D3
Mercers Row CB5 . . . . . . .84 B4
Mercian Ct PE2 . . . . .187 D7
Mere Cl PE26 . . . . .221 A4
Mere Dro
Ramsey PE26 . . . . .221 D4
Yaxley PE7 . . . . .181 F4
Merelade Gr PE4 . . . . .204 B5
Mere Mill Dro CB6 . . . . . .210 F4
Mere Side CB7 . . . . .212 A4
Mere Side Dro PE26 . . . . .221 B4
Mere View PE7 . . . . .182 A6
Mere View Ind Est PE7 . . . .182 A6
Mere Way
Cambridge CB4 . . . . .83 E6
Hemingford Grey PE28 . . . .120 B5
Houghton & Wyton PE28 . . .143 A6
Meridian Cl 12 PE28 . . . . .215 C1
Meridian Dr CB23 . . . . . . .101 C4
Meridian Prim Sch CB23 . . .62 C5
Meridian Sch The SG8 . . . . .5 E7
Meriton PE2 . . . . .185 F3
Merle Way CB23 . . . . .79 A4
Merlin Cl
Huntingdon PE29 . . . . .142 B7
St Neots PE19 . . . . .75 B7
Merlin Dr 4 CB6 . . . . .240 B5
Merritt St PE29 . . . . .141 C5
Merryland PE27 . . . . .144 A3
Merryvale CB2 . . . . .64 D1
Merton Grange SG19 . . . .41 F5
Merton Rd CB24 . . . . .104 B3
Merton St CB3 . . . . .64 C7
Mertoun Paddocks CB8 . . .90 A8
Metcalfe Rd CB4 . . . . .83 D5
Metcalfe Way CB6 . . . . . .210 A5
Metro Ctr The PE2 . . . . . .186 D6
Mewburn PE3 . . . . .204 A1
Mews Cl PE26 . . . . .172 B7
Meynell Gdns CB8 . . . . . .111 A5
Meynell Wlk PE3 . . . . .197 B3
Michael's Cl CB3 . . . . .103 E1
Michigan PE28 . . . . .151 E4
Michigan Rd PE27 . . . . . .143 E6
Mickle Gate PE3 . . . . .197 A1
Mickle Hill PE28 . . . . .135 D7
Mid Career Coll CB21 . . . . .67 B4
Middle Broad Dro PE13 . .237 D5
Middle Cl 5 CB6 . . . . .210 F5
Middledrift SG8 . . . . .5 C6
Middle Dro
Newton PE13 . . . . .237 E3
Ramsey PE26 . . . . .171 A7
Soham CB7 . . . . .211 F3
Wimblington PE15 . . . . . . .223 C5
Middlefield Prim Sch
PE19 . . . . .74 F2
Middlefield Rd PE28 . . . . .168 B3
Middleham Ct PE7 . . . . . . .151 E4
Middlemiss View PE29 . . .118 F8
Middlemoor Rd
Ramsey PE26 . . . . .220 D3
Whittlesford CB22 . . . . .32 A5
Middle Pasture PE4 . . . . .204 B5
Middle Rd
Crowland PE6 . . . . .207 E7
March PE15 . . . . .227 E4
Newborough PE6 . . . . .205 C7
Middle St
Elton PE8 . . . . .178 D8
Farcet PE7 . . . . .187 C2
Great Gransden SG19 . . . . .58 E4
Litlington SG8 . . . . .12 A2
Thriplow SG8 . . . . .31 B1
Middleton PE15 . . . . .197 A4
Middleton Prim Sch PE15 .197 A4
Middletons Rd PE7 . . . . . .181 E5
Middleton Way CB24 . . . .121 E4
Middle Watch CB24 . . . . .122 E5
Middle Way CB22 . . . . . . .50 A1
Mid Fenton PE29 . . . . . . .221 B3
Midfield CB24 . . . . .103 D4
Midgate PE1 . . . . .198 A2
Midhurst PE7 . . . . .84 A5

Midland Rd PE3 . . . . .197 E3
Midloe Grange PE19 . . . . .95 A6
Mikanda Cl PE14 . . . . . . .245 C2
Milburn Dro CB8 . . . . .112 E5
MILDENHALL 239 A6
Mildenhall Airfield IP28 . .239 B8
Mildenhall Coll of Tecnology
IP28 . . . . .239 E4
Mildenhall Ind Est IP28 . .239 B6
Mildenhall Mus* IP28 . .239 C4
Mildenhall Pl CB9 . . . . . . .24 B8
Mildenhall Rd
Barton Mills IP28 . . . . .239 C2
Beck Row, Holywell Row & Kenny
Hill IP28 . . . . .239 C8
Ely CB7 . . . . .219 E8
Fordham IP28 . . . . .213 A2
Freckenham IP28 . . . . .213 D3
Icklingham IP28 . . . . .214 E4
Littleport CB7 . . . . .242 F6
Mildenhall Swimming Pool
IP28 . . . . .239 C4
Mildmay Rd PE4 . . . . .197 D8
Mile Dro
Glinton PE6 . . . . .231 F5
Yaxley PE7 . . . . .182 B5
MILE END 219 C5
Mile End Rd CB7 . . . . .219 C6
Mile Rd CB22 . . . . .50 C4
Miles Hawk Way IP28 . . .200 A5
Mile Tree La PE13 . . . . . . .235 E7
Milford St CB1 . . . . .84 A1
Military Rd CB7 . . . . .212 C2
Militia Way CB7 . . . . .240 C4
Milking Nook Rd PE6 . . . .206 E1
Milking Slade Rd PE28 . . .167 A4
Milk & Water Dro PE7 . . .188 A4
Millards La CB25 . . . . .107 D2
Millbank CB8 . . . . .110 F4
Mill Cl
Burwell CB25 . . . . .130 B1
Exning CB8 . . . . .110 B8
Hemingford Grey PE28 . . . .143 D2
Huntingdon PE29 . . . . .142 A6
Murrow PE13 . . . . .234 D5
Peakirk PE6 . . . . .206 B1
The Stukeleys PE28 . . . . . .151 D3
Wisbech PE13 . . . . .245 D6
Mill Cnr CB7 . . . . .212 A4
Mill Comm PE29 . . . . .141 C3
Mill Cres PE2 . . . . .185 E4
Mill Croft CB7 . . . . .212 B3
Mill Ct CB22 . . . . .49 A5
Mill Dro
Crowland PE6 . . . . .207 F7
Lode CB25 . . . . .128 A1
Ramsey PE26 . . . . .221 A2
Soham CB7 . . . . .212 A3
Southery PE38 . . . . .226 E8
MILL END 72 E5
Mill End SG19 . . . . .25 A4
Mill End Cl
Cambridge CB1 . . . . .65 F5
Warboys PE28 . . . . .165 A5
Mill End Rd CB1 . . . . .65 E6
Miller Cl
2 Doddington/Wimblington
PE15 . . . . .222 F5
Godmanchester PE29 . . . . .118 F8
Offord Cluny PE19 . . . . . . .118 A2
Millers Cl CB21 . . . . .35 D3
Miller's Rd CB23 . . . . .61 D5
Miller's Way PE28 . . . . . . .173 C3
Miller Way
Brampton PE28 . . . . .140 C3
Cambourne CB23 . . . . .79 B3
Mill Farm La CB22 . . . . . .32 F4
MILLFIELD 197 F5
Millfield
Littleport CB6 . . . . .242 C6
Upwell PE14 . . . . .236 E2
Willingham CB24 . . . . .128 A8
Mill Field 8 CB6 . . . . .216 E2
Millfield Cl PE16 . . . . .241 B2
Millfield La CB6 . . . . .210 C5
Millfield Pl CB6 . . . . .210 D5
Millfield Prim Sch CB6 . .242 C3
Millfield Rd
Market Deeping PE6 . . . . . .231 F8
Peterborough PE1 . . . . .231 D8
Millfields
Ramsey PE26 . . . . .172 B8
Stetchworth CB8 . . . . .89 F1
Millfields Way CB9 . . . . . .24 B8
Millfield Way PE7 . . . . . . .189 F6
Mill Gn PE28 . . . . .165 A5
MILL GREEN 22 D7
Mill Hill
Conington PE7 . . . . .177 C1
Downham CB6 . . . . .217 F7
Glatton PE28 . . . . .175 E1
Haverhill CB9 . . . . .23 F7
Newmarket CB8 . . . . .111 A4
Royston SG8 . . . . .5 E4
Swaffham Prior CB25 . . . . .108 E5
Steeton Colville CB21 . . . . .54 B1
Mill Hill End PE28 . . . . . .120 B1
Mill Hill Rd 7 PE19 . . . . . .74 D5
Mill Hole CB23 . . . . .33 E8
Millington Rd CB3 . . . . . . .64 C7
Mill La
Arrington SG8 . . . . .44 C3
Barrington CB22 . . . . .29 E8
Bassingbourn SG8 . . . . . . .12 D5
Bluntisham/Colne PE28 . . .208 D5
Burwell CB25 . . . . .130 B1

Mill La continued
Cambridge CB2 . . . . .246 A2
Castor PE5 . . . . .184 F7
Duxford CB22 . . . . .32 E1
Exning CB8 . . . . .110 B8
Fordham CB7 . . . . .212 F1
Gorefield PE13 . . . . .235 B8
Hauxton CB22 . . . . .48 A6
Hemingford Grey PE28 . . . .143 D3
Hinxton CB10 . . . . .18 A7
Histon CB4 . . . . .104 D6
Ickleton CB10 . . . . .18 B4
Impington CB24 . . . . .104 D5
Linton CB21 . . . . .35 C2
Little Paxton PE19 . . . . . . .95 E1
Newton PE13 . . . . .237 F5
Peterborough PE7 . . . . .185 A5
Potton SG19 . . . . .40 D1
Ramsey PE26 . . . . .172 B8
Sawston CB22 . . . . .32 E7
Shingay cum Wendy SG8 . . .27 B4
Stetchworth CB8 . . . . .89 F1
St Neots PE19 . . . . .74 F6
Swaffham Bulbeck CB25 . .108 B3
Tallington PE9 . . . . .230 F7
Toft CB23 . . . . .61 D5
Water Newton PE8 . . . . . . .184 C7
West Walton PE14 . . . . . . .238 F4
Whittlesford CB22 . . . . .32 D5
Mill Pit Furlong CB6 . . . . .242 D3
Mill Quern CB23 . . . . .80 C2
Mill Rd
Alconbury PE28 . . . . .150 E4
Ashley CB8 . . . . .91 F8
Barnack PE9 . . . . .230 C3
Buckden PE19 . . . . .117 C3
Cambridge CB1 . . . . .246 C2
Emneth PE14 . . . . .236 D6
Fen Drayton CB24 . . . . . . .121 D5
Glatton PE28 . . . . .175 E1
Great Gidding PE28 . . . . . .166 E3
Great Wilbraham CB21 . . . .67 F7
Harston CB22 . . . . .47 D2
Haverhill CB9 . . . . .24 A7
Histon CB24 . . . . .104 B1
Huntingdon PE29 . . . . .142 A6
Kirtling CB8 . . . . .72 E5
Little Gransden SG19 . . . . .58 E4
Little Stukeley PE28 . . . . . .151 D4
Little Wilbraham CB1 . . . . . .86 D1
Lode CB25 . . . . .107 C2
Maxey PE6 . . . . .231 C2
Nassington PE8 . . . . .183 A7
Oakington/Longstanton
CB24 . . . . .103 D6
Royston SG8 . . . . .5 F4
Stilton PE7 . . . . .175 F8
Walpole PE14 . . . . .238 F6
Waterbeach CB25 . . . . . . .106 A7
West Walton PE14 . . . . . . .238 D4
West Wickham CB21 . . . . . .36 E8
West Wratting CB21 . . . . . .53 F2
Whittlesey PE7 . . . . .189 E6
Willingham CB24 . . . . .124 A8
Wisbech St Mary PE13 . . . .234 C5
Wittering PE8 . . . . .163 F6
Mill Reef Cl CB24 . . . . . . .110 D7
Mills La
Longstanton CB24 . . . . . . .124 A1
Witchford CB6 . . . . .217 D1
Mill St
Ashwell SG7 . . . . .2 D4
Cambridge CB1 . . . . .246 C1
Gamlingay SG19 . . . . .41 D5
Isleham CB7 . . . . .213 A5
Mildenhall IP28 . . . . .239 B3
St Ives PE28 . . . . .143 A5
Millstone La PE9 . . . . . . .230 D3
Mill View
March PE15 . . . . .243 D4
Peterborough PE7 . . . . .185 A5
Sawtry PE28 . . . . .168 A4
Mill View Ct PE19 . . . . . . .74 C2
Mill Way
Grantchester CB3 . . . . .64 A3
Holywell-cum-Needingworth
PE27 . . . . .144 F3
Stretham CB6 . . . . .210 E6
Swavesey CB24 . . . . .122 C6
Wisbech PE14 . . . . .236 A4
Millyard PE28 . . . . .210 A6
Mill Yd PE19 . . . . .141 E2
Milner Cl
March PE15 . . . . .243 D5
Sawston CB22 . . . . .32 E7
Milner Rd
Comberton CB23 . . . . .62 D6
Wisbech PE13 . . . . .245 C4
Milners Row 13 PE9 . . . . .244 C5
Milnyard Sq PE2 . . . . .185 C2
MILTON 105 E2
Milton Ave PE19 . . . . .74 C6
Milton CE Prim Sch
CB24 . . . . .105 C2
Milton Cl
Huntingdon PE29 . . . . .141 E6
Ramsey PE26 . . . . .171 F5
Royston SG8 . . . . .13 C1
St Ives PE27 . . . . .143 F6
Milton Ctry Pk* CB24 . . .105 D1
Milton Dr PE13 . . . . .238 B1
Milton Rd
Cambridge CB4 . . . . .246 B4
Impington CB24 . . . . .104 F4
Peterborough PE2 . . . . .187 A7
Milton Rd Prim Sch CB4 . .83 E5
Milton Way PE3 . . . . .196 E3
Mina Cl PE2 . . . . .187 D4

Minden Ct 8 PE19 . . . . . . .74 C5
Minerva Cl CB9 . . . . .24 D6
Minerva Way CB4 . . . . . . .83 E8
Mingle La CB22 . . . . .49 B5
Minster Pl 4 CB7 . . . . . . .240 D4
Minster Precincts PE1 . . .198 B2
Minster Rd
Haverhill CB9 . . . . .39 A1
Royston SG8 . . . . .5 C8
Minter Cl CB25 . . . . .86 A5
Mint La PE19 . . . . .96 E4
Minton Ent Pk CB8 . . . . . .110 F7
Missleton Ct CB1 . . . . .65 C5
Misterton PE2 . . . . .185 E3
Misty Mdws CB5 . . . . .84 D4
Mitchell Cl PE1 . . . . .198 C2
Mitchells CB10 . . . . .20 B1
Mitchells Cotts CB10 . . . . .20 B1
Mitchell's Yd CB6 . . . . . . .210 C5
Moat Cl PE28 . . . . .208 D7
Moat La
Abbots Ripton PE28 . . . . . .152 C8
Melbourn SG8 . . . . .14 D7
Perry PE28 . . . . .115 D1
Moats' Way PE28 . . . . . . .119 E7
Moat Way CB24 . . . . .122 E6
Moat Wlk CB9 . . . . .23 E8
Mobb's Hole SG7 . . . . . . .10 C4
Moggswell La PE2 . . . . . .186 B4
Mole Dro PE12 . . . . .233 F8
MOLESWORTH 147 A5
Molewood Cl CB4 . . . . . . .83 C6
Molls Dro PE6 . . . . .236 C3
Monarch Ave PE2 . . . . . . .187 A6
Monarch Rd PE19 . . . . . . .74 B4
Moncrieff Cl 1 CB4 . . . . . .83 E7
Mondela Pl PE7 . . . . .176 A7
Monet Cl PE27 . . . . .144 A7
Money Bank PE13 . . . . . .245 E4
Money Hill (Tumulus)*
CB23 . . . . .47 B3
Moneypiece Cl 1 CB9 . . . .38 F1
Monk Dr CB23 . . . . .79 C4
Monkfield La CB23 . . . . . . .79 C3
Monkfield Park Prim Sch
CB23 . . . . .79 B4
Monks Cl PE7 . . . . .189 D8
Monks Dr 17 PE6 . . . . . . .232 A1
Monks Gr PE4 . . . . .204 A5
Monks Hardwick PE19 . . . .75 E8
Monks Mdw PE6 . . . . .232 A1
Monks Way PE28 . . . . . . .168 B2
Monkswell CB2 . . . . .64 D3
Monkswood CB6 . . . . .242 C5
Monks Wood National
Nature Reserve* PE28 . .161 B4
Montagu Ct 2 PE19 . . . . . .74 E4
Montague Rd
Brampton PE28 . . . . .117 D8
Cambridge CB4 . . . . .84 A3
Montagu Gdns PE28 . . . .113 E5
Montagu Rd
Huntingdon PE29 . . . . .141 E4
Little Stukeley PE28 . . . . . .151 F2
Peterborough PE4 . . . . .197 D8
Montagu Sq PE19 . . . . . . .74 E4
Montagu St PE19 . . . . .74 E4
Monte Long Cl PE15 . . . . .243 E1
Montford Cl CB25 . . . . . . .130 C4
Montfort Ct 9 CB9 . . . . . . .23 F7
Montfort Way CB23 . . . . . .83 E6
Montgomery Rd CB4 . . . . .83 E6
Montreal Rd CB1 . . . . .65 C7
Montrose Cl CB4 . . . . .83 E7
Monument St PE1 . . . . . . .198 A3
Monument View PE15 . . .243 D1
Moonhall Bsns Pk CB9 . . .24 A5
Moon Hall La CB9 . . . . . . .24 A6
Moore Cl CB4 . . . . .84 A6
Moor End SG8 . . . . .29 D3
Moore's La 4 PE6 . . . . . . .232 A1
Moores Wlk PE16 . . . . . . .206 F3
Moorfield Rd
Duxford CB22 . . . . .32 E3
Peterborough PE3 . . . . .197 D3
Moorfield Way PE28 . . . . .151 F2
Moorhen Rd PE7 . . . . .201 A1
Moorhouse Dr PE29 . . . . .141 E7
Moor Pasture Way PE6 . . .39 B4
Moor Rd
Great Staughton MK44 . . . .93 B1
Newborough PE6 . . . . .206 E2
Moor The SG8 . . . . .14 C7
Moory Croft Cl PE19 . . . . .94 A6
Moot Way PE28 . . . . .155 A5
MORBORNE 180 B3
Morborne Cl PE2 . . . . .187 D6
Morborne La PE7 . . . . . . .180 D4
Morborne Rd PE7 . . . . . . .180 C2
MORDEN GREEN 11 C1
Morden Rd CB23 . . . . .99 B3
More's Mdw CB22 . . . . . . .48 F6
Moreton Cl PE7 . . . . .189 F8
Moretons Cl PE7 . . . . .190 A8
Morgan Cl PE7 . . . . .181 E6
Morgans CB24 . . . . .125 D4
Morland Way PE27 . . . . . .144 A7
Morley Cl 1 IP28 . . . . .213 F8
Morley Dr CB6 . . . . .242 E4
Morley Meml Prim Sch
CB1 . . . . .65 B5
Morley Way
17 Eastwood End PE15 . .223 B7
Peterborough PE2 . . . . .186 D5
Morpeth Cl PE2 . . . . .186 C6
Morpeth Rd PE3 . . . . .197 C3
Morrice Gn SG8 . . . . .1 A3

Morris Cl PE19 . . . . 117 A3
Morris Ct PE7 . . . . 181 E6
Morris St PE1 . . . . 198 B3
Mortimer La IP28 . . . . 213 C3
Mortimer Rd
Cambridge CB1 . . . . 246 C2
Royston SG8 . . . . 5 E6
Mortimer Row [11] PE28 . . 208 C8
Mortimers La CB22 . . . . 30 C5
Mortlock Ave CB4 . . . . 84 B6
Mortlock Cl SG8 . . . . 14 C6
Mortlock Gdns CB21 . . . . . . 34 C5
Mortlock St SG8 . . . . 14 C6
Morton Ave PE15 . . . . 243 E3
Morton Cl CB6 . . . . 240 E8
Morton's Leam* PE7 . . . 200 C1
Morton St SG8 . . . . 5 D7
Morton Way [6] PE15 . . . . . 223 B7
Mosquito Rd PE26 . . . . 171 E3
Moss Bank CB4 . . . . 84 C5
Moss Cl PE26 . . . . 171 B1
Moss Dr CB23 . . . . 47 C5
Moss-Nook CB23 . . . . 79 B3
Mostyn Cl [2] CB6 . . . . 216 E1
Moules La CB21 . . . . 20 C6
Moules Yd SG7 . . . . 2 D3
MOULTON 112 E6
Moulton Ave CB8 . . . . 134 A2
Moulton CE Prim Sch
CB8 . . . . 112 E6
Moulton Coll PE1 . . . . 198 A1
Moulton Gr PE3 . . . . 197 C6
Moulton Paddocks CB8 . . 111 F6
Moulton Rd
Ashley CB8 . . . . 112 D1
Cheveley CB8 . . . . 91 D8
Newmarket CB8 . . . . 111 D4
Moulton Rd or Kennett Rd
CB8 . . . . 112 F7
Mountbatten Ave
Stamford PE9 . . . . 244 A6
Yaxley PE7 . . . . 181 D5
Mountbatten Ct [6] PE19 . . 74 C4
Mountbatten Dr PE13 . . . 245 A7
Mountbatten Way
Peterborough PE3 . . . . 197 B6
Whittlesey PE7 . . . . 190 A6
Mount Dr PE13 . . . . 245 E4
Mounteagle [2] SG8 . . . . 5 D5
Mountford Cl CB22 . . . . 48 C4
Mountfort Cl [3] PE19 . . . . . 74 F3
Mount Pleasant
[3] Cambridge CB3 . . . . 83 C3
Great Paxton PE19 . . . . 96 E4
Peterborough PE2 . . . . 187 C7
Spaldwick PE28 . . . . 137 E6
Mount Pleasant Rd PE13 245 C7
Mount Pleasant Wlk [2]
CB3 . . . . 83 C3
Mount Rd CB9 . . . . 24 A7
Mountsteven Ave
Gunthorpe PE4 . . . . 204 D2
Peterborough PE4 . . . . 204 C1
Mount The
Barley SG8 . . . . 6 E1
Toft CB23 . . . . 61 D5
Mouth La PE13 . . . . 235 B4
Mowbray Cl [4] PE13 . . . . . 235 B7
Mowbray Rd
Bretton PE3 . . . . 203 F1
Cambridge CB1 . . . . 65 C4
Mowfen Rd CB6 . . . . 242 D5
Mowlam Cl CB24 . . . . 104 C2
Mowlands PE29 . . . . 142 A1
Moyne Cl CB4 . . . . 83 D7
Moyne Rd PE28 . . . . 168 C3
Moyse's Bank PE14 . . . . . . 236 F6
Muchwood La PE26 . . . . . . 221 B1
Mudd's Dro PE14 . . . . 229 F6
Muggleston La PE26 . . . . . 172 B6
Mulberry Cl
Bottisham CB25 . . . . 86 F6
Cambridge CB4 . . . . 83 F5
Mildenhall IP28 . . . . 239 E4
Whittlesey PE7 . . . . 189 F5
Yaxley PE7 . . . . 182 A5
Mulberry Way CB7 . . . . 240 E5
Mullard Radio Astronomy
Obsy* CB23 . . . . 46 E7
Mullein Cl [4] PE19 . . . . 74 C5
Mumby's Dro PE14 . . . . . . 229 E6
Mumford Theatre* CB1 . 246 C2
Muncey Wlk CB24 . . . . 104 C5
Munday Way [16] PE13 . . . 238 B2
Munnings Cl
Haverhill CB9 . . . . 38 D1
Newmarket CB8 . . . . 111 A4
Muntjac Cl
[3] Bretton PE3 . . . . 197 A5
[5] Eaton Socon PE19 . . . . . . 74 B5
Murfitt's La CB7 . . . . 212 E2
Murfitt Way SG19 . . . . 41 D6
Muriel Cl CB23 . . . . 99 B2
Murrell Cl PE19 . . . . 74 F7
Murrell Ct PE19 . . . . 74 F7
MURROW 234 D5
Murrow Bank PE13 . . . . . . 234 D6
Murrow La PE13 . . . . 234 F5
Murrow Prim Sch PE13 . 234 D5
Murton Cl CB25 . . . . 130 A3
Murton Slade [5] CB9 . . . . . 24 A8
Museum of Archaeology &
Anthropology* CB2 . . . . 246 B2
Museum of Classical
Archaeology* CB3 . . . . . . 64 C8
Museum of Flag Fen The*
PE6 . . . . 199 B2
Museum of Tech* CB5 . . . . 84 B3
Museum Sq [22] PE13 . . . . 245 C5
Musgrave Way
Fen Ditton CB5 . . . . 84 F6
[7] St Neots PE19 . . . . 74 F5
Musker Pl CB23 . . . . 99 B1
Muskham PE3 . . . . 196 F4
Mustards Gapp [5] CB9 . . . . 24 C7
Musticott Pl PE13 . . . . 245 F6
Mustill's La CB24 . . . . 123 B8
Muswell Rd PE3 . . . . 197 E4
Mutlow Hill (Tumulus)*
CB21 . . . . 67 F1
Myles Way PE13 . . . . 245 C8
Myrtle Ave PE1 . . . . 198 C7
Myrtle Cl CB25 . . . . 130 B3
Myrtle Ct PE1 . . . . 198 C7
Myrtle Gn PE27 . . . . 144 A5
Myrtle Gr PE1 . . . . 198 C7
Myrtle House Cvn Pk
PE1 . . . . 198 E5
Myrtle Way PE27 . . . . 144 A5

N

Nansicles Rd PE2 . . . . 186 D6
Napier Pl PE2 . . . . 185 C6
Napier St CB1 . . . . 246 C3
Narrow Dro
Whittlesey PE7 . . . . 188 C5
Yaxley PE7 . . . . 182 C5
Narrow La CB24 . . . . 104 B4
Naseby Cl PE3 . . . . 197 C5
Naseby Gdns PE19 . . . . 75 A4
Nash Rd [7] SG8 . . . . 5 D5
Natal Rd CB1 . . . . 65 C7
Nat Flatman St CB8 . . . . . 111 B3
Nathan Cl PE3 . . . . 197 B2
National Extension Coll
CB2 . . . . 64 F5
National Horseracing Mus*
CB8 . . . . 111 A3
Natures Way PE7 . . . . 186 B2
Navigation Wharf [6] PE19 74 E5
Nayland Rd CB9 . . . . 23 E6
Neal Dr CB4 . . . . 83 E8
Neale Cl CB1 . . . . 65 F7
Neale Wade Com Coll
PE15 . . . . 243 D1
Neaverson Rd PE6 . . . . 203 F7
Nedderworth Rd PE27 . . . 144 B3
Needham Bank PE14 . . . . 236 C4
Needham Ct PE7 . . . . 181 E4
NEEDINGWORTH 208 B3
Needingworth Rd PE27 . . . 144 B4
Nelson Gdns PE13 . . . . . . 245 D6
Nelson Rd
Eaton Socon PE19 . . . . 74 B3
Huntingdon PE29 . . . . 142 A6
Nelson's La CB6 . . . . 210 A5
Nene Cl
Wansford PE8 . . . . 194 A3
Whittlesey PE7 . . . . 189 F6
[2] Wittering PE8 . . . . 230 B1
Nene Inf Sch PE13 . . . . . . 245 D4
Nene Par
March PE15 . . . . 243 E4
Wisbech PE13 . . . . 245 B7
Nene Parkway PE3 . . . . 196 F1
Nene Quay PE13 . . . . 245 C5
Nene Rd
Eaton Socon PE19 . . . . 74 C4
Ely CB6 . . . . 240 C6
Huntingdon PE29 . . . . 141 E8
Kimbolton PE28 . . . . 114 A7
Whittlesey PE7 . . . . 189 E6
Neneside [1] PE15 . . . . 222 A5
Nene St PE1 . . . . 198 B2
NENE TERRACE 232 D6
Nene Way
St Ives PE27 . . . . 144 A7
Sutton PE5 . . . . 194 F2
Warmington PE8 . . . . 178 A2
Neptune Cl CB4 . . . . 83 E7
Ness Rd CB25 . . . . 130 C3
Netherby Dr PE14 . . . . 245 E1
Nether Gr CB24 . . . . 123 F2
Netherhall Sch The CB1 . . . 65 E4
Netherhall Way CB1 . . . . . . 65 D4
Nettle Bank PE14 . . . . 235 C4
Neve Gdns IP28 . . . . 213 E6
Neville Rd CB1 . . . . 65 C6
NEWARK 198 E6
Newark Ave PE1 . . . . 198 C6
Newark Cl SG8 . . . . 5 C8
Newark Hill Prim Sch
PE1 . . . . 198 D6
Newark Rd PE1 . . . . 198 F4
New Barn Dro PE28 . . . . . . 173 D4
New Barns Ave CB7 . . . . . 240 D6
New Barns Rd CB7 . . . . . . 240 D5
Newbey Cl PE3 . . . . 197 B3
Newbolt SG8 . . . . 5 D8
Newborn Cl PE2 . . . . 187 E5
NEWBOROUGH 207 D1
Newborough Prim Sch
PE6 . . . . 207 C1
Newborough Rd PE4 . . . . . 205 C2
Newboults La PE9 . . . . 244 A5
New Bridge La
Elm PE14 . . . . 235 F6
Wisbech PE14 . . . . 245 A1
New Bridge Rd PE14 . . . . . 236 E1
New Broadpool PE28 . . . . . 173 F1
New Cangle Com Prim Sch
CB9 . . . . 38 F1
Newcastle Dr PE2 . . . . 186 D6
New Cheveley Rd CB8 . . . 111 C2
New Cl SG8 . . . . 12 B2
New Close Rd CB6 . . . . 211 A7
Newcomb Ct PE9 . . . . 244 B5
Newcombe Way PE2 . . . . . 185 D2
New Cross Dro CB6 . . . . . . 216 B3
New Cross Rd PE9 . . . . 244 B5
New Cut
Newmarket CB8 . . . . 111 A3
Thorney PE6 . . . . 233 D5
New Dro
Soham CB7 . . . . 211 E4
[3] Wisbech PE13 . . . . 245 D2
Wisbech St Mary PE13 . . . 235 C5
Newell Cl SG8 . . . . 44 D1
Newell Wlk CB1 . . . . 65 F7
NEW ENGLAND 197 E7
New England PE28 . . . . 120 B2
New Farm Cl SG8 . . . . 15 E8
New Farm Cotts CB1 . . . . . . 20 E7
New Fen Dike PE12 . . . . . 237 A6
New Fen Rd La PE26 . . . . . 171 C8
New Field
Gorefield PE13 . . . . 237 D2
Newton PE13 . . . . 237 F4
NEWFIELDS 237 D1
New Fields Cvn Pk CB4 . . . 84 D6
NEW FLETTON 187 B8
Newgate Rd PE13 . . . . 237 F6
Newgates [1] PE9 . . . . 244 C5
Newgate St PE15 . . . . 222 F5
Newghant Dro PE15 . . . . . . 223 F4
New Hall CB3 . . . . 83 C3
New Hall La CB23 . . . . 79 C4
Newham Rd PE9 . . . . 244 A7
Newington CB24 . . . . 124 B8
New La PE8 . . . . 183 C8
New Lakeside PE7 . . . . 186 B1
Newlands Ave PE15 . . . . . . 243 D5
Newlands Bldgs SG19 . . . . . 42 D4
Newlands Rd
Chatteris PE16 . . . . 241 E6
Parson Drove PE13 . . . . . . 234 D7
Whittlesey PE7 . . . . 190 A8
New London Rd
(Peterborough United FC)
PE2 . . . . 187 A8
New Long Dro PE7 . . . . 177 F6
Newman Ave SG8 . . . . 5 F6
Newman Cl [16] PE8 . . . . . 230 B1
NEWMARKET 111 B5
Newmarket Bus Pk CB8 . . 110 E7
Newmarket Cl PE1 . . . . 198 B6
Newmarket Coll CB8 . . . . . 110 F4
Newmarket Hospl CB8 . . . 111 A5
Newmarket Leisure Ctr
CB8 . . . . 110 F4
Newmarket Rd
Ashley CB8 . . . . 91 E8
Barton Mills IP28 . . . . 239 D1
Burwell CB25 . . . . 130 C1
Cambridge CB5 . . . . 246 C3
Cheveley CB8 . . . . 91 C8
Cowlinge CB8 . . . . 73 D3
Fen Ditton CB1 . . . . 85 D3
Fordham CB7 . . . . 131 D7
Great Chesterford CB10 . . . . 18 C3
Lidgate CB8 . . . . 73 C6
Moulton CB8 . . . . 112 E5
Royston SG8 . . . . 5 F6
Snailwell CB8 . . . . 132 B2
Stow cum Quy CB25 . . . . . . 85 F4
Stretham CB6 . . . . 211 A3
Newmarket Sta CB8 . . . . . 111 A2
Newmarket Swimming Pool
CB8 . . . . 110 F3
NEW MEADOW 187 F2
New Meadow Dro PE7 . . . 187 D1
NEWNHAM 64 C8
Newnham Cl
Huntingdon PE29 . . . . 142 A7
Mildenhall IP28 . . . . 239 D5
Newnham Coll CB3 . . . . 64 C8
NEWNHAM CROFT 64 D7
Newnham Croft Prim Sch
CB3 . . . . 64 C7
Newnham Croft St [2]
CB3 . . . . 64 C7
Newnham Dro CB25 . . . . . 129 C5
Newnham La CB25 . . . . 130 B3
Newnham Rd CB3 . . . . 64 C7
Newnham St [7] CB7 . . . . 240 D4
Newnham Terr
Cambridge CB1 . . . . 246 A1
Newnham CB3 . . . . 64 C8
Newnham Way SG7 . . . . 2 B2
Newnham Wlk CB3 . . . . 64 C8
New Orchard Pk CB6 . . . . 242 E4
New Park St CB5 . . . . 246 A4
New Path CB7 . . . . 212 E1
New Pk PE15 . . . . 243 E5
Newport Ave CB7 . . . . 213 A1
Newport Way PE9 . . . . 230 F2
New Rd
Barton CB23 . . . . 63 B4
Burwell CB25 . . . . 130 B3
Chatteris PE16 . . . . 241 E5
Cottenham CB24 . . . . 125 E4
Exning CB8 . . . . 110 B8
[15] Eye PE6 . . . . 232 A1
Girton CB3 . . . . 103 E4
Great & Little Chishill SG8 . . 15 B1
Guilden Morden SG8 . . . . . . 11 A5
Haddenham CB6 . . . . 210 A6
Harston CB22 . . . . 47 F3
Haslingfield CB23 . . . . 47 B5
Hemingford Abbots PE28 . . 143 A1
Hinxton CB10 . . . . 18 B6
Histon CB24 . . . . 104 C3
New Rd *continued*
Littleport CB6 . . . . 242 D5
March PE15 . . . . 243 E4
Melbourn SG8 . . . . 14 E4
Mepal CB6 . . . . 216 E3
Offord Cluny PE19 . . . . 118 A2
Outwell PE14 . . . . 236 E1
Over CB24 . . . . 208 D1
Peterborough PE2 . . . . 185 E4
Ramsey PE26 . . . . 172 B7
Sawston CB22 . . . . 32 E8
Shudy Camps CB21 . . . . 22 C7
St Ives PE27 . . . . 144 B3
Upwell PE14 . . . . 229 E8
Warboys PE28 . . . . 165 A4
Whittlesey PE7 . . . . 189 F6
Woodston PE2 . . . . 186 F7
Wood Walton PE28 . . . . 161 E7
New River Bank CB7 . . . . . 242 F5
New River Gn CB8 . . . . 110 B8
New Road Prim Sch PE7 . 189 F6
New Row [8] PE6 . . . . 231 E8
New School Rd CB24 . . . . . 104 B3
New Sq CB1 . . . . 246 B3
New St
Cambridge CB1 . . . . 84 A2
Chippenham CB7 . . . . 132 E8
Doddington/Wimblington
PE15 . . . . 222 F5
Godmanchester PE29 . . . . . 141 F1
Mildenhall IP28 . . . . 239 C4
Stamford PE9 . . . . 244 C6
St Neots PE19 . . . . 74 E5
NEWSTEAD 244 E6
Newstead Cl PE6 . . . . 232 A2
Newstead La PE9 . . . . 244 F8
Newstead Rd PE9 . . . . 230 A8
NEWTON
Harston 31 C7
Wisbech 238 A5
Newton Fen PE13 . . . . 237 E4
Newton Pl [9] CB9 . . . . 24 B8
Newton Prim Sch PE19 . . . . 77 E3
Newton Rd
Cambridge CB2 . . . . 64 E5
Great Shelford CB22 . . . . . . 48 D3
Harston CB22 . . . . 47 F1
Newton CB22 . . . . 31 A8
Sawtry PE28 . . . . 168 C4
Newtons Ct PE29 . . . . 141 E4
Newton Way PE1 . . . . 198 D2
NEWTOWN 64 E7
Newtown PE19 . . . . 74 B8
NEWTOWN
Huntingdon 141 E5
Kimbolton 114 A5
Newtown
Kimbolton PE28 . . . . 113 F5
Stamford PE9 . . . . 244 C4
New Town CB24 . . . . 125 D3
Newtown La PE28 . . . . 113 F5
Newtown Rd PE26 . . . . 172 B7
New Town Rd CB6 . . . . 209 F6
Next Odsey SG7 . . . . 3 C3
Nicholas Taylor Gdns
PE3 . . . . 196 F3
Nicholls Ave PE3 . . . . 197 E3
Nicholson Way CB4 . . . . 83 E6
Nigel Rd CB6 . . . . 240 E8
Nightall Dr PE15 . . . . 243 D7
Nightall Rd CB7 . . . . 212 A4
Nightingale Ave
Bassingbourn SG8 . . . . 13 A5
Cambridge CB1 . . . . 65 C3
Nightingale Cl IP28 . . . . . . 239 D4
Nightingale Ct PE4 . . . . . . 205 A2
Nightingale Dr PE7 . . . . . . 181 D6
Nightingale Way
Royston SG8 . . . . 5 E8
[1] St Neots PE19 . . . . 75 B7
Nightingale Wlk PE15 . . . . 224 B4
Nimbus Way CB8 . . . . 110 E8
Nimrod Dr PE28 . . . . 143 A8
Nine Chimneys La CB21 . . . 53 B2
Nipcut Rd PE6 . . . . 232 C2
Nixhill Rd PE15 . . . . 223 B6
Noahs Way CB6 . . . . 242 B5
Noble Gdns PE15 . . . . 243 E3
Nobles Cl PE7 . . . . 190 F8
Nobles La PE28 . . . . 208 C5
Noel Murless Dr CB8 . . . . . 110 F5
Nook The PE6 . . . . 231 C4
Norburn PE3 . . . . 197 B8
Norfolk Ave CB8 . . . . 110 E5
Norfolk Rd
Ely CB6 . . . . 240 A3
Huntingdon PE29 . . . . 141 E8
St Ives PE27 . . . . 144 A8
Wyton Airfield PE28 . . . . . . 143 B8
Norfolk Sq [3] PE9 . . . . . . 244 B6
Norfolk St
Cambridge CB1 . . . . 84 A1
Doddington/Wimblington
PE15 . . . . 223 B7
Peterborough PE1 . . . . 197 F4
Wisbech PE13 . . . . 245 C4
Norfolk Terr CB1 . . . . 84 A1
Norgett's La SG8 . . . . 14 D6
Norham Ct PE7 . . . . 188 A5
Norico Bay PE15 . . . . 243 E2
Norman Cl PE7 . . . . 189 E8
NORMAN CROSS 180 F2
Norman Dr PE7 . . . . 175 F8
Norman Pk CB23 . . . . 102 C4
Norman Rd PE1 . . . . 198 C4
Norman's La [8] SG8 . . . . 5 D5
Normanton Rd PE1 . . . . . . 198 D7
Normanton Way CB24 . . . . 104 B5
Norman Way
Cherry Hinton CB1 . . . . 65 E7
[9] Doddington/Wimblington
PE15 . . . . 223 B7
Over CB24 . . . . 123 B7
Normoor Dro PE16 . . . . 223 B2
Nornea La CB7 . . . . 211 F8
Norris Mus The* PE27 . . . 144 A3
Norris Rd PE27 . . . . 144 A4
Northam Cl PE6 . . . . 232 A2
Northampton Cl [4] CB6 . 240 A3
Northampton St CB3 . . . . . . 83 C2
North Ave CB9 . . . . 23 E8
North Bank PE6 . . . . 199 D1
North Bank Rd [4] PE1 . . . 198 D3
NORTHBOROUGH 231 F7
Northborough Prim Sch
PE6 . . . . 231 F6
Northborough Rd PE6 . . . . 206 F1
North Brink PE13 . . . . 245 A4
North Brook End SG8 . . . . . 11 B6
North Cambridgeshire Hospl
PE13 . . . . 245 D5
North Cl SG8 . . . . 5 C8
North Cotts CB2 . . . . 64 D4
North Dr
March PE15 . . . . 243 E4
Newmarket CB8 . . . . 110 F5
Soham CB7 . . . . 212 B5
North End
Bassingbourn cum Kneesworth
SG8 . . . . 12 D6
Exning CB8 . . . . 130 F3
Meldreth SG8 . . . . 29 B2
Wisbech PE13 . . . . 245 B6
North End Rd CB10 . . . . 18 A8
Northey Rd PE6 . . . . 199 C2
North Fen Dro CB6 . . . . . . 218 B8
North Fen Rd PE6 . . . . 231 F5
Northfield
Fulbourn CB21 . . . . 67 A5
Girton CB3 . . . . 103 E2
Northfield Cl SG19 . . . . 41 C6
Northfield Pk CB7 . . . . 212 A5
Northfield Rd
Ashwell SG7 . . . . 2 C7
Peterborough PE1 . . . . 197 F7
Soham CB7 . . . . 212 A5
Wyboston PE19 . . . . 74 A1
NORTHFIELDS 244 C6
Northfields Ave CB4 . . . . 83 E7
Northfields Ct PE9 . . . . 244 C6
Northfields Rd CB25 . . . . . 107 D2
Northgate PE7 . . . . 189 D8
Northgate Cl PE7 . . . . 189 D8
NORTH GREEN 190 E8
North La SG19 . . . . 41 B7
North Lodge Dr CB23 . . . . . 99 B2
Northminster PE1 . . . . 198 A3
North Pl IP28 . . . . 239 C4
North Rd
Alconbury Weston PE28 . . . 150 E5
Brampton PE28 . . . . 140 D1
Great Abington CB21 . . . . . . 33 F5
St Ives PE27 . . . . 144 A4
Whittlesford CB22 . . . . 32 B6
NORTH SIDE 200 F4
North Side PE6 . . . . 200 F5
North St
Burwell CB25 . . . . 130 B4
Cambridge CB4 . . . . 83 C4
Folksworth & Washingley
PE7 . . . . 181 A1
Freckenham IP28 . . . . 213 C3
Huntingdon PE29 . . . . 141 E5
March PE15 . . . . 243 D5
Peterborough PE1 . . . . 198 A2
Stamford PE9 . . . . 244 B5
Stilton PE7 . . . . 176 A8
Wicken CB7 . . . . 211 E1
Wisbech PE13 . . . . 245 C5
North Terr
Cambridge CB1 . . . . 246 C3
Mildenhall IP28 . . . . 239 C4
Peterborough PE1 . . . . 198 E7
Sawston CB22 . . . . 32 F5
Northumberland Ave [4]
PE9 . . . . 244 A6
Northumberland Cl [2]
CB4 . . . . 83 D6
Northumbria Cl CB6 . . . . . 210 A7
Northwold CB6 . . . . 240 C5
Norton Cl
Cambridge CB5 . . . . 84 D3
Papworth Everard CB23 . . . . 99 A2
Norton Rd
Haverhill CB9 . . . . 23 E6
Peterborough PE1 . . . . 197 F6
Norwalde St PE15 . . . . 243 C6
Norwich Rd PE13 . . . . 245 D5
Norwich St CB2 . . . . 64 E7
Norwood Ave PE15 . . . . 243 D5
Norwood Cres PE15 . . . . . . 243 C6
Norwood La PE4 . . . . 205 B2
Norwood Prim Sch PE4 . . 204 F3
Norwood Rd
March PE15 . . . . 243 D7
[10] Somersham PE28 . . . . . 215 C1
NORWOODSIDE 243 C7
NOSTERFIELD END 22 F5
Notley Dr CB9 . . . . 38 C1
Nottingham Way PE1 . . . 198 C6
Nuffield Cl CB4 . . . . 84 B7
Nuffield Hospl CB2 . . . . 64 E6

Nuffield Rd
Cambridge CB4 84 B6
St Ives PE27 144 C6
Nunns Way 4 CB6 216 E1
Nun's Orch CB24 104 B4
Nuns Way CB4 83 F7
Nursery Cl
Isleham CB7 212 F4
Mildenhall IP28 239 D4
Peterborough PE1 198 A4
Nursery Dr
March PE15 243 B5
Wisbech PE13 245 E8
Nursery Gdns
Little Paxton PE19 96 A2
St Ives PE27 144 B5
Whittlesey PE7 189 F6
Nursery La PE1 198 D2
Nursery Rd
Huntingdon PE29 141 E4
St Neots PE19 74 F4
Nursery Way 2 CB23 62 C5
Nursery Wlk
Brampton PE28 140 C3
Cambridge CB4 83 C5
Nutholt La CB6 240 D5
Nutters Cl CB3 64 A4
Nuttings Rd CB1 84 D1

O

Oak Ave PE7 186 B2
Oak Cl PE19 75 A5
Oak Ct PE7 182 A6
Oakdale Ave PE2 187 D4
Oakdale Prim Sch PE7 187 C4
Oak Dr
Brampton PE28 140 C4
Huntingdon PE29 141 E8
Little Stukeley PE28 151 F3
Mildenhall IP28 213 F8
Outwell PE14 236 F3
Oak End PE28 150 F4
Oakery The CB7 240 D6
Oak Farm Cl PE7 176 A7
OAKINGTON 103 B5
Oakington Barracks CB24 124 B1
Oakington CE Prim Sch CB24 103 C5
Oakington Rd
Cottenham CB24 125 B1
Dry Drayton CB23 102 D2
Girton CB3 103 E3
Oakington & Westwick CB24 103 E7
Oak La
Cheveley CB8 91 C4
Littleport CB6 242 A2
Oaklands
Fenstanton PE28 121 B5
Peterborough PE1 198 B4
Oaklands Ave PE28 163 F7
Oaklands Dr PE13 245 F7
Oakleaf Rd PE1 198 C6
Oakleigh Cres PE29 141 F1
Oakleigh Dr PE2 186 C6
Oakley Cl PE13 245 E4
Oakley Dr PE28 168 B3
Oak Rd
Glinton PE6 231 E5
Stilton PE7 176 A7
Oakrits SG8 14 B8
Oakroyd Cres PE13 245 C6
Oaks Bsns Pk The CB8 110 F7
Oaks Dr CB8 110 F7
Oaks The
15 Elm PE14 236 A5
Milton CB24 105 C2
Soham CB7 212 B3
Oak Tree Ave CB4 83 F5
Oaktree Cl PE15 222 F5
Oak Tree Cl
March PE15 243 C5
St Ives PE27 143 F5
Oaktree Rd CB24 121 D6
Oak Tree Way CB24 104 B3
Oak View PE3 196 F2
Oak Way PE26 220 D3
Oakwood Dr CB23 79 B2
Oasthouse Way PE26 172 A5
Oates' La CB6 216 E1
Oates Way PE26 172 C7
Oatlands Ave CB23 102 B4
Occupation Rd
Cambridge CB1 84 A2
Peterborough PE1 197 E6
Ockendon Cl PE19 74 B3
Octagon Dr PE13 245 A6
Octavia Cl PE13 245 F6
Octavia Hill Birthplace House* PE13 245 B5
Odecroft PE3 197 C7
Odin Cl PE7 189 E8
ODSEY 3 C1
Offa Lea CB22 31 B7
OFFORD CLUNY 118 F3
OFFORD D'ARCY 118 F1
Offord Prim Sch PE19 118 A2
Offord Rd PE19 97 F6
O Furlong Dro CB6 224 F1
Ogden Cl SG8 14 D6
Oil Mill La PE13 245 B5
Oilmills Dro PE26 220 F4
Oilmills Rd PE26 220 E6
Oklahoma PE28 151 F4
Old Allots The MK44 93 A1
Old Auction Yd PE16 241 C5
Old Bailey Rd PE7 181 C8
Old Bank CB7 219 B4
Old Brewery Cl CB7 240 E4
Old Broadpool PE28 173 D2
Oldbrook PE3 204 A1
Old Bull Yd PE19 74 E5
Old Church La PE28 208 C7
Old Clements La 7 CB9 23 F7
Old Court Hall PE29 141 E1
Oldeamere Way PE7 190 A7
Old Farm Cl
Histon CB24 104 B5
3 Needingworth PE27 208 A3
Old Fen Dike PE12 237 B8
Old Field PE13 237 F4
Oldfield Ave PE14 236 B5
Oldfield Gdns PE7 189 D7
Oldfield La PE13 245 B4
OLD FLETTON 187 A6
Old Fletton Prim Sch PE2 186 F6
Old Ford La PE19 114 B2
Oldforge Gdns PE16 241 C5
Old Forge Way CB22 32 E8
Old Glebe PE28 150 E5
Old Great North Rd PE8 194 C2
Old Haverhill Rd CB9 39 E4
Old Houghton Rd PE29 142 B6
Old House Rd CB21 53 C2
OLD HURST 154 E7
Oldhurst Rd PE28 155 E8
Old Knarr Fen Dro PE6 233 C2
Old Leicester Rd PE8 194 A3
Old Lynn Dro CB6 217 C7
Old Lynn Rd PE13 245 E7
Old Mill Ave PE28 165 A5
Old Mill Cl CB22 29 D7
Old Mill La IP28 239 F2
Old Mkt PE13 245 C5
Old North Rd
Bassingbourn cum Kneesworth SG8 13 B4
Longstowe CB23 60 A3
Royston SG8 5 C7
Sawtry PE28 168 D4
Wansford PE8 194 A3
Old Orch The PE15 222 A5
Old Oundle Rd PE8 193 A6
Old Pinewood Way CB23 99 B4
Old Pond La PE5 195 E2
Old Pools Dro CB6 225 C4
Old Pound Cl PE28 143 D2
Old Priory Farm PE6 231 F8
Old Railway Ind Est PE27 144 D4
Old Ramsey Rd
St Ives PE28 143 E8
Woodhurst PE28 154 E2
Old Rectory Dr
Dry Drayton CB23 102 B1
4 Tallington PE9 230 F7
Thornhaugh PE8 194 A6
Old Rope Wlk CB9 23 E7
Old Rorge Gdns PE16 241 C5
Old School Cl
Burwell CB25 130 C3
Littleport CB6 242 D5
1 Soham CB7 212 B5
Old School Dr PE16 241 C5
Old School Gdns 3 PE19 74 C2
Old School La
Brinkley CB8 70 E1
Milton CB24 105 D2
Whittlesford CB22 32 C5
Wicken CB7 211 B1
Old South Eau Bank PE6 233 E8
Old Stable Wlk PE26 172 A4
Old Station Pl PE16 241 B5
Old Station Rd
Newmarket CB8 111 B4
Ramsey PE26 172 A6
Old West Est PE15 222 A5
OLD WESTON 148 A8
Old Weston Rd PE28 158 A5
OLD WIMPOLE 44 F3
Oliver Cl PE26 171 F6
Oliver Cromwell's House* CB7 240 C4
Olive Rd PE1 198 C7
Oliver Rd PE27 144 B3
Olivers Way PE15 243 D2
Olivia Rd PE28 140 C3
Ollard Ave PE13 245 D7
Ongar Ct CB5 84 F4
Onyx Ct 9 PE13 245 C4
Opeford Cl PE19 118 A3
Open Univ in East of England 1 CB2 246 C1
Opportune Rd PE13 245 C6
Orange Gr 1 PE13 245 C4
Orchard Ave CB4 83 E5
Orchard Cl
Balsham CB21 52 F3
Bassingbourn SG8 13 A5
Cottenham CB24 125 C3
Eaton Socon PE19 74 C4
Elsworth CB23 100 B4
Girton CB3 103 E1
Hail Weston PE19 95 A1
Haverhill CB9 23 F7
Lidgate CB8 73 E8
Littleport CB6 242 D4
Little Wilbraham CB1 86 E2
Manea PE15 224 B4
Orchard Cl *continued*
March PE15 243 E3
9 Market Deeping PE6 231 E8
Peterborough PE3 197 D3
Stamford PE9 244 B5
Stilton PE7 176 A7
Warboys PE28 164 F6
Warmington PE8 178 B3
15 Wisbech PE13 238 B2
9 Wisbech PE14 236 A5
Orchard Cres PE28 208 E6
Orchard Ct PE6 232 F3
Orchard Dr
Girton CB3 82 E7
Waterbeach CB25 127 B1
Wisbech PE13 245 E4
Orchard End
Bluntisham/Colne PE28 208 C5
Rampton CB24 124 E4
Orchard Est
Cambridge CB1 65 F7
1 Little Downham CB6 218 B7
Orchard Gate SG8 14 C6
Orchard Gdns
Fenstanton PE28 121 B5
Gaultree PE14 236 D5
Leverington PE13 238 A1
Orchard Gr PE6 231 C7
Orchard La
Brampton PE28 140 E3
Huntingdon PE29 141 E4
Orchard Mews PE2 186 F8
Orchard Park Prim Sch CB4 83 D8
Orchard Pightle CB21 20 B6
Orchard Rd
Barnack PE9 230 E4
Eaton Socon PE19 74 C4
Great Shelford CB22 49 B6
Haslingfield CB23 47 B5
Histon CB24 104 C5
March PE15 243 E3
Melbourn SG8 14 C5
Royston SG8 5 B7
Sawston CB22 32 F7
Stamford PE9 244 B5
Orchard Road S PE15 243 E3
Orchard Row CB7 212 C2
Orchards CE Prim Sch PE13 245 D8
Orchard St
Cambridge CB1 246 B3
Peterborough PE2 186 F7
Stow cum Quy CB25 85 F5
Whittlesey PE7 189 D7
Orchards The
Cambridge CB1 65 F5
Chatteris PE16 241 D5
Great Shelford CB22 49 B6
Peterborough PE2 185 F4
Sutton CB6 216 E2
1 Wilburton CB6 210 C6
Witcham CB6 217 A2
Orchard Terr
St Ives PE27 144 A4
Whittlesford CB22 32 C4
Orchard The
Ashley CB8 91 F7
Fen Drayton CB24 121 F5
Little Paxton PE19 95 F2
Peterborough PE4 204 C3
Orchard View
Ashwell SG7 3 A3
Waterbeach CB25 127 B1
Orchard Way
Burwell CB25 130 B3
Cambourne CB23 79 A3
4 Doddington/Wimblington PE15 223 B7
Godmanchester PE29 141 F2
Haddenham CB6 210 A5
Manea PE15 224 B4
Melbourn SG8 14 D6
Oakington/Longstanton CB24 103 C5
Offord Cluny PE19 97 A8
Ramsey PE26 172 A7
Royston SG8 5 C8
Orchid Cl
13 Eaton Socon PE19 74 C6
Yaxley PE7 181 F7
Orchid Fare CB23 80 C2
Oregon PE28 151 E4
Orford Rd CB9 23 F6
Orkney Cl CB9 24 D7
Orme Rd PE3 197 D4
Orthwaite PE29 141 B6
Orton Ave PE2 186 E7
ORTON BRIMBLES 185 D5
Orton Dr CB6 217 D1
Ortongate Sh Ctr PE2 185 E3
ORTON GOLDHAY 185 F3
ORTON LONGUEVILLE 186 B5
Orton Longueville Sch PE2 186 A5
ORTON MALBOURNE 186 B5
Orton Mere PE2 186 B7
Orton Parkway PE2 185 D4
ORTON SOUTHGATE 185 C2
ORTON WATERVILLE 185 E4
ORTON WISTOW 185 C6
Orton Wistow Prim Sch PE2 185 C6
ORWELL 45 E1
Orwell Cl PE27 144 A6
Orwell Dr PE15 243 B5
Orwell Furlong CB4 84 C7
Orwell Gr PE4 204 F1
Orwell Rd CB22 29 C8
Orwell Terr CB22 29 D8
Osborn Cl 3 CB24 209 A1
Osborne Pk PE13 245 C8
Osborne Rd PE13 245 B7
Osbourne Cl 3 PE4 204 F1
Osier Ave PE7 186 D2
Osier Cl CB7 240 E4
Osier Ct 4 PE19 74 C6
Osier Holt PE28 208 D6
Osiers The PE19 117 A3
Osier Way CB23 79 C5
Oslar's Way CB21 66 E5
Osprey PE2 185 F2
Osprey Cl PE29 142 A7
Osprey Ct PE29 141 A5
Osprey Rd CB9 24 C7
Osric Ct PE1 198 C5
Oswald Rd PE2 186 D7
Otago Cl PE7 189 F8
Otago Rd PE7 189 E8
Othello Cl PE29 142 A7
Otterbrook PE2 185 D5
Otter Cl CB23 102 B4
Otter Way 9 PE19 74 B5
Oundle Rd
Elton PE8 183 F1
Peterborough PE2 185 E6
Ouse Fen Rd Or Bank CB24 208 D3
Ouse Rd
Eaton Socon PE19 74 C4
Kimbolton PE28 114 B7
St Ives PE27 144 A7
Ouse Valley Way PE19 117 E4
Ouse Washes Nature Reserve* CB6 224 D2
Ouse Wlk PE29 141 E4
Outfield PE3 204 A1
OUTWELL 236 F3
Outwell Rd
Boyces Bridge PE14 236 D4
Elm PE14 236 C5
Outwell PE14 236 E3
OVER 208 E1
Overchurch Cl CB9 23 F7
Overcote La PE27 208 B2
Overcote Rd CB24 208 D1
Overend PE8 178 D8
OVER END 178 E7
Overhall Grove Nature Reserve* CB23 100 F3
Over Hall La CB10 21 D2
Overhills Prim Sch PE28 113 F5
Over Prim Sch CB24 208 D1
Over Rd
Swavesey CB24 122 F8
Willingham CB24 208 F1
Overstone Ct PE3 197 C6
Overstone Dr 1 PE14 235 D1
Overstone Rd 2 PE14 235 D1
Overton Way PE2 185 F4
Overwater Cl PE29 141 A6
Ovington Pl 3 CB9 24 B8
Owall Wlk 8 SG8 5 E8
Owen Cl 3 PE9 230 D3
Owen Dr SG8 13 D1
Owens Gdns PE7 189 C8
OWL END 152 A3
Owl End PE28 151 F2
Owl End Wlk PE7 181 D5
Owls End PE26 172 A4
Owlstone Rd CB3 64 C7
Owl Way PE29 142 B7
Oxbow Cres PE15 243 C4
Oxburgh Cl
Peterborough PE7 187 F5
Wisbech PE13 245 A7
Ox Cl PE3 197 A8
Oxclose PE3 197 A8
Ox Field PE13 237 F3
Oxford Cl
Bassingbourn SG8 12 F7
Mildenhall IP28 239 A5
Wyton PE29 143 B8
Oxford Gdns PE7 189 C7
Oxford Rd
Cambridge CB4 83 B4
Peterborough PE1 197 F5
Stamford PE9 244 A7
St Ives PE27 144 A4
Oxford St CB8 110 B8
Oxholme Dro CB24 209 F1
OXLODE 224 C1
Oxney Rd PE1 198 D5
Oyster Row CB5 84 B3

P

Pacific Cl PE15 243 C6
Paddock Cl CB24 104 C4
Paddock Row CB23 100 B4
Paddocks Chase PE19 118 A3
Paddocks Dr CB8 111 A1
Paddocks Prim Sch CB8 110 E4
Paddock St CB7 212 B4
Paddocks The
Alconbury PE28 150 F5
Burwell CB25 130 B1
Cambridge CB1 84 C1
Eastwood End PE15 223 B7
Folksworth PE7 175 D8
Hilton PE28 120 B2
Little Wilbraham CB8 68 F6
Peterborough PE4 204 A5
Whittlesey PE7 189 E7
Woodhurst PE29 155 B4
Paddocks The *continued*
Worlington IP28 213 F4
Paddock The
Bluntisham PE28 208 C5
Eaton Socon PE19 74 D4
Ely CB6 240 D5
Harston CB22 47 F2
Huntingdon PE29 141 E5
15 Somersham PE28 215 C1
Stamford PE9 244 A5
Paddock Way
Haddenham CB6 210 A6
Sawston CB22 32 F7
Padgetts Cl PE28 165 A5
Padgett's Rd PE14 229 C3
Padholme Rd PE1 198 C3
Padholme Road E PE1 198 E3
Padlock Rd CB21 53 F4
Padnal Bank CB7 219 B6
Padnal Dro CB6 242 E3
Padney Dro CB7 211 D5
Page Ct CB7 240 D6
Pages Way 3 PE28 140 C3
Paget Cl CB2 64 E3
Paget Pl CB8 111 A6
Paget Rd CB2 64 D2
Painter's La CB6 216 D1
Pakenham Cl CB4 84 A5
Pakenham Pl CB9 24 B7
Palace Gdns SG8 5 C6
Palace Gn CB7 240 C4
Palace La CB7 132 D8
Palace St CB8 111 A3
PALE GREEN 23 D1
Palisade Ct 3 CB6 211 B7
Palm Ct PE1 198 B8
Palmer Cl PE7 189 F6
Palmers Cl CB21 35 B3
Palmers La
Alconbury PE28 150 F4
Chrishall SG8 8 C4
Palmers Rd PE1 198 F5
Palmerston Rd PE2 186 F7
Palmers Way SG8 14 D6
Palmers Wlk
Cambridge CB1 246 C2
Chatteris PE16 241 D5
Pamment's La IP28 213 D6
PAMPISFORD 33 B5
Pampisford Rd CB21 34 C5
Pamplin Ct 1 CB1 65 F6
Panswell La PE13 235 C8
Panther Way CB1 66 A7
Pantile La CB25 130 A3
Pantiles CB21 20 B7
Pantiles The PE7 189 D8
Panton St CB2 246 B1
PAPLEY 174 A6
Papley Grove Farm Cotts PE19 77 E7
Papley Hollow PE19 77 F8
PAPWORTH EVERARD 99 B3
Papworth Hospl CB23 99 C2
Papworth Rd
Graveley PE19 98 A5
March PE15 243 F4
PAPWORTH ST AGNES 98 D5
Papworth's Cl CB24 208 D1
PAPWORTH VILLAGE SETTLEMENT 99 A2
Papyrus Rd PE4 203 F3
Papyrus Way PE28 168 B4
Parade La CB7 240 C4
Paradise La
Northborough PE6 231 F6
3 Whittlesey PE7 189 D6
Paradise Nature Reserve* CB1 246 A1
Paradise Sports Ctr & Pool CB7 240 D5
Paradise St CB1 246 C3
Paragon Rd PE27 144 A5
Parcell Wlk PE29 118 F8
Parish Bush Dro CB7 219 C1
Park Ave
Histon CB24 104 A4
Little Paxton PE19 95 F1
Newmarket CB8 111 B3
St Ives PE27 144 B4
Wisbech PE13 245 C6
Park Cl
Bassingbourn SG8 12 E5
Holme PE7 176 F4
Little Paxton PE19 95 E1
Moulton CB8 112 F5
Thorney PE6 233 B3
Yaxley PE7 181 F5
Park Cotts 1 CB8 111 B3
Park Cres
Little Paxton PE19 95 F2
Peterborough PE1 198 B5
Thorney PE6 233 B3
Waterbeach CB25 106 C8
Park Dr
Histon CB24 104 C3
Little Paxton PE19 95 F1
Park End CB25 87 B8
Parker Cl PE19 74 E2
Parker Rd PE8 230 B1
Parker's Cl PE16 241 B5
Parker's Dro IP28 213 D6
Parkers Mill IP28 239 C4
Parker St CB1 246 B2
Parker's Terr 2 CB1 84 A2
Park Est 1 PE6 231 F8
Park Farm Cotts CB10 18 F6
Park Farm Cres PE7 187 F5
Park Farm Dr IP28 214 A2

Park Farm La SG8 . . . . 1 A2
Park Farm Rd PE6 . . . . 196 E5
Park Farm Way PE7 . . . . . . 187 F6
Parkfield La PE15 . . . . 223 B6
Parkgate PE29 . . . . 141 C6
Parkhall Rd PE28 . . . . 215 C2
Park Hill CB21 . . . . 37 C2
Park Home Rd PE7 . . . . . . 186 D1
Parkinson's La ■ PE7 . . 189 D6
Park La
 Brampton PE28 . . . . 117 D8
 Castle Camps CB21 . . . . . . .22 F3
 Cottenham CB24 . . . . 125 D4
 Dry Drayton CB23 . . . . 81 A1
 Fen Drayton CB24 . . . . . . 121 F6
 Gamlingay SG19 . . . . .41 C5
 Godmanchester PE29 . . . 141 F2
 Histon CB24 . . . . 104 D4
 Kimbolton PE19 . . . . 113 F2
 Langley CB11 . . . . 1 F2
 Leverington PE13 . . . . 238 A3
 Little Downham CB6 . . . . 217 F6
 Longstowe CB23 . . . . .59 F3
 Madingley CB23 . . . . .81 F6
 Newmarket CB8 . . . . 111 B3
 Newton PE13 . . . . 237 F3
 Peterborough PE1 . . . . . . 198 C4
 Stamford PE9 . . . . 244 C4
 Whittlesey PE7 . . . . 189 C7
Parklands SG8 . . . . 5 E6
Park Lane Prim Sch PE7 189 C6
Park Par CB5 . . . . 246 A4
Park Rd
 Brampton PE28 . . . . 140 C2
 Buckden PE19 . . . . 117 B4
 Burwell CB25 . . . . 130 B2
 Cheveley CB8 . . . . .91 C6
 Great Chesterford CB10 . . .18 E5
 Haverhill CB9 . . . . .23 D8
 Manea PE15 . . . . 224 B4
 Market Deeping PE6 . . . . 231 E8
 Peterborough PE1 . . . . . . 198 A3
 Ramsey PE26 . . . . 171 F6
 Sawston CB22 . . . . .32 F5
 Sawtry PE28 . . . . 168 B5
 St Ives PE27 . . . . 144 B4
 St Neots PE19 . . . . .74 F6
 Sutton CB6 . . . . 214 D3
 Tydd St Giles PE13 . . . . . 237 D7
 Wisbech PE13 . . . . 245 D5
Parkside
 Cambridge CB1 . . . . 246 C2
 Chatteris PE16 . . . . 241 D4
 Chippenham CB7 . . . . 132 E8
 Haverhill CB9 . . . . .23 F6
 Mildenhall IP28 . . . . 214 A8
 Peterborough PE2 . . . . . . 186 B6
Park Side
 Little Paxton PE19 . . . . . . .95 E1
 St Ives PE27 . . . . 144 B4
Parkside Coll CB1 . . . . 246 C2
Parkside Pools CB1 . . . . . 246 C2
Park St
 Cambridge CB5 . . . . 246 A3
 Chatteris PE16 . . . . 241 C4
 Dry Drayton CB23 . . . . . . 102 C1
 Peterborough PE2 . . . . . . 186 F7
 ☑ Wisbech PE13 . . . . . . 245 D5
Parks The PE15 . . . . 243 F5
Park Street Prim Sch
 CB5 . . . . 246 A3
Park Terr
 Cambridge CB1 . . . . 246 B2
 Peterborough PE1 . . . . . . 198 A6
Park The PE28 . . . . 146 A3
Park View
 Bassingbourn SG8 . . . . . . .12 E5
 Little Stukeley PE28 . . . . . 151 F1
 Needingworth PE27 . . . . . 208 A2
Park View E PE15 . . . . 243 C4
Park View W PE15 . . . . . . 243 C4
Parkway
 Shudy Camps CB21 . . . . . .22 C6
 St Ives PE27 . . . . 144 B4
 The Stukeleys PE29 . . . . . 141 A5
Park Way
 Little Paxton PE19 . . . . . . .95 F1
 Offord Cluny PE19 . . . . . . 118 A2
 St Neots PE19 . . . . .74 F7
Parkway Mid Sch PE9 . . . .23 D8
Parliament St PE1 . . . . 197 F5
Parlour CI CB24 . . . . 104 B5
Parnwell Prim Sch PE1 . . 198 E7
Parnwell Way PE1 . . . . . . 198 F6
Parr CI CB24 . . . . 104 C3
Parrens Rd PE28 . . . . 208 E6
Parr Rd PE9 . . . . .23 D6
Parsonage Barns CB25 . . .86 F5
Parsonage CI
 Burwell CB25 . . . . 130 B2
 Duxford CB22 . . . . .17 E8
Parsonage Farm La CB8 . .90 F2
Parsonage Gdns ☑ CB9 . . .23 E7
Parsonage La CB25 . . . . . . 130 B2
Parsonage St
 Cambridge CB5 . . . . 246 C3
 Wistow PE28 . . . . 163 F6
Parsonage Way CB21 . . . . .35 D2
Parson Dro La PE13 . . . . . 238 B2
PARSON DROVE 234 D7
Parson's Ct CB2 . . . . 246 A2
Parson's Dr PE28 . . . . 139 A4
Parsons Gn PE27 . . . . 144 C4
Parson's La CB6 . . . . 242 C4
Parson's Land Dro PE15 . 222 D6
Parthia CI SG8 . . . . 5 E6
Partridge CI PE7 . . . . 181 D5
Partridge Dr CB23 . . . . . . 102 B3
Partridge Gr PE4 . . . . 204 A5
Partridge Hill SG7 . . . . .2 C3
Paske Ave CB9 . . . . .23 F7
Passage The ■ CB7 . . . . . 240 D4
PASTON 204 B4
Paston La PE4 . . . . 197 D8
Paston Parkway PE4 . . . . 204 B4
Paston Ridings PE4 . . . . . 204 E1
Paston Ridings Prim Sch
 PE4 . . . . 204 F1
Pasture CI PE28 . . . . 165 A5
Pasture Gr ☑ CB6 . . . . . . 240 A3
Pasture La PE21 . . . . 231 F6
Pastures The CB23 . . . . . . .81 A1
Pasture The ☑ PE28 . . . . 208 B8
Pates CI CB23 . . . . .47 A6
Pathfinder Way
 Ramsey PE26 . . . . 171 F5
 Warboys PE28 . . . . 164 F4
 Wyton PE28 . . . . 143 A8
Patterdale Dr PE4 . . . . 205 A2
Patterdale Rd PE4 . . . . . . 205 A2
Paulsgrove PE1 . . . . 185 D5
Pavement The PE27 . . . . . 144 A3
Pavilion CI PE29 . . . . 141 F2
Pavilion Ct
 Haverhill CB9 . . . . .24 B7
 ☑ Kings Hedges CB4 . . . .83 E8
Paxton CI CB4 . . . . 125 E3
Paxton Hill PE19 . . . . .96 D2
Paxton Pitts Nature
 Reserve* PE19 . . . . .96 A3
Paxton Rd
 Offord Darcy PE19 . . . . . . .96 F7
 Peterborough PE2 . . . . . . 185 D4
Payne Ave PE13 . . . . 245 D7
Paynells PE2 . . . . 186 A3
Payne Prim Sch PE13 . . . 234 D7
Paynesholm PE4 . . . . 205 A1
Paynes Mdw CB21 . . . . . . .35 C3
Payton Way CB25 . . . . 106 B7
Peacock Dr CB25 . . . . .86 F7
Peacocks CB22 . . . . .49 A4
Peacock Way
 Littleport CB6 . . . . 242 E4
 Peterborough PE2 . . . . . . 196 F2
Peake CI PE2 . . . . 186 F6
Peakes Dr PE7 . . . . 201 F1
PEAKIRK 206 B1
Peakirk cum Glinton Prim
 Sch PE6 . . . . 203 E8
Peakirk Rd
 Deeping Gate PE6 . . . . . . 231 F8
 Glinton PE6 . . . . 203 F8
 Northborough PE6 . . . . . . 206 A4
Peaks Ct PE29 . . . . 141 A5
Pearce CI CB24 . . . . .64 B8
Pearces Rd PE6 . . . . 199 B5
Pearl CI CB4 . . . . .84 A4
Pearmain CI CB4 . . . . .84 C5
Pearmains CI SG8 . . . . .45 E1
Pearson CI
 Milton CB24 . . . . 105 D1
 St Neots PE19 . . . . .74 E2
Pear Tree CI CB13 . . . . 234 C2
Pear Tree CI
 Fenstanton PE28 . . . . 121 A5
 Haddenham CB6 . . . . 210 A5
Pear Tree Cres PE13 . . . . 238 A2
Peartree Way ■ PE14 . . 236 A5
Pease Way CB24 . . . . 103 F4
PEAS HILL 243 B6
Peas Hill CB2 . . . . 246 A2
Peas Hill Rd PE15 . . . . 243 A5
Peas Mkt Hill CB9 . . . . .24 A8
Peate CI PE29 . . . . 141 F1
Peatlings La PE15 . . . . 243 A4
Peckover CI PE7 . . . . 187 F5
Peckover Dr PE13 . . . . 245 E4
Peckover House & Gdn*
 PE13 . . . . 245 B5
Peckover Prim Sch PE13 245 B6
Pecks CI PE28 . . . . 120 C1
Pecks Yd PE16 . . . . 141 C5
Peddars Way PE3 . . . . 197 A2
Pedley La PE13 . . . . 245 A6
Peer Rd PE19 . . . . .74 B4
Pegler CI ☑ CB24 . . . . . . 209 A1
Peldon Dr PE13 . . . . 245 E5
Pelham CI
 Cottenham CB24 . . . . 125 D3
 Peterborough PE3 . . . . . . 196 F2
Pelham Ct CB4 . . . . .83 C6
Pelham Way CB24 . . . . 125 D3
Pelican Pre-Prep Sch The
 CB1 . . . . .65 B4
Pemberton PI CB2 . . . . . . 246 B1
Pemberton Terr CB2 . . . . 246 B1
Pembroke Ave
 Peterborough PE2 . . . . . . 185 F5
 ☑ St Neots PE19 . . . . . . .74 F2
 Waterbeach CB25 . . . . . . 105 F8
Pembroke CI
 Huntingdon PE29 . . . . 141 F7
 Mildenhall IP28 . . . . 239 C5
 ☑ Newmarket CB8 . . . . . 111 B2
Pembroke Coll CB2 . . . . . 246 A2
Pembroke Gr PE6 . . . . 203 F8
Pembroke La CB2 . . . . .35 E2
Pembroke Rd PE9 . . . . . . 244 A7
Pembroke St CB2 . . . . 246 A2
Pembroke Way CB1 . . . . . .85 B1
Penarth Dr CB21 . . . . .64 A8
Pen CI CB1 . . . . .66 A6
Pendleton PE1 . . . . 197 B6
Pendragon Cty Prim Sch
 CB23 . . . . .99 A3
Pendragon Hill CB23 . . . . .99 A4
Pendula Rd PE13 . . . . 245 E7
Pen Hills Nature Reserve*
 SG8 . . . . 1 A4
Pennine Way PE4 . . . . 204 D2
Pennington PE2 . . . . 185 E3
Pennington Rd PE29 . . . . 142 A7
Pennway ■ PE28 . . . . . . 215 C1
Penrith Gr PE4 . . . . 205 A2
Penrose Gdns PE13 . . . . . 245 E4
Penrwyn Ct ☑ PE19 . . . . .74 F1
Pentelowes The PE28 . . . 135 D2
Pentlands CI CB4 . . . . 246 C4
Pentlands CI CB1 . . . . 246 C4
Pentlands The PE4 . . . . . . 204 E2
Pentland Way PE15 . . . . . 243 B5
Pentlow Hawke CI CB9 . . .24 B7
Penwald CI ☑ PE6 . . . . . . 232 B8
Penwald Ct PE6 . . . . 206 B1
Penyale PE3 . . . . 197 A1
Pepper CI SG8 . . . . .12 F4
Peppercorn CI PE1 . . . . . . 197 B6
Peppercorns La ☑ PE19 . .74 C2
Peppersdale CB22 . . . . . . .31 F1
Pepys House* PE28 . . . . 140 F2
Pepys Rd
 Brampton PE28 . . . . 140 F2
 St Neots PE19 . . . . .75 A4
Pepys Terr CB24 . . . . 104 C1
Pepys Way CB3 . . . . .82 E8
Percheron CI CB24 . . . . . . 104 D3
Percheron Dr PE15 . . . . . . 243 E2
Percival St PE3 . . . . 197 E2
Peregrine CI PE29 . . . . . . 142 A7
Peregrine St ■ PE7 . . . . 186 D1
Perkins La ☑ PE6 . . . . . . 231 C7
Perne Ave CB1 . . . . .65 C6
Perne Rd CB1 . . . . .65 C6
Pernys CI PE7 . . . . 186 D3
Perry CI CB6 . . . . 210 A6
Perry Ct CB3 . . . . .83 A2
Perry Dr SG8 . . . . .5 E7
Perry Rd
 Buckden PE19 . . . . 116 F3
 Leverington PE13 . . . . 238 B2
Perry Wood View PE28 . . 115 D2
Perse Prep Sch CB2 . . . . . .64 E4
Perse Sch The CB2 . . . . . . .65 A4
Perse Way CB4 . . . . .83 D5
Pershore Rd CB23 . . . . .81 A3
Pershore Way PE2 . . . . . . 232 B2
Persimmon Wlk CB8 . . . . 110 E8
PETERBOROUGH 197 D5
Peterborough Airport
 (Conington) PE7 . . . . . . 176 F3
Peterborough Bsns Pk
 PE2 . . . . 185 C5
Peterborough Cath*
 PE1 . . . . 198 A2
Peterborough Coll of Adult
 Ed PE1 . . . . 198 B3
Peterborough District Hospl
 PE3 . . . . 197 E2
Peterborough Dr
 Bretton PE6 . . . . 196 E2
 Castor PE6 . . . . 196 D3
Peterborough High Sch
 PE3 . . . . 197 D2
Peterborough Mus & Art
 Gall* PE3 . . . . 197 F2
Peterborough Nene Valley
 Sta PE3 . . . . 197 F2
Peterborough Rd
 Castor PE5 . . . . 195 E1
 Crowland PE6 . . . . 232 B8
 Eye PE6 . . . . 205 F1
 Newborough PE6 . . . . 205 D8
 Peterborough PE7 . . . . . . 187 C3
 Wansford PE8 . . . . 194 A3
 Warmington PE8 . . . . 178 B4
 Whittlesey PE7 . . . . 187 B4
Peterborough Regional Coll
 PE1 . . . . 198 B5
Peterborough Regional Pool
 & Fitness Ctr PE1 . . . . . 198 B1
Petergate ■ PE7 . . . . 244 B4
Peter Goodin CI CB24 . . . 105 C2
Peterhouse CI
 Mildenhall IP28 . . . . 239 D4
 Peterborough PE3 . . . . . . 197 E3
 Stamford PE9 . . . . 244 B7
Peterhouse Coll CB2 . . . . 246 A1
Peterhouse Cres PE15 . . 243 E4
Peterhouse Dr CB88 . . . . 111 A2
Peterhouse Tech Pk CB1 .66 A4
Petersfield ☑ CB1 . . . . . . 246 C2
Petersfield CE Prim Sch
 CB1 . . . . 246 C2
Petersfield Rd CB22 . . . . . .17 D8
Petingo CI CB8 . . . . 110 D7
Pettis Rd PE7 . . . . 143 E6
Pettit Rd PE7 . . . . 142 A1
Pettits CI CB23 . . . . .66 F4
Pettitt's CI CB23 . . . . 102 C2
Pettitt's La CB23 . . . . 102 C1
Pettitt's St PE13 . . . . 245 E7
Petts La CB10 . . . . .19 E1
Petty Cury CB2 . . . . 246 A2
Petworth St CB1 . . . . .84 A2
Peverel CI CB3 . . . . .84 D3
Peverel Rd CB5 . . . . .84 D3
Peveril Rd PE1 . . . . 197 F6
Peyton Ave PE15 . . . . 243 B6
Peyton CI PE15 . . . . 223 A5
Pheasant Gr PE4 . . . . 204 B1
Pheasant Rise CB3 . . . . . . 102 A3
Pheasant Way PE7 . . . . . . 181 D5
Philip Gdns PE19 . . . . .74 F2
Philippa CI CB6 . . . . 240 E7
Philipps CI
 Exning CB8 . . . . 110 B8
 Newmarket CB8 . . . . 110 D4
Phillips Ave SG8 . . . . .5 C8
Phillips Chase PE15 . . . . . 243 C4
Phillips Ct PE4 . . . . 244 C4
Phillips' Fen Dro CB7 . . . 219 B6
Phoenix Rd CB9 . . . . .24 A5
Phoenix Sch PE2 . . . . 186 B4
Phoenix Way PE6 . . . . .74 E6
Phorpres CI PE7 . . . . 186 D3
Phorpres Houses PE2 . . . 186 F4
Phorpres Way PE7 . . . . . . 186 E4
Pickards Way PE13 . . . . . 245 A6
Pickle Fen Dro PE16 . . . . 215 E6
Picknage Rd SG8 . . . . .7 A2
PIDLEY 155 E8
Pidley Hill PE28 . . . . 208 A8
Pidley Sheep La PE28 . . . 155 F7
Pieces La CB25 . . . . 106 B8
Pieces Terr CB25 . . . . 106 B7
Pierce Ct PE8 . . . . 178 C3
Pierce La CB21 . . . . .66 F5
Pigeons CI SG8 . . . . .31 C2
Pightle CI
 Harston CB22 . . . . .47 D2
 Royston SG8 . . . . .5 C7
Pightle The
 Bottisham CB25 . . . . .86 E6
 Grafham PE28 . . . . 116 A7
 Haverhill CB9 . . . . .24 A8
Pig La PE27 . . . . 144 B5
Pike's Wlk CB1 . . . . 246 B3
Piketts CI PE7 . . . . 189 D7
Pilgrims CI CB10 . . . . .18 D4
Pilgrims Way CB6 . . . . 240 A3
PILSGATE 230 C4
Pilton CI ☑ PE4 . . . . 204 F2
Pinder CI PE29 . . . . 118 F7
Pine Gr CB24 . . . . 122 E3
Pines Ind Est The CB8 . . . 131 F4
Pines The CB21 . . . . .66 E6
Pine Tree CI PE1 . . . . 198 B8
Pine Trees Ave IP28 . . . . 239 E4
Pine View CB24 . . . . 126 A7
Pinewood Ave
 Whittlesey PE7 . . . . 189 E7
 Wittering PE8 . . . . 230 B1
Pinfold La
 Godmanchester PE29 . . . 141 F1
 ■ Somersham PE28 . . . 208 B8
 Stamford PE9 . . . . 244 A5
Pinfold Rd PE14 . . . . 236 E1
Pingle Bank PE7 . . . . 177 A4
Pingle CI PE7 . . . . 189 C7
Pingle Dro CB6 . . . . 216 E6
Pingle La
 Haddenham CB6 . . . . 210 B8
 Northborough PE6 . . . . . . 231 F6
Pingle The PE6 . . . . 231 F6
Pingle Wood & Cutting
 Nature Reserve* PE28 . 165 A8
Pinhoe Dr CB9 . . . . .23 C8
Pinkneys SG8 . . . . .8 D5
Pioneer Ct CB24 . . . . 104 B2
Pioneer Way PE6 . . . . 232 B1
Pipe La PE1 . . . . 198 B2
Piperell Way CB9 . . . . .24 A5
Pipers CI CB9 . . . . .24 C7
Pipistrelle CI PE19 . . . . . . .96 A2
Pipistrelle Ct ☑ PE4 . . . 204 C3
Pipit CI SG8 . . . . .5 E8
Pippin CI
 Offord Darcy PE19 . . . . . . 117 F1
 Over CB24 . . . . 208 D1
 ☑ Sutton CB6 . . . . 216 E1
Pippin Dr CB4 . . . . .84 C6
Pippin PI PE13 . . . . 245 E2
Pippin Wlk CB23 . . . . .81 A3
Pitfield CI PE28 . . . . 121 C5
Pitsdean Rd PE19 . . . . .57 A4
Pits La PE15 . . . . 243 D1
Pits The CB7 . . . . 213 A4
Pitneys PE4 . . . . 204 F1
Place Farm Com Prim Sch
 CB9 . . . . .23 F8
PLACE HOUSE 93 E6
Plains La CB6 . . . . 225 C3
Plaistow Way SG8 . . . . .7 E2
Plane Tree CI SG19 . . . . . .41 C6
Plank Dro PE6 . . . . 232 B8
Plantation Gate CB6 . . . . 210 E7
Plantation Rd CB22 . . . . . .33 A7
Plantation Dro PE15 . . . . 227 D5
Plash Dro PE13 . . . . 234 F4
Playles Yd SG8 . . . . .12 E5
Playsteds La CB23 . . . . . . .79 C4
Plough CI SG8 . . . . .12 F4
Plough Cres ■ PE7 . . . . . 189 C8
Plough La PE6 . . . . 232 D7
Plough Rd PE7 . . . . 189 D8
Plover CI PE16 . . . . 241 C5
Plover Dr PE15 . . . . 243 F5
Plover Rd PE7 . . . . 189 F8
Plowright CI PE15 . . . . . . 243 B3
Plumian Way CB21 . . . . . . .35 C5
Plumpton Ave IP28 . . . . . 239 C5
Plum Tree CI ■ CB8 . . . . .83 D7
Polecat La PE6 . . . . 150 E5
Poles Ct PE7 . . . . 189 D7
Pollards La IP28 . . . . 213 D7
Pond CI
 Eastwood End PE15 . . . . 223 B6
 Pidley cum Fenton PE28 . 165 D1
 The Stukeleys PE29 . . . . 140 F5
PONDERSBRIDGE 220 D7
Pond Gn CB7 . . . . 211 E1
Pond La CB6 . . . . 218 A6
Pond The CB6 . . . . 210 A7
Ponsonby Dr PE2 . . . . 186 D8
Pont's Hill CB6 . . . . 242 D5
Pooley Way PE7 . . . . 181 D6
Pools Rd CB6 . . . . 210 D8
Pool Way CB5 . . . . .84 C2
Poorsfield Rd ☑ CB25 . . 106 A7
Poor's Land SG8 . . . . .6 D4
Pope Rd PE19 . . . . .74 E4
Popes Ct ☑ CB9 . . . . .24 C5
Popes La
 Thetford CB8 . . . . 211 B7
 Warboys PE28 . . . . 164 E4
Pope's La PE13 . . . . 238 A2
Pope Way PE11 . . . . 197 E8
Popham CI PE19 . . . . 174 A3
Pophams Eau* PE14 . . . 229 C7
Poplar Ave PE1 . . . . 198 C8
Poplar CI
 Great Gransden SG19 . . . .58 D4
 Great Shelford CB22 . . . . .49 A5
 Haverhill CB9 . . . . .38 D1
 Huntingdon PE29 . . . . 141 E7
 March PE15 . . . . 243 C5
 Royston SG8 . . . . .5 E7
Poplar Dr SG8 . . . . .5 E7
Poplar Dro CB6 . . . . 242 F8
Poplar Farm CI SG8 . . . . . .12 D4
Poplar Rd CB24 . . . . 104 B3
Poplars CI CB25 . . . . 130 B2
Poplars The
 Bluntisham/Colne PE28 . . 208 C6
 Stukeley PE29 . . . . 140 F5
Poplar Way CB22 . . . . .49 C4
Popple Dro PE13 . . . . 235 A8
Poppy CI
 Ramsey St Mary's PE26. . 220 D3
 Yaxley PE7 . . . . 182 A2
Poppy Fields ☑ CB7 . . . . 212 B5
Poppyfields Ave PE15 . . . 224 B4
Porch CI PE29 . . . . 141 F1
Porson Ct CB2 . . . . .64 E4
Porson Rd CB2 . . . . .64 D5
Portchester CI PE2 . . . . . 187 F5
Porters Yd PE16 . . . . 241 C6
Port La PE5 . . . . 195 E1
Portland Ave PE1 . . . . 197 F7
Portland Gn CB88 . . . . 110 E3
Portland PI
 Cambridge CB1 . . . . 246 C3
 Whittlesey PE7 . . . . 189 E6
Portland Rd CB88 . . . . 110 E3
Portman Ct PE15 . . . . 197 C4
Portobello La CB22 . . . . . .32 E7
Portugal PI CB2 . . . . 246 A3
Portugal St CB5 . . . . 246 A3
Portway SG8 . . . . .14 E7
Portway Rd CB23 . . . . .81 A1
Post Office La ☑ PE13 . . 245 C5
Post St PE29 . . . . 141 E2
Potter's La CB7 . . . . 240 D3
Potters Way PE1 . . . . 198 B1
Pott Hall Rd IP28 . . . . 213 E6
Potton End PE19 . . . . .77 E3
Potton Rd
 Everton SG19 . . . . .40 C3
 Fenstanton PE28 . . . . 120 C3
 Gamlingay Great Heath
 SG19 . . . . .39 A4
 Gamlingay SG19 . . . . .41 D3
 Guilden Morden SG8 . . . . .10 F6
 Hilton PE28 . . . . .99 B8
 St Neots PE19 . . . . .74 F2
 Wrestlingworth SG19 . . . . .25 B4
Potton Wood* SG19 . . . . .25 A8
Poulter Ave PE2 . . . . 187 D5
Poulter's Dro PE14. . . . . . 229 D5
Pound CI
 Bottisham CB25 . . . . .86 E7
 Burwell CB25 . . . . 130 B2
 Hail Weston PE19 . . . . . . .95 B1
 Spaldwick PE28 . . . . 137 F6
Pound Gn SG8 . . . . .10 F5
Pound Hill CB6 . . . . .83 C3
Pound Hill CI PE27. . . . . . 144 F5
Pound La
 Isleham CB7 . . . . 213 A5
 Kimbolton PE28 . . . . 113 F4
 Sutton CB6 . . . . 216 E2
 ■ Willingham CB24 . . . . 209 A1
Pound Rd
 Chatteris PE16 . . . . 241 B6
 Hemingford Grey PE28 . . 143 D1
 Ramsey PE26 . . . . 172 A4
Pound The PE27 . . . . 144 A5
Pound Way CB25 . . . . 108 B2
Powell CI CB23 . . . . .61 D5
Powis PI ☑ PE19 . . . . .74 F1
Pratt Ave PE4 . . . . 204 F2
Pratt St ☑ PE13 . . . . 212 B4
Prentice CI CB24 . . . . 123 F2
Presses CI PE28 . . . . 208 C5
Preston CI CB23 . . . . .61 D5
Pretoria Rd CB4 . . . . 246 C4
Priam's Way CB22 . . . . . . .49 B4
PRICKWILLOW 219 B5
Prickwillow Drainage Engine
 Mus* CB7 . . . . 219 B5

Prickwillow Rd
Ely CB7 .... 240 F5
Isleham CB7 ....212 F7
Soham CB7 .... 219 D3
Priestgate **4** PE1 .... 198 A2
Priest La CB24 ......209 A1
Priests Meadow Ct CB6 . 240 C5
Primary Ct CB4 ......84 B5
Primrose Cl SG8 ......14 C6
Primes Cl CB22 ....29 D7
Primrose Cl
Cambridge CB1 ......66 A5
Peterborough PE1 .... 198 A8
Ramsey St Mary's PE26 .220 D3
Primrose Dr PE7.....181 F7
Primrose Farm Rd CB1...86 E2
Primrose Hill
Doddington PE15.....222 E5
Haverhill CB9.........23 F7
Little Gransden SG19.....58 E3
Primrose La
Huntingdon PE29.....141 E5
5 Soham CB7........212 B5
Waterbeach CB25 .... 106 A8
Primrose St CB4.......83 D4
Primrose View SG8......5 F5
Prince Andrew's Cl **1** SG8 .5 D5
Prince Cl PE19..........74 B5
Prince of Wales Cl PE13 .245 D8
Princes Cl CB21 ....53 C1
Princes Dr PE19 ....75 A6
Princes Gate PE1.....198 B4
Princes Gdns PE1.....198 B4
Princes Mews SG8 ......5 C6
Prince South Rd PE13....245 C4
Princes Rd
Peterborough PE2 ....187 A7
Stamford PE9........244 B6
Princess Ave PE15 ....243 C2
Princess Ct CB1 ......246 B1
Princess Dr CB22 ......49 F1
Princess of Wales Hospl
CB6................240 E7
Prince's St
Huntingdon PE29.....141 D4
Peterborough PE1....198 A4
Ramsey PE26........172 A8
Princess Way
Haverhill CB9.........23 E8
Newmarket CB8.......110 E4
Prince St PE13........245 D5
Prince Wlk PE15......243 D4
Prince William Ct **8** CB4 .83 C4
Prince William Way CB22 .32 F6
Pringle Ct PE28.......151 D4
Pringle Way PE28.....151 D4
Prins Ave PE13 ....245 D7
Prins Ct **3** PE13 .....245 D7
Prior's Cl CB24 ....104 B4
Priors Ct CB6.........240 B5
Prior's Ct **5** CB6 .....216 E2
Priors Gate PE4 ......204 A4
Priors Rd
Hemingford Grey PE28 ...143 C1
Whittlesey PE7 ......189 C7
Priory Ave
Haverhill CB9.........23 F7
Swavesey CB24.......122 E5
Priory Cl
Burwell CB25.........130 B2
Ickleton CB10 ....18 A3
7 Market Deeping PE6 .231 F8
Royston SG8 ....5 E6
Priory Dro CB25 ......129 D7
Priory Gdns
Peterborough PE7....184 F3
Stamford PE9........244 D5
Waterside CB7........213 A5
Priory Gr PE29.......141 E5
Priory Hill PE19.......75 B7
Priory Hill Rd PE19 ....75 A7
Priory Jun Sch PE19....75 A6
Priory La
Huntingdon PE29.....141 E5
Royston SG8 ....5 D5
St Neots PE19.........74 E5
Priory Mews
St Ives PE27.........144 A3
St Neots PE19.........74 E6
Priory Park Inf Sch PE19..74 F6
Priory Rd
Cambridge CB5........84 A3
Holywell-cum-Needingworth
PE27..............208 A3
Horningsea CB25.....106 A1
Huntingdon PE29.....141 E5
Needingworth PE27...144 F5
Peterborough PE3....197 E3
Stamford PE9........244 D5
St Ives PE27.........144 A2
St Neots PE19.........74 E6
Priory St **3** CB4......83 C4
Priory The PE19.......74 F6
Priory Wlk CB23 ....79 C3
Proby Cl PE7.........181 D5
Prospect Pl PE13 .....245 C3
Prospect Rd PE15.....243 B5
Prospect Row
Cambridge CB1 ......246 C2
9 St Neots PE19.....74 F5
Prospect Way PE16....241 C6
Prospero Pl PE2......186 F6
Prospero Way PE29...141 F7
Provence Pl **2** PE13 ...245 A5
Provence Rd PE29 ....141 A6

Providence Cl **16** PE28 ..215 C1
Providence Pl PE15 ....224 B4
Providence Way CB25...127 A1
Pryor Cl CB24 ....105 D2
Puddingbag Dro PE7 ...190 D5
Pudding Bag La PE9....230 C4
Pudding La SG8 ....7 A1
Puddock Hill PE28 ....165 A8
Puddock Rd
Ramsey PE28........221 F1
Warboys PE28.......165 A8
Pudgell The SG8 ....7 E2
Puffin La PE7........181 D8
Puma La
2 Hardwick CB23.....81 A3
4 Stretham CB6.....210 F5
Purbeck Cl PE13 ......245 A4
Purbeck Rd CB2 ....65 A5
Purley Rd **1** CB23 .....79 A4
Purls Bridge PE15.....224 B2
Purl's Bridge Dro PE15..224 B3
Putney Hill Rd CB7 ....213 A5
Pycecroft PE1........198 B6
Pye Terr CB4 ....84 A4
Pyhill PE1...........197 B8
PYMOOR.............224 E1
Pymore (Pymoor) La
CB6................224 E1
Pyrecroft CB2 ....224 E1
Pyrethrum Way **2** CB24 .209 A1

Q

Quadrangle The PE28 .. 208 D7
Quadrant The
Royston SG8 ....5 C8
St Ives PE27.........144 B3
Quail Wlk **8** SG8 ......5 E8
Quainton Cl CB25......84 D3
Quaker Cl PE28 ......153 C6
Quaker La PE13.......245 E3
Quaker's Bro PE27....191 F5
Quaker's La CB9.......24 A7
Quaker Way PE16.....241 C5
Quanea Dro CB7......240 F1
Quarry La
Haslingfield CB23 .....47 B4
Maxey PE6..........231 C6
Swaffham Bulbeck CB25 ..108 B1
Quay Ct PE27.........144 A3
Quay Hill CB6........242 E4
Quayside
Cambridge CB1 ......246 A3
Chatteris PE16.......241 C6
Ely CB7.............240 E3
Quay The PE27.......144 A3
QUEEN ADELAIDE 218 D4
Queen Adelaide Way
CB7................240 E3
Queen Ann Terr CB1 ..246 B1
Queen Charlotte Mews
PE1................198 A6
Queen Edith Prim Sch
CB1................65 C4
Queen Edith's Way CB1..65 D4
Queen Eleanor Cl PE7...176 A8
Queen Eleanor Tech Coll
PE9................244 B6
Queen Elizabeth Dr
PE13...............245 D3
Queen Emma Wlk CB6..240 E6
Queenholme Way CB24 .209 C2
Queen Mary Cl PE26 ...172 A6
Queensberry Rd CB8...111 A3
Queens Cl
Balsham CB21........52 F2
Harston CB22.........48 A3
St Ives PE27.........144 A5
Queen's Cl
Holme PE7...........176 F4
1 Over CB24.......208 D1
Queens' Coll CB3 .....246 A2
Queens Ct
Eaton Socon PE19 .....74 B3
7 Haverhill CB9......23 E8
Queens Dr PE29......141 F5
Queen's Dr
Mildenhall IP28......239 B4
1 Haverhill CB9......24 A3
Queens Drive Inf Sch
PE1................198 A5
Queen's Drive W PE1 ..198 A5
Queensgate Ctr PE1...198 A2
Queens Gdns PE1.....198 A5
Queen's Gdns PE1....198 A5
Queens' La CB22......246 A2
Queen's Marlborough Coll
CB8................64 E7
Queen's Mdw CB1......65 F7
Queens Rd
Littleport CB6.......242 B5
Peterborough PE3....187 B7
Royston SG8 ....5 C7
Somersham PE28.....215 C1
Wisbech PE13.......245 C4
Queen's Rd CB3 ....64 C8
Queens St CB15......243 D6
Queens Sq CB9........24 A8
Queens St
March PE15.........243 D6
Stamford PE9........244 B6
Withersfield CB9......38 C4
Queen St
Cowlinge CB8.........73 C1
Haverhill CB9.........24 A8
Newmarket CB8.......111 B3
2 Peterborough PE1 ..198 A2

Queen St *continued*
Whittlesey PE7 ......189 D7
Wisbech PE13 ....245 C6
Yaxley PE7..........181 F6
Queens View CB8 .....110 A8
Queensway
Cambridge CB2 ....64 E6
Chatteris PE16.......241 D5
Exning CB8..........110 B8
Haverhill CB9.........23 E8
Mildenhall IP28......239 B4
Royston SG8 ....5 D7
Sawston CB22........32 E8
Soham CB7..........212 B4
St Neots PE19........74 F7
Queens Way CB24.....103 D6
Queens Wlk PE2 ......186 F8
Queen's Wlk PE9 .....244 A5
Quendon Pl CB9.......24 B8
Quickset Rd CB11......9 B5
Quidditch La CB23.....79 A4
Quince Rd CB23 ....41 A3
Quinion Cl PE7.......189 F6
Quinton Garth PE3....197 C5
Quorn Cl PE6........205 C8
Quy Ct CB25..........86 A6
Quy Rd CB25..........86 B8

R

Raceys CB14 ....236 D6
Racey's Cl PE14.......236 D6
Rachel Cl **1** CB5 ......84 E4
Rackham CE Prim Sch The
CB6................217 E1
Rackham Cl CB4.......83 C4
Radcliffe Cl **9** PE9 ....244 B5
Radcliffe Rd PE9 .....244 A5
Radegund Rd CB1......65 B7
Radegunds CB22.......32 C5
Radford Cl PE8.......230 C1
Radwinter Rd CB10....21 B1
RAF Molesworth PE28...147 C8
RAF Witchford Display of
Memorabilia CB6....217 F1
RAF Wyton PE28......143 A8
Ragdale Cl PE1.......198 E7
Railway Cl CB25......109 B8
Railway La PE16......241 C5
Railway Rd PE13......245 C3
Railway St CB1........65 F7
Railworld Ex Ctr & Mus
PE2................197 F1
Raine Ave CB9.........23 D8
Raleigh Cl PE19........74 B3
Raleigh Way PE3......197 B6
RALINGHAM HALL.....229 E6
Ramnoth Jun Sch PE13..245 D4
Ramnoth Rd PE13.....245 D4
Rampart The CB6.....210 A6
Ramper Rd CB24......123 A3
Rampley La PE19.......95 F2
Rampleys The PE28 ...143 D2
Ramply Cl PE19.......95 F1
RAMPTON...........125 F4
Rampton Drift
Oakington/Longstanton
CB24..............124 B2
Westwick CB24......103 A8
Rampton End CB24 ....209 A1
Rampton Rd
Cottenham CB24.....125 B4
Longstanton CB24....124 A2
Oakington/Longstanton
CB24..............123 F1
Willingham CB24......124 B7
Ramsden Sq CB4.......84 A7
RAMSEY.............172 B6
Ramsey Abbey Gatehouse
PE26...............172 C7
Ramsey Adult Ed Ctr
PE26...............172 C6
RAMSEY FORTY FOOT . 221 C2
RAMSEY HEIGHTS 171 A7
Ramsey Hollow Dro
PE26...............173 B7
Ramsey Hts Nature Reserve
PE26...............170 E6
Ramsey Jun Sch PE26...172 A7
Ramsey Leisure Ctr
PE26...............172 D6
RAMSEY MERESIDE ...221 A4
Ramsey Rd
Benwick PE15.......221 F4
Ely CB7.............240 E6
Kings Ripton PE28....153 C5
Old Hurst PE28.......154 D6
Peterborough PE26...221 C2
St Ives PE27.........143 F7
Upwood & The Raveleys
PE26..............171 D2
Warboys PE28.......164 E6
Whittlesey PE7 ......187 E4
Ramsey Rural Mus
PE26...............172 D7
RAMSEY ST MARY'S...220 D3
Ramsey Way PE27 ....187 F6
Ramshill Cotts PE6....203 A2
Randalls La CB24......208 D1
Rangefield PE2.......185 E4
Range The CB7.......240 C4
Ransome's Cl PE14....236 E2
Ransonmoor Dro PE15..222 D7
Ransonmoor Grange
PE26...............222 F8
Raptor Foundation The
PE28...............155 E4

Rasen Ct **2** PE1......198 D3
Ratcliffe Ct PE1......198 D7
Ratfords Yd CB21 ......68 A8
Rathmore Cl CB1......65 A6
Rathmore Ct CB1 .....65 A6
Ravel Cl PE9.........244 A6
Raveley Fen Rd PE28...162 D8
Raveley Rd PE28......161 F6
Raven Cl
Mildenhall IP28......239 D4
St Neots PE19........75 B7
Ravenhill Dr PE15.....243 C3
Ravenscourt **6** PE27...208 A3
Ravenscroft PE16.....241 C6
Ravens Ct CB24.......240 C5
Ravensdale
Landbeach CB25.....105 D7
Stilton PE7..........175 F7
RAVENSTHORPE......197 C6
Ravensthorpe Prim Sch
PE3................197 C7
Ravensworth Gdns CB1..65 A7
Rawlyn Cl CB5.........84 D3
Rawlyn Ct CB5.........84 D3
Rawlyn Rd CB5........84 D3
Rayes La CB8........111 A4
Rayleigh Cl CB2.......64 E5
Raymond St **14** PE13 ..245 C4
Rayner Ave PE2.......187 E5
Rayner's Ct SG8 ....30 D1
Rays Ct PE15.........223 B6
Ray's Dro PE26.......220 B1
Rayson Way CB5.......84 D3
REACH..............130 C1
Reach Dro PE7.......189 B5
Reaches The PE4.....204 C3
Reach Rd
Burwell CB25.......109 B8
Reach CB25.........129 F1
Read's Sch CB6......210 F5
Ream Cl PE19..........74 E2
Recreation Cl CB24....105 D1
Recreation Ground Rd
PE9................244 B6
Recreation Rd CB9......23 F7
Recreation Way IP28...239 C4
Rectors Way **3** PE4...204 F2
Rectory Cl
Brampton PE28......140 E2
Great Paxton PE19....96 E4
Oakington/Longstanton
CB24..............123 F1
Rectory Dr PE15......243 D1
Rectory Farm Cl PE28..162 C1
Rectory Farm Rd CB1...86 F2
Rectory Fields CB6....216 E3
Rectory Gdns
Glinton PE6.........203 E8
Godmanchester PE29 ..141 F2
Peterborough PE7....187 B7
Wisbech PE13.......245 E6
Rectory La
Abbots Ripton PE28...152 B8
Ashdon CB10 ....21 A1
Etton PE6...........231 E5
Fowlmere SG8........15 E8
Kingston CB23 ....61 B3
Peakirk PE6.........206 B2
Somersham PE28.....215 B1
Southoe & Midloe PE19..95 D6
St Ives PE27.........142 F5
St Neots PE19........117 E2
Rectory Rd
Bluntisham/Colne PE28..208 D5
Duxford CB22........17 E8
Newton PE13.........238 B5
Outwell PE14........236 F2
Rectory Way PE7......175 F7
Red Barn PE7........191 E6
Redbridge PE4.......204 A6
Redcaps La CB4......217 E6
Redcot Gdns **8** PE9 ..244 B6
Redcott Gdns PE4....244 B5
Red Cross La CB2......65 B3
Red Dock La CB8.......73 F1
Redebourne La PE26...171 F4
Red Fen Rd CB6......210 F7
Redfern Cl CB4........83 E6
Redgate Ct PE1.......198 E7
Redgate Rd
Girton CB3..........84 E8
Tydd St Giles PE13...238 C8
Red Hall Cl CB22 ......48 E8
Red Hill La CB22......48 E8
Redhouse Gdns **3** CB7..212 B3
Redit La CB7.........211 E1
Redlands La CB22 .....49 F8
Redlands Rd CB23....101 E5
Red Lion Cl PE28.....150 F4
Red Lion La CB6......216 E1
Red Lion St **12** PE9 ..244 B5
RED LODGE...........49 A7
Redman Cl CB7.......240 F7
Redmile Wlk PE1.....198 D8
Redmoor Bank PE14...235 F4
Redmoor La PE14......73 F4
Redmoor La PE14.....235 F5
Redroofs CB6.........211 B7
Red Roofs CB6.......210 B8
Redshank Cl
Haverhill CB9.........23 F8
6 Soham CB7.......212 A5
Whittlesey PE7 ......201 A1
Redwell St PE27......143 E5
Redwing Cl PE2.......187 E7

Redwing Dr
Royston SG8 ....5 E8
5 Wisbech PE14.....245 D2
Redwing Pl **2** PE19....75 B7
Redwing Rise SG8 ......5 E8
Redwongs Way PE29...141 D7
Reed Cl
Cambridge CB2 ....64 E1
Chatteris PE16.......241 C3
Reedland Way PE7....186 C1
Reedmace Cl PE6.....205 C8
Reeds La CB9..........24 A8
Reedway PE1.........198 E7
Reeve Hill SG8 ....8 A6
Reeves Pightle SG8......7 F3
Reeves Way PE1 .....198 D5
Regal Dr CB7.........212 C3
Regal La CB7.........212 C3
Regal Pl PE2.........187 A8
Regal Rd PE13.......245 B2
Regatta Cl CB5 ....85 B4
Regency Sq CB1.......65 A7
Regency Way PE3 ....197 E1
Regent Ave PE15.....243 D5
Regent Cl PE19........74 B4
Regent Pl **1** CB7 .....212 B3
Regents Ct CB8......110 F3
Regent St CB2 ....246 B1
Regent Terr CB2......246 B1
Reidy Gdns **2** PE7 ...189 D8
Reilly Way CB1........65 F7
Rembrandt Way PE27...144 A7
Renoir Cl PE27.......144 A7
Resbury Ct CB22......50 A1
Retreat The **8** PE6...231 C7
Reubens Rd CB25.....105 C7
Reynolds Cl PE27.....144 A7
Reynold's Cl CB9......38 D1
Reynolds Ct **3** PE19...74 C6
Reynolds Dr PE19......95 F1
Reynolds' Dro CB24...124 D3
Rhee Lane Dro PE28...208 E8
Rhee Mdw CB22........29 E7
Rhees The PE28......208 D6
Rhine Ave PE2........186 B8
Rhoda Pk PE15.......222 C7
Rhone Pl **8** PE13....245 E3
Rhugarve Gdns CB21...35 D2
Rhymers Gate PE28...142 F5
Ribble Cl PE27.......144 B6
Ribe Ct CB6..........240 C4
Ribes Cl PE7.........186 D3
Ribston Way CB4.......84 C6
Richard Foster Rd PE28..64 F6
Richards Cl PE15.....243 B5
Richardson Way PE7...189 E7
Richard Young Cl PE13..245 C8
Richmond Ave
March PE15.........243 C3
Peterborough PE4....204 C2
Richmond Cl
Huntingdon PE29.....141 E8
3 St Neots PE19......74 F1
Richmond Ct CB1.....245 A4
Richmond Field PE13...237 E2
Richmond Rd CB4......83 D5
Richmond Terr CB1....246 A4
Richmond Way **6** PE13..238 B2
Rickard Cl CB1........65 E6
Rickards CB22.........32 B4
Rickwood Cl CB6.....216 C5
Rickyard The SG7......2 D3
Riddiford Cres PE28...140 C2
Riddy Cl CB22.........48 B5
Riddy La CB23.........60 C5
Rideaway PE28.......143 D2
Ridgefield Prim Sch CB1..65 C7
Ridge The PE7.......186 D1
Ridgeway
Papworth Everard CB23..99 A4
Perry PE28..........115 D2
Peterborough PE7....187 B8
St Neots PE19........74 F2
Ridgeway The CB21....35 E2
Ridley Hall Rd CB3.....64 C8
Rigg Cl PE13.........245 B3
Rightwell **1** PE3.....197 A6
Rightwell E PE3......197 A5
Rightwell W PE3.....197 A5
Riley Cl PE7.........181 D6
Ringers La PE13......238 B8
Ring Fort Rd CB4......83 D7
RING'S END..........234 F1
Ringstead Rd PE4.....204 B3
Ringwood PE3........196 F3
Ringwood Cl PE26....142 C1
Ripon Cl PE4.........204 B3
Rippons Dro PE15.....231 F7
Risby PE3............197 B8
Riseholme PE2.......185 E3
Rivar Pl CB1..........48 B8
Rivendale PE4........204 B2
River Bank CB7.......128 C6
Riverbank Cl
Guyhirn PE13........234 F2
2 Market Deeping PE6..231 F8
River Cl
2 Haverhill PE15...222 A5
Little Paxton PE19.....95 F1
Mepal CB6..........216 E4
Riverdown PE15......243 F5
River Dr PE15........245 C6
River Dro PE7........191 C5
River End PE28.......178 C8
Rivergate **3** PE1.....198 A1
Rivergate Sh Ctr PE1...198 A1

River La
Brampton PE28 . . . . **140** E1
Cambridge CB5 . . . . **84** A3
Elton PE8 . . . . **178** C8
Fordham CB7 . . . . **212** E1
Great Paxton PE19 . . . .**96** D3
Haslingfield CB23 . . . . **47** C5
Peterborough PE3 . . . . **197** F2
River Mdw PE28 . . . . **142** F3
Rivermill Gall * PE19 . . . . . **74** C2
River Pl PE27 . . . . **144** A4
River Rd
Eaton Socon PE19 . . . . **74** C4
Kimbolton PE28 . . . . **114** B7
West Walton PE14 . . . . . . **238** D4
Riverside
Cambridge CB5 . . . . **84** B3
II Market Deeping PE6 . . **231** F8
Riverside Cl
Ely CB7 . . . . **219** B5
Mildenhall IP28 . . . . **239** B4
Whittlesey PE7 . . . . **189** D6
Riverside Ct CB1 . . . . **246** B4
Riverside Gdns
Parson Drove PE13 . . . . . . **234** C7
Peterborough PE3 . . . . **197** D1
Riverside KS2 Ctr PE2 . . **186** D8
Riverside Mead PE2 . . . . **187** B8
Riverside Mid Sch IP28 . . **239** A4
Riverside Pl CB5 . . . . **84** A3
Riverside Rd PE29 . . . . . . **141** E4
Riverside Spinney PE8 . . **194** A3
Riverside Way PE13 . . . . **245** B3
Riverside Wlk
Ely CB7 . . . . **240** E3
Moulton CB8 . . . . **112** F6
Riversmead PE19 . . . . **74** E6
River Terr
II St Neots PE19 . . . . **74** E5
Wisbech PE13 . . . . **245** A8
Rivey Cl CB21 . . . . **35** D3
Rivey Way CB21 . . . . **35** D2
Roan Wlk **II** SG8 . . . . **5** E6
Robbs Wlk PE27 . . . . **144** A3
Robden Ct PE2 . . . . **197** E1
Robert Arkenstall Prim Sch
CB6 . . . . **210** A6
Robert Ave
Peterborough PE1 . . . . **197** F8
I Somersham PE28 . . . . . **215** C1
Robert Jennings Cl CB4 . . **84** A6
Robert May Cl CB1 . . . . **65** D7
Robert Rayner Cl PE2 . . **186** D6
Roberts Cl PE19 . . . . **74** B2
Robertson Dr PE28 . . . . . . **152** E1
Robertson Way PE29 . . . **152** E1
Robin Cl
Bar Hill CB23 . . . . **102** C4
Haverhill CB9 . . . . **24** C7
Mildenhall IP28 . . . . **239** D4
Robingoodfellow's La
PE15 . . . . **243** C6
Robin Goodfellow's La
PE15 . . . . **243** D5
Robin Hood Cl PE3 . . . . . . **196** F2
Robin Mews **II** PE14 . . . . **245** D2
Robins Cl
Ely CB6 . . . . **240** B5
II Isleham CB7 . . . . **213** A5
Peterborough PE2 . . . . **186** E8
Robins Field PE8 . . . . **194** A4
Robins' La CB23 . . . . **101** F5
Robinson Coll CB3 . . . . **83** B1
Robinson Ct CB22 . . . . **49** A4
Robinson Way CB2 . . . . . . **65** A3
Robins Wood PE8 . . . . . . **194** A4
Robshaw Cl **II** PE15 . . . . **243** E4
Rocester Way SG8 . . . . **5** D8
Rochford Wlk **II** PE13 . . **245** E5
Rochfort Ave CB8 . . . . . . **110** E5
Rockall Cl CB9 . . . . **24** D7
Rockingham Gr PE4 . . . . . **204** C2
Rockingham Rd PE28 . . . . **168** B3
Rockingham Way CB8 . . . . **90** D8
Rockmill End CB24 . . . . . **209** A1
Rock Rd
Cambridge CB1 . . . . **65** A6
Peterborough PE1 . . . . **197** F6
Royston SG8 . . . . **5** C8
Stamford PE9 . . . . **244** B5
Rodham Rd PE15 . . . . **228** F5
Rodings The CB5 . . . . **84** E4
Rodney Rd PE29 . . . . **142** A6
Roedeer Cl CB1 . . . . **66** A7
Roe Gn PE19 . . . . **74** B5
Roe's Cl CB22 . . . . **32** F8
Roger's Cl CB23 . . . . **100** B4
Rogers End CB10 . . . . **21** B1
Rogers Rd CB25 . . . . **108** E6
Rogues La CB23 . . . . **99** D5
Roland Cl CB4 . . . . **83** E5
Rolfe Cl IP28 . . . . **213** C7
Rolleston Garth PE1 . . . . **198** C8
Rolls Cl PE7 . . . . **181** E7
Rollys La SG7 . . . . **2** D1
Roman Bank
Newton PE13 . . . . **238** B4
Stamford PE9 . . . . **244** A4
Roman Cl
Burwell CB25 . . . . **130** A2
Whittlesey PE7 . . . . **189** F8
Roman Courts CB4 . . . . . . **83** E8
Roman Dr PE28 . . . . **194** D2
Roman Drift CB23 . . . . **80** C1
Roman Hill CB23 . . . . **63** C4
Roman Way
Godmanchester PE29 . . . . **142** A1
Haverhill CB9 . . . . **24** D7

Roman Way *continued*
March PE15 . . . . **243** E6
Perry PE28 . . . . **115** D2
Stilton PE7 . . . . **176** A8
Roman Way Fst Sch SG8 . . . **5** D8
Romany Gdns PE2 . . . . . . **187** D5
Romney Cl PE27 . . . . **144** A7
Romney Ct **II** PE19 . . . . . . **74** C5
Romsey Mews CB1 . . . . **65** B7
Romsey Rd CB1 . . . . **65** C8
Romsey Terr CB1 . . . . **65** B7
ROMSEY TOWN **65** B8
Ronaldsway **II** PE15 . . . . **222** F5
Ronalds Way PE16 . . . . . . **241** C5
Rookery Cl
Great Chesterford CB10 . . **18** D3
St Ives PE27 . . . . **144** C4
Waterbeach CB25 . . . . . . **106** A8
Rookery Pl PE28 . . . . **121** C5
Rookery Rd PE19 . . . . **74** A1
Rookery The
Balsham CB21 . . . . **53** A2
Little Paxton PE19 . . . . **95** F2
II Newmarket CB8 . . . . . **111** A3
Peterborough PE2 . . . . **185** C7
Yaxley PE7 . . . . **181** D5
Rookery Way PE28 . . . . . . **121** B5
Rook Gr CB24 . . . . **209** A1
Rooks St CB24 . . . . **125** E4
Rookswood Rd PE15 . . . . **243** C4
Rookwood Way CB9 . . . . . . **24** A6
Rosary The CB24 . . . . **121** F5
Roscrea Terr PE29 . . . . . . **141** D4
Rose Ave PE2 . . . . **187** C2
Rosebay Gdns **II** CB7 . . . **212** B5
Roseberry Rd PE14 . . . . . **236** B5
Roseberry Way CB8 . . . . . **110** E5
Rose Cres CB2 . . . . **246** A3
Rose Croft PE28 . . . . **115** E2
Rose & Crown Rd CB24 . . **122** C3
Rose & Crown Yd **II**
CB24 . . . . **209** A1
Rose Ct PE7 . . . . **181** F7
Rosedale PE14 . . . . **236** E8
Rosedene Dr PE15 . . . . . . **243** D3
Rosefinch Cl CB9 . . . . **24** C7
Roseford Rd CB4 . . . . **83** D6
Rose Gn La **II** IP28 . . . . . **213** F8
Rose Hill CB9 . . . . **38** D5
Rose La
II Elm PE14 . . . . **236** A5
Great Chesterford CB10 . . **18** E2
Melbourn SG8 . . . . **14** C6
Roselea CB24 . . . . **104** C3
Rosemary Cl **II** PE28 . . . **214** A1
Rosemary Gdns PE1 . . . . **197** F8
Rosemary Greene Cl
CB23 . . . . **78** E2
Rosemary La
Cambridge CB1 . . . . **65** E7
Chatteris PE16 . . . . **241** B4
Sutton CB6 . . . . **216** C1
Rosemary Rd CB25 . . . . . **106** B7
Rosemeadows **II** PE28 . . **208** B8
Rose's Cl PE15 . . . . **243** D2
Rose Wlk
Royston SG8 . . . . **5** C7
Wisbech PE13 . . . . **245** A6
Wittering PE8 . . . . **230** B1
Rosewood Cl PE7 . . . . **181** E5
Rosie Maternity Hospl
CB2 . . . . **65** A3
Ross Cl CB9 . . . . **24** D6
Ross Peers Sports Ctr
CB7 . . . . **212** B3
Ross St CB1 . . . . **65** B8
Roswell View CB7 . . . . . . **240** E5
Rosyth Ave PE2 . . . . **185** D3
Rotherby Gr **II** PE1 . . . . **198** D7
Rotherwick Way CB1 . . . . . **65** C3
Rothleigh Rd **II** CB1 . . . . . **65** D5
Rothwell Way PE2 . . . . . . **186** C7
Round Church St CB2 . . . **246** A3
Roundhills View PE28 . . . **167** E8
Round Hills Way PE28 . . . **168** A5
Roundhouse Cl PE1 . . . . . **198** D3
Round House Cl CB23 . . . . **80** C2
Round House Com Prim Sch
The PE19 . . . . **75** C6
Roundhouse Dr PE28 . . . **115** D3
Round House Dro PE28 . . **222** A1
Rous Rd CB8 . . . . **111** B3
Rowan Ave
Peterborough PE1 . . . . **198** C6
Sawston CB22 . . . . **32** F6
Rowan Cl
Bottisham CB25 . . . . **86** F6
Haddenham CB6 . . . . **210** A5
Hanchet End CB9 . . . . **38** E1
Huntingdon PE29 . . . . **141** C5
Wisbech PE13 . . . . **245** F7
Rowans The
II Doddington/Wimblington
PE15 . . . . **223** A6
Milton CB24 . . . . **105** C1
Rowan Wlk IP28 . . . . **239** E5
Rowe Ave PE2 . . . . **186** D7
Rowell Cl
Haverhill CB9 . . . . **39** A2
Newborough PE6 . . . . **207** C1
Rowells The CB24 . . . . . . **125** C3
Rowell Wlk PE26 . . . . **172** A4
Rowland Ct PE4 . . . . **204** B5
Rowlands Cl CB22 . . . . **30** C5
Rowles Way CB24 . . . . . . **101** D8
Rowley Ct
Newmarket CB8 . . . . **110** C3
II Sturmer CB9 . . . . **24** E5

Rowley Dr CB8 . . . . **110** F4
Rowley Gdns CB25 . . . . . . **86** E6
Rowley Rd PE19 . . . . **75** B7
Rowlinson Way CB4 . . . . . **84** B3
Row The CB8 . . . . **110** F3
Row The CB6 . . . . **216** E1
Roxburgh Rd CB4 . . . . **83** E7
Royal Anglian Regiment Mus
The* CB22 . . . . **16** F8
Royal Cl **II** PE19 . . . . **74** B4
Royal Oak La PE28 . . . . . . **143** A2
Royal Palace Cl CB8 . . . . **110** D7
Royal Pl **II** PE13 . . . . **245** C4
Royce Cl PE7 . . . . **181** E6
Royce Ct PE27 . . . . **144** B7
Royce Rd
Alwalton PE7 . . . . **185** A4
Eastfield PE1 . . . . **198** D3
Royle Cl PE2 . . . . **186** C5
Royse Gr SG8 . . . . **5** D4
Roysia Mid Sch SG8 . . . . . . **5** D8
ROYSTON **5** B6
Royston Ave
Peterborough PE2 . . . . **186** C6
Spaldwick PE28 . . . . **137** F6
Royston & District Mus
SG8 . . . . **5** D4
Royston Hospl SG8 . . . . **5** D4
Royston La
Comberton CB23 . . . . **62** C3
Elmdon CB11 . . . . **9** C6
Royston Rd
Barley SG8 . . . . **6** F3
Caxton CB23 . . . . **59** F7
Duxford CB22 . . . . **32** C4
Foxton CB22 . . . . **30** A5
Harston CB22 . . . . **47** D1
Litlington SG8 . . . . **12** B1
Royston Sta SG8 . . . . **5** C7
Rubens Way PE27 . . . . . . **144** A7
Ruddles La PE28 . . . . **142** E6
Rudlands Cl **II** CB7 . . . . . **213** A5
Rudyard Gr PE4 . . . . **204** C7
Ruffles Rd CB9 . . . . **24** C7
Rupert Brooke Mus * CB2 **64** A3
Rushbrook Cl CB23 . . . . . . **59** F3
Rush Gr CB1 . . . . **66** A6
Rushington Cl PE27 . . . . **144** B5
Rushmere PE2 . . . . **185** F6
Rushmere Cl PE26 . . . . . **171** B1
Rushton Ave PE4 . . . . **204** A4
Ruskin Cl **II** CB9 . . . . **38** D1
Russel Cl PE26 . . . . **172** A8
Russell Ave PE15 . . . . . . **243** B6
Russell Cl
Steeple Morden SG8 . . . . . **11** B2
II Thorney PE6 . . . . **233** A3
Russell Ct
Cambridge CB2 . . . . **64** E7
St Neots PE19 . . . . **74** F6
Stamford PE9 . . . . **244** C3
Russell Hill PE8 . . . . **193** F6
Russell St
Cambridge CB2 . . . . **246** C1
Peterborough PE1 . . . . **197** F3
St Neots PE19 . . . . **74** E6
Wisbech PE13 . . . . **245** C6
Russet Cl PE27 . . . . **144** B5
Russet Ct CB4 . . . . **84** A8
Russets The PE14 . . . . . . **236** E2
Russett Ave PE27 . . . . . . **208** A2
Russet Way SG8 . . . . **14** C6
Russet Wlk **II** CB23 . . . . . **81** A3
Rustat Ave CB1 . . . . **65** A7
Rustat Cl CB1 . . . . **65** A6
Rustat Rd CB1 . . . . **65** A6
Ruster Way PE7 . . . . **186** B2
Ruston Ct PE16 . . . . **241** D4
Rustons Rd PE14 . . . . **236** F7
Rustons The CB22 . . . . **32** D1
Rusts La PE28 . . . . **150** F4
Ruther Cl PE2 . . . . **186** D8
Rutherford Rd CB2 . . . . . . **64** E4
Rutland Cl
Cambridge CB4 . . . . **83** D6
St Ives PE27 . . . . **143** F7
Rutland Ct **II** CB9 . . . . **23** B7
Rutland Dr PE28 . . . . **120** B1
Rutland Rd PE9 . . . . **244** D7
Rutland Terr PE9 . . . . **244** A4
Rutland Way PE15 . . . . . . **224** B4
Rutner Cl PE2 . . . . **186** D8
Rycroft Ave
II Deeping St James
PE6 . . . . **231** F8
St Neots PE19 . . . . **74** E6
Rydal Cl PE29 . . . . **141** B6
Rydal Ct PE4 . . . . **204** E3
Rye Cl
Littleport CB6 . . . . **242** C3
II St Neots PE19 . . . . **74** F1
Rye Ct CB8 . . . . **110** E5
Rye Gdns CB6 . . . . **218** A6
Ryhall Rd PE9 . . . . **244** D6

S

Saberton Cl CB25 . . . . . . **106** B8
Sable Cl CB1 . . . . **66** A7
Sackville Cl CB4 . . . . **83** E7
Sackville St CB8 . . . . **111** B4
Sackville Way CB23 . . . . . . **79** C4
Sacred Heart RC Prim Sch
PE3 . . . . **119** F6
Sacrewell Farm & Ctry Ctr *
PE8 . . . . **194** C5

Saddle Ct PE4 . . . . **197** E8
Saddlers Cl PE6 . . . . **203** E8
Saddlers Pl SG8 . . . . **5** C7
Saddlers Way **II** PE16 . . . **241** D5
Sadlers Cl
Coton CB23 . . . . **82** B2
Hardwick CB23 . . . . **81** A1
Sadlers Way PE28 . . . . . . **143** D1
Saffron Cl CB6 . . . . **242** C2
Saffron Piece **II** CB6 . . . . **216** E1
Saffron Rd
Histon CB24 . . . . **104** B3
Sawston CB22 . . . . **33** A8
Saffron St SG8 . . . . **5** F5
Sage's La PE4 . . . . **197** C8
Saggers Cl SG8 . . . . **12** D6
Sainfoin Cl CB22 . . . . **33** A8
Sainsfoins CB22 . . . . **48** F1
St Alban's Cl CB8 . . . . **111** A6
St Alban's Dr **20** PE6 . . . . **232** A1
St Albans RC Prim Sch
CB2 . . . . **246** B1
St Albans Rd CB4 . . . . **83** D6
St Andrew CB8 . . . . **111** A4
St Andrew's CE Prim Sch
CB7 . . . . **212** B3
St Andrews Cl
II Isleham CB7 . . . . **213** A5
Sutton CB6 . . . . **216** E2
St Andrew's Cl CB22 . . . . . **49** C4
St Andrew's Hill CB25 . . . **106** B7
St Andrew's Hill CB25 . . . **106** B7
St Andrews Pk **II** CB7 . . . **212** B4
St Andrew's Pk CB24 . . . . **104** B5
St Andrew's Pl PE7 . . . . . **189** D6
St Andrews Rd **II** PE6 . . . **231** F7
St Andrew's Rd CB4 . . . . . **84** A3
St Andrew's St
Cambridge CB2 . . . . **246** B2
Mildenhall IP28 . . . . **239** C4
St Andrews Way
Histon CB24 . . . . **104** E4
Sawtry PE28 . . . . **168** C4
St Andrew's Way CB6 . . . **240** B6
St Annes CE Prim Sch
PE29 . . . . **118** F8
St Anns Dr IP28 . . . . **239** B4
St Ann's La PE29 . . . . **141** F1
St Anselm Pl **II** PE19 . . . . **74** E5
St Anthony **2** CB8 . . . . . . **111** A4
St Anthonys Wlk CB2 . . . . **64** F7
St Audleys La PE27 . . . . . **144** A5
St Audrey Cl
Peterborough PE2 . . . . **187** D6
St Ives PE27 . . . . **144** B5
Saint Audrey La PE27 . . . **144** A5
St Audrey's Cl CB24 . . . . . **104** A4
St Audrey's Way CB6 . . . . **240** D6
St Augustines CE Jun Sch
PE2 . . . . **186** F8
St Augustines RC (Aided)
Prim Sch PE9 . . . . **244** C7
St Augustines Rd CB3 . . . **245** C5
St Augustine's Wlk PE2 . **186** E8
St Barnabas Ct **II** PE29 . . **141** F7
St Barnabas Rd CB1 . . . . . **65** A8
St Barnabus Ct CB1 . . . . . . **65** A8
St Bartholomew's Ct CB5 . **84** B3
St Bede's Cres CB1 . . . . . . **65** E6
St Bede's Gdns CB1 . . . . . . **65** E6
St Bede's Inter Church Comp
Sch CB1 . . . . **65** D6
St Bee's Dr **10** PE6 . . . . . . **232** A1
St Benedict's Cl PE6 . . . . **203** F7
St Benedicts Ct **10** PE29 . **141** D4
St Benedict's Ct PE20 . . . . **65** D8
St Benet's Gdns **8** PE6 . . **232** A1
St Botolph La PE2 . . . . . . **186** C6
St Botolphs CE Prim Sch
PE2 . . . . **186** B6
St Botolph's Gn PE28 . . . . **178** E7
St Botolphs Pl CB9 . . . . . . **23** E7
St Botolph's Way
Haverhill CB9 . . . . **23** F8
II Thorney PE6 . . . . **233** A2
St Catharines Coll CB2 . . **246** A2
St Catharines Hall CB23 . . **82** C2
St Catharines Sq
Arbury CB4 . . . . **83** C7
II Kings Hedges CB4 . . . . **83** D7
St Catherine's CB6 . . . . . **240** C5
St Catherines Cl IP28 . . . **239** D6
St Catherines Ct SG8 . . . . **11** F2
St Catherines Prep Sch
CB2 . . . . **64** E7
St Christophers Ave **2**
CB4 . . . . **83** C4
St Clement Cl PE14 . . . . . **236** F2
St Clement's PE29 . . . . . . **144** A5
St Clements Gdns CB1 . . **246** A3
St Clements Pas PE29 . . . **141** E4
St Colettes Prep Sch CB1 . **66** F7
St David Cl CB1 . . . . **111** A4
St David's Sq CB1 . . . . . . **198** D1
St David's Way PE28 . . . . **168** C4
St Denys CB3 . . . . **111** A4
St Edmunds Coll CB3 . . . . . **83** C3
St Edmunds Dr PE14 . . . . **236** D5
St Edmunds Way PE7 . . . **186** D2
St Edwards Pas **4** CB1 . . **246** A2
St Ethelwolds Cl CB6 . . . **240** B4
St Fabians Cl CB8 . . . . . . **110** F5
St Faith's Sch CB2 . . . . **64** E6
St Felix CE VC Mid Sch
CB7 . . . . **110** F6
St Felix Cl CB7 . . . . **212** B5
St Felix RC Prim Sch CB9 . **23** D7

St Felix Rd PE26 . . . . **221** C2
St Francis Dr **2** PE16 . . . . **241** D5
St George **II** CB8 . . . . **111** A4
St George Ave PE2 . . . . . . **187** E6
St Georges Ave PE19 . . . . **244** D6
St Georges CE Prim Sch
PE9 . . . . **244** C7
St Georges Cl PE28 . . . . . **140** E1
St Georges Ct **II** PE29 . . . **141** D4
St George's Rd
St Ives PE27 . . . . **144** A4
II Wittering PE8 . . . . **230** B1
St George's Sq **5** PE2 . . . **244** C5
St George's St PE9 . . . . . **244** C5
St Georges Way CB24 . . . **104** E4
St Germain St PE29 . . . . . **141** D4
St Germain Walk Sh Ctr
PE29 . . . . **141** D4
St Germain Wlk **8** PE29 . **141** D4
St Gilberts CE Prim Sch
PE6 . . . . **244** B5
St Giles Cl PE7 . . . . **176** F4
St Giles Gr PE14 . . . . **236** B5
St Goerges Ct CB24 . . . . . **104** E4
St Helena Farm IP28 . . . . **239** F6
St Helena Wlk PE28 . . . . **239** C7
St Helens Prim Sch
PE28 . . . . **208** D6
St Hugh's Rd PE19 . . . . . . **117** A4
ST IVES **143** E7
St Ives Rd
Eltisley PE19 . . . . **77** E6
Hemingford Grey PE28 . . **143** D2
Old Hurst PE28 . . . . **144** B7
Papworth Everard CB23 . . **98** F2
Somersham PE28 . . . . **208** B8
St Ives PE28 . . . . **143** A5
St Ivo Leisure Ctr PE27 . . **143** F4
St Ives Sch PE27 . . . . **143** F5
St James CB8 . . . . **111** A4
St James Ave PE1 . . . . . . **197** F7
St James Cl
Newton PE13 . . . . **238** A5
3 Stretham CB6 . . . . . . **210** F5
St James Ct **9** CB9 . . . . . . **23** E8
St James Rd CB8 . . . . **99** F3
St John Fisher RC Sch
PE1 . . . . **198** C4
St Johns Sq **14** C5
St Johns Ave CB8 . . . . . . **111** A1
St Johns Bsns Pk PE29 . . **141** C8
St John's CE Prim Sch
PE29 . . . . **141** E7
St John's Chase PE15 . . . **243** D5
St Johns Church Sch
PE2 . . . . **185** E3
St John's Cl PE28 . . . . **155** B5
St John's Cl
Mildenhall IP28 . . . . **239** D6
7 Needingworth PE27 . . **208** A3
Waterbeach CB25 . . . . . . **106** B7
St Johns Coll CB2 . . . . . . **246** A3
St John's Innovation Ctr
CB4 . . . . **84** C8
St Johns La CB23 . . . . **99** B2
St John's La CB25 . . . . . . **106** A2
St Johns Mews PE19 . . . . . **96** E4
St John's Pl
Cambridge CB4 . . . . **83** C3
Wistow PE28 . . . . **163** F7
St Johns Prim CE Sch
PE1 . . . . **187** C7
St Johns Rd
Cambridge CB5 . . . . **246** A4
Peterborough PE1 . . . . **187** B7
St John's Rd
Coton CB23 . . . . **82** B2
Ely CB6 . . . . **240** A4
March PE15 . . . . **243** D5
13 Wittering PE8 . . . . **230** B1
St John's St PE29 . . . . **141** D5
St John's St
Beck Row, Holywell Row &
Kenny Hill IP28 . . . . . . **214** A8
Cambridge CB2 . . . . **246** A3
Duxford CB22 . . . . **32** D1
Mildenhall IP28 . . . . **213** F8
Peterborough PE1 . . . . **198** B2
St Johns Way CB23 . . . . . . **79** A4
St Judith's La PE28 . . . . . **160** B6
St Katherines Mews PE7 **186** C3
St Kilda Ave CB4 . . . . **84** A7
St Kyneburgha Cl PE5 . . . **195** E2
St Laurence Rd CB22 . . . . . **30** C5
St Laurences RC Prim Sch
CB4 . . . . **83** D7
St Lawrence Way **2** PE9 **230** F7
St Leger Dr CB8 . . . . **110** E5
St Leonard's Rd **II** PE13 . **238** B2
St Leonard's St **4** PE9 . . **244** C5
St Louis RC Prim Sch
PE29 . . . . **111** A4
St Lukes CE Prim Sch
CB4 . . . . **83** C4
St Lukes Cl PE29 . . . . **141** D5
St Lukes Mews CB4 . . . . . . **83** D4
St Lukes St CB4 . . . . **246** A4
St Margarets PE2 . . . . **186** F6
St Margarets Rd PE2 . . . . **186** F6
St Margaret's Rd CB3 . . . . **82** F6
St Margaret's Sq CB1 . . . . **65** B5
St Marks Ct CB3 . . . . **64** C8
St Mark's Ct **3** PE1 . . . . . **198** A3

St Marks Rd PE13. . . . . 237 E3
St Marks St PE1 . . . . 198 A3
St Martin's Cl
  Chatteris PE16. . . . . 241 D5
  Exning C88. . . . . 110 C7
  Stamford PE9. . . . . 244 C4
St Martin's Rd
  Chatteris PE16. . . . . 241 D4
  Newborough PE6. . . . . 205 B8
  Wisbech PE13 . . . . 245 E7
St Martin's St PE1 . . . . 197 F5
St Martins Wlk CB7 . . . . . . 240 D5
St Mary's
  Earith PE28. . . . . 208 E6
  Gamlingay SG19 . . . . 41 E5
St Mary's Ave PE8 . . . . 230 B1
St Marys CE Prim Sch
  Mildenhall IP28. . . . . 239 C5
  St Neots PE19 . . . . .75 A5
St Marys Cl CB6 . . . . 216 E3
St Mary's Cl
  Bainton PE9. . . . . 230 F5
  Bluntisham PE28 . . . . 208 D5
  Farcet PE7. . . . . 187 C2
  Mildenhall IP28. . . . . 239 C4
  Peterborough PE1. . . . . 198 B4
  Thorney PE6. . . . . 233 A2
  Wisbech St Mary PE13 . . . . 235 C7
St Marys Ct
  Ely CB7 . . . . 240 C4
  Peterborough PE1 . . . . 198 B2
St Mary's Dr
  March PE15. . . . . 243 C5
  Peterborough PE2. . . . . 185 F4
St Mary's Gn PE28 . . . . 164 E6
St Mary's Hill 9 PE9. . . . . . 244 C5
St Marys Pas PE1. . . . . 246 A2
St Mary's Pas 2 CB1 . . . . . 246 A2
St Marys Pk SG8. . . . . .5 D6
St Mary's RC JMI Sch SG8 . .5 D7
St Mary's Rd
  Bluntisham/Colne PE28. . . . 208 C5
  Ramsey PE26. . . . . 220 E2
  Sawston CB22 . . . . .33 A7
  Stilton PE7. . . . . 175 F8
  West Walton PE14. . . . . . . 238 E4
St Marys Sen Sch CB2 . . . . .64 E7
St Marys Sq 7 CB8 . . . . . . 111 A3
St Marys St 9 PE29. . . . . . 141 D4
St Mary's
  1 Cambridge CB1 . . . . . . 246 A2
  Ely CB7 . . . . 240 C4
  Farcet PE7. . . . . 187 C2
  Stamford PE9. . . . . 244 C5
  St Neots PE19 . . . . .74 E4
  Whittlesey PE7 . . . . 189 D6
St Marys View CB25. . . . . . 130 C1
St Mary's Wlk
  Everton SG19 . . . . .40 C3
  Fowlmere SG8. . . . . .15 E8
St Matthew's Cl CB1 . . . . . .84 A2
St Matthew's Gdns CB1 . . . .84 A2
St Matthews Prim Sch
  CB1 . . . . 246 C2
St Matthew's St CB1 . . . . . .84 A2
St Michaels CB24 . . . . 103 A8
St Michael's Ave PE13 . . . . 245 C7
St Michael's Gate PE1. . . . . 198 F7
St Michaels La
  Longstanton CB24 . . . . 124 A1
  Oakington/Longstanton
    CB24 . . . . 103 A8
St Michael's Rd 12 PE8 . . . 230 B1
ST NEOTS 74 E4
St Neots Com Coll PE19 . . . .74 E3
St Neots Comm Nature
  Reserve* PE27. . . . . .74 E2
St Neots Leisure Ctr PE19 . . .74 E2
St Neots Mus* PE19 . . . . . . .74 E5
St Neots Rd
  Abbotsley PE19 . . . . .57 A7
  Comberton CB23 . . . . .81 D3
  Coton CB23 . . . . .82 B3
  Eaton Socon PE19 . . . . .74 C4
  Eltisley PE19 . . . . .57 D4
  Hardwick CB23 . . . . .80 E4
  Knapwell CB23. . . . . .79 D5
  Madingley CB23. . . . . .81 F3
  St Neots Sta PE19 . . . . .75 B6
St Olave's Dr 10 PE6 . . . . . 232 A1
St Ovins Gn CB6. . . . . 240 B5
St Patrick 8 CB8 . . . . 111 A4
St Paul's CE Prim Sch
  CB2 . . . . 246 B1
St Paul's Cl
  Gorefield PE13. . . . . 237 E2
  5 Wisbech PE13. . . . . 245 C4
St Pauls Dr PE16. . . . . 241 D6
St Paul's Rd
  Cambridge CB1 . . . . 246 C1
  Peterborough PE1. . . . . 197 F7
St Paul's Sq PE1 . . . . 197 F7
St Pauls Wlk CB1. . . . . 246 C1
St Pega's Rd PE6. . . . . 204 A8
St Peters Ave CB8 . . . . 112 F4
St Peter's CE Jun Sch
  PE13. . . . . 245 E6
St Peters Cl CB8. . . . . 112 F5
St Peters Ct 9 PE9 . . . . . . 244 B5
St Peter's Dr PE15 . . . . 223 B7
St Peter's Field CB25 . . . . . .86 E5
St Peter's Hill 8 PE9 . . . . . 244 B5
St Peter's Pl CB7. . . . . 212 F1

St Peters Rd
  Outwell PE14. . . . . 236 E1
  Peterborough PE1. . . . . 198 A2
St Peter's Rd
  Coton CB23 . . . . .82 B2
  Huntingdon PE29. . . . . 141 D7
  March PE15. . . . . 243 D3
  4 Wisbech PE13. . . . . 245 C4
St Peters Sch Prim PE1 . . . 141 D6
St Peter's St
  Cambridge CB3 . . . . .83 C3
  Caxton CB23 . . . . .59 E8
  Duxford CB22 . . . . .17 D8
  Stamford PE9. . . . . 244 B3
St Peters Terr CB1 . . . . 246 B1
St Peter's Vale PE9 . . . . . . 244 B4
St Peter's Way
  Ellington PE28 . . . . 139 A4
  Thorney PE6. . . . . 233 A2
St Philips CE Prim Sch
  CB1. . . . . .84 C1
St Philips Rd
  Cambridge CB1 . . . . .65 C8
  Newmarket CB8. . . . . 110 C4
St Philip's Rd CB1 . . . . .65 B8
St Regis CB4 . . . . .83 F4
St Stephen's Dr PE16 . . . . . 241 C6
St Stephen's Pl 1 CB4 . . . . .83 C4
St Thomas PE12. . . . . .77 E4
St Thomas Cl CB23 . . . . . . .62 D6
St Thomas Dr PE15. . . . . . . 243 C3
St Thomas Moore RC Prim
  Sch PE1 . . . . 198 D4
St Thomas' Pl CB7 . . . . 240 C4
St Thomas's Sq CB1. . . . . . .65 D6
St Tibb's Row CB2 . . . . 246 B2
St Vigor's Rd CB21. . . . . . . .66 F4
St Vincent's Cl CB3 . . . . . . .82 E8
St Wendreda's Dr PE15 . . . . 243 C1
St Wendred's Way CB8. . . . 110 B7
Salcott Dr PE13. . . . . 245 E5
Salem Ct PE16. . . . . 241 C4
Salgasson Wlk CB23 . . . . . .79 B2
Salisbury Cl PE27. . . . . 143 F8
Salisbury Ct 1 CB9 . . . . . . .23 F7
Salisbury Rd PE4 . . . . 204 B3
Salisbury Villas CB1. . . . . . .64 F7
Salk Rd PE7 . . . . 186 B2
Sallowbush Rd PE29 . . . . . . 141 D6
Sallows PE28 . . . . 121 C6
Sallows Rd PE1. . . . . 198 B6
Salmon La CB1 . . . . 246 C3
Salon Way PE29 . . . . 141 B7
Saltergate PE1. . . . . 198 E7
Saltersgate PE4 . . . . 198 F7
Salters Way
  Sawtry PE28. . . . . 168 B5
  Wisbech PE13. . . . . 245 A2
Saltmarsh PE2. . . . . 186 C4
Salts Rd PE14. . . . . 238 F4
Sambar Cl 3 PE19. . . . . . . .74 B5
Sames Ct CB24 . . . . 125 E5
Samphire Cl CB24 . . . . .60 C2
Samuel Pepys Sch PE19. . . .75 A4
Samuels Cl PE28. . . . . 164 E4
Samuels Way CB6. . . . . 240 C4
Samuel Ward Art & Tech Coll
  CB9 . . . . .39 B1
Samworths Cl PE5 . . . . 195 F2
Sancton Wood Sch CB1. . . . 246 C1
Sand Acre Cl IP28 . . . . 239 D5
Sandall Rd PE13 . . . . 245 C1
Sand Bank PE13 . . . . 235 A7
Sand Dro CB25 . . . . 127 C8
Sanderling Cl IP28. . . . . . . 239 D4
Sanderlings The PE6. . . . . . 206 B1
Sanders Cl PE28 . . . . 151 D3
Sanders La CB21. . . . . .67 A4
Sandfields Rd PE19 . . . . . . .74 F4
Sandford PE3. . . . . 197 B5
SANDHILL 242 E3
Sandhill CB8. . . . . 242 F3
Sandhurst Rd PE7 . . . . 186 C1
Sand La CB6. . . . . 209 E4
Sandown Rd PE13 . . . . 245 A2
Sandpiper Cl
  Haverhill CB9. . . . . .24 B7
  St Neots PE19 . . . . .74 B1
  Whittlesey PE7 . . . . 190 A8
Sandpiper Dr PE2. . . . . 198 B7
Sandpit Rd PE6. . . . . 233 A3
Sand Rd SG19 . . . . .58 F5
Sandringham Ave PE13 . . . . 245 D6
Sandringham Cl PE9 . . . . . . 244 B7
Sandringham Dr PE26. . . . . 221 C2
Sandringham Rd PE4 . . . . . 197 C8
Sand Road Ind Est SG19. . . .58 F5
Sand St CB7 . . . . 212 B3
Sandwich Cl
  Huntingdon PE29. . . . . 141 E7
  St Ives PE27 . . . . 143 F8
Sandwich Rd
  Brampton PE28 . . . . 140 D1
  St Neots PE19 . . . . .75 A5
Sandwick Cl 2 CB4 . . . . . . .83 E8
Sandy Dro IP28 . . . . 214 D3
Sandy Gate PE12. . . . . 237 A7
Sandy La
  Cambridge CB4 . . . . .83 F4
  Kimbolton PE28 . . . . 113 C6
  Tydd St Giles PE13. . . . . . . 238 B7
  Wisbech PE13. . . . . 245 F4
Sandyland PE13 . . . . 245 B5
Sandy Rd
  Everton SG19. . . . . .40 B2
  Lode CB25 . . . . 107 C6
Sandys Cres CB23. . . . . 242 E3
Sanfoin Cl 5 IP28 . . . . 214 A1

Sapcote Way PE28 . . . . 168 B3
SAPLEY 141 F8
Sapley Pk PE29 . . . . 141 F8
Sapley Rd PE29 . . . . 141 F8
Sapley Sq PE29 . . . . 152 F1
Sapley Spinneys Nature
  Reserve* PE28. . . . . 152 E1
Sapley Sq PE29 . . . . 141 E7
Sapperton PE4 . . . . 204 B6
Sarah Ct CB9 . . . . .24 A5
Sargent's Ct PE9. . . . . 244 A6
Saracen Way PE1. . . . . 198 F4
Saunders Cl
  Huntingdon PE29. . . . . 141 D6
  Peterborough PE2. . . . . 186 E8
Saunders Ct CB23. . . . . .79 B3
Savile's Cl PE19 . . . . .74 D7
Savile Way SG8. . . . . .15 E8
Saville Rd PE3 . . . . 197 D5
Saville Road Ind Est PE3 197 D5
Savory Rd PE13 . . . . 245 B7
Sawpit La PE28 . . . . 159 A4
SAWSTON. 33 A7
Sawston Rd CB22 . . . . .33 D8
Sawston Village Coll
  CB22. . . . . .32 E8
SAWTRY. 168 A4
Sawtry Com Coll PE28 . . . . 168 C4
Sawtry Jun & Inf Sch
  PE28. . . . . 168 A3
Sawtry Leisure Ctr PE28. . . 168 B3
Sawtry Rd
  Conington PE28. . . . . 167 F8
  Sawtry PE28 . . . . 168 A6
  Sawtry Roughs PE28. . . . . . 168 F2
Sawtry Way PE28 . . . . 153 E2
Sawtry Way Cotts PE28. . . . 143 C6
Saxby Gdns PE1 . . . . 198 C8
Saxham Ct PE9 . . . . .38 B1
Saxon Cl
  Ely CB6 . . . . 240 C5
  Exning C88. . . . . 110 D8
  Godmanchester PE29 . . . . . 141 F1
  Oakington CB24 . . . . 103 D6
  Peterborough PE2. . . . . 185 F8
Saxon Dr CB25. . . . . 130 B1
Saxone Com Learning Ctr
  PE29. . . . . 141 E4
Saxon Pl PE19 . . . . .74 F4
Saxon Rd
  5 Barnack PE9. . . . . 230 D3
  Cambridge CB5 . . . . .84 A3
  Peterborough PE2. . . . . 198 C4
  Whittlesey PE7 . . . . 189 C7
Saxon St Rd CB8. . . . . .91 D4
Saxon St CB22. . . . . .91 B3
SAXON STREET 91 B3
Saxon Way
  Bar Hill CB23 . . . . 102 B2
  Knights End PE15 . . . . 228 B1
  Melbourn SG8 . . . . .14 C4
  3 Waterbeach CB25. . . . . . 106 A7
  Willingham CB24 . . . . 209 A1
Sayer Ct PE21 . . . . 141 D4
Sayers Ct PE28 . . . . 208 C5
Sayer St PE28 . . . . 141 C5
Scaldgate PE7 . . . . 189 C6
Scalesgate Rd PE12 . . . . . . 237 A8
Scalford Dr PE1 . . . . 198 C8
Scaltback Cl CB8 . . . . 110 E6
Scaltback Mid Sch CB8 . . . 110 E5
Scarfield La PE14 . . . . 236 C6
Scargell's La CB21 . . . . .53 D4
Scarlett's La CB21 . . . . .53 D4
Scarsdale Cl CB4 . . . . .84 B6
Sch of Clinical Medicine
  CB2 . . . . .65 B3
Scholars Ave PE29 . . . . 141 C4
Scholars Cl PE15 . . . . 224 B4
Schole Rd CB24 . . . . 209 A1
School Cl
  Cheveley CB8. . . . . .91 C6
  Gamlingay SG19 . . . . .41 D5
  5 Maxey PE6 . . . . 231 C7
  Peterborough PE3. . . . . 197 A5
  2 Whittlesey PE7. . . . . 189 B1
School Dro PE26. . . . . 171 A7
School Farm Dro PE26 . . . . 171 E8
School Hill CB24. . . . . 104 B4
School La
  Alconbury PE28 . . . . 150 F5
  Barley SG8. . . . . .7 A1
  Barton CB23 . . . . .63 B4
  Bourn CB23 . . . . .79 B3
  Boxworth CB23 . . . . 101 B5
  Buckden PE19 . . . . 117 B4
  Burwell CB25. . . . . 130 B1
  Bythorn & Keyston PE28 . . . .89 F5
  Conington CB23 . . . . 121 C1
  Coveney CB6 . . . . 217 D5
  Downham CB6. . . . . 218 A7
  Elton PE8 . . . . 178 D8
  Fenstanton PE28. . . . . 121 B6
  Fulbourn CB21. . . . . .66 F4
  Glinton PE6 . . . . 203 E8
  Haslingfield CB23. . . . . .47 B5
  Haverhill CB9. . . . . .24 B6
  Histon CB24 . . . . 104 C3
  Kings Ripton PE28 . . . . 153 C6
  Little Paxton PE19 . . . . .96 A2
  Longstanton CB24 . . . . 123 F1
  Longstowe CB23 . . . . .60 A3
  Manea PE15. . . . . 224 B4
  Mepal CB6 . . . . 216 E3
  Pymoor CB6. . . . . 224 D1
  Ramsey PE26. . . . . 172 B7

School La continued
  St Neots PE19 . . . . .74 E4
  Swavesey CB24. . . . . 122 E6
  Thriplow SG8 . . . . .31 B2
  Toft CB23. . . . . .61 D4
  1 Uffington PE9 . . . . 230 C6
  Warmington PE8 . . . . 178 B3
  Waterbeach CB25. . . . . 127 B8
  Wilburton CB6. . . . . 210 C5
  1 Wisbech PE13. . . . . 245 C5
School Rd
  5 Barnack PE9. . . . . 230 D4
  Broughton PE28 . . . . 153 F8
  Earith PE28. . . . . 208 E6
  Great Wratting CB9. . . . . . . .39 E5
  Moulton CB8 . . . . 112 F6
  Newborough PE6. . . . . 205 D8
  Outwell PE14. . . . . 229 D8
  Warboys PE28. . . . . 164 F5
  West Walton PE14. . . . . . . 238 E4
  Wooddition CB8. . . . . .91 A3
School St CB10 . . . . .18 D2
School Wlk CB23 . . . . .99 A2
Scolding Dro PE6. . . . . 233 E5
Scorney PE28 . . . . 121 C6
Scotendon PE2 . . . . 185 E3
Scotenoon PE2 . . . . 185 E3
Scotgate PE9. . . . . 244 A5
Scotland Cl CB4. . . . . .84 B5
Scotland End CB7. . . . . 213 C1
Scotland Rd
  Cambridge CB4 . . . . .84 A5
  Dry Drayton CB23 . . . . .81 A6
Scotney St PE1 . . . . 197 E7
Scotney Way PE28 . . . . 168 C3
Scotred Cl CB25 . . . . 109 B8
Scotsdowne Rd CB2 . . . . . . .64 D3
Scott Ave IP28. . . . . 239 C5
Scott Cl
  Peterborough PE2. . . . . 187 E6
  Royston SG8 . . . . .13 D1
Scotts Cl PE13 . . . . 120 B1
Scotts Cres PE28 . . . . 120 B1
Scotts Gdns CB22 . . . . .32 C5
Scotts Rd PE6. . . . . 203 F8
Scott's Rd PE14. . . . . 229 C2
Scotts Yd CB23 . . . . .47 B5
Scrafons PE27 . . . . 143 E6
Seabank Rd PE13 . . . . 245 F6
SEADYKE 234 F6
Seadyke Bank PE13 . . . . . . 235 A7
Seadyke Rd PE13 . . . . 234 F6
Seafield Rd 7 PE13. . . . . . . 238 B2
Sealey's La PE13. . . . . 234 D8
Sealodes Rd CB7. . . . . 211 E5
Seargeants Cl PE6 . . . . 207 F5
Seargeant St PE11. . . . . 197 E5
Searles Ct PE7. . . . . 189 D8
Searles Mdw CB23 . . . . 102 B1
Searle St CB4. . . . . .83 D4
Sears Cl PE29 . . . . 118 F8
Searson Cl PE9 . . . . 230 F7
Seathwaite PE29 . . . . 141 B6
Seaton Cl PE7 . . . . 181 D6
Sebrights Way PE3. . . . . 196 F3
Second Ave
  Warboys PE28. . . . . 164 E6
  Wisbech PE13. . . . . 245 D4
Second Broadpool Dro
  PE28. . . . . 165 F8
Second Drift PE9 . . . . 244 B2
Second Dro
  Downham CB6. . . . . 218 A8
  Ely CB7 . . . . 218 F5
  Littleport CB6 . . . . 225 B1
  Peterborough PE1. . . . . 198 D1
  St Ives PE27 . . . . 144 C2
Second Drove Ind Est
  PE1. . . . . 198 D1
Second Marsh Rd PE14 . . . . 238 C3
Sedge Fen Rd PE38 . . . . . . 226 E7
Sedge Way CB6. . . . . 217 D2
Sedgwick Mus of Earth
  Sciences* CB2. . . . . 246 B2
Sedgwick St CB1 . . . . .65 B8
Sedley Taylor Rd CB2 . . . . . .64 F4
Sefton Ave PE13 . . . . 245 E6
Sefton Cl CB2 . . . . .64 D3
Sefton Way CB8 . . . . 110 D5
Selby Ct 2 PE29. . . . . 141 F7
Sellers Grange PE2 . . . . 186 B4
Selsingen Way CB22 . . . . . . .32 F7
Selwyn Cl
  Great Shelford CB22 . . . . . . .49 A5
  Mildenhall IP28 . . . . 239 D6
  Newmarket CB8. . . . . 111 A1
Selwyn Coll CB3 . . . . .64 B8
Selwyn Gdns CB3 . . . . .64 B8
Selwyn Rd
  Cambridge CB3 . . . . .64 B7
  Stamford PE9. . . . . 244 A7
Senate House Hill 6
  CB2 . . . . 246 A2
Senate House Pas CB2 . . . . 246 A2
Senes Calls 9 PE27 . . . . . . 208 A3
Sennitt Way CB6. . . . . 210 F5
Seppings Cl 2 CB6 . . . . 210 C6
Serby Ave SG8 . . . . .5 C8
Serjeants Cl PE26 . . . . 172 A6
Serby Gdns PE3. . . . . 197 B3
Serpentine Green Sh Ctr
  PE7. . . . . 186 D3
Setchel 11 PE19 . . . . .74 C6
Setchel Dro CB24 . . . . 125 F7
Setchell Cl PE19 . . . . .97 F5
Setchfield Pl PE22 . . . . 186 F7
Sevenacres PE2 . . . . 185 E5
Seven Rides SG8. . . . . .5 D3

Seventh Ave PE13. . . . . 245 E4
Seventh Dro CB6 . . . . 225 A3
SEVERALS THE 111 B5
Severn Cl PE4 . . . . 204 E1
Severn Pl CB1. . . . . .84 A2
SEWELLS BARN 138 A2
Seymore Dr CB9 . . . . .23 D7
Seymour Cl CB8 . . . . 111 C3
Seymour Ct PE1. . . . . .65 C8
Seymour Cl CB8 . . . . .65 C8
Seymour Pl PE4 . . . . 205 B2
Seymour St CB1 . . . . .65 C8
Seynory Dro PE7. . . . . 177 F7
Shade The CB7 . . . . 212 A5
Shadowbush Cl 2 CB9. . . . . .38 F1
Shady Wlk 2 PE19 . . . . .74 F5
Shaftenhoe End Rd SG8. . . . .7 A1
Shaftesbury Ave
  March PE15. . . . . 243 C5
  St Neots PE19 . . . . .74 F5
Shaftesbury Ct CB21 . . . . . .23 E7
Shaftesbury Rd CB2. . . . . . . .64 F6
Shaftesbury Way SG8 . . . . . . .5 E6
Shaftsbury Ct PE15 . . . . . . 243 E3
Shakespeare SG8 . . . . .5 D8
Shakespeare Ave PE1 . . . . . 197 F7
Shakespeare Rd
  Eaton Socon PE19 . . . . .74 C3
  St Ives PE27 . . . . 143 F6
Shamrock Cl PE2 . . . . 187 C7
Shannon Cl CB9 . . . . .24 D7
Shardlow Cl 1 CB9. . . . . . . .38 C1
Sharma Leas PE4 . . . . 204 A3
Sharman's Rd CB21. . . . . . . 212 E1
Sharnbrook Ave PE7 . . . . . . 186 C1
Sharp Cl PE27 . . . . 143 E5
Sharps La PE28. . . . . 150 F3
Shaw Dr PE15 . . . . 243 C3
Shawley Rd PE28 . . . . 168 A4
Shearling Dr CB23 . . . . .79 A4
Shearwater PE2 . . . . 185 D6
Sheepfold PE27. . . . . 144 C5
Sheepfold La CB23. . . . . . . .79 B5
Sheep Mkt
  6 Stamford PE9. . . . . 244 B5
  St Ives PE27 . . . . 144 B3
Sheep St PE28 . . . . 148 D3
Sheepwalk PE4 . . . . 205 A1
Sheepwash Way CB24 . . . . . 123 E2
Sheldrick's Rd CB7 . . . . 213 B5
Shelford Mill CB22 . . . . .48 F4
Shelford Park Ave CB22 . . . . .49 A5
Shelford Rd
  Cambridge CB22 . . . . .48 E8
  Fulbourn CB21. . . . . .66 C3
  Harston CB22 . . . . .48 C3
  Whittlesford CB22 . . . . .32 A6
Shelford Sta CB22 . . . . .49 B5
Shelley Cl
  Huntingdon PE29. . . . . 141 F6
  Peterborough PE1. . . . . 197 E8
  Royston SG8 . . . . .13 D1
Shelley Pl 5 PE19 . . . . .74 D1
Shelly Gdns CB3 . . . . .83 C3
Shelly Row 4 CB3 . . . . .83 C3
Shelton Rd PE2 . . . . 187 D6
Shepherd Cl SG8 . . . . .5 E5
Shepherd Dr PE19 . . . . .74 E2
Shepherds Cl PE4 . . . . 204 C4
Shepherd's Cl
  Cambridge CB1 . . . . .66 A6
  Fen Ditton CB5. . . . . .84 F5
Shepherds Ct 9 CB9. . . . . . .23 E7
Shepherd's Dro CB7 . . . . . . 226 B2
Sheppard's Dro PE6 . . . . . . 232 D8
Sheppard Way CB1. . . . . . . .85 B1
Sheppersons Gr 2 PE15 . . 243 E4
SHEPRETH. 29 F5
Shepreth L-Moor Nature
  Reserve* SG8. . . . . .29 D3
Shepreth Rd
  Barrington CB22 . . . . .30 A7
  Foxton CB22. . . . . .30 D4
Shepreth Sta SG8. . . . . .29 E5
Shepreth Wildlife Pk*
  SG8 . . . . .29 E5
Sheralds Croft La SG8 . . . . .31 A4
Sherborne Rd PE1. . . . . 198 D6
Sherbourne Cl CB4. . . . . . . .84 B6
Sherbrooke Cl PE15. . . . . . 243 D1
Sheridan Rd PE1. . . . . 197 F8
Sheriffs Ct CB8 . . . . .70 F3
Sheringham Way PE13 . . . . 186 C6
Sherlock Cl CB3 . . . . .83 B4
Sherlock Cl CB3 . . . . .83 B4
Sherlock Rd CB3. . . . . .83 B5
Sherwood Ave
  4 Peterborough PE2. . . . . . 186 F7
  Wisbech PE13. . . . . 245 D7
Shetland Rd CB9 . . . . .24 D8
Shillow Mill PE26 . . . . 172 B1
SHINGAY 26 F2
Shingay La CB22. . . . . .32 F7
Ship Gdns IP28 . . . . 239 B3
Ship La CB7 . . . . 240 D3
Shippea Hill Rd IP28. . . . . . .23 E8
Shirdley Rd PE19 . . . . .74 F4
Shire Cl CB9. . . . . .23 E7
Shire Gr PE1 . . . . 198 C5
Shires The
  Bluntisham/Colne PE28. . . . 208 C5
  March PE15. . . . . 243 E2
  Royston SG8 . . . . .5 E6
Shirley Cl CB24 . . . . 105 C2
Shirley Gr CB4 . . . . .83 E4
Shirley Inf Sch CB4. . . . . . . .84 B5
Shirley Rd CB4 . . . . .84 B5
Shooter's Hollow PE19. . . . . 116 D3

Shores Cl IP28 . . . . 213 C3
Shore View PE7 . . . . 186 C2
Shortacres Rd PE2 . . . . 186 F7
Short Cl PE8 . . . . 178 B3
Short Cswy CB6 . . . . 217 C4
Short Dr PE15 . . . . 224 B5
Short Dro
 Cottenham CB24 . . . . 125 F2
 Downham CB6 . . . . 224 F3
 Earith PE28 . . . . 208 F6
 Holme PE7 . . . . 177 A4
 Little Downham CB6 . . . . . . 217 F5
 Pymore CB6 . . . . 217 C8
 Ramsey PE26 . . . . 221 A2
 Somersham PE28 . . . . 215 D3
Shortfen PE2 . . . . 186 C4
Short La
 Bluntisham/Colne PE28. . 208 C5
 Coveney CB6 . . . . 217 C4
 Papworth Village Settlement
  CB23 . . . . 99 A2
 Willingham CB24 . . . . 209 A1
 Wisbech PE13 . . . . 238 A1
Shortland **6** PE28 . . . . . . 215 C1
Short Nightlayer's Dro
 PE16. . . . . 241 C6
Short North Dro CB6. . . . . 216 B4
Short Rd
 Exning CB8 . . . . 131 F2
 Snailwell CB8 . . . . 132 A3
 Stretham CB6 . . . . 210 E5
Shortsands Yd **3** PE19. . . .75 A5
Short St
 Bourn CB23 . . . . 60 C5
 Cambridge CB1 . . . . 246 B3
Shrewsbury Ave PE2 . . . . . 186 D5
Shropshire Pl PE1 . . . . 198 B2
Shrubberies The CB8. . . . . 111 D1
Shrubbery Gr SG8 . . . . 5 D4
Shrubbery The PE16 . . . . . 241 D4
Shrub House Cl IP28. . . . . . 213 F8
Shrublands IP28. . . . . 239 C4
Shrub Rd PE7 . . . . 186 C1
Shubbery The PE29 . . . . . . 140 F5
SHUDY CAMPS 22 B5
Shudy Camps Pk CB21. . . . 22 C6
SIBSON 183 C8
Sibson Aerodrome PE8. . . 183 E6
Sidgwick Ave CB3 . . . . 64 C8
Siding Dro PE28 . . . . 215 C5
Sidings The PE26 . . . . 172 B6
Sidney Farm Rd CB1 . . . . . . 65 E6
Sidney Gdns CB23 . . . . 47 B6
Sidney St CB2 . . . . 246 A3
Sidney Sussex Coll CB1. 246 B3
Siggin's La CB1. . . . . 20 D6
Signal Rd PE26 . . . . 172 B6
Silhalls Cl CB8. . . . . 91 F7
Silt Rd
 Littleport CB6 . . . . 242 D5
 March PE15 . . . . 243 F4
 Upwell PE14. . . . . 229 F5
Silvan Cl PE19 . . . . 95 E1
Silver Birch Ave PE27 . . . 143 F6
Silver Birch Cl PE19 . . . . . 141 E7
Silver Ct SG2 . . . . 2 D4
Silverdale Ave CB23. . . . . . 82 B2
Silverdale Cl CB23 . . . . 82 A2
Silver Hill PE7 . . . . 186 D3
Silver La PE27 . . . . 208 A3
Silverley Way CB8 . . . . 91 F7
Silver Lodge IP28 . . . . 239 F3
Silvers Cl CB7 . . . . 212 B5
Silver's La PE13 . . . . 234 E7
Silver St
 Ashwell SG7. . . . . 2 D4
 Buckden PE19 . . . . 117 B4
 Burwell CB25. . . . . 130 B4
 Cambridge CB3 . . . . 246 A1
 Ely CB7 . . . . 240 C4
 Godmanchester PE29 . . . . 118 E8
 Guilden Morden SG8 . . . . . 10 F4
 Littlington SG8 . . . . 12 A2
 March PE15 . . . . 243 C7
 Peterborough PE2 . . . . 186 F7
 Ramsey PE26 . . . . 172 B7
 St Neots PE19 . . . . 74 E4
 Willingham CB24 . . . . 209 A1
 Wisbech PE13 . . . . 245 C6
 Wisbech PE13 . . . . 238 A4
 Withersfield CB9 . . . . 38 A4
Silverweed PE19 . . . . 74 C5
Silverwood Cl CB1. . . . . 84 B2
Silverwood Rd PE1 . . . . . . 197 F5
Silvester Rd PE5. . . . . 195 E2
Simeon Cl CB6 . . . . 240 F7
Simmer Piece PE28 . . . . . . 121 C5
Simpkin Cl PE19 . . . . 74 B2
Singerfre Rd PE15. . . . . 243 C7
Sir Harry Smith Com Coll
 PE7. . . . . 189 F7
Sir James Black Rd CB7 240 C2
Siskin Cl SG8 . . . . 5 E8
Sissley PE2 . . . . 185 E2
Sitch Rd CB23 . . . . 79 C2
Six Bells **14** PE28 . . . . . . 215 C1
SIX MILE BOTTOM 68 F7
Six Mile Bottom Rd CB21. 69 A1
Sixteen Foot Bank
 Christchurch PE14. . . . . . . 229 C4
 Wimblington PE15 . . . . 223 E5
Sixth Ave PE13. . . . . 245 E4
Skaters Way PE4. . . . . 204 C4
Skeaping Cl CB8. . . . . 111 A4
Skeels Ct PE26. . . . . 141 F7
Skeggles Cl PE29 . . . . 141 B5
Skeifs Row **4** PE15 . . . . . . 222 A5
Skelton Pl PE27. . . . . 144 B5

Skelton's Dro IP28. . . . . . . 213 F8
Skipper's La
 West Wickham CB21 . . . . . . 37 F8
 West Wratting CB21 . . . . . . 54 E1
 Withersfield CB9. . . . . 38 A5
Skiver Cl CB22. . . . . 32 F6
Skylark Pl **9** SG8. . . . . 5 E8
Skylarks Cl PE7. . . . . 186 D3
Slade Cl PE26 . . . . 172 A7
SLADE FIELD 241 B7
Slade Mews PE26 . . . . 172 A7
Slade The
 Witcham CB6 . . . . 217 A2
 Wrestlingworth & Cockayne
  Hatley SG19 . . . . 25 B3
Slade Way PE14 . . . . 241 C5
Slatebarn Dro PE7 . . . . . . 221 C8
Slaters Dr CB9. . . . . 38 E2
Sleaford St CB1. . . . . 84 A1
Sleford Cl CB21. . . . . 53 B2
Sleights Dr **4** PE14. . . . . . 238 F1
Slid La CB22. . . . . 29 F8
Slipe Cotts PE28 . . . . 146 A6
Small Lode PE14. . . . . 236 F1
Smallwood PE3. . . . . 197 B5
Smeefield PE28. . . . . 99 B8
Smeeth Rd
 Emneth PE14. . . . . 236 E6
 Marshland St James PE14. 236 F7
Smith Dr PE19. . . . . 117 B3
Smithey Fen Engine Dro
 CB24. . . . . 209 E2
Smithfield PE6. . . . . 233 B3
Smiths Chase PE15 . . . . . . 243 B5
Smith's Dr PE15 . . . . 243 F3
Smith's Dro PE38 . . . . 226 F4
Smith's End La SG8 . . . . . . 6 F1
Smith St CB23. . . . . 100 A4
Smiths Yd PE19 . . . . 94 A6
Smithy Way CB23 . . . . 79 C4
Snail Croft PE13 . . . . 238 A2
SNAILWELL 133 B4
Snailwell Rd
 Fordham CB8. . . . . 131 F5
 Newmarket CB8. . . . . 111 B6
Snailwell Short Rd CB8 . 131 A1
Snoots Rd PE7. . . . . 189 B7
Snowberry Way **3** CB7 . . 212 B5
Snowden Cl **1** PE6 . . . . . . 232 C8
Snowdon Cl **9** CB9 . . . . . . 23 E6
Snowdonia Way PE29 . . . . 141 A4
Snowley Pk PE7 . . . . 189 B8
Snowy Way PE29. . . . . 142 B6
Sobrite Way PE4. . . . . 204 B7
SOHAM 212 B4
Soham Cotes CB7. . . . . 211 F5
Soham Mere CB7 . . . . 211 F4
Soham Rd
 Ely CB7 . . . . 211 D8
 Fordham CB8 . . . . 212 D2
Soham Village Coll CB7. 212 B3
Sokemans Way PE28 . . . . . 117 D8
Soke Parkway PE3 . . . . 197 A3
Soke Rd PE6. . . . . 207 B1
Somerby Cl PE9 . . . . 244 B7
Somerby Garth **1** PE1 . . 198 D7
Somerset Cl CB4. . . . . 83 D7
Somerset Cl **16** CB9 . . . . . . 23 E7
Somerset Rd
 Histon CB24. . . . . 143 F4
 Wyton Airfield PE28. . . . . . 143 B8
SOMERSHAM 215 B1
SOMERSHAM PARK 208 C8
Somersham Prim Sch
 PE28. . . . . 215 C1
Somersham Rd
 Bluntisham PE28 . . . . 155 E2
 Colne PE28 . . . . 208 C8
 Holywell-cum-Needingworth
  PE27. . . . . 144 C7
Somers Rd PE13. . . . . 245 B4
Somervell Ct **5** CB4. . . . . . 83 E7
Somerville PE4 . . . . 204 A5
Somerville Rd **1** PE9 . . . . 244 A6
Somes Cl **1** PE9. . . . . 230 C6
Sorbus Cl PE7 . . . . 186 D3
Sorrel Cl SG8 . . . . 5 F5
Sorrell Cl SG8 . . . . 5 F5
Sorrel Wlk CB9. . . . . 38 D1
Southacre Cl CB22. . . . . . . 64 E6
Southacre Dr CB22. . . . . . . 64 E6
Southampton Pl PE16. . . . 241 C3
South Brink
 Elm PE14. . . . . 235 B4
 Wisbech PE13 . . . . 245 A3
Southbrooke Cl **2** CB2. . . 64 D3
Southbrook Field CB23. . . 99 A2
Southcl Cl SG8 . . . . 5 B7
Southcourts CB22. . . . . 48 F3
Southdown Rd PE7 . . . . . . 181 F5
South Dr
 March PE15. . . . . 243 E4
 Newmarket CB8. . . . . 110 F4
South End Cl SG8 . . . . 12 E3
Southerns The **7** CB6. . . 216 E1
Southey Wood* PE9. . . . . . 231 A1
Southfield CB10. . . . . 18 A3
Southfields Ave PE2 . . . . . 187 A5
Southfields Cl
 Newmarket CB8. . . . . 110 E4
 Wisbech PE13 . . . . 245 A3
Southfields Dr PE2. . . . . . . 187 D6
Southfields Jun & Inf school
 PE2. . . . . 187 D5
Southgate Ave PE28. . . . . . 239 B7
Southgate Way CB2. . . . . . 185 C2
SOUTH GREEN 190 F7
South Green Rd CB3 . . . . . 64 C7

South La **3** CB23. . . . . 62 C5
Southlands Ave PE1. . . . . . 198 A6
SOUTHOE. 95 E5
Southoe Rd PE7 . . . . 187 D2
SOUTHORPE 230 D2
Southorpe Meadow Nature
 Reserve* PE9. . . . . 230 E2
Southorpe Paddock Nature
 Reserve* PE9. . . . . 230 E1
South Par PE3. . . . . 197 E3
South Park Dr CB23. . . . . . 99 B1
South Park St PE16. . . . . . 241 C4
South Rd
 Brampton PE28 . . . . 117 D8
 Great Abington CB21. . . . . 33 F4
 Histon CB24. . . . . 104 B1
Southside Ct CB4. . . . . 84 A5
South St
 Comberton CB23 . . . . 62 C4
 Great Chesterford CB10 . . 18 D2
 Huntingdon PE29. . . . . 141 F5
 Littlington SG8 . . . . 12 A2
 Peterborough PE1. . . . . . . 198 B2
 St Neots PE19 . . . . 74 E5
 Woodhurst PE28 . . . . 155 A4
South Terr CB22 . . . . 32 F5
South View PE2. . . . . 186 F7
South View Rd PE4. . . . . . . 197 D8
Southwell Ave PE29 . . . . . 204 A4
Southwell Cl PE15 . . . . 243 C6
Southwell Rd PE13. . . . . . . 245 C8
Southwick Cl **5** PE4. . . . . 204 F1
Sovereign Cl CB13 . . . . 245 A6
Sovereign Ct PE29 . . . . 141 B8
Sovereign Pl PE2 . . . . 197 E2
Sovereign Way CB24 . . . . . 125 E3
Spaldings La CB25. . . . . . . 105 D7
Spalding Way CB1. . . . . 65 D4
SPALDWICK 137 F6
Spaldwick Prim Sch
 PE28. . . . . 137 F5
Spaldwick Rd PE28 . . . . . . 137 C3
Spar Cl CB23 . . . . 79 A4
Sparkes Cl **2** CB7 . . . . . . 213 A5
Sparrow Cl PE29. . . . . 141 E5
Sparrow Dr PE28 . . . . 158 E4
Sparrowgate Rd PE14. . . . 238 F1
Sparrowhawk Way PE29. 142 B7
Sparrow Rd **2** PE7 . . . . . . 186 D1
Sparrows Cl PE28 . . . . 117 D8
Sparrow Way PE28. . . . . . . 120 B1
Spartan Cl
 Haverhill CB9. . . . . 23 C8
 Wisbech PE13 . . . . 245 E2
Speechley Rd PE7 . . . . 181 F6
Speechley's Dro PE7 . . . . 207 F2
Speed La CB7 . . . . 212 B4
Speedwell Cl CB1. . . . . 66 A6
Spencer Ave PE2 . . . . 187 D5
Spencer Cl
 Eaton Socon PE19 . . . . . . 74 B4
 West Walton PE14. . . . . . . 238 E4
Spencer Croft CB7. . . . . . . 240 E6
Spencer Dro
 Melbourn SG8 . . . . 14 C6
 St Ives PE27 . . . . 144 A7
Spencer Rd
 Guyhirn PE13. . . . . 235 A2
 Soham CB7 . . . . 212 A4
Spencer Rd CB10 . . . . 18 D3
Spens Ave CB7. . . . . 64 B8
Spenser Cl SG8 . . . . 13 D1
Sperside Cl **9** PE2 . . . . . . 185 D4
Spicer's Cl CB21. . . . . 53 F4
Spiggots Cl CB24 . . . . 123 E2
Spindle Rd CB9 . . . . 38 D1
Spinney Abbey **2** PE1 . . 211 D2
Spinney Cl
 Brampton PE28 . . . . 140 D3
 Warboys PE28 . . . . 164 F5
 Warmington PE8 . . . . 178 B2
Spinney CP Sch The CB1. 65 E6
Spinney Dr CB22. . . . . 49 A4
Spinney Field PE28. . . . . . 138 F3
Spinney Fields PE7 . . . . . . 176 F4
Spinney La PE28 . . . . 150 F5
Spinney The
 Bar Hill CB23. . . . . 102 B3
 Cottenham CB24 . . . . 125 E5
 Huntingdon PE29. . . . . 142 B6
Spinney Way
 Needingworth **5** PE27 . . 208 A3
 St Ives PE27 . . . . 144 A6
Spinning Inf Sch PE26 . . 172 B7
Spires End PE28 . . . . 150 D6
Spitfire Cl PE29. . . . . 141 B8
Spittals Way
 Huntingdon PE29. . . . . 141 C7
 The Stukeleys PE29. . . . . . 152 C1
Splash La
 Castor PE5. . . . . 184 E8
 St Ives PE28 . . . . 142 F6
Split Dro CB25. . . . . 129 A4
Spong Dro CB24 . . . . 209 B1
Spooners Cl CB8 . . . . 70 F8
Sprignall PE3. . . . . 196 F4
Springall Rd PE7. . . . . 186 B2
Spring Ave PE7 . . . . 186 B1
Springbrook PE19 . . . . 74 F4
Spring Cl
 Burwell CB25. . . . . 130 B1
 Histon CB24. . . . . 104 A1
 Huntingdon PE29. . . . . 141 E6
 Spring Comm Sch PE29. . 141 F6
 Spring Dr PE7 . . . . 187 B2
Springfield
 Huntingdon PE29. . . . . 141 C7

Springfield continued
 Peterborough PE1 . . . . . . 187 A7
 Somersham PE28. . . . . . . 215 C1
Springfield Ave PE15. . . . 243 C2
Springfield Rd
 Buckden PE19 . . . . 117 A3
 Great Cambourne CB23. . . 79 C2
 2 St Neots PE19 . . . . 75 A5
Springfield Rd
 Alconbury Weston PE28. . 150 D5
 Cambridge CB4 . . . . 83 E4
 1 Parson Drove PE13 . . 234 D7
 Peterborough PE1. . . . . . . 197 F5
 Sawston CB22 . . . . 32 F5
 Yaxley PE7 . . . . 181 F5
Springfields PE7 . . . . 190 C7
Springfield Terr **1** CB4 . . 83 E4
Springhead SG7 . . . . 2 D4
Springhead La CB7 . . . . . . 240 E5
Spring Hill MK44. . . . . 93 A3
Springfield Rd CB24. . . . . . 121 E6
Spring La
 Bassingbourn SG8. . . . . . . 12 F3
 Bottisham CB25. . . . . 86 F6
Spring Meadow Inf Sch
 CB7 . . . . 240 E6
Spring Pl PE19 . . . . 95 A1
Spruce Dr PE28. . . . . 151 F2
Spurgeons Ave CB25. . . . . 106 B8
Spurgeon's Cl CB1. . . . . . . 85 B1
Spurling Cl CB8. . . . . 91 C5
Square The
 6 Barnack PE9. . . . . 230 D4
 Stow cum Quy CB25. . . . . 86 A6
Squires Cl **17** PE28. . . . . . 215 C1
Squires Ct
 3 Eaton Socon PE19 . . . 74 B4
 Haverhill CB9. . . . . 23 E7
Squire's Dr PE14. . . . . 229 F7
Squire's Field The CB1. . . 67 F7
Squires Gate PE4 . . . . 204 F3
Squires The PE2 . . . . 186 F8
Stables Cl PE13. . . . . 238 B2
Stables The PE7 . . . . 189 C7
Stable Yd CB23. . . . . 79 B3
Stackyard The
 Ickleton CB10 . . . . 18 A3
 Peterborough PE2. . . . . . . 185 E5
Stafford Rd PE7 . . . . 189 F6
Staffordshire Gdns **8**
 CB1. . . . . 84 A1
Staffordshire St CB1 . . . . . 84 A2
Stagsden PE2. . . . . 185 F4
Stagshaw Dr PE2 . . . . 187 B8
STAGS HOLT 228 D7
Stagshaw Dr
 Cl CB7 . . . . 240 D4
Staithe Rd CB25 . . . . 245 E5
Stake Piece Rd SG8. . . . . . . 5 C5
Stakings The CB22 . . . . 32 D7
Stallebrass Cl PE2 . . . . 187 E5
STAMFORD 244 D4
Stamford Arts Ctr* PE9 . 244 D5
Stamford Ave SG8 . . . . 5 D7
Stamford Cl SG8. . . . . 5 D7
Stamford Coll PE9 . . . . 244 D6
Stamford Dr SG8. . . . . 5 D7
Stamford High Sch PE9 . 244 C4
Stamford Jun Sch PE9 . 244 B3
Stamford La PE8 . . . . 178 B3
Stamford Leisure Ctr
 PE9 . . . . 244 D6
Stamford Mus* PE9 . . . . . 244 C5
Stamford Rd
 Barnack PE9 . . . . 230 C4
 Easton on the Hill PE9. . . 244 A1
 Helpston PE6. . . . . 231 C1
 Marholm PE6 . . . . 203 B2
 Market Deeping PE6. . . . . 231 D8
 Peterborough PE1 . . . . . . 172 A7
 Stamford Ret Pk PE9. . . . 244 D6
Stamford & Rutland Hospl
 PE9. . . . . 244 D6
Stamford Sch PE9 . . . . 244 C5
Stamford St **3** CB9. . . . . . 111 B2
Stamford Sta PE9. . . . . 244 B4
Stamford Theatre* **14**
 PE9 . . . . 244 D5
Stamford Wlk **11** PE9 . . . . 244 C5
Stamford Yd SG8 . . . . 5 C6
Stamper St PE1 . . . . 196 F3
Stanbury Cl CB25. . . . . 84 E6
Stanch Hill Rd PE28. . . . . . 168 C3
Standish Ct PE2 . . . . 186 D8
Stanegate **3** PE28. . . . . . . 168 D2
Stanesfield Rd CB5 . . . . . . 84 B3
Stamford Bus Pk PE9. . . . 244 D7
Stanground PE2 . . . . 187 C5
Stanley Rd
 Cambridge CB5 . . . . 84 B3
 Great Chesterford CB10 . . 18 E3
 Newmarket CB8. . . . . 111 C3
 Peterborough PE1. . . . . . . 198 A3
Stanley St PE1 . . . . 198 A3
Stanley Webb Cl CB22. . . . 33 A8
Stanpoint Way PE27 . . . . . 144 A5
Stan Rowing Ct PE2 . . . . . 187 C7

Stansfield Gdns CB21 . . . . .66 F5
Stansgate Ave CB2. . . . . . . 65 B3
Stanton Mere Way CB24. 124 A6
Stantons CB21. . . . . 35 B2
Stanton Sq PE7. . . . . 186 D2
Stanwick Ct PE3 . . . . 197 F2
Stapledon Rd PE1 . . . . 185 D2
Staplee Way PE1. . . . . 198 F6
STAPLEFORD 49 D4
Stapleford Com Prim Sch
 CB22. . . . . 49 C4
Staples La CB7 . . . . 212 B3
Staploe Mews **18** CB7 . . 212 B4
Star Cl PE1 . . . . 198 C3
Star & Garter La CB8 . . . . . 91 C7
Stargoose Cl CB23 . . . . 80 B1
Star La
 Ramsey PE26 . . . . 172 A8
 Stamford PE9. . . . . 244 C5
Starling Cl
 Alconbury PE28 . . . . 150 E4
 Milton CB24. . . . . 105 D3
Starlock Cl CB6. . . . . 210 E4
Star Mews PE1 . . . . 198 C2
Star Rd PE1 . . . . 198 C2
Stathern Rd PE1 . . . . 198 D7
Station App
 March PE15 . . . . 243 D6
 Newmarket CB8. . . . . 111 A2
 Somersham PE28. . . . . . . 208 C8
Station Ave PE13. . . . . 234 D5
Station Dr
 Wisbech PE13 . . . . 245 C4
 Wisbech St Mary PE13 . . 235 C7
Station Gate CB25 . . . . 109 B8
Station Gdns PE26 . . . . . . 172 A8
Station La PE19. . . . . 117 F3
Station Rd
 Abbots Ripton PE28. . . . . 162 B1
 Ailsworth PE5 . . . . 184 C8
 Ashwell SG7. . . . . 2 E4
 Barnack PE9 . . . . 230 E4
 Bluntisham PE28 . . . . 208 C4
 Cambridge CB1. . . . . 64 F7
 Catworth PE28. . . . . 136 D5
 Chatteris PE16. . . . . 241 C4
 Deeping St James PE6 . . 206 E6
 Dullingham CB8. . . . . 89 C2
 Elm PE14. . . . . 235 C2
 Ely CB7 . . . . 240 D3
 Fordham CB7. . . . . 131 A8
 Foxton CB22. . . . . 30 B6
 Fulbourn CB21 . . . . 67 A5
 Gamlingay SG19 . . . . 41 E5
 Gedney Hill PE12 . . . . 233 F8
 Great Shelford CB22. . . . . 49 A1
 Haddenham CB6 . . . . 210 A6
 Harston CB22 . . . . 47 F2
 Haverhill CB9. . . . . 24 A8
 Histon CB24. . . . . 133 F5
 Holme PE7 . . . . 177 A4
 Isleham CB7 . . . . 213 A4
 Kennett CB8. . . . . 133 F5
 Kimbolton PE28 . . . . 113 F5
 Linton CB21. . . . . 132 B3
 Littleport CB6 . . . . 242 E4
 Lode CB25 . . . . 107 C2
 Longstanton CB24 . . . . . . 123 F4
 Manea PE15 . . . . 224 B5
 March PE15. . . . . 243 D5
 Meldreth SG8 . . . . 14 B6
 Mildenhall IP28. . . . . 239 B3
 Oakington & Westwick
  CB24. . . . . 103 D7
 Over CB24 . . . . 122 F8
 Pampisford CB21. . . . . 33 F6
 Peterborough PE2 . . . . . . 197 F2
 Ramsey PE26. . . . . 172 A7
 Shepreth SG8. . . . . 29 E5
 Soham CB7 . . . . 212 B4
 Stamford PE9. . . . . 244 B4
 Steeple Morden SG8 . . . . . 3 B7
 St Ives PE27 . . . . 144 B3
 St Neots PE19 . . . . 75 B5
 Stow cum Quy CB25. . . . . 86 A5
 Sutton CB6. . . . . 216 F1
 Swaffham Bulbeck CB25 . 108 A2
 Swaffham Prior CB25. . . . 108 C5
 Swavesey CB24 . . . . 122 F7
 Thorney PE6 . . . . 183 A4
 Tilbrook PE28. . . . . 113 B7
 Walsoken PE14 . . . . 241 F6
 Warboys PE28 . . . . 164 F7
 Waterbeach CB25 . . . . . . 106 B7
 Whittlesey PE7 . . . . 189 E5
 Wilburton CB6 . . . . 210 C7
 Willingham CB24 . . . . 124 A7
 Wisbech St Mary PE13 . . 235 C7
 Yaxley PE7. . . . . 182 A7
Station Road E CB22. . . . . 32 E3
Station Road W CB22. . . . 32 E3
Station St PE16. . . . . 241 B4
Station Yd PE28 . . . . 239 B3
STAUGHTON GREEN 93 F7
STAUGHTON HIGHWAY . . . 94 A5
Staughton Pl **2** PE19. . . . 74 C4
Staunch Hill PE28. . . . . . . 148 C3
Staverton Rd PE4 . . . . 204 A3
Staxton Cl PE6. . . . . 203 C1
Stearne's Yd CB23 . . . . 47 B5
Steeple PE15 . . . . 74 B2
STEEPLE GIDDING 159 B7
STEEPLE MORDEN 3 E8
Steeple Morden CE Prim Sch
 SG8 . . . . 11 B2

Steeple Row 13 CB7 .... 240 D4
Steeple View
  March PE15. . . . . 243 C1
  Wisbech PE13 . . . . . . 245 F7
Stephen Cl CB9 . . . . . . 23 F8
Stephenson Cl
  1 March PE15 . . . . . . 243 D7
  Royston SG8 . . . . 5 B7
  Yaxley PE7 . . . . 181 D6
Stephenson Ct PE1 . . . 198 B2
Stephenson Rd PE27 . . 144 B6
Stephens Way 15 PE6 . 231 F8
Stepping Stones PE28. . 143 D1
Stermyn St 14 PE13 . . 245 C5
Sterndale Cl CB3 . . . . . 82 E8
Sterne Cl CB1 . . . . 65 B6
Sternes Way CB22 . . . . 49 C4
STETCHWORTH 90 A2
STETCHWORTH LEY . . . 71 B7
Stetchworth Rd
  Dullingham CB8. . . . . . 70 F8
  Stetchworth CB8 . . . . 71 B4
Stevens Cl CB24 . . . . . 125 D4
Stevenson Ct
  Cambridge CB5 . . . . . . 84 A3
  Eaton Socon PE19 . . . 74 D6
Stevensons Rd CB24 . . 123 E2
Stevens Way PE15 . . . 243 D6
STEVENTON END. 21 C2
Steward Cl CB7. . . . . . 211 D8
Stewards Field 16 CB7 212 E1
Steward's La CB5 . . . . 216 E1
Stewart Cl PE28 . . . . . 140 C2
Steynings The PE4 . . . 204 C3
STIBBINGTON 194 C2
Stickle Cl PE29 . . . . . . 141 B7
Stile Plantation SG8 . . . 5 E6
Stiles The PE29 . . . . . 141 F1
Still The PE13. . . . . . . 238 B1
STILTON 176 A7
Stilton CE Prim Sch PE7 175 F7
Stirling Cl
  Beck Row, Holywell Row &
    Kenny Hill IP28. . . . 213 D6
  Cambridge CB4 . . . . . 84 A5
  Warboys PE28 . . . . . 164 F4
Stirling Dr CB8 . . . . . . 23 E8
Stirling Gdns CB8. . . . 110 E4
Stirling Rd PE27 . . . . 144 A7
Stirling Way
  Papworth Village CB23 . 99 C1
  Peterborough PE3 . . . 204 A1
  3 Sutton CB6 . . . . . . 216 E2
  Witchford CB6. . . . . . 217 F1
STIRTLOE 118 B2
Stirtloe La PE19 . . . . . 117 A2
Stitch The PE14. . . . . 236 B4
Stocker Way 2 PE19. . . 74 E2
Stocking Cl PE28 . . . . 161 C4
Stocking Dro
  Chatteris PE16. . . . . . 241 B1
  Ferry Hill PE16. . . . . . 215 E6
Stocking Fen Rd PE26. 221 A1
Stocking La
  Nuthampstead SG8 . . . . 1 A2
  Spaldwick PE28 . . . . 114 E8
Stockley Cl CB9. . . . . . 24 C7
Stocks Bridge Way PE27 144 C5
Stocks Cl CB25 . . . . . . 86 E5
Stocks Hill PE5 . . . . . 195 F1
Stocks La
  Gamlingay SG19 . . . . 41 D4
  Orwell SG8. . . . . 45 E1
Stockwell St CB1 . . . . . 65 B8
Stokesay Ct PE3 . . . . 197 B1
Stokes Cl CB24 . . . . . 123 F1
Stonald Ave PE7 . . . . 189 D8
Stonald Rd PE7 . . . . . 189 C8
Stonea Camp* PE15 . . 223 E8
Stonebridge PE2. . . . 186 C5
Stonebridge La CB21. . 67 A4
Stonebridge Lea PE2. . 186 C5
Stonecross Way PE15 . 243 D3
Stone Field CB23 . . . . 102 A3
Stonehill
  Huntingdon PE29 . . . 141 C7
  St Neots PE19 . . . . . 75 C5
Stonehill Rd CB22 . . . . 48 E7
Stonehouse Rd
  Upwell PE14. . . . . . . 236 E1
  Yaxley PE7 . . . . 181 E5
Stone La
  Meldreth SG8. . . . . . 29 C3
  Peterborough PE1 . . . 197 F5
Stoneleigh Ct PE3 . . . 197 B2
STONELY. 115 B3
Stonely Rd PE28 . . . . 138 B3
Stone St CB1. . . . . . . 84 B1
Stone Terr CB1 . . . . . . 84 B1
Stoney Cl PE29 . . . . . 141 E8
Storbeck Rd 8 PE13. . 245 D7
Storers Wlk PE7 . . . . 190 C6
Stores Hill CB8 . . . . . . 92 E8
Storey's Bar Rd PE6 . . 199 A3
Storey's Way CB3. . . . 83 B3
Storrington Way PE4. . 204 C3
Stott Gdns CB4 . . . . . 84 A6
Stott St CB23 . . . . 99 A2
STOURBRIDGE COMMON. 84 B4
Stourbridge Gr CB1. . . 84 C1
Stour Cl PE27 . . . . . . 144 A6
Stour Gn CB6. . . . . . . 240 E8
Stour Valley Rd CB9. . . 24 B7
STOW CUM QUY 86 A6
Stowehill Rd PE4 . . . . 204 F2

Stowgate Rd PE6 . . . . 206 B7
Stow Gdns PE13 . . . . 245 E4
Stow La PE13. . . . . . . 245 E4
STOW LONGA 137 C2
Stow Rd
  Kimbolton PE28. . . . . 113 F5
  Spaldwick PE28 . . . . 137 F6
  Stow cum Quy CB25 . . 85 F5
  Wisbech PE13 . . . . . . 245 F5
Straight Dro
  Bury PE28 . . . . 172 D3
  Coveney CB6 . . . . . . 217 C7
  Farcet PE7 . . . . 187 E1
  Sawtry PE28 . . . . 168 D3
  Wistow PE28 . . . . . . 172 E2
Straight Furlong CB6 . . 224 C2
Straight Rd PE15 . . . . 224 B3
Strangeways Rd CB1. . 65 D4
Strasbourg Sq 6 CB9. . 24 B8
Stratfield Cl CB4. . . . . 83 B5
Stratford Pl PE19 . . . . 74 C3
Strathcarron Cl CB4 . . 83 C7
Strawberry Cl PE13 . . 245 A6
Strawberry Fields CB6 . 23 D7
STREETLY END 37 A5
Streetly End CB21. . . . 37 B5
Street The
  Barton Mills IP28 . . . 239 C2
  Beck Row, Holywell Row &
    Kenny Hill IP28 . . . 214 A8
  Dalham CB8. . . . . . . 92 E8
  Freckenham IP28 . . . 213 C3
  Great Bradley CB8. . . 55 F7
  Great Wratting CB9. . 39 E6
  Kirtling CB8 . . . . 72 D6
  Lidgate CB8 . . . . 73 D8
  Mildenhall IP28 . . . . 213 E8
  Moulton CB8 . . . . . . 112 F5
  Snailwell CB8. . . . . . 124 F5
  Westley Waterless CB8. 70 C5
  Woodditton CB8. . . . 91 B2
  Worlington IP28 . . . . 213 F4
Streetways CB8. . . . . . 68 E7
STRETHALL 9 F4
STRETHAM 213 D6
Stretham Com Prim Sch
  CB6 . . . . 210 F5
Stretham Old Engine*
  CB6 . . . . 210 F4
Stretham Rd
  Wicken CB7 . . . . 211 D2
  Wilburton CB6 . . . . . 210 D5
Stretten Ave CB4 . . . . 83 D4
Stretton Ave CB8 . . . . 111 B2
Stricklands Dr 4 PE6 . 232 B8
Strollers Way CB8 . . . . 90 A2
Stroud Hill PE28 . . . . 165 E2
Strympole Way CB23. . 80 B1
Stuart Cl
  Godmanchester PE29 . 142 A1
  Peterborough PE2 . . . 187 C6
Stuart Ct PE1. . . . . . . 198 B4
Stuart Dr SG8 . . . . 5 D8
Stubbs Cl
  9 Haverhill CB9 . . . . 38 D1
  St Ives PE27 . . . . . . 144 A7
Studland Ret Pk CB8. . 110 F7
STUDLANDS PARK. . . 110 F8
Studlands Park Ave CB8. 110 D6
Studlands Rise SG8 . . . 5 E6
Studlands Rise Fst Sch
  SG8. . . . . 5 E6
STUKELEY 141 B6
Stukeley Cl
  Cambridge CB4 . . . . . 64 A8
  Peterborough PE2 . . . 187 D5
Stukeley Meadows Com Prim
  Sch PE29. . . . . 141 C6
Stukeley Meadows Ind Est
  PE29. . . . . 141 C6
Stukeley Pk PE28 . . . . 152 A2
Stukeley Rd PE29 . . . 141 C6
Stulp Field Rd CB3. . . . 64 A4
Stumpacre PE3 . . . . . 197 A8
Stumpcross 3 PE28 . . 168 C2
Stump Cross CB10 . . . 18 D5
STUNTNEY. 218 D1
Stuntney Cswy CB7 . . 240 E2
STURMER. 24 F4
Sturmer Cl CB9 . . . . . 24 C7
Sturmer Rd CB9 . . . . . 23 C7
Sturmer Road Ind Est
  CB9 . . . . 24 C6
Sturrock Way PE3 . . . 197 C8
Sturton St CB1 . . . . . . 84 A1
Sudbury Ct
  Peterborough PE7 . . . 187 F5
  Whittlesey PE7 . . . . . 189 D8
Sudeley Gr CB23 . . . . 81 A3
Suet Hills Dro PE7 . . . 188 E1
Suez Rd CB1. . . . . 65 C7
Suffolk Cl
  5 Ely CB6. . . . . 240 A3
  Huntingdon PE29 . . . 141 F6
  Peterborough PE3 . . . 197 B2
  St Ives PE27 . . . . . . 144 A8
Suffolk Rd 5 SG8 . . . . 5 E6
Suffolk Way
  March PE15. . . . . . . 243 E2
  Newmarket CB8. . . . 110 E5
Sugar Way PE2 . . . . . 186 D8
Sulehay Rd PE8. . . . . 193 C1
Summerling Way PE28. 208 C6
Summerfield CB3 . . . . 64 C8
Summerfield Cl
  Burwell CB25. . . . . . 130 C1
  Wisbech PE13 . . . . . 245 A6
Summerfield Rd PE1. . 197 F4

Summerhayes 1 CB7 . 240 F6
Sunderland Ave CB22 . 33 A8
Sundew Cl PE19 . . . . . 74 B6
Sunfield Rd PE26. . . . 172 A4
Sunflower St CB4. . . . 83 D7
Sun Hill SG8. . . . . 5 C5
Sun La 6 CB8. . . . . . 111 A3
Sunmead Wlk CB1 . . . 66 A6
Sunningdale PE2 . . . . 185 E6
Sunningdale Ave IP28. 239 B4
Sunningdale Cvn Pk CB4. 84 D6
Sunnybank 1 PE19 . . 75 A5
Sunnymead PE2 . . . . 204 A6
Sunnymead Orch SG7 . 3 A3
Sunnyside CB5 . . . . . . 84 E2
Sunnyville Rd PE7 . . . 190 F8
Sunset Gdns PE13 . . . 245 E2
Sunset Sq 2 CB4 . . . . 83 D7
Sun St
  1 Cambridge CB1 . . . 84 A2
  Isleham CB7 . . . . . . 213 A5
Surrey Rd PE29 . . . . . 141 E8
Sussex Rd
  Stamford PE9. . . . . . 244 B6
  Wyton Airfield PE28. . 143 B8
Sussex St CB2 . . . . . . 246 B3
Sutcliffe Rd PE8 . . . . 193 D8
SUTTON
  Ailsworth 194 F2
  Ely 216 E2
Sutton CE Prim Sch CB6 216 E1
Sutton Cl CB24 . . . . . 105 D3
Sutton Ct 6 CB6 . . . . 216 E2
Sutton Gate PE12 . . . 237 D8
Sutton Heath Rd PE9 . 194 D7
Sutton Mdws PE13. . . 245 A8
Sutton Pk CB6. . . . . . 216 E2
Sutton Rd
  Eyeworth SG19 . . . . . 10 A8
  Haddenham CB6 . . . . 210 A8
  Mepal CB6. . . . . 216 E3
  Newton PE13 . . . . . . 238 B6
  Wentworth CB6 . . . . 217 C1
  Wisbech PE13 . . . . . 245 A7
  Witchford CB6. . . . . . 217 C1
Suttons Cl PE14 . . . . . 77 D8
Sutton's La PE6. . . . . 231 E8
Sutton Way 1 PE15. . 223 A5
Svenskaby PE2 . . . . . 185 C6
SWAFFHAM BULBECK . 108 E3
Swaffham Bulbeck CE Prim
  Sch CB25 . . . . 108 B1
Swaffham Heath Rd
  CB25. . . . . 108 C1
SWAFFHAM PRIOR . . 108 E4
Swaffham Prior CE Prim Sch
  CB25. . . . . 108 D5
Swaffham Rd
  Bottisham CB25. . . . . 107 E1
  Burwell CB25. . . . . . 109 A7
  Reach CB25. . . . . . . 108 E8
Swain Ct PE2. . . . . . . 186 F8
Swain's Dro PE13. . . . 238 C8
Swale Ave PE4 . . . . . 204 E1
Swallow Cl PE7 . . . . . 201 A1
Swallow Ct
  Manea PE15. . . . . . . 224 B4
  3 St Neots PE19 . . . . 75 B6
Swallowfield PE4 . . . 204 A4
Swallow La PE13 . . . . 238 B8
Swallow Way PE15. . . 243 F5
Swan Cl
  St Ives PE27 . . . . . . 143 F7
  Whittlesey PE7 . . . . . 189 F8
Swan Ct PE15. . . . . . . 243 D6
Swan Dr PE16 . . . . . . 241 D5
Swan End PE19 . . . . . 117 B4
Swan Gdns
  Fenstanton PE28 . . . 121 B5
  Parson Drove PE13 . . 234 C7
  Peterborough PE1 . . . 198 E6
Swan Gr CB8 . . . . 110 B8
Swanhill PE8 . . . . 194 A4
Swan La
  Exning CB8. . . . . . . 110 B8
  Guilden Morden SG8 . . 10 F4
  Haverhill CB9. . . . . . 24 A8
Swann Rd CB5. . . . . . 84 C4
Swann's Cl SG8. . . . . 26 A3
Swann's Rd CB5. . . . . 84 B4
Swann's Terr 4 CB1 . . 65 A8
Swan Rd
  Fenstanton PE28 . . . 121 B5
  Whittlesey PE7 . . . . . 189 F8
Swansley La CB23. . . . 79 A4
Swanspool PE3 . . . . . 197 B6
Swan St SG7 . . . . 2 C4
Swanton Cl PE15 . . . . 243 D7
Swavesdale Dro CB7 . 219 A5
SWAVESEY. 123 E6
Swavesey Prim Sch
  CB24. . . . . 122 E6
Swavesey Rd CB24 . . 122 A4
Swavesey Village Coll
  CB23. . . . . 79 A4
Swayne's La CB23 . . . 62 C5
Sweetbriar La PE4 . . . 204 B6
Sweetentree Way 3
  CB23. . . . . 79 A4
Sweeting Ave PE19 . . 95 F1
Sweetings Rd PE29 . . 118 F8
Swift Cl
  March PE15. . . . . . . 243 F5
  Market Deeping PE6 . 231 E8
  Royston SG8 . . . . . . 13 D1
  St Neots PE19 . . . . . 75 B6
Swifts Cnr CB21. . . . . 66 F5

Swinburne Cl SG8 . . . 13 D1
SWINGBROW. 222 D3
Swinnell Cl SG8 . . . . . 13 A5
Sybil Rd PE13. . . . . . . 245 C6
Sycamore Ave PE1. . . 198 C6
Sycamore Cl
  4 Cambridge CB1 . . . 65 D5
  March PE15. . . . . . . 243 C3
Sycamore Dr PE29 . . . 141 E8
Sycamore La CB7 . . . . 240 F5
Sycamore Pl CB6 . . . . 242 D4
Sycamore Rd PE7 . . . 189 F6
Sycamores The
  Bluntisham/Colne PE28. 208 C6
  Little Paxton PE19 . . 95 F2
Sydney Rd PE2 . . . . . 187 D5
Syers La PE7 . . . . 189 D7
Sylton Cl PE29. . . . . . 141 F1
Sylvden Dr PE13. . . . . 245 F6
Sylvester Rd CB3 . . . . 83 B1
Symmington Cl PE2. . 186 F8
Symonds Cl CB24 . . . 104 B4
Symonds La
  Grantchester CB3 . . . 64 A4
  Linton CB21. . . . . . . 35 B3
Sywell Gr 5 PE14 . . . 236 A5

T

Tabor Ct PE7 . . . . 186 D2
Tabrum Cl CB23 . . . . . 63 F4
Tadlow Cl CB23 . . . . . 25 C3
Tadlow Rd SG19 . . . . . 25 C3
Tait Cl PE1 . . . . 198 C5
Talbot Ave PE2 . . . . . 186 D6
Talbot Cl PE6 . . . . 175 F8
Talbot Dro CB6. . . . . . 216 E2
TALLINGTON 230 E7
Tallington Dry Ski Slope
  PE9. . . . . 230 F8
Tallington Lakes Leisure
  Pk* PE9. . . . . 231 A8
Tallington Rd PE9. . . . 230 F5
Tall's La PE28. . . . . . . 121 B6
Tall Trees 3 SG8. . . . . . 5 E6
Tamar Cl PE27. . . . . . 144 B6
Tamarin Gdns CB1. . . 66 A6
Tanglewood
  Alconbury Weston PE28. 150 E6
  Peterborough PE4 . . . 204 B6
Tanhouse PE2 . . . . . . 186 C5
Tan House La PE25. . . 109 B8
Tannersfield Way CB8. 110 F4
Tanners La CB7 . . . . . 212 B3
Tanners La CB24. . . . . 5 C6
Tannery Drift SG8. . . . 5 C2
Tannery Drift Fst Sch SG8. 5 C6
Tannery Rd CB22. . . . 32 F6
Tansor Garth PE3 . . . 197 C5
Tansor Grange PE3 . . 178 A1
Tansur Ct PE19 . . . . . 74 F8
Tansy Cl 1 PE19 . . . . 74 B5
Tantallon Ct PE3 . . . . 197 B1
Tanyard The SG8. . . . 112 E1
Tan Yd PE19 . . . . 74 F5
Tarrant PE4. . . . . 204 A6
Taskers Field CB23. . . 78 E2
Tasman Rd CB9 . . . . . 24 C7
Tates Field
  Caxton CB23 . . . . . . 78 E1
  Great Grandsen CB23 . 59 E8
Tatwin Dr 8 PE6 . . . . 232 B8
Taunton Cl CB1 . . . . . 65 D7
Taverners Dr PE26 . . . 171 F5
Taverners Rd PE1. . . . 197 F4
Tavistock Cl 8 PE6 . . 233 A3
Tavistock Rd
  Cambridge CB4 . . . . . 83 C6
  Wisbech PE13 . . . . . 245 D5
Tawny Cres PE29 . . . . 142 B7
Tay Cl PE27 . . . . 144 B7
Taylor's Dro PE12 . . . 237 C8
Taylors Field CB8 . . . . 70 F8
Taylors Gn PE8 . . . . . 178 A2
Taylor's La PE19 . . . . 116 F5
Taylor's La CB24 . . . . 122 D6
Taymor Pl PE14. . . . . 225 A8
Teachers Cl PE15 . . . . 224 B4
Tea Kettle La CB8 . . . . 89 F1
Teal Ave CB7 . . . . 212 A5
Teal Cl
  Chatteris PE16. . . . . 241 C6
  St Ives PE27 . . . . . . 143 F7
Teal Rd PE7 . . . . 189 F8
Teanby Ct PE1. . . . . . 196 F3
Teasdale Cl SG8 . . . . . 13 D1
Teasel Cl
  Eaton Socon PE19 . . . 74 C6
  1 Haverhill CB9. . . . . 38 D1
  2 Royston SG8 . . . . . 5 E5
Teasel Dr CB8. . . . . . 240 B5
Teasel Way CB1. . . . . 66 A5
Tebbutts Rd PE19. . . . 74 E5
Tedder Way CB4 . . . . 83 C6
Telegraph St CB24 . . . 125 E4
Telford Dr PE7. . . . . . 181 D6
Templars Cl PE29. . . . 141 E4
Temple Cl
  Duxford CB22 . . . . . . 32 D1
  Huntingdon PE29 . . . 141 E4
Temple Ct 4 CB24 . . . 88 E7
Templemore Cl CB1. . 65 B4

Temple Pl PE29. . . . . 141 E4
Temple Rd CB7 . . . . . 212 F4
Temples Ct PE6. . . . . 231 B4
Tempsford Rd SG19 . . 40 A4
Ten Acre Dro PE7 . . . 220 C8
Ten Bell La 3 CB7. . . . 212 B4
Tenby Cl CB1. . . . . . . 66 A6
Tenby Way 9 PE19 . . 74 F1
Tenison Ave CB1 . . . . 64 F7
Tenison Manor CB24 . 125 D4
Tenison Rd CB1. . . . . 65 A8
Ten Mile Bank CB6. . . 242 F6
Tennis Court Ave PE29. 141 E5
Tennis Court Rd CB2 . 246 B3
Tennis Court Terr CB22 246 A1
Tennyson Ave PE27 . . 143 F6
Tennyson Cl
  Huntingdon PE29 . . . 141 F6
  Royston SG8 . . . . . . 13 D1
Tennyson Pl
  Eaton Socon PE19 . . . 74 D6
  Ely CB6 . . . . 240 A5
Tennyson Rd PE1 . . . . 197 F7
Tenter La PE9 . . . . . . 244 C5
Tenterleas PE27 . . . . 144 B3
Tern Cl PE14 . . . . 24 C7
Tern Gdns PE16. . . . . 241 C6
Tern Rd PE7. . . . . 186 C2
Tern Way 4 PE19. . . . 75 B6
Terrill Cl PE29 . . . . . . 141 C5
Terrington Cl PE14 . . . 236 D6
Terr The
  Little Shelford CB22. . 48 E3
  Newmarket CB8. . . . 111 A3
TETWORTH 40 F7
Tetworth Hill SG19. . . 41 A7
TEVERSHAM 85 C1
Teversham CE Prim Sch
  CB5 . . . . 85 B2
Teversham Drift CB1. . 66 A7
Teversham Rd CB21. . 66 E6
Teversham Way CB22 . 50 A1
Texas PE28 . . . . 151 E4
Teynham Cl CB1 . . . . 65 D7
Thackeray Cl SG8. . . . 13 D1
Thackers Cl PE8 . . . . 194 A4
Thackray Cl PE29 . . . 141 E7
Thames Rd PE29 . . . . 141 F8
Thaw Way CB7 . . . . . 213 C1
Thatchers Cl
  Ramsey PE26. . . . . . 171 B2
  Yelling PE19. . . . . . . 95 B2
Thatcher Stanfords Cl
  SG8 . . . . 14 C7
Thatchers Wood CB24. 123 F1
Thatchwood Ave PE14. 236 C6
Thetford Cnr CB6. . . . 211 A7
Thetford Rd IP28 . . . . 239 E4
Thetford Terr CB5. . . . 84 F3
Thicket Rd PE28 . . . . 143 B4
Thickwillow 8 PE29 . . 118 F8
Thimble Cl PE28. . . . . 208 D6
Third Ave
  Warboys PE28 . . . . . 164 E6
  Wisbech PE13 . . . . . 245 E5
Third Dro
  Downham CB6. . . . . . 225 B1
  Peterborough PE1 . . . 198 E2
Third Marsh Rd PE14 . 238 C3
Thirlby Gdns CB7 . . . 240 E7
Thirleby Cl CB4. . . . . 83 D5
Thirlmere Gdns PE4 . . 204 E3
Thirlmere Rd PE29 . . 141 B6
Thirlwall Dr CB7 . . . . 213 A1
Thistle Cnr CB7 . . . . . 218 D4
Thistle Dr PE2 . . . . . . 187 C7
Thistle Gn CB24 . . . . 122 E6
Thistlemoor Rd PE1. . 197 E7
THISTLEY GREEN. . . . 213 C7
Thodays Cl CB24 . . . . 209 A1
Thoday St CB1. . . . . . 84 B4
THOLOMAS DROVE. . . 235 A5
Thomas Christian Way
  CB25. . . . . 86 E7
Thomas Cl PE13 . . . . 196 F3
Thomas Clarkson Com Coll
  PE13. . . . . 245 C3
Thomas Deacon Acad
  PE1. . . . . 198 B3
Thomas Eaton Prim Sch The
  PE15. . . . . 225 B7
Thomas King Dr PE29. 141 C6
Thomas Parsons Sq CB7 240 C4
Thomas Rd CB25 . . . . 66 D5
Thomas Way SG8 . . . 13 D1
Thompsons Gd PE7 . . 186 D3
Thompson's La CB2 . . 246 A3
Thompsons Mdw SG8 . 11 A4
Thongsley PE29 . . . . . 141 F7
Thongsley Fields Prim Sch
  PE29. . . . . 141 F7
Thorby Ave PE15. . . . 243 A7
Thorley Cres PE2 . . . . 186 D8
Thorley Rd CB5. . . . . 84 E2
Thordon Cl CB7 . . . . . 62 D5
Thorn Cl CB7 . . . . 212 A4
Thorndown Cl PE27. . 143 D6
Thorndown Inf Sch PE27 143 D6
Thorndown Jun Sch
  PE27. . . . . 143 D6
THORNEY. 233 A3
Thorney Dyke PE6 . . . 201 C6
Thorney Heritage Mus*
  PE6 . . . . 233 A3

Thorney Rd
Eye PE6 . . . . 232 B1
Newborough PE6 . . . . 206 E2
Wisbech St Mary PE13 . . . 234 C3
THORNEY TOLL 234 A3
Thornham Way PE7 . . . . 190 C6
THORNHAUGH 193 F5
Thornhill Pl CB24 . . . . 123 F2
Thornleigh Dr PE2 . . . . 186 C6
Thornmead PE4 . . . . 204 D4
Thorn Rd PE7 . . . . 186 C2
Thornton Cl
Girton CB3 . . . . 82 F6
Peterborough PE4 . . . . 204 E3
Thornton Rd
Girton CB3 . . . . 82 F7
March PE15 . . . . 243 D6
Thornton Way CB3 . . . . 83 A6
Thorolds Way PE5 . . . . 195 D2
Thoroughfare La CB7 . . . . . 218 F1
Thoroughfare Way CB6 . . 242 E4
Thorpe Ave PE3 . . . . 197 C2
Thorpe Lea Rd PE3 . . . . . . 197 F1
Thorpe Mdws PE3 . . . . 197 D1
Thorpe Park Rd PE3 . . . . . 197 C3
Thorpe Prim Sch PE3 . . . . 197 B3
Thorpe Rd PE3 . . . . 197 B1
Thorpe The PE28 . . . . 143 B1
Thorpe Way CB5 . . . . 84 F4
Thorpe Wood PE3 . . . . 196 F1
Thorpe Wood Nature
Reserve* PE3 . . . . 196 F1
Thorseby Cl PE3 . . . . 197 B3
Thrapston Rd
Brampton PE28 . . . . 140 B4
Catworth PE28 . . . . 147 C2
Ellington PE28 . . . . 139 A4
Kimbolton PE28 . . . . 150 E3
Spaldwick PE28 . . . . 137 F6
Three Cups Wlk CB7 . . . . 240 D4
Three Hills 21 A7
THREE HOLES 229 E7
Three Shires Way PE28 . 135 E4
Thrifts Wlk CB4 . . . . 84 A4
THRIPLOW 31 C2
Thriplow CE Prim Sch
SG8 . . . . 31 B2
Thriplow Rd SG8 . . . . 30 F1
THROCKENHOLT 234 B8
Throckmorton PE28 . . . . . 164 E5
Throckmorton Rd PE28 . . 117 D8
Throstlenest PE7 . . . . 187 C3
Thruffle Way CB23 . . . . . . 102 C3
Thulborn Cl CB1 . . . . 85 B1
Thurland's Dro PE14 . . . . 229 C8
Thurlaston Cl PE3 . . . . 197 B2
Thurley Cl PE19 . . . . 95 E5
Thurloe Cl PE13 . . . . 245 C2
Thurlow Rd
Great Wratting CB9 . . . . . . 39 C6
Withersfield CB9 . . . . 38 D4
Thurnall Ave SG8 . . . . 5 D5
Thurning Ave PE2 . . . . 187 C6
Thurning Rd PE28 . . . . 119 C7
Thur Gr PE2 . . . . 186 A3
Thursfield PE4 . . . . 204 C4
Thurston Gate PE3 . . . . . . 197 A1
Tiberius Cl CB9 . . . . 24 D7
TILBROOK 114 B7
Tilbrook Mill MK44 . . . . . . 113 A7
Tilbrook Rd PE28 . . . . 113 D6
Tillbrooks Hill CB8 . . . . 73 C1
Tilling Way CB6 . . . . 242 D3
Tillyard Way CB1 . . . . 65 D4
Tilton Ct PE1 . . . . 198 C8
Tindall Cl PE13 . . . . 245 C8
Tinker's Dro PE13 . . . . 245 D8
Tinkers La PE28 . . . . 168 B4
Tinker's La CB23 . . . . 61 C2
Tintagel Ct
Peterborough PE3 . . . . 197 B1
☑ St Neots PE19 . . . . 74 F2
Tintern Rise ☑ PE6 . . . . . 232 A1
Tinus Ave PE7 . . . . 186 C1
Tinwell Rd PE9 . . . . 244 A4
Tinwell Rd La PE9 . . . . 244 A4
Tipplers' Rd CB24 . . . . 122 E2
TIPPS END 229 F2
Tiptree Cl CB5 . . . . 84 F4
Tirrington PE2 . . . . 187 A2
Titchmarsh Cl SG8 . . . . 5 D7
Tithe Ave PE28 . . . . 213 F8
Tithe Cl PE28 . . . . 120 B2
Tithe Rd PE16 . . . . 241 C2
Tithe Way CB23 . . . . 79 C3
Tiverton Rd PE3 . . . . 197 C3
Tiverton Way CB1 . . . . 65 C7
Toates Cl CB6 . . . . 210 C6
TOFT 61 C4
Toft La CB21 . . . . 67 F7
Toftland PE2 . . . . 186 D5
Tointons Rd PE14 . . . . 229 F8
Tolethorpe Sq ☑ PE9 . . . 244 B6
Toll Bar La PE28 . . . . 146 B5
Toll Dro PE15 . . . . 224 A3
Tollfield PE28 . . . . 113 F4
Tollgate PE3 . . . . 197 A5
Toll House Rd PE2 . . . . . . 203 A2
Toll Rd PE7 . . . . 188 A5
Tom Jennings Cl CB8 . . . . 110 F5
Tomlins Cl SG8 . . . . 6 F1
Tomlinson Ct PE29 . . . . . . 141 F8
Toneham La PE4 . . . . 226 F1
Topcliffe Way CB1 . . . . 65 C3
TOP END 93 B1
Topham Cres ☑ PE6 . . . . 233 A3
Topham Way PE19 . . . . 74 F7
Topham Way CB4 . . . . 83 D6

Top La PE19 . . . . 57 B5
Topmoor Way PE4 . . . . . . 204 F1
Topper St CB4 . . . . 83 E8
Top St CB6 . . . . 210 F5
Torkington Gdns ☑ PE9 . 244 B5
Torold Dr PE7 . . . . 186 E2
Torpel Way ☑ PE6 . . . . . . 231 C7
Tort Hill PE28 . . . . 168 C5
TOSELAND 97 D2
Toseland Rd PE19 . . . . 97 E4
Tothill Rd CB25 . . . . 108 D4
Touthill Cl PE1 . . . . 198 A2
Tower Cl
Bassingbourn SG8 . . . . 12 F5
Cottenham CB24 . . . . 125 D3
Huntingdon PE29 . . . . 141 D8
Ⅲ Over CB24 . . . . 208 D1
Ramsey PE26 . . . . 172 C7
Whittlesey PE7 . . . . 189 B8
Tower Ct
Ely CB6 . . . . 240 B3
Haverhill CB9 . . . . 23 E7
Peterborough PE2 . . . . . . 186 F8
Tower Rd
Downham CB6 . . . . 217 F7
Elm PE14 . . . . 236 A3
Ely CB7 . . . . 240 B3
Sawston CB22 . . . . 33 A8
Sutton CB6 . . . . 216 E2
Tower Sq PE29 . . . . 152 D1
Tower St PE2 . . . . 186 F8
Tower View CB21 . . . . 35 D3
Towgood Way PE19 . . . . . . 96 D4
Towler St PE1 . . . . 198 A3
Town Bridge PE13 . . . . . . 245 B5
Town Cl CB22 . . . . 32 E7
TOWN END 243 D1
Town End PE15 . . . . 243 D1
Town End Cl CB9 . . . . 38 F1
Towne Rd SG8 . . . . 5 D5
Town Farm Cl SG8 . . . . 10 F4
Town Green Rd SG8 . . . . . . 28 D8
Town La CB22 . . . . 33 B5
Townley Cl PE14 . . . . 236 E1
Townley Prim Sch PE14 . 229 D3
Town Orch PE19 . . . . 95 E5
Townsend
Little Downham CB6 . . . . . 217 F6
Soham CB7 . . . . 212 A5
Townsend Cl CB24 . . . . . . 105 D3
Townsend Rd
Needingworth PE27 . . . . . 208 A3
Upwell PE14 . . . . 229 E7
Wittering PE8 . . . . 230 B1
Townsend Way PE7 . . . . . . 175 D8
Townsend Rd PE13 . . . . . . 245 C6
Town St
Newton CB22 . . . . 31 B7
Outwell PE14 . . . . 236 E1
Town The PE19 . . . . 93 E6
Toyse Cl CB25 . . . . 130 C4
Toyse La CB25 . . . . 130 B4
Trafalgar Rd
Cambridge CB4 . . . . 246 B4
Eaton Socon PE19 . . . . 74 C5
Trafalgar St CB4 . . . . 246 B4
Trafalgar Terr PE9 . . . . . . 244 B6
Trafalgar Way CB23 . . . . 102 B5
Trafford Est PE14 . . . . 238 F4
Trafford Pk ☑ PE13 . . . . . 245 D5
Trafford Rd PE13 . . . . 245 D5
Tramar Dr ☑ PE28 . . . . . . 246 A2
Tram Station La PE14 . . . 236 B6
Tramway The PE14 . . . . . . 236 F2
Trap Rd SG8 . . . . 11 A4
Treading Bank PE13 . . . . 237 C4
Treading Field PE13 . . . . . 237 C4
Tredegar Cl CB4 . . . . 83 E6
Tredgold La CB1 . . . . 246 C3
Treeway PE16 . . . . 241 B5
Trefoil Ct ☑ CB9 . . . . 23 F7
Trent Cl PE27 . . . . 144 A7
Trent Rd PE8 . . . . 193 D8
Tresham Rd PE2 . . . . 185 D3
Trevone PI CB1 . . . . 65 D7
Tribune Cl PE16 . . . . 241 D3
Tribune Ct CB4 . . . . 83 E7
Trienna PE2 . . . . 186 B5
Trigg Way SG8 . . . . 14 D6
Trinity Ave PE19 . . . . 239 C5
Trinity Cl
Balsham CB21 . . . . 53 B2
Bottisham CB25 . . . . 46 F5
Ely CB6 . . . . 240 C5
Fordham CB7 . . . . 212 F1
Great Paxton PE19 . . . . . . 96 E4
Haslingfield CB23 . . . . 47 B5
Trinity Coll CB2 . . . . 246 A3
Trinity Dr CB8 . . . . 111 B2
Trinity La CB2 . . . . 246 A2
Trinity Link CB9 . . . . 39 A1
Trinity Pl PE29 . . . . 141 E4
Trinity Rd
Stamford PE9 . . . . 244 A6
Wisbech PE13 . . . . 245 E6
Trinity St
Cambridge CB2 . . . . 246 A2
☑ Peterborough PE1 . . . . 198 A2
Triplow Meadows Nature
Reserve* SG8 . . . . 31 B2
Trotwood Mews CB3 . . . . 245 D3
Troughton Way ☑ PE13 . 238 B2
Troutbeck Cl PE4 . . . . 204 F3
Truman Ave PE15 . . . . 243 A5
TRUMPINGTON 64 C2
Trumpington High St CB2 . 64 E5
Trumpington Rd CB2 . . . . 64 E5
Trumpington St CB2 . . . . 246 A2

Trundle Mere PE7 . . . . . . 182 B2
Trundle The PE28 . . . . 215 C1
Trundley Cl CB9 . . . . 38 F1
Tuckers Nook ☑ PE6 . . . . 231 C7
Tuckers Yd PE2 . . . . 187 C7
Tuck's Yd PE15 . . . . 224 B4
TUDDENHAM 214 D2
Tuddenham CE Prim Sch
IP28 . . . . 214 E2
Tuddenham Rd IP28 . . . . . 239 F2
Tudor Ave PE7 . . . . 186 C1
Tudor Cl PE4 . . . . 204 E2
Tudor Ct
Bassingbourn cum Kneesworth
SG8 . . . . 13 B4
Kimbolton PE28 . . . . 113 F5
Tudor Rd PE29 . . . . 141 F2
Tulyar Wlk CB8 . . . . 110 E8
Tunbridge Cl
Bottisham CB25 . . . . 86 E6
Burwell CB25 . . . . 130 B2
Tunbridge La CB25 . . . . . . 86 E6
Tunkers La PE26 . . . . 171 F4
Tunwells Cl CB22 . . . . 49 A5
Tunwells La CB22 . . . . 49 A5
Turberville Ct PE28 . . . . . 143 C1
Turf Dro PE7 . . . . 191 C5
Turf Fen La PE15 . . . . 222 F5
Turf Fen Rd PE26 . . . . 170 F3
Turf Lot Dro PE14 . . . . . . 229 E1
Turf Maze* PE28 . . . . 120 C1
Turlough Rd PE15 . . . . . . 243 B3
Turner Cl CB9 . . . . 38 D1
Turner Rd
Eaton Socon PE19 . . . . 74 C5
St Ives PE27 . . . . 144 A7
Turners La PE7 . . . . 189 D6
Turnerspike Rd PE7 . . . . . 190 A3
Turnover Bank PE13 . . . . 237 D2
Turnpike Cl ☑ PE13 . . . . . 245 E6
Turnpike Hill CB9 . . . . 38 C4
Turnpike Rd IP28 . . . . 133 E8
Turnpike The CB7 . . . . 240 B3
Turnpole Cl PE9 . . . . 244 D7
Turnstone Cl IP28 . . . . . . 239 D4
Turnstone Way PE2 . . . . . 187 D7
Turpin's Ride
☑ Royston SG8 . . . . 5 D5
Stilton PE7 . . . . 176 A7
Turpyn Ct CB4 . . . . 83 E6
Turvers La PE26 . . . . 172 B7
TURVES 191 F6
Turves Rd PE6 . . . . 232 A2
Tuyar Wlk CB8 . . . . 110 E8
Tweedale CB1 . . . . 65 F5
Twelvetree Ave PE4 . . . . . 204 A5
Twenty Foot Rd PE15 . . 227 F8
Twenty Pence Rd
Cottenham CB24 . . . . 125 F6
Wilburton CB6 . . . . 210 B3
Two Pole Dro
Farcet PE7 . . . . 187 F1
Ramsey PE26 . . . . 211 E7
Two Tree Hundred Dro
PE15 . . . . 228 A6
Twyford Gdns PE1 . . . . . . 198 D7
TYDD ST GILES 237 F7
Tydd St Giles Golf & Leisure
Ctr PE13 . . . . 238 A7
Tyesdale PE3 . . . . 197 A4
Tylers Mews PE4 . . . . 204 B3
Tyrrell Pk PE1 . . . . 198 D2
Tythe PE28 . . . . 121 C5

Uffen Way CB22 . . . . 32 E8
UFFINGTON 230 C6
Uffington CE (Cont) Prim
Sch PE9 . . . . 230 C6
Uffington Rd
☑ Barnack PE9 . . . . 230 D4
Stamford PE9 . . . . 244 D5
UFFORD 230 F3
Ufford Pl ☑ CB9 . . . . 24 B8
Ugg Mere Ct Rd PE26 . . . 220 D1
Uldale Way PE4 . . . . 204 F2
Ullswater PE2 . . . . 186 D5
Ullswater Ave PE4 . . . . . . 204 D2
Underwood Cl PE7 . . . . . . 190 D7
Union Cl
Union La CB4 . . . . 83 F5
Union Pl ☑ PE13 . . . . 245 C5
Union Rd CB2 . . . . 246 B1
Union St ☑ PE13 . . . . 245 C5
Univ Arts Sch CB2 . . . . . . 246 B2
University Concert Hall
CB3 . . . . 83 C1
University Music Sch CB3 83 C1
Univ Mus of Zoology*
CB2 . . . . 246 B2
Univ of Cambridge
Cambridge CB2 . . . . 84 A2
Cambridge CB2 . . . . 246 B2
Madingley CB3 . . . . 82 D7
Univ of Cambridge
Biotechnology Ctr CB3 . 82 D7
Univ of the 3rd Age in
Cambridge CB2 . . . . 246 A3
Unwin's La ☑ CB24 . . . . . 208 D1
UPEND 92 A1
UPEND GREEN 91 F2
Uphall Rd PE14 . . . . 236 F6
Upherd's La CB6 . . . . 240 C5
Uplands PE4 . . . . 204 C5
Upper Delph Dro PE6 . . . 209 A5
Upper Gatley End SG8 . . . . 3 D6

Upper Gwydir St ☑ CB1 . . 84 A1
UPTON
Ailsworth 195 B6
Alconbury 160 C1
Upton Cl
Longthorpe PE3 . . . . 197 A2
Stanground PE2 . . . . 187 E5
Upton Hill PE28 . . . . 160 C1
Upton La CB6 . . . . 242 D4
Upton Pl CB6 . . . . 242 C4
UPWARE 211 B1
Upware Rd
Swaffham Prior CB7 . . . . 128 D8
Wicken CB7 . . . . 211 C1
UPWELL 236 D1
Upwell Pk PE15 . . . . 243 F3
Upwell Prim Sch PE14 . . 229 D8
Upwell Rd
Christchurch PE14 . . . . . . 229 C4
March PE15 . . . . 243 E3
UPWOOD 171 C2
Upwood Airfield PE26 . . 171 D4
Upwood Meadows National
Nature Reserve* PE26. 171 A2
Upwood Prim Sch PE26 . 171 D3
Upwood Rd PE26 . . . . 171 B5
Utah PE28 . . . . 151 F4

Valarian Cl ☑ PE19 . . . . 74 C6
Vale Dr PE7 . . . . 186 C1
Valence Rd PE2 . . . . 185 F4
Valerian Ct CB1 . . . . 66 A5
Vale The PE29 . . . . 152 B6
Valiant Rd PE27 . . . . 143 F7
Valiant Sq PE26 . . . . 171 F3
Valley Rise SG8 . . . . 5 E6
Valley The CB23 . . . . 62 D6
Valley Way CB8 . . . . 110 E4
Valparaiso Univ CB3 . . . 83 C3
Van Diemans Way PE28 . 116 A7
Van Dyke Pl PE2 . . . . . . 144 A7
Van Gogh Pl PE27 . . . . . 144 A7
Vanners Rd CB9 . . . . 24 A7
Varrier Jones Dr CB23 . . 99 A3
Varrier Jones Pl CB23 . . 99 A3
Vars Rd PE7 . . . . 186 B2
Veasey Rd PE29 . . . . 142 A7
Velos Wlk CB5 . . . . 244 B8
Vence Cl PE9 . . . . 244 A5
Ventress Cl CB1 . . . . 65 D5
Ventress Farm Ct CB1. . . 65 E5
Verdun Rd PE13 . . . . 245 D5
Vere Rd PE1 . . . . 197 F7
Vergette Rd PE13 . . . . . . 245 D5
Vergette St PE1 . . . . 198 B4
Vermont Gr PE3 . . . . 197 E1
Vermuyden PE28 . . . . . . 164 E8
Vermuyden Way ☑ CB6 . 206 E2
Vermuyden Way CB24 . . 121 F5
Verulam Way CB4 . . . . . . 83 D6
Vester's Hill Dro PE26 . . 171 B7
Vetchfield PE2 . . . . 185 E5
Vetch Wlk CB9 . . . . 38 D1
Vicarage Ave CB22 . . . . . 32 F7
Vicarage Cl
Chatteris PE16 . . . . 241 D5
Dullingham CB8 . . . . 89 C1
Holme PE7 . . . . 177 A4
Melbourn SG8 . . . . 14 C6
Oakington/Longstanton
CB24 . . . . 103 D6
Swaffham Bulbeck CB25 . 108 A1
Waterbeach CB25 . . . . . 106 A7
Vicarage Dr CB3 . . . . 64 A3
Vicarage Farm Rd ☑
PE1 . . . . 198 D3
Vicarage Farm Rd PE19 . 57 B6
Vicarage Gdns
Mildenhall IP28 . . . . 239 B4
☑ St Neots PE19 . . . . 74 B3
Vicarage La
Swaffham Prior CB25 . . . 108 D4
Whittlesford CB22 . . . . . . 32 B5
Woodditton CB8 . . . . 90 D3
Vicarage Rd
Newmarket CB8 . . . . 111 B3
Waresley SG19 . . . . 58 A2
Vicarage Terr CB1 . . . . . . 84 A1
Vicarage Way PE7 . . . . . 181 D5
Vicarage Wlk PE19 . . . . . 93 F6
Viceroy Cl PE19 . . . . 74 A3
Victor Cl PE27 . . . . 144 A7
Victoria Ave CB5 . . . . . . 246 B3
Victoria Cres
Royston SG8 . . . . 5 D7
St Ives PE28 . . . . 143 A5
Victoria Gdns CB6 . . . . . 242 D4
Victoria Gn ☑ CB6 . . . . . 217 D1
Victoria Pk CB4 . . . . 83 D4
Victoria Pl
Peterborough PE1 . . . . . 197 F4
Sutton CB6 . . . . 216 D1
☑ Wisbech PE13 . . . . . . 245 C4
Victoria Rd
Cambridge CB4 . . . . 83 D4
Haverhill CB9 . . . . 23 D7
Stamford PE9 . . . . 244 B6
Wisbech PE13 . . . . 245 C4
Victoria Sq PE29 . . . . . . 141 E4
Victoria St
Cambridge CB1 . . . . 246 B2
Chatteris PE16 . . . . 241 C4
Ely CB7 . . . . 240 D3
Littleport CB6 . . . . 242 E4

Victoria St *continued*
Old Fetton PE2 . . . . 186 F6
Peterborough PE1 . . . . . 198 A5
Victoria View CB24 . . . . . 125 F7
Victoria Way
Melbourn SG8 . . . . 14 D5
Newmarket CB8 . . . . 110 E7
Victor St PE28 . . . . 154 A1
Victory Ave PE7 . . . . 189 F7
Victory Rd PE13 . . . . 245 B3
Victory Way CB24 . . . . . . 125 D4
Victory Wlk ☑ SG8 . . . . . . 5 E5
Viersen Platz PE1 . . . . . . 198 A1
Viking Cl CB21 . . . . 53 E5
Viking Way
Bar Hill CB23 . . . . 102 B4
Whittlesey PE7 . . . . 189 E8
Villa Ct CB4 . . . . 83 E8
Village The PE2 . . . . 186 B5
Village Way SG7 . . . . 3 A3
Villa Pl CB24 . . . . 104 C2
Villa Rd CB24 . . . . 104 C2
Vincent Cl CB8 . . . . 110 E7
Vines Cl CB6 . . . . 240 C4
Vine Cl
Great Shelford CB22 . . . . 49 C4
Hemingford Grey PE27 . . 143 E2
Vinegar Hill PE28 . . . . . . 150 E2
Vine Inter-Church Prim Sch
The CB23 . . . . 79 E3
Vinery Ct PE26 . . . . 172 B7
Vinery Pk CB1 . . . . 66 A5
Vinery Rd CB1 . . . . 65 C8
Vinery Way CB1 . . . . 84 C1
Vine St PE9 . . . . 244 C5
Vine Wlk PE3 . . . . 197 B4
Vineyard Rd PE1 . . . . . . 198 B2
Vineyards The CB7 . . . . . 240 D4
Vineyard The PE28 . . . . 208 D7
Vineyard Way
Buckden PE19 . . . . 117 B3
Ely CB7 . . . . 240 E5
Vineyard Wlk CB25 . . . . . 86 F6
Viney Cl PE1 . . . . 198 D5
Vintner Cl CB23 . . . . 99 A3
Vintners Cl PE3 . . . . 197 D3
Violet Cl CB1 . . . . 66 A5
Violet Way PE7 . . . . 182 A7
Virginia Cl PE3 . . . . 197 A2
Virginia Rd PE28 . . . . . . 213 E8
Virginia Way PE27 . . . . . 143 E6
Viscount Ct PE9 . . . . 73 F6
Viscount Rd PE19 . . . . . . 187 A6
Vixen Cl PE7 . . . . 181 F6
Vokes St PE2 . . . . 186 D8
Voyager Sch PE4 . . . . . . 204 C1
Vulcan Way PE7 . . . . 74 B1

Waddelow Rd CB25 . . . . 106 A8
Wade Park Ave ☑ PE6 . . 231 E8
Wadloes Rd CB5 . . . . 84 D4
Waggoners Way ☑ PE15 223 B7
Wagstaff Cl PE3 . . . . 83 F7
Wainman Rd PE2 . . . . . . 186 D5
Wainwright PE4 . . . . 204 A5
Waits The PE27 . . . . 144 A3
Wake Ave IP28 . . . . 239 C5
Wakefield Cl CB10 . . . . . . 18 D3
Wakelin Ave CB22 . . . . . . 49 F1
Wakelyn Rd PE7 . . . . . . 189 C7
Wake Rd
March PE15 . . . . 243 C6
Peterborough PE2 . . . . . 198 B2
Wakerley Dr PE2 . . . . . . 186 C7
Walcot Rd PE9 . . . . 230 E2
Walcot Wlk PE3 . . . . 197 B3
Walden St ☑ PE15 . . . . 223 A5
Walden Gr PE29 . . . . 141 D4
Walden Rd
Great Chesterford CB10 . 18 E3
Hadstock CB21 . . . . 20 D6
Huntingdon PE29 . . . . . . 141 D4
Walden Way CB22 . . . . . . 48 F6
Wales Bank PE14 . . . . . . 236 A5
Walgrave PE2 . . . . 186 B4
Walkden's SG7 . . . . 2 E4
Walker Ct CB4 . . . . 83 E6
Walker Rd PE26 . . . . 203 F7
Walkers Way PE3 . . . . . 196 F3
Walking Way CB24 . . . . . 105 D1
Walks E The ☑ PE29 . . . 141 D4
Walks N The PE29 . . . . . 141 D4
Wallace Ct PE29 . . . . . . 142 A8
Wallace's Dro PE6 . . . . . 233 D4
Waller's Cl SG8 . . . . 7 F2
Wallman's La CB24 . . . . . 122 C6
Walnut Cl
Milton CB24 . . . . 105 C2
Newborough PE6 . . . . . . 205 C8
Royston SG8 . . . . 5 D6
Wisbech St Mary PE13 . 235 B6
Walnut Dr CB22 . . . . 48 E7
Walnut Gr
Gunthorpe PE4 . . . . 204 D2
Worlington IP28 . . . . . . 213 E4
Walnut Rd PE13 . . . . . . 234 A3
Walnut Tree Cl
Bassingbourn SG8 . . . . . 12 E5
Little Downham CB6 . . . 218 A6
☑ Stretham CB6 . . . . . . 237 A4
Walnut Tree Cres PE28 . 121 B5
Walnut Tree Dr PE29 . . 141 C6

Walnut Tree Gr PE28 .... 140 D3
Walnut Tree Way CB4 ... .83 C7
Walnut Way PE7 . . . . .175 F7
Walpole Bank PE14 . . . . . .238 F7
Walpole Ct CB7. . . . . .240 C4
WALPOLE MARSH 238 F8
Walpole Rd CB1 . . . . .65 D6
Walsham Rd PE7 . . . . .181 D8
Walsingham Ct PE13. . . . .245 A7
Walsingham Way
  Ely CB6. . . . . .240 B5
  10 Eye PE6 . . . . .232 A1
WALSOKEN 245 F6
Walsoken Rd PE14 . . . . . .236 E7
Waltham Cl PE1 . . . . .198 D8
WALTON 204 D1
Walton Cl CB7. . . . . .212 E1
WALTON DAM 238 D4
WALTON HIGHWAY 238 F4
Walton Hill PE28. . . . . . . .161 D5
Walton Pk PE4. . . . . .204 C1
Walton Prim Sch PE4 . . . .204 C1
Walton Rd
  9 Leverington PE13. . . . .238 B2
  Marholm PE6. . . . . .203 E1
  Wisbech PE13 . . . . .245 E7
Waltons CB10. . . . . .21 C3
Wamil Rd IP28 . . . . .213 F5
Wamil Way IP28 . . . . .239 B4
Wandlebury Ctry Pk*
  CB22 . . . . .50 B8
WANSFORD 194 A4
Wansford Pasture Nature
  Reserve* PE8. . . . . .193 F3
Wansford Rd
  Elton PE8. . . . . .183 D5
  Wansford PE8 . . . . .194 A3
  Yarwell PE8 . . . . .193 F2
Wantage Gdns PE19. . . . . .96 A2
Warbon Ave PE1 . . . . .197 F7
WARBOYS 165 A5
Warboys Airfield Ind Est
  PE28. . . . . .164 D2
Warboys Cl CB23. . . . . .61 D5
Warboys CP Sch PE28. . . .164 E5
Warboys Rd
  Bury PE26. . . . . .172 B6
  Old Hurst PE28 . . . . .154 D8
  Pidley cum Fenton PE28 . .155 E8
Ward Cl
  Peterborough PE1 . . . . . .198 B3
  Ramsey PE26. . . . . .172 A5
  St Ives PE28 . . . . .143 A5
Warden Hill SG19. . . . . . . .40 C3
Ward Rd CB1 . . . . .65 D6
Ward Way CB6. . . . . .217 D1
WARDY HILL 217 B4
Ware La PE28. . . . . .142 F5
Wareley Rd PE2. . . . . .197 F1
Ware Rd PE19 . . . . .74 E6
WARESLEY 57 E2
Waresley & Gransden Woods
  Nature Reserve* SG19 . .58 C2
Waresley Rd
  Gamlingay SG19 . . . . .41 D6
  Great Gransden SG19 . . . .58 B3
Warkworth St CB1 . . . . . .246 C2
Warkworth Terr CB1 . . . . .246 C2
WARMINGTON 178 A3
Warmington Sch PE8 . . . .178 B3
Warner's Dro
  Pidley cum Fenton PE28 . .215 B3
  Somersham PE28. . . . . . .215 C2
Warners Gr PE27 . . . . .144 A4
Warren Cl
  St Ives PE28 . . . . .142 F6
  Wilburton CB6. . . . . .210 C5
Warren Croft PE28. . . . . . .168 B5
Warren Ct **6** CB9. . . . . . .23 E7
Warren La
  Bythorn & Keyston PE28 . .146 D4
  Titchmarsh PE28 . . . . . . .156 F1
Warrenne Keep PE9. . . . . .244 B4
Warren Pl CB28. . . . . .111 F5
Warren Rd
  Cambridge CB4 . . . . .84 A6
  Herringswell CB8. . . . . . .134 A7
  Red Lodge IP28. . . . . . . .214 A1
  St Ives PE27 . . . . .144 B4
  Wothorpe PE9 . . . . .244 B1
Warren The
  3 Royston SG8. . . . . .5 D5
  St Neots PE19 . . . . .75 C5
  Witchford CB6. . . . . .217 E1
Warren Twrs CB8 . . . . .111 E4
Warrington St CB8. . . . . . .111 A2
Warwick Cl
  Eaton Socon PE19 . . . . . .74 C3
  2 Haverhill CB9 . . . . . . .23 E8
Warwick Dr CB6 . . . . .240 A3
Warwick Rd
  Cambridge CB4 . . . . .83 C5
  Peterborough PE4 . . . . . .204 C1
Wasdale Gdns PE4. . . . . . .205 A2
Washbank Rd **3** CB14 . . . .69 A7
Washingley La PE7. . . . . . .175 B7
Washingley Rd
  Folksworth PE7 . . . . .175 D8
  The Stukeleys PE29. . . . . .141 C8
Washington Cl CB6 . . . . . .242 D5
Washington St IP28. . . . . .213 E8
Wash La PE7 . . . . .189 E8
Washpit La CB23. . . . . .46 D7
Washpit Rd CB13 . . . . .82 C8
Wash Rd PE14 . . . . .225 B8

Wastwater PE29 . . . . .141 B6
WATERBEACH 106 C7
Waterbeach CP Sch
  CB25. . . . . .106 B8
Waterbeach Rd CB25. . . . .105 E7
Waterbeach Sta CB25. . . . .106 C6
Watercourse The CB8 . . . .111 A4
WATER END 25 B3
Water End
  Alwalton PE7 . . . . .185 A5
  Marholm PE6. . . . . .203 D1
  Peterborough PE3 . . . . . .197 D2
  Wrestlingworth SG19 . . . . .25 B3
Waterfall Gdns PE6 . . . . . .207 C1
Waterfields PE16. . . . . . . .241 B3
Waterfurlong PE28. . . . . . .244 A4
Watergall PE3 . . . . .197 B8
Watergall Prim Sch PE3. . .197 A8
Water Gdns The PE13 . . . .245 A5
Watergrove La CB23 . . . . . .79 C5
Water La
  Bourn CB23 . . . . .60 D6
  Cambridge CB4 . . . . .84 B5
  Castor PE5. . . . . .195 F1
  Cottenham CB24 . . . . . . .126 A7
  Great Bradley CB8. . . . . . .55 F8
  Histon CB24. . . . . .104 C3
  Oakington/Longstanton
    CB24. . . . . .103 C5
  Sturmer CB9. . . . . .24 F5
Waterlees Rd **2** PE13. . . .245 E7
Waterloo Cl
  Brampton PE28 . . . . .140 D3
  Newmarket CB8. . . . . . . .110 D8
Waterloo Dr **2** PE19. . . . .74 F3
Waterloo Rd PE1 . . . . .198 A5
Watermead CB23 . . . . .102 C3
Watermead Cres CB23 . . . .79 A3
WATER NEWTON 184 C7
WATERSIDE 213 A6
Waterside
  Ely CB7 . . . . .240 E4
  Isleham CB7 . . . . .213 A5
Waterside Gdns
  March PE15. . . . . .243 E5
  Whittlesey PE7 . . . . .189 D8
Waterslade Rd PE7 . . . . . .181 C4
Watersmead PE19 . . . . . . .117 E3
Waters Meet PE29 . . . . . . .141 D3
Water St
  Cambridge CB4 . . . . .84 B4
  Stamford PE9. . . . . .244 C4
Waterton Cl **6** PE6. . . . . .231 F8
Waterwick Hill CB11 . . . . . .1 F1
Waterworks La PE6 . . . . . .203 D6
Waterworks Rd IP28. . . . . .213 E8
Watsons La **1** CB6. . . . . .213 B7
Wattl Cl PE4 . . . . .204 E2
Wattle Cl CB23 . . . . .79 A4
Wavell Way CB4 . . . . .83 E6
Waveney Dr PE15. . . . . . . .243 B5
Waveney Gr PE4 . . . . .204 E2
Waveney Rd PE27. . . . . . . .144 A7
Waveney Terr CB9. . . . . . . .24 B7
Waverley Cl PE13 . . . . . . .235 A3
Waverley Gdns **3** PE9 . . .244 A6
Wayford Cl PE13 . . . . .197 A2
WAY HEAD 217 C6
Way Head Dro CB6. . . . . . .217 C6
Way La
  Waterbeach CB25 . . . . . . .106 B8
  Wicken CB7 . . . . .211 D2
WAYSIDE 138 C5
Way The SG8 . . . . .30 E1
WEALD 76 B4
Weasenham La **1** PE13 . .245 D7
Weatheralls Cl CB47 . . . . .212 B4
Weatheralls Prim Sch The
  CB7 . . . . .212 B4
Weatherthorn PE2 . . . . . . .186 C5
Weavers Field CB13. . . . . . .82 E7
Webbs Mdw SG19. . . . . . . .58 D4
Webb's Rd CB21. . . . . .36 F5
Websters Cl PE6. . . . . .203 F8
Webster's Way CB24 . . . . .208 D1
Weddell Rd CB8 . . . . .24 C6
Wedgewood Dr CB1. . . . . . .65 F6
Wedgwood Dr CB13. . . . . .245 D5
Weedon Cl **4** PE4 . . . . . .204 F1
Weir Cl
  Buckden PE19 . . . . .117 A3
  Hemingford Grey PE28 . . .143 D1
Weir Rd PE28 . . . . .143 D1
Weirs Dro CB25. . . . . .129 F1
Welbeck Rd PE13 . . . . . . .245 E4
Welbeck Way PE6. . . . . . . .186 D7
Welbourne PE4 . . . . .204 C4
Welbourne Prim Sch
  PE4. . . . . .204 C4
Welby Cl PE28 . . . . .115 D3
WELCHES DAM 224 A1
Welches Dam Visitor Ctr*
  CB6 . . . . .217 A8
Welland Bank PE6 . . . . . . .207 D7
Welland Cl
  Peterborough PE1. . . . . . .198 A7
  St Ives PE27 . . . . .144 A7
Welland Ct **8** PE19 . . . . . .74 C4
Welland Mews PE9 . . . . . .244 C4
Welland Pl CB6. . . . . .240 D6
Welland Prim Sch PE1 . . . .198 C8
Welland Rd
  Peterborough PE1 . . . . . .198 B8
  Wittering PE8. . . . . .230 B1
Welland Way **5** PE6 . . . .231 F8
Well Bottom CB8. . . . . . . .112 B8
Wellbrook Way CB3. . . . . . .82 F7

Wellcome Trust Genome
  Campus CB10 . . . . .18 B6
Well Creek Rd PE14 . . . . . .236 F2
Well End PE14 . . . . .236 A3
Wellingly Ct CB23 . . . . .79 A3
Wellington Ave PE27 . . . . .143 F7
Wellington Cl
  Old Hurst PE28 . . . . .154 E7
  Thistley Green IP28. . . . . .213 D6
Warboys PE28 . . . . .164 F4
  Waterbeach CB25 . . . . . . .106 B7
Wellington Ct **3** CB1 . . . . .84 A2
Wellington Pl SG8 . . . . . . .13 B5
Wellington Rd
  Ely CB6 . . . . .217 F1
  Mildenhall IP28. . . . . . . .213 E8
Wellington St
  4 Cambridge CB1 . . . . . .84 A2
  Littleport CB6 . . . . .242 D4
  4 Newmarket CB8. . . . . .111 A3
  Peterborough PE1. . . . . . .198 B2
  St Ives PE27 . . . . .144 A3
Wellington Terr
  16 Haverhill CB9 . . . . . . .23 E7
  10 Wisbech PE13. . . . . . .245 C5
Wellington Way PE28. . . . .154 A1
Well Rd PE14 . . . . .236 D4
Wells Bridge PE26 . . . . . . .221 C3
Wells Cl
  Haslingfield CB23 . . . . . . .47 A5
  Peterborough PE4 . . . . . .204 B3
Wells Ct
  Mildenhall IP28. . . . . . . .239 B5
  Peterborough PE2 . . . . . .187 D6
Wellsfield PE29 . . . . .141 E6
Wells Way PE7 . . . . .177 A5
Wellum Cl **18** CB9. . . . . . .23 E7
Welmore Rd PE6. . . . . .203 F8
WELNEY 225 B8
Welstead Rd CB1 . . . . .66 A6
WENDY 27 C4
WENNINGTON 162 D4
Wenny Ct PE16 . . . . .241 C4
Wenny Est PE16 . . . . .241 D3
Wenny Rd PE16. . . . . .241 E3
Wenny Severals PE16. . . . .216 B7
Wensum Cl PE27. . . . . . . .144 B6
WENTWORTH 217 B1
Wentworth Dr IP28 . . . . . .239 B4
Wentworth Rd CB4 . . . . . . .83 C4
Wentworth St **1** PE1. . . . .198 A1
Wentworth Terr **6** CB9. . . .23 E8
Wenvoe Cl CB1. . . . . .65 F6
WERRINGTON 204 B4
Werrington Bridge Rd
  PE6. . . . . .204 E7
Werrington Ctr PE4. . . . . .204 B5
Werrington Gr PE4. . . . . . .204 B2
Werrington Grove Cvn Pk
  PE4. . . . . .204 B2
Werrington Mews **5**
  PE4. . . . . .204 C3
Werrington Park Ave **2**
  PE4. . . . . .204 C3
Werrington Parkway
  PE4. . . . . .203 B5
Werrington Prim Sch
  PE4. . . . . .204 C3
Werrington Sports & Recn
  Ctr PE4. . . . . .204 B4
Wertheim Way PE29 . . . . .141 B6
Wesleyan Rd PE1 . . . . .198 A7
Wesley Dr PE16. . . . . .241 D5
Wesley House CB5. . . . . . .246 B3
Wessex Cl PE4 . . . . .204 D2
West Ave PE26. . . . . .171 F6
Westberry Ct CB3. . . . . .64 B8
Westbourne Cl PE16 . . . . .241 B3
Westbourne Ct CB9 . . . . . . .24 A8
Westbourne Dr PE6 . . . . . .203 E8
Westbourne Rd PE16. . . . .241 B4
West Brook PE28 . . . . .120 B2
Westbourne Ave **1** PE2 . .186 F7
Westbrook Cl
  1 Brampton PE28 . . . . .140 C3
  Steeple Morden SG8 . . . . . .3 B8
West Brook Ct PE28. . . . . .120 B2
Westbrook Park Cl **2**
  PE2. . . . . .186 F7
Westbrook Park Rd PE2. . .186 F7
Westbury Rd PE27 . . . . . . .143 F4
West Cl
  Alconbury Weston PE28. . .150 D6
  March PE15. . . . . .243 B6
  Waresley SG19 . . . . .57 F2
Westcombe Sq PE1 . . . . . .198 D4
WESTCOTE 211 F6
Westcott House Theological
  Coll CB1. . . . . .246 B3
Westcroft **4** CB23 . . . . . . .62 B4
WEST DEEPING 231 B8
West Delph PE7. . . . . .189 D8
West Dr
  Friday Bridge PE14 . . . . . .236 A4
  Highfields CB23. . . . . .80 C2
  March PE15. . . . . .243 F4
  Mildenhall IP28. . . . . . . .239 B4
  Soham CB7 . . . . .212 B4
West Drive Cres CB7 . . . . .212 A4
West Drive Gdns CB7 . . . . .212 A4
West Drove S PE12 . . . . . .233 E8
WEST END 155 A5
West End
  Ashwell SG7. . . . . .2 C3
  Brampton PE28 . . . . .140 C3
  Ely CB6 . . . . .240 C4
  Gorefield PE13. . . . . .237 E3
  Haddenham CB6 . . . . .209 F6

West End **continued**
  March PE15. . . . . .243 B4
  Somersham PE28. . . . . . .208 B8
  Whittlesey PE7 . . . . .189 C7
  Whittlesford CB22. . . . . . .32 B4
  Wilburton CB6. . . . . .210 B5
  Woodditton CB8. . . . . .71 D8
  Yaxley PE7 . . . . .181 D4
West End Cl PE16. . . . . . . .241 B4
West End La CB9 . . . . .38 E8
West End Rd
  Fenstanton PE28 . . . . . . .121 A5
  Maxey PE6. . . . . .231 C7
West End Villas PE9. . . . . .244 A5
Westering The CB5. . . . . . . .84 E2
Westerley Cl PE3 . . . . .197 C4
Westerman Cl PE28 . . . . . .168 B5
Western Ave
  Haverhill CB9. . . . . .38 E1
  Peterborough PE1. . . . . . .198 B7
West Fen Dro
  Downham CB6 . . . . .218 A6
  March PE7. . . . . .227 A1
  Whittlesey PE7 . . . . .191 F3
West Fen Rd
  Coveney CB6. . . . . .217 E4
  Ely CB6. . . . . .240 B5
  Willingham CB24. . . . . . .208 F2
  Witchford CB6. . . . . .218 A3
Westfield CB24 . . . . .124 A6
West Field CB21 . . . . .34 B7
Westfield Com Prim Sch
  CB9. . . . . .24 B7
Westfield Jun Sch PE27. . .144 A4
Westfield La CB4 . . . . .83 C4
Westfield Rd
  Fowlmere SG8. . . . . .15 D8
  Great Shelford CB22. . . . . .48 E7
  Newton PE13. . . . . .237 F5
  Peterborough PE3 . . . . . .197 E4
  Ramsey PE26. . . . . .171 F7
  Sawtry PE28 . . . . .168 B4
  Wisbech PE13 . . . . .245 E7
  Yaxley PE7 . . . . .181 D5
West Field Rd PE15 . . . . . .224 A3
Westfields CB23 . . . . .99 A2
Westgate
  Cambridge CB1 . . . . .65 E5
  Peterborough PE1. . . . . . .198 A2
Westgate Arc PE1 . . . . . . .198 A2
West Gn CB22 . . . . .29 D7
Westhawe PE3. . . . . .196 F7
West Hill Rd CB22 . . . . .30 B4
West Lodge La PE13. . . . . . .99 C3
West Lodge La CB24 . . . . .216 D1
Westmead Ave PE13 . . . . .245 E2
Westmeadow Cl CB24 . . . .208 F1
West Meadowgate La PE14.245 E2
Westminster & Cheshunt
  Colleges CB3. . . . . .83 C3
Westminster Gdns **10**
  PE6. . . . . .232 A1
Westminster Pl PE1. . . . . .198 F5
West Moor Ave CB22 . . . . . .32 E8
Westmoor Comm CB6. . . . .217 E8
Westmoor Dro
  Chatteris PE16. . . . . .222 D2
  Littleport CB6 . . . . .225 B4
Westmoreland Gdns PE1.198 B2
Westmorland Ave PE28. . .143 A8
West Newlands **3** PE28. .208 B8
Weston Ave SG8 . . . . .5 C7
Weston Cl PE19 . . . . .95 A1
WESTON COLVILLE 54 B7
Weston Colville Rd CB8 . . .70 D1
Weston Ct PE19 . . . . .74 C4
WESTON DITCH 213 C7
Weston Gr CB21. . . . . .66 E5
WESTON GREEN 54 D5
Weston Miller Dr PE13 . . .245 C7
Weston Rd PE13 . . . . .245 C3
Weston Way CB8. . . . . .110 F6
West Par
  Peterborough PE3 . . . . . .197 D3
  Wisbech PE13. . . . . .245 B7
West Park St PE16 . . . . . . .241 C4
WEST PERRY 116 D2
West Perry PE28 . . . . .115 D2
West Rd
  Cambridge CB3 . . . . .83 C1
  Gamlingay SG19 . . . . .41 C4
  Histon CB24. . . . . .104 B3
  3 Tallington PE9. . . . . . .230 F7
  Tydd St Giles PE13. . . . . .238 B8
WEST ROW 211 F4
West Row Com Prim Sch
  IP28. . . . . .213 D7
West Row Rd
  Beck Row, Holywell Row &
    Kenny Hill IP28. . . . . .213 F6
  Mildenhall IP28. . . . . . . .239 A5
WESTRY 227 F5
Westry Ave PE15 . . . . .243 A7
Westry Cl **3** PE14 . . . . . .238 F1
West St Gdns PE9. . . . . . . .244 A5
West St
  Chatteris PE16. . . . . .241 B3
  Godmanchester PE29 . . . .141 E1
  Great Gransden SG19 . . . .58 D4
  Helpston PE6. . . . . .196 B1

West St **continued**
  Huntingdon PE29. . . . . . .141 E5
  Isleham CB7 . . . . .212 F5
  Over CB24 . . . . .123 A8
  Stamford PE9. . . . . .244 B4
  St Ives PE27 . . . . .144 A4
  St Neots PE19 . . . . .74 E5
  Toft CB23 . . . . .62 B5
  Wisbech PE13 . . . . .245 C4
West Stonebridge PE2 . . .186 C5
West Town Prim Sch
  PE3. . . . . .197 E3
West View
  Cambridge CB3 . . . . .64 C7
  Stukeley PE28. . . . . .151 F1
WEST WALTON. 238 E4
WEST WALTON CHURCH
  END. 238 D5
West Water Cres PE7 . . . . .186 C1
West Way
  Meldreth SG8. . . . . .28 F1
  Sawston CB22 . . . . .50 A1
Westway Pl CB6 . . . . .217 A2
WESTWICK 103 E7
WEST WICKHAM 37 B7
West Wickham Rd
  Balsham CB21. . . . . .53 C1
  Horseheath CB21. . . . . . . .37 A3
West Wlk CB25 . . . . .86 F6
WESTWOOD 197 B4
Westwood PE3. . . . . .197 C8
Westwood Ave PE15 . . . . .243 C5
Westwood Com Jun Sch
  PE15. . . . . .243 C5
Westwood Ind Est PE3 . . .197 D7
Westwood Park Cl PE3 . . .197 C3
Westwood Park Rd PE3 . . .197 D2
Westwood Rd PE27 . . . . . .144 A4
WEST WRATTING. 53 E5
West Wratting Rd CB21 . . . .53 B2
Wetenhall Rd CB1. . . . . . . .65 B8
Wetherby Way **1** PE1. . . .198 D3
Wether Rd CB23 . . . . .79 C2
Weymouth Way PE1. . . . . .198 D6
WHADDON. 28 C1
Whaddon Gap SG8. . . . . . .28 A1
Whaddon Rd SG8. . . . . . . .28 E2
Whaddons The PE29 . . . . .141 D5
Whalley St PE1 . . . . .198 B3
Wharf Rd PE9 . . . . .244 C4
Wheat Croft CB21. . . . . . . .35 D3
Wheatdole PE2. . . . . .186 A3
Wheatfield Cres **2** SG8. . . .5 E6
Wheatfield Dr PE26 . . . . . .171 F5
Wheatfields PE27. . . . . . . .144 A6
Wheatfields Prim Sch
  PE27. . . . . .144 A6
Wheatley Bank PE14 . . . . .238 F7
Wheatley Cres PE28. . . . . .208 C6
Wheats Cl **1** CB6. . . . . . .217 D1
Wheatsheaf Cl **1** CB6. . . .242 A4
Wheatsheaf Dro PE14 . . . .229 C3
Wheatsheaf Rd
  Alconbury Weston PE28. . .150 D6
  Eaton Socon PE19 . . . . . .74 C3
  Woodhurst PE28 . . . . . . .155 D4
Wheatsheaf Way CB21 . . . .35 D3
Wheatsheaves **2** PE28 . .168 C2
Wheel Ctr The PE15 . . . . .243 D4
Wheelers CB22 . . . . .49 B6
Wheeler's Cl CB23 . . . . .46 A7
Wheeler St CB22. . . . . .246 A2
Wheeler's Way CB23. . . . . .46 A7
Wheelwright Way CB25 . . .86 A5
Wheel Yd PE1. . . . . .198 A2
Whellams Yd PE26 . . . . . . .172 C7
Wherry Cl PE15. . . . . .243 D4
Whetstone Ct **5** PE1. . . .198 D7
Whetstone Way PE14 . . . . .236 E2
Whichcote Rd PE6. . . . . . .206 E6
Whincups Yd PE9 . . . . . . .244 C4
Whines La CB24 . . . . .123 B8
Whinfell Cl PE29 . . . . .141 A4
Whipple Mus of the History
  of Science* CB1. . . . . . .246 A2
Whippletree Rd CB22 . . . . .32 A5
Whiskins CB22. . . . . .32 C5
Whistler Rd **5** PE19 . . . . .74 C5
Whistlers The PE7 . . . . . . .144 A7
Whiston Cl
  Peterborough PE4. . . . . . .204 F2
  4 Somersham PE28. . . .208 C8
Whitacre PE1. . . . . .198 E6
Whitby St **3** PE13 . . . . . .245 C5
White Acres PE7. . . . . .189 E8
Whitebeam Cl **3** PE7 . . . .186 D3
White Caville CB9 . . . . .23 C8
Whitecroft Rd SG8. . . . . . . .14 A8
Whitecross PE27 . . . . .144 A4
White Cross PE15. . . . . . . .197 B6
White Cross Hill CB6 . . . . .210 C2
White Cross Rd CB6 . . . . . .210 E7
White Droveway CB25. . . .108 A3
White Fen Droveway
  CB25. . . . . .107 B5
White Hall Way CB22. . . . . .32 D8
Whitefriars CB4 . . . . .84 B5
Whitegate Cl
  Girton CB3. . . . . .82 E8
  Sawaway CB24 . . . . .122 D6
Whitegates CB8 . . . . .111 C3
WHITE HALL 235 E6
White Hall Cl **21** PE28. . .215 C1
White Hart Gdns PE9 . . . . .244 A5
Whitehall Gdns CB22. . . . .231 E1
Whitehall Sch PE28. . . . . .215 B1
Whitehall Way PE28. . . . . .115 D2
Whitehall Wlk PE19 . . . . . .74 F4
White Hart Ct PE27 . . . . . .144 A3

White Hart Dr 5 PE15 222 A5
White Hart La
Godmanchester PE29 142 A1
6 Littleport CB6 242 D4
13 Soham CB7 212 B4
St Ives PE27 144 A3
Whitehill Cl CB1 84 D2
Whitehill Rd CB5 84 C2
White Horse Gdns PE15 243 C4
White Horse La CB6 218 A6
Whitehouse La CB3 83 A5
Whitehouse Rd PE28 168 A4
White House Rd CB7 226 C2
White Lion Cl 1 PE15 243 D2
Whitemill Rd PE16 241 C3
Whitemoor Rd PE15 227 C4
Whitepost Rd
Borough Fen PE6 207 F1
Newborough PE6 205 F6
White Rose Wlk 5 CB4 83 D7
Whiteway Dro CB25 107 F8
White Wr PE2 185 D6
Whitfield Cl CB4 83 E7
Whitgift Rd CB1 85 B1
Whitlocks CB2 64 D2
Whitman Cl 7 PE9 230 D3
Whitmore St PE7 189 D7
Whitmore Way CB25 106 B6
Whitsed Rd PE6 207 D1
Whitsed St PE1 198 B3
Whittets Cl SG19 58 D4
Whittington PE1 198 E7
Whittlesea Sta PE7 189 F5
WHITTLESEY 189 D5
Whittlesey Mus* PE7 189 D7
Whittlesey Rd
Benwick PE15 221 E6
March PE15 243 A5
Peterborough PE2 187 B7
Thorney PE6 200 F7
WHITTLESFORD 32 B5
Whittlesford Rd
Little Shelford CB22 48 F2
Newton CB22 31 D7
Whittlesford Sta CB22 32 E3
Whitton Cl CB24 122 E5
Whitwell PE4 205 A2
Whitwell Way CB23 82 A2
Whybrows La PE28 208 E6
Whydale Rd 4 SG8 5 E5
Whytefield Rd PE26 172 A7
Whytford Cl CB4 84 A3
WICKEN 211 F1
Wicken Fen National Nature Reserve* CB7 211 D1
Wicken Rd CB7 212 B1
Wicken Way PE3 197 C6
Wickfield Ct PE13 245 D4
Wick Rd PE7 186 B2
Widgham Gn CB8 71 D3
WIGGENS GREEN 23 E1
Wiggin Cl IP28 239 D2
Wigmore Cl PE29 141 E1
Wigmore Dr PE7 187 F5
Wigsted Cl CB23 99 A2
Wigstone's Rd PE15 243 E5
Wilberforce Rd
Cambridge CB3 83 B2
Peterborough PE1 197 E7
Wisbech PE13 245 D5
Wilbraham Rd
Bottisham CB1 86 F3
Fulbourn CB21 67 C7
Wilbraham Temple CB21 68 A8
WILBURTON 210 B5
Wilburton CE Prim Sch CB6 210 C6
Wilburton Rd CB6 210 A6
Wild Acres CB25 130 B1
Wildber Cl PE19 74 F4
Wilderness The PE27 144 B3
Wilderspin Cl CB3 82 F6
Wild Goose Leys PE28 152 D5
Wilding Wlk CB4 84 A5
Wildlake PE2 186 C5
Wildmere La IP28 214 A8
Wiles Cl
Cambridge CB4 84 A7
Waterbeach CB25 106 A8
Wilff Cl PE29 152 E1
Wilford Dr CB7 240 E6
Wilford Furlong CB24 209 A1
Wilfred Sherman Cl 7 CB8 111 A4
Wilkinson Cl
Eaton Socon PE19 74 B3
March PE15 243 E5
Wilkinson Pl CB2 64 F6
Wilkins Rd PE14 236 D7
Wilkin St 1 CB1 65 A8
Willan Ct PE2 186 F8
Willesden Ave PE4 197 D8
William Blake Ct CB9 38 E1
William Ct PE9 244 A7
William de Yaxley CE Jun Sch PE7 181 E6
William Dr 8 PE19 74 F1
William Law CE Prim Sch PE4 204 B5
William Rd PE13 245 C5
Williams Cl
Brampton PE28 140 C3
Ely CB6 240 E7
Great Gransden SG19 58 E4
Newborough PE6 207 C1
William Smith Cl CB1 65 A7
Williamson Ave PE3 197 E3
Williams Way PE15 224 B4
William's Way IP28 213 D6
William Westley CE Prim Sch CB22 32 D5
Willie Snaith Rd CB8 110 F6
WILLINGHAM 209 B1
WILLINGHAM GREEN 54 D8
Willingham Green Rd CB8 54 D8
Willingham Prim Sch CB24 209 A1
Willingham Rd CB24 208 E1
Willis Rd CB1 246 C2
Willmott Rd SG8 12 F5
Willock La PE13 235 A5
Willonholt PE3 197 C7
Willoughby Ct PE1 198 E8
Willoughby Rd PE9 244 C7
Willow Ave PE1 198 B7
Willowbrook Dr PE7 201 F1
Willow Cl
Beck Row, Holywell Row & Kenny Hill IP28 214 A8
Brampton PE28 140 C2
Doddington PE15 222 A5
Haverhill CB9 38 D1
Little Paxton PE19 95 F1
Stilton PE7 175 F7
St Neots PE19 74 F3
Willow Cres
Milton CB24 105 D2
Newmarket CB8 111 B2
Willow Ct CB6 242 E4
Willow Dr
Manea PE15 224 C5
March PE15 243 B3
Willow Dro PE6 207 D4
Willow End PE28 150 F4
Willow Farm Cl PE28 150 D7
Willow Gate PE6 198 D6
Willow Gn PE27 208 A3
Willow Gr
Ely CB7 240 E4
Lode CB25 107 C2
Willow Hall La PE6 199 D6
Willow Holt PE7 186 C3
Willow La CB23 79 C3
Willow Rd PE7 182 A6
Willow Row Farms CB6 226 A5
Willowside Way SG8 5 C8
Willows The
Glinton PE6 203 F8
Great Chesterford CB10 18 D3
Highfields CB23 80 C3
Mildenhall IP28 239 B3
Willow Tree Cl PE16 241 B4
Willow Way
Bottisham CB25 86 F6
Hauxton CB22 48 B4
Ramsey PE26 172 B7
St Ives PE27 144 C4
Wisbech PE13 245 D3
Willow Wlk
Cambridge CB1 246 B3
Ely CB7 240 E4
Wilson Cl CB4 84 A7
Wilsons La SG7 2 C4
Wilson's Rd CB24 103 A8
Wilson Way
Brampton PE28 117 E8
Milton CB24 105 D2
Wilthorne PE28 165 A5
Wilton Cl PE3 197 C4
Wilton Dr PE3 197 C4
Wilton Gdns CB6 216 E3
Wiltshire Rd PE28 154 B1
Wimbish Rd CB23 99 A2
WIMBLINGTON 223 A6
Wimblington Rd
Doddington/Wimblington PE15 223 A5
March PE15 243 C1
Wimblington PE15 223 E6
Wimborne Dr PE1 198 E7
Wimbridge Cl SG8 27 F6
WIMPOLE 128 B8
Wimpole Hall* SG8 44 F3
Wimpole Home Farm* SG8 44 F3
Wimpole Pk* SG8 44 E3
Wimpole Rd
Barton CB23 63 A2
Great Eversden CB23 45 E7
Wimpole St PE16 241 B4
Winchester Way PE3 197 E1
Winchfield SG19 58 E5
Winchmore Dr CB2 64 C3
Winderemere Cl CB1 66 A7
Windermere PE29 141 B6
Windermere Way PE4 204 E3
Winders La CB24 104 B5
Windgate Way PE8 194 A6
Windlesham Cl CB4 83 E6
Windmill Cl
Ellington PE28 138 F4
2 Ely CB6 240 B3
Sawston CB22 32 F8
Soham CB7 212 C2
Windmill Hill CB8 110 C8
Windmill La
Fulbourn CB21 66 E4
Histon CB24 104 B4
8 Sutton CB6 216 E1
Windmill St
Peterborough PE1 197 F5
Whittlesey PE7 189 D8
Windmill Wlk CB6 216 E1
Windover Rd PE29 141 D7
Windrush Dr PE4 204 F1
Windsor Ave PE4 197 C8
Windsor Cl
Chatteris PE16 241 E5
Stamford PE9 244 B7
St Ives PE27 143 F8
10 St Neots PE19 74 F2
Windsor Dr
March PE15 243 B5
Peterborough PE2 187 D6
Ramsey PE26 221 C2
Wisbech PE13 245 D8
Windsor Gdns 9 PE28 208 C8
Windsor Pl PE7 190 A7
Windsor Rd
Cambridge CB4 83 C5
Godmanchester PE29 142 A1
Newmarket CB8 110 E4
Royston SG8 5 F6
Sawtry PE28 168 B3
Yaxley PE7 181 F6
Windsors The PE15 243 A5
Windsor Terr CB9 23 D8
Winfold Rd CB25 106 A8
Wingate Cl CB2 64 D3
Wingate Way CB2 64 D3
Wingfield PE2 185 F3
Winhills Prim Sch PE19 75 A4
Winship Rd CB24 105 C1
Winslow Rd PE3 197 C3
Winston Way PE7 187 C2
WINTRINGHAM 75 F4
Wintringham Rd 8 PE19 74 F5
WINWICK 158 B6
Winwick Pl PE3 197 C5
Winwick Rd PE28 158 B8
Winyates PE2 185 F3
Winyates Prim Sch PE2 186 A3
WISBECH 245 A6
Wisbech Castle* PE13 245 C4
Wisbech & Fenland Mus* 24 PE13 245 C4
Wisbech Gram Sch PE13 245 B5
Wisbech Rd
Lakes End PE14 229 F3
Littleport CB6 242 A6
Manea PE15 224 C5
March PE15 243 A7
Outwell PE14 236 F3
Thorney PE6 233 A3
Walsoken PE13 245 E8
Welney PE14 229 E2
Whittlesey PE7 191 C8
Wisbech St Mary PE13 234 A2
WISBECH ST MARY 235 C6
Wisbech St Mary Prim Sch PE13 235 B7
Wisbey's Yd CB23 47 B5
Wissey Way CB6 240 C6
Wistaria Rd PE13 245 F7
Wisteria Rd PE7 181 D4
WISTOW 163 F6
Wistow Ct 3 PE19 74 C6
Wistow Fen Dro PE28 173 B4
Wistow Fen La PE28 164 C8
Wistow Way PE2 185 D6
Wistow Wood Nature Reserve* PE28 172 D1
WITCHAM 217 A2
Witcham Bridge Dro CB6 217 A5
Witcham Rd CB6 216 E3
WITCHFORD 217 D1
Witchford Rd
Ely CB6 240 A3
Witchford CB6 217 F1
Witchford Village Coll CB6 217 E2
Witham Cl PE9 244 C6
Witham Way PE4 204 F1
WITHERSFIELD 38 C4
Withersfield Rd
Haverhill CB9 38 E1
Withersfield CB9 38 F7
Withers Pl CB7 212 E1
WITTERING 230 C1
Wittering Airfield PE8 230 A2
Wittering Ford Rd PE9 230 C2
Wittering Prim Sch PE8 230 B1
Wittering Rd PE9 230 D3
Woburn Cl
Cambridge CB4 83 E7
Peterborough PE3 197 A1
Woburn Ct PE7 176 A7
Woburn Dr PE6 233 A2
Woburn Pl CB22 31 F1
Wolf Cl PE28 152 E1
Wolf La
Gorefield PE13 237 F1
Wisbech PE13 235 C8
Wolfson Coll CB3 64 B8
Wollaston Rd
Cambridge CB1 246 C1
Peterborough PE3 197 C6
Wolseley Cl PE7 181 E6
Wolsey Gdns PE19 117 A5
Wolsey Way CB1 65 F7
Woodbine St PE2 187 A8
Woodbrook Cl CB23 99 B2
Woodbyth Rd PE1 198 A6
Woodcock Cl
Haverhill CB9 24 C7
Histon CB24 104 D3
Woodcock Rd 10 SG8 5 E8
Woodcote Cl PE1 198 A7
Woodcote Pk PE13 245 A4
Woodcroft Castle* PE6 203 C5
Woodcroft Rd
Etton PE6 203 B7
Woodcroft Rd *continued*
Glinton PE6 203 C3
Marholm PE6 203 D1
WOODDITTON 90 E3
Woodditton Rd
Kirtling CB8 72 B5
Newmarket CB8 111 A1
Woodditton CB8 90 B8
Wood End
Bluntisham/Colne PE28 208 C6
Pertenhall MK44 113 D1
Woodfen Rd CB6 242 A2
Woodfield Ave PE26 172 A4
Woodfield Dr PE28 168 A3
Woodfield La CB23 79 A3
Woodfield Rd PE3 197 D3
Woodforde Cl SG7 2 E4
Woodgate PE6 231 C4
Woodgate La PE6 231 D7
Woodgate Rd 3 PE13 238 B2
Wood Green Animal Ctr* PE29 119 C5
Woodhall La CB21 53 A1
Woodhall Rise PE4 204 B6
Woodhead Cl PE9 244 D7
Woodhead Dr CB4 83 F6
Woodhead Pl CB23 99 B3
Woodhouse Way CB4 84 A7
WOODHURST 155 B4
Woodhurst Rd PE2 187 D6
Wood La
Abbots Ripton PE28 162 E2
Broughton PE28 163 A2
Papworth Everard CB23 99 A4
Ramsey PE26 172 C8
Stretham CB6 210 F5
WOODLAND GREEN 24 E7
Woodland Lea PE6 231 B4
Woodland Rd CB22 32 F8
Woodlands
1 Royston SG8 5 E6
St Neots PE19 75 A7
Stukeley PE29 140 F5
Warboys PE28 164 F5
Woodlands Ave PE15 243 D2
Woodlands Cl
Girton CB3 103 D1
Great Shelford CB22 49 A4
Woodlands Ct PE13 245 F7
Woodlands Dr SG8 14 B8
Woodlands Pk CB3 103 D1
Woodlands Rd CB22 49 A4
Woodlands The
Linton CB21 35 B4
Peterborough PE1 198 D5
Woodlands Way IP28 239 F5
Woodland Wlk 2 CB23 79 C3
Woodlark Dr CB24 125 D4
Woodlark Rd CB3 83 B5
Woodmans Way CB24 105 D2
Woodpecker Way CB23 79 C3
Woodroffe Rd PE8 193 D8
Woods Cl CB9 24 E5
Woodside
Chatteris PE16 241 C4
Oakington/Longstanton CB24 123 F1
Woodside Way PE27 144 B5
Wood St
Chatteris PE16 241 C4
Doddington/Wimblington PE15 223 A6
Huntingdon PE29 141 E4
Wisbech PE13 245 B6
WOODSTON 186 E7
Woodstone Gate PE2 186 D6
Woodston Ind Est PE2 186 E6
Woodston Prim Sch PE2 186 F7
Wood View PE28 140 B4
WOOD WALTON 161 F6
Woodwalton Fen National Nature Reserve* PE26 170 B6
Woodwalton Marsh Nature Reserve* PE28 161 E7
Woodward Cl PE7 176 A8
Woodysfield 2 PE15 223 B7
Woolcroft Cl PE13 238 A1
Woolfellhill Rd PE6 205 F3
Woolgard PE3 197 A3
Woollards La CB22 49 A4
WOOLLEY 149 E1
Woolley Cl PE28 140 D3
Woolley Hill PE28 138 D6
Woolley Rd PE28 149 B3
Woolpack La
St Ives PE27 144 A3
2 Whittlesey PE7 189 D6
Woolpack Way SG8 29 B1
Woolthwaite La CB23 79 A4
Wooton Field SG19 41 D4
Woottens Cl CB23 62 C5
Wootton Ave PE2 186 F6
Wootton Way CB3 64 A8
Worboys Ct SG8 10 F5
Worcester Ave CB23 81 A4
Worcester Cres 2 PE9 244 B6
Worcester Rd PE13 245 C7
Worcester Way SG8 14 E6
Wordsworth Ave PE19 74 D6
Wordsworth Cl
Peterborough PE4 197 E8
Royston SG8 13 D1
Wordsworth Gr CB3 64 C8
Workhouse La PE14 229 D8
WORLINGTON 213 E4
Worlington Rd
Barton Mills IP28 214 C3
Worlington IP28 239 A3
Worsley PE2 186 A4
Worsley Chase PE15 243 D2
WORSTED LODGE 51 B4
Wortham Pl 2 CB9 24 A8
Wortham Rd SG8 5 E4
Worthington Cl PE7 176 A7
Worts' Cswy CB1 65 C2
WOTHORPE 244 B2
Wothorpe Hill PE9 244 A1
Wothorpe Mews 5 PE9 244 B4
Wothorpe Rd PE9 244 B4
Wragg Dr CB8 111 A6
Wratting Rd
Great Thurlow CB9 39 B8
Haverhill CB9 24 A8
Wren Cl
Little Stukeley PE28 150 E4
Mildenhall IP28 239 D4
Wren Pk CB22 32 B4
Wrens Cl CB6 240 B5
WRESTLINGWORTH 25 C4
Wrestlingworth Lower Sch SG19 25 B3
Wrexham Terr SG8 5 D7
Wright Ave PE2 187 D5
Wright's Cl CB5 84 E6
Wrights Dro PE7 220 B8
Wright's Dro PE6 232 B7
Wrights Gr CB21 66 F4
Wrights Way PE28 140 E2
Wroe The PE14 236 C5
Wulfric Sq PE3 197 C8
Wulfstan Ct CB1 65 C4
Wulfstan Way CB1 65 C4
Wyatt Cl PE26 172 B6
Wyboston Ct 1 PE19 74 C4
Wycliffe Gr PE4 204 A5
Wycliffe Rd CB1 65 C8
Wydham Pk PE2 185 D6
Wye Pl PE4 204 E1
Wye Valley Rd PE2 186 E8
Wykes Dr 3 PE13 235 B7
Wykes Rd PE7 181 D4
Wyman Way PE2 185 F5
Wynborne Cl CB4 83 E5
Wyndham Way CB8 111 A6
Wynemares CB22 32 E7
Wynford Way CB4 83 F7
Wype Dro PE7 191 A5
Wype Rd PE7 190 C7
Wysing Arts Ctr* CB23 60 C3
Wytches The CB6 211 A7
WYTON 142 F5
Wyton Airfield PE28 153 F2
Wyton Prim Sch PE28 143 B8
Wyvern The PE28 116 A7

Y

Yardy Cl PE15 243 B4
Yarmouth Pl 1 CB9 24 A8
Yarrow Cl PE15 243 B5
Yarrow Rd CB1 66 A5
YARWELL 183 A8
Yarwell Cl PE2 186 D7
Yarwells Headlands PE7 189 D8
Yarwells Wlk PE7 189 D8
YAXLEY 181 F4
Yaxley Inf Sch PE7 181 E4
Yaxley Rd PE7 177 B4
Yeats Cl SG8 13 D1
Yeldham Pl CB9 24 A8
YELLING 98 C1
Yellowgate Rd PE28 154 A1
Yeomans Cl PE28 136 D7
Yerril Gdn 3 CB9 23 E7
Yew Tree Wlk PE4 197 A2
Yokine Gdns PE13 235 A3
York Cl
Godmanchester PE29 141 F1
Mildenhall IP28 213 D8
Yorke Way CB6 240 B3
York Gdns PE13 245 D6
York Rd
Chatteris PE16 241 C4
Haverhill CB9 23 E7
Peterborough PE1 197 F6
9 Stamford PE9 244 B6
Sutton CB6 216 D1
Wisbech PE13 245 D6
Wyton Airfield PE28 143 A8
York Row 23 PE13 245 C5
York Sq PE28 143 B8
York St CB1 84 A1
York Terr
Cambridge CB1 84 A1
Wisbech PE13 245 C6
York Way
Royston SG8 5 B8
St Ives PE27 144 A8
Youngman Ave CB24 104 C5
Youngman Cl CB24 104 C5
Young St CB1 84 A2

Z

Zara Ct PE9 244 B6
Zetland Wlk CB1 65 D7

Addresses

Name and Address	Telephone	Page	Grid reference

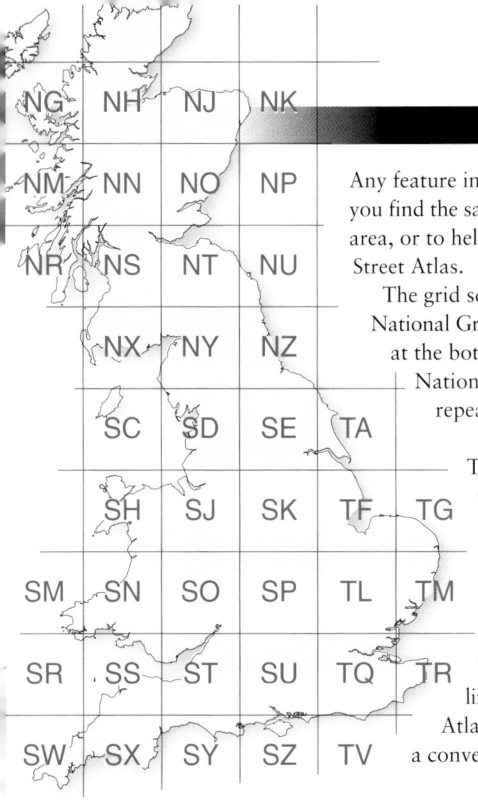

The map grid squares are labelled:

NG NH NJ NK
NM NN NO NP
NR NS NT NU
NX NY NZ
SC SD SE TA
SH SJ SK TF TG
SM SN SO SP TL TM
SR SS ST SU TQ TR
SW SX SY SZ TV

Any feature in this atlas can be given a unique reference to help you find the same feature on other Ordnance Survey maps of the area, or to help someone else locate you if they do not have a Street Atlas.

The grid squares in this atlas match the Ordnance Survey National Grid and are at 500 metre intervals. The small figures at the bottom and sides of every other grid line are the National Grid kilometre values (**00** to **99** km) and are repeated across the country every 100 km (see left).

To give a unique National Grid reference you need to locate where in the country you are. The country is divided into 100 km squares with each square given a unique two-letter reference. Use the administrative map to determine in which 100 km square a particular page of this atlas falls.

The bold letters and numbers between each grid line (**A** to **F**, **1** to **8**) are for use within a specific Street Atlas only, and when used with the page number, are a convenient way of referencing these grid squares.

Example   *The railway bridge over DARLEY GREEN RD in grid square B1*

Step 1: Identify the two-letter reference, in this example the page is in **SP**

Step 2: Identify the 1 km square in which the railway bridge falls. Use the figures in the southwest corner of this square: Eastings **17**, Northings **74**. This gives a unique reference: **SP 17 74**, accurate to 1 km.

Step 3: To give a more precise reference accurate to 100 m you need to estimate how many tenths along and how many tenths up this 1 km square the feature is (to help with this the 1 km square is divided into four 500 m squares). This makes the bridge about **8** tenths along and about **1** tenth up from the southwest corner.

This gives a unique reference: **SP 178 741**, accurate to 100 m.

Eastings (read from left to right along the bottom) come before Northings (read from bottom to top). If you have trouble remembering say to yourself "Along the hall, THEN up the stairs"!

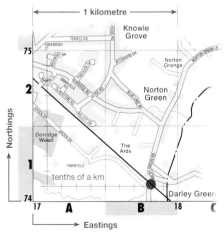

PHILIP'S MAPS

the Gold Standard for drivers

- ◆ **Philip's street atlases cover every county in England, Wales, Northern Ireland and much of Scotland**

- ◆ Every named street is shown, including alleys, lanes and walkways
- ◆ Thousands of additional features marked: stations, public buildings, car parks, places of interest
- ◆ Route-planning maps to get you close to your destination
- ◆ Postcodes on the maps and in the index
- ◆ Widely used by the emergency services, transport companies and local authorities

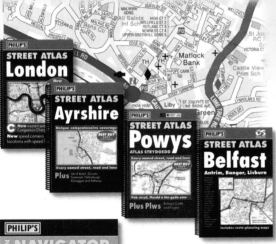

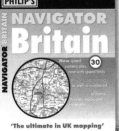

For national mapping, choose
Philip's Navigator Britain
the most detailed road atlas available of England, Wales and Scotland. Hailed by Auto Express as 'the ultimate road atlas', the atlas shows every road and lane in Britain.

'The ultimate in UK mapping'
The Sunday Times

Street atlases currently available

England
Bedfordshire and Luton
Berkshire
Birmingham and West Midlands
Bristol and Bath
Buckinghamshire and Milton Keynes
Cambridgeshire and Peterborough
Cheshire
Cornwall
Cumbria
Derbyshire
Devon
Dorset
County Durham and Teesside
Essex
North Essex
South Essex
Gloucestershire and Bristol
Hampshire
North Hampshire
South Hampshire
Herefordshire Monmouthshire
Hertfordshire
Isle of Wight
Kent
East Kent
West Kent
Lancashire
Leicestershire and Rutland
Lincolnshire
Liverpool and Merseyside
London
Greater Manchester
Norfolk
Northamptonshire
Northumberland
Nottinghamshire
Oxfordshire
Shropshire
Somerset
Staffordshire
Suffolk

Surrey
East Sussex
West Sussex
Tyne and Wear
Warwickshire and Coventry
Wiltshire and Swindon
Worcestershire
East Yorkshire Northern Lincolnshire
North Yorkshire
South Yorkshire
West Yorkshire

Wales
Anglesey, Conwy and Gwynedd
Cardiff, Swansea and The Valleys
Carmarthenshire, Pembrokeshire and Swansea
Ceredigion and South Gwynedd
Denbighshire, Flintshire, Wrexham
Herefordshire Monmouthshire
Powys

Scotland
Aberdeenshire
Ayrshire
Dumfries and Galloway
Edinburgh and East Central Scotland
Fife and Tayside
Glasgow and West Central Scotland
Inverness and Moray
Lanarkshire
Scottish Borders

Northern Ireland
County Antrim and County Londonderry
County Armagh and County Down
Belfast
County Tyrone and County Fermanagh

How to order
Philip's maps and atlases are available from bookshops, motorway services and petrol stations. You can order direct from the publisher by phoning **0207 531 8473** or online at **www.philips-maps.co.uk**
For bulk orders only, e-mail philips@philips-maps.co.uk